OXFORD THEOLOGICAL MONOGRAPHS

OXFORD THEOLOGICAL MONOGRAPHS

THE PRINCIPLE OF RESERVE IN THE WRITINGS
OF JOHN HENRY NEWMAN
By R. C. Selby. 1975

THE COSMIC CHRIST IN ORIGEN AND
TEILHARD DE CHARDIN
A Comparative Study
By J. A. Lyons. 1982

THE HIDDEN GOD
By Samuel E. Balentine. 1983

PROTESTANT REFORMERS IN ELIZABETHAN
OXFORD
By C. M. Dent. 1983

GOD IN HIMSELF
Aquinas' Doctrine of God
as Expounded in the
Summa Theologiae
By W. J. Hankey. 1987

REVELATORY POSITIVISM?
Barth's Earliest Theology and
the Marburg School
By Simon Fisher. 1988

THE COMMUNION OF SAINTS
Radical Puritan and Separatist Ecclesiology 1570–1625
By S. Brachlow. 1988

PROBABILITY AND THEISTIC EXPLANATION
By Robert Prevost. 1990

Verbal Aspect in
New Testament Greek

BUIST M. FANNING

CLARENDON PRESS · OXFORD
1990

Oxford University Press, Walton Street, Oxford OX2 6DP

Oxford New York Toronto
Delhi Bombay Calcutta Madras Karachi
Petaling Jaya Singapore Hong Kong Tokyo
Nairobi Dar es Salaam Cape Town
Melbourne Auckland

and associated companies in
Berlin Ibadan

Oxford is a trade mark of Oxford University Press

Published in the United States
by Oxford University Press, New York

British Library Cataloguing in Publication Data
Fanning, B. M.
Verbal aspect in New Testament Greek.
1. Bible. N. T. Greek. Linguistic aspects
I. Title
225.4'8'014.
ISBN 0–19–826729–0

Library of Congress Cataloging-in-Publication Data
Fanning, Buist M.
Verbal aspect in New Testament Greek
Buist M. Fanning.
Includes Bibliographical references.
1. Greek language, Biblical–aspect.
2. Bible. N. T.–Language, Style. I. Title. II. Series
PA847.F36 1990 487'.4–dc20 89-38663
ISBN 0–19–826729–0

Typeset in Greece by
Fotron S.A. 31, Tsacaloff St., Athens

Printed in Great Britain by
Bookcraft Ltd., Midsomer Norton, Avon

PREFACE

THIS book is the presentation, with minor revisions, of a D.Phil. thesis accepted by the Faculty of Theology in the University of Oxford in 1987. The thesis was prepared under the supervision of the late Prof. G. B. Caird and Dr John Ashton. The examiners of the thesis were Prof. James Barr and Dr Robert Murray. I am grateful to all of them for their encouragement and valuable criticisms of my work. Thanks also to Prof. J. P. Louw, who read a portion of the thesis at an early stage and gave helpful advice. The thesis was completed in the summer of 1986 and revised for publication in the spring of 1988.

The literature on verbal aspect in various languages and in general linguistics has been voluminous over the past hundred years, and the volume shows no sign of abating. I cannot claim to have utilized all the studies which have appeared, but I have attempted to find the works which seem to be most significant and weigh what contributions they make towards asking the right questions and pointing to the most workable answers. The reader will see that I have learnt a great deal from numerous writers, and nothing that I have said by way of disagreement with their views should be understood to diminish my appreciation for their work. It will be clear that I follow an approach to aspect advanced most clearly by Carl Bache, and I am grateful to him in particular for insights which helped to bring a number of other details into place. Of course, none of these people should be held responsible for the use which I make of their ideas and criticisms.

I have struggled in writing this book with the difficulties of working across two or three fields of specialized research (linguistics, Greek philology, and NT studies), each of which

has its own terminology, history of research, and questions of
method that form the setting for the treatment of issues such
as verbal aspect. I hope that students of each of these fields
will find something of value in this book, but it will be clear to
linguists and philologists that a NT student has ventured as
an amateur into their domain. I ask for their patience where I
have failed to set the issues within the larger framework of
research in these fields, and I hope that this has not vitiated
my conclusions.

On the other hand, research on linguistic or philological
topics is not common in contemporary NT studies, and my
book is clearly linguistic rather than theological or exegetical.
In addition, though I have studied NT texts and cited them
extensively as illustrations of some point or other, one will not
find in this book detailed exegetical discussions of NT passages or exciting new solutions of old cruces ready-made,
based on my treatment of aspect. My conviction is that verbal
aspect is too dependent on other features of the context for it
alone to be determinative in interpretation. However, in combination with other features, verbal aspect is a significant
linguistic element to be weighed in interpreting a number of
texts in the NT, and I hope to offer some new insights and
clearer approaches to this linguistic element to aid the interpreter in his larger task. In this connection I should say that in
treating the various features of usage I have tried to cite by
way of illustration a *number* of NT texts (rather than only a
few), so that the reader can obtain a broader view of the
linguistic patterns which I believe are there. If my idea about
an individual text appears not to be valid, perhaps the point
can be seen in the other texts cited. In this way I hope to have
provided a group of examples which one may consult for
linguistic comparison and contrast when one is pondering a
feature of aspectual usage in a text which I have not included.

It remains for me to express appreciation to several others
who have contributed to this work in special ways. I am
grateful to Dallas Theological Seminary for providing study-
leaves from my faculty duties in 1979–81 and 1987–8, financial

support during these times, and an atmosphere conducive to Christian scholarship. To Harold Hoehner I owe a special word of thanks: as my department chairman, colleague, and friend, he has given encouragement and support throughout the process of completing this project. I am thankful also to a group of friends in Irving, Texas, who provided financial assistance in 1979–81, to Gene Saur for his friendship and generous financial support, to Conrad and Barbara Koch for a special favour in the summer of 1983, to the Park family of Huntsville, Alabama, for their financial support in 1988, and to the Faßheber family for their kind hospitality towards my family and me during our stay in Göttingen in 1987–8.

Most importantly, I express my love and gratitude to my wife Jan and our four children for their support and encouragement. I am especially thankful to Jan, whose patience and remarkably good attitude about this project all along have helped me immensely.

B. M. F.

CONTENTS

ABBREVIATIONS   x

INTRODUCTION   1

I GENERAL MATTERS

1. A Definition of Verbal Aspect   8

2. The Meaning of the Verbal Aspects in New
   Testament Greek   86

3. The Effect of Inherent Meaning and Other
   Elements on Aspectual Function   126

II SPECIFIC AREAS OF ASPECT-USAGE

4. The Aspects in the Indicative Mood   198

5. The Aspects in Commands and Prohibitions   325

6. The Aspects in the Other Non-Indicative Forms
   of the Verb   389

CONCLUSION   420

BIBLIOGRAPHY   423

INDEX OF BIBLICAL PASSAGES   449

SUBJECT INDEX   463

ABBREVIATIONS

Abel, *Grammaire*	F.-M. Abel, *Grammaire du grec biblique suivie d'un choix de papyrus*, 2nd edn. (Paris: J. Gabalda et Fils, 1927)
AJP	*American Journal of Philology*
AL	*Archivum Linguisticum*
Aspectology (1979)	Thore Pettersson (ed.), *Aspectology* (Stockholm: Almqvist and Wiksell, 1979)
BAGD, *Lexicon*	Walter Bauer, *A Greek–English Lexicon of the New Testament and Other Early Christian Literature*, trans. and adapted by William F. Arndt and F. Wilbur Gingrich, 2nd edn., rev. and augmented by F. Wilbur Gingrich and Frederick W. Danker (Chicago: University of Chicago Press, 1979)
BDF, *Grammar*	F. Blass and A. Debrunner, *A Greek Grammar of the New Testament and Other Early Christian Literature*, trans. and rev. of the 9th–10th German edn., by Robert W. Funk (Chicago: University of Chicago Press, 1961)
BDR, *Grammatik*	F. Blass, and A. Debrunner, *Grammatik des neutestamentlichen Griechisch*, ed. Friedrich Rehkopf, 15th edn. (Göttingen: Vandenhoeck and Ruprecht, 1979)
BGDSL	*Beiträge zur Geschichte der deutschen Sprache und Literatur*
BICS	*Bulletin of the Institute of Classical Studies*
BSL	*Bulletin de la Société de Linguistique de Paris*
BT	*Bible Translator*
Burton, *MT*	Ernest De Witt Burton, *Syntax of the Moods and Tenses in New Testament Greek*, 3rd edn. (Edinburgh: T. and T. Clark, 1898)
Buttmann, *Grammatik*	Alex Buttmann, *Grammatik des neutes-*

tamentlichen Sprachgebrauchs (Berlin: Ferd. Dümmler, 1859)

BW, *Syntax*   James A. Brooks and Carlton L. Winbery, *Syntax of New Testament Greek* (Washington, DC: University Press of America, 1979)

Comrie, *Aspect*   Bernard Comrie, *Aspect: An Introduction to the Study of Verbal Aspect and Related Problems* (Cambridge: Cambridge University Press, 1976)

CQ   *Classical Quarterly*

CR   *Classical Review*

DM, *Grammar*   H. E. Dana and Julius R. Mantey, *A Manual Grammar of the Greek New Testament* (New York: Macmillan, 1927)

Exp. T.   *Expository Times*

FL   *Foundations of Language*

Friedrich, *Aspect Theory* Paul Friedrich, *On Aspect Theory and Homeric Aspect* (International Journal of American Linguistics, Memoir 28; Chicago: University of Chicago Press, 1974)

Gildersleeve, *Syntax* Basil Lanneau Gildersleeve, *Syntax of Classical Greek, from Homer to Demosthenes*, 2 vols. (New York: American Book Co., 1900–11)

HS, *Grammatik*   Ernst G. Hoffmann and Heinrich von Siebenthal, *Griechische Grammatik zum Neuen Testament* (Riehen: Immanuel-Verlag, 1985)

ICC   International Critical Commentary

IF   *Indogermanische Forschungen*

IE   Indo-European

JBL   *Journal of Biblical Literature*

JEGP   *Journal of English and Germanic Philology*

JL   *Journal of Linguistics*

JTS   *Journal of Theological Studies*

KG, *Satzlehre*   Raphael Kühner and Bernhard Gerth, *Ausführliche Grammatik der griechischen Sprache*, pt. 2. *Satzlehre*, i, 3rd edn. (1898; repr. edn. Hanover: Verlag Hahnsche Buchhandlung, 1976)

KZ   [*Kuhns*] *Zeitschrift für vergleichende Sprachforschung*

Lg.   *Language*

Lloyd, *Verb*   Albert L. Lloyd, *Anatomy of the Verb: The Gothic Verb as a Model for a Unified Theory of Aspect, Actional Types, and Verbal Velocity* (Amsterdam: John Benjamins, 1979)

Lyons, *Semantics*   John Lyons, *Semantics* (Cambridge: Cambridge University Press, 1977)

Mandilaras, *Verb*   Basil G. Mandilaras, *The Verb in the Greek Non-Literary Papyri* (Athens: Hellenic Ministry of Culture and Sciences, 1973)

Mateos, *Aspecto verbal*   Juan Mateos, *El aspecto verbal en el nuevo testamento* (Estudios de nuevo testamento, 1; Madrid: Ediciones Cristiandad, 1977)

Mayser, *Grammatik*   Edwin Mayser, *Grammatik der griechischen Papyri aus der Ptolemäerzeit*, ii. *Satzlehre*, pt. 1 (Berlin: Walter de Gruyter and Co., 1926)

MH, *Accidence*   James Hope Moulton, *A Grammar of New Testament Greek*, ii. *Accidence and Word Formation*, by Wilbert Francis Howard (Edinburgh: T. and T. Clark, 1929)

Moorhouse, *Syntax*   A. C. Moorhouse, *The Syntax of Sophocles* (Leiden: E. J. Brill, 1982)

Moule, *Idiom Book*   C. F. D. Moule, *An Idiom Book of New Testament Greek*, 2nd edn. (Cambridge: at the University Press, 1959)

Moulton, *Proleg.*   James Hope Moulton, *A Grammar of New Testament Greek*, i. *Prolegomena*, 3rd edn. (Edinburgh: T. and T. Clark, 1908)

MT, *Syntax*   James Hope Moulton, *A Grammar of New Testament Greek*, iii. *Syntax*, by Nigel Turner (Edinburgh: T. and T. Clark, 1963)

MT, *Style*   James Hope Moulton, *A Grammar of New Testament Greek*, iv. *Style*, by Nigel Turner (Edinburgh: T. and T. Clark, 1976)

Mussies, *Morphology*   G. Mussies, *The Morphology of Koine Greek as Used in the Apocalypse of John: a Study in Bilingualism* (Leiden: E. J. Brill, 1971)

NEB   *New English Bible*

NGG   *Nachrichten der Gesellschaft/Akademie der Wissen-*

	schaften zu Göttingen, philologisch-historische Klasse
NIV	New International Version
Nov. T.	*Novum Testamentum*
NT	New Testament
NTS	*New Testament Studies*
OT	Old Testament
Rijksbaron, *SSV*	Albert Rijksbaron, *The Syntax and Semantics of the Verb in Classical Greek: An Introduction* (Amsterdam: J. C. Gieben, 1984)
Robertson, *Grammar*	A. T. Robertson, *A Grammar of the Greek New Testament in the Light of Historical Research* (Nashville, Tenn.: Broadman Press, 1914)
SD, *Syntax*	Eduard Schwyzer, *Griechische Grammatik*, vol. ii. *Syntax und syntaktische Stilistik*, ed. Albert Debrunner (Munich: C. H. Beck, 1950)
Smyth, *Grammar*	Herbert Weir Smyth, *Greek Grammar*, rev. Gordon M. Messing (Cambridge, Mass.: Harvard University Press, 1956)
Stahl, *Syntax*	J. M. Stahl, *Kritisch-historische Syntax des griechischen Verbums der klassischen Zeit* (Heidelberg: Carl Winter, 1907)
Stork, *Aspectual Usage*	Peter Stork, *The Aspectual Usage of the Dynamic Infinitive in Herodotus* (Groningen: Bouma, 1982)
Tense and Aspect (1981)	Philip J. Tedeschi and Annie Zaenen (eds.), *Syntax and Semantics*, xiv. *Tense and Aspect* (New York: Academic Press, 1981)
Tense-Aspect (1982)	Paul J. Hopper (ed.), *Tense-Aspect: Between Semantics and Pragmatics* (Amsterdam and Philadelphia: John Benjamins, 1982)
Winer, *Grammatik*	G. B. Winer, *Grammatik des neutestamentlichen Sprachidioms*, 2nd edn. (Leipzig: F. C. W. Vogel, 1825)
WL, *Grammatik*	G. B. Winer, *Grammatik des neutestamentlichen Sprachidioms*, 7th edn., ed. Gottlieb Lünemann (Leipzig: F. C. W. Vogel, 1867)
WM, *Grammar*	G. B. Winer, *A Treatise on the Grammar of New Testament Greek*, trans. with additions, by W.

	F. Moulton, 3rd edn. (Edinburgh: T. and T. Clark, 1882)
RSV	Revised Standard Version
ZAW	*Zeitschrift für die alttestamentliche Wissenschaft*
Zerwick, *Biblical Greek*	Maximilian Zerwick, *Biblical Greek: Illustrated by Examples*, trans. and adapted by Joseph Smith (Rome: Scripta Pontificii Instituti Biblici, 1963)
ZNW	*Zeitschrift für die neutestamentliche Wissenschaft*

INTRODUCTION

VERBAL aspect, according to one commonly cited description, is concerned 'not with the location of an event in time, but with its temporal distribution or contour'.[1] It is usually distinguished in some way from the 'tenses' (i.e. past, present, and future), and is said to be concerned rather with features like duration, progression, completion, repetition, inception, current relevance, and their opposites. Illustrations of aspect which are frequently cited are: the simple and progressive forms in English; perfectives and imperfectives in Russian and other Slavic languages; perfect and imperfect in Hebrew; present, aorist, and perfect forms in ancient Greek; and to a lesser degree, differences between past tenses in French, Spanish, and German. This is, of course, rather a broad spread of languages and features of meaning, and the exact limits of the category of 'aspect' are quite vague. Over the last century, however, many writers have given attention to this topic and a vast literature of aspectology has been built up to shed light on aspectual usage and meaning in various languages.[2]

For an introduction to this grammatical category in NT Greek one can turn to the standard grammars. In most NT grammars 'aspect' or 'Aktionsart' (a common synonym in these works) is defined in quite general terms. It will be helpful to cite several definitions at length to facilitate comparison:

BLASS (1896)[3]

. . . jedes Tempus [hat] wenigstens im Indik. im allgemeinen eine

---

[1] Charles Hockett, *A Course in Modern Linguistics* (New York: Macmillan, 1958), 237.

[2] See ch. 1.

[3] Grammars of NT Greek will be cited in this Introduction by author's name and publication date only. See Bibliography for full publication data.

doppelte Funktion: es drückt zugleich eine *Aktion* aus (der Dauer, der Vollendung, der Dauer in der Vollendung), und eine *Zeitstufe* (Gegenwart, Vergangenheit, Zukunft).

Das *Präsens* bezeichnet also eine Handlung . . . als in ihrer *Dauer* (ihrem Verlaufe) angeschaut.

Was im Aorist als vollendet (geschehen) berichtet wird, braucht durchaus nichts Momentanes zu sein, sondern kann sich thatsächlich und auch nach ausdrücklicher Angabe über eine beliebig lange Zeit erstreckt haben, wofern nur die *Vollendung* und der *Abschluß* hervorzuheben ist, was eben durch den Aorist geschieht.

Das *Perfectum* . . . vereinigt in sich gleichsam Präsens und Aorist, indem es die *Dauer* des *Vollendeten* ausdrückt. (pp. 182-3, 188, 194).

BURTON (1898)

The action denoted by a verb may be defined by the tense of the verb . . . as respects its *progress*. Thus it may be represented as *in progress*, or as *completed*, or *indefinitely*, i.e. as a *simple event* without reference to progress or completion. . . . The *chief* function of a Greek tense is thus not to denote time, but progress. (p. 6)

MOULTON (1908)

The first topic to be discussed under the verb is . . . *Aktionsart*, or the 'kind of action' denoted by different verbal formations. . . . the Aorist has a 'punctiliar' action, that is, it regards action as a *point*: it represents the point of entrance . . . or that of completion . . . or it looks at a whole action simply as having occurred, without distinguishing any steps in its progress. . . . The present has generally a durative action — 'linear', we may call it, to keep up the same graphic illustration. . . . The *Perfect* action is a variety by itself, denoting what began in the past and still continues. . . . The present stems which show an ι-reduplication . . . are supposed to have started with an *Iterative* action. (pp. 108–9)

ROBERTSON (1914)

Aktionsart ('kind of action') must be clearly understood. . . . The three essential kinds of action are thus momentary or punctiliar when the action is regarded as a whole and may be represented by a dot (●), linear or durative action which may be represented by a continuous line ——, the continuance of perfected or completed action which may be represented by this graph ●——. (p. 823)

MOULTON–TURNER (1963)

. . . essentially the tense in Greek expresses the kind of *action*, not time, which the speaker has in view and the *state* of the subject, or, as the Germans say, the *Aspekt*. In short, the tense-stems indicate the point of view from which the action or state is regarded. . . . The aorist stem expresses punctiliar, and the present expresses linear action. Sometimes however the aorist will not even express momentary or punctiliar action but will be non-committal; it regards the action as a whole without respect to its duration.

The[se] rules must be viewed with great caution. . . . Nevertheless, assuming as a working hypothesis the essential punctiliar and momentary meaning of the aorist stem, one will find various ways of using the indicative. (pp. 59, 71)

BLASS–DEBRUNNER–REHKOPF (1979)

Die ursprüngliche Funktion der sogenannten Tempusstämme des Verbums war in den indogermanischen Sprachen nicht die von Zeitstufen (Gegenwart, Vergangenheit, Zukunft), sondern die von *Aktionsarten* (Arten der Handlung) oder *Aspekten* (Betrachtungs-weisen) . . .

Die wichtigsten im Griech. (auch des NT) erhaltenen Aktionsarten sind:

1. die *momentane (punctuelle)* im Aoriststamm: die Handlung ist als Moment gedacht, und zwar wird entweder der Anfangs- oder der Endpunkt hervorgehoben . . . oder die Handlung wird an sich als Ganzes ohne Rücksicht auf die Dauer ins Auge gefaßt . . .

2. die *durative* (*lineare* oder *kursive*) Aktionsart im Präsensstamm: die Handlung ist in ihrer Dauer (in ihrem Verlauf) vorgestellt . . .

3. die *iterative* ebenfalls im Präsensstamm . . .

4. die *perfektische* im Perfektstamm: sie bezeichnet einen Zustand als Resultat einer vergangenen Handlung . . .

These definitions, though simple, are nevertheless useful as introductions to this feature of grammar, and in a rough and ready way they serve the interpreter well, if used with common sense and attention to significant contextual factors. It is true also that the grammars include extensive discussion of individual uses of the aspects in the NT, which aid the interpreter in his work.

Useful general definitions can be easily given, but it is more difficult to specify what aspect is in a precise way. When one probes further, one discovers disparate definitions of what the aspects actually involve and begins to question what contribution this category of grammar should make to interpretation. For example, do the aspects in NT Greek indicate whether an action was durative or momentary, as Robertson, Turner, and Blass–Debrunner–Rehkopf imply? Or do they pertain more to the completion or lack of completion, as Blass and Burton indicate? Is progressive/non-progressive a better way to describe the aspects? What can they tell about the repetition or single occurrence of an action? How do imperfective, indefinite, stative, simple, or habitual relate to these categories? Are these really different from the tense-distinctions (past, present, future), which are more familiar and with which they are closely associated? Such issues, since they involve a feature so central to the entire verb-system, can often be significant for interpretation of particular NT texts.

Generally speaking, these disparate definitions and uncertainties are due to the intermingling of aspect with other closely related categories of meaning. As a matter of fact, verbal aspect is part of an immensely complex system of interactions between various elements of meaning, and simple definitions are not sufficient for guiding one through such a tangle, however much they may help to give general orientation to it. One writer on aspect (outside the field of NT) has commented: 'The history of aspect studies is, apart from the interminable arguing about terminology, essentially a process of broadening horizons and increasing recognition of the immense complications inherent in the concept of predication, beside which the early ideas of aspect seem almost childishly naive'.[4]

Part of the difficulty for the NT interpreter is that, when he turns to his grammars for help in handling verbal aspect, he is turning to works which do not reflect the wealth of more

---

[4] Lloyd, *Verb*, pp. 2–3.

recent study in aspectology. The standard reference-grammars of NT Greek reflect the state of aspect studies as they stood in approximately 1920,[5] and their statements about verbal aspect, while not inaccurate, must be described as 'early ideas of aspect' which are rather simplistic and to some degree misleading. This is unfortunately part of a general paucity of current research in NT Greek grammar, which was lamented over a decade ago by Rydbeck: 'There is a prevalent but false assumption that everything in NT Greek scholarship has been done already. "You have all the facts in Blass–Debrunner's Grammar and Bauer's Dictionary, even if you don't care very much to look them up." In the long run this outlook will prove detrimental to N.T. exegesis . . .'[6]

In the light of these factors, the purpose of this book is to present a more detailed analysis of NT verbal aspect[7] than is given by the standard grammars, using insights from contemporary research in linguistics and in NT studies. Three subsidiary goals are included in this purpose: (1) to evaluate and utilize the results of broader work in aspectology, as a background for analysing aspect in the NT; (2) to assess the contributions of various studies concerned with individual

---

[5] One should notice that many standard works pre-date 1920: e.g. Burton (1898), Moulton (1906–8), Robertson (1914, with only reprints subsequent). Several others have been issued in more recent editions, but reflect essentially the same treatment of aspect as the pre-1920 editions: this is true of Nunn (1912–38) and most notably of Blass–Debrunner–Funk (1961) and Blass–Debrunner–Rehkopf (1976/9), in which the introduction to the aspects in § 318 and much of the subsequent discussion of specific uses are virtually unchanged from Debrunner's 1913 edition. In regard to other standard grammars produced since 1920 (e.g. Radermacher [1925], Moule [1959], Moulton–Turner [1963]), the survey of aspect studies in the next chapter will illustrate that their treatments do not show detailed acquaintance with developments in aspectology since 1920. Of course, in a general grammar one does not expect the detailed treatment which a monograph can give.

[6] Lars Rydbeck, 'What Happened to New Testament Greek Grammar after Albert Debrunner!', *NTS* 21 (1975), 424.

[7] The question of which forms to include as 'aspects' is debated. Here it should be said that all the forms sometimes called 'aspects' will be discussed in the book: the *present* forms (including the imperfect tense), the *aorist* forms, the *perfect* forms (including the pluperfect tense), and the *future* forms. The validity of regarding the latter two as aspects must be discussed in due course.

issues relating to verbal aspect in the NT; and (3) to show in summary the possibilities to be considered and questions to be asked when interpreting aspectual forms in the NT. Because NT verbal aspect has received no recent comprehensive treatment, it is necessary to include all of the verbal aspects of NT Greek in the discussion, though the topic is rather large for the limits of one book. In addition, it is necessary to limit the analysis to NT usage and not attempt to study other bodies of ancient Greek usage. Research done by others in literature outside the NT will be cited whenever possible for comparison. Perhaps the appearance of the material in this form will stimulate further research into the details of aspectual usage within more specific limits.

The book will be structured in two major parts: a section covering *general* matters, including the definition of aspect, the meaning of the major aspects in NT Greek, and the effect of lexical meaning and other features on aspectual function (Chapters 1–3); and a section on *specific* areas of usage, including aspect in the indicative mood, in commands and prohibitions, and in other forms of the verb (Chapters 4–6).

The Greek text of the United Bible Societies (3rd edn.) and Nestle–Aland (26th edn.) has been followed as a standard text, with discussion of textual variants in only a few places. In the citations of Greek texts to illustrate verbal usage, the relevant verb is usually evident; in places where it may not be so, letter-spacing has been used to highlight the relevant word or phrase. At times the citations are divided into more than one group separated by a blank line; the different groups illustrate more than one variation of usage, as described in the paragraph above the citations.

I

GENERAL MATTERS

1

A DEFINITION OF VERBAL ASPECT

THE purpose of this chapter is twofold: (1) to discuss basic issues of the meaning of aspect and formulate a general theory of aspect as a foundation for more specific discussion in later chapters; and (2) to provide a survey of aspectology over the last century to give perspective for the discussion of problems of aspect-usage in the NT.[1] The history of aspect studies has shown that the major problem in understanding verbal aspect involves two interrelated issues: first, to distinguish aspect from other features of meaning with which it is commonly intertwined (e.g. tense, procedural character of verbs, structural contrasts between aspects, and discourse functions), and second, to note the variable function of aspect in connection with these other features.[2] This chapter will discuss these distinctions and interconnections with other categories of meaning and propose a preliminary definition of verbal aspect.

1. 1 Aspect and Tense

Modern studies of verbal aspect began with the contribution of nineteenth-century comparative philologists, whose study of the IE languages led them to distinguish aspect from tenses.[3]

---

[1] Since this field may not be familiar to NT students, fuller quotations of significant literature will be given in this chapter to provide background.

[2] See the comment by Lyons, *Semantics*, p. 714: 'Few parts of a language–system illustrate better than its aspect–system does the validity of the structuralist slogan: *Tout se tient* ("Everything hangs together . . .")'.

[3] Insights into aspect were achieved before this time by grammarians of Slavic languages, but remained unknown to scholars outside their circles and exerted little

1. 1. 1 *Origin of the distinction*

In earlier works Greek aspectual distinctions had been masked by an analysis of the verb-system based on temporal distinctions of 'past, present, future' and similar values centring on temporal *sequence* (simultaneity, previous past, etc.). Alexandrian grammarians had observed aspect-values in Greek, but their rudimentary descriptions were lost in the Latin grammatical tradition of the medieval and early modern eras.[4]

Typical of this older approach was the treatment of Buttmann in his *Ausführliche griechische Sprachlehre* (1819–27), a standard work of the early nineteenth century. In his analysis the basic division of the Greek tenses is that of present, past, and future time, and the Greek tenses correspond in meaning to the tenses of Latin and German, except for the richer range of *past* tenses in Greek. The past tenses likewise are distinguished essentially by differences of temporal sequence: the perfect represents a past event in regard to its connection to present time; the aorist leaves the present out of view and, within the past-time frame, narrates events in sequence; the imperfect presents events occurring at the same time as other past events; and the pluperfect mentions events which happened previous to the past time already in view.[5] Buttmann goes on to describe a type of aspect-distinction, 'durative vs. momentary', which he observes in imperfect and aorist indicatives and in present and aorist forms of the non-indicative

influence until later in the century. For a survey of these works see Jan Gonda, *The Aspectual Function of the Ṛgvedic Present and Aorist* (The Hague: Mouton, 1962), 8–10; and André Mazon, 'La notion morphologique de l'aspect des verbes chez les grammariens russes', in *Mélanges offerts à Émile Picot*, 2 vols. (Paris: E. Rahir, 1913), i. 343–67.

[4] See Gustav Herbig. 'Aktionsart und Zeitstufe: Beiträge zur Funktionslehre des indogermanischen Verbums', *IF* 6 (1896), 172–8; R. H. Robins, *A Short History of Linguistics*, 2nd edn. (London: Longman, 1979), 29–35, 51–2, 59–62; and Francis P. Dinneen, *An Introduction to General Linguistics* (New York: Holt, Rinehart, and Winston, 1967), 93–123.

[5] Philipp Buttmann, *Ausführliche griechische Sprachlehre*, 2 vols. (Berlin: in der Myliussischen Buchhandlung, 1819–27), §§ 81 (4), 137 (2).

moods. But this is regarded as secondary to the more important difference of temporal sequence: that which is simultaneous with another event must have some duration, while sequenced events are either momentary or represented as momentary.[6] With some variations, this approach to the Greek tenses was the predominant one in published grammars up until the mid-nineteenth century.[7]

The breakthrough to a different approach under the influence of comparative philology began with the work of Curtius, who was perhaps the first to attempt a union between the new comparative linguistics and Greek philology as it was more traditionally conceived. In an early book (1846), Curtius argued that, in contrast to Latin, *temporal* meaning is limited in Greek to the indicative mood and a different type of meaning is expressed by the present and aorist verbal stems: that of durative vs. 'quickly-passing' action.[8] He described his new approach more fully in a later work:

Die ältere Grammatik behandelt den Aorist durchaus, zum Theil auch das Perfect als ein Tempus der Vergangenheit. Die Analyse der Formen aber ergibt . . . auf das schlagendste, daß die Sprache zur Bezeichnung der Vergangenheit überhaupt gar kein anderes Mittel besitzt, als das Augment, daß mithin Bezeichnung der Vergangenheit ursprünglich nur da angenommen werden kann, wo das Augment steht, das heißt im Imperfect, Plusquamperfect und *Indicativ* des Aorists, mithin überhaupt *nur* im Indicativ. An diesen Indicativen können wir nun aber auch am deutlichsten sehen, daß die Sprache neben der Vergangenheit in solchen Formen noch etwas ganz anderes bezeichnet. ἐ-γέν-ε-το, ἐ-γίγν-ε-το, ἐ-γεγόν-ει unter-

---

[6] Ibid. § 137 (4–5).

[7] Some writers developed variations of the 'durative vs. momentary' distinction, but this was derived from the primary values of temporal sequence. See G. Bernhardy, *Wissenschaftliche Syntax der griechischen Sprache* (Berlin: Duncker and Humbolt, 1829), 369–82; and V. C. F. Rost, *Griechische Grammatik*, 3rd edn. (Göttingen: Vandenhoeck and Ruprecht, 1826), 440–50. For NT see Winer, *Grammatik*, p. 114; and Buttmann, *Grammatik*, pp. 170–4.

[8] Georg Curtius, *Die Bildung der Tempora und Modi im Griechischen und Lateinischen sprachvergleichend dargestellt* (Berlin: Wilhelm Besser, 1846), 148–52.

scheiden sich untereinander durch etwas ganz anderes als ἐγίγνετο
von γίγνομαι, ἐγεγόνει von γέγονα.[9]

He went on to state that new terms were needed to describe
these differing categories of the tense–system, and he explained his choice of terms based on the significance which he
discerned in the categories:

Da stellte sich nun heraus, daß die *eine* temporale Unterscheidung
eine mehr äußerliche, die andere eine innere war. Der Unterschied
zwischen Gegenwart, Vergangenheit und Zukunft beruft nur auf
dem Verhältniß der Handlung zu dem Sprechenden. Ich nenne also
diesen Unterschied, bei dem es nur auf den Standpunkt ankommt,
den der Zeitstufe. . . . Offenbar mußte nun aber die Differenz
zwischen γενέσθαι, γίγνεσθαι, γεγονέναι durch ein Wort bezeichnet
werden, das sofort andeutet, daß es sich hier um eine *innerhalb* der
Handlung selbst liegende Differenz, nicht bloß um das Verhältniß
zu etwas außer ihr liegendem handelt. In diesem Sinne wählte ich
den Ausdruck *Zeitart*, indem wir ja das Wort Art recht eigentlich da
verwenden, wo wir specifische, innere Eigenthümlichkeiten benen-
nen wollen.[10]

Finally, the characteristics of the three categories of Zeitart
are listed. Two are described quickly: 'Die Handlung des
Präsensstammes ist die *dauernde*, Perfectstammes die *vollendete*.'[11] The aorist takes longer, because, as Curtius laments, it
is more difficult to characterize in a brief expression. He
suggests 'momentan' and rejects that term because it implies
that the distinction between aorist and present is merely one of
time-measurement, but in fact the difference is much deeper
and quite different from mere time-lapse, he argues. So he
adopts the term 'eintretend' and attempts to explain the sense
he intends. But he confesses that the sense of 'eintreten' is
somewhat ambiguous and indefinite, and he concludes by

[9] Id. *Erläuterungen zu meiner griechischen Schulgrammatik* (Prague: F. Tempsky, 1863),
171.
[10] Ibid. 172. See also his *Das Verbum der griechischen Sprache* (Leipzig: S. Hirzel,
1873), 2–3.
[11] Curtius, *Erläuterungen*, p. 172.

saying that no one can describe the aorist with a single, unequivocal term.[12]

1. 1. 2 *Early consensus and its results*

This clear distinction between two elements of meaning in the Greek tense-system, 'Zeitstufe' and 'Zeitart',[13] and the assertion that Greek tenses are different from the Latin system, marked a departure in the description of Greek tenses. Curtius' presentation of these distinctions was widely accepted in the latter half of the century and became the dominant viewpoint.[14]

Widespread agreement among Indo-European scholars concerning the distinction of temporal sequence and aspect in the Greek verb led *c.*1890–1910 to a flowering of aspect studies which assumed this distinction.[15] The new issue for discussion in these later works centres instead on what range of aspect-values occur in Greek or in the IE languages in general. However, the tendency of these discussions was towards the multiplying of categories and of conflicting terminology to describe them. An early listing was given by Streitberg (1889):

    1. Die *imperfective* actionsart, auch *durative* oder *continuative* a.

---

[12] Ibid. 172–4. It is interesting to note his use of the figure of 'point vs. line' to illustrate the difference between 'aoristic' and 'continuing' aspect (pp. 174–5). He uses this illustration in the *Schulgrammatik* (1855) and develops it more fully here (describing it as though it is original with him). This is perhaps the earliest specific use of 'Punkt' vs. 'Linie' in this way, a figure which later became a commonplace in descriptions of aspect.

[13] Later the term 'Aktionsart' was substituted for Curtius' *Zeitart*. Herbig cites Karl Brugmann for this change in terminology. See Herbig, 'Aktionsart und Zeitstufe', pp. 185–8.

[14] Later writers who develop these ideas and cite Curtius as the pioneer are: Delbrück (1879), Hultsch (1893), Miller (1895), and Herbig (1896). Mahlow (1883) and Mutzbauer (1893) present these ideas as axiomatic without reference to Curtius' work.

[15] See Blass (1889), Streitberg (1889, 1896), Mutzbauer (1893), Hultsch (1893), Miller (1895), Herbig (1896), Delbrück (1897), Purdie (1898), Meltzer (1901, 1904–5), Pedersen (1901, 1904), Brugmann (1902–4), Lindroth (1905), Stahl (1907), Rodenbusch (1907, 1908), Hentze (1907–8), and Schlachter (1907–9).

genannt. Sie stellt die handlung in ihrer ununterbrochenen dauer oder continuität dar. . . .

2. Die *perfective* actionsart, auch *resultative* a. geheißen. Sie fügt dem bedeutungsinhalt, der dem verbum innewohnt, noch den nebenbegriff des vollendet werdens hinzu. Sie bezeichnet also die handlung des verbums nicht schlechthin in ihrem fortgang, ihrer continuität, sondern stets im hinblick auf den *moment der vollendung*, die erziehlung des resultates. . . . [*The perfective verbs are then subdivided into two:*]

(*a*) Sie sind *momentan*, wenn sie den schwerpunkt einzig und allein auf den moment der vollendung, den augenblick des resultates legen, alles andere unberücksichtigt lassen. . . .

(*b*) Den gegensatz hierzu bilden die *durativ-perfectiven* verba. Auch sie heben den moment der vollendung hervor, setzen ihn aber in ausdrücklichen gegensatz zu der vorausgehenden *dauer* der handlung. . . .

3. Die *iterative* actionsart. Sie bezeichnet die handlung in ihrer widerholung. Die handlung selbst, die widerholt wird, kann entweder imperfectiv oder perfectiv sein. Wir erhalten demnach:

(*a*) *imperfectiv-iterative* verba. . .

(*b*) *perfectiv-iterative* verba. . .[16]

A later survey of Aktionsarten which utilized different nomenclature for the first two (more significant) categories was given by Brugmann (1902–4):

(1) *Punktuelle* (momentane, perfektive, aoristische) *Aktion* d. h. etwa: die Handlung wird mit ihrem Eintritt zugleich vollendet oder durch eine einzige Bewegung vollendet vorgestellt. . . .

(2) *Kursive* (durative, imperfektive) *Aktion:* die Handlung wird verlaufend vorgestellt ohne Rücksicht auf einzelne Akte innerhalb derselben und so, daß Anfangs- und Endpunkt aus dem Gesichtskreis bleiben. . . .

(3) *Perfektische Aktion*, d. h. Aktion des Perfektstamms: es wird ein

---

[16] Wilhelm Streitberg, 'Perfective und imperfective Actionsart im Germanischen', *BGDSL* 15 (1889), 70–2. In a similar listing of Aktionsarten in his *Urgermanische Grammatik* (Heidelberg: Carl Winter, 1896), 277–80, Streitberg includes these three categories virtually unaltered and adds two others: *inchoative* ('Sie drückt den ganz allmählichen Übergang von einem Zustand in den Andern aus') and *perfektische* ('bezeichnet die Handlung im Zustand des Vollenden– und Fertigseins').

Zustand des Subjekts bezeichnet, der sich aus einer vorhergehenden Handlung desselben ergeben hat. . . .

(4) *Iterative Aktion:* die Handlung wird als aus wiederholten gleichen Akten bestehend vorgestellt. . . .

(5) *Terminative* (durativ-perfektive) *Aktion:* eine Handlung wird vor sich gehend vorgestellt, doch so, daß ein Terminus, der Ausgangs- oder der Endpunkt, ins Auge gefaßt wird.[17]

These representative lists reflect the differences of opinion which existed at that time concerning the true nature of the distinctions in Aktionsart which were being presented. All agreed that these were not distinctions of *Zeitstufe*, but the further question of the specific nature of the Aktionsarten was not settled. To many writers of this period the primary Aktionsarten (e.g. present and aorist in Greek) reflected a distinction of 'incompletion versus completion'.[18] To others the issue of extension in time (i.e. durative vs. momentary) was still a primary consideration, though they emphasized that perceived duration is the point rather than actual duration or lack of it.[19] Others presented a third option, especially for the aorist, by arguing that it has primarily a constative, summarizing, or 'concentrating' meaning (with any perfective or momentary sense as subsidiary).[20] As a counterpart to this third view of the aorist, the present was thought to be cursive (i.e. viewing the action in its development or course of occurrence) rather than strictly incomplete or durative.[21]

These distinctions and where they fit in a general theory of aspect will be discussed in section 1.2. Here it is enough to

[17] Karl Brugmann, *Kurze vergleichende Grammatik der indogermanischen Sprachen* (Strasburg: Karl J. Trübner, 1902–4), 493–4.

[18] Friedrich Blass. 'Demosthenische Studien, III: Aorist und Imperfekt', *Rheinisches Museum für Philologie*, 44 (1889), 406–30; C. W. E. Miller, 'The Imperfect and the Aorist in Greek', *AJP* 16 (1895), 141–85; and Herbig, 'Aktionsart und Zeitstufe'.

[19] Friedrich Hultsch, 'Die erzählenden Zeitformen bei Polybios: Ein Beitrag zur Syntax der gemeingriechischen Sprache', *Abhandlungen der philologisch–historischen Classe der königlich Sächsischen Gesellschaft der Wissenschaften*, 13 (1893), 6–8.

[20] Eleanor Purdie, 'The Perfective "Aktionsart" in Polybius', *IF* 9 (1898), 67–8; Carl Mutzbauer, *Die Grundlagen der griechischen Tempuslehre und der homerische Tempusgebrauch* (Strasburg: Karl J. Trübner, 1893), 10–12, 21; and Stahl, *Syntax*, pp. 74–9.

[21] Mutzbauer, *Grundlagen*, pp. 25–7.

take note of this variety in approaches simply to illustrate the flowering of aspect study which occurred around the turn of the century as a result of Curtius' distinction of aspect from tense or temporal sequence.[22]

1. 1. 3 *Evaluation of the distinction*

The question which must now be considered is the validity of this distinction. Although the predominant opinion over the past hundred years has been that Curtius was right and that his distinction marked a major step forward,[23] others have dissented. Most of the dissent came later, since during the period just discussed Curtius' views were accepted almost without dispute.[24] Discussion of these ideas will help to clarify important questions about aspect.

The distinction of aspect from tense was supported in the early period by two lines of argument advanced by Curtius and others. The first support cited was *morphology* of the Greek verb-system. The discovery that the augment was associated with past-time value and that among the three normally augmented forms (aorist, imperfect, pluperfect) there remained a further distinction of aspect associated with the verbal stems[25] was regarded as firm evidence of this distinction. While it is recognized today that Greek verbal morphology is not this simplistic,[26] the general tenor of this argument

---

[22] One will notice how similar these ideas are to the treatment of aspect given in the standard reference–grammars for NT Greek, which also came essentially from this era of linguistic study. See Introduction, n. 5.

[23] See the recent standard discussions of aspect in Comrie, *Aspect*, pp. 1–6; and Lyons, *Semantics*, pp. 703–18; both treatments begin by affirming the distinction made by Curtius.

[24] A few writers objected to some features of Curtius' work but agreed with the basic distinction of aspect from tense: cf. Othon Riemann, 'La question de l'aoriste grec', in *Mélanges Graux: Recueil de travaux d'érudition classique* (Paris: Libraire du Collège de France, 1884), 585–7, 598; and C. Thurot, 'Observations sur la signification des radicaux temporaux en grec', *Mélanges de la Société de Linguistique de Paris*, 1 (1868), 111–25.

[25] Cf. Curtius, *Erläuterungen*, p. 171, as cited earlier.

[26] For example, the verbal suffixes (in addition to the augment) reflect a distinction

remains valid. Non-indicative verbs of present, aorist, and perfect form are distinct from each other not in terms of temporal sequence or of temporal relation to some *outside* reference-point, but reflect a difference in regard to the *internal* nature of the action itself.[27] Even though tense and aspect interact in complicated ways, there are morphological distinctions between these two in the Greek verb.[28]

The second line of argument presented by the early supporters of this distinction was the comparison of Greek usage to that of other languages in which aspect-differences were predominant and tense-differences were only secondary if they appeared at all. An increasing awareness of languages other than Latin, Greek, and the Western European languages led to significant advances in nineteenth-century language study, and this contributed to the analysis of Greek verbs as distinct from the traditional Latin tense-system. A most significant aid in this regard was comparison with the Slavic languages, which reflect an unmistakable category of *aspect* predominating over tense-values.[29] Curtius, who spent his early career in Prague,[30] cites the Slavonic languages in support of his distinction, and seems to have been helped greatly by a study published in 1851 by Kobliska, comparing the Greek aorist with Czech verb-forms.[31] Herbig too included a lengthy treatment of Slavic aspects in order to support such catego-

---

of past and non–past, which intersects in a complicated way with indications of mood, voice, person, and number. Also, the augment was optional in some eras of ancient Greek usage, though past-time value was apparently retained.

[27] SD, *Syntax*, pp. 248, 254, 269, 294. This distinction of external relationship vs. internal constituency is developed by Comrie, *Aspect*, pp. 1–4, and will be discussed later in this section. It was originally suggested by Curtius, *Erläuterungen*, p. 172.

[28] Comrie, *Aspect*, pp. 95–8.

[29] Even those who reject aspect–values for Greek and IE in general accept this analysis of Slavic languages. See Oswald Szemerényi, 'Review Article: Unorthodox Views of Tense and Aspect', *AL* 17 (1965), 166.

[30] SD, *Syntax*, p. 251, date his activity in Prague as 1849–54, during which his ideas became more clearly defined.

[31] Curtius, *Erläuterungen*, p. 174. The Czech work referred to is A. Kobliska, *Über das Verhältnis des Aorists zu den Formen des čechischen Verbums* (Königgräz, 1851), which I have not seen.

ries in the Greek verb.[32] The other language-family to which reference was made was the Semitic group, cited as lacking time-distinctions and operating with aspect-values instead.[33]

However, a line of argument based on comparison with other languages must always be of limited value. Comparison with other aspectual languages has some value, if only for illustrative purposes and for establishing the *plausibility* of an aspectual analysis of Greek, but it cannot, of course, finally prove that such a system is valid for Greek itself.

Adequate consideration of a distinction between aspect and tense requires the introduction of a further distinction within the category of tense. It has long been a commonplace of traditional grammar that tense can be regarded on two levels. One level is that of so-called primary or absolute tense, indicating the normal distinction of past, present, and future. The other level involves secondary or relative tense, which relates one event within an utterance to other events, indicating notions like antecedence, simultaneity, and subsequence. It is obvious that both levels involve matters of temporal relationship or sequence: relating the time of the event described by the verb to the time of some other event which serves as the reference-point. The only difference between primary and secondary tense is the nature of the reference-point; for the former the reference-point is the time of speaking (either in reality or rhetorically), while for the latter the reference-point is some other event within the utterance.

---

[32] Herbig, 'Aktionsart und Zeitstufe', pp. 186–92.

[33] Ibid. 161. In a later era, Jakob Wackernagel also cites Hebrew usage as illustrative of Greek aspects, in his *Vorlesungen über Syntax*. 2nd edn., 2 vols. (Basle: Emil Birkhäuser, 1926), i. 153. An aspectual description of the Semitic verb-system— i.e. one which emphasizes aspect over tense—is questioned by some, most recently Beat Zuber, *Das Tempussystem des biblischen Hebräisch: Eine Untersuchung am Text* (Beiheft zur ZAW 164; Berlin: Walter de Gruyter, 1986). but it appears to be the most widely accepted view among Semitic grammarians. See the surveys by Tryggve N. D. Mettinger. 'The Hebrew Verb System: A Survey of Recent Research', *Annual of the Swedish Theological Institute*, 9 (1973), 65–84; and Leslie McFall, *The Enigma of the Hebrew Verbal System; Solutions From Ewald to the Present Day* (Sheffield: Almond Press, 1982).

Another way of phrasing this would be to say, with Lyons, that primary tenses are 'deictic', secondary tenses are 'non-deictic'. Deixis is the function of various linguistic features (e.g. personal pronouns, demonstrative pronouns, definite article) to relate the utterances in which they occur to the time and place of the act of utterance.[34] Primary tense serves to indicate the temporal relationship of the *event described* to the *speech-event*, a situation outside of the utterance itself. The temporal relations expressed by secondary tense are all within the utterance itself and are thus non-deictic.[35]

The value of introducing this distinction in tense is to note that verbal aspect bears very little similarity to *primary* tense. In Lyons's terms, aspect is non-deictic, and does nothing to relate the event described to the time of the utterance.[36] However, aspect does at times involve features of meaning which are similar to *secondary* tenses. Progressive or continuous aspect (to speak generally) is parallel in some ways to 'simultaneous' or 'contemporaneous' tense, while aspects of completion or termination have parallels with 'antecedent' tenses. Thus, it is more difficult to distinguish aspects from relative or secondary tenses,[37] because there is an overlap in function. This overlap is evident in sentences with temporal clauses, where the parallels just mentioned go hand in hand. For example, in Acts 10: 7–8 and 10: 17 there are temporal

---

[34] Lyons, *Semantics*, pp. 636–7, 677–8.

[35] Roman Jakobson, *Shifters, Verbal Categories, and the Russian Verb* (Cambridge, Mass.: Harvard University Press, 1957), repr. in *Roman Jakobson: Selected Writings*, ii. *Word and Language* (The Hague: Mouton, 1971), 134–5, makes the same observations in slightly different terms. Using the word 'tense' to mean primary tense and coining the word 'taxis' for secondary tense, he writes: 'Tense characterizes the narrated event with reference to the speech event;' and 'Taxis characterizes the narrated event in relation to another narrated event and without reference to the speech event'.

[36] Lyons, *Semantics*, p. 705. In Jakobson's words, aspect 'characterizes the narrated event itself . . . without reference to the speech event' (*Shifters*, p. 134).

[37] Lyons, *Semantics*, pp. 689, 705. The same point is made by Yurij S. Maslov, 'An Outline of Contrastive Aspectology', in Yurij S. Maslov (ed.), *Contrastive Studies in Verbal Aspect*, trans. and annotated by James Forsyth in collaboration with Josephine Forsyth (Heidelberg: Julius Groos, 1985), 2–6, and by Östen Dahl, *Tense and Aspect Systems* (Oxford: Basil Blackwell, 1985), 24–5.

clauses parallel in structure, but differing in the tense used. In the first, the aorist occurs and the meaning is a combination of 'summary or indefinite' aspect and the secondary tense-value of 'antecedent' time:

Acts 10: 7-8 ὡς δὲ ἀπῆλθεν ὁ ἄγγελος ὁ λαλῶν αὐτῷ, φωνήσας δύο τῶν οἰκετῶν . . . ἀπέστειλεν αὐτοὺς εἰς Ἰόππην.

In the second, the present aspect (i.e. imperfect indicative) is used and the sense combines 'progressive or continuous' aspect with a time-value of 'simultaneous' occurrence:

Acts 10: 17 ὡς δὲ ἐν ἑαυτῷ διηπόρει ὁ Πέτρος τί ἂν εἴη τὸ ὅραμα ὁ εἶδεν, ἰδοὺ οἱ ἄνδρες . . . ἐπέστησαν ἐπὶ τὸν πυλῶνα . . .

This overlap is also observable in some chains of narrative clauses, in which perfective (aorist) verbs indicate sequenced events occurring one after another as the 'main line' of the narrative, while imperfect verbs indicate simultaneous occurrences, which fill in background circumstances of the narrative. Although it is only a brief bit of narration, 1 Cor. 3: 6 appears to be best explained in this way: ἐγὼ ἐφύτευσα, Ἀπολλῶς ἐπότισεν, ἀλλὰ ὁ θεὸς ηὔξανεν. Illustrations of this in a more extended passage can be seen in Acts 7: 20–5.[38]

Comrie discusses an example of the former kind ('John was reading when I entered') and argues that the aspects in such cases serve to indicate the temporal relation of one action to another only as a *secondary* consequence of the more important non-temporal (i.e. unrelated to time-sequence) value of the aspects.[39] Others have studied examples like these and arrived at different conclusions, which lead them to call into question the entire distinction of tense and aspect which began with Curtius. The ideas of these writers must now be discussed.

The influential distinction of tense and aspect by Curtius has been questioned from two different viewpoints, broadly

---

[38] These meanings for the aspects are discussed in sects. 1.4 and 3.4.1.

[39] Comrie, *Aspect*, p. 5. This overlap in meaning between aspect–function and secondary tense is undeniable; either could produce the same contextual effect. The question to be decided is one of priority: which is more basic and which is secondary.

considered. These objections are associated with two approaches to aspect which emphasize insights from other disciplines: a psychological-philosophical approach, and an approach seeking the meaning of the aspects in the wider literary context.

The former set of objections are derived from approaches to aspect based on psychological and philosophical analyses of the nature of time and how the human mind encounters the flow of time. Two writers in particular have taken this approach, and they are sometimes thought to object to Curtius' distinction: E. Koschmieder and G. Guillaume.

Erwin Koschmieder has been a very prolific writer on the subject of aspect over the years.[40] His views are distinctive and are often mentioned in surveys of aspectology, usually in order to register disagreement with him.[41] But several later scholars have argued that his ideas should be followed, especially in his view that aspect is essentially time-based at its root.[42] In brief, Koschmieder argues that aspects are distinctions in how the mind encounters the *temporal direction* of an event: aspect is a grammatical category for reflecting the relationship of the event to the 'I' on a time-line *(Zeitrichtungsbezug).* If the mind conceives the 'I' moving from past to future towards the event, an imperfect aspect is used; if the mind conceives the event moving from future to past towards the 'I', a perfect aspect is used.[43] Szemerényi argues that these ideas show the primarily *temporal* nature of IE 'aspect' and that this is not aspect in the Slavic sense. In discussing the work of Galton, who (according to Szemerényi) has followed Koschmieder's view in an

---

[40] See the following works: 'Studien zum slavischen Verbalaspekt', *KZ* 55 (1927), 280–304; ibid. 56 (1928), 78–95; *Zeitbezug und Sprache: ein Beitrag zur Aspekt- und Tempusfrage* (Leipzig: B. G. Teubner, 1929); 'Zu den Grundfragen der Aspekttheorie', *IF* 53 (1935), 280–300; 'Aspekt und Zeit', in M. Braun and E. Koschmieder (eds.), *Slawistische Studien zum V. Internationalen Slawistenkongreß in Sofia 1963* (Göttingen: Vandenhoeck and Ruprecht, 1963), 1–22.

[41] Cf. Jens Holt, *Études d'aspect* (Acta Jutlandica, 15. 2; Copenhagen: Munksgaard, 1943), 9–13. Gonda, *Aspectual Function*, p. 19; and Lloyd, *Verb*, p. 13.

[42] Cf. Ružić (1943), Schlachter (1959), and Raith (1969).

[43] Koschmieder, *Zeitbezug*, pp. 47–8.

adapted form, Szemerényi insists, 'Surely the whole point of his [Galton's] book was to show that the difference between aor. and impf.—the main prop of current views on IE, i.e. Greek "aspect"—is temporal not aspectual.[44]

However, Koschmieder himself agrees with Curtius' distinction of aspect from *Zeitstufe*, and the practical result of his views is much like the description of aspect which will be given in this book, even though he bases his ideas in a time-oriented approach theoretically. For example, when Koschmieder discusses the meaning of the Slavic (and Greek) aspects in his 1929 book, he articulates a fairly standard distinction of imperfect (or present) as 'geschehend' vs. perfective (or aorist) as 'geschehen'. Although he does centre his theoretical description on *Zeitrichtungsbezug* and say that the aspects are concerned with 'the course of the activity in time', he goes on to say that these meanings are expressed '. . . ganz ohne Rücksicht auf die Zeitstufe.'[45] It seems quite correct to understand some sort of distinction in reference-point in the meaning of the IE aspects (to be discussed later), but this does not deny the distinction from *Zeitstufe*. However, Koschmieder's focus on *Zeitrichtungsbezug* is unconvincing and unnecessary.[46] A simpler description of the aspects without appeal to this feature is generally accepted today, and such an approach will be presented and validated below.

Another scholar whose views should be mentioned here is Gustave Guillaume. Like Koschmieder, he describes aspect in philosophical and psychological terms and associates it with differing ways in which an individual encounters the flow of time. However, he also accepts the distinction of aspect from *Zeitstufe*, and describes the aspects (of French, Latin, Greek,

---

[44] Szemerényi, 'Unorthodox Views', p. 166. In his *Einführung in die vergleichende Sprachwissenschaft* (Darmstadt: Wissenschaftliche Buchgesellschaft, 1970), 286–8, Szemerényi argues that aspect (as it exists in Slavic languages) is absent from IE and Greek.

[45] *Zeitbezug*, pp. 46–7.

[46] Cf. Nils B. Thelin, *Towards a Theory of Aspect, Tense and Actionality in Slavic* (Uppsala: Acta Universitatis Upsaliensis, 1978), 12–14.

and Russian) in quite traditional terms.[47] This is seen also in a
more recent writer who follows the Guillaumean approach,
W. H. Hirtle. In two books on English aspect Hirtle supports
a clear dichotomy between aspect and time by speaking of
event-time ('contained in the event expressed by the verb')
and universe-time ('containing the event'). Universe-time is
the realm of temporal differences like past, present, and
future, while event-time is the domain of aspect.[48] When
Hirtle comes to define the simple/progressive opposition, it
sounds very much like aspect in the tradition of Curtius:

The opposition between simple and progressive is therefore basically
one between whole and part. An event whose material significate
strikes the mind as being complete, as permitting of no further
additions, will be expressed by the simple form. One which gives the
impression of lacking something, of leaving room for something to
come, will be expressed by the progressive. In grammatical terms
this opposition can be stated thus: the simple form is *perfective*, the
progressive *imperfective*.[49]

Jacob (1967) and Martin (1971)[50] have also followed
Guillaume in their books on aspect. However, it must be
reiterated in conclusion that the views of both Koschmieder
and Guillaume do not call into question the basic difference
suggested by Curtius.

A more serious objection to the distinction of aspect and
tense has been advanced by writers who emphasize the
function of aspect in the wider literary context and define

---

[47] See Gustave Guillaume, *Temps et verbe: Théorie des aspects, des modes et des temps*
(Paris: Champion, 1929; repr. by Champion, 1984), and the essays collected in
Langage et science du langage (Quebec: Les Presses de L'Université Laval, 1964).

[48] W. H. Hirtle, *The Simple and Progressive Forms: An Analytical Approach* (Quebec:
Les Presses de l'Université Laval, 1967), 14–16; and id. *Time Aspect and the Verb*
(Quebec: Les Presses de l'Université Laval, 1975), 22–31.

[49] Hirtle, *Simple and Progressive Forms*, pp. 26–7.

[50] André Jacob, *Temps et langage* (Paris: Libraire Armand Colin, 1967); and Robert
Martin, *Temps et aspect: Essai sur l'emploi des temps narratifs en moyen français* (Paris:
Klincksieck, 1971). A critique of Jacob's book (and of the Guillaumean school) on
wider linguistic grounds is given by M. G. Worthington, 'In Search of Linguistic
Time', *Romance Philology*, 22 (1969), 515–30.

aspect as essentially an indication of 'relative time'. Bakker advances this idea in a limited way in *The Greek Imperative* (1966). Taking a suggestion from Seiler (1952),[51] he argues that the present or imperfect aspect denotes 'coincidence' with the action of another verb, or 'the assumption of a close connection with another verbal notion', while the aorist presents the action absolutely, without noting such coincidence.[52] Bakker adds that the other verbal notion with which the present aspect is connected will either occur nearby or 'if not explicitly expressed, must be implied', and he further explains that the connection or coincidence need not be temporal, but may be causal or some other logical relation.[53] However, it is clear that his starting-point for defining the aspects is the notion of relative time (coincidence), and he moves out from there to include related notions of non-temporal connection.[54]

This view is advanced more forcefully by Ruijgh and Hettrich (who bases his work on Ruijgh). Ruijgh argues that aspect is fundamentally a matter of temporal relationship. He writes: 'Il ne faut pas oublier qu'au fond, l'aspect est lui aussi une catégorie d'ordre temporel. . . . Il n'est donc pas correct de dire, comme on le fait souvent, que les thèmes du présent, de l'aoriste et du parfait n'expriment pas le temps mais l'aspect.'[55] Later he summarizes as follows:

---

[51] Hansjakob Seiler, *L'Aspect et le temps dans le verbe neo–grec* (Paris: Les Belles Lettres, 1952).

[52] W. F. Bakker, *The Greek Imperative: An Investigation into the Aspectual Differences between the Present and Aorist Imperatives in Greek Prayer from Homer up to the Present Day* (Amsterdam: Adolf M. Hakkert, 1966), 23–7. This view is presented also in his article 'A Remark on the Use of the Imperfect and Aorist in Herodotus', *Mnemosyne* 4th ser. 21 (1968), 22–8.

[53] Bakker, *Greek Imperative*, pp. 23–4.

[54] Though Bakker states that Seiler's notion of coincidence 'will provide us with an aspect theory on which the rest of this study is based' (p. 22), and though he cites this idea as the basic value of the aspects later in his study (pp. 31, 65–6), it is reported by Mussies, *Morphology*, 268 n. 3, that Bakker did not intend this notion as an exhaustive description of the aspects in ancient Greek.

[55] C. J. Ruijgh, *Autour de 'τε épique': Études sur la syntaxe grecque* (Amsterdam: Adolf M. Hakkert, 1971), 231.

Après tout, nous avons donc le droit de conclure que le système des thèmes temporels du grec sert à l'expression des rapports temporels, tout comme celui du latin, du français et des langues germaniques, bien que les valeurs exprimées par les différents éléments du système grec ne coïncident pas avec celles du latin, du français, etc.; l'aspect, lui aussi, est donc un rapport temporel.[56]

Taking this view of aspect, Ruijgh must posit a reference-point to which the verbal action may be temporally related. This he describes as 'the moment given by the context or by the situation', and he proceeds from there to give definitions of the present and aorist aspects: 'Le thème du présent signale que le procès verbal continue au-delà d'un moment donné par le contexte ou la situation. . . . Le thème de l'aoriste signale que le procès verbal est un fait accompli à un moment donné.'[57]

Hettrich takes this view as his starting-point and sets out to show its validity in a large number of temporal clauses in Herodotus. He emphasizes that too many treatments of aspect look at the verb-form alone or only at the sentence in which it occurs, and he rightly argues that the wider context must be considered in analysis of aspect-usage. In a study of Herodotus, Hettrich finds Ruijgh's view to be valid for aspect-usage in temporal clauses, and he suggests a broader applicability to other situations, though he does not examine others in detail.[58]

Another who argues for this approach to aspect is Rijksbaron, who defines the Greek present and aorist as follows: '. . . the present stem signifies that the verbal action continues through a point in time given in context or situation and is,

---

[56] Ibid. 233.

[57] Ibid. 235. A more recent, wide–ranging treatment of aspect by Ruijgh is given in 'L'emploi "inceptif" du thème du présent du verbe grec: Esquisse d'une théorie de valeurs temporelles des thèmes temporels', *Mnemosyne*, 4th ser. 38 (1985), 1–61. This reiterates his basic temporal approach to aspect, while adjusting it in some details and discussing examples of infinitive and imperative usage in classical usage, especially in response to the work of Stork, *Aspectual Usage*.

[58] Heinrich Hettrich, *Kontext und Aspekt in der altgriechischen Prosa Herodots* (Göttingen: Vandenhoeck and Ruprecht, 1976), 12–24, 94–7.

therefore, *not-completed* (imperfective value) . . . the aorist stem signifies that the verbal action is *completed* at a point in time given in context or situation (confective value)'.[59] He states that these stems have various senses in specific contexts, but emphasizes temporal relation above other features of meaning.[60]

One final writer to mention here is Galton, who combines elements of the philosophical-psychological approach (of Koschmieder and Guillaume) with the wider contextual perspective (of Ruijgh *et al.*). Galton rejects much of recent aspect theory and offers in its place a system suggested by the metaphysical reflections of Kant and Whitehead as to the nature of time and our experience of it. Galton argues that time involves both succession and simultaneity, motion and rest, change and permanence:

Now the flow of time, to be perceived by us, does not only require a succession of changing events, but also a background of unchanging states against which the former can be set. Unchanging states and changing events lie, therefore, at the basis of our perception of time. . . . and although reality only presents us with a constant flow of events, the only way we can handle it and them is by marking imaginary fixed points in the eternal flow of time and effecting artificial delimitations in it. . . . I emphasize especially the point that only the flow, the succession, is given in reality, whereas the underlying, immutable perserverance represents a necessary fiction that constitutes its dialectic counterpart.[61]

These two, he argues, are the basic distinctions between the perfective and imperfective aspects in Slavic: the perfective is

---

[59] Rijksbaron *SSV*, p. 1. See similar ideas in T. Givón, *Syntax: A Functional–Typological Introduction*, i (Amsterdam and Philadelphia: John Benjamins, 1984), 272–6.

[60] Ibid. 1–3.

[61] Herbert Galton, *The Main Functions of the Slavic Verbal Aspect* (Skopje: Macedonian Academy of Sciences and Arts, 1976), 9–10. These ideas were presented also in his earlier book, *Aorist und Aspekt im Slavischen: Eine Studie zur funktionellen und historischen Syntax* (Wiesbaden: Harrassowitz, 1962).

[62] Galton, *Slavic Verbal Aspect*, pp. 11–12. See also id. 'A New Theory of the Slavic Verbal Aspect', *AL* 16 (1964), 143–4.

used to show the succession of events, and the imperfective to stop the flow of time and dwell on an unchanging state or durative process in disregard of the temporal sequence.[62] The aspects thus are a matter of time-sequence within a context, and other distinctions in aspect are developments of these temporal meanings, in his view.

The ideas advanced by these writers illustrate the overlap in function between aspect and 'relative' or 'secondary' tenses, as noted above. However, it is reductionistic to argue from this overlap that aspect is nothing more than relative time, or that it is only a matter of a temporal nature. There is a temporal meaning (of a non-deictic sort) which can be involved in aspect-function: the underlying logic of notions such as duration, progression, completion, and some other functions of the aspects show that temporal meanings of a sort can be produced. It is true also that the aspects function *within a context* in ways similar to relative tenses. All of these functions should be noted and described in our discussion of aspect-usage. But the various functions of aspect (to be detailed later) are very difficult to explain on the theory that this is all there is to aspect or that this temporal element is primary. Instead it is the argument of this book that such meanings are a *secondary* function of aspect when combined with other elements like the verb's inherent lexical meaning, adverbs, and so forth. It seems better to argue, as Comrie does, that these meanings are secondary effects of the aspects, rather than a reflection of the essential nature of the aspects as temporal.[63]

But what value do the aspects express which allows this parallel in meaning between aspect- and 'relative' tense-values? Comrie suggests that it is the feature of 'viewpoint', or whether the action is viewed from from *within* or from *outside*.[64] But the further point which must be developed is that this viewpoint feature implicitly involves the relationship between

[63] Comrie, *Aspect*, p. 5.
[64] Ibid. This distinction appears prominently in E. Hermann, 'Objektive und subjektive Aktionsart', *IF* 45 (1927), 213–14; and 'Aspekt und Aktionsart', *NGG* (1933), 477–8.

the *action described* and a *reference-point* or vantage-point from which the action is viewed.[65] The crucial distinction, then, is whether the reference-point is *internal* or *external* to the action. The action can be viewed from a reference-point *within* the action, without reference to the beginning or end-point of the action, but with focus instead on its internal structure or make-up. Or the action can be viewed from a vantage-point *outside* the action, with focus on the whole action from beginning to end, but without reference to its internal structure.[66] The former viewpoint is naturally compatible with a 'relative' tense-value of contemporaneous occurrence, since the event is viewed from within. The latter viewpoint is often associated with antecedence, since the view includes the end-point of the action.[67]

However, this relationship between the action and the reference-point from which it is viewed is not primarily a *chronological* one, even though it can produce that effect. If the relationship must be pictured in any dimension, a *spatial* one fits better, since the distinction is one of proximity vs. distance.[68] In order to view the action from within and ignore

[65] This is like Marion R. Johnson's proposal in 'A Unified Temporal Theory of Tense and Aspect', in *Tense and Aspect* (1981), 145–8, that three temporal reference-points are important for verbal predication: the point of speech (when the act of speaking takes place), the point of the event (when the action described takes place), and the point of reference (some other point of time to which these can be related). These are based on suggestions by Hans Reichenbach, *Elements of Symbolic Logic* (New York: Macmillan, 1947). The function of aspect, in Johnson's view, is to show the relationship of the event–time to some point of reference. The weakness of this approach is that it gives too much emphasis to the *temporal* relation of the event to the reference–point. See the critique of this in the following discussion.

[66] The best development of these ideas is found in Lloyd, *Verb*, pp. 71–6, 79, 88. See also the very clear treatment in Carlota S. Smith, 'A Theory of Aspectual Choice', *Lg.* 59 (1983), 479–82.

[67] This connection is suggested by A. Rijksbaron, Review of H. Hettrich, *Kontext und Aspekt in der altgriechischen Prosa Herodots*, in *Lingua*, 48 (1979), 228, 251; Rijksbaron, *SSV*, pp. 1–2; and Roland Harweg, 'Aspekte als Zeitstufen und Zeitstufen als Aspekte', *Linguistics*, 181 (1976), 5–28.

[68] Harweg (op. cit. 6–8) recognizes both the spatial and temporal options for explaining this relationship, but argues for the temporal one. Gernot L. Windfuhr, 'A Spatial Model for Tense, Aspect, and Mood', *Folia Linguistica*, 19 (1985), 415–61, discusses both and decides for a spatial approach. He argues that even *tense*-categories

the initial and final limits, the vantage-point must be *near*, an internal perspective; on the other hand, viewing the whole action from beginning to end without focus on the internal make-up of the action most naturally fits a *remote* or distanced perspective. If the relationship of the reference-point to the action were primarily a chronological or temporal one, the Greek aorist should appear only as an occurrence *antecedent* to some reference-point (as Ruijgh argues). In many cases this is acceptable, but in many others the aorist is presented as an action yet to take place (especially in the subjunctive and imperative forms): the reference-point from which the action is regarded is the present (the time of speaking), not some hypothetical time in the future when the action will actually stand completed. The action can be viewed as a whole from beginning to end in any chronological arrangement as long as the action is *remote* so that the whole act can be viewed in perspective: the act will more naturally be antecedent or subsequent since both of these are distanced from the reference-point, but it could even be simultaneous as long as the act is viewed 'from afar', as a total occurrence without regard to any specific internal details of action which are actually contemporaneous with the reference-point.[69] Thus, the aspectual relationship of event and reference-point is not essentially or primarily chronological, but as described here it is easily compatible with and closely parallel to the 'relative' tense-values so important to the theories of Ruijgh, Rijksbaron, and others. The relative time-values are a secondary effect of the aspects in context rather than a feature central to what the aspects themselves denote.

are better seen as focusing on (e.g.) the 'here' than on the 'now'. John Anderson, *An Essay Concerning Aspect* (The Hague: Mouton, 1973), esp. 39–40, has developed the spatial/local conception of aspect extensively, and his view of the imperfective is similar to the one given in this book. But his analysis of the perfective/aorist aspect (to locate an event *at* a certain point in time) is not as helpful as the option taken here.

[69] The idea of remoteness as a necessity for the perfective/aoristic aspect is discussed by Carl Bache, 'Aspect and Aktionsart: Towards a Semantic Distinction', *JL* 18 (1982), 67, who suggests rightly that the remoteness may be either temporal or *modal:* 'the situation must be placed in the past, in the future or be conceived of as hypothetical, necessary etc'.

1. 1. 4 *Summary of the relationship of aspect and tense*

In conclusion to this treatment of the relationship of aspect and tense, it must be stated that Curtius was essentially correct in distinguishing aspects in Greek from 'primary' tenses such as past, present, and future. Though aspect does produce temporal meanings of a certain sort (e.g. duration, termination), these are the effect of aspect's combination with other factors and are related to the *internal* nature of the verbal action. They have no connection with the *external* relationship of the action to the time of speaking (i.e. deictic temporal reference or primary tense-meaning).[70]

There is also the overlap in meaning between aspect and 'secondary' or non-deictic tense-meaning, as discussed above. This results in the subsidiary function of the aspects to show temporal relations between events in a narrative and perhaps other functions involving the larger context.[71]

1. 2 Aspect and Procedural Characteristics of Verbs, Verb-Phrases, and Actual Situations

The next major advance in aspect studies after the distinction from tense involved the insight that aspect should be distinguished from another closely related feature of verbal meaning: the procedural characteristics of actual occurrences and of other linguistic elements. This advance came, broadly speaking, in three steps: the distinction from Aktionsart, from lexical characteristics of verbs, and from the meaning of words and phrases used in composition with the verb (e.g. adverbs, prepositional phrases, objects).

---

[70] Comrie, *Aspect*, pp. 1–3. This contrast of 'internal constituency (aspect) vs. external relationship (tense)' was suggested earlier by Holt, *Études d'aspect*, p. 46.

[71] It is true, moreover, that in the Greek *indicative* the aspects of 'present', aorist, and perhaps the perfect and future (associated in form with the verb–stems) are linked with tense–values of present, past, and future (meanings associated with the augment and verbal suffixes). This interference of primary tense with aspect affects the function of the aspects in various ways, which will be detailed in ch. 4.

1. 2. 1 *Aspect and Aktionsart*

In the period from Curtius until the 1920s the words 'Zeitart', 'Aktionsart', and 'aspect' were used with few exceptions as synonymous terms to label the feature of verbal meaning which Curtius and others had distinguished from *Zeitstufe* or tense. Aspect or Aktionsart (the term 'Zeitart' fell into disuse in the late nineteenth century) was described as concerned with the *nature* of the action or the *kind* of action portrayed by the verb, and matters such as duration, repetition, completion, momentariness, inception, and so forth were cited as illustration. A few writers pointed out that Aktionsart or aspect involved the *perceived* nature of the action rather than the *actual* external nature of the action itself.[72] But until the 1920s most spoke of Aktionsart or aspect interchangeably as something to do with the nature of the action (with its duration, repetition, etc.).

One writer who was an exception to this pattern, although he became influential only later, was Sigurd Agrell. In a treatment of the Polish tenses he drew a distinction between aspect and Aktionsart as follows:

Unter *Aktionsart* verstehe ich . . . nicht die beiden Hauptkategorien des slavischen Zeitwortes, die unvollendete und die vollendete Handlungsform (das Imperfektivum und das Perfektivum)—diese nenne ich *Aspekte*. Mit dem Ausdruck Aktionsart bezeichne ich bisher fast gar nicht beachtete—geschweige denn klassifizierte— *Bedeutungsfunktionen* der Verbalkomposita (sowie einiger Simplicia und Suffixbildungen), *die genauer ausdrücken* wie *die Handlung vollbracht wird*, die *Art und Weise* ihrer Ausführung markieren.[73]

Agrell states that the aspects simply note *that* an action is fulfilled, while the Aktionsarten tell *how* it is carried out. He follows his basic distinction with a discussion and listing of twenty types of Aktionsarten. These include categories like resultative, effective, momentary, durative, terminative, cur-

---

[72] e.g. Hultsch, 'Die erzählenden Zeitformen bei Polybios', pp. 6–7.

[73] Sigurd Agrell, *Aspektänderung und Aktionsartbildung beim polnischen Zeitworte* (Lunds Universitets Årsskrift, 4. 2; Lund: H. Ohlsson, 1908), 78 (his emphasis).

sive, and inchoative,[74] which had been commonly cited as aspect/Aktionsart categories before then. He does not, however, discuss *aspect* in the new sense, but simply illustrates it by reference to the Slavic aspects of 'fulfilled' vs. 'unfulfilled'.

This distinction was not picked up by others until the mid-1920s, when it was articulated and expanded in a series of influential articles by Jacobsohn, Porzig, and Hermann.[75] The difference traced in these articles between Aktionsart and aspect was, in summary, as follows:

Aktionsart involves how the action actually occurs; reflects the external, objective facts of the occurrence; focuses on something outside the speaker. This is usually expressed lexically, either in the inherent meaning of the lexical form or in the derivational morphology (i.e. by means of prefixes or suffixes which affect the meaning of the verb).

Aspect involves a way of viewing the action; reflects the subjective conception or portrayal by the speaker; focuses on the speaker's representation of the action. This is usually expressed grammatically, by contrasting verb-pairs as in Slavic languages or by tense-inflexion and tense-stems as in Greek.[76]

---

[74] Ibid. 2, 82, 121–7.

[75] Wackernagel referred to Agrell's distinction in his *Vorlesungen über Syntax*, i. 153, but he does not explain it or adhere to it in his treatment. In a review of Wackernagel, Hermann Jacobsohn, *Gnomon*, 2 (1926), 369–95, developed this distinction extensively and attempted to define aspect accordingly, thus moving the discussion beyond Agrell's suggestive beginning, although he later asserted that he knew nothing of Agrell's work when writing the review. Influenced by Jacobsohn, Walter Porzig carried such ideas further in his 'Zur Aktionsart indogermanischer Präsensbildungen', *IF* 45 (1927), 152–67. Eduard Hermann suggested the same distinctions (using different terms and initially without knowledge of the work of Agrell, Jacobsohn, or Porzig) in 'Objektive und subjektive Aktionsart'. In later interaction between Jacobsohn, Hermann, and Koschmieder these ideas were refined further: Jacobsohn, 'Aspektfragen', *IF* 51 (1933), 292–318; Hermann, 'Aspekt und Aktionsart'; Koschmieder, 'Zu den Grundfragen der Aspekttheorie'; and Hermann, 'Aspekt und Zeitrichtung', *IF* 54 (1936), 262–4.

[76] e.g. Jacobsohn, Review of Wackernagel, *Vorlesungen über Syntax* p. 379, writes concerning aspect: 'Es handelt sich... um subjektive Anschauungsformen, d. h. es wird in ihnen zum Ausdruck gebracht, wie der Sprecher den Verlauf der Handlung

This distinction is a very important one to make, for several reasons which these writers pointed out. First, some of the differences between Aktionsarten or aspects (in the older sense) were not actually differences in the grammatical form, but were inherent in the lexical meaning or in the effect of prefixed elements.[77] For example, 'terminative' and 'intensive' meanings are expressed frequently by prepositions prefixed to the verb-root, as seen in cases like κατεσθίω and ἐκδιώκω, and do not come directly from the perfective/aoristic forms. Durative meaning is often a matter of lexical sense rather than grammatical function, as verbs like μένω and οἰκέω in any tense-form show.[78] Second, it is clear that the aspects (in the newer sense) involve some degree of subjectivity, since in some cases the same external actions can, depending on the speaker's choice, be described by either of the primary aspect-forms.[79] The variation in Mark 12: 41 and 12: 44 from imperfect ἔβαλλον to aorist ἔβαλον is just such a case. Also, some problems in aspectology which defied solution in earlier discussions are closer to being solved when seen in the light of

ansieht. Im Gegensatz dazu aber liegt den Kategorien wie Iterativ, Intensiv, Kausativ [i.e. *Aktionsarten*] ein objektiv anderer Tatbestand zugrunde als beim Simplex'. See also Porzig's description in 'Zur Aktionsart', p. 152: 'Die *Aktionsart* ist die Art, wie eine Handlung oder ein Vorgang verläuft. . . . der *Aspekt* dagegen ist der Gesichtspunkt, unter dem ein Vorgang betrachtet wird nämlich *ob* als Verlauf *oder* als Ereignis'.

[77] Otto Jespersen, *The Philosophy of Grammar* (London: George Allen and Unwin, 1924), 286–9, noted a host of lexical, prefixal, and adverbial meanings (e.g. conclusion, duration, finished action, repetition, change of condition, implication of a result; and their opposites) which he felt had been indiscriminately included under the one category of aspect/Aktionsart, and he suggested that such meanings be classified separately from the grammatical distinction of the Slavic perfective and imperfective forms.

[78] Cf. Jacobsohn, 'Aspektfragen', pp. 315–16; and Hermann, 'Aspekt und Aktionsart', pp. 477–9.

[79] Hermann, 'Objektive und subjektive Aktionsart', pp. 207–8. He cites Hdt. 1. 16 ἐβασίλευσεν ἔτεα δυώδεκα, and argues that the Greek imperfect could have been used: 'Der Unterschied zwischen ἐβασίλευον "ich war König" und ἐβασίλευσα "ich war König" liegt lediglich in der Auffassung des Sprechenden; denn es kommt nur darauf an, ob man sich das Königsein als im Verlauf begriffen vorstellt oder ob man es zusammenfaßt. . . . Der Unterschied zwischen der komplexiven und der kursiven Aktionsart [*i.e. aspect*] ist demnach nur durch die Auffassung gegeben, nicht durch zwei verschiedene außerhalb des Sprechenden liegende Tatsachen'.

this distinction. Disagreement over the basic significance of the Greek aorist and over how to accommodate so-called 'extended' aorists[80] in one's view has been a perennial problem, but a solution is closer when the sense of the aorist is regarded separately from the inherent meaning of the verb.

These distinctions were developed primarily by the group of scholars mentioned above, but their ideas were quickly adopted and followed by a wider range of writers,[81] and in some form they are accepted by virtually all aspectologists to this day.[82] The distinction between aspect and Aktionsart in this general sense will be adopted in this book as a basic axiom, and its usefulness will be demonstrated in later chapters.

While agreeing with this basic distinction, several writers in the initial discussion made significant corrections to the way in which the difference had been portrayed. Koschmieder agreed that Aktionsart centres on lexical meaning as opposed to the grammatical meaning of the verbal form, but he noted that the lexical sense should not be limited to the verb alone. The sense of the whole phrase in which the verb occurs must be considered in assessing the Aktionsart meaning of a particular verb.[83] More importantly, Koschmieder and Jacob-

---

[80] e.g. aorists which involve an extended or durative meaning due to some combination of factors, such as Acts 28: 30 ἐνέμεινεν δὲ διετίαν ὅλην ἐν ἰδίῳ μισθώματι and Rev. 20: 4 ἐβασίλευσαν μετὰ τοῦ Χριστοῦ χίλια ἔτη.

[81] See F. Stiebitz, 'Aspekt und Aktionsart', *Listy filologicke*, 55 (1928), 1–13; N. Van Wijk, '"Aspect" en "Ationsart"', *Die nieuwe taalgids*, 22 (1929), 225–39; B. Faddegon, 'The Categories of Tense; or Time, Manner of Action, and Aspect, as Expressed by the Verb', in *Donum Natalicium Schrijnen* (Nijmegen: N. V. Dekker and Van de Vegt, 1929) 116–29; Eugen Seidel, 'Zu den Funktionen des Verbalaspekts', *Travaux du Cercle Linguistique de Prague*, 6 (1936), 111–29; Else Hollmann, *Untersuchungen über Aspekt und Aktionsart, unter besonderer Berücksichtigung des Altenglischen* (Ph.D. thesis, University of Jena, 1935; Würzburg: Konrad Triltsch, 1937); H. M. Sørensen. 'Om definitionerne af verbets aspekter', in *In Memoriam Kr. Sandfeld* (Copenhagen: Gyldendalske Boghandel Nordisk Forlag, 1943) 221–33; and J. Brunel, 'L'aspect et "L'ordre de procès" en grec', *BSL* 42 (1946), 43–75. See Hollmann, pp. 3–17, for a survey of the development of this distinction from Agrell to Hermann and Jacobsohn.

[82] Lloyd, *Verb*, p. 10, says of Jacobsohn and Hermann: 'their basic assumption that aspect is not the same as *Aktionsart* is universally accepted today'. This is not entirely correct, as shown below.

[83] Koschmieder, 'Zu den Grundfragen der Aspekttheorie', pp. 285–6. This is certainly correct and will be developed later.

sohn argued that the suggested difference in *subjectivity* and *objectivity* between aspect and Aktionsart must not be seen in absolute terms. This point was made in two ways. First, the 'objectivity' of the Aktionsarten had been exaggerated.[84] The degree to which linguistic features like lexical meaning, derivational morphology, and adverbial adjuncts reflect the *actual* situations which they describe varies greatly, and they also inevitably involve some degree of subjectivity, although perhaps less so than the aspects.[85] Second, the 'subjectivity' of the aspects had been exaggerated. The fully free choice of the speaker to portray an action by any aspect occurs only in a limited range of situations. Jacobsohn argues that examples such as those cited by Hermann (ἐϐασίλευον 'ich war König' and ἐϐασίλευσα 'ich war König') are indeed subject to the free choice of the speaker, but that such cases are rare. In most uses of the aspects the speaker's choice is restricted by other factors, including the external facts of the occurrence, and as a result the line between the 'subjective' aspects and the 'objective' Aktionsarten is a very fluid one.[86] For example, an action perceived as non-durative effectively limits the speaker's options to a compatible aspect (i.e. he would avoid an imperfective or progressive form, unless an iterative sense is intended).

These corrections, however, highlight a larger issue in aspectology which divided scholars in the 1920s and 1930s, and is still not clearly settled today. This issue focuses on the question of the exact semantic nature of 'aspect', even in the new sense, when various Aktionsart differences have been

---

[84] This was argued also by Hollmann, *Untersuchungen über Aspekt und Aktionsart*, pp. 13–22.

[85] Koschmieder notes ('Zu den Grundfragen der Aspekttheorie', p. 286) that Aktionsart features regarded as 'non–durative' merely concern acts which our normal sense–perception cannot conceive as extended in time. As Comrie, *Aspect*, pp. 42–3, discusses, even such momentary acts as 'to cough' can under some situations of heightened perception (e.g. slow–motion film) be regarded as durative or extended in time.

[86] Jacobsohn, 'Aspektfragen', pp. 308, 315–16; also his review of Wackernagel, *Vorlesungen über Syntax*, p. 386.

separated from it. Two views were suggested in the early discussion (these two approaches are still debated today), differing in regard to the degree of semantic parallelism which one sees between the aspects and the Aktionsarten. One approach is that developed initially by Jacobsohn, which sees the aspects as semantically *equivalent* to the Aktionsarten: both categories are concerned with matters such as duration, profession, fulfilment, termination, accomplishment, and so forth. In this approach the only difference between aspect and Aktionsart is the *linguistic means* used to express the semantic values of durativity, fulfilment, and so forth: aspect expresses such meanings grammatically, while Aktionsart reflects them lexically. This view holds that objective differences in the external state of affairs described by the verb (e.g. its actual temporal duration, its accomplishment) play a more important role in the speaker's choice of aspects, even though it is acknowledged that a measure of subjectivity enters in. Based on this approach, Jacobsohn labels the primary aspects in IE as 'durativ' vs. 'perfektiv' (emphasizing the fulfilment).[87]

The other approach was suggested initially by Porzig and Hermann, who took the aspects as semantically *different* from the Aktionsarten. In this view the Aktionsarten are concerned with matters like duration and fulfilment, and are thus more dependent on the objective, external facts of the situation; in contrast, the aspects have nothing inherently to do with duration, fulfilment, and so on. Instead, they reflect whether the speaker chooses to view or portray the action (1) as in its development, as in process of being carried out; or (2) as a single whole, as summarized in one event from beginning to end.[88] In this approach the question of duration (or lack of it) and the question of fulfilment (or lack of it) are left out of view in the choice of aspects. Hermann expresses these two in

---

[87] Jacobsohn, review of Wackernagel, *Vorlesungen über Syntax*, p. 386; and 'Aspektfragen', pp. 308–9, 313–18.

[88] See Hermann's discussion in 'Objektive und subjektive Aktionsart', pp. 207–14, and his definition of the two aspects, pp. 213–14.

another way by referring to an 'inner' viewpoint on the action (seeing it in regard to its various stages of development) and to an 'outer' viewpoint (seeing it from the outside as a total entity without regard to its development).[89] Although this approach recognizes the larger distinction of lexical vs. grammatical means of expression (i.e. Aktionsart vs. aspect), it sees the semantic nature of the two as quite different. Based on this, Hermann labels the primary aspects in IE as 'kursiv' (viewing the action in its development) vs. 'komplexiv' (viewing the action as a summarized whole).[90]

This issue of the exact nature of 'aspect' was diverted for a time when attention in aspectology shifted to the question of the relationship between the aspects themselves (see section 1.3). However, the issue has been taken up here and there in the interim, and it has recently surfaced again in aspectology. The question is set forth in clearest terms by Bache,[91] who reviews the approach to this issue taken by Comrie and Lyons, two of the most comprehensive recent treatments of aspect and related phenomena. His article makes it plain that the two earlier views of the nature of 'aspect' have reappeared (albeit in more sophisticated form) in the contrast between his approach to aspect and that taken by Comrie and Lyons.

Comrie and Lyons stand together in their presentation of aspect and Aktionsart, and their view is essentially that of

---

[89] Ibid. 213–14.

[90] Ibid. Later Hermann dropped these terms in favour of the more usual 'imperfective' and 'perfective', but he maintains his definitions focusing on 'development/inner view' vs. 'summary/outer view'. See his 'Aspekt und Aktionsart', pp. 477–8; and 'Aspekt und Zeitrichtung', pp. 263–4. Porzig, 'Zur Aktionsart', p. 152, does not develop this in detail, but explains the two aspects as portraying the action either 'als Verlauf oder als Ereignis'. In the same period Hollmann, *Untersuchungen über Aspekt und Aktionsart*, pp. 2–6, 16–20, argued for this approach, distinguishing aspect and Aktionsart more sharply than Jacobsohn did.

[91] Bache, 'Aspect and Aktionsart', pp. 57–72. See also id. *Verbal Aspect: A General Theory and its Application to Present–Day English* (Odense: Odense University Press, 1985), 5–31, 145–52; and 'The Semantics of Grammatical Categories: A Dialectical Approach', *JL* 21 (1985), 51–77. Lloyd, *Verb*, pp. 8–14, 71–88, discusses this issue and arrives at the same conclusions as Bache.

Jacobsohn,[92] in that they regard aspect and Aktionsart categories as operating in the *same* semantic plane. They do note that there is a need to distinguish what languages communicate *grammatically* from what they communicate *lexically*, and they point out the more subjective nature of grammatical aspect. They also mention that the terms 'aspect' and 'Aktionsart' were suggested by earlier scholars to label these differences (i.e. 'grammatical vs. lexical' and 'subjective vs. objective'). But both of them drop the term 'Aktionsart' after the initial mention, and use 'aspect' thereafter to refer to both categories of meaning. Thus, 'aspect' is the term used to describe features of meaning from both sides of the earlier dichotomy: aspects (perfective, summarizing, imperfective, cursive) and Aktionsarten (durative, iterative, momentary, inceptive, terminative, etc.).[93] Even for features like these which are reflected lexically (which earlier writers would have called 'Aktionsarten'), Lyons uses the phrase *'aspectual* charac-

---

[92] This is true despite the fact Comrie defines aspect and explains the perfective and imperfective aspects in a way plainly reminiscent of the approach taken by Porzig and Hermann. He writes (*Aspect*, p. 3): 'As the general definition of aspect, we may take the formulation that "aspects are different ways of viewing the internal temporal constituency of a situation"'. And he explains the perfective and imperfective as follows (p. 4): 'the perfective looks at the situation from outside, without necessarily distinguishing any of the internal structure of the situation, whereas the imperfective looks at the situation from inside, and as such is crucially concerned with the internal structure of the situation'. Lyons, *Semantics*, p. 709, makes a similar reference to aspect as the speaker's concern with the internal make up of the action.

[93] Comrie, *Aspect*, pp. 4–13; and Lyons, *Semantics*, pp. 705–18. Others also have used the term 'aspect' to denote both types of meaning. Friedrich, *Aspect Theory*, pp. 1–5, uses 'aspect' to label all such meanings whether expressed grammatically, lexically, or otherwise, and he defines the focus of aspect as duration (p. 1): 'Aspect, by one general definition, signifies the relative duration or punctuality along a time line that may inhere in words or constructions. . . . DURATIVE/NONDURATIVE was *the* basic aspectual opposition in Homeric Greek and Proto–Indo–European'. Paul J. Hopper, 'Aspect between Discourse and Grammar: An Introductory Essay for the Volume', in *Tense–Aspect* (1982), 4, commends Comrie's approach as follows: 'it is not always clear where the boundary between aspect and Aktionsart is to be drawn, and Comrie . . . sensibly eschews the distinction altogether. The tendency among most linguists who have written about aspect, especially non–Slavists, in the West has beeen the same, that is, to regard all phenomena which are not clearly tense or modality as aspectual'. Surely this includes too much in the category.

ter', and Comrie speaks of 'inherent *aspectual* . . . properties of various classes of lexical items'.[94]

Bache, on the other hand, feels that Comrie and Lyons have conflated two categories which ought to be kept separate, and he tries to show 'that a strict distinction between aspect and Aktionsart must be insisted on . . . and that failure to recognize the necessity of this distinction is responsible for some confusion on the part of both Comrie and Lyons'.[95] In fact, what he desires is the recognition that certain features of verbal meaning formerly labelled 'Aktionsarten' (e.g. durative, momentary, iterative, semelfactive, accomplished, incomplete, inceptive, etc.) are of an entirely different order semantically to other features labelled 'aspects' (e.g. complexive, cursive). In other words, he argues basically for the approach to aspect articulated earlier by Porzig and Hermann. However, he does this in a more sophisticated way and meets some of the objections raised against the earlier formulations. He mentions the suggestions made by earlier scholars that 'aspect is a more or less SUBJECTIVE category in that it involves the speaker/writer's choice between a "perfective" or "imperfective" description of the situation referred to by a verb, whereas Aktionsart is an OBJECTIVE category in that it involves the actual constituency of the situation described'.[96] Bache then proceeds to show that this distinction must be modified on both sides, although it does reflect an important general difference in the two.

He argues first that Aktionsart is not always objective in the sense of 'applying to the real world', since it frequently involves not actual differences in external facts but rather

---

[94] Lyons, *Semantics*, pp. 706; Comrie, *Aspect*, p. 41 (my emphasis). A similar conflation of the categories is found in Horst G. Klein, *Tempus, Aspekt, Aktionsart* (Tübingen: Max Niemeyer, 1974), 78–114; and, among more recent works: Taina Duţescu–Coliban, 'Towards a Definition of Aspect', *Revue roumaine de linguistique*, 26 (1981), 263–74; Alfred F. Majewicz, 'Understanding Aspect', *Lingua Posnaniensis*, 24 (1982), 29–61; ibid. 25 (1983), 17–40; and Maslov, 'An Outline of Contrastive Aspectology', pp. 6–26.

[95] Bache, 'Aspect and Aktionsart', p. 59.

[96] Ibid. 64.

differing perceptions by the speaker (or by his speech-community) whereby the action is *conceived* as durative or momentary and so on. Thus, he concludes that the category of Aktionsart should be seen as follows:

it refers to the time opposition of durative vs. punctual as well as to kinetic or 'procedural' oppositions . . . like dynamic vs. stative, telic vs. atelic, semelfactive vs. iterative, etc. These notions are not to be regarded as physically measurable, 'objective' characteristics of situations but rather as psychological classifications of (objective and other) situations based on intuitive belief or conception.[97]

He argues, on the other side, that aspect is not always subjective in the sense of 'offering an optional choice', since the aspects are incompatible with certain other features of verbal meaning, thus forcing a speaker to one particular aspect in many situations. For example, a perfective/aoristic aspect can be used to refer to a *past* or *future* process or activity, but not to one occurring in the immediate *present* (i.e. one in progress at the time of speaking). The correlation of aspect with *tense* in this case leads to a certain restriction in the speaker's optional choice. He suggests other restrictions based on the speaker's perception of objective differences in the *action itself* (essentially 'Aktionsart' distinctions, as described by Bache).[98] He argues, however, that this interaction between aspect and Aktionsart should not lead one to conflate the two categories but rather to note more carefully the difference 'between PURE ASPECTUAL OPPOSITION and ASPECTUAL FUNCTION in relation to other categories such as Aktionsart and tense'. Taking this distinction as a starting-point, he proposes

that in our definition of aspect we depart from the optional nature of aspectual choice, i.e. from what I refer to as 'pure aspectual opposition', and then proceed to the distribution of aspects, i.e. to aspectual functions, especially in relation to Aktionsart and tense.

---

[97] Ibid. 64–5, 70.

[98] Ibid. 65–9. For example, he argues that a fully free choice of aspects is possible only in regard to actions which are perceivable as objectively (1) durative, (2) atelic, and (3) non–stative. These will be discussed in ch. 3.

By adopting this approach it is possible, I think, to provide reasonable justification for the view that aspect is basically 'subjective' but may have various 'objectively' determined functions.[99]

Thus, he concludes that the category of aspect 'reflects the situational focus with which a situation is represented', and as examples he cites descriptions of the perfective as 'holistic', 'summarizing', or 'unifying' and of the imperfective as being concerned for the internal structure of the action.[100] He goes on to add, however, that a 'subjective choice' between these two representations of an action is possible only in a limited range of circumstances and that in a larger number of instances the choice of aspect is restricted to one or the other by the *function* of the aspects in combination with tense or Aktionsart.[101]

A more recent writer who develops the same semantic distinction as Bache (though independently from him) is Smith.[102] She notes also that both categories are subjective to a degree, in that they involve a speaker's choice to present an actual occurrence in one of perhaps several possible ways, which may be idealized representations rather than objective descriptions of the actual situation. In addition, Smith insists that the interpretation of aspect must be done both by *maintaining a distinction* between the two categories and by *examining the interaction* between the two. However, she uses the term 'aspect' to describe both areas of meanings (aspect and Aktionsart in Bache's sense), with further qualification to indicate reference to one or the other. Her distinction is between 'viewpoint aspects' and 'situation aspects' as follows.

Viewpoint aspects—simple vs. progressive (e.g. English forms):

In the perspective of simple aspect, an event is presented as a whole. The focus includes both initial and final endpoints; internal struc-

[99] Ibid. 67.
[100] See the discussion in sect. 1.1.3 and 1.1.4.
[101] Ibid. 70–1.
[102] Smith, 'Aspectual Choice', pp. 479–501.

ture is ignored. . . . Progressive aspect presents an interior perspective, from which the endpoints of an event are ignored. Thus the progressive indicates a moment or interval of an event that is neither initial nor final.[103]

Situation aspects:

Specific situations can be classified according to whether they have properties such as agency, activity, duration, stability, or completion (this is not an exhaustive list). One familiar classification, focusing on temporal properties, recognizes four main types of situation: ACTIVITY, ACHIEVEMENT, ACCOMPLISHMENT, and STATE.[104]

It is clear that these ideas are in essential agreement with Bache's approach; only the labels are different. The problem of nomenclature in aspectology has always been a vexed one, and technical definitions of aspect and Aktionsart are difficult to maintain. Nevertheless, it seems more workable to use the term 'aspect' in the later chapters of this book for the category of meaning which Bache has outlined for that term (Smith's viewpoint aspect), and to use 'Aktionsart' for the other category (Smith's situation aspect). However, because of the frequent use of 'Aktionsart' in NT grammars to mean some combination of both categories, that term will generally be avoided in later chapters except in quotations, and Bache's Aktionsart category will normally be referred to by the phrase *procedural character* or some variation of it.

In summary of this section, the view of aspect advanced by Porzig and Hermann, and more clearly by Bache and Smith, appears to hold more potential for accurate and clear analysis of the NT Greek aspects. In this approach the aspects are semantically *different* from the various Aktionsarten or procedural characteristics, although they interact with these in important and somewhat predictable ways which ought to be noted clearly.[105] Further discussion and validation of this

---

[103] Ibid. 482.

[104] Ibid. 481.

[105] See Lloyd, *Verb*, pp. 8–10, 14, in which he argues for a distinction ('"aspect" and *"Aktionsart"* are two entirely different things') but concedes that the two must be

conclusion will need to be done in connection with the analysis of the individual aspects in NT Greek and their usage in actual texts.

1. 2. 2 *Aspect and lexical classes of verbs*

After the initial contribution of Jacobsohn, Porzig, and Hermann in distinguishing aspect from Aktionsart, the emphasis of the discussion shifted away from analysing the precise nature of aspect (as distinct from Ationsart); instead, scholars examined the basic distinction itself and expanded it in two important ways. On the one hand, greater stress was laid on the 'grammatical vs. lexical' difference between aspect and Aktionsart; and on the other, attention was given to expanding and classifying the list of possible Aktionsarten.

As scholars came to understand and accept the basic distinction of aspect and Aktionsart in the period 1935–55, it became commonplace to articulate this difference more clearly as 'grammatical vs. lexical' in nature. Goedsche, for example, in comparing Slavic, English, and Gothic verbal usage, distinguished between (1) 'word content', 'semantic analysis of verbs (Aktionsart)', or 'lexical meaning, found in simple verbs and expressed in compound verbs by means of the semantic function of prefixes'; and (2) 'verbal aspect', 'grammatical forms . . . [telling] how an action takes place', or 'a syntactical meaning expressed by a special set of forms'.[106]

Others, while emphasizing this grammatical/lexical distinction, gave attention at the same time to expanding the list of possible Aktionsarten and classifying them into various subcategories.[107] Renicke, for example, distinguishes three main

---

studied together: 'Since aspect is so closely related to actional types (*Aktionsarten*) . . . a theory limited to aspect alone is neither possible nor desirable'.

[106] C. R. Goedsche, 'Aspect versus *Aktionsart*', *JEGP* 39 (1940), 189, 191, 196. Erich Hofmann also expresses the distinction in these terms in 'Zu Aspekt und Aktionsart', in *Corolla Linguistica: F. Sommer Festschrift* (Wiesbaden: Otto Harrassowitz, 1955), 86–7.

[107] Max Deutschbein, 'Aspekte und Aktionsarten im Neuenglischen', *Neuphilologi-*

types of 'Phasenaktionsarten', with subcategories of each: 'die initive Sphäre' (including 'inchoativ-punktuell', 'inchoativ-progressiv', 'ingressiv-punktuell', and 'ingressiv-progressiv'), 'die prozedente Sphäre' (including 'progressiv' and 'kontinuativ'), and 'die finitive Sphäre' (including 'konklusiv', 'effektiv', and 'resultativ').[108] These are distinct, of course, from the aspects, which Renicke lists as 'kursiv', 'komplexiv', and 'prospektiv'.[109]

These attempts to analyse the varieties of possible Aktionsart distinctions of verbs were an important contribution to aspectology, because variations in the lexical character of verbs produce significant and predictable patterns of meaning when combined with the grammatical aspects.[110] However, the tendency to multiply categories of Aktionsarten and draw over-fine (and idiosyncratic) differences proved to be a hindrance to their usefulness. A more workable approach to the significant variations in this area was needed, and such an approach began to appear in the 1950s.

This new approach involved the formulation of fewer, more comprehensive classes of lexical characteristics which are significant for predicting variation in the function of the aspects. The most important contributions along this line were made by Vendler and Kenny,[111] whose treatments of the

sche Monatsschrift, 10, (1939), 135–40; Eduard Hermann, 'Die altgriechischen Tempora: Ein strukturanalytischer Versuch', NGG 15 (1943), 591–601; Horst Renicke, 'Die Theorie der Aspekte und Aktionsarten', BGDSL 72 (1950), 152–73; and Walther Azzalino, 'Wesen und Wirken von Aktionsart und Aspekt', Neuphilologische Zeitschrift, 2 (1950), 105–10, 192–203.

[108] Renicke, 'Aspekte und Aktionsarten', pp. 152–73.

[109] This third aspect is taken from the work of Deutschbein, 'Aspekte und Aktionsarten im Neuenglischen', 145–7, and is suggested to cover the English verb–phrase with 'going to' as in 'I am/was going to write'.

[110] A survey of significant literature from this period and later work following the same pattern is given by Jacques François, 'Aktionsart, Aspekt und Zeitkonstitution', in Christoph Schwarze and Dieter Wunderlich (eds.), Handbuch der Lexikologie, (Königstein: Athenäum, 1985) pp. 229–49. He also discusses the Vendler–Kenny system and its refinements (see next section).

[111] Zeno Vendler, 'Verbs and Times', Philosophical Review, 66 (1975), 43–60; and Anthony Kenny, Action, Emotion and Will (London: Routledge and Kegan Paul, 1963),

topic arose out of philosophical discussion rather than from grammar or philology. But their work has been followed by many subsequent writers in the field of aspectology.

Vendler suggested a four-part scheme of verb-classes in English, and he proposed that they reflect more universal characteristics of occurrences in general. The four classes (of verbs and verb-phrases) with brief descriptions and examples are as follows:

1. CONTINUOUS VERBS (which admit continuous tenses in English): 'processes going on in time, that is, roughly, that they consist of successive phases following one another in time'.

(*a*) *Activities* 'go on in time in a homogeneous way: any part of the process is of the same nature as the whole' (e.g. running, walking, swimming, pushing a cart).

(*b*) *Accomplishments* 'also go on in time, but they proceed toward a terminus which is logically necessary to their being what they are'; 'have a "climax", which has to be reached if the action is to be what it is claimed to be' (e.g. running a mile, drawing a circle, painting a picture, making a chair, building a house, writing or reading a novel, delivering a sermon, giving or attending a class, playing a game of chess, growing up, recovering from illness, getting ready for something).

2. NON-CONTINUOUS VERBS (which do not admit continuous tenses) 'do not indicate processes going on in time'.

(*a*) *Achievements* 'can be predicated only for single moments of time'; 'occur at a single moment' (e.g. reaching the hill-top, winning the race, crossing the border, spotting or recognizing something, realizing, identifying, losing, finding, starting, stopping, resuming, being born, dying).

(*b*) *States* 'can be predicated for shorter or longer periods of time'; 'last for a period of time'; are not done deliberately or

151–86. A revised version of Vendler's essay 'with only minor changes' was issued in his *Linguistics in Philosophy* (Ithaca, NY: Cornell University Press, 1967), 97–121. The later version will be cited here.

carefully – in fact, not 'done' at all (e.g. knowing, believing, loving, dominating, having, possessing, desiring, wanting, liking, disliking, hating, ruling).[112]

Without reference to Vendler's work, Kenny set forth a similar taxonomy of verbs in three main classes, putting accomplishments and achievements together in one class, which he called 'performances', but maintaining similar classes of activities and states.[113]

Although these essays did not use the label 'Aktionsart', such categories obviously involve what earlier writers had meant by that term. Subsequent treatments of aspect have made extensive use of these lexical classes to shed light on the function of the aspects in relation to such verbal types. The important point to be grasped is that such categories are not themselves 'aspects' in the sense developed above. They should be distinguished from the aspects, but the interaction of aspect with such characteristic types must be carefully studied.

The most detailed treatment of NT verbal aspect to be published to date takes this area of analysis as its predominant emphasis. Juan Mateos's *El aspecto verbal en el nuevo testamento* (1977) divides factors that express 'aspect' into three areas:

El aspecto expresado por una forma verbal en contexto depende de tres factores que se combinan entre sí:

(1) del sema o semas de aspecto incluidos en el núcleo sémico de cada lexema verbal (*aspecto lexemático*).

(2) del aspecto propio de la forma verbal en que se presenta el lexema (*aspecto morfemático*).

(3) de las relaciones sintácticas que establece la forma verbal con otros elementos del sintagma (*aspecto sintagmático*).

---

[112] This is a summary from Vendler, 'Verbs and Times', pp. 99–108. Another article appearing at the same time as Vendler's original essay (1957) gave a more extensive treatment of 'accomplishment' verbs, but labelled them 'telic' verbs; see J. B. Garey, 'Verbal Aspect in French', *Lg.* 33 (1957), 91–110.

[113] Kenny, *Action, Emotion and Will*, pp. 172–86. Kenny refers along the way to passages in Aristotle which suggest similar divisions.

El aspecto lexemático puede llamarse *lexical*, los aspectos morfemático y sintagmático, *gramaticales*.[114]

Mateos then notes that 'aspecto leximático' is divided into
four classes, which he names 'lexemas estáticos', 'lexemas de
acción continua', 'lexemas de acción instantánea', and 'lexemas de acción resultativa' (with the last three grouped as
'lexemas dinámicos').[115] His treatment of the morphological
expressions of aspect in NT Greek is rather brief, while the
major portion of the book (pp. 41–133) is spent discussing
these lexical classes and the aspectual usage of NT verbs
which fit into each class. As is obvious, his classes of verbs are
very close to the Vendler–Kenny scheme, although he does
not refer to their work.

A detailed presentation of the important lexical classes of
verbs (based on Vendler, Kenny, and Mateos) and their
impact on aspectual function will be given in section 3.1.

1. 2. 3 *Aspect and compositional elements*

The third step in clarifying the meaning of the aspects in
relation to procedural characteristics involved distinguishing
them from other elements used 'in composition with verbs'[116]
which also interact in significant ways with the aspects.
Observations of a general sort were made by earlier writers in
the field,[117] but detailed treatment of these elements has come
more recently.

---

[114] Mateos, *Aspecto verbal*, p. 20. His approach to aspect is like that of Comrie and
Lyons, in labelling features on both sides of the aspect/Aktionsart distinction as
'aspect'. Another extensive treatment of ancient Greek aspect which utilizes the
Vendler–Kenny scheme is Stork, *Aspectual Usage*.

[115] Ibid. 22–3.

[116] This phrase is used here to mean 'as an adjunct of verbs' or 'along with a verb',
not in the sense of 'as a prefix or suffix of a verb'.

[117] Herbig, 'Aktionsart und Zeitstufe', p. 219, noted that the presence of a plural
object or subject often accompanies an iterative nuance of the imperfective aspect; a
number of later writers have observed this pattern (see sect. 3.2.1.1). Koschmieder,
'Zu den Grundfragen der Aspekttheorie', pp. 285–6, observed that the sense of the
entire phrase used with the verb (not just the lexical nature of the verb) must be

Verkuyl made observations about the effect of *durational* or *non-durational* adverb-phrases (e.g. 'for hours', 'until 1965', 'yesterday', 'at that time', 'in a moment') and about the effect of *specified quantity* vs. *unspecified quantity* in the object- or subject-phrases used with the verb ('to play cello music', 'to play a cello concerto', 'to deliver a letter', 'to deliver letters').[118] In sentences with such phrases the function of aspect varies depending on the nature of phrases combined with it. It is also true that certain phrases do not occur with some aspects due to the unnatural collocation of elements which would be produced. For example, one does not usually say 'I delivered a letter for hours', but it makes good sense to say 'I delivered letters for hours', since the object-references relate differently with a durational phrase. However, durationals are compatible with some objects of specified quantity (e.g. 'I kicked a ball for hours'), if an iterative meaning is possible.[119]

Others have developed these ideas further, particularly the effect produced by variation between 'count'- vs. 'mass'-nouns as subject or object.[120] Some nouns are 'countable' and do not normally accord well with durationals, unless an iterative idea is in view ('she played the concerto all day'). Other nouns are 'mass'-terms, which are not counted and do not occur as plurals, except in some different sense of the word (e.g. 'wines'

analysed when one is examining the Aktionsart distinctions. Jacobsohn, 'Aspekt-fragen', pp. 297–300, went further and discussed differences produced by the presence of an *effected object* as opposed to an affected object (e.g. 'Der Mann schlug den Hund' vs. 'Die Maurer bauten das Haus'), and of a *partitive* vs. non-partitive phrase used with the verb ('Ich schrieb an dem Brief' vs. 'Ich schrieb den Brief').

[118] H. J. Verkuyl, *On the Compositional Nature of the Aspects* (FL Supplementary Series, 15; Dordrecht: D. Reidel Publishing Co., 1972), 40–97. He assumes in his discussion that aspect and procedural characteristics like duration and repetition are of the same semantic order, an assumption which is disputed in this book.

[119] Mateos, *Aspecto verbal*, pp. 33–6, 39, has a brief treatment of the effect of singular vs. plural nouns and of various adverb–expressions used with a verb.

[120] See A. P. D. Mourelatos, 'Events, Processes, and States', *Linguistics and Philosophy*, 2 (1978), 415–34 (repr. in *Tense and Aspect* [1981], 191–212); David Armstrong, 'The Ancient Greek Aorist as the Aspect of Countable Action', ibid. 1–12; Lauri Carlson, 'Aspect and Quantification', ibid. 31–64; and Jakob Hoepelman, *Verb Classification and the Russian Verbal Aspect* (Tübingen: Gunter Narr, 1981), 14–15, 113–17, 190–3.

as 'types of wine'). Mass-nouns fit quite easily with durationals ('she played music all day'), but do not fit well with expressions of accomplishment or termination (cf. 'we drank [a bottle of] wine at lunch'; without the count-phrase added, the mass-noun cancels any sense of completion or accomplishment). Similar features of compositional meaning have been treated under the topic of 'bounded' vs. 'unbounded' expression, an issue closely related to the lexical category of 'accomplishment'-verbs mentioned in the previous section.[121]

Other elements besides durational adverb-phrases and specified subject- or object-phrases[122] may interact in meaningful ways with aspect. Some which have been suggested are directional adverb-expressions,[123] the presence of an *effected accusative*,[124] negatives[125] and other categories like voice and mood.[126]

Many of these are, of course, common-sense observations and are covered in traditional exegetical discussion under the general rubric of 'context'. But to focus attention on these elements and attempt to specify their precise effect as far as possible is the goal of those who have worked on the interconnections between aspect and compositional elements. Again the point to be emphasized is that the meaning of the aspects themselves must be distinguished from such factors, although

[121] See Rennat Declerck, 'Aspect and the Bounded/Unbounded (Telic/Atelic) Distinction', *Linguistics*, 17 (1979), 761–94; and Östen Dahl, 'On the Definition of the Telic/Atelic (Bounded/Nonbounded) Distinction', in *Tense and Aspect* (1981), 79–90.

[122] These include the variation between partitive and non-partitive phrases, as suggested by Jacobsohn, 'Aspektfragen', pp. 299–300, and treated further by Verkuyl, *Compositional Nature*, pp. 53, 71–9.

[123] Declerck, 'Bounded/Unbounded', pp. 785–8; and Verkuyl, *Compositional Nature*, pp. 41–6, 93–7.

[124] Jacobsohn, 'Aspektfragen', pp. 297–9; Verkuyl, *Compositional Nature*, pp. 85–90; and Hoepelman, *Verb Classification*, pp. 100–3.

[125] Hettrich, *Kontext und Aspekt*, pp. 45–51; and Stephen Wallace. 'Figure and Ground: The Interrelationships of Linguistic Categories', in *Tense-Aspect* (1982), 203–4.

[126] Bernard Comrie, 'Aspect and Voice: Some Reflections on Perfect and Passive', in *Tense and Aspect* (1981), 65–78; Scott Delancey, 'Aspect, Transitivity and Viewpoint', in *Tense-Aspect* (1982), 167–83; Wallace, 'Figure and Ground', pp. 201–23; and G. de Boel, 'Aspect, Aktionsart und Transitivität', *IF* 92 (1987), 33–57.

the function of the aspects in combination with them must be noted. Further treatment of these elements will be given in the third chapter.

1. 2. 4 *Summary of the relationship of aspect and procedural characteristics*

Forsyth points out that the term 'action' is used in confusing ways in discussions of aspect-usage. In general treatments the term 'action' is used in at least four senses:

(*a*) the objective reality described, the actual performance of the given type of action on a specific occasion or occasions. . . .

(*b*) the general lexical meaning of a given verb—'write' as distinct from 'run', 'think', etc. as a general, potential phenomenon. . . .

(*c*) the view or presentation of the type of action, which is inherent in the lexical meaning of a given verb [*e.g. repetition, limited duration*]. . . .

(*d*) the subjective view of a specific objective fact: the speaker may choose to present an event as a single indivisible whole, or not.[127]

These four provide a clear path for summarizing the distinctions traced above. The point of this section has been that a significant part of defining and interpreting aspect as a grammatical category involves distinguishing it from the closely related feature of 'procedural character' which is inherent in actual situations (i.e. Forsyth's first item above), in the lexical nature of the verb itself (Forsyth's third item), and in verbal phrases or wider expressions which occur with the verb (not listed by Forsyth but similar to the third item). The argument of this book is that aspect is semantically distinct from these procedural characteristics: it is not to be equated with various characteristics of the *actual occurrence* (e.g. duration, repetition, completion, inception, and their opposites); nor is it to be equated with the same features when they are reflected in various more subjective ways in the *lexical*

---

[127] James A. Forsyth, *A Grammar of Aspect: Usage and Meaning in the Russian Verb* (Cambridge: at the University Press, 1970), 16.

meaning of the verb or in the larger *expressions in which the verb occurs*. The aspects are of a different semantic order from procedural oppositions such as durative/momentary, repeated/single, dynamic/stative, completed/incomplete, inceptive/terminative, and so forth.

Aspects pertain instead to the focus of the speaker with reference to the action or state which the verb describes, his way of viewing the occurrence and its make-up, without any *necessary* regard to the (actual or perceived) nature of the situation itself. It was noted earlier that fully subjective choices between aspects are not common, since the nature of the occurrence or the procedural character of the verb or verb-phrase sometimes restricts the way a situation can be viewed or is normally viewed. But the argument of this section is that analysis of these interactions is best done by attempting to separate the sense of the aspects from the procedural character of the verb or phrase in which it occurs.

It ought to be reiterated, however, that the interpretation of aspect-usage must be achieved by analysing carefully the interaction of aspect with these procedural characteristics. Aspect operates so closely with such features and is so significantly affected by them that no treatment of it can be meaningful without attention to these interactions.

1. 3 Structural Relations between Aspects

A third major trend in modern discussion of verbal aspect has been the consideration of how the aspects of a language relate to *one another* in their meaning and usage. As the general emphasis in language study shifted in the first half of this century from comparative philology to descriptive linguistics, the focus of interest in aspectology also shifted and questions of a different sort were asked. One of the primary features of this change was an emphasis on structural relationships between the aspects and a certain impatience with earlier writers who neglected this issue. Some have felt that this is the answer to previously insoluble problems in aspectology.

1. 3. 1 *The need to define the aspects in terms of their mutual relationships*

Speaking about past 'confusions' in analysing aspect, Friedrich attributes such confusion in part to 'linguists in the item-inventory tradition [who] have often been content simply to list aspectual and aspectoidal features without inferring the structure of their interrelationships'.[128] Gonda also comments on this weakness of earlier aspect studies:

The earlier literature on the phenomenon under consideration neglected the requirement of more modern methods that linguistic categories should not be defined separately: if there are, in a given language, a 'perfective' and an 'imperfective' aspect these two should not be considered in isolation but studied in mutual connection, because they are each other's counterparts or complements—or if one would prefer another formulation—because they constitute a 'system'.[129]

This call for a system or a 'structure of interrelationships' between aspects is characteristic of the approach adopted by virtually all contemporary linguists.[130] The idea of language as a system of interrelated entities each of which must be defined in reference to their mutual relationships is traceable primarily to the lectures of the Swiss linguist Ferdinand de Saussure,[131] founder of modern linguistics. Though others spoke in similar terms before him, Saussure's forceful presentation of this idea and of its implications has led to this

[128] Friedrich, *Aspect Theory*, p. 28.

[129] Gonda, *Aspectual Function*, p. 29.

[130] This is not to say that all modern linguists are 'structuralists' or 'structural linguists', since these terms have been used in various ways (some of them pejorative) and of various schools of thought. But in broad terms all would agree concerning the nature of language itself as a system whose elements cannot be analysed properly apart from their relationships within the total system. Cf. Giulio C. Lepschy, *A Survey of Structural Linguistics* (London: Faber and Faber, 1970), 33–8; and Lyons, *Semantics*, pp. 230–2.

[131] See e.g. Ferdinand de Saussure, *Course in General Linguistics*, ed. Charles Bally and Albert Sechehaye in collaboration with Albert Reidlinger, trans. by Wade Baskin, rev. edn. (London: Peter Owen, 1974), 22–3, 114–27, 133.

concept being regarded as distinctly 'Saussurean' and being accepted as axiomatic.[132]

This structural principle has been applied in beneficial ways to phonology, to grammar, and to the lexical stock of languages. In regard to grammar, the concept is significant both in reference to the *syntactical* relationships within an utterance (i.e. each part of a sentence has meaning only in mutual interaction with the others) and in reference to the *paradigmatic* relationships within a particular grammatical category (i.e. the interdependent or contrastive meanings of the tenses, cases, voices, numbers, etc.).[133] It is, of course, the paradigmatic structure which is of interest in this section, since the concern here is to define the mutual relations between the various members of the category of aspect.

As scholars have moved to consider the aspects in regard to their relationships to each other, they have cited three general points by way of informal justification for adopting this structural or relational approach. Apart from the theoretical principles presented above, these points also demonstrate the need for such an approach:

1. In using the category of aspect in Greek (which is obligatory throughout the verbal system),[134] the native speaker does not have the choice of any conceivable 'aspect-value' which he desires. Rather he is to some degree 'kept within the limits set by the language itself which—to mention only this—does not provide him with the realization of all theore-

---

[132] Roman Jakobson, *Main Trends in the Science of Language* (London: George Allen and Unwin, 1973), 18: 'in the *Cours* . . . an effective emphasis was placed on the mutual solidarity of the system and its constituents, on their purely relative and oppositive character, and on the basic antinomies which we face when we deal with language'. See also Winfred P. Lehmann, *Descriptive Linguistics: An Introduction* (New York: Random House, 1972), 270.

[133] Cf. Lyons, *Semantics*, pp. 234–5: 'Each term in a grammatical category (e.g. past in the English category of tense, or plural in the category of number) is in contrast with other terms in the same category. . . . The units of grammatical description derive their linguistic validity from the place they occupy in a network of functional relations and cannot be identified independently of these interrelations.'

[134] Except perhaps in the *future* and *perfect* forms, a question to be considered later.

tical possibilities'.[135] That is, he must select one of the Greek aspects—the one which most nearly expresses what he wishes to say or, perhaps, the one which least obstructs his intentions. Of course, he may go on to qualify or alter this choice of aspect by additional phrases and modifiers, or he may choose to recast his expression entirely to communicate his meaning. But the verb-forms which he uses will reflect a choice of one of the Greek aspects and must conform in some way to the limits of that set of choices.

2. As intimated in the previous point, the choice of aspects may be motivated not so much by the positive value of one aspect as by the desire to *avoid* the value of another. Since the speaker does not have all theoretical possibilities to choose from, 'an aspectual category may be resorted to because its opposite would be still less suitable to convey the speaker's intentions'.[136] If the language lacks an aspect which produces the desired meaning, the speaker may resort to the aspect which does the least damage to his intended sense.

3. To speak more generally, the choice of one aspect over another, as with all meaningful linguistic variation, is not a random or illogical choice. Some linguistic motivation or underlying logic governs the speaker's choice in this matter, even though this rationale may be an unconscious one and the selective principles may be complex. The grammarian should attempt to discover, as far as he is able, the reasons for one choice over another. In the formulation of such reasons, some sort of governing relationship between the aspects seems inevitable in the light of Saussurean principles. In regard to the baffling usage of the aspects in Russian, Forsyth writes:

There is a logical basis underlying the choice of aspect. A Russian selects one or the other form for some (albeit unconscious) *reason,*

---

[135] Gonda, *Aspectual Function*, p. 27. See also Friedrich, *Aspect Theory*, p.3: 'Systems of thematic aspect [i.e. grammatical aspect] force the speaker to code all (or nearly all) verbal expressions in terms of obligatory and usually binary choices between aspects'.

[136] Gonda, *Aspectual Function*, p. 28.

and the relationship between the aspects depends upon an opposition of meanings and grammatical functions which constitutes part
of the *system* of the Russian verb. The essential thing is to establish
the nature of this opposition.[137]

To sum up, the view of language as a self-contained system
of interrelated entitities requires that these individual units of
language be defined and their meanings interpreted not
autonomously, but in terms of their mutual relationships.
More particularly, the individual verbal aspects of a language
(perfective, imperfective, etc.) must be examined as interrelated entities, since they are mutually interchangeable as
members of the category of aspect. However, to argue for a
structural definition of the aspects does not dictate what *kind*
of structure one will find when studying the aspects relation-
ally. This question must now be considered.

1. 3. 2 *The types of aspectual relationships*

Early analyses of structural relations between aspects were led
to these ideas by structural work done in phonology and other
areas of grammar. Jakobson, for example, took a phonological
correlation from Trubetzkoy[138] and produced a study which
made a significant theoretical contribution to the structural
definition of the verbal aspects, though it dealt with aspect
only in a cursory manner. In this article, Jakobson writes:

Eine der wesentlichen Eigenschaften der phonologischen Korrela-
tion besteht darin, daß die beiden Glieder eines Korrelationspaares

---

[137] Forsyth, *Grammar of Aspect*, p. 2.
[138] Cf. N. S. Trubetzkoy. 'Die phonologischen Systeme', *Travaux du Cercle Linguistique de Prague*, 4 (1931), 97: 'Die zwei Glieder eines korrelativen Gegensatzes sind nicht
gleichberechtigt: das eine Glied besitzt das betreffende Merkmal (oder besitzt es in
seiner positiven Form), das andere besitzt es nicht (oder besitzt es in seiner negativen
Form). Wir bezeichnen das erste als *merkmalhaftig*, das zweite—als *merkmallos*'.
Trubetzkoy's ideas on linguistic oppositions were developed further and expressed in
fullest form in his *Grundzüge der Phonologie* (Prague: Cercle Linguistique de Prague,
1939), 66–7, in which he presents three types of oppositions: privative, gradual, and
equipollent. These are very much like the relationships cited by these names later in
this section.

nicht gleichberechtigt sind: das eine Glied besitzt das betreffende Merkmal, das andere besitzt es nicht; das erste wird als *merkmalhaltig* bezeichnet, das zweite—als *merkmallos* . . . Dieselbe Definition kann zur Grundlage der Charakteristik der *morphologischen Korrelationen* dienen.[139]

Later in the article, Jakobson applies this model to the Russian aspects (taking the perfective as marked and the imperfective as unmarked), but he does not develop this idea in any detail.[140] This concept of 'marked vs. unmarked' members of a category (later known as the 'privative' opposition) has been applied to numerous features of language since the 1930s: phonological, grammatical, and lexical features. It has been used by a number of authors to explain the category of verbal aspect in various languages, as will be shown below.

Another important work using a structural approach was Holt's monograph *Études d'aspect* (1943), which adapted several concepts derived from Louis Hjelmslev's treatment of the noun-cases.[141] Holt describes aspectual relations in terms of 'participative' oppositions. The oppositions may relate the members to each other in a 'contradictory' way or in a 'contrary' way. On the other hand, the opposition may be 'purely participative', in which case one member will be intensive (positive value) and the other extensive (neutral value).[142]

These ideas concerning types of oppositions have exercised considerable influence on aspect studies as they have been taken up and utilized in the grammatical realm. It is now time

---

[139] Roman Jakobson, 'Zur Struktur des russischen Verbums', in *Charisteria Guilelmo Mathesia* (Prague: Cercle Linguistique de Prague, 1932, pp. 74–83, repr. in Roman Jakobson, *Selected Writings*, ii. *Word and Language*); (The Hague: Mouton, 1971, pp. 3–15, cited henceforth from this reprinted edition); quotation taken from *Selected Writings*, ii. 3.

[140] Ibid. 6.

[141] Louis Hjelmslev, *La Catégorie des cas*, pt. 1 (Acta Jutlandica, 7. 1; Copenhagen: C. A. Reitzel, 1935), and 'Essai d'une théorie des morphèmes', in *Actes du Quatrième Congrès International de Linguistes (1936)* (Copenhagen: Munksgaard, 1938) 140–51.

[142] Holt, *Études d'aspect*, pp. 23–7. These ideas will be developed later in this section.

to take these seed-thoughts and combine them with other suggestions to construct a list of *possible* relationships which may be sustained in aspectual oppositions. These relationships are not merely theories, divorced from linguistic study, but have been suggested in one form or another as a model for understanding the relationship of the aspects of a given language. They are given here as possible tools for comprehending aspectual usage more clearly.

It seems best to follow Comrie[143] in adopting a twofold division in the types of oppositions. The primary dichotomy, in this approach, divides the *privative* opposition (with marked vs. unmarked members) from the *equipollent* opposition (in which both members are marked). But several subtypes may also be distinguished.

The privative opposition was suggested by Trubetzkoy and Jakobson in the 1930s, as described above.[144] The essential characteristics of this relationship are that it is a binary (two-part)[145] opposition, with one member 'marked' and the other 'unmarked' (in some sense), and the marking is in reference to one particular issue or 'basic feature' of the opposition (e.g. duration, completion, totality). Within this overall framework, one can distinguish two types of privative oppositions, depending on the nature of the unmarked member.

1. *The purely privative opposition.* This is the privative type first

---

[143] Comrie, *Aspect*, p. 111.

[144] Holenstein finds a hint of this concept as early as 1921 in a brief footnote given in a Russian monograph by Jakobson, but the more fruitful development of this idea came in the 1930s. See Elmar Holenstein, *Roman Jakobson's Approach to Language: Phenomenological Structuralism*, trans. Catherine Schelbert and Tarcisius Schelbert (Bloomington, Ind.: Indiana University Press, 1976), 123–31.

[145] The privative opposition is limited to *two* members; multiple members may be incorporated into one or more of the equipollent types of oppositions. Jakobson argues that *all* linguistic oppositions are ultimately reducible to binary oppositions, and binary oppositions are indeed the most frequent; but it seems that room should be left for the possibility of muliple-membered oppositions in the equipollent type. For a discussion of Jakobson's viewpoint see Linda R. Waugh, *Roman Jakobson's Science of Language* (Lisse: Peter de Ridder Press, 1976), 65–7.

elaborated with reference to grammar by Jakobson, who explained the sense as follows:

Indem der Forscher zwei einander entgegengesetzte morphologische Kategorien betrachtet, geht er oft von der Voraussetzung aus, diese beiden Kategorien seien gleichberechtigt, und jede besitze ihre eigene positive Bedeutung: die Kategorie I bezeichne A, die Kategorie II bezeichne B. Oder mindestens: I bezeichne A, II bezeichne das Nichtvorhandensein, die Negation von A. In Wirklichkeit verteilen sich die allgemeinen Bedeutungen der korrelativen Kategorien anders: falls die Kategorie I das Vorhandensein von A ankündigt, so kündigt die Kategorie II das Vorhandensein von A nicht an, d.h. sie besagt nicht, ob A anwesend ist oder nicht. Die allgemeine Bedeutung der merkmallosen Kategorie II im Vergleich zu der merkmalhaltigen Kategorie I beschränkt sich auf den Mangel der 'A-Signalisicrung'.[146]

The crucial point to be noted here is the *neutral* value of the unmarked member: it does not state the *opposite* of the marked member; rather it simply says nothing in regard to the basic feature of the opposition. As Comrie puts it: 'the marked category signals the presence of some feature, while the unmarked category simply says nothing about its presence or absence'.[147] Holt, referring to Jakobson's work, discusses this type of opposition under the terms 'intensive' (marked) and 'extensive' (unmarked), and argues that the extensive, since it is neutral, may be used without contradiction in contexts where the intensive can also be used.[148]

At least two treatments of the aspects of individual languages adopt this structure to explain aspectual usage in that language. Forsyth develops this position in great detail in regard to the Russian aspects, with specific citation of Jakobson's 'Zur Struktur'. He defines the perfective (marked) as 'presentation of the action as an indivisible whole, a total event summed up with reference to a single juncture',[149] while

---

[146] Jakobson, 'Zur Struktur', p. 3.
[147] Comrie, *Aspect*, p. 112.
[148] Holt, *Études d'aspect*, pp. 24–7.
[149] Forsyth, *Grammar of Aspect*, p. 15.

the imperfective (unmarked) is simply neutral in regard to that sense.

This approach is adopted also by Stagg in his treatment of the NT Greek aorist, although he makes no reference to privative oppositions or markedness theory of any sort. He describes the aorist as 'undetermined or undefined. . . . It tells nothing about the nature of the action under consideration. . . . The action is viewed without reference to duration, interruption, completion, or anything else.' Later he writes: 'The aorist "presents" an action, of whatever nature, without respect to its nature. It does not as such reflect the nature of the action itself . . . . The presence of the aorist does not in itself give any hint as to the nature of the action behind it. . . . It simply points to the action without describing it.'[150] It must be added that Stagg does not place the aorist in binary opposition but seems to set its 'undefined sense' over against a positive definition of the other aspects (present and perfect).

In addition to the defining features of the 'purely privative' opposition which have been presented above, several other characteristics have been alluded to and should be made more explicit at this point.

a. With this type of opposition, the two members can frequently be interchangeable in specific contexts, because the unmarked member may substitute for the marked one without introducing an opposing sense.[151] Since the unmarked member is neutral, it can be used to refer to the same action as the

---

[150] Frank Stagg, 'The Abused Aorist', *JBL* 91 (1972), 223, 231. A writer who goes further in denying aspect–marking of any kind for the NT aorist is Charles R. Smith, 'Errant Aorist Interpreters', *Grace Theological Journal*, 2 (1980), 205–26; however, he is apparently unaware of issues of structural relations between aspects and explicitly denies that the aorist is in contrast or opposition to any other aspect in Greek (pp. 217–20). Another work which suggests a purely privative opposition for Greek (imperfect marked as durative; aorist unmarked) is Fred W. Householder and Gregory Nagy, *Greek: A Survey of Recent Work* (Janua Linguarum, Series Practica, 211; The Hague: Mouton, 1972), 42–3.

[151] Cf. Comrie, *Aspect*, p. 112: 'The meaning of the unmarked category can encompass that of its marked counterpart. . . . The unmarked category can always be used, even in a situation where the marked category would also be appropriate.'

marked member: though it does not explicitly communicate the positive feature of the marked member, neither does it bring in an opposing sense, so the two can display this partial overlapping of usage.

b. In a purely privative opposition, any attempt to define the unmarked aspect in positive terms will prove futile, since its essence is merely to avoid the value of the marked member (or, more correctly, to refrain from comment in regard to that value). Forsyth says about his treatment of Russian aspects:

The definition given above of the relationship between the aspects . . . makes no attempt to define the meaning of the imperfective verb (which has been shown above to be too indefinite and wide to be adequately covered by any combination of positive characteristics). It simply opposes the imperfective negatively to the single positive meaning of the perfective.[152]

c. Since it has no positive aspectual value, the unmarked member could be described as non-aspectual, and Forsyth indeed describes it in this way.[153] However, in the light of its usage in a linguistic opposition paired with the aspectually marked member, it seems more accurate to regard the unmarked member as displaying a *neutral* aspectual meaning, instead of a non-aspectual meaning.

d. Because it has a neutral aspectual sense, the unmarked member is often thought of as more appropriate for referring to the mere occurrence of the action or for simply *naming* the action concerned (i.e. making the lexical distinction of 'walk' vs. 'ride', 'run', etc.) without adding any further elements of meaning (duration, completion, etc.).[154] This is probably a

---

[152] Forsyth, *Grammar of Aspect*, p. 11.

[153] See ibid. 14. 'A logical conclusion to be drawn from the explanation of the aspect system in terms of a privative opposition is that, since positive aspectuality is expressed only in perfective verb forms, the imperfective is in a sense "non-aspectual", i.e. that the meaning of a perfective form includes as one of its elements the expression of aspect, while an imperfective form carries no such element of meaning.'

[154] See ibid. 15, and Stagg, 'The Abused Aorist', pp. 228–9. Smith, 'Errant Aorist Interpreters', p. 207, writes: 'Other tenses should be recognized as for the purpose of *adding* time or aspect considerations. *As it relates to the matter of aspect*, the aorist is

valid inference, but one should not go further and assume that the unmarked member will thus be more normal or statistically more frequent than the marked one.[155] Any conclusion on these latter points must take into account the nature of the markedness involved as well as other factors which may influence the aspectual contrast.

2. *The modified privative opposition.* While the purely privative opposition was a salutary contribution to the structural treatment of the aspects, it did not long stand as an unaltered model. Observations about actual usage soon led to refinements within the overall framework of the privative opposition. The primary refinement came in regard to a possible *contrastive* meaning for the unmarked member. Comrie describes the sort of linguistic usage which led to such a suggestion:

. . . where the [Russian] Imperfective and Perfective are explicitly contrasted, then the [unmarked] Imperfective may well take on the opposite semantic value of the [marked] Perfective, as in *on mnogo delal* (Ipfv.), *no malo sdelal* (Pfv.) 'he did (Ipfv., i.e. tried to do, undertook) a lot, but did (Pfv., i.e. accomplished) little'; but on its own the Imperfective *delal* does not imply that the action was attempted but unsuccessful.[156]

The use of the unmarked member to reflect a *contrastive* sense can be explained in two ways: it can be regarded as a strictly 'contextual' meaning and not attributed to the unmarked member directly (thus maintaining the purely privative opposition with its *neutral* unmarked member).[157] Or the analysis of the unmarked member can be altered to describe it as possessing *two* possible meanings: the *neutral* sense or the *contrastive* sense (with reference to the value of the marked member).

transparent, it leaves the verbal idea "naked" by adding *nothing* to the basic vocabulary concept. It merely labels or titles the act.'

[155] Comrie, *Aspect*, p. 111, seems open to criticism on this point.

[156] Ibid. 113.

[157] This is the argument of Hansjakob Seiler, 'Zur Problematik des Verbalaspekts', *Cahiers Ferdinand de Saussure*, 26 (1969), 130–1.

Most aspectologists who use the privative opposition in their system have not followed the former explanation of 'contextual' meaning alone, but have attributed the contrastive sense to the unmarked member directly and thus speak of a *dual* value for the unmarked aspect. This approach, which is here referred to as the 'modified privative' opposition, has been adopted by at least four writers on aspect: Ruipérez (1954) for classical Greek, Rundgren (1961) for biblical Hebrew, Johanson (1971) for modern Turkish, and Mussies (1971) for Koine Greek.[158] Ruipérez is sometimes credited with introducing this idea, as an innovation within the overall Jakobsonian framework.[159] What is not commonly stated is that Jakobson himself actually discussed these two values for the unmarked member in his 1932 article:

Die Asymmetrie der korrelativen grammatischen Formen kann als *Antinomie der Signalisierung von A und der Nicht-Signalisierung von A* charakterisiert werden. . . .

Aus der Asymmetrie der korrelativen Formen folgt eine weitere Antinomie—die der allgemeinen und der partiellen Bedeutung der merkmallosen Form, oder mit anderen Worten, die *Antinomie der Nicht-Signalisierung von A und der Signalisierung von Nicht-A. Ein und dasselbe Zeichen* kann *zwei verschiedene Bedeutungen* besitzen.[160]

However, Jakobson seems to view this contrastive sense as the product of the *context* primarily, while the basic sense or the 'general sense' of the unmarked member is the *neutral* value.[161]

In any case, credit must be given to Ruipérez and later writers for the elaboration of the modified privative opposition

---

[158] Martin Sánchez Ruipérez, *Estructura del sistema de aspectos y tiempos del verbo griego antiguo: Análisis funcional sincrónico* (Salamanca: Consejo Superior de Investigaciones Científicas, 1954), recently issued in French trans.: *Structures du système des aspects et des temps du verbe en grec ancien*, trans. M. Plenat and P. Serça (Paris: Les Belles Lettres, 1982); Frithiof Rundgren, *Das althebräische Verbum: Abriß der Aspektlehre* (Stockholm: Almqvist and Wiksell, 1961); Lars Johanson, *Aspekt im Türkischen* (Uppsala: Acta Universitatis Upsaliensis, 1971); and Mussies, *Morphology* (1971).

[159] See e.g. N. E. Collinge, review of Ruipérez, *AL* 7 (1955), 60; and Rundgren, *Aspektlehre*, pp. 35–9.

[160] Jakobson, 'Zur Struktur', p. 15.

[161] Cf. Jakobson, *Shifters, Verbal Categories, and the Russian Verb*, p. 136.

and its detailed application to the analysis of specific languages. Ruipérez's work is of particular interest since he applied this model in detail to ancient Greek (although he deals with the language only up to 300 BC and does not treat NT usage *per se*). He describes the aspects of present and aorist in classical Greek as follows:

Tema de presente y tema de aoristo son términos de una oposición simple privativa, cuya noción básica es la consideración del contenido verbal en su duración.

El tema de presente, como término caracterizado, expresa positivamente la noción básica.

El tema de aoristo, como término no-caracterizado, expresa la puntualidad (*valor negativo*) y la indiferencia a las nociones de duración y de puntualidad (*valor neutro*).[162]

Mussies' view of the aspects of Koine Greek is not developed fully, but his suggestions follow the modified privative approach. He structures three aspects in a double binary hierarchy, with the perfect opposed to the present and aorist in one modified privative opposition, and then the present opposed to the aorist in another. The first opposition is described as follows: 'The non-perfective section of the verb system [i.e. present and aorist aspects] is unmarked as opposed to the perfective section [i.e. perfect or "perfectisch"]. It depends on the context whether the former are to be evaluated as negative with regard to perfectivity (conatives; ingressive aorist) or as indifferent.'[163] The second opposition is viewed as a modified privative type as well: 'According to context the aoristics are therefore either indifferent as to the progression of the action, or they are negative with regard to it ... the aoristic subsystem is unmarked as opposed to the durative subsystem'.[164]

---

[162] Ruipérez, *Estructura*, p. 89. His view of the Greek perfect is that it stands in a purely privative opposition as the marked term contrasting with the present/aorist together, with the basic marking being 'consideración del contenido verbal después de su término' (p. 65).

[163] Mussies, *Morphology*, p. 261.

[164] Ibid. 271.

Since it preserves the neutral meaning of the unmarked member, the modified privative opposition has essentially the same feature mentioned above for the purely privative opposition: overlapping usage of the marked and unmarked members; a largely indefinable sense for the unmarked member (when seen in isolation); and the use of the unmarked member simply to *name* the action in view without further qualification of progress, completion, and so forth.

The further point which needs to be discussed in regard to the modified privative opposition is the question of 'actualizing' the negative or contrastive sense for the unmarked member: that is, attempting to identify the conditions under which one should interpret the unmarked member as *opposite* rather than *neutral* in reference to the value of the marked member.[165]

One case which seems clear is the situation described in the quotation from Comrie at the start of this section,[166] in which the two members are used in close connection with each other; in such a close correlation of the *positive* marked member with the unmarked one, a *negative* value for the latter seems to be the sense intended by the speaker. In these cases a neutral sense misses the point of the correlation. However, beyond this situation (which is difficult to describe in itself), other conditions for 'actualizing' the opposite sense are difficult to delineate in a systematic way. Rundgren says: 'Der Grad der Positivität ist beim merkmallosen Term von der Situation oder der Kontext abhängig. Wird die betreffende Opposition infolge einer besonders engen Kombination des merkmallosen Terms mit dem merkmalhaften *aktualisiert*, schlägt der negative Wert durch, sonst wohl grundsätzlich nicht oder doch weniger deutlich.'[167] Johanson, describing the distinction of negative vs. neutral values for the unmarked member, writes:

---

[165] Rundgren, *Aspektlehre*, p. 39, and Johanson, *Aspekt im Türkischen*, pp. 32–4, 40–1, use the terms *aktualisieren, Aktualisierung* in this way. Ruipérez and Mussies do not discuss this question directly.

[166] Comrie, *Aspect*, p. 113.

[167] Rundgren, *Aspektlehre*, p. 39.

'Diese theoretisch einleuchtende Distinktion ist selbstver-
ständlich in der Praxis oft undurchführbar. . . . Demnach
erheben wir mit den Termini "neutral" und "negative" für
diese doppelte Funktion nicht unbedingt Anspruch darauf, die
proportionale Verteilung der Werte untereinander in jedem
konkreten Falle klar bestimmen zu können.'[168]

To phrase this in terms of 'actualizing the contrastive sense'
immediately suggests that the neutral idea is more normal or
expected and the contrastive sense is abnormal and so must be
indicated by overt features in the utterance. Thus, if no clear
indicators of the contrastive sense are present, the neutral
sense should be understood. Given the nature of this distinction, such an assumption seems plausible. However, the
structure may be reversed in a given language to favour the
contrastive sense, requiring the neutral one to be actualized by
overt indicators. Or the two may be regarded as equal in
likelihood of occurrence, and one would need to look for
actualization of one or the other in every case.

To summarize, the privative opposition is that in which one
member is marked and the other member is unmarked in
some sense (either neutral or negative) in regard to the basic
feature of the opposition. Normally when reference is made to
markedness or non-markedness, this type of opposition is in
view. Although this aproach to aspect in the IE languages has
been followed quite frequently over the last half-century, there
has been no general agreement as to which aspect is marked or
unmarked, nor as to what the basic feature of the opposition
might be. Writers who have regarded the present/imperfective
member as the marked one (with the basic feature they
suggest in parentheses) include Ruipérez (duration), Galton
('desire to dwell on a process in disregard of the flux of time'),
and Bakker ('coincidence').[169] Others who regard the aoristic/
perfective as the marked member include Jakobson ('die

---

[168] Johanson, *Aspekt im Türkischen*, p. 32.
[169] Ruipérez, *Estructura*, p. 89; Galton, 'A New Theory of the Slavic Verbal Aspect',
pp. 143–4; and Bakker, *Greek Imperative*, pp. 24–7.

absolute Grenze der Handlung'), Forsyth ('total event'), and Armstrong ('countability').[170] One other variation which should be mentioned is the double binary opposition, with three members set in two pairs of privative contrasts. Thus, Collinge suggested that the IE present and perfect are opposed as to *completion* (with the perfect as marked), while the present and aorist are opposed as to *duration* (with the present as marked).[171]

Several writers have expressed doubts about whether the privative opposition has any place in aspectology, especially in regard to Greek aspects. It is thought that a phonological structure such as this cannot be valid in the grammatical realm,[172] but surely it should not be ruled out for grammar a priori; the real test is whether it helps to explain the actual usage of forms. A more persuasive reason for rejecting this structure would be cases where each aspect of a language appears in usage to possess a positive value rather than a positive-neutral opposition.[173] This issue will be taken up again at the end of this section.

In contrast to the privative opposition, the other major type of linguistic opposition is the *equipollent* one. The general characteristic of this type of opposition is that all members are *marked* in some way,[174] and thus they stand as more or less equal terms. Trubetzkoy's term 'equipollent' is adopted here, although two of his opposition-types (*graduell* and *äquipollent*) are included under the one term.[175]

---

[170] Jakobson, 'Zur Struktur', p. 6; Forsyth, *Grammar of Aspect*, p. 15; and Armstrong, 'The Ancient Greek Aorist as the Aspect of Countable Action', p. 11.

[171] N. E. Collinge, 'Some Reflections on Comparative Historical Syntax', *AL* 12 (1960), 95–6. John Lyons, *Introduction to Theoretical Linguistics* (Cambridge: at the University Press, 1968), 314–15, suggests the same structure for ancient Greek. This is similar to the view of Ruipérez mentioned earlier.

[172] L. Jenaro MacLennan, *El problema del aspecto verbal* (Madrid: Editorial Gredos, 1962), 56–7, 137–42.

[173] Comrie, *Aspect*, pp. 113–14; and Lloyd, *Verb*, pp. 12, 84.

[174] Cf. Comrie, *Aspect*, p. 111: 'It is not, at least not necessarily, the case that all oppositions will have an unmarked member and a marked member or members; in some oppositions, all members may be equally marked.'

[175] See Trubetzkoy, *Grundzüge der Phonologie*, p. 67.

The linguistic evidence which gives rise to this structural model is seen in situations where change from one form to another produces a different sense, not just a neutral one or the loss of the value of the parallel form.[176] In such cases it seems that both (or all) members have some positive or negative meaning; there are no *neutral* members, as in the privative opposition.

However, within this general framework the members of the opposition can bear somewhat different logical relationships to each other. To reflect this, the equipollent category will be divided into three subtypes: the *contradictory*, the *contrary*, and the *mixed* opposition. The first two are based on suggestions made by Jakobson[177] and also bear some affinities, as will be seen, to the linguistic structures which Lyons calls 'complementarity' and 'antonymy'.[178] The third subtype is based on ideas advanced by Friedrich.[179]

1. *The contradictory opposition*. In this equipollent opposition there are *two* members only, and both are marked somehow in regard to the same basic feature; furthermore, the two 'markings' are opposed in such a way that the members are mutually exclusive and yet include all possible situations in one or the other. Thus, both cannot be true, nor can both be false, in regard to a particular situation to which the opposition is applicable (much like 'contradictory propositions' in logic). Lyons describes this type of opposition under the label of 'complementary' or 'ungradable' opposites:

Ungradable opposites . . . divide the universe of discourse (i.e. the objects of which they are predicable . . .) into two complementary

---

[176] Cf. Comrie, *Aspect*, p. 114: 'The replacement of an Aorist by an Imperfect or vice versa usually implies a different meaning altogether, not merely the loss of some information by use of an unmarked category.'

[177] Roman Jakobson, 'Observations sur le classement phonologiques des consonnes' (1939), repr. in Roman Jakobson, *Selected Writings*, i. *Phonological Studies*, (The Hague: Mouton, 1962), 273. The terms 'contradictoire' and 'contraire' were used also by Holt, *Études d'aspect*, pp. 26–7, but in a very different model of structural relations and thus in a different sense from their use in this book.

[178] Lyons, *Semantics*, pp. 270–80.

[179] Friedrich, *Aspect Theory*, pp. 14, 37.

subsets. It follows from this, not only that the predication of either one of the pair implies the predication of the negation of the other, but also that the predication of the negation of either implies the predication of the other.[180]

Under a scheme of *contradictory* oppositions, one could analyse the aspects according to two variations of the same pattern.

a. The two members are seen as marked with *positive* and *negative* values with reference to the same basic feature (e.g. durative vs. non-durative, punctual vs. non-punctual, completed vs. non-completed).

b. The two members are complementary opposites, not reducible to a 'positive vs. negative' schema but otherwise having the same logical relationship (e.g. 'male vs. female', which is neither 'male vs. non-male' nor 'female vs. non-female'—yet the two are nevertheless contradictory). In aspect, this could be exhibited by an opposition of 'durative vs. instantaneous or momentary', since these are usually regarded as complementary opposites.

Many older treatments of the Greek aspects seem to regard the aspectual distinction of present vs. aorist as a contradictory opposition in the sense described here. The two aspects were seen to possess a positive or negative value, not a neutral one, and were regarded as contradictory. This distinction in Greek was commonly described as durative vs. non-durative or continuing vs. momentary. Winer-Moulton, for example, explain the distinction between aorist and present imperatives in NT Greek in the following way:

The aorist imperative . . . is used in reference either to an action which rapidly passes and should take place at once, or at any rate to an action which is to be undertaken once only. . . . The present imperative is used in reference to an action which is already commenced and is to be continued, or which is lasting and frequently repeated.[181]

---

[180] Lyons, *Semantics*, pp. 271–2.
[181] WM, *Grammar*, pp. 393–4.

Holt presents a variation on this opposition when he treats the three Greek aspects as a contradictory opposition of two members, with the third member neutral to this opposition:

Par l'aspect du parfait le procès est regardé après son terme, par celui du présent il est considéré avant son terme, ou plus précisément: l'aspect du parfait désigne le procès avec son terme, *celui du présent sans son terme.* . . .

L'essentiel de la notion de l'aspect en grec ancien est d'indiquer si le procès est regardé après que son terme est passé ou non, et il s'ensuit que l'aoriste, qui est indifférent quant à cette distinction, indique *un procès qui n'est considéré ni avant ni après le terme.*[182]

This is something of a combination of privative opposition (aorist neutral to the basic feature) and equipollent opposition (contradictory present and perfect).

Adrados criticized Holt's treatment for opposing the present directly to the perfect; in its place he presents a system in which the perfect is opposed to the present and aorist together (as 'stative/non-stative'), while the present and aorist are opposed as to whether the action has reached its end ('término') or not.[183] In his view there are contradictory oppositions operating in Greek, but the present and perfect are not systematically opposed to each other. These options will be evaluated in section 2.5.

2. *The contrary opposition.* This opposition generally contains more than two members, all of which are marked in some way in regard to the same basic feature. This basic feature, however, is a 'gradable' quality, so that the various members are marked for differing degrees of the quality and are arranged like points on a continuum, with two extreme members (at the opposite poles) and one or more mediate members ranged along the continuum between them. The members of this opposition are mutually exclusive, but not *contradictory* in the sense described above. The relationship

---

[182] Holt, *Études d'aspect,* pp. 31–3.
[183] F. R. Adrados, 'Observaciones sobre el aspecto verbal', *Estudios clásicos,* 1 (1950), 11–15, 19–22.

between any two members, and especially between the extreme members, could be described as *contrary:* that is, both
cannot be true, but both can be false (since there are other
members) in regard to a situation to which the opposition is
applicable.[184]

This model is not as common in aspect studies. Turner's
analysis of the NT Greek aspects fits this scheme in some
sense, although it is not an exact fit and he would perhaps
describe the relationships differently. He describes the present
as continuous or 'linear' and the aorist as instantaneous or
'punctiliar', with the perfect standing somewhat between the
two, combining both these features: 'The *Aktionsart* belonging
properly to the [perfect] is either fulfilment in the present of a
process begun in the past or else the contemplation of an event
having taken place in the past with an interval intervening. . . . It is therefore a combining of the *Aktionsarten* of aorist
and present.'[185]

3. *The mixed opposition.* This structure, described by Friedrich
under the term 'equivalent',[186] is more promising for aspect
studies. The mixed opposition will normally be binary, with
both members marked, but the markings will be for *divergent*
values: that is, they are not distinct in regard to one *precise*
'basic feature', although the markings both fit within the
overall framework of aspect-meaning. Thus, the two markings
operate on differing planes and are not necessarily contradictory or contrary to each other. This is generally the approach

---

[184] Cf. Lyons's description of 'gradable opposites' or 'antonymy' in *Semantics,* pp.
272, 279. This is also similar to Trubetzkoy's 'gradual' opposition; cf. Trubetzkoy,
Grundzüge der Phonologie, p. 67.

[185] MT, *Syntax,* pp. 81–2. Holt, *Études d'aspect,* p. 28, mentions such a view but does
not prefer it.

[186] Friedrich, *Aspect Theory,* pp. 14, 37. Friedrich's analysis of Homeric aspect
presents another double contrast, but with variations from those cited earlier. He
contrasts (p. 27) the present with the perfect and aorist as durative/non-durative',
and then the perfect and aorist as 'realized/non-realized'. Both of these are regarded
as equipollent oppositions, but he suggests that the basic contrasts are not single but
multiple, since the aorist is thus both non-durative and non-realized, the perfect is
non-durative and realized, and the usage of all three is affected by other secondary
contrasts.

which Burton adopts to the Greek present and perfect: the two represent action as 'in progress' vs. 'completed'. These two, properly understood, are not incompatible, although combined with other linguistic factors they produce secondary distinctions which are clearly contrastive. The aorist meanwhile is indifferent to these values, or 'indefinite', 'without reference to progress or completion'.[187]

A different way to view this opposition is to see it with *two* or more 'basic features' which are at issue, and to see the members as alternately marked and unmarked in regard to these basic features in a multiple privative relationship. Thus, one member could be *marked* for durativity but *unmarked* for totality while the other is conversely *unmarked* for durativity and *marked* for totality. Again, this multi-featured opposition produces contrastive pairs of verb-forms in given contexts, but the markings themselves are not contrary or contradictory.

This scheme can be illustrated by several treatments of the NT Greek present and aorist, although the grammarians in view define these with certain positive but divergent meanings and do not emphasize the structural relation between the aspects. Robertson and Blass-Debrunner-Funk, for example, define the present essentially as a durative or continuative aspect and the aorist as a 'summary' one, presenting the action as an indivisible whole without regard for any duration or progress which may have been involved.[188] The aorist in this scheme is not simply unmarked or neutral in regard to the feature of duration, but instead is positively marked for 'totality': presenting the action as a whole, summing it up as though it were *single*, although it may objectively include various parts or extended actions within this totality. In this way both aspects are marked but the two markings operate on divergent planes and are thus contradictory or contrary.

---

[187] Burton, *MT*, §§ 5–6, 35, 95.
[188] Robertson, *Grammar,* pp. 823, 831–5; and BDF, *Grammar,* § 318.

1. 3. 3 *Summary of the relationships of the aspects to each other*

In this section it has been argued that there is a need to view aspects in a structure of oppositions. In addition, the question of what relationships may exist between the aspects has been considered, and a number of subtypes have been surveyed. The two major types are the *privative* opposition (one member marked, one unmarked) and the *equipollent* opposition (all members marked). In broad terms these provide ideas for the analysis undertaken in Chapter 2 of this book. But two points of summary can be mentioned here.

First, it should be noticed that many studies of aspect which emphasize oppositions have not clearly distinguished aspect from procedural character in the sense described in section 1.2. In some cases this structural approach has given a means for explaining difficulties which arise from intermingling the two areas of meaning. For example, Ruipérez's privative treatment of the Greek present and aorist as 'marked vs. unmarked for duration' provides a device for avoiding problems that come when *durativity* is taken as an aspect-value. Such problems can be solved apart from privative marking theory if one separates aspect from procedural characteristics like duration. However, some who emphasize structural oppositions (e.g. Forsyth) have also distinguished aspect from procedural character, so the two approaches are not mutually exclusive. Whatever the aspect values, there is a need to view them within the system of oppositions which the language exhibits.

Second, a preliminary preference should be recorded here for the *equipollent* type of opposition over the privative one in the analysis of aspect in NT Greek. In the places in which the aspects are most clearly in contrast (i.e. in the non-indicative forms of the verb, and in the past-time oppositions of aorist vs. imperfect indicative), the evidence of usage suggests that both the aspects have a positive marking, rather than one being merely the neutral or negative foil for the other.[189] Full

---

[189] As suggested for ancient Greek by Comrie, *Aspect*, pp. 113–14; and Lloyd, *Verb*,

validation for this claim will be developed in the examination of the use of the aspects in Chapters 4-6.

1. 4. Aspect and Discourse-Functions

The fourth major step in modern discussion of verbal aspect has been the consideration of how the aspects may play a *discourse* role in a language: that is, how they may function to communicate meaning not only at phrase level or at sentence level but in regard to larger segments of language. A number of recent linguists have stressed the importance of investigating linguistic categories in the light of this larger perspective, and verbal aspect has been included in this investigation. Hopper, for example, writes:

This introduction has related a view of Aspect as an essentially discourse-level, rather than a semantic, sentence-level phenomenon. I have presented it in this way out of a conviction that morphological and local-syntactic accounts of aspect are either incomplete or, to the extent that they are valid, essentially show the sentence-level correlates of discourse structures. . . . Our understanding of aspect should be rooted in the last resort in discourse.[190]

It is the contention of the present book, however, that such discourse-functions do not exhaust the meanings of the aspects, nor are they the primary meanings. Aspectual meaning in and of itself must be distinguished from these uses, although it is important to analyse the ways in which aspect secondarily contributes to the ability of a language to structure extended texts. Three major functions of the aspects at discourse level have been suggested.

pp. 12, 84, and for oppositions in many languages by Dahl, *Tense and Aspect Systems*, pp. 69–72.

[190] Hopper, 'Aspect between Discourse and Grammar' p. 16. See also Wallace, 'Figure and Ground', pp. 207–8, who emphasizes 'that verbal categories are important components in the structure of discourses, and indeed, that one does not truly understand "the meaning" of a verbal category in a particular language unless one understands its place in discourse'.

1. 4. 1 *To show the nature of the speech-situation*

An early writer who emphasized a discourse-function for the verb was Weinrich. Along the way, however, he rejected both time and aspect as the significance of the 'tenses' in language, and argued that a discourse function of the tense is the true meaning. In his view, aspect was 'invented' by linguists who observed correctly that the tenses indicated something far different from past, present, and future, but it was a wrong turn from the start to posit the traditional aspect-distinctions.[191] The most significant function of the tenses, according to Weinrich, is to inform the hearer (or reader) about the nature of the speech-situation in which he finds himself: whether it is a 'discursive' or a 'narrative' speech-situation. Present, perfect, and future tenses, for example, indicate the former, while preterite and pluperfect tenses show the latter situation.[192] The difference between these two situations centres primarily on the listener's degree of involvement in the events described: whether they touch him immediately and directly or are remote from him. As Weinrich develops it, the tenses are an important marker to the listener of the attitude he should take towards a spoken (or written) utterance:

If, by means of certain tenses, we know that what is said is discursive, as listeners we have to adopt the non-relaxed attitude which corresponds to a situation that touches upon our own existence. If, on the other hand, by means of other tenses, we know that what is said is merely narrated, we can listen with a great deal of relaxation. . . . These two different categories of speech situation are like different levels of alarm in the discourse.[193]

It is true that, in terms of general frequency, there is in most

---

[191] Harald Weinrich, 'Tense and Time', *AL*, NS 1 (1970), 31–2. In his book *Tempus: Besprochene und Erzählte Welt* (Stuttgart: Kohlhammer, 1964), 152, Weinrich labels aspect 'ein unglücklicher Begriff'.

[192] Weinrich, *Tempus*, pp. 44–59; and 'Tense and Time', pp. 32–5. He suggests a secondary distinction among the preterite tenses, to be treated in the following section.

[193] Weinrich. 'Tense and Time', p. 35.

languages a correlation of certain tenses with narration, and other tenses with discursive material following the pattern suggested by Weinrich. To a limited degree it is plausible that the tenses serve as rough markers of one type of discourse or the other. But one must recognize that so much overlap in discourse-type occurs (e.g. narrative mixed with dialogue, argument based on narrative material) and tenses so often appear contrary to the normal pattern (e.g. historical presents, perfects used in narration) that it seems unlikely that Weinrich's view is correct in its full form. The tenses and aspects surely mean more than he suggests, although their more central meanings are perhaps secondarily useful as indicators of the general discourse-type.

1. 4. 2 *To show prominence in narrative*

Along with his primary distinction of speech-situations. Weinrich proposed a secondary distinction among preterite tenses: between tenses which relate *foreground* narration and those relating *background* narration. This is the difference between aorist and imperfect in Greek, in his view.[194] Others have advanced this idea, both before Weinrich[195] and after him.[196] The distinction between the two types of narration is put succinctly by Wallace: 'Included in the foreground, for in-

---

[194] Ibid. 37–8. See also his *Tempus*, 292, where he writes: 'Alle Anzeichen sprechen dafür, daß auch im Griechischen die Tempora Imperfekt und Aorist Hintergrund und Vordergrund der Erzählung unterscheiden.'

[195] Smyth, *Grammar*, §§ 1898–9, 1909, 1929. Also a very brief mention (in connection with the more 'descriptive' use of the imperfect) in Jespersen, *Philosophy of Grammar*, pp. 275–6; and SD, *Syntax*, pp. 276–7.

[196] William Diver, 'The System of Relevance of the Homeric Verb', *Acta Linguistica Hafniensia*, 12 (1969), 45–68; Forsyth, *Grammar of Aspect*, pp. 9–10; Paul J. Hopper, 'Aspect and Foregrounding in Discourse', in T. Givón (ed.), *Syntax and Semantics*, xii. *Discourse and Syntax* (New York: Academic Press, 1979), 213–41; Paul J. Hopper and Sandra A. Thompson, 'Transitivity in Grammar and Discourse', *Lg*. 56 (1980), 283–6; Hopper, 'Aspect between Discourse and Grammar', pp. 3–18; Wallace, 'Figure and Ground', pp. 208–9; and Linda R. Waugh and Monique Monville–Burston. 'Aspect and Discourse Function: The French Simple Past in Newspaper Usage', *Lg*. 62 (1986), 846–77.

stance, are the more important events of a narrative, the more important steps of a procedure, the central points of an exposition, the main characters or entities involved in an episode. The background includes events of lesser importance, subsidiary procedures, secondary points, descriptions, elaborations, digressions, and minor characters or things'.[197]

Most writers who discuss the use of the aspects in this regard present it as a *subsidiary* function in narrative of the more basic aspectual meanings. However, some have argued that this is the primary meaning of the aspects and any other senses of completion, progression, and so forth are secondary manifestations of this discourse-level meaning.[198] Several lines of evidence point to the former view as a more accurate reflection of the linguistic usage in ancient Greek. The aspects are used often in non-narrative ways exhibiting clear aspectual values quite apart from any foreground/background distinction (in dependent forms such as subjunctives and infinitives: e.g. συμπαραλαβεῖν vs. συμπαραλαμβάνειν in Acts 15: 37-8: and in imperatives and other discursive forms). Also, studies of language-acquisition in children have shown that, even before they are able to structure connected discourses, they can use aspect to reflect different descriptions in individual statements.[199] It is better to conclude that the primary aspectual values (e.g. perfective and imperfective) serve in a *secondary* way to reflect the prominence of events recorded in a narrative, with perfective verbs used of the foreground events and imperfective verbs of the background ones.[200] This distinction appears to be a valid function of the aspects in narration, and NT illustrations of this will be given in section 3.5.1.

---

[197] Wallace, 'Figure and Ground', p. 208.
[198] See articles by Hopper (1979; with Thompson, 1980; and 1982) cited in the preceding notes.
[199] Delancey, 'Aspect, Transitivity and Viewpoint', pp. 179–80.
[200] This is the view of Wallace, 'Figure and Ground', p. 209.

1. 4. 3 *To show temporal sequence in narrative*

A final discourse-function suggested for the aspects is closely related to the previous one: their use to reflect temporal sequence in narrative. It is a long-standing view of the Greek aorist and imperfect (and of related aspects in other languages) that aorist (or perfective) aspect commonly denotes *sequential* events, while imperfective aspect denotes *simultaneous* occurrences.[201] This is thought to be true of the aspects in main clauses and in subordinate ones.

In main clauses the contrast of aorist and imperfect often reflects (alongside other differences) this pattern of temporal ordering: aorists denoting events in sequence one after another, with imperfects inserted here and there to relate events which occurred concurrently with the aorists.[202] A brief example of this in the NT is 1 Cor. 3:6 ἐγὼ ἐφύτευσα, Ἀπολλῶς ἐπότισεν, ἀλλὰ ὁ θεὸς ηὔξανεν. In over-translated form this is 'I planted, *then* Apollos watered, but *all the while* God was causing the growth'. This temporal sequencing can be seen also in close combination with the distinction of foreground and background in Acts 7: 20-5. Background or descriptive features are often events or conditions which occur simultaneously with the main (usually sequenced) events.

In subordinate clauses as well the aspects frequently reflect an element of temporal sequence in their usage in context. This is especially true in temporal clauses, but can be valid for other types of dependent clauses. Thus, present and imperfect verbs are frequently simultaneous with the action of the main clause, and aorist verbs are normally antecedent to the main verb.[203] Examples of this in NT usage can be seen in lexicon entries for the temporal conjunctions ὅταν, ὅτε, and ὡς, which report precisely this temporal sequencing.[204]

---

[201] Buttmann, *Ausführliche griechische Sprachlehre*, §§ 81 (4) and 137 (2).

[202] Bakker, *Greek Imperative*, pp. 24–7; Ruijgh, *Autour de 'τε épique'*, pp. 235–49; and Forsyth, *Grammar of Aspect*, pp. 9–10.

[203] Hettrich, *Kontext und Aspekt*, pp. 94–7; and Rijksbaron, Review of Hettrich, *Kontext und Aspekt*, pp. 231–4.

[204] BAGD, *Lexicon*, pp. 287–8, 898.

As mentioned in section 1.1.3, several writers advance the opinion that aspect in its essence is concerned with nothing more than temporal ordering of events relative to each other. The view presented in that section is that this is a secondary function of the aspects, whose primary meanings concern the perspective or focus of the speaker with reference to the internal make-up of the action. Here it is sufficient to add the points noted in the foreground/background discussion: that various non-narrative uses of the aspects are difficult to explain on a 'temporal-sequence' theory. However, a comprehensive aspectual approach must reflect this function of the aspects in narrative material.

1. 4. 4 *Summary of the relationship of aspect- and discourse-functions*

The point of this section is that aspect can play a role at the discourse level of language, as a device for structuring narrative and for reflecting other features of meaning in regard to the larger units of language in which it occurs. More particularly, it can reflect the difference between foreground and background events in a narrative, and it can show the temporal sequence of events between main clauses and some types of subordinate clauses. These discourse-level meanings do not, however, exhaust the meaning of the aspects, nor are they the primary values. Instead, they are secondary functions of the basic aspect-values in relation to the larger contexts in which they occur.

To sum up the argument of the chapter to this point, understanding verbal aspect involves two issues: distinguishing aspect from other features of meaning with which it is commonly connected, and noting its variable function in relation to these other features. The four features of meaning which are closely related to aspect are: tense, procedural characteristics of verbs and actions, structural oppositions among the aspects, and discourse-functions. This section has surveyed these features in order to propose a definition of verbal aspect which takes such relationships into account.

1. 5 Concluding Observations on Method in Defining Aspect

1. 5. 1 *Levels of complexity in defining aspect*

In defining aspect one should operate on two levels. At a basic level, one can give simple, general descriptions of aspect which are useful for many purposes. A number of serviceable definitions of this sort have been given, usually focusing on the *nature* of the action, the *kind* of occurrence involved, *how* it takes place, or the make-up of the action itself, in contrast to its temporal location or *when* it occurs. Moorhouse gives a useful definition of this kind: 'Aspect represents the manner in which the action etc. is envisaged as occurring by the speaker. This "way of looking at the action" is itself basically temporal, showing not *when*, but *how* the action occurs in relation to time.'[205] Mitchell states such a definition as well: 'the view adopted in this essay is of Aspect concerned with extension or spread, in time certainly but also often enough in space, while Tense and associated deictic categories relate rather to location in these dimensions'.[206] Such descriptions are certainly the best place to begin a definition of aspect, and in many cases there is no need to go beyond these to more complicated discussion, which may only frustrate rather than clarify. If one is merely introducing the category, simple descriptions will serve quite well.

However, there is at times a need to define aspect more rigorously, especially if one wishes to interpret finer nuances of textual meaning based on aspect-distinctions. In this case one must move to a different level of discussion. It is at this more complex level that one encounters several problems of method apart from the difficulties involved in the phenomena themselves.

---

[205] Moorhouse, *Syntax*, p. 181.

[206] T. F. Mitchell, 'The English Appearance of Aspect', in D. J. Allerton, Edward Carney, and David Holdcroft (eds.), *Function and Context in Linguistic Analysis: a Festschrift for William Haas* (Cambridge: Cambridge University Press, 1979), 159–60.

1. 5. 2 *Problems in defining aspect*

The difficulties which will be considered here are all related to the complex interactions of aspect with other features of meaning which have been presented in this chapter. When one investigates a definition of aspect at a more complex level, it is necessary to resolve these problems of method.

In attempting to define aspect more clearly, one discovers a welter of disparate ideas of what the category actually involves, and this in itself presents problems of method. As shown in this chapter, differing analyses of aspect include definitions centring on:

1. the temporal relationship of the action to some reference-point: occurrence *during* or *before* some other point;
2. procedural or situational characteristics of the action itself or inherent in the speaker's presentation of the action: durative/momentary, repeated/single, dynamic/ stative, completed/incomplete, inceptive/terminative, and so on;
3. differences arising from relating the aspects to each other in variant structural oppositions: markedness or non-markedness for various features;
4. discourse-related features: prominence and sequencing in narrative;
5. The viewpoint or perspective which the speaker takes towards an action: viewed in progress (inner view focusing on make-up of the action, ignoring beginning and end-points) or viewed as a whole (outer view including beginning and end-point, ignoring internal make-up).

These disparate definitions of aspect arise from the complex interconnections of aspect with other closely related categories of meaning. In the face of such complexities, it is easy to tolerate confusion of meanings (refusing to differentiate between the various elements) or to be reductionistic (collapsing all the distinctions of meaning into one).

In contrast to this, the argument of this book is that there is a need (1) to distinguish aspect from these other features by stating a primary or invariant meaning for aspect apart from secondary effects produced by its combination with other elements; and (2) to define the function (or secondary effects) of the invariant in combination with these other elements.[207] The latter of these two is a task to be undertaken in the third chapter of this book, and then supported further in Chapters 4-6. The former requires investigation of an invariant meaning both for *aspect* as a general category and for the *aspects* as individual members of that category in a given language. Investigation of the individual aspects will be done in the next chapter, but stating an invariant meaning for the general category of aspect must be done here.

Stating a primary meaning for aspect apart from secondary effects, however, is vexed by two further difficulties of method: the doubtful validity of stating an invariant meaning for aspect,[208] and uncertainty concerning which feature of meaning to focus upon as primary.

Some writers on aspect, especially more recent ones, despair of ever arriving at a useful invariant meaning of aspect in

---

[207] See this approach in Lloyd, *Verb*, pp. 8–10, 14; Bache, 'Aspect and Aktionsart', p. 67; Hopper, 'Aspect between Discourse and Grammar', pp. 4–5, 15; Alan Timberlake, 'Invariance and the Syntax of Russian Aspect', in *Tense–Aspect* (1982), 327–8; Smith, 'Aspectual Choice', pp. 491–5; and Dahl, *Tense and Aspect Systems*, pp. 3–11, 22–3. Bache, *Verbal Aspect*, pp. 5–25, 145–52. Working with two levels of aspectual analysis is the approach taken in contemporary Soviet aspectology as well, though the distinction between viewpoint aspect and procedural character is not clearly maintained. See Aleksandr V. Bondarko, 'Stand und Perspektiven der Aspektologie in der UdSSR', in Wolfgang Girke and Helmut Jachnow (eds.), *Theoretische Linguistik in Osteuropa* (Tübingen: Niemeyer, 1976), 123–39. For Greek usage, K. L. McKay, 'Aspects of the Imperative in Ancient Greek', *Antichthon*, 20 (1986), 41–2, makes reference to a 'basic significance' for each aspect, as well as an 'interplay between this and the context' which produces 'a range of realizations'.

[208] See the comment by Jeffrey Heath, 'Aspectual "Skewing" in Two Australian Languages: Mara, Nunggubuyu', in *Tense and Aspect* (1981), 93, in discussing the aspectual contrast in an aboriginal language: 'it is difficult or impossible to find a single core meaning *(Grundbedeutung)* for a particular morpheme'. Later he says (p. 97): 'the search for a "unified" analysis of this opposition is a fundamentally misguided research strategy, and . . . the details we have provided make sense in functional terms even without discovering invariant semantic properties of each morpheme'.

general or of the aspects of a language in particular.[209] Their opinion is that attempts at stating an invariant meaning are inevitably plagued by being (1) too general or ingenious to be of value, or (2) not sufficiently central or transparent in the various uses of the aspect, so that the secondary meanings are of more practical use anyway.[210]

Thus, it is thought better to state subrules or descriptions of how aspects combine with other elements to produce various meanings. This, of course, must be done, but how is one to give a useful description of aspect's interaction and combination with other categories if one has no general conception of what the category is itself? Before one can meaningfully evaluate this interaction, it is essential to have in mind at least a heuristic and provisional estimate of the semantic value which is central to the category. This general idea may be only an estimate of the 'internal consistency' which can be discovered between the various secondary meanings,[211] a hypothesis derived from investigating what meaning could plausibly produce the multiple secondary senses when combined with other distinguishable elements. An estimate of the invariant meaning apart from other features is important for interpreting aspect when it is combined with them in a given context.

The validity of stating an invariant meaning for the category of aspect is based ultimately on the conviction that such a widespread grammatical feature (as it is in Greek) cannot derive all its meaning from the context.[212] There must be

---

[209] Cf. Ranjit Chatterjee, 'On Cross-Linguistic Categories and Related Problems', in *Tense–Aspect* (1982), 337: 'we have not succeeded in isolating or defining a tense/aspect category (giving it Gesamtbedeutungen) in the most studied languages [e.g. Slavic languages and Homeric Greek]'. He speaks also (p. 343) of 'the possible indefinability of the category' and agrees (p. 340) with a suggestion that 'aspect is related to the unconscious and beyond direct analysis'.

[210] Timberlake, 'Invariance and the Syntax of Russian Aspect', pp. 305–8, 317, 327–8. His subtitle on p. 305, 'Stalking the Wild Invariant', though picturesque, reflects his pessimism about this.

[211] This is the conclusion that Timberlake himself comes to, despite his pessimism about the status of the invariant (ibid. 327–8).

[212] Hopper, 'Aspect between Discourse and Grammar', p. 4.

something there to interact with the context in the first place. To be sure, one can expect aspect, like any linguistic feature, to be maximally redundant in a context—that is, it will correlate with other elements of a sentence, and there will be little of importance which the aspect alone contributes to the overall meaning. But aspect in Greek can be investigated in various ways by which the effect of the context is minimized and the meaning of the category itself thrown into sharper focus. For example, one can examine 'minimal pairs' of contrasting forms, testing what meaning remains when. as many other variables as possible are eliminated (e.g. comparing present, aorist, and perfect *infinitives* of the same verb in similar constructions). Or one can examine the same aspect *across* a single feature of contextual variation (e.g. the aorist used with stative vs. active verb).[213] When this is done, one discovers that there is clearly an invariant sense for aspect in Greek apart from contextual effects.[214]

However, one concession must be made to those who question the value of an invariant meaning: the invariant sense of aspect in Greek is not so primary or dominant over the secondary meanings that it is transparent or obvious in all its usage. The secondary distinctions do at times supersede in the writer's choice of a form, so that they are indispensable to the correct interpretation of the sense: one cannot refer only to the invariant meaning in such cases.[215] This may occur in a

[213] This is what Smith has done for a 'unified analysis' of simple aspect in English in 'Aspectual Choice', pp. 491–5.

[214] This will be demonstrated in later chapters, though virtually no one disputes this conclusion for Greek. A most detailed treatment of aspectual function in ancient Greek following this method is given by Stork, *Aspectual Usage* (see esp. 23–5, 360–95). His description of the secondary or combinatory meanings of the Greek aspects is very similar to the results presented in this book, but his conclusions about the invariant meaning of aspect itself combine what I would label a 'viewpoint' feature with what I consider to be a secondary function of the aspects. He concludes that aspect as a category involves two basic oppositions (p. 395): (1) 'the primary relevancy of the process/activity' vs. 'the primary relevancy of the actualization/effectuation' of the situation denoted by the verb (clearly a viewpoint distinction); and (2) non-specific vs. specific reference (a valid distinction, but secondary, in my view).

[215] Cf. Timberlake, 'Invariance and the Syntax of Russian Aspect', pp. 305–8,

given context only (e.g. συνήλλασσεν in Acts 7: 26 with a conative meaning), with all uses of a verb in a particular lexical sense (e.g. different senses of οἶδα and γινώσκω depending on the aspect used),[216] or in a wider range of uses of a certain form (e.g. 'general precept vs. specific command' as the normal distinction in the present vs. aorist imperative).[217]

The final issue of method concerns uncertainty about which feature is regarded as primary. At various places in this chapter it has been argued that the central or invariant meaning of aspect is 'the viewpoint or perspective which the speaker takes in regard to the action'. The chapter has been concerned with distinguishing this from certain other features of meaning (i.e. temporal sequence, procedural character, structural oppositions, and discourse functions) which have been confused with aspect because they relate so closely and affect its sense in various ways. However, many have argued that one of these other features is central to aspect, and viewpoint is secondary if observed at all.

Apart from the arguments advanced earlier, it is important to state at this point why, in terms of general method, the feature of 'viewpoint', and not one of the others, should be regarded as central or invariant in aspect. The fundamental reason for this is that viewpoint or perspective appears to be the residue of meaning left when the other features are stripped away or minimized by various means. This is the best articulation of the aspect-value in a variety of situations where one can study the aspects without interference from the other features: examining the pair of past-tense forms (aorist and imperfect) where primary tense is not a distinctive factor, examining the sense of individual present and aorist impera-

---

326–8. As Timberlake notes (pp. 306–7), Forsyth (*Grammar of Aspect*, p. 118) makes this observation also, despite his advocacy of a clear invariant statement for Russian aspect: 'these secondary criteria are so firmly associated with the imperfective that to some extent they act in the mind of the Russian speaker as criteria for the positive choice of the imperfective'.

[216] This is the argument of Richard J. Erickson, 'Oida and Ginōskō and Verbal Aspect in Pauline Usage', *Westminster Theological Journal*, 44 (1982), 110–22.

[217] To be developed in ch. 5.

tives in direct speech where narrative sequence and relative time are not factors, examining aspect-function within the same procedural character of actual occurrences or lexical and phrasal meaning (e.g. aorist vs. present with 'achievement' verbs), or examining the same aspect with variant procedural characteristics (e.g. aorist in stative vs. active verbs). While certain of the other features can provide an explanation for individual variations in function, 'viewpoint' distinctions as the primary value of aspect can account for all of them.[218] Thus, the argument of this book is that 'viewpoint' is the most plausible invariant meaning to explain the full range of secondary senses which are produced in aspect-usage. It must be reiterated, however, that the real usefulness of this invariant meaning comes when it serves as the starting-point for analysing aspect's interaction with the other elements. As stated earlier, the invariant sense of aspect in Greek is not so dominant over the secondary senses that it is transparent throughout. Combinatory meanings at times supersede in the speaker's choice, so that they are indispensable to correct interpretation: one cannot refer only to the invariant in such cases.[219]

1. 6 Summary Definition of Aspect

Verbal aspect in NT Greek is that category in the grammar of the verb which reflects the focus or viewpoint of the speaker in regard to the action or condition which the verb describes. It shows the perspective from which the occurrence is regarded

---

[218] The rest of the book will attempt to validate this view.

[219] This is why Hoepelman's objection to the 'viewpoint' approach to aspect is not a telling critique. He cites Comrie's definition and says: 'To my mind it cannot be said meaningfully that in these examples the imperfective describes the situation more from the inside than does the perfective. . . . A more precise treatment of the phenomena concerned is needed' (*Verb Classification*, p. 17). A more precise treatment should be given, but the starting point is an accurate view of the invariant, with a clear grasp of how it combines with other features to produce various phenomena of meaning.

or the portrayal of the occurrence apart from the actual or perceived nature of the situation itself.

To be more specific, aspect is concerned with the speaker's viewpoint concerning the action in the sense that it implicitly sets up a relationship between the action described and a reference-point from which the action is viewed. The crucial aspectual distinction is whether this reference-point is internal or external to the action. The action can be viewed from a reference-point *within* the action, without reference to the beginning or end-point of the action, but with focus instead on its internal structure or make-up. Or the action can be viewed from a vantage-point *outside* the action, with focus on the whole action from beginning to end, without reference to its internal structure.

Thus, aspect has nothing inherently to do with temporal sequence, with procedural characteristics of actual situations or of verbs and verb-phrases, or with prominence in discourse. It is instead a rather subjective category, since a speaker may choose to view or portray certain occurrences by one aspect or another without regard to the nature of the occurrence itself. However, fully subjective choices between aspects are not common, since the nature of the action or the procedural character of the verb or verb-phrase can restrict the way an action is viewed by a speaker. In fact, aspect interacts so closely with such features and is so significantly affected by them that no analysis of aspect can be fully meaningful without attention to these interactions.

2

THE MEANING OF THE VERBAL ASPECTS IN NEW TESTAMENT GREEK

IN the previous chapter verbal aspect in Greek as a *general* category was discussed and defined. In this chapter the *particular* aspects of NT Greek will be examined to define the meaning which they communicate. There is no presumption that all of the forms to be covered here are in fact 'aspects' in the sense described in the first chapter; instead what will be done is to study the meaning of all of the forms sometimes labelled 'aspects' in NT grammar, to see whether they are 'viewpoint' aspects or some combination of aspect, Aktionsart, tense, and so forth. The purpose of this chapter is to examine the verbal forms in NT Greek which are labelled 'aspects', in order to define their individual meanings and relationships to each other.

It was argued in the first chapter that understanding the aspects requires an interpreter to understand *both* the basic meaning of the aspects themselves *and* their function in combination with other linguistic features. It is the first of these which must be examined in this chapter—the basic or invariant sense of the individual aspects of NT Greek. It will be more convenient to take up the aorist first and then the 'present', perfect, and future forms in order. In each case suggested meanings for the forms will be evaluated and an invariant meaning which best fits the linguistic usage will be stated.

2. 1 The Significance of the Aorist Aspect

The meaning of the aorist forms has been more widely disputed than that of the other aspects. In the years that it has been studied as an *aspect* (rather than as a pure tense), there have been four general suggestions made for the general or basic sense of the aorist.

2. 1. 1 *Instantaneous or momentary aspect*

Most of the earlier grammars of NT Greek, when they venture an aspect-meaning at all, give this significance for the aorist. Winer-Lünemann describes the aorist as follows: 'der *Aoristus* die reine Vergangenheit (das einstmalige Geschehensein schlechthin und als momentan) bezeichnet . . . der Imper. *aor* . . . steht von einer entweder schnell vorübergehenden und unverzüglich eintreten sollenden . . . oder doch nur einmal vorzunehmenden Handlung'.[1] Buttmann also describes the aorist as expressing a 'momentary' action.[2]

Some later grammars as well emphasize a momentary or instantaneous value for the aorist. Turner speaks in terms of 'the essential punctiliar and momentary meaning of the aorist stem'. He does mention that at times the aorist 'regards the action as a whole without respect to its duration', but he appears to regard this as an exception to the rule of instantaneous action: 'the rules appear to collapse with the "linear" aorists'.[3] Moule is somewhat ambiguous, but repeatedly uses the term 'instantaneous' in describing the aorist: action conceived of as 'virtually instantaneous', 'focused into a point', 'action viewed as instantaneous', 'instantaneous or "punctiliar" action'.[4]

A variation on this view is given by Pistorius, though he specifically denies that the aorist expresses momentary action. He writes: 'The first and most important point to remember is that the aorist refers to a point in an action and not to a

---

[1] WL, *Grammatik*, pp. 248, 293.

[2] Buttmann, *Grammatik*, pp. 173, 182.

[3] MT, *Syntax*, pp. 59, 71. He notes also (p. 72) 'it must not be supposed that punctiliar *Aktionsart* necessarily involves a brief space of time', but he seems to consider non-momentary uses exceptional.

[4] Moule, *Idiom Book*, pp. 5, 10.

momentary action . . . [it is wrong to imply] that the aorist can indicate a momentary action. Its function is not to indicate a momentary action, but a moment in an action.'[5] But the major thrust of his argument is to deny that the aorist is used to portray durative or repeated actions in a summary or constative way: 'In all these cases the aspect is either ingressive aorist or effective aorist. In no instance is there an attempt to condense a durative action into a single point, which is supposed to be the function of the "constative aorist".'[6] Instead he argues that the aorist is always used to refer to a moment of an action, either the beginning or end-point. Thus, the aorist in itself is always momentary or instantaneous, in his view. Any duration or repetition is added by other phrases, which indicate that the action continued for a time after its inception (e.g. John 1: 39 παρ' αὐτῷ ἔμειναν τὴν ἡμέραν ἐκείνην) or leading up to its termination (John 2: 20 τεσσεράκοντα καὶ ἓξ ἔτεσιν οἰκοδομήθη). For a repeated action, the aorist indicates that the act was commenced or completed on various occasions (e.g. 2 Cor. 11: 25 τρὶς ἐρραβδίσθην 'the act of whipping was completed on three occasions').[7]

In evaluating this basic meaning for the aorist, it must be said that whether the action itself is momentary or not does not seem to affect the use of the aspect. To judge from actual usage, the aorist is quite tolerant of actions which are instantaneous and of verbs and phrases which portray actions as instantaneous. When the lexical sense of the verb or phrase is momentary,[8] this sense is certainly valid for the overall aorist function (e.g. Mark 3: 5 ἀπεκατεστάθη ἡ χεὶρ αὐτοῦ; Acts 5: 5 ὁ Ἀνανίας . . . πεσὼν ἐξέψυξεν). On the other hand, the aorist is also compatible with durative or iterative actions, verbs, and phrases (e.g. Heb. 11: 7, 9, 12, 13 κατεσκεύασεν κιβωτόν;

---

[5] P. V. Pistorius, 'Some Remarks on the Aorist Aspect in the Greek New Testament', *Acta Classica*, 10 (1967), 33, 35.

[6] Ibid. 37. He refers to one grammarian's category of 'aorist of long duration' as 'a total denial of the essential force of the aorist' (p. 35).

[7] Ibid. 36.

[8] See sect. 3.1.2.4.

παρῴκησεν εἰς γῆν τῆς ἐπαγγελίας; ἐγενήθησαν . . . καθὼς τὰ ἄστρα τοῦ οὐρανοῦ τῷ πλήθει; ἀπέθανον οὗτοι πάντες). The momentary, durative, or iterative sense thus appears to come from some element outside of the aspect itself, usually the lexical character of the verb either by itself or in combination with the aspect.

In addition, it does not seem valid to argue, as Pistorius does, that the aorist indicates only the point of completion or inception in cases like John 1: 39, 2: 20, 2 Cor. 11: 25, Rom. 5: 12 (πάντες ἥμαρτον), and Mark 12: 44 (πάντες ἔβαλον). Especially in the last two verses and others like them (Mark 12: 22-3 οἱ ἑπτὰ οὐκ ἀφῆκαν σπέρμα . . . οἱ γὰρ ἑπτὰ ἔσχον αὐτὴν γυναῖκα; examples could be multiplied), a better explanation is needed than 'inception' or 'the act completed on various occasions': these acts were not done in a moment or on a single occasion, and it is highly unlikely that the aspect focuses only upon the final moment when the composite acts were 'completed'. The momentary or instantaneous meaning for the aorist must be regarded as an over-simplification of the linguistic usage. Most recent treatments of the aorist rightly begin by rejecting this sense as the basic meaning.

2. 1. 2 *Completed or accomplished aspect*

Another analysis of the Greek aorist originated in treatments of the Slavic aspects and came to be applied to Greek during the period when comparative philology flourished in language study. In this view the aorist emphasizes the accomplishment of an effort or the fulfilment of the action as opposed to the incomplete or unfulfilled nuance of the present. The major exponent of this view for NT Greek was Blass. The first three editions of his grammar present this as the primary value of the aorist: 'Was im Aorist als vollendet (geschehen) berichtet wird, braucht durchaus nichts Momentanes zu sein, sondern kann sich thatsächlich und auch nach ausdrücklicher Angabe über eine beliebig lange Zeit erstreckt haben, wofern nur die *Vollendung* und der *Abschluß* hervorzuheben ist, was eben durch

den Aorist geschieht'.[9] This view did not gain wider accept-
ance among NT grammars, but several studies presented this
idea for various bodies of extra-biblical Greek.[10]

Most notable of the works on extra-biblical Greek which
have espoused this view of the aorist is the major reference-
grammar by Schwyzer–Debrunner (1950). This work uses the
term 'konfektiv' to describe the aorist (as opposed to the
present as 'infektiv'), and these terms are initially explained as
follows:

Die beiden Hauptaspekte sind hier als der *infektive* und der *konfektive*
benannt: der *konfektive* sieht einen Vorgang oder eine Handlung als
Ereignis, als schlechthin geschehen, vollendet (confit oder confec-
tum est); der *infektive* betrachtet den Verbalinhalt ohne das Moment
der Vollendung, einen Zustand als lediglich zuständlich, einen
Vorgang oder eine Handlung als noch unabgeschlossen, noch
geschehend, verlaufend.[11]

It is not entirely clear that the meaning of the term 'konfektiv'
here is the sense of completed action; it is possible that their
approach to the aorist fits better under one of the next two
categories of meaning to be presented in this chapter.
However, the contrast with the description of the present
indicates that 'completed' action is the fundamental meaning
of the aorist offered by Schwyzer–Debrunner. This is confirmed a few pages later in further discussion of the aorist
aspect: 'Eine abschwächung des konfektiven Gebrauchs im
eig. Sinne scheint der *faktive* zu sein (gewöhnlich konsta-
tierend, komplexiv, auch konzentrierend, totalitär gennant),

---

[9] Quotation from Friedrich Blass, *Grammatik des neutestamentlichen Griechisch* (Göttingen: Vandenhoeck and Ruprecht, 1896), 188. A rudimentary form of this view is
given in Thomas Sheldon Green, *A Treatise on the Grammar of the New Testament*, new
edn. (London: Samuel Bagster and Sons, 1862), 133.

[10] Friedrich Blass, 'Demosthenische Studien, III: Aorist und Imperfect', *Rheinisches Museum für Philologie*, 44 (1889), 406–30; Felix Hartmann, 'Aorist und Imperfektum', *KZ* 49 (1919), 31–4, and 'Aorist und Imperfektum im Griechischen', *Neue
Jahrbücher für das klassische Altertum*, 43 (1919), 316–39; and A. Poutsma, *Over de tempora
van de imperativus en de conjunctivus hortativus-prohibitivus in het grieks* (Amsterdam: Uitgave
van de Koninklijke Akademie van Wetenschappen, 1928), 69–74.

[11] SD, *Syntax*, p. 252.

der nicht so sehr den Moment des Abschlußes betont als den Vollzug einer Handlung oder eines Geschehnisses schlechthin, also nicht so sehr konfektiv als nicht-infektiv ist'.[12]

This sense for the aorist is certainly valid in some cases, especially when used with verbs of the 'accomplishment' type, which denote a process leading to a goal, an action with a terminus or climax which must be reached if the action is to be 'truly done' (see discussion of this type in section 3.1.2.3). With such verbs the aorist clearly signifies that the goal has been reached (e.g. Matt. 27: 20 'they *persuaded* [ἔπεισαν] the crowd to ask for Barabbas and to condemn Jesus'; 1 Thess. 2: 18 'we wanted to come to you . . . but Satan *hindered* [ἐνέκοψεν] us'). With any verb denoting a 'bounded' action (cf. sections 3.1.2.3–4) the aorist can express some idea of *completed* occurrence.

However, with verbs denoting simply a homogeneous activity without such a bounded sense, the aorist denotes not fulfilment or completion but mere 'termination'.[13] Though the aorist denotes an entire 'occurrence' of the action, the end of the action is an *arbitrary* limit, not a culminating or natural conclusion such as this view suggests for the aorist:

Matt. 12: 1 ἐπορεύθη ὁ Ἰησοῦς . . . διὰ τῶν σπορίμων

Acts 11: 12 ἦλθον δὲ σὺν ἐμοὶ καὶ οἱ ἓξ ἀδελφοὶ οὗτοι

Phil. 2: 22 σὺν ἐμοὶ ἐδούλευσεν εἰς τὸ εὐαγγέλιον

Compared to the instantaneous view, this approach is perhaps closer to the true sense of the aorist, since some reference to an end-point seems to be included in the meaning of the aspect. But as an invariant meaning for the aspect it is too restricted, since it describes the effect of one particular lexical type on the aorist's function but fails to do justice to others.

[12] Ibid. 261. F. R. Adrados, 'Observaciones sobre el aspecto verbal', *Estudios clásicos*, 1 (1950), 11–15, discusses the view of Schwyzer-Debrunner concerning the aorist and interprets it as 'action seen as reaching its terminus or end'.

[13] Cf. Carlota S. Smith, 'A Theory of Aspectual Choice', *Lg.* 59 (1983), 482, who discusses English examples of these differing verbal types.

Two other views of the aorist arose along with this one, and have survived as widely accepted alternatives among recent grammarians.

2. 1. 3 *Constative or summary aspect*

In an attempt to correct the weaknesses of the strictly 'momentary' view of the aorist, many grammarians began to explain its use as *subjectively* punctiliar; that is, they realized the important distinction between the nature of the action as an objective fact and the presentation of the action in the speaker's subjective portrayal of it. Thinking along this line, grammarians began to describe the aorist as a constative or 'summary' aspect, presenting the action in its totality, as a whole, without regard to its actual constituency. The action may be continued or repeated but this is left out of view and the aorist presents it 'as a whole', in summary of all the parts which may be involved.

This view is found in three of the most widely used grammars of NT Greek. Moulton, Robertson, and Blass–Debrunner espouse this definition of the aorist:

MOULTON

. . . the Aorist has a 'punctiliar' action, that is, it regards action as a *point*: it represents the point of entrance . . . or that of completion . . . or it looks at a whole action simply as having occurred, without distinguishing any steps in its progress . . .[14]

ROBERTSON

. . . the action is regarded as a whole. . . . The 'constative' aorist just *treats* the act as a single whole entirely irrespective of the parts or time involved.[15]

BLASS–DEBRUNNER

. . . die *momentane* (*punctuelle*) im Aoriststamm: die Handlung ist als Moment gedacht, und zwar wird entweder der Anfangs- oder der

---

[14] Moulton, *Proleg.*, p. 109.
[15] Robertson, *Grammar*, pp. 823, 831.

Endpunkt hervorgehoben . . . oder die Handlung wird an sich als Ganzes ohne Rücksicht auf die Dauer ins Auge gefaßt.[16]

Other grammars also take this approach. A particularly useful definition is that given by McKay in his most recent treatment of NT aspects; he states that the aorist 'represents an activity as a total action, in its entirety without dwelling on its internal details'.[17]

The advantage of this view is that it allows for the so-called 'linear' or durative aorists, but also explains the sense of instantaneous or accomplished action which the aorist often carries. In combination with a lexically instantaneous verb or phrase, the portrayal of totality naturally reflects the momentary sense which Winer and others observed. With a verb or phrase denoting a process leading to a goal, the aspectual sense of totality (since it includes the *end-point* of the action) results in the overall meaning of accomplishment or completed effect which Blass and others observed.

The ingressive nuance which the aorist sometimes reflects is also explained by this concept. This sense occurs with stative verbs, and the aorist aspect of totality alters the overall meaning from *stative* (existence in the state or condition denoted by the verb) to *transformative* (the event of entering the state or condition denoted; e.g. Rev. 18: 3, 15, 19 ἐπλούτησαν, οἱ πλουτήσαντες, ἐπλούτησαν 'they got wealthy'). The aorist does this by adding an end-point to a verb which does not usually imply such a limit, since a state or condition normally 'goes on' without limits in view. Using an aorist aspect with such a verb alters the sense to a related meaning in which 'the total

---

[16] F. Blass and A. Debrunner, *Grammatik des neutestamentlichen Griechisch*, 4th edn. (Göttingen: Vandenhoeck and Ruprecht, 1913), 185. The same idea is presented in the current edition (Blass–Debrunner–Rehkopf, 1979) and in the current English translation (Blass–Debrunner–Funk, 1961).

[17] K. L. McKay, 'Aspect in Imperatival Constructions in New Testament Greek', *Nov. T.* 27 (1985), 203–4. See also his other articles on aspect in NT: 'Syntax in Exegesis', *Tyndale Bulletin*, 23 (1972), 44, 46; and 'On the Perfect and Other Aspects in New Testament Greek', *Nov. T.* 23 (1981), 290, 307–9; also Gottfried Steyer, *Handbuch für das Studium des neutestamentlichen Griechisch*, ii. *Satzlehre* (Berlin: Evangelische Verlagsanstalt, 1968), 57–8.

entity from beginning to end' is a natural feature: the event of *entering* the state or condition.[18]

Similar to this approach is the fourth view of the aorist which must now be presented.

2. 1. 4 *Unmarked or undefined aspect*

Largely in response to the linear aorists which seemed to devastate the view of the aorist as momentary or instantaneous, this analysis was advanced quite early and has gained adherents increasingly over the last century. In this view the aorist is essentially non-aspectual and, rather than portraying the nature of the action in any way, it simply records the mere 'happening' or undefined occurrence of the action without aspectual definition of any kind. It does not portray the action as momentary or completed or as total but merely passes on the lexical idea of the verb stated as an event or process or state which takes place or took place in some way.

In the statements of this view found in grammars, it is often difficult to distinguish it from the previous view, and indeed they are quite similar. But the small conceptual difference can produce a significant alteration when one comes to apply it in the interpretation of specific instances. It seems that in the apparent intention and application of their definitions, the following NT grammars adopt this interpretation of the aorist:

BURTON (1898)

. . . it represents the action denoted by it indefinitely; i.e. simply as an event, neither on the one hand picturing it in progress, nor on the other affirming the existence of its result.[19]

NUNN (1938)

. . . denotes that the action is regarded simply as an event without any account being taken of its progress or of the existence of its

---

[18] See discussion and other examples in sect. 3.1.2.1.
[19] Burton, *MT*, § 35.

result. . . . The name aorist means *without boundaries* or *indefinite,* and denotes that the action expressed by the verb is not defined with regard to its time, progress, or result.[20]

ZERWICK (1963)

. . . the action of the verb is presented by the speaker . . . as a simple realization (e.g. in the indicative for the mere statement of historical fact) without reference to continuation or repetition, but simply 'globally'.[21]

Others who advance this view are Cuendet (1924) and Abel (1927);[22] Radermacher (1925);[23] Louw (1959);[24] and Stagg (1972), Kuehne (1976, 1978), and Smith (1980).[25] The clearest exposition of this view is by Stagg. Emphasizing the derivation of the term 'aorist' as a guide to its meaning, he writes:

It is 'a-oristic', i.e., undetermined or undefined. The aorist draws no boundaries. It tells nothing about the nature of the action under consideration. It is 'punctiliar' only in the sense that the action is

[20] H. P. V. Nunn, *A Short Syntax of New Testament Greek,* 5th edn. (Cambridge: at the University Press, 1938), 68.

[21] Zerwick, *Biblical Greek,* p. 77.

[22] Georges Cuendet, *L'Impératif dans le texte grec et dans les versions gotique, arménienne et vieux slave des Évangiles* (Paris: Geuthner, 1924), 19; and Abel, *Grammaire,* p. 254. These works are related in that they use the same phrase in describing the aorist: it expresses 'l'action pure et simple' or 'l'idée verbale pure et simple'. This description of the aorist is a standard phrase in many French works on Greek grammar from this time.

[23] Ludwig Radermacher, *Neutestamentliche Grammatik: Das Griechisch des Neuen Testament im Zusammenhang mit der Volkssprache,* 2nd edn. (Tübingen: J. C. B. Mohr, 1925), 149. This is his approach for the indicative, but for the non-indicative forms he states that the aorist indicates momentary or non-recurring action.

[24] J. P. Louw, 'On Greek Prohibitions', *Acta Classica,* 2 (1959), 50–2, 57. In this article Louw is very close to the view that the aorist focuses on the *completion* of the action (pp. 46, 49, 57).

[25] Frank Stagg, 'The Abused Aorist', *JBL* 91 (1972), 222–31; C. Kuehne, 'Keeping the Aorist in its Place', *Journal of Theology,* 16 (1976), 2–10, 'The Viewpoint of the Aorist', ibid. 18 (1978), 2–10; and 'Translating the Aorist Indicative', ibid. 18 (1978), 19–26; and Charles R. Smith, 'Errant Aorist Interpreters', *Grace Theological Journal,* 2 (1980), 205–26. These are cited together because Kuehne and Smith are dependent upon Stagg to a great degree. However, Smith more than any other emphasizes that the aorist simply passes on the bare lexical idea of the verb, without aspectual modification of any kind.

viewed without reference to duration, interruption, completion, or anything else. What is 'aoristic' belongs to semantics and not necessarily to the semantic situation. The aorist can properly be used to cover any kind of action: single or multiple, momentary or extended, broken or unbroken, completed or open-ended. The aorist simply refrains from describing.[26]

As developed in the first chapter of this book, this type of aspectual value is known in wider linguistic circles as 'unmarked' or neutral aspect, in opposition to a contrasting 'marked' or positive aspect, such as the present or the perfect. Of the writers who hold that the NT aorist is 'undefined', most do not show an acquaintance with 'markedness' theory. However, there are two writers who, in holding this view of the aorist, phrase the meaning of the aspect in terms of markedness: Mussies (1971)[27] and Louw (1975).[28] Their view of the aorist itself is essentially the same as that of the other grammarians mentioned here, but the opposition with the present is emphasized.

This fourth view has some attractiveness, since it seems to be true to actual usage that the aorist presents the action as an occurrence, without in itself dictating the character of the action. Thus, if the verb or phrase is instantaneous in meaning, the aorist allows that sense to appear. If the sense is durative, that idea appears without difficulty. An unmarked or undefined aspect handles such linguistic evidence very well.

However, other evidence from usage is not as consistent with this view. For example, one might expect *stative* verbs to appear regularly in the aorist as forms denoting the 'mere existence of the state' (in the past or other times, depending on the mood and context). But the far more frequent pattern is the ingressive meaning, denoting the entrance into the condi-

---

[26] Stagg, 'Abused Aorist', p. 223. Stagg does not consider alternatives to this view, but presents it as something beyond question, which every 'grammarian' already knows (p. 222).

[27] Mussies, *Morphology*, pp. 227, 266, 271.

[28] J. P. Louw, 'Verbal Aspect in the First Letter of John', *Neotestamentica*, 9 (1975), 98–104.

tion (see section 3.1.2.1 for evidence). What in the context, if not the aorist aspect, produces this pattern of meaning? With *accomplishment* verbs in the aorist, the sense of completion is consistently stronger than one might expect if the action is presented 'totally without regard for completion' (see section 3.1.2.3). As it is actually employed, the aorist is not simply an aspectual blank without any positive aspect-meaning. In the uses in which the aorist and the present aspects are most clearly in contrast (i.e. in the non-indicative forms of the verb and in the past-time contrast of aorist and imperfect indicative), the evidence suggests that the aorist has a positive meaning and is not merely the contrastive foil for the other aspects.[29]

2. 1. 5 *Summary of the aspectual meaning of the aorist*

The argument of this book, here and in the following chapters, is that the third view of the aorist presented above gives the best analysis of its aspectual value. According to this approach, the aorist is a viewpoint aspect (see section 1.2.1), in that it reflects the speaker's or writer's focus or *perspective* on the occurrence and not the actional character of the occurrence itself (duration–momentariness, process–event, etc.). Nor does it give the speaker's *portrayal* of the actional character (i.e. 'viewed as an event', 'viewed as momentary'). Instead the aorist presents an occurrence *in summary, viewed as a whole from the outside, without regard for the internal make-up of the occurrence.* This 'external, summarizing' viewpoint concerning the occurrence is what is invariant in the meaning of the aorist itself. Other nuances of meaning (instantaneous occurrence, completed action, ingressive action, etc.) come from combinations of the aorist with the lexical nature of the verb or from other features of the context—and these 'combinatory variants' or functions of the aorist in interaction with other features must be studied—but the aorist itself does not bear

---

[29] Cf. Comrie, *Aspect*, pp. 113–14. Development of this point will appear in chs. 4–6.

these meanings. The relationship of this aspectual value to the rest of the aspect-system of Greek will be described in the last section of this chapter.

2. 2 The Significance of the Present Aspect

With the foundation given above, the present aspect will be treated more briefly. Three general suggestions have been made for its basic sense.

2. 2. 1 *Durative or extended aspect*

This was one of the earliest aspectual descriptions of the present forms, and it has been held in some form by almost all NT grammars of the past hundred years. Standard works which adopt this view of the present are: Winer-Lünemann (1867), Blass (1896), Moulton (1908), Robertson (1914), Radermacher (1925), Nunn (1938), Moule (1959), Turner (1963), and Mateos (1977).[30] Blass-Debrunner-Funk (1961) may be quoted as typical of the others. The second Aktionsart listed is: 'The *durative* (*linear* or *progressive*) in the present stem: the action is represented as durative (in progress) and either as timeless. . . or as taking place in present time (including, of course, duration on one side or the other of the present moment. . .).'[31] Thus, the action is seen as protracted over some length of time, although the duration may take differing forms: continuous activities, habitual acts, or universal occurrences. Most of these grammars regard the iterative or repeated sense as simply one type of duration, since the continuation need not be uninterrupted. In others, repeated or iterative action is given a separate but subsidiary status as another value of the present, distinct from the durative.[32] But the durative sense is regarded as foremost for the present, no matter what is done with the iterative meaning.

---

[30] See Bibliography for details.
[31] BDF, *Grammar*, § 318 (2).
[32] Cf. ibid., § 318 (3).

From the earlier discussion, one will notice immediately that this definition of the present is phrased primarily in terms of *actional character:* the feature of temporal duration is made central to the present aspect. It is possible that the term 'durative' in these grammars is meant to serve as a more general description of progress, development, and so on, without emphasis on the *temporal* extension, but this is not made clear, and in fact temporal duration is often stressed. Grammars will sometimes state that the present is 'subjectively durative' or '*portrays* the occurrence as durative', but the focus remains on actional character none the less.

The argument of this book is that defining the Greek present in terms of an actional characteristic, such as duration, is an erroneous step from the start. While the present is quite compatible with the feature of duration and virtually all presents can be seen as 'continuing' for some extent of time, it is questionable whether this is the invariant value of the present itself. Is it instead the product of an aspect-value of a different sort in combination with lexical or contextual features which add the durative sense? The parallel with the aorist suggests that the latter is true, since many aorists also denote an extended occurrence (when the verb itself has a durative lexical sense). For example, Acts 20: 25 διῆλθον κηρύσσων τὴν βασιλείαν; 2 Thess. 2: 15 τὰς παραδόσεις ἃς ἐδιδάχθητε; 1 Pet. 5: 2 ποιμάνατε τὸ ἐν ὑμῖν ποίμνιον τοῦ Θεοῦ. The combination of present aspect with such a verb may emphasize the verb's inherent durative sense more than an aorist could, but this emphasis appears to come from the *viewpoint* difference between the two; it seems wrong to attribute duration to the present itself in such cases.

In addition, with verbs of a 'bounded' sort (see sections 3.1.2.3–4) the present usually denotes the action as 'in progress but not carried to completion' (e.g. Matt. 3: 14 ὁ δὲ Ἰωάννης διεκώλυεν αὐτόν; Luke 5: 7 ἔπλησαν ἀμφότερα τὰ πλοῖα ὥστε βυθίζεσθαι αὐτά). This is difficult to account for on the basis of the durative view of the present, since there is nothing in the concept of *duration* which is inimical to completion:

extended actions are often brought to conclusion. A better explanation for this pattern of usage must be sought.

Thus, while one can say that duration is a common secondary characteristic of the present aspect, it is not the best definition of the primary or invariant meaning of the present itself.

2. 2. 2 *Incompleted or unaccomplished aspect*

This meaning for the present, corresponding to the 'accomplishment' view of the aorist, has never gained much of a following among grammarians of NT Greek, although it has been proposed in the wider literature on aspect in the IE languages. T. S. Green (1862) is consistent with his ideas on the aorist as 'accomplishment' and describes the present as action 'in process' as opposed to the 'fulfilled' meaning of the aorist. He appears to regard the durative sense as a secondary nuance of the incomplete meaning.[33] Webster (1864) emphasizes the idea of incompletion for the imperfect indicative ('denotes an incomplete action, one that is in its course, and is not yet brought to its intended accomplishment') but articulates the durative view for the present aspect in general.[34] Even Blass, who argues for the sense of completion as the basic value for the aorist, describes the present as essentially durative rather than incomplete.[35] Other writers have advanced the 'incomplete' meaning for the present in extra-biblical Greek,[36] but for NT Greek, grammars have largely avoided this position.

---

[33] Green, *Grammar of NT*, pp. 128–30.

[34] William Webster, *The Syntax and Synonyms of the Greek Testament* (London: Rivingtons, 1864), 87, 107. Turner, in MT, *Syntax*, pp. 60–8, also makes much of the incomplete action expressed by the imperfect but emphasizes linear or continued action for the present.

[35] Blass, *Grammatik*, pp. 182–3.

[36] J. Donovan, 'Greek Jussives', *CR* 9 (1895), 289–93, 342–6; E. Rodenbusch, 'Beiträge zur Geschichte der griechischen Aktionsarten', *IF* 21 (1907), 116–45; and Hartmann, 'Aorist und Imperfektum', pp. 31–4, and 'Aorist und Imperfektum im Griechischen', pp. 316–39.

This view of the present must also be seen as reflecting a valid *secondary function* of the present aspect but not its basic sense. It is true that the present forms, when used with a verb of 'bounded' lexical sense, display a meaning of incomplete or unaccomplished action, but this sense is not appropriate for actions and states which are 'unbounded' (see section 3.1.2.2). The primary or invariant meaning must be sought elsewhere.

2. 2. 3 *Cursive or progressive aspect*

A third approach to defining the basic sense of the present aspect is taken by those who describe it as *progressive* and avoid emphasizing duration or incompletion. This approach is adopted by Burton, who says that the present denotes 'action in progress' and does not use the term durative.[37] When he refers to a sense of incompletion in the present, he takes pains to portray this as secondary to the more basic meaning of progressive action.[38] Zerwick describes the present aspect as progressive, habitual, repeated, or 'activity tending toward a given end', and he also avoids references to duration and makes incompletion a secondary sense.[39]

Mussies views the present in this way as well. Even though he uses the term 'durative', he clarifies it as follows: 'This does not imply . . . that the action lasted for a long time . . . the period implied . . . may be short or long . . . [the durative] does therefore not express any objective difference in duration.'[40] He notes that the term 'durative' has been retained as a traditional term, though, like many traditional terms, it is not strictly correct. In addition, he divides the 'durative' aspect into two subcategories, the 'cursive durative' and the 'iterative durative'. Mussies' progressive view of the present becomes clear in his description of these categories:

---

[37] Burton, *MT*, §§ 5, 8–34, 96.
[38] Ibid. § 11.
[39] Zerwick, *Biblical Greek*, pp. 77, 91–3. Perhaps Abel, *Grammaire*, pp. 249–52, should be included here, but his position is not clear.
[40] Mussies, *Morphology*, pp. 266–7.

Cursive durative

The speaker fixes the attention of the addressee on the progression of the action during a period either long or short. This period need not, and very often does not, include the beginning and the end of the action.[41]

Iterative durative

. . . likewise implies two points in time, but in contrast to the cursive durative the implication may be here that these points are separated from each other by a not too short, often by a considerable lapse of time. The action need not be seen as going on for the whole period between these two points, but may repeatedly be interrupted (iterative), or less often (customary-general).[42]

McKay likewise takes this view of the present, and shows that it is naturally associated with the third view of the aorist listed above. He summarizes the distinction between the two: 'The difference between the aorist and imperfective [i.e. present] aspects is that the former represents an activity as a total action, in its entirety without dwelling on its internal details; while the latter represents an activity as a process going on, with the focus on its progress or development'.[43] He adds: 'Duration and repetition are not restricted to the imperfective: a long drawn out activity or a series of repeated activities may be represented as a totality in relation to the context and so be expressed by the aorist'.[44]

Taking this approach to the present aspect, one is better equipped to account for the various secondary senses produced by combinations of the aspect with lexical and contextual features. If the present focuses on the development or progress of an occurrence and thus sees the occurrence in regard to its internal make-up without beginning or end in view, then it is understandable that an expression durative in itself will reflect such duration, and an occurrence which has a

[41] Ibid. 266.
[42] Ibid. 267. Earlier he defined the present as 'action seen while going on' (p. 227).
[43] McKay, 'Aspect in Imperatival Constructions', pp. 203–4.
[44] Ibid. 204.

natural end-point will display a sense of incompletion, and so forth.

2. 2. 4 *Summary of the aspectual meaning of the present*

The most workable definition of the invariant meaning of the present aspect in NT Greek is to see it also as a viewpoint aspect, concerned with the perspective of the speaker in regard to the occurrence and not directly with actional characteristics such as duration or incompletion. The present reflects an *internal* viewpoint concerning the occurrence which *focuses on its development or progress* and sees the occurrence *in regard to its internal make-up, without beginning or end in view*. Combinatory variants such as duration, incompletion, repetition, and other functions can be explained more readily as secondary effects of this invariant meaning.

2. 3 The Significance of the Perfect Forms

There is a remarkable consistency in the way that grammars of NT Greek have treated the perfect forms. Though individual points of emphasis exist in the grammars, there is no ground for surveying differing views of the perfect here, since NT grammars for the last 150 years have presented a uniform view of these forms. What must be done instead is to examine this traditional approach to determine how far it is valid, and consider along the way some issues raised by general linguistic studies of the perfect which may lead down a different path of analysis for the Greek perfect.

2. 3. 1 *The traditional view of the Greek perfect*

The analysis of the perfect forms presented by grammars of NT Greek in recent times can be summarized as follows: the perfect is an *aspect* (parallel to the present and aorist), which denotes *a state or condition resulting from a completed action*. Most grammars present both of these features (state and completed

action) and underscore its dual significance. Blass–Debrunner–Rehkopf include the perfect as one of the major aspects
and describe it as follows: 'sie bezeichnet einen Zustand als
Resultat einer vergangenen Handlung'.[45] Zerwick explains
the perfect in the same terms: 'it is not a past tense but a
present one, indicating not the past action as such but the
present state of affairs resulting from the past action'.[46] Burton
emphasizes the dual sense: 'The reference of the tense is . . .
double; it implies a past action and affirms an existing
result'.[47] Other grammars describe the perfect in these terms
also.[48]

Some grammars, while presenting this view in general,
place more emphasis on one or the other of these features. For
example, Mussies and Radermacher put the stress on the
completed action, but note the resulting state as well.[49] On the
other hand, McKay puts the focus of the perfect on the
resulting state: 'The ancient Greek perfect expresses the state
or condition of the subject of the verb, as the result of a prior
action, but most often with comparatively little reference to
that action itself'.[50] Louw and Abel also focus on the stative
feature.[51] However, it is clear that these are only differences of
emphasis within the same basic view and do not reflect
differing analyses of the perfect. This view of the perfect can be
found in virtually all of the reference-grammars of NT Greek
produced in the past century and a half.[52]

---

[45] BDR, *Grammatik*, § 318 (4).

[46] Zerwick, *Biblical Greek*, p. 96.

[47] Burton, *MT*, § 74.

[48] Robert W. Funk, *A Beginning-Intermediate Grammar of Hellenistic Greek*, 2nd edn., ii. *Syntax* (Missoula, Mont.: Society of Biblical Literature, 1973), 626–30; Mateos, *Aspecto verbal*, pp. 31–2; Moule, *Idiom Book*, pp. 6, 13; Nunn, *Short Syntax*, pp. 70–1; Robertson, *Grammar*, pp. 823, 892–4; Steyer, *Handbuch* ii. 59.

[49] Mussies, *Morphology*, pp. 227, 261–5; and Radermacher, *Grammatik*, p. 154 ('*Das Perfekt* bezeichnet die Handlung als abgeschlossen vorliegend'). See also WL, *Grammatik*, pp. 248, 254.

[50] McKay, 'On the Perfect and Other Aspects', p. 296.

[51] Louw, 'Verbal Aspect in the First Letter of John', pp. 101–3; and Abel, *Grammaire*, pp. 257–9.

[52] Moulton and Turner take this approach as well, although their phrasing of it is

Thus, according to this view the perfect 'aspect' is in general terms different from the present on the one hand and from the aorist on the other. Compared to the present, the perfect refers not only to the present state, but to the action which produced the condition as well (e.g. κοιμᾶται 'he is asleep' vs. κεκοίμηται 'he is/has fallen asleep'). In contrast to the aorist, which in itself refers only to a past occurrence, the perfect denotes not only the occurrence but also its present consequence. Zerwick cites Col. 1: 16a ἐκτίσθη used of the 'historical fact', vs. 1: 16b ἔκτισται used of 'the present (and future) . . . state of affairs' produced by the action.[53]

The same explanation of the perfect is found in most grammars of extra-biblical ancient Greek as well. Moorhouse summarizes the perfect as follows: 'This aspect has reference to a state which results from a preceding, and completed, action'.[54] This is the approach taken by many others.[55]

The background to this general analysis of the Greek perfect is found in the pattern of development which the Greek perfect seems to have undergone in the course of its history from Homer to the Hellenistic period. According to the work of Wackernagel and Chantraine,[56] the perfect in Homer has a predominantly *stative* sense, usually with passive or intransitive verbs, denoting a state or condition of the subject without clear allusion to the action which produced it. As it developed

---

rather infelicitous in places. Moulton, *Proleg.*, p. 109, states: '*Perfect* action is a variety by itself, denoting what began in the past and still continues'. Turner, in MT, *Syntax*, pp. 81–2, says: 'The Aktionsart belonging properly to the [perfect] is either fulfilment in the present of a process begun in the past or else the contemplation of an event having taken place in the past with an interval intervening'.

[53] Zerwick, *Biblical Greek*, p. 97.

[54] Moorhouse, *Syntax*, p. 181; cf. pp. 197–202.

[55] Satya Ranjan Banerjee, *Indo-European Tense and Aspect in Greek and Sanskrit* (Calcutta: Sanskrit Book Depot, 1983), 57–60; Jean Humbert, *Syntaxe grecque*, 3rd edn. (Paris: Klincksieck, 1960), 135–6; Rijksbaron, *SSV*, pp. 34–8; SD, *Syntax*, pp. 263–4; Smyth, *Grammar*, §§ 1945–51; and Stahl, *Syntax*, pp. 107–8.

[56] Jacob Wackernagel, 'Studien zum griechischen Perfectum', *Programm zur akademischen Preisverteilung* (1904), 3–24, repr. in *Kleine Schriften* (Göttingen: Vandenhoeck and Ruprecht, [1953]), 1000–21; and Pierre Chantraine, *Histoire du parfait grec* (Paris: H. Champion, 1927).

during the classical period, it began to be used with transitive actives and occurred with more attention paid to the *action* which produced a particular result. In these uses the 'result' in focus is often the state of the *object* rather than the subject of the verbal action, and the emphasis is often on the *past* implication, by which the perfect eventually comes to be used in narrative as a general equivalent for the aorist. Thus, by the late classical period and through the Hellenistic period, the Greek perfect had a range of meaning from denoting a *state* (of either subject or object), with varying degrees of emphasis on the action which produced it, to expressing completed *action*, with varied implications of existing results.

There is a wide consensus that the ancient Greek perfect, in general, is an aspect denoting 'a state resulting from a completed action'. However, exceptions to this consensus can be found in several monographs which comment on the Greek perfect, and these works raise questions to be considered in evaluating the traditional view and analysing the perfect itself.

2. 3. 2 *Objections to the traditional view*

Some who question this consensus object to the label 'aspect' being applied to the perfect but accept the basic sense for the perfect which it presents. Friedrich states the meaning of the perfect as 'a state of the subject resulting from a realization of the process referred to by the verb', but he goes on to say that the perfect is 'semantically quite different from the basic aspects DURATIVE and COMPLETIVE [i.e. present and aorist]'.[57] A similar opinion is adopted by Schwyzer–Debrunner, Crisafulli, and Comrie.[58] Lloyd expresses himself more strongly: 'Attempts . . . to identify the IE perfect as a third aspect, contrasting with the "perfective" (aorist stem) and "imperfec-

---

[57] Friedrich, *Aspect . Theory*, pp. 16–17. He prefers to see the perfect as an 'intersection' of aspect, Aktionsart, tense, and voice (p. 19).

[58] SD, *Syntax*, pp. 263–4; Virgil Santi Crisafulli, 'Aspect and Tense Distribution in Homeric Greek' (Ph.D. dissertation, University of North Carolina at Chapel Hill, 1968), 4, 9–11, 31; and Comrie, *Aspect*, pp. 52–3.

tive" (present stem) are not consistent with the basic function of aspect and must be rejected'.[59] Nevertheless, these writers adopt the meaning of 'state resulting from a previous action', although they object to the label 'aspect' to describe this meaning.

Others object to the label 'aspect' as well as the meaning attached to the perfect by the traditional approach, and they suggest a different path of analysis for discovering and describing the meaning of the ancient Greek perfect. Mourelatos, for example, emphasizes that the perfect is a tense, not an aspect: 'The function of the [perfect] is not to provide a categorization of the type of action . . . it is rather to encode the "phase" of time reference, specifically, to mark a certain action, occurrence, or situation as temporally prior and relevant to a given reference point'.[60]

At this point it is useful as background to bring into this discussion some recent works analysing the *English* perfect forms, since several writers mentioned here (e.g. Comrie, Mourelatos, Bybee) come to the Greek perfect with concepts and questions drawn from debate over the English perfect.

2. 3. 3 *Recent views of the English perfect*

Issues raised in recent studies of the English perfect can be most easily presented by surveying a book by McCoard, who summarizes the voluminous literature on the subject under four basic analyses of its meaning. According to McCoard, the four common views of the English perfect, with his summary label, are:

1. current relevance: 'expresses a present state resulting from past action';

---

[59] Lloyd, *Verb*, pp. 117–18.

[60] A. P. D. Mourelatos, 'Events, Processes, and States', *Linguistics and Philosophy*, 2 (1978), 415–34, repr. in *Tense and Aspect* ((1981), 195. Similar ideas are expressed by David Armstrong, 'The Ancient Greek Aorist as the Aspect of Countable Action', in *Tense and Aspect* (1981), 1, 3; and Joan Bybee, *Morphology: A Study of the Relation between Meaning and Form* (Amsterdam and Philadelphia: John Benjamins, 1985), 141, 159–61.

2. indefinite past: 'expresses a past event which is unidentified as to time';

3. extended now: 'expresses a past event within a time span which is continuous with the present, not differentiated into "then" versus "now" ';

4. embedded past: 'is made up of a past-tense sentence embedded as sentential subject of a present-tense predicate'.[61]

It will be useful to mention each of these views separately and focus on points of discussion which may be important for analysing the Greek perfects. They will be surveyed here in reverse order.

The 'embedded past' approach to the English perfect is associated with the transformational-generative model of grammatical description, and it appears as a somewhat undeveloped link in broader attempts to analyse English sentence structure. According to this approach, the perfect 'have . . .' phrase is a combination of two simple tenses: it is a present with a past tense embedded within it. Although this general idea by itself is unobjectionable, this is usually the starting-point for moving to either the 'current relevance' view or the 'indefinite past' view.[62] This approach by itself is motivated so directly by the verb-phrase structure of English that it has no apparent validity in defining the Greek perfect.

The 'extended now' view of the English perfect is the approach which McCoard himself espouses, and it seems to be the most workable understanding of the English perfect forms.[63] According to this analysis, the English perfect is a *tense*, not an aspect, but it is a tense in a different sense from

---

[61] Robert W. McCoard, *The English Perfect: Tense Choice and Pragmatic Inferences* (Amsterdam: North-Holland, 1978), 17–18.

[62] See discussion ibid. 165–215, and literature cited there.

[63] This is the view taken by W. F. Bryan, 'The Preterite and Perfect Tense in Present-Day English', *JEGP* 35 (1936), 363–82; and Gero Bauer, 'The English "Perfect" Reconsidered', *JL* 6 (1970), 189–98. See also the brief explanation of the English perfect along this line in Funk, *Beginning-Intermediate Grammar*, ii. 627–8; and Burton, *MT*, § 52.

simply past, present, and future (i.e. deictic time-reference). What is 'invariant' in the meaning of the perfect (i.e. what is due to the perfect itself and not to contextual or pragmatic information easily associated with the perfect) is 'an identification of prior events with the "extended" now which is continuous with the moment of coding. The preterite contrasts in identifying prior events with "then"-time which is conceived as separate from the present, the "now" of speaking. We may think of this as a contrast of temporal inclusion versus exclusion, continuity versus discontinuity.'[64]

For the Greek perfect, however, this approach is not workable, since the Greek perfect and preterite (i.e. aorist) are not distinct in this way. The Greek perfect has no restrictions on occurring with adverbs denoting a time separate from the time of speaking (e.g. 1 Cor. 15: 4 ἐγήγερται τῇ ἡμέρᾳ τῇ τρίτῃ; Heb. 10: 9 τότε εἴρηκεν), while the aorist can occur with 'now' adverbs, unlike the English preterite (Luke 5: 26 εἴδομεν παράδοξα σήμερον). However, awareness of this meaning for the English perfect (to the degree that it is valid) may affect the way one would translate the Greek tenses into English: an aorist or imperfect (or present)[65] which interposes no interval between the 'then' and the extended 'now' would be translated as an English perfect (e.g. Luke 5: 26 'we have seen strange things today'), while a Greek perfect which is not continuous with the present of the text should not be translated as an English perfect (e.g. 1 Cor. 15: 4 'he arose/was raised on the third day').

The view of the English perfect as 'indefinite past' has a degree of validity[66] but is thought by McCoard to be a poor synthesis of the general meaning of the perfect. The English

[64] McCoard, *The English Perfect*, p. 19; see also pp. 73, 83, 123–7.

[65] Cf. the Greek present used of 'past action still in progress' (e.g. in Burton, *MT*, § 17), which in English must be phrased as a perfect: e.g. Luke 15: 29 'for so many years I have served you (δουλεύω)'.

[66] This approach is espoused by Allen (1966), Leech (1971), and Macauley (1971). Related to it is the view of Reichenbach (1947), whose ideas are followed by Classen (1979) and Johnson (1981).

preterite and perfect are sometimes in contrast as 'occurring at a definite time' vs. 'occurring at an indefinite time', but according to McCoard this is a secondary and incidental distinction produced by the more basic difference of nearer and further past.[67] For ancient Greek usage this meaning for the perfect must be rejected also, since the perfect is clearly used of actions which occur at definite points and the aorist can be used of indefinitely occurring actions: e.g. Rev. 5: 7 καὶ ἦλθεν καὶ εἴληφεν 'and he went and took (the scroll)' (also perfects in 1 Cor. 15: 4, Heb. 11: 28); Mark 12: 26 οὐκ ἀνέγνωτε; 'Have you not read?' (also aorists in Rom. 3: 23, 1 Thess. 2: 9–10). Again, it is true that on occasion this difference in English usage (even if secondary) may affect the translation of a Greek form into English. Along this line, one must be careful not to label a Greek perfect 'aoristic' simply because it resists translation as an English perfect due to this distinction of definite and indefinite action.[68]

Finally the 'current relevance' view of the English perfect must be considered. In McCoard's synthesis of this view, the following meanings for the English perfect are included as varieties of the 'current relevance' approach:

recency (a)
present existence (b)
  of the surface-subject referent;
  of the deep-subject referent;
  of a certain state of the subject referent;
  of a 'posthumous personage';
  of a belief in the subject referent or in some kind of validity;
  of the object referent;
unspecified 'connection with the present' (c)
continuance of a state into the present (d)
iterativity (e)
experientiality (f)
present possibility (g)[69]

---

[67] McCoard, *The English Perfect*, pp. 75–86.

[68] This use of the Greek perfect will be discussed in ch. 4.

[69] McCoard, *The English Perfect*, pp. 64–5. Letters in parentheses refer to itemizing of these meanings in his preceding discussion (pp. 32–65).

In spite of this variety. McCoard argues that these agree on the general point that 'the defining function of the perfect in English is to express the pastness of the event(s) embodied in the lexical verb, together with a certain applicability, pertinence, or relevance of said past event(s) to the context of coding—the "now" of the speaker or writer'. Another summary which he suggests is: 'some state resulting from a prior event continues to hold'.[70] Obviously, this is the approach which most nearly resembles the traditional analysis of the ancient Greek perfect, as presented above.

McCoard's criticism of the current-relevance approach for English is that it fails to distinguish between information inherent in the perfect itself and information gained from the linguistic *context* (the verb's lexical sense and adverbial features) or from *pragmatic inferences* (the interpreter's knowledge of the real world and its affairs).[71] Basing his argument on this idea, he argues that many *preterites* substituted in utterances in place of perfects would carry the same sense of continuing relevance. Thus, 'he has died' certainly denotes a past action which has current relevance, but 'he died' has the same implication ('he is now dead'), and in both cases the current relevance is drawn from pragmatic information.[72] In other cases, he feels that the sense of 'current relevance' seen in the perfect is so vague that it is worthless as an explanatory tool.[73]

These difficulties for the 'current-relevance' view of the English perfect suggest problems also for the traditional view of the Greek perfect. These issues must now be investigated along with other questions which have been raised about the perfect as 'an aspect denoting a state resulting from a completed action'.

---

[70] Ibid. 31–2.
[71] Ibid. 1, 3–4, 20, 38, 65. This distinction is called for also by Bauer. 'The English "Perfect" Reconsidered', pp. 189–98; and Wolfgang Zydatiß, "Continuative" and "Resultative" Perfects in English?', *Lingua*, 44 (1978), 339–62.
[72] McCoard, *The English Perfect*, pp. 44–5, 56–60.
[73] Ibid. 39–44.

2. 3. 4 *Re-analysis of the New Testament Greek perfect*

As a result of a study of the perfect forms in NT Greek in the light of these issues, it seems justifiable to conclude that the perfect is a category in which three elements of meaning combine: it consists of *tense, Aktionsart,* and *aspect* features working together. This conclusion must now be discussed and defended in regard to each of these elements.

One element of meaning in the perfect which is clear from a study of usage is the dual 'time'-reference inherent in virtually all its occurrences. The perfect forms, with few exceptions,[74] juxtapose two related situations: an occurrence and a consequence of that occurrence. Juxtaposing these produces an inherent temporal sense, since the occurrence is anterior to its consequence. Although one could regard this anteriority as, at its heart, a *logical* rather than chronological relationship, it works its way out in actual expression as a *temporal* one, producing a dual time-reference of 'past and present' together.[75]

The evidence for this inherent time-reference is the temporal comparison and contrast which the perfect displays when placed alongside the present or the aorist. Like the *present*, the perfect displays a present-time value, in denoting a consequence simultaneous with some reference-point. But at the same time it contrasts with the present in referring also to a past occurrence which produced the consequence.

---

[74] Exceptions to this pattern lie at either end of the historical spectrum. Some perfects preserve an older sense of 'present state', without any allusion to a past occurrence which produced the state (e.g., οἶδα, ἕστηκα). This was a common meaning of the perfect in Homeric usage. On the other hand, there are a few perfects in the NT which display a tendency to become virtual equivalents of the aorist in denoting simply a past action without reference to its present consequence (e.g. εἴληφα, εἴρηκα, ἔσχηκα). This tendency is clearly documented in later Greek. Cf. BDF, *Grammar,* §§ 341, 343; and Burton, *MT,* §§ 80–8.

[75] This temporal feature of the perfect has been noted by others: Comrie, *Aspect,* p. 52 ('it expresses a relation between two time-points, on the one hand the time of the state resulting from a prior situation, and on the other the time of that prior situation'); Friedrich, *Aspect Theory,* pp. 17–19; Lyons, *Semantics,* pp. 714–15; Mourelatos, 'Events, Processes, and States', pp. 415–34; and Bybee, *Morphology,* pp. 141, 159–61.

Matt. 8: 6 ὁ παῖς μου βέβληται . . . παραλυτικός (present distress with idiomatic reference to the point when the affliction struck)

John 11: 27 ἐγὼ πεπίστευκα (in answer to πιστεύεις τοῦτο; this describes her present state of faith, but includes also a reference to its past beginning-point)

Rom. 5: 5 ἡ ἀγάπη τοῦ θεοῦ ἐκκέχυται ἐν ταῖς καρδίαις ἡμῶν (a present resource with allusion to the time when it was given)

On the other hand, the perfect has a past sense like the *aorist* in denoting an occurrence which is antecedent to some reference-point, but differs from it in referring at the same time to a present consequence of the occurrence.

Matt. 22: 4 τὸ ἄριστόν μου ἡτοίμακα . . . καὶ πάντα ἕτοιμα (statement about what has been done, but reference also to the present consequence as reinforced in the summary phrase at the end)

Acts 21: 28 κεκοίνωκεν τὸν ἅγιον τόπον τοῦτον (past act with present responsibility for it in view)
  25: 11 εἰ . . . ἀδικῶ καὶ ἄξιον θανάτου πέπραχά τι (supposition about existence of a past occurrence, but referring in addition to a present responsibility for the deed if such was done; the present nuance is reinforced by the preceding and following clauses)

It should be emphasized that this inherent or 'internal' temporal sense of the perfect is totally apart from the *external* time-value which it, like the present and aorist, picks up when used in the indicative mood. External or deictic time-value relates a situation to an external reference-point (e.g. the time of speaking), and the perfect indicative does this by portraying its consequence as simultaneous and its occurrence as antecedent to the time of speaking (as seen in the examples given above). An external tense-meaning like this comes into play in the pluperfect and future perfect forms as well, since these indicative forms reflect the same basic sense as the perfect indicative but move it either into the past or the future respectively. But, just as for the present and aorist aspects, this deictic time-value of the perfect in the indicative does not carry over to the other moods and is not basic to the meaning of the perfect itself.

However, even outside of the indicative the perfect has the internal temporal sense of *anteriority,* in its dual reference to 'occurrence with its consequence'. This can be seen, for example, in the perfect infinitive and subjunctive forms, which have no external time-value but which differ from present and aorist forms in the sense of anteriority which they display.

John 17: 23 ἵνα ὦσιν τετελειωμένοι εἰς ἕν (state and prior action)
19: 28 ἵνα τελειωθῇ ἡ γραφή (action only)

2 Cor. 5: 10–11 τοὺς γὰρ πάντας ἡμᾶς φανερωθῆναι (action) δεῖ ἔμπροσθεν τοῦ βήματος . . . θεῷ δὲ πεφανερώμεθα· ἐλπίζω δὲ καὶ ἐν ταῖς συνειδήσεσιν ὑμῶν πεφανερῶσθαι (state and action in view)

Thus, the perfect must be seen in its basic meaning as, in part,[76] a *tense*-form. It has the internal time-value of anteriority, since basic to its sense is the implicit temporal relation of 'a consequence with its related anterior occurrence'.

A second element of meaning in the perfect which seems evident from usage is the *stative* sense which it carries. Many grammars of ancient Greek have noted this, as seen in their almost universal description of the perfect as denoting 'a state resulting from a completed action' (see section 2.3.1 for citations). What must be considered, however, is the possibility that the stative idea is derived from other factors in the linguistic or pragmatic context, and not from the perfect itself. This has been argued in regard to the English perfect by McCoard and a few others, as noted in 2.3.3, but no one seems to have discussed this issue in treating the Greek perfect forms.

One of the primary points which McCoard argues is that many verbs denote a resultative idea by their lexical meaning and that such verbs imply just as much 'resulting state' when used in the English *preterite* as they do in the perfect.[77] This point can be tested for Greek by comparing the aorist and perfect of verbs which seem to have such a sense. When one

---

[76] Anteriority is one element of the perfect's sense, and not its entire meaning, as will be developed below. Cf. Friedrich, *Aspect Theory,* pp. 17–19.

[77] McCoard, *The English Perfect,* pp. 44–5, 56–60.

does this, one finds that there *is* a distinct difference between the Greek forms. In such cases the perfect consistently denotes an *existing condition* as the result of a previous occurrence, while the aorist portrays just the occurrence without implying the stative idea. A stative sense may be possible when the aorist is used (the aorist is not antithetical to such), but the use of the aorist form does not 'trigger' a stative sense, whereas the perfect of such verbs seems to denote, and not just allow, such a meaning. Consider these examples:

Matt. 22: 4 τὸ ἄριστόν μου ἡτοίμακα
    26: 19 ἡτοίμασαν τὸ πάσχα

John 17: 23 ἵνα ὦσιν τετελειωμένοι εἰς ἕν
    19: 28 ἵνα τελειωθῇ ἡ γραφή

Acts 1: 18 ἐξεχύθη πάντα τὰ σπλάγχνα αὐτοῦ
    10: 45 καὶ ἐπὶ τὰ ἔθνη ἡ δωρεὰ τοῦ ἁγίου πνεύματος ἐκκέχυται

Rom. 5: 5 ἡ ἀγάπη τοῦ θεου ἐκκέχυται ἐν ταῖς καρδίαις ἡμῶν

Titus 3: 5–6 πνεύματος ἁγίου, οὗ ἐξέχεεν ἐφ᾽ ἡμᾶς

2 Cor. 5: 10 τοὺς γὰρ πάντας ἡμᾶς φανερωθῆναι δεῖ ἔμπροσθεν τοῦ βήματος
    5: 11 θεῷ δὲ πεφανερώμεθα· ἐλπίζω δὲ καὶ ἐν ταῖς συνειδήσεσιν ὑμῶν πεφανερῶσθαι

Heb. 7: 19 οὐδὲν γὰρ ἐτελείωσεν ὁ νόμος
    10: 14 μιᾷ γὰρ προσφορᾷ τετελείωκεν εἰς τὸ διηνεκές

It is noticeable that variations in *voice* make a difference in the stative force of both perfect and aorist.[78] As many have observed, a stative sense is more likely if the form appears in the passive (especially for the aorist forms), while an active-voice form is more likely to emphasize the occurrence and not the resulting condition (even with the perfect, although here the state is still implied).[79] However, even after allowances are

---

[78] It is also true that variations in the lexical sense make a difference, a fact that does not show up as clearly in these examples. Verbs with stative meaning already or with some other type of active sense exhibit predictable variations which will be treated in the next chapter, but the stative element of meaning in the perfect is maintained with these other lexical types.

[79] Mateos, *Aspecto verbal*, p. 121.

made for voice variations, the perfect maintains a stronger stative meaning, which thus appears to be due to the perfect itself and not merely the lexical character of the verb. One must acknowledge that the aorist can combine with lexical factors to produce a combinatory sense which is similar to a perfect, but the stative element does not derive from the aorist itself, as it seems to do with the perfect.[80]

It is possible to say, along the lines of McCoard's arguments for English, that the difference seen above is due not to a variation in the stative or resultative sense of the perfect and aorist, but is due simply to a *tense*-change of some sort in which the aorist is pure past (i.e. a 'then' past) and the perfect is some sort of phasal present–past combination (a 'now' past). But though this seems valid for English usage and it may affect the translation into English, it does not explain the variation in Greek itself. For example, the aorist and perfect with νῦν in Greek violate the pattern suggested by McCoard, yet the perfect still maintains its dual 'occurrence with consequence' sense, while the aorist focuses on the occurrence which has taken place within a period of time which includes the present (e.g. Rom. 3: 21 νυνὶ δὲ χωρὶς νόμου δικαιοσύνη θεοῦ πεφανέρωται vs. 16: 26 μυστηρίου χρόνοις αἰωνίοις σεσιγημένου, φανερωθέντος δὲ νῦν and Col. 1: 26 νῦν δὲ ἐφανερώθη). Also in the non-indicative uses cited above (John 17: 23, 19: 28; 2 Cor. 5: 10 –11) one can see the same distinction, even though the deictic temporal differences of aorist and perfect disappear entirely.

In summary, the long tradition of seeing a stative sense for the perfect forms seems true to actual usage: part of the invariant meaning of the perfect is the reference to a state or condition resulting from the occurrence denoted by the verb. A later discussion must take up the more specific question of what sort of 'state' to expect with perfect verbs, since some predictable patterns do appear. The kind of result denoted by

---

[80] See the similar argument by McKay, 'On the Perfect and Other Aspects', pp. 316–22.

the perfect is related closely to the verb's lexical sense, as will be developed in the next chapter.[81] The final point to be noted here is that this stative sense should be labelled an Aktionsart-value, rather than an aspect.[82] The reasons for this will now be developed.

The issue of an aspect-meaning for the Greek perfect is bedevilled, of course, by differences in understanding what 'aspect' is. There are many who seem to regard as 'aspectual' any feature of meaning which does not fit under the more common categories of tense and mood. Thus, the perfect becomes an aspect by default.[83] Others have narrowed the definition of aspect and include only those features which centre on 'kind of action'. Within this point of view, the perfect as traditionally described can be easily labelled an aspect, since the combination of 'state and completed action' is clearly within the realm of kinds of action.[84] However, for those who distinguish Aktionsart (process, state, event, etc.) from aspect, as argued in Chapter 1 of this book, the traditionally conceived perfect is more difficult to fit into the aspect category.[85]

It is tempting, if only to simplify description, to regard the perfect as entirely non-aspectual and see it as only a sort of tense,[86] or as a combination of tense and Aktionsart.[87] There is, however, a feature of the perfect as described above

[81] There is also the issue of whether the consequence focuses on the state of the *subject* or that of the *object*, as discussed extensively in the secondary literature. This will be taken up in ch. 3 as well.

[82] As noted by Lloyd, *Verb*, pp. 117–18; and in part by Friedrich, *Aspect Theory*, p. 19.

[83] See McCoard's comments, *The English Perfect*, pp. 6–11, about the English perfect labelled an 'aspect' because it does not fit neatly into the more familiar categories.

[84] This is the approach taken by most grammars of ancient Greek (see 2.3.1).

[85] This is why Lloyd, for example, in *Verb*, pp. 117–22, vehemently rejects the label 'aspect', even though he accepts the stative meaning for the perfect in IE. Even Comrie, *Aspect*, p. 52, and Friedrich, *Aspect Theory*, pp. 16–19, who intermingle aspect with Aktionsart, state that the perfect is an 'aspect' of a different sort.

[86] Bybee, *Morphology*, pp. 141, 159–61; Mourelatos, 'Events, Processes, and States' p. 418.

[87] Lloyd, *Verb*, pp. 117–22; and Armstrong, 'Aorist as the Aspect of Countable Action', in *Tense and Aspect* (1981), 1, 3.

('occurrence with its resulting state') which could fit within the bounds of even the narrowest definition of aspect— namely, its reference to the *occurrence* of an action. This feature of the perfect may be like the aorist aspect, viewing the occurrence as a whole without regard to internal make-up of the situation itself. On the other hand, it may be regarded as merely referring to the occurrence as an anterior event, in the way that a simple tense-form does, without involving aspectual or viewpoint meaning (cf. the future forms, to be discussed next). It seems that the only way to decide between these options is to test instances of the perfect to see whether they exhibit the characteristics of the aorist aspect or of a non-aspectual expression.

When one investigates the perfect in the way just proposed, it is seen that the perfect, in regard to this one element (reference to an occurrence), displays the aspect-value of the aorist, and not a simple tense-reference to a prior occurrence. It views the occurrence as a whole including its beginning and end-point but without regard to internal make-up of the situation itself. This can be seen, for example, with stative verbs; with statives both the aorist and perfect (in its reference to the prior 'occurrence') carry an *ingressive* sense.[88] The perfect with stative verbs does not display a mere tense-reference to the past situation without aspectual modification.

John 8: 52 νῦν ἐγνώκαμεν ('we have *come to know* and now know')[89]

　11: 11 κεκοίμηται ('he has *fallen* asleep', not 'he has been asleep')

1 Tim. 6: 4 τετύφωται ('he is puffed up' as a result of becoming puffed up)

Rev. 3: 17 πλούσιός εἰμι καὶ πεπλούτηκα καὶ οὐδὲν χρείαν ἔχω (repetition of ideas for emphasis: 'I am prosperous and have become wealthy and need nothing')

This can be seen also with verbs denoting an unbounded

---

[88] To be developed further in 3.1.2.1.

[89] Cf. McKay, 'On the Perfect and Other Aspects', p. 299: 'While in many respects very similar to οἶδα, ἔγνωκα, the perfect of γινώσκω, normally seems to differ in having an inbuilt reference to the event of acquisition of knowledge'.

action as opposed to those denoting a bounded action.[90] With the former type, the aorist presents a whole period of the action as 'done' but with an *arbitrary* rather than a *natural* end-point, since an unbounded action has no natural end-point. For occurrences such as these the description 'completed' is not appropriate, although one can speak of them as finished. The same sense appears with the perfects of such verbs (in regard to the *occurrence* referred to by the perfect):

John 4: 38 ἄλλοι κεκωπιάκασιν ('others have laboured')

Heb. 2: 18 πέπονθεν ('he has suffered')

Rev. 18: 3 ἐκ τοῦ οἴνου . . . πέπωκαν πάντα τὰ ἔθνη ('all nations have drunk from the wine')

With verbs of the latter type (bounded actions), aorists more naturally denote the completion of the action, and the same is true for perfects of such verbs:

Matt. 9: 22 ἡ πίστις σου σέσωκέν σε ('your faith has delivered you')

John 1: 41 εὑρήκαμεν τὸν Μεσσίαν ('we have found the Christ')

Heb. 12: 2 κεκάθικεν ('he is seated at the right hand')

12: 22 προσεληλύθατε Σιὼν ὄρει ('you have come to Mount Zion')

Because of this similarity to the aorist, it seems best to conclude that the perfect also possesses an *aspect*-value as part of its composite meaning. The aspect meaning of 'summary, external' view is reflected in the reference which the perfect makes to a prior occurrence.

2. 3. 5 *Summary of the meaning of the perfect forms*

The perfect in NT Greek is a complex verbal category denoting, in its basic sense, a state which results from a prior occurrence. Thus, it combines three elements within its invariant meaning: the Aktionsart-feature of stative situation, the tense-feature of anteriority, and the aspect of summary

---

[90] See 3.1.2.2.

viewpoint concerning the occurrence.[91] In individual texts one can observe degrees of emphasis on one or the other of these features due to variety of contextual factors, but some allusion to all three elements is normally preserved even if one is highlighted over the others.

2. 4 The Significance of the Future Forms

Three meanings have been proposed for the future in NT Greek.

2. 4. 1 *Dual significance: future tense and punctiliar aspect*

A common interpretation of the future is that it possesses a dual significance of tense and aspect. In this approach the future is regarded as a category expressing both future time and an aspect-value of *punctiliar* action.[92] However, many grammars hold that the aspect-value of the future is 'chiefly punctiliar', but can express a durative or linear sense on occasion.[93] Moulton says: 'the action of the future is in usage mixed. Ἄξω is either "I shall lead" or "I shall bring"—the former durative, the latter effective'; and he notes other verbs which can occur in either sense in the future.[94]

However, this mixture of usage in the future (punctual *or* durative sense) appears to indicate not the *flexible* aspectual meaning of the future but its *non-aspectual* character. The variation between punctiliar and durative seems to be dependent upon the lexical sense and contextual features, totally apart from an aspectual value for the future. For example, the range of futures in John 14: 12–25 includes several durative, continuing occurrences (e.g. ἀγαπήσω, τηρήσει), but also some punctual or momentary ones (e.g. ἀφήσω, πέμψει). This variation, however, appears to derive from the lexical sense

---

[91] This is similar to the view of the perfect in Friedrich, *Aspect Theory*, pp. 16–19, 36.

[92] This is the view expressed by Moule, *Idiom Book*, p. 10, and less definitely by MT, *Syntax*, p. 86.

[93] Moulton, *Proleg.*, pp. 148–50; and Robertson, *Grammar*, pp. 870–2.

[94] Moulton, *Proleg.*, p. 149.

and contextual application of the verbal meaning, without alteration by aspect-value. Thus, 'punctiliar' does not appear to be the aspectual value of the future, unless punctiliar means 'unmarked' or aspectually undefined; this is, however, tantamount to saying that it is non-aspectual, since it is not opposed to any marked form in order to produce aspectual variation in expressions about the future.

2. 4. 2 *An aspect expressing 'intention'*

In his comments about the future Zerwick takes a common line (see next section) and states that the future lies outside the aspect-system, expressing only future time. He goes on to suggest, however, that it could be regarded as an aspect of 'intention' or 'end in view', which would have some affinity with the moods rather than with the tenses. But he leaves the idea undeveloped.[95] The point is taken up independently by McKay, who sees the future as primarily an *aspect* parallel with the present, aorist, and perfect, and only secondarily a tense-form. He writes that the Greek future is 'usually regarded simply as a tense . . . but . . . is probably best regarded as a fourth aspect, expressing intention', and he states that it is 'used to express *intention*, and consequently simple *futurity*'.[96]

There is no question that the future has something of this sense about it. But one must wonder whether this may rightly be labelled an *aspect*. Even in the general terms in which McKay defines aspect,[97] the future is only questionably included in parallel to the other aspects which he lists: imperfective ('an activity as in process'), aorist ('whole action

---

[95] Zerwick, *Biblical Greek*, p. 93.

[96] K. L. McKay, *Greek Grammar for Students: A Concise Grammar of Classical Attic with Special Reference to Aspect in the Verb* (Canberra: Department of Classics, The Australian National University, 1974), 136, 140–1. In 'On the Perfect and Other Aspects in New Testament Greek', p. 290, he takes the same view about the future in the NT: that it views the event or activity 'as intention'.

[97] Cf. McKay, *Greek Grammar for Students*, p. 136: 'One of the most important category systems of the ancient Greek verb . . . by which the author (or speaker) shows how he views each event or activity in relation to its context'.

or simple event'), and perfect ('the state consequent upon an action'). 'Intention' is more justifiably a *modal* value or perhaps some hybrid of temporal and modal meanings. But in the terms in which aspect has been defined in this book intention stretches the bounds of the category too far. The meaning of intention which he observes in usage can be better accommodated as part of the next view of the future.

2. 4. 3 *A tense expressing future time*

The most widely held view in NT grammars is that the future is simply a tense-form, without aspectual meaning. Blass–Debrunner–Funk write: 'In meaning, time is practically the only significance of the future (even in the optative, infinitive and participle); *Aktionsart* is expressed only occasionally at most and then only in a secondary way.'[98] Later it is phrased more strongly: 'the future is the only tense which expresses only a level of time and not an Aktionsart so that completed and durative action are not distinguished.'[99] This is the sense given by many NT grammars and is adopted by Schwyzer–Debrunner for ancient Greek in general.[100]

According to this view, the future is a deictic or primary tense, which tells the *temporal relation* of the verbal action to some reference-point, usually the time of speaking: the action is presented as *subsequent* (i.e. yet to take place). Even in the non-indicative forms this value for the future holds, though the reference-point is the time of the main verbal action (infinitives: Acts 11: 28, 24: 15, 27: 10; Heb. 3: 18; participles: Matt. 27: 49; Luke 22: 49; Acts 24: 11; 1 Cor. 15: 37; Heb. 3: 5). In some indicative forms as well the reference-point of the

---

[98] BDF, *Grammar*, § 318.

[99] Ibid., § 348.

[100] Burton, *MT*, §§ 58–73; Nunn, *Syntax*, p. 66; Zerwick, *Biblical Greek*, p. 93; Mussies, *Morphology*, pp. 255–6; Funk, *Beginning-Intermediate Grammar* ii. 634–5; HS, *Grammatik*, pp. 82, 333; and SD, *Syntax*, pp. 264–5. See this view also in Felix Hartmann, 'Zur frage der Aspektbedeutung beim griechischen Futurum', *KZ* 62 (1934), 116–31.

future is some occurrence in the context itself rather than the time of writing or speech (e.g. John 21: 19; possibly Rom. 6: 5).

This view does not deny that, in origin, the future is perhaps a late development from the subjunctive or earlier potential mood. This is likely to be true. But the future as one finds it in ancient Greek functions primarily as a tense, not as a mood. Nor does the view deny that the Greek future can secondarily express various non-indicative modal forces (i.e. potentiality, intention, command). These uses certainly occur; but they appear to stem from the natural connection between future time and non-factual mood. As Lyons points out, the nature of future-time reference is inherently bound up with contingency, possibility, intention, and other non-assertive modal forces, and this is reflected in the grammatical function of futures in many languages.[101] This is true of the future in NT Greek (e.g. Matt. 11: 16; Luke 1: 31, 22: 49; John 6: 68; Rom. 5: 7; 1 Cor. 16: 5, 12). Such 'modal' uses occur, however, as a secondary function of the future-time reference, according to this third view.

2. 4. 4 *Summary of the meaning of the future forms*

Since the future form in Greek is sometimes understood as an aspect, it was necessary to include it in the investigation of possible aspects undertaken in this chapter. However, as seen above, the future must be taken as a non-aspectual *tense*-category, indicating occurrence *subsequent* to some reference-point. What is invariant about the future through all its forms is the temporal meaning of 'future occurrence', which can have secondary· nuances of intention, potential, command, and so forth as a consequence of this time-reference. Thus, it

---

[101] Lyons, *Semantics*, pp. 814–18. This is treated in more detail in Suzanne Fleischman, *The Future in Thought and Language: Diachronic Evidence from Romance* (Cambridge: Cambridge University Press, 1982), 1–31; and Östen Dahl, *Tense and Aspect Systems* (Oxford: Basil Blackwell, 1985), 103–10.

contrasts with the aorist and present forms not on the basis of aspect-distinctions but in regard to the time-values which are attached to their indicative forms. Since the future is not an aspect, it will not be treated in the later chapters of this book.

2. 5 Conclusion: The Relationship of the Aspects to Each Other

In section 1.3.2 different schemes for relating the Greek aspects to each other were surveyed. There now remains, in conclusion to this chapter, the need to state which of those structures best represents the relationship of the NT Greek aspects as discussed here. The *primary* aspectual relationship is that which obtains between the present and aorist aspects. The place of the perfect in relation to these is secondary, since it has an aspect-value like that of the aorist, along with two non-aspectual elements of meaning in its basic sense. Thus, in regard to the primary opposition of aspect-meaning, the perfect can be omitted. Its relationship to the present and aorist in broader terms will be developed in later chapters.

It has been argued above that invariant values for the primary aspects are best expressed in terms of the viewpoint of the speaker concerning the occurrence. Specifically, the *present* reflects an internal viewpoint which focuses on the development or progress of the occurrence and sees it in regard to its internal make-up, without beginning or end in view. On the other hand, the *aorist* presents an external viewpoint, seeing the occurrence in summary without regard for the internal details, but viewed as a whole, including its end-points. When analysed in this way, the aspects form an equipollent opposition[102] rather than a privative one, since they are both marked with a distinctive meaning. Thus, the use of one aspect rather

---

[102] More specifically, this is a 'contradictory' or 'complementary' opposition (cf. 1.3.2). This structure involves two members, both marked in regard to the same basic feature and opposed in such a way that the use of one implies the negative of the other.

than the other constitutes, in regard to aspect itself, the choice of a different meaning and not just a shift to a neutral value.

However, the difference between the aspects in actual usage is always overlaid with various distinctions added by other features. These include the lexical character of the verb itself, adverbial and nominal adjuncts, and other contextual factors which combine with the invariant aspectual meanings. As a result, the contrast between aspects in a specific text may take on a different structure from that reflected by the basic opposition, moving from privative oppositions (e.g. completion vs. 'neutral to completion') to other types of equipollent ones (gradable or mixed oppositions: e.g. single vs. repeated action). The interaction of aspect with these other features is the topic to be treated in Chapter 3.

3

THE EFFECT OF
INHERENT MEANING AND OTHER
ELEMENTS ON ASPECTUAL
FUNCTION

IT was argued in the first chapter that interpreting the aspects requires an understanding of the basic meaning of the aspects themselves as well as their function in combination with other linguistic features. Aspect interacts so closely with other features and is so significantly affected by them that no analysis of it can be meaningful without attention to these elements. It is the goal of this chapter to examine and define what these other features are and to describe in general terms what effect they have on aspectual function when combined with the aspect-values delineated in Chapter 2.

The primary features which affect aspect-function are: procedural character of verbs (i.e. inherent lexical meaning), compositional elements (other elements occurring with the verb: adverbial modifiers, subject- and object-phrases, and negatives), general vs. specific reference, tense-reference (past, present, future), and discourse-related factors (e.g. showing prominence and sequence in a narrative). The most important of these appears to be the inherent lexical meaning carried by the verb itself. As suggested in Chapter 2, this produces several clear-cut distinctions (e.g. durative vs. punctual, incomplete vs. complete) which have often been identified with the aspects themselves. It is the argument of this book that such contrasts are due rather to the combinations of lexical meanings with the viewpoint-oriented values for the aspects themselves. The effect of inherent lexical meaning will be treated first in this chapter, followed by the other factors listed above.

3. 1 The Effect of the Procedural Characteristics of Verbs on Aspectual Function

Many have observed that the verb's lexical meaning is central in its aspectual function, and several systems of classification have been suggested focusing on actional characteristics of the verb. The most widely used approach is that put forth by Vendler and Kenny, which divides verbs into three or four classes: (1) states, (2) activities, and (3) performances; or (3) accomplishments and (4) achievements.[1] These categories are useful in many ways and serve as a base for the approach taken here. But improvements of various kinds to the Vendler–Kenny scheme have been proposed, and these will be utilized also.

In this section a taxonomy will be presented which attempts to categorize the lexical features most important for aspectual function. At the outset, however, three limiting factors must be stated. First, it must be noted that these features of meaning are characteristic ultimately of entire *propositions* or sentences, and not of the verb alone, although the verb is central. Later it will be seen how other features of the sentence combine with the verb to influence the sense. Thus, even though loose reference may be made to 'verb-types' or to 'activity-verbs' (for example), these are shorthand references to 'proposition-types' or to 'propositions which describe activities'.[2] Second, it is important to emphasize that no verb is

---

[1] Zeno Vendler, 'Verbs and Times', *Philosophical Review*, 66 (1957), 43–60 repr. in id. *Linguistics in Philosophy* (Ithaca, NY: Cornell University Press, 1967), 97–121; and Anthony Kenny, *Action. Emotion and Will* (London: Routledge and Kegan Paul, 1963), 151–86. The four categories of Vendler's scheme are elaborated in regard to NT usage by Mateos, *Aspecto verbal* (1977), and for a selection of classical Greek usage (the 'dynamic' infinitive in Herodotus) by Stork, *Aspectual Usage* (1982).

[2] It is also worth noting that this taxonomy does not classify the characteristics of actual situations, but the *linguistic portrayals* of situations, which reflect the actual occurrences only indirectly. Cf. the comments on this point in Renaat Declerck,

entirely uniform in its actional behaviour, although some verbs are more stable than others. What is listed here, when specific examples are given, is an estimate of the *normal* character of some verbs, and how this may affect aspectual function. Verbs may occur in exceptional uses, but even then they appear to shift merely to another category within this system, rather than to some characteristic outside of the system altogether. Third, these categories apply primarily to propositions describing *specific* situations.[3] Statements about repetitions and general occurrences behave differently in regard to aspect-function and will be discussed separately (section 3.3).

3. 1. 1 *Overview: a hierarchy of distinctions based on actional features of verbs in propositions*

For aspectual function there are *four* elements of propositional meaning which are primary: whether a situation is seen as involving *change* or not (action vs. state), whether an action is viewed as '*bounded*' or not (performance vs. activity), whether a performance is viewed as *durative* or not (accomplishment vs. achievement), and whether an achievement is seen as '*prefaced*' by another action or not. These elements of meaning centre on the verb, but they may also involve other features of the sentence, as will be developed in later sections. It should be noted that the four features of meaning do not operate on the same plane, but must be seen in a succession of *parallels* and *contrasts*. In Fig. 3.1 and the discussion which follows, the five individual groups of verbs are noted in small capital letters and the more general groups which link several of them together are given in normal type. The names of the categories, except for the last two, originated with Vendler and

---

'Aspect and the Bounded/Unbounded (Telic/Atelic) Distinction', *Linguistics*, 17 (1979), 764–5.

[3] See the same qualification for these verb-classes given by A. P. D. Mourelatos, 'Events, Processes, and States', *Linguistics and Philosophy*, 2 (1978), 421; and Carlota S. Smith, 'A Theory of Aspectual Choice', *Lg.* 59 (1983), 481.

Kenny and have become a common tradition in aspectology. The primary feature of meaning which distinguishes each type is listed beneath it. These features of meaning and their combinations in various ways in the different classes have a significant impact on the function of the aspects, as the rest of this section will show.

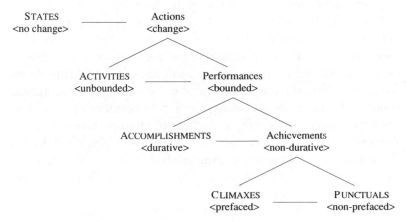

STATES ——————— Actions
<no change>   <change>

ACTIVITIES ——————— Performances
<unbounded>   <bounded>

ACCOMPLISHMENTS ——————— Achievements
<durative>   <non-durative>

CLIMAXES ——————— PUNCTUALS
<prefaced>   <non-prefaced>

FIG. 3.1. Overview of distinctions in actional character

3. 1. 2 *Definition and examples of specific classes of verbs*

The individual classes listed above will now be defined and illustrated,[4] and a brief description of their influence on aspectual function will be given.

3. 1. 2. 1 STATES *versus actions*

1. *Definition of* STATES. The first distinction to be made is that between *stative* verbs and *active or dynamic* verbs. Even though

_____

[4] The classification of word-meanings into discrete classes is a difficult task. Some items fit nicely into the categories, while others defy precise labelling. See Stork, *Aspectual Usage*, pp. 36–37, for discussion of some of the difficulties involved. The classification of individual verbs given here cannot claim to be correct in every case. What is claimed is that the description of these classes as a whole is legitimate and that these characteristics of meaning are significant in their effect on aspect-function. I have attempted to include as many verbs as possible in the lists and have given special attention to classifying verbs which occur more frequently in the NT. But

STATES share some features of meaning with the four active classes of verbs (e.g. they are 'durative' like both ACTIVITIES and ACCOMPLISHMENTS and 'unbounded' like ACTIVITIES), they are in other ways quite distinct, and the other four classes share a basic feature of meaning which STATES do not possess. This basic feature which distinguishes actions from STATES appears to be the feature of *change* in the meaning of the verb: actions involve some sort of change in the condition (or relation or location) of the subject or object, either as a momentary event or as occurring through successive stages, while STATES involve no change in condition.[5] As Mourelatos says, 'A state, as the name implies, involves no dynamics. Though it may arise, or be acquired, as a result of change, and though it may provide the potential of change, the state itself does not constitute a change.[6] Thus, for example, verbs like *to be*, *to have*, and *to know* are normally *states*, while *to become*, *to get*, and *to discover* are *actions* (along with other more clearly 'active' ideas: *go*, *build*, *take*, *hit*).[7]

There are two other incidental features of meaning characteristic of STATES: they are always durative and 'unbounded' (to be explained below). But these are not *determinative* of STATES, since they are true of some types of actions as well. The distinctive feature of meaning is 'lack of change', as

---

verbs whose classification seemed too tenuous have simply been omitted, and no systematic attempt has been made to validate the classifications.

[5] This is the distinction suggested by Comrie, *Aspect*, pp. 48–9; Lyons, *Semantics*, p. 483; Smith, 'Aspectual Choice', p. 481; and Christer Platzack, *The Semantic Interpretation of Aspect and Aktionsarten: A Study of Internal Time Reference in Swedish* (Dordrecht: Foris Publications, 1979), 68–70, 108–14. Platzack puts this more specifically: 'In order to have a change, we require at least two different situations, one valid before the change, the other valid after the change. When we have no change, only one situation is involved. Following a well-established practice, we will use the term *state* for situations not involving a change'.

[6] Mourelatos, 'Events, Processes, and States', p. 416.

[7] Mateos, *Aspecto verbal*, p. 22, gives a definition of STATES which is more general than these, and is strictly meaning-based: 'No denotan realización, sino condiciones o situaciones no momentáneas que se conciben como un continuo indiviso'. His treatment is more valuable in suggesting subgroups of STATES and in classifying individual NT verbs.

described above.[8] This feature seems valid, since it appears to reflect the intuitive distinction which most discern between STATES and actions, but it has certain limitations. Since the distinction is strictly *meaning*-based, it is subject to a wider range of subjective estimates as to whether a given verb fits the criterion. For this reason, many have suggested other criteria related less to meaning and more to syntactic behaviour and acceptable usage with certain words or phrases. The most important of these will be evaluated here.

(*a*) STATES cannot occur in the progressive form.[9] In linguistic discussions based on English usage this criterion is often noted first, since English utilizes an easily observed syntactic pattern: STATES do not normally occur in the progressive (or 'expanded') form, while most active verbs occur readily in this form. This has some usefulness, since it brings to the surface an element of meaning in the English progressive form (process, successive stages of occurrence?) which is incompatible with stative meaning. But as a language-general criterion it will not work, since it is not necessarily true that other languages (e.g. NT Greek) have this restriction.[10]

---

[8] Antony Galton, *The Logic of Aspect: An Axiomatic Approach* (Oxford: Clarendon Press, 1984), 24–8, 68–72, disputes this. He prefers to distinguish states from *events* in a way similar to the distinction between mass- and count-nouns: i.e. states are homogeneous and dissective, while events are inhomogeneous and unitary. Thus, Galton includes as 'states' most of the verbs here classed as STATES and ACTIVITIES, and speaks of them as 'states of rest' and 'states of change'. It is certainly true that STATES and ACTIVITIES share these features as distinct from the other classes of actions (see the discussion to follow and the summary in 3.1.3), but the distinction based on change/lack of change is far more useful for predicting aspectual usage in NT Greek than Galton's taxonomy.

[9] Vendler, 'Verbs and Times', pp. 99, 102-3; Kenny, *Action, Emotion and Will*, pp. 172–5; Ronald Kerr Steven Macauley, 'Aspect in English' (Ph.D. Dissertation, University of California at Los Angeles, 1971), 26–34; and David Dowty, *Studies in the Logic of Verb Aspect and Time Reference in English* (Studies in Linguistics, 1; Austin: Department of Linguistics, University, of Texas, 1972), 20–1.

[10] There appears to be no idiomatic avoidance of STATES in the NT Greek periphrastic construction, which is comparable in other ways to the English progressive. Of the 86 NT examples of the type 'imperfect of εἰμί with present participle' as listed by MH, *Accidence*, p. 452, at least 20 occur with the participle of a

(b) STATES cannot occur in the imperative mood or as complements of verbs of 'persuading' or 'forcing'.[11] This suggestion works fairly well for English, but is not valid for NT Greek. STATES do commonly occur in the imperative and in all types of indirect commands, with their stative sense preserved.[12] However, this criterion (no imperative etc.), even for English usage, appears to focus on a cardinal feature *not* of stativity/activity, but of the related distinction 'agentive/non-agentive'. In other words, episodes which can be commanded, persuaded, or compelled must involve an *agent* (i.e. an animate being capable of acting or producing an effect) who is influenced to engage in the episode in question. However, even though there is a common association of agentive episodes with actions (e.g. 'The man struck the boulder') and non-agentive episodes with STATES ('The boulder lay on the canyon floor'), this is not a necessary connection ('The boulder rolled down and struck the man, as he lay on the canyon floor').[13] Thus, this criterion has limited usefulness for discerning stativity itself.

(c) STATES cannot occur with manner adverbials like 'reluctantly', 'carefully', 'deliberately', 'willingly', or 'for someone's sake'.[14] This criterion must be seen in the same way as the preceding one, since these adverbials cannot be associated with an inanimate subject: agency is the focus, not stativity.

STATE — e.g. Mark 10: 22~Matt. 19: 22 (ἦν γὰρ ἔχων κτήματα πολλά) John 11: 1 (ἦν . . . ἀσθενῶν); and other verbs which are clearly STATES (κάθημαι, καθεύδω, κατάκειμαι, δύναμαι, ἀγνοέω). This occurs also with the less frequent 'present periphrastic' as in Rev. 1: 18 ζῶν εἰμι.

[11] Kenny, *Action, Emotion and Will*, pp. 183–4; Macauley, 'Aspect in English', p. 34; and Dowty, *Verb Aspect and Time Reference*, p. 21.

[12] See stative indirect commands after πειθω and παρακαλέω in Acts 11: 23, 13: 43, 14: 22, 28: 14; Phil. 4: 2; 1 Tim. 1: 3; Tit. 2: 6. For usage in the imperative mood in general, see ch. 5.

[13] Lennart Nordenfelt, *Events, Actions, and Ordinary Language* (Lund: Doxa, 1977), 54–7, shows that the feature of agency is not essential to activity nor inimical to stativity.

[14] Macauley, 'Aspect in English', p. 34; and Dowty, *Verb Aspect and Time Reference*, p. 21.

(*d*) STATES cannot be used as substitute or parallel for the active proverbs 'do' or 'happen'.[15] This criterion is phrased as a linguistic frame which the STATE cannot fit: 'what he *did* was _____'; 'I _____, though he told me not to *do* so'; or as the answer to the question 'What happened?' These are helpful tools for evaluating individual verbs, but the focus of these tests is the *meaning* of the verb, as discerned by a competent speaker. STATES do not fit the frames because they do not contain some element of meaning common to the active verbs used in parallel. Thus, this criterion is meaning-based like the feature 'change/no change' suggested above, and in fact this may be the unnamed feature which the frames put in focus. It is difficult to apply this test to ancient Greek, since no native speakers are available to discern the acceptability of a verb in such a frame.[16]

(*e*) STATES can occur with temporal phrases of the sort '*for* x time', but not with adverbials like '*in* x time', 'quickly', 'slowly' (the latter two in the sense of 'in a short/long time').[17] These are certainly true of STATES, but they are not *distinctive* of them: ACTIVITIES share these characteristics. So these temporal phrases narrow the field somewhat, but do not by themselves indicate stativity, in English or in Greek.

In summary, the first distinction to be made separates STATES from actions, based on whether a verb expresses *no change* or *change* in the condition, relation, or location of the subject or object. For NT Greek this must be discerned from estimating the meaning of the verb, rather than from syntactically based tests.

---

[15] Macauley, 'Aspect in English', p. 34; Dowty, *Verb Aspect and Time Reference*, p. 21; and Platzack, *Semantic Interpretation*, p. 68.

[16] Problems of studying a 'dead' language are discussed by H. Pinkster, *On Latin Adverbs* (Amsterdam: North-Holland, 1972), 9–16. He argues that one must base such a study on attested examples, with additional insight from knowledge of other languages known to him. One cannot, of course, bring categories over from another language without justification.

[17] Kenny, *Action, Emotion and Will*, pp. 176–7; Platzack, *Semantic Interpretation*, pp. 68–70; and Lars Heltoft, 'Information about Change', in *Aspectology* (1979), 145–6.

An emphasis on the unchanging nature of STATES, however, leads to an area of ambiguity which now needs to be clarified. If a STATE by nature involves no change, one would assume that, when left to itself, it will continue with no effort needed to maintain it. But an action, since it involves change, requires effort or exertion to produce its inherent change.[18] This association of *effort* with *change,* and the lack of it with no change, produces two types of ambiguity between STATES and actions: (1) change which requires no effort, and (2) resistance to change (or maintenance of a condition) which does require effort. The former situation, which is less frequent, can be seen in these examples: the ball stopped rolling, the fire died out, the man became old. These cases, on linguistic grounds at least, should be considered actions, since they have more parallels with actions than with STATES.[19]

The cases of resistance to change or maintenance of a condition (by exerted effort) are more frequent and more difficult. Examples of these are: verbs of 'active possession' (e.g. *keep, hold tight*), verbs of 'active perception' (*look at, listen*: 'where the perceiver is actively directing his attention towards some object'[20]), and verbs of 'active cognition' ('I am thinking of my friend').[21] Even though these involve no change, they also (on linguistic grounds) are closer to actions than to STATES and will be classed as actions in this book.

2. *Illustrations of* STATES. Based on the definition given

[18] Cf. Comrie, *Aspect,* p. 49: 'With a state, unless something happens to change that state, then the state will continue: this applies equally to standing and to knowing. With a dynamic situation, on the other hand, the situation will only continue if it is continually subject to a new input of energy. . . . To remain in a state requires no effort, whereas to remain in a dynamic situation does require effort'.

[19] For example, they take progressive form in English, they occur with 'in *x* time' rather than 'for *x* time', and they fit frames like 'What it/he did was ____'.

[20] Geoffrey N. Leech, *Meaning and the English Verb* (London: Longman, 1971), 20. See his discussion of several of these cases, pp. 20–7.

[21] Parallel to each of these are cases of *passive or inert* possession (have, own), perception (see, hear), and cognition ('I think that he is my friend'); these are all unchanging and are clearly STATES. Many verbs, of course, shift from one sense to the other depending on context.

above, several types of verbs, in their normal usage, should be listed as STATES:

(a) Verbs of 'being': predication of *qualities, conditions*, or *attributes* associated with the subject (these may be permanent or temporary)

εἰμί with adjective predicate (ἅγιος, μέγας, etc.)
γίνομαι (in sense of εἰμί)[22] with adjective predicate
ἔχω with adverb (εὖ, κακῶς, καλῶς, ἑτοίμως, etc.)

Other verbs with lexicalized predication of qualities, etc. as above:

ἀσθενέω	διψάω	εἰρηνεύω
ζάω	ἰσχύω	κάμνω
μεθύω	πεινάω	πλουτέω
πτωχεύω	σιγάω	σιωπάω
ὑγιαίνω	ὑστερέω	

(b) Verbs of *existence, identity, or class-membership*

εἰμί as intransitive (not as copula or with location phrase)
εἰμί with noun predicate (υἱός, ἄνθρωπος, etc.)
γίνομαι (in sense of εἰμί) with noun predicate
ὑπάρχω with noun predicate

(c) Verbs of passive or inert *possession:* no focus on exertion to maintain possession

ἔχω   γέμω (=be full of, contain)
χωρέω (=hold, contain)

(d) Verbs of passive *perception:* not actively directing attention but passively receptive[23]

ἀκούω   βλέπω   θεωρέω
ὁράω/εἶδον

(e) Verbs of passive *cognition*, mental attitude, or emotional

---

[22] See BAGD, *Lexicon*, p. 160.
[23] Verbs in this group can shift back and forth from passive perception to active perception, depending on the contextual sense: e.g. βλέπω with the active meaning 'take care'; ἀκούω with the active meaning 'listen, give attention, obey'.

state: no focus on exertion to maintain knowledge/attitude or to act in keeping with it

ἀγρυπνέω	ἀναπαύομαι	ἀρκέομαι
βδελύσσομαι	γινώσκω[24]	γρηγορέω
δοκέω	ἐλπίζω	ἐξίσταμαι
ἐξουθενέω	ἐπιθυμέω	ἐπίσταμαι
εὐαρεστέω	εὐδοκέω	ἡγέομαι
θέλω	θυμέομαι	καθεύδω
καταφρονέω	κοιμάομαι	μαίνομαι
μεριμνάω	μιμνήσκω	μνημονεύω
νομίζω	οἶδα	ὀργίζομαι
ὀρέγομαι	πιστεύω	πλανάομαι
προσδοκάω	φοβέω	φρονέω

(f) Verbs of location and corporeal position

εἰμί+ἐκεῖ, ὧδε, ἐγγύς
εἰμί+preposition of location: ἐν, σύν, μετά, πρός, etc.

ἄπειμι	καθέζομαι	κάθημαι[25]
κεῖμαι+compounds	μένω+compounds	οἰκέω+compounds
πάρειμι	σκηνόω	στήκω

(g) Impersonal states

δεῖ	ἔξεστιν	καθήκει
πρέπει	συμφέρει	χρή

3. *Influence of* STATES *on aspectual function.* The importance of distinguishing STATES from actions can be seen in their unique effect on aspectual function compared to that of action-verbs. Conversely, the different meanings of the aspects can seen more clearly when *aorist* use of STATES is contrasted with *present* use of STATES.

---

[24] Cf. Richard J. Erickson, 'Oida and Ginōskō and Verbal Aspect in Pauline Usage', *Westminster Theological Journal*, 44 (1982), 110–22, who shows from contextual semantic evidence in Paul that γινώσκω denotes a stative sense in the present, but normally an ingressive meaning in the aorist. His treatment rightly suggests the importance of noting verbal aspect in discerning contextual verb-meaning, but he misconstrues the value of the aspects in NT Greek.

[25] This verb is normally a STATE ('sit; live'), but uses of the imperative and a few other forms exhibit the active sense 'sit down'. See BAGD, *Lexicon*, p. 389.

(a) *Present*: the present aspect[26] with STATES denotes the *continuing existence* of the subject in the condition indicated by the verb. This is the most compatible aspect for use with STATES, since the aspectual sense of 'the situation viewed from within, focusing on the internal make-up, without regard for beginning or end-point' gives a very natural reference to the unchanging condition.[27] For example:

Luke 22: 2 ἐφοβοῦντο γὰρ τὸν λαόν 'they were fearful . . .' (*contra*
  20: 19 ἐφοβήθησαν τὸν λαόν 'they became fearful . . . [as a result of the parable just told]')
Acts 9: 26 πάντες ἐφοβοῦντο αὐτόν (not 'became afraid', but 'were afraid')
Cf. φρονέω (occurs in present/imperfect 25 times in the NT, all denoting the unchanging state 'to think, to hold an opinion'); καθεύδω (19 times in present/imperfect, all stative); ἐπίσταμαι (14 times in present/imperfect, all stative).

In contrast to actions, STATES with present aspect will, by definition, never denote a 'process' occurring through time or something 'in progress', since STATES are not amenable to such notions.

(b) *Aorist:* the aorist aspect with STATES denotes most frequently the *entrance* of the subject into the condition denoted by the verb.[28] Thus, it makes a shift in sense and in effect becomes a type of *active* verb when the aorist is used. This use is best explained according to the definition of the aorist given in Chapter 2: 'the situation viewed from the outside, without regard for internal make-up, but with focus on beginning and end-point'. The focus on the *terminal points* of the situation

---

[26] Including all forms of the Greek 'present' as well as the imperfect indicative.

[27] Alternative definitions of present aspect do not work as well with STATES. Defining the present as 'incomplete' makes no sense with stative meaning, while the 'durative' definition is possible here but not as workable in other classes of verbs.

[28] As noted by William W. Goodwin, *Syntax of the Moods and Tenses of the Greek Verb* (Boston: Ginn and Co., 1890), § 55, and many NT grammars: Moulton, *Proleg.*, p. 130; MT, *Syntax*, pp. 71–2; H. P. V. Nunn, *A Short Syntax of New Testament Greek*, 5th edn. (Cambridge: at the University Press, 1938), 69; and Zerwick, *Biblical Greek*, pp. 81–2.

normally produces the shift to an ingressive, active sense: the 'event' of entering the state.[29]

For example, the verb ζάω in the NT occurs eight times in the aorist indicative, seven of which have the ingressive sense ('came to life'), with one having the past stative idea (Acts 26: 5 ἔζησα, summarizing an extended past condition as described below). In contrast, ζάω occurs twenty-nine times in the present or imperfect indicative, all of which have a stative sense (e.g. Rom. 7: 9 ἐγὼ δὲ ἔζων χωρὶς νόμου ποτέ). The verbs πλουτέω and σιωπάω together occur eleven times in the present aspect, and all these are best interpreted as stative, while their ten aorists are all best taken as ingressives. The verb ἔχω, used hundreds of times in the present aspect (usually with the stative sense 'have, possess'), occurs only twenty times in aorist form (base σχ-) in the NT; twelve of these are ingressive, while seven denote a summary of a series of states, as in Mark 12: 23 (and parallels): οἱ ἑπτὰ ἔσχον αὐτὴν γυναῖκα.

Less frequently, the aorist of a STATE may take a summary view of the entire situation (especially in the indicative) and denote the (past) *existence* of the subject in the state, or a summary of repeated (past) states:

Matt. 25: 35–6, 42–3 ἐπείνασα, ἐδίψησα, ἠσθένησα (paraphrased in the passage by present participles and adjectives)

Mark 12: 23 (+parallels) οἱ ἑπτὰ ἔσχον αὐτὴν γυναῖκα

Luke 9: 36 (cf. Acts 15: 12) καὶ αὐτοὶ ἐσίγησαν 'now they kept silent'

(*c*) *Perfect*: the perfect verb-forms with STATES denote most frequently a meaning which combines the present and aorist senses noted above: they describe an existing state and imply

[29] If the aorist were 'unmarked' or aspectually blank in keeping with one alternative theory discussed in ch. 2 (e.g. Charles R. Smith, 'Errant Aorist Interpreters', *Grace Theological Journal*, 2 [1980], 207–8, feels that the aorist simply passes on the lexical idea without aspectual alteration of any kind), it is hard to explain why the aorist does not refer to the *existence* of the subject in the state, especially in the non-indicative uses where temporal or discourse factors are less important. Yet in the non-indicative uses the ingressive sense for STATES is even more pronounced than in the indicative.

the act of entrance which led into that state, with the emphasis usually on the former. Thus, they contrast with the present and aorist, which refer only to the continuing state or to the beginning of it, respectively.[30]

John 8: 52 νῦν ἐγνώκαμεν ὅτι δαιμόνιον ἔχεις.[31]

11: 11–12 (cf. Matt. 27: 52, 1 Cor. 15: 20) Λάζαρος ὁ φίλος ἡμῶν κεκοίμηται . . . κύριε, εἰ κεκοίμηται σωθήσεται.

11: 27 (occurs 7 other times in Johannine material, 11 others in NT, all with this sense) πιστεύεις τοῦτο; λέγει αὐτῷ· ναὶ κύριε, ἐγὼ πεπίστευκα ὅτι σὺ εἶ ὁ χριστός

14: 7, 9 καὶ ἀπ᾽ ἄρτι γινώσκετε αὐτὸν καὶ ἑωράκατε αὐτόν . . . ὁ ἑωρακὼς ἐμὲ ἑώρακεν τὸν πατέρα[32]

Rom. 5: 2 δι᾽ οὗ καὶ τὴν προσαγωγὴν ἐσχήκαμεν [τῇ πίστει] εἰς τὴν χάριν ταύτην

16: 25 κατὰ ἀποκάλυψιν μυστηρίου χρόνοις αἰωνίοις σεσιγημένου

2 Cor. 1: 10 (cf. John 5: 45; 1 Cor. 15: 19; 1 Tim. 4: 10, 5: 5, 6: 17) ἠλπίκαμεν [ὅτι] καὶ ἔτι ῥύσεται

Rev. 3: 17 πλούσιος εἰμι καὶ πεπλούτηκα καὶ οὐδὲν χρείαν ἔχω (parallel clauses repeating essentially the same idea for emphasis)

With some verbs the perfect denotes instead a stative sense *without* reference to a previous occurrence which began the state, and thus it is no different in meaning from the present stative idea. These do not appear to have a more 'intensive' meaning.

---

[30] Cf. K. L. McKay, 'On the Perfect and Other Aspects in New Testament Greek', *Nov. T.* (1981), 297: 'The perfect of a stative verb . . . mostly has in some respects the same basic implication as the imperfective: the state is continuing, but it has either an intensified meaning or an inbuilt reference to the commencement of the state, or both'.

[31] Cf. McKay, ibid. 299–303, esp. 299: 'ἔγνωκα . . . normally seems to differ [from οἶδα] in having an inbuilt reference to the event of acquisition of knowledge'.

[32] The perfect of ὁράω is very common in Johannine writings. It is thought to have a sense similar to the other perfects listed here: 'I have seen and thus retain the vision in mind'. See Morton S. Enslin, 'The Perfect Tense in the Fourth Gospel', *JBL* 55 (1936), 127–31.

Acts 1: 11 τί ἑστήκατε βλέποντες εἰς τὸν οὐρανόν;[33]

1 Cor. 11: 2 (cf. 2 Tim. 1: 4) ἐπαινῶ δὲ ὑμᾶς ὅτι πάντα μου μέμνησθε

In summary, the first distinction to be made separates STATES from actions, based on whether a verb expresses *no change* or *change* in the condition, relation, or location of the subject or object. STATES are different in this regard from all the active classes of verbs, and the function of the aspects with STATES reflects this procedural characteristic.

3. 1. 2. 2 ACTIVITIES *versus performances*

1. *Definition of* ACTIVITIES. The next distinction of procedural characteristics operates only within the larger group of *actions*,[34] to distinguish actions which are 'unbounded' (ACTIVITIES) from those which are 'bounded' (performances). This difference, which is very significant for aspectual function, has been observed by many writers,[35] and more than any other distinction it involves the entire sentence, including subject- and object phrases and temporal or directional adverbials, as well as the lexical character of the verb. Put very simply, the difference between bounded and unbounded expression focuses on whether the expression includes a *limit*

---

[33] This seems the best place to include ἵστημι, though its present is not a stative but a transitive active. However, the perfect serves always as an intransitive stative present, without implication of a previous act of 'taking one's stand' (cf. Matt. 12: 47~Luke 8: 20; Matt. 20: 3; Acts 26: 6, 22).

[34] This is discussed briefly in Östen Dahl, *Tense and Aspect Systems* (Oxford: Basil Blackwell, 1985), 28–9. STATES share with ACTIVITIES the characteristic of being unbounded, but they should be kept separate since their lack of *change* leaves them on an entirely different plane.

[35] Aristotle appears to note this distinction in *Metaphysics*, 1048[b] 18–35, and in *Nicomachean Ethics*, 1140[a] 1–24. See references to his treatment, in Timothy C. Potts, 'States, Activities and Performances, I', *Proceedings of the Aristotelian Society*, Supp. vol 39 (1965), 65–84; C. C. W. Taylor, 'States, Activities and Performances, II', ibid. 85–102; and J. L. Ackrill, 'Aristotle's Distinction between Energeia and Kinesis', in Renford Bambroagh (ed.) *New Essays on Plato and Aristotle* (London: Routledge and Kegan Paul, 1965), 121–41. Modern discussions of this distinction (up to 1979) are surveyed by Declerck, 'Bounded/Unbounded', pp. 761–7. See also the extensive survey of research given in Sven-Gunnar Andersson, *Aktionalität im Deutschen: Eine Untersuchung unter Vergleich mit dem russischen Aspektsystem*, i (Uppsala: Acta Universitatis Unsaliensis, 1972), 69–184.

or terminus for the action or not. A bounded expression involves, either as part of the inherent lexical meaning of the verb or as part of a nominal or adverbial complement used with the verb, a terminal point at which the action is 'finished', not just 'ended'.[36] Unbounded actions or ACTIVITIES have no such terminus. In Vendler's terms, unbounded expressions have 'no set terminal point', while bounded expressions have 'a "climax" which has to be reached if the action is to be what it is claimed to be'.[37] Several formal characteristics have been proposed to distinguish unbounded and bounded expressions, and these will now be surveyed.

(a) One clear criterion is the acceptability of temporal adverbials like 'for x time'.[38] This temporal phrase can occur with *unbounded* expressions using simple aspect (e.g. Greek aorist), but it cannot occur with *bounded* ones using simple aspect.[39] Thus, 'he walked in the park', 'he read poetry', and 'he ate noisily' are unbounded, and one can easily add 'for hours/for five minutes' and so on. With such unbounded expressions, these temporal phrases simply tell how long the

[36] Smith, 'Aspectual Choice', p. 481, speaks of natural vs. arbitrary end-points as a way of expressing this distinction: 'Achievements and accomplishments have different stages, from beginning to completion, e.g. in winning a race or building a wall. These are events with natural endpoints, because the beginnings and endings are intrinsic to the event. Activities, such as laughing or swimming in a pond, are homogeneous: their stages do not differ, and they can begin or end arbitrarily, at any stage'. The difference of 'homogeneity' between ACTIVITIES and performances is developed by Barry Taylor, 'Tense and Continuity', *Linguistics and Philosophy*, 1 (1977), 199–220.

[37] Vendler, 'Verbs and Times', p. 100. Mateos, *Aspecto verbal*, p. 65, also describes ACTIVITIES (his 'lexemas dinámicos de acción continua') in these terms: 'Dentro de los lexemas dinámicos, los de acción continua son lexemas no efectivos; denotan una actividad (o su correlativa pasividad) que se concibe como un continuo indiviso, sin término, efecto o resultado previsto'.

[38] The early treatments of the topic all mention this but do not develop it. Cf. Gilbert Ryle, *The Concept of Mind* (London, Hutchinson and Co., 1949), 149; Vendler, 'Verbs and Times', pp. 100–1; and Kenny, *Action, Emotion and Will*, p. 176. More extensive discussion of this is given by Lauri Carlson, 'Aspect and Quantification', in *Tense and Aspect* (1981), 37–9; and Declerck, 'Bounded/Unbounded', p. 763.

[39] This assumes, as mentioned earlier, a non-iterative reading. The test must be applied to the simple verb, since the progressive distorts the results in assuming an iterative sense, which is durative.

action continued before it came to some arbitrary end. On the other hand, bounded expressions like 'he walked two miles', 'he read a sonnet', and 'he ate his supper' will not tolerate phrases like 'for hours/for five minutes', except in an iterative reading (which makes them unbounded) or in an instance where the duration-phrase refers not to the occurrence itself but to its result (e.g. Luke 4: 25 ἐκλείσθη ὁ οὐρανὸς ἐπὶ ἔτη τρία καὶ μῆνας ἕξ). See other examples from NT usage in section 3. 2. 2. 2.

(b) A second criterion suggested is the entailment difference between an *imperfective* verb in an unbounded expression compared to a bounded one. This entailment difference works two ways:

(i) The *past imperfective* of an unbounded expression entails the parallel preterite or perfect verb, but for bounded express-ions there is no such entailment. In other words, to say 'he was V-ing' entails 'he V-ed/he has V-ed' with unbounded phrases, but not with bounded ones.[40] For Greek this means that the imperfect entails the aorist or perfect if the expression is unbounded, but not if it is bounded: Acts 3: 3, 5 ἠρώτα ἐλεημοσύνην λαβεῖν . . . ὁ δὲ ἐπεῖχεν αὐτοῖς ... (entails 'he asked', 'he gave attention') *contra* Acts 7: 26 συνήλλασσεν αὐτοὺς εἰς εἰρήνην (does not entail 'he reconciled').

(ii) The *present imperfective* entails the *negative* perfect verb for bounded expressions ('he is V-ing' implies 'he has not [yet] V-ed'), but not for unbounded expressions.[41] Thus, 'he is building the house' entails 'he has not (yet) built the house' and is a bounded expression; but 'he is building houses' does not necessarily entail 'he has not (yet) built houses' and is

---

[40] J. B. Garey, 'Verbal Aspect in French', *Lg.* 33 (1957), 105; Kenny, *Action, Emotion and Will,* p. 172; and Declerck, 'Bounded/Unbounded', p. 763. Garey's oft-cited illustration of a bounded action is the verb 'drown' in English: if a man *was drowning* and he got rescued from his plight, one does not say 'he drowned/has drowned'. The terminus must be reached before it is said to be 'truly' done. For an unbounded verb, however, the case is different: if a man *was running* and got stopped along the way, one can still say, 'he ran/has run'.

[41] Kenny, *Action, Emotion and Will,* p. 175; Macauley, 'Aspect in English', p. 119; Lyons, *Semantics,* p. 711.

unbounded.[42] These entailment criteria work quite well for determining bounded and unbounded expressions, except that some bounded phrases (specifically 'punctual' ones) do not easily fit the imperfective form in a non-iterative sense: 'he hit the ball' is bounded, and 'he is/was hitting the ball' (as non-iterative) suits the entailment tests, but such progressive phrases are unusual for punctuals.

(c) The third criterion is that only bounded expressions (performances) can appropriately be used as complements of the verb *finish*, as in 'I have finished _____' or 'I have not yet finished _____'. Unbounded actions (i.e. ACTIVITIES) fit more naturally with a verb like *stop*: 'I have stopped _____'.[43] For example, 'reading the novel' (not in the sense 'reading *from* the novel') is something one 'finishes', while 'reading poetry' is just 'stopped'. As Taylor says of ACTIVITIES, they are 'impossible to finish doing in any sense other than simply stopping doing them'.[44] This criterion, like the second, fits more naturally with performances which are non-punctual, but it works with punctuals as well.

In summary, ACTIVITIES are 'unbounded' in that they are verbs or expressions which do not involve a *limit* or terminus for the action. A bounded expression (i.e. performance) involves, either as part of the inherent lexical meaning of the verb or as part of a nominal or adverbial complement used with the verb,[45] a terminal point at which the action is 'finished', not just 'ended'. Classifying a Greek verb or expression as an ACTIVITY is thus ultimately a matter of estimating its meaning, though a classification may be validated to a degree by syntactic tests like those given above.

[42] This illustrates the fact that many bounded expressions involve the whole verbal proposition along with the verb: the adjuncts of the verb must be specific and limited in reference, or the proposition will be unbounded.

[43] Kenny, *Action, Emotion and Will*, p. 177; Dowty, *Verb Aspect and Time Reference*, p. 23; Macauley, 'Aspect in English', pp. 118–19; and Galton, *Logic of Aspect*, pp. 66–8.

[44] Taylor, 'States, Activities and Performances, II', p. 91. This is what Kenny means in *Action, Emotion and Will*, p. 177, when he says. 'Only performances can be complete or incomplete'.

[45] See sect. 3.2 concerning the effect of compositional elements.

2. *Illustrations of* ACTIVITIES. Based on the definition given above, several types of verbs, in their normal usage, should be listed as ACTIVITIES:

(*a*) Verbs of movement (transitive or intransitive): verbs which lexically denote a change in the location of the subject or object (these are unbounded unless they are used with a prefix or adverbial phrase denoting *source* or *destination* or some other sort of limit to the movement)[46]

ἄγω	ἀκολουθέω	ἀναβαίνω
διέρχομαι (='go about')	ἔρχομαι	κυλίομαι
περιάγω	περιέρχομαι	περιπατέω
πορεύομαι	τρέχω	φέρω

(*b*) Gradable transitions (transitive or intransitive): verbs which lexically denote a change in the subject or object, but with a *relative* terminal point—there is no definite end at which the action must cease[47]

αὐξάνω	διδάσκω	ἑτοιμάζω
κοσμέω	παλαιόω	στηρίζω
φθείρω	φυσιόω	

(ἐπ)οικοδομέω (fig. meaning only)

(*c*) Other transitive or intransitive verbs with unbounded meaning

ἀγωνίζομαι	ἀλείφω	ἀναγινώσκω
γογγύζω	γράφω	δακρύω
διακονέω	διαλογίζομαι	διώκω
δουλεύω	ἐνεργέω	ἐργάζομαι
ἐσθίω	εὐαγγελίζομαι	ζητέω
θησαυρίζω	κηρύσσω	κλαίω
κοπιάω	κράζω	λαλέω
λατρεύω	λέγω	λειτουργέω
μαρτυρέω	νηστεύω	πάσχω
πίνω	ποιέω	πράσσω
στρατεύομαι	τρέφω	χράομαι

---

[46] Compare this with 3.1.2.3 regarding ACCOMPLISHMENT expressions.
[47] Cf. Declerck, 'Bounded/Unbounded', p. 783, n. 33; Wolfgang Zydatiß, ' "Con-

(d) Verbs of active *possession*: focus on exertion to *maintain* possession

κατέχω   κρατέω   τηρέω

(e) Verbs of active *perception*: not passively receptive but actively directing attention

ἀτενίζω   εἰσακούω   ἐμβλέπω
ἐνωτίζω   ἐπακούω   ἐπακροάομαι
περιβλέπω

(f) Verbs of active *cognition*, mental attitude, or emotional state: focus on exertion to maintain knowledge/attitude or to act in keeping with it

ἀγαλλιάομαι   ἀγαπάω   ἐγκρατεύομαι
εὐφραίνω   λογίζομαι   μισέω
φιλέω   χαίρω

3. *Influence of* ACTIVITIES *on aspectual function*. ACTIVITIES bear some resemblance to STATES, since both are durative and unbounded, but they differ from STATES in that they denote continuing change of some sort on the part of the subject. On the other side, ACTIVITIES differ from all performances (i.e. all the other active verb-types) in being unbounded, while they are bounded. The aspects are influenced by these characteristics in these ways:

(a) *Present*: the present aspect with ACTIVITIES denotes a continuing process as occurring, an action progressing without a termination being reached. This lexical type combines easily with the aspectual value of 'viewing the situation from within, without regard for beginning or end-point', and the result is a sense of cutting into a process at some point as it is unfolding, with part of the process stretching out before and part running on after the point at which it is viewed. The combination is always durative in some way since this is inherent in the nature of this verb-type. When the verb in

tinuative" and "Resultative" Perfects in English?', *Lingua*, 44 (1978), 343; Platzack, *Semantic Interpretation*, pp. 96–7; and Lloyd, *Verb*, pp. 198–200.

context refers to a specific action, it is quite descriptive and vivid: 'the action occurring before one's eyes'. Even though there is no end-point indicated, the action is not thought of as 'incomplete', since an ACTIVITY does not have a natural or expected end-point. For example:

Matt. 28: 5 (+parallels) Ἰησοῦν . . . ζητεῖτε

Mark 2: 16 (~Matt. 9: 11) ἐσθίει μετὰ τῶν τελωνῶν καὶ ἁμαρτωλῶν

Mark 5: 32 καὶ περιεβλέπετο ἰδεῖν τὴν τοῦτο ποιήσασαν
   9: 20 πεσὼν ἐπὶ τῆς γῆς ἐκυλίετο ἀφρίζων

Luke 5: 18 ἐζήτουν αὐτὸν εἰσενεγκεῖν

John 12: 2 ἡ Μάρθα διηκόνει
   20: 4 ἔτρεχον δὲ οἱ δύο ὁμοῦ

Acts 5: 26 ἦγεν αὐτοὺς οὐ μετὰ βίας (pictures the 'leading' vividly as though occurring before us; οὐ μετὰ βίας adds to the description; the action is pictured 'in progress' rather than in summary, since v. 27 notes the conclusion: ἀγαγόντες αὐτούς . . .)

At times an imperfect indicative verb refers to a specific action and the same effect would be gained (i.e. action going on before and after the point of observation), except that the process stretching out *before* the reference-point is 'crowded' by the narration of an immediately preceding occurrence. In these cases the narrative sequence[48] produces an *inceptive* sense, since the verb in sequence denotes the process as beginning and then proceeding on without limit, usually with a descriptive nuance maintained:

Matt. 8: 15 καὶ ἠγέρθη καὶ διηκόνει αὐτῷ
   26: 16 (+parallels) καὶ ἀπὸ τότε ἐζήτει εὐκαιρίαν ἵνα αὐτὸν παραδῷ

When the verb refers to a general or indefinite action, it is less vivid but maintains the sense of a process running on before and after a point of reference, without a limit being

---

[48] Cf. Mateos, *Aspecto verbal*, pp. 36–7, 76, who likewise attributes the inceptive sense to 'la sucesión narrativa'. This point is taken up again in sect. 3.5.2.

envisaged (the action is occurring not just 'now', but in a broader scope of time).[49]

Matt. 15: 27 τὰ κυνάρια ἐσθίει ἀπὸ τῶν ψιχίων

Luke 15: 29 τοσαῦτα ἔτη δουλεύω σοι[50]

(b) *Aorist:* the aorist aspect with ACTIVITIES denotes a period in which the action is/was carried out and perhaps ended, but it does not indicate an *accomplishment* or consummation of the action as a similar use of a bounded verb would. The action is not 'successfully done' or 'done to completion'; it is just 'done', and even though the aorist denotes the action in its entirety, the end of the action is an *arbitrary* limit, not a culminating or absolute conclusion.

Matt. 12: 1 ἐπορεύθη ὁ Ἰησοῦς . . . διὰ τῶν σπορίμων

Luke 20: 19 ἐζήτησαν . . . ἐπιβαλεῖν ἐπ᾽ αὐτόν

Acts 3: 17 κατὰ ἄγνοιαν ἐπράξατε

   11: 12 ἦλθον δὲ σὺν ἐμοὶ καὶ οἱ ἀδελφοὶ οὗτοι

Phil. 2: 22 σὺν ἐμοὶ ἐδούλευσεν εἰς τὸ εὐαγγέλιον

(c) *Perfect:* the perfect forms with ACTIVITIES are similar in one feature to the aorist, in indicating that the action is/was carried out to an arbitrary end (summary, external view of the action itself). But the perfect adds to this a reference to some kind of continuing *consequence* of the action, which the aorist itself does not suggest. With this class of verbs, however, the 'result' indicated by the perfect is not nearly as obvious as with the other lexical groups, since there is no sense of 'completion' involved. Nevertheless, the result envisaged is often the *effect* of the ACTIVITY on the subject or object. McKay argues that perfects in the NT always refer to the condition of the subject and not that of the object.[51] However,

---

[49] The effects of general reference are discussed in sect. 3.3

[50] The grammars refer to examples like this as 'the present of a past action still in progress', used of a present which has a temporal modifier referring to past time. It denotes an action in progress, but the beginning of it is stretched further into past time by the modifier. Cf. Burton, *MT*, § 17.

[51] McKay, 'On the Perfect and Other Aspects in NT Greek', pp. 311–14.

it seems better to leave open the possibility of both and evaluate individual cases on their own merits. But there is one very helpful suggestion made by McKay in regard to the state of the subject: that the result may lie in the realm of *responsibility* on the part of the subject for having done the action, whether for credit or for blame, or it may emphasize his *authority* to act in such a way.[52]

Matt. 22: 4 τὸ ἄριστόν μου ἡτοίμακα . . . καὶ πάντα ἕτοιμα (result emphasized by adjective in the following clause)

Luke 1: 45 καὶ μακαρία ἡ πιστεύσασα ὅτι ἔσται τελείωσις τοῖς λελαλημένοις αὐτῇ παρὰ κυρίου (faith in continuing validity of what was uttered)

John 4: 38 ἄλλοι κεκοπιάκασιν (to their credit: μισθόν, v. 36)
     15: 3 ἤδη ὑμεῖς καθαροί ἐστε διὰ τὸν λόγον ὃν λελάληκα ὑμῖν (state of subject or object?)
     17: 6 τὸν λόγον σου τετήρηκαν (to their credit; here the meaning of the verb suggests 'action up to the time of speaking', but this is unusual for the perfect)

Acts 25: 11 εἰ . . . ἀδικῶ καὶ ἄξιον θανάτου πέπραχά τι (present responsibility for the past act is in view)

1 Thess. 1: 4 ἀδελφοὶ ἡγαπημένοι ὑπὸ τοῦ θεοῦ (present condition based on prior acts of God's love; similar uses in Col. 3: 12, 2 Thess. 2: 13, Jude 1)

Heb. 2: 18 ἐν ᾧ γὰρ πέπονθεν αὐτὸς πειρασθείς, δύναται τοῖς πειραζομένοις βοηθῆσαι (state of subject shown in 18b)
     8: 13 ἐν τῷ λέγειν καινὴν πεπαλαίωκεν τὴν πρώτην (state of object)

Rev. 18: 3 ὅτι ἐκ τοῦ οἴνου . . . πέπωκαν πάντα τὰ ἔθνη (they have drunk . . .)

In summary, the first type of *action* which should be distinguished is the ACTIVITY, an action which is unbounded, in contrast to other actions which are portrayed as limited in some way. Kenny and a few others end their classification at this point, with three major groups of verbal expressions: STATES, ACTIVITIES, and performances.[53] There seems to be

---

[52] Ibid. 296–7, 311–14.
[53] Kenny, *Action, Emotion and Will*, pp. 151–86; Macauley, 'Aspect in English',

good reason, however, for going further in subdividing performances (as many have done), as is attempted in the next section.

3. 1. 2. 3 ACCOMPLISHMENTS *versus achievements*

1. *Definition of* ACCOMPLISHMENTS. The third distinction to be surveyed operates only within the group of *bounded action* (i.e. performances), and it separates ACCOMPLISHMENTS from achievements by the criterion of perceived *temporal duration*. ACCOMPLISHMENTS are *durative*[54] bounded actions, while achievements are non-durative bounded actions.[55] This difference is very important for aspectual function, as will be shown below. It must be remembered, however, that 'duration' as an actional characteristic is not a factual, strictly objective feature; it is affected by subjective notions of how the action in its temporal duration is normally viewed by the speaker or his speech-community.[56] There are two interrelated tests to measure bounded duration and thus distinguish ACCOMPLISHMENTS from achievements.

(*a*) 'Inclusive durational' phrases like 'in *x* time' (where *x* is viewed as durative: e.g. 'in five hours', 'in ten minutes'; but

---

pp. 100–22; Mourelatos, 'Events, Processes, and States', pp. 415–34; and Cathrine Fabricius–Hansen, *Transformative, intransformative und kursive Verben* (Linguistische Arbeiten, 26, Tübingen: Max Niemeyer, 1975), 17–38.

[54] Thus ACCOMPLISHMENTS have this temporal feature in common with STATES and ACTIVITIES though they differ on the features of change and boundedness. They differ also in that those two are homogeneous in nature (the duration involves the same state or activity wherever one cuts into it), while ACCOMPLISHMENTS are non-homogeneous—a durative process concluded by an event or terminal point, with both parts integral to the action.

[55] Mateos, *Aspecto verbal*, pp. 85, 97, focuses on this distinction by dividing his 'lexemas dinámicos efectivos' into 'lexemas de acción resultativa' ('cuyo efecto . . . se concibe . . . como resultado de algún proceso') and 'lexemas de acción instantánea' ('en que el efecto de la acción . . . se concibe . . . como realizado en un momento de tiempo').

[56] Cf. Carl Bache, 'Aspect and Aktionsart: Towards a Semantic Distinction', *JL* (1982), 65–6; Galton, *Logic of Aspect*, pp. 59–66; and Wesley M. Jacobsen, 'Lexical Aspect in Japanese', in David Testen, Veena Mishra, and Joseph Drago (eds.), *Papers from the Parasession on Lexical Semantics* (Chicago: Chicago Linguistic Society, 1984), 151–5.

not in the sense of 'within x time')[57] *can* occur with ACCOM-
PLISHMENT expressions which have a verb with simple (e.g.
aorist) aspect, but not with achievement expressions with
simple aspect: 'I read this book in five hours'; but not 'I
bought this book in five hours'.[58]

(*b*) 'Point' temporal phrases like 'at x time' *can* occur with
achievement expressions which have a verb with simple (e.g.
aorist) aspect, but not with ACCOMPLISHMENT expressions
with simple aspect: 'I bought this book at five o'clock'; but not
'I read this book at five o'clock'.[59] Some expressions which
usually denote ACCOMPLISHMENTS can contain a point-
temporal, but this alters the sense to 'begin to ____', which is
an achievement: 'I gave the lecture at five o'clock'; 'I went to
town at five o'clock'.

The classification of verbs in the following list has been
done by considering the basic meaning of each verb in the
light of these criteria, but no systematic examination of these
temporal phrases in the NT has been attempted. See section
3.2.2.2 for some NT examples.

2. *Illustrations of* ACCOMPLISHMENTS. Based on the definition given above, several types of verbs, in their normal usage,
can be listed as ACCOMPLISHMENTS:

(*a*) Verbs of movement: these are bounded if used with a
phrase or prefix denoting *source* (e.g. ἀπό, ἐκ, ἐκεῖθεν), *destination*
(*e.g.* πρός, εἰς, ἐπί [+acc.], ἄχρι, ἕως, ἐκεῖ, ὧδε; a dative or ἔξω in
this sense), or *extent* (διά with a specific object in the genitive or
an accusative of extent)

---

[57] 'Within x time' is ambiguous, but can denote a *point* of time coming inside
certain boundaries, rather than duration of action for the whole inclusive period; the
phrase actually denotes the time during which one did *not* do the action: 'John spotted
the plane (with)in ten minutes'. Cf. Jakob Hoepelman, *Verb Classification and the
Russian Verbal Aspect* (Tübingen: Gunter Narr, 1981), 9 (the illustration is his);
Declerck, 'Bounded/Unbounded', pp. 773, 790 nn. 16, 20.

[58] Declerck, 'Bounded/Unbounded', p. 770; Carlson, 'Aspect and Quantification',
pp. 37–9; and Platzack, *Semantic Interpretation*, pp. 93–4.

[59] Vendler, 'Verbs and Times', pp. 102–4; Carlson, 'Aspect and Quantification',
pp. 37–9.

All the verbs of movement included above as ACTIVITIES can occur as ACCOMPLISHMENTS when accompanied by one of the features listed above; in addition these prefixed verbs are usually ACCOMPLISHMENTS:

διέρχομαι (='go through')

εἰσάγω	ἐκπορεύομαι	προσέρχομαι
εἴσειμι	ἐκφέρω	προστρέχω
εἰσέρχομαι	ἐξάγω	προσφέρω
εἰσπορεύομαι	ἐξαποστέλλω	
εἰσφέρω	ἔξειμι	
	ἐξέρχομαι	

(*b*) Durative verbs with bounded *effected* or *abolished* object (i.e. the action brings the object into, or puts it out of, 'existence')[60]

$$\text{κατασκευάζω} \quad \text{κτίζω} \quad \text{ποιέω}$$

(*c*) Other durative verbs with bounded lexical meaning

ἀλλάσσω+compounds	ἀναγκάζω	ἀποκρύπτω
γεμίζω	γνωρίζω	δηλόω
θάπτω	ἱματίζω	κερδαίνω
κωλύω	μανθάνω	παρασκευάζω
πείθω	πληρόω	φανερόω

(*d*) Other verbs with perfectivizing prefix (the simple forms are generally homogeneous ACTIVITIES)

ἐκβάλλω	κατακρίνω
ἐκδιώκω	καταπίνω
ἐκκόπτω	κατεργάζομαι
ἐκχέω	κατεσθίω

3. *Influence of* ACCOMPLISHMENTS *on aspectual function.*

---

[60] In addition to the verbs listed, some other expressions (which can be described as metaphorical extensions of the category) behave in similar ways linguistically: e.g. 'speak a word', 'preach a sermon', 'write a letter', 'eat a meal'. The object in phrases of this sort produces a bounded sense, because there is a certain point at which the action is 'done' and can continue no further, apparently in a way similar to the effected expressions listed.

ACCOMPLISHMENTS bear some resemblance to ACTIVITIES in that both these active types are durative, and this resemblance appears at times in usage. On this point both types are distinct from achievements, which are non-durative. But ACCOMPLISHMENTS differ from ACTIVITIES on the criterion of boundedness, and this characteristic influences its aspectual function as well.

(a) *Present:* the present aspect with ACCOMPLISHMENTS denotes a process occurring without its termination being reached. It envisages a durative action as running on before and after the point at which it is viewed, but not reaching its natural end-point. Thus, the action is viewed as *incomplete.* This incompletion may be a minor feature (e.g. to indicate temporal overlap of this process with something else occurring alongside), or it may assume greater significance: if the lexical meaning or the context implies an effort or a note of difficulty, opposition, or resistance to the action, the sense of incompletion will be that of unfulfilled or unsuccessful action.[61]

Luke 19: 1 καὶ εἰσελθὼν διήρχετο τὴν Ἰεριχώ

Acts 13: 25 ὡς δὲ ἐπλήρου Ἰωάννης τὸν δρόμον

1 Pet. 3: 20 ὅτε ἀπεξεδέχετο ἡ τοῦ θεοῦ μακροθυμία ἐν ἡμέραις Νωε κατασκευαζομένης κιβωτοῦ

Matt. 3: 14 ὁ δὲ Ἰωάννης διεκώλυεν αὐτόν

Mark 9: 38 (Luke 9: 49) εἴδομεν τινα ἐν τῷ ὀνόματί σου ἐκβάλλοντα δαιμόνια . . . καὶ ἐκωλύομεν αὐτόν

Acts 7: 26 συνήλλασσεν αὐτοὺς εἰς εἰρήνην
    13: 43 (cf. 26: 28) ἔπειθον αὐτοὺς προσμένειν τῇ χάριτι τοῦ θεοῦ

Gal. 6: 12 οὗτοι ἀναγκάζουσιν ὑμᾶς περιτέμνεσθαι

Heb. 11: 17b τὸν μονογενῆ προσέφερεν (but cf. 11: 17a προσενήνοχεν)

(b) *Aorist:* the aorist aspect with ACCOMPLISHMENTS indi-

---

[61] This use corresponds to the 'conative' present or imperfect listed by the grammars. Cf. BDF, *Grammar,* §§ 319, 326.

cates that a process occurs and runs all the way to its termination or limit, at which it ceases. Duration is implied but the more important point is that the action is viewed as *completed*. Again, this completion may be of minor significance (showing a sequenced event in narrative) or it may reflect a major point of the description. If the context or verbal meaning highlights an effort or if there is an idea of opposition or resistance, the completed action can become a successful effort or a fulfilled process.[62]

Luke 2: 15 ὃ ὁ κύριος ἐγνώρισεν ἡμῖν

John 1: 42 ἤγαγεν αὐτὸν πρὸς τὸν Ἰησοῦν

Eph. 3: 3 κατὰ ἀποκάλυψιν ἐγνωρίσθη μοι τὸ μυστήριον

Matt. 3: 8 ποιήσατε οὖν καρπὸν ἄξιον τῆς μετανοίας

25: 16–22 ἐκέρδησεν ἄλλα πέντε . . . ἐκέρδησεν ἄλλα δύο . . .
ἄλλα πέντε τάλαντα ἐκέρδησα . . . ἄλλα δύο τάλαντα ἐκέρδησα

27: 20 οἱ δὲ ἀρχιερεῖς καὶ οἱ πρεσβύτεροι ἔπεισαν τοὺς ὄχλους ἵνα . . .

Acts 5: 39 (cf. 17: 4) ἐπείσθησαν δὲ αὐτῷ

7: 36 οὗτος ἐξήγαγεν αὐτούς

27: 43 ὁ δὲ ἑκατοντάρχης βουλόμενος διασῶσαι τὸν Παῦλον ἐκώλυσεν αὐτοὺς τοῦ βουλήματος

Rom. 1: 13 πολλάκις προεθέμην ἐλθεῖν πρὸς ὑμᾶς, καὶ ἐκωλύθην ἄχρι τοῦ δεῦρο

2 Cor. 12: 11 γέγονα ἄφρων, ὑμεῖς με ἠναγκάσατε

Phil. 4: 11 ἐγὼ γὰρ ἔμαθον ἐν οἷς εἰμι αὐτάρκης εἶναι

Heb. 11: 7 (similar in 9: 2) κατεσκεύασεν κιβωτόν

(*c*) *Perfect:* the perfect with ACCOMPLISHMENTS also indicates that the action is carried to its completion and highlights, in addition, continuing consequence from the action, which the aorist does not suggest. With ACCOMPLISHMENTS the result of the verbal action is clearer than with ACTIVITIES. Again it can be said that the result may focus on the effect of the action on subject or object or it may lie in the realm of the

---

[62] This is usually included in the grammars as an 'effective' or 'consummative' aorist. Cf. MT, *Syntax*, p. 72.

responsibility of the subject for having done the action or in the realm of his *authority* to act in such a way.

John 7: 15 πῶς οὗτος γράμματα οἶδεν μὴ μεμαθηκώς;

Acts 5: 28 (cf. Luke 4: 21; Rom. 1: 29, 13: 8) πεπληρώκατε τὴν Ἰερουσαλὴμ τῆς διδαχῆς ὑμῶν (their responsibility for the act is in view)

  10: 45 ἐξέστησαν . . . ὅτι καὶ ἐπὶ τὰ ἔθνη ἡ δωρεὰ τοῦ ἁγίου πνεύματος ἐκκέχυται

Rom. 3: 21 (cf. 2 Cor. 5: 10–11) νυνὶ δὲ χωρὶς νόμου δικαιοσύνη θεοῦ πεφανέρωται

  14: 23 ὁ δὲ διακρινόμενος ἐὰν φάγῃ κατακέκριται

2 Cor. 9: 2 Ἀχαΐα παρεσκεύασται ἀπὸ πέρυσι

Col. 1: 16 τὰ πάντα δι' αὐτοῦ καὶ εἰς αὐτὸν ἔκτισται

Heb. 12: 22 ἀλλὰ προσεληλύθατε Σιὼν ὄρει

At least one verb of this type displays a present stative use of its perfect passive and (intransitive) active, without allusion to a previous action which produced the state.

Rom. 8: 38 πέπεισμαι γὰρ ὅτι οὔτε θάνατος . . .

  14: 14 πέπεισμαι ἐν κυρίῳ Ἰησοῦ ὅτι . . .

Gal. 5: 10 ἐγὼ πέποιθα εἰς ὑμᾶς ἐν κυρίῳ ὅτι . . .

(21 similar instances of the perfect of πείθω in NT)

Vendler's classification of verbal expressions stops at these four classes (STATES, ACTIVITIES, ACCOMPLISHMENTS, achievements),[63] and most writers on this topic follow his lead. There is, however, a further distinction among achievements which is valuable for predicting aspectual function, and this will be explored now.

3. 1. 2. 4 CLIMAXES *versus* PUNCTUALS

1. *Definition of* CLIMAXES *and of* PUNCTUALS. The final distinction suggested here is drawn between two types of achievements (i.e. bounded, non-durative actions). This dis-

---

[63] Vendler, 'Verbs and Times', pp. 97–121.

tinction is based on the feature of 'prefacing'. Some achievements are 'prefaced': they occur as the result of a closely
related process or effort which culminates in this event but is
regarded as a separate action; others are 'unprefaced': they
are truly momentary and imply no other action.[64] In this book
these classes will be labelled CLIMAXES and PUNCTUALS
respectively.

A CLIMAX, then, is an action which occurs *in a moment* as the
culmination of a separate process which is its preface: e.g. 'he
arrived just in time', 'she found her coat'. These imply a
separate approach-phase which affects their aspectual function: 'going towards and then arriving', 'searching and then
finding'. CLIMAXES are similar to ACCOMPLISHMENTS in that
both involve a process leading to a terminus, but for ACCOM-
PLISHMENTS the process is an integral part of the action,
while for CLIMAXES the process is to some extent separate and
the culmination or terminal point is emphasized. This is why
CLIMAXES can take momentary adverbial modifiers (e.g. 'at
five o'clock', 'at that moment'), but not inclusive durational
modifiers (e.g. 'in five hours', 'in ten minutes'), while ACCOM-
PLISHMENTS are the opposite. CLIMAXES do occur with 'in *x*
time' modifiers like ACCOMPLISHMENTS, but the phrase
denotes rather 'within *x* time', the time during which the
action actually is *not* done, leading up to the moment when it is
done: 'she found her coat in five minutes'. ACCOMPLISH-
MENTS occurring with such phrases denote the time during
which the action proceeds and then culminates: 'I read the
book in five hours'.[65]

---

[64] This distinction is suggested by Frede Østergaard, 'The Progressive Aspect in
Danish', in *Aspectology* (1979), 90–1, who uses the labels 'transitional' vs. 'momentary'
for achievements which 'presuppose an approach phase' vs. those which do not, but
instead are 'truly momentary'. Carlson, 'Aspect and Quantification', pp. 37–9, posits
such a distinction among Vendler's achievements, but does not develop or explain the
difference. Galton, *Logic of Aspect*, pp. 65–6, observes the distinction but gives a
different account of it.

[65] For some CLIMAXES the approach-phase cannot be described by the verb itself
unless the culmination is eventually reached, while for ACCOMPLISHMENTS the
approach-phase can be labelled with the verb itself whether or not the terminus is

PUNCTUALS are also done in a moment, but the event is not linked with another action as its preface. They are more truly *momentary* compared with CLIMAXES, since they have no approach-phase, and it is difficult to conceive of them in a single occurrence as having any duration whatever: for example, 'I kicked the ball', 'she nodded in agreement'.

The primary criterion for distinguishing these two types of achievements is their different sense when used in progressive/imperfective form (referring to specific occurrences): CLIMAXES in this use denote the preface or approach-phase leading up to but not including the climax, while PUNCTUALS normally denote instead the *iterative* occurrence of the momentary action. For example, 'he was arriving at the door', 'she was finding her coat' in contrast to 'I was kicking the ball', 'she was nodding in agreement'.[66]

2. *Illustrations of* CLIMAXES. Based on the definition given above, several types of verbs, in their normal usage, should be listed as CLIMAXES:

(*a*) Verbs denoting an instantaneous transition of the subject or object from one absolute (ungradable) state or location to another[67]

ἁγιάζω	ἁγνίζω	ἀθετέω
ἀνακλίνομαι	ἀνατρέπω	ἀνίστημι

reached. One would not say 'she was finding her coat' unless she searched *and* found, but one could say 'I was reading the book' even if only half of it was ever completed. Cf. Comrie, *Aspect*, pp. 47–8. Other CLIMAXES, however, are not restricted in this way: e.g. 'die', 'stop', 'persuade'.

[66] CLIMAXES and PUNCTUALS are very close in sense and one could operate quite well without this further distinction. Mateos, for example, includes many of the verbs in this CLIMAX list under his 'lexemas dinámicos de acción instantánea' (*Aspecto verbal*, p. 85), The advantage of preserving this distinction is that it accounts for the similarity in *present* aspect of CLIMAXES to ACCOMPLISHMENTS (denoting a process leading to but not yet reaching a terminus), and accounts also for their similarity in *aorist* aspect to PUNCTUALS (denoting instantaneous occurrence).

[67] These are called 'bordercrossings' by Zydatiß, ' "Continuative" and "Resultative" Perfects in English?', p. 343, who cites Jessen (1974), which I have not seen. The difference between gradable and ungradable transitions for aspect-usage is noted also by Declerck, 'Bounded/Unbounded', p. 783 n. 33; Platzack, *Semantic Interpretation*, pp. 96–7; and Lloyd, *Verb*, pp. 198–9.

ἀποθνήσκω   ἀποκτείνω   ἀπόλλυμι
ἀπολύω   ἀποστέλλω   ἀρνέομαι
ἄρχομαι   ἀφαιρέω   ἀφίημι
βαπτίζω   βυθίζω   γαμίζω
δέω   δικαιόω   δοκιμάζω
ἐγείρω   ἐκλέγομαι   ἐλευθερόω
ἐπαίρω   ἐπιτίθημι   ἐπιτρέπω
εὑρίσκω   ἰάομαι   καθαρίζω
καθίζω   κάμπτω   καταλείπω
καταλύω   καταντάω   καταργέω
καταρτίζω   κλείω   κοινόω
λύω   μερίζω   μεταβαίνω
νεκρόω   νικάω   παύομαι
πέμπω   περιτέμνω   ῥύομαι
σβέννυμι   σκανδαλίζω   σφραγίζω
στρέφω   σχίζω   σώζω
τελέω   τίθημι   φιμόω
χωρίζω

(b) Verbs of instantaneous 'receiving/giving' or 'getting/losing'

ἀγοράζω   ἁρπάζω   δέχομαι
δίδωμι   λαμβάνω   παραλαμβάνω
πιάζω   πιπράσκω   πωλέω

(c) Verbs with object-complement constructions[68] denoting an instantaneous naming, appointing, or constituting of the object 'as' or 'to be' something (i.e. 'as' the complement)

καθίστημι/καθιστάνω   καλέω
ποιέω (instantaneous, not process)
τίθημι   φωνέω

3. *Illustrations of* PUNCTUALS. Based on the definition given above, several types of verbs, in their normal usage, should be listed as PUNCTUALS:

βάλλω   ἐκψύχω   κλάω
πατάσσω   πίπτω   προσκόπτω
πταίω   πτύω   ῥίπτω

[68] Cf. BDF, *Grammar*, § 157.

4. *Influence of* CLIMAXES *on aspectual function.* CLIMAXES function in some ways like ACCOMPLISHMENTS and in some ways like PUNCTUALS. They are like ACCOMPLISHMENTS (especially with present forms) in that both involve an action leading to a *terminal* point, and can thus be viewed as complete or (with present aspect) incomplete. In this regard these differ from ACTIVITIES and STATES, which are unbounded and thus are indifferent to the notion of completion. But CLIMAXES differ from ACCOMPLISHMENTS on the criterion of duration, since CLIMAXES (especially in the aorist) emphasize the moment of transition and thus are instantaneous in sense. In this way CLIMAXES approach the character of PUNCTUALS, and denote (in the aorist) a complete occurrence of the action in a moment. The aspects combine with CLIMAXES as follows.

(*a*) *Present:* the present aspect with CLIMAXES focuses on the *prefaced action* as continuing or in progress, without the termination (i.e. the climax itself) being reached. Thus, they have a sense of incompletion and are subject to the same range of nuances described above for ACCOMPLISHMENTS: the incompletion may be a minor feature or it may assume a sense of failure in an effort or that of imminent occurrence (both traditionally 'conative' senses).

Matt. 8: 25 κύριε, σῶσον, ἀπολλύμεθα
  25: 8 αἱ λαμπάδες ἡμῶν σβέννυνται
Mark 15: 23 ἐδίδουν αὐτῷ ἐσμυρνισμένον οἶνον· ὃς δὲ οὐκ ἔλαβεν
Luke 5: 7 ἔπλησαν ἀμφότερα τὰ πλοῖα ὥστε βυθίζεσθαι αὐτά (at the point of going under)
  8: 42 αὐτὴ ἀπέθνῃσκεν
  19: 33 λυόντων δὲ αὐτῶν τὸν πῶλον εἶπαν οἱ κύριοι αὐτοῦ πρὸς αὐτούς· τί λύετε τὸν πῶλον; (simultaneous with εἶπαν)
Acts 27: 41 ἡ δὲ πρύμνα ἐλύετο ὑπὸ τῆς βίας τῶν κυμάτων
Gal. 5: 4 οἵτινες ἐν νόμῳ δικαιοῦσθε ('. . . but justification cannot be accomplished thus')

(*b*) *Aorist:* the aorist aspect with CLIMAXES focuses on the instantaneous climax without the prefaced action in view. It denotes the moment of transition only and leaves out the approach-phase. Thus, CLIMAXES have much the same sense as PUNCTUALS when used in the aorist, denoting the complete occurrence of the action in a moment. This completion then may have the sense of success or fulfilment of an effort, or it may be a simple report that the action is done.

Matt. 25: 10 ἐκλείσθη ἡ θύρα

Mark 7: 35 ἐλύθη ὁ δεσμὸς τῆς γλώσσης αὐτοῦ
15: 38 (+parallels) καὶ τὸ καταπέτασμα τοῦ ναοῦ ἐσχίσθη εἰς δύο ἀπ' ἄνωθεν ἕως κάτω

Acts 5: 1 ἀνὴρ δέ τις . . . ἐπώλησεν κτῆμα
8: 39 πνεῦμα κυρίου ἥρπασεν τὸν Φίλιππον

Rev. 5: 5 ἐνίκησεν ὁ λέων ὁ ἐκ τῆς φυλῆς Ἰούδα

(c) *Perfect:* the perfect with CLIMAXES focuses, as the aorist does, on the climax of the action being reached without focus on the prefaced action. It denotes the *completion* of the action and a *state* or condition which is the consequence of the action. However, as Mateos points out, the perfect with this type of verb may accentuate one of these features and only allude to the other. The emphasis may be on the *completion* (or actual occurrence)[69] of the action, with the result referred to only secondarily. Emphasis on completion of the action is often the case when the perfect verb occurs in the active voice with transitives.[70]

Matt. 13: 46 εὑρὼν δὲ ἕνα πολύτιμον μαργαρίτην ἀπελθὼν πέπρακεν πάντα ὅσα εἶχεν καὶ ἠγόρασεν αὐτόν

Mark 5: 34 (+parallels) θυγάτηρ, ἡ πίστις σου σέσωκέν σε

John 1: 41 εὑρήκαμεν τὸν Μεσσίαν
16: 33 (cf. 1 John 2: 13–14) ἀλλὰ θαρσεῖτε, ἐγὼ νενίκησα τὸν κόσμον

---

[69] This is similar in many cases to the use of the perfect which Comrie, *Aspect*, pp. 58–9, calls 'experiential perfect'. This use 'indicates that a given situation [i.e. action or state] has held at least once during some time in the past leading up to the present'. The point is that the action has *actually* occurred: it *has* taken place at least once, or (with the negative) it has never occurred. See examples in text above.

[70] Mateos, *Aspecto verbal*, pp. 121–2.

Acts 8: 14 ἀκούσαντες . . . ὅτι δέδεκται ἡ Σαμάρεια τὸν λόγον τοῦ θεοῦ
(stative nuance stronger here?)

On the other hand, the emphasis may be on the resulting *state* of the subject or object, with less attention paid to the action which produced the condition. This is often the case with passive or intransitive perfects.

Matt. 2: 20 τεθνήκασιν γὰρ οἱ ζητοῦντες τὴν ψυχὴν τοῦ παιδίου

Luke 5: 23 ἀφέωνταί σοι αἱ ἁμαρτίαι σου

16: 18 ὁ ἀπολελυμένην ἀπὸ ἀνδρὸς γαμῶν μοιχεύει

John 5: 24 (cf. 1 John 3: 14) μεταβέβηκεν ἐκ τοῦ θανάτου εἰς τὴν ζωήν

11: 34 ποῦ τεθείκατε αὐτόν; (state of object, despite being active?)

11: 57 δεδώκεισαν δὲ οἱ ἀρχιερεῖς καὶ οἱ Φαρισαῖοι ἐντολὰς (pluperf.; seems stative despite being transitive active—perhaps to be expected in John)

19: 28 ἤδη πάντα τετέλεσται

Acts 21: 28 κεκοίνωκεν τὸν ἅγιον τόπον τοῦτον (state of the subject from having done this deed: his guilt is proclaimed)

Rom. 4: 14 (cf. Gal. 5: 11) εἰ γὰρ οἱ ἐκ νόμου κληρονόμοι . . . κατήργηται ἡ ἐπαγγελία

1 Cor. 1: 13 μεμέρισται ὁ Χριστός;

7: 27 δέδεσαι γυναικί, μὴ ζήτει λύσιν· λέλυσαι ἀπὸ γυναικός, μὴ ζήτει γυναῖκα

Heb. 12: 2 ἐν δεξιᾷ τε τοῦ θρόνου τοῦ θεοῦ κεκάθικεν

Rev. 14: 3 οἱ ἠγορασμένοι ἀπὸ τῆς γῆς

5. *Influence of* PUNCTUALS *on aspectual function.* PUNCTUALS are similar to all other performances (ACCOMPLISHMENTS and CLIMAXES) in being bounded, and so in the aorist PUNCTUALS describe completed actions. But their instantaneous temporal character (unlike ACCOMPLISHMENTS) and 'unprefaced' phasal character (unlike CLIMAXES) cause them to function differently with the aspects than these other two.

(*a*) *Present:* the present aspect with PUNCTUALS denotes repeated occurrences of the momentary act. It does not denote the single act 'in progress' or 'as occurring', since a single act conceived of as *instantaneous* cannot be viewed 'from within, with regard to the internal constituency of the action'. So when a PUNCTUAL verb occurs in the present aspect in Greek, it must denote multiple occurrences of the act, because only in this way can the situation possess internal structure and be compatible with the viewpoint of the present.[71] The multiple occurrences, when viewed together and conceived as occurring in series over an extent of time, can have something of a progressive sense, but this is different from the progressive nuance shown by the other active verb-types.

Matt. 27: 35 (~Mark 15: 24) σταυρώσαντες δὲ αὐτὸν διεμερίσαντο τὰ ἱμάτια αὐτοῦ βάλλοντες κλῆρον

Mark 12: 41 πολλοὶ πλούσιοι ἔβαλλον πολλά
14: 35 ἔπιπτεν ἐπὶ τῆς γῆς καὶ προσηύχετο (perhaps means 'he repeatedly fell to the ground and prayed')[72]

Luke 3: 9 (+parallels) πᾶν οὖν δένδρον μὴ ποιοῦν καρπὸν καλὸν ἐκκόπτεται καὶ εἰς πῦρ βάλλεται[73]

(*b*) *Aorist:* the aorist aspect with PUNCTUALS denotes most naturally the *single* occurrence of the momentary act. Less frequently, the aorist of these verbs will indicate a summary or composite of repeated occurrences of the act. Like other performances (i.e. bounded actions), PUNCTUALS in the aorist

---

[71] See the helpful discussion of this in Comrie, *Aspect*, pp. 41–4. The only exception to this in normal speech is the use of the present to denote simultaneity with another action, in which case the other action is presented as occurring *at* (if not *during*) the time of the momentary act, e.g. Luke 21: 2 'he saw a poor widow put in [βάλλουσαν] two coins'. This is discussed in sect. 3.4.

[72] This may, however, be a *descriptive* use, picturing the act as occurring before one's eyes (though it is odd to picture an instantaneous act as a process). This is suggested by H. B. Swete, *The Gospel According to St. Mark*, 3rd edn. (London: Macmillan and Co., 1909), 343. Another possibility is that Mark is unskilled in his use of Greek tenses and should have used another tense. This is the view of C. H. Turner, *The Gospel According to St. Mark: Introduction and Commentary;* repr. from *A New Commentary on Holy Scripture*, ed. C. Gore H. L. Goudge, and A. Guillaume (London: SPCK, 1931), 77, on Mark 15: 23 ἐδίδουν. Issues concerning Mark's frequent use of the imperfect will be discussed in ch. 4.

[73] Note that this text, though phrased in the singular, makes a general statement of 'distributive' plurality: a reference to the act done by/upon *each* of a group of individuals. Such references are discussed further in sect. 3.2 and 3.3.

indicate a *completed* action. However, with their momentary meaning, aorist PUNCTUALS very rarely occur in any sort of consummative or effective sense, in contrast to ACCOMPLISHMENTS and CLIMAXES.

Matt. 7: 27 ἔπνευσαν οἱ ἄνεμοι καὶ προσέκοψαν τῇ οἰκίᾳ ἐκείνῃ, καὶ ἔπεσεν

Mark 9: 22 πολλάκις καὶ εἰς πῦρ αὐτὸν ἔβαλεν καὶ εἰς ὕδατα

Luke 22: 50 ἐπάταξεν εἷς τις ἐξ αὐτῶν τοῦ ἀρχιερέως τὸν δοῦλον

John 21: 6 βάλετε εἰς τὰ δεξιὰ μέρη τοῦ πλοίου τὸ δίκτυον . . . ἔβαλον οὖν

Acts 12: 23 παραχρῆμα δὲ ἐπάταξεν αὐτὸν ἄγγελος κυρίου

   27: 19 καὶ τῇ τρίτῃ αὐτόχειρες τὴν σκευὴν τοῦ πλοίου ἔρριψαν

(c) *Perfect:* the perfect with PUNCTUALS indicates, as the aorist does, the *single* occurrence of the momentary act. It denotes the *completion* of that action and a *state* or condition which is its consequence, with the emphasis usually on the continuing state.

Matt. 8: 6 ὁ παῖς μου βέβληται ἐν τῇ οἰκίᾳ παραλυτικός

   9: 36 ἦσαν ἐσκυλμένοι καὶ ἐρριμμένοι ὡσεὶ πρόβατα . . .

Luke 16: 20 πτωχὸς δέ τις ὀνόματι Λάζαρος ἐβέβλητο πρὸς τὸν πυλῶνα αὐτοῦ

   17: 2 (~Mark 9: 42 βέβληται) λυσιτελεῖ αὐτῷ εἰ . . . ἔρριπται εἰς τὴν θάλασσαν

John 3: 24 οὔπω γὰρ ἦν βεβλημένος εἰς τὴν φυλακὴν ὁ Ἰωάννης

   13: 2 τοῦ διαβόλου ἤδη βεβληκότος εἰς τὴν καρδίαν

Acts 15: 16 ἀνοικοδομήσω τὴν σκηνὴν Δαυὶδ τὴν πεπτωκυῖαν

Rev. 2: 5 μνημόνευε οὖν πόθεν πέπτωκας καὶ μετανόησον

3. 1. 3 *Summary of verb-classes based on procedural character*

The actional characteristics of verbs which are most important for aspect-function can be summarized in five groups, distinguished hierarchically by four criteria. These classes (given in small capitals) are set forth in Fig. 3.2, with the distinctive feature of each noted beneath it and incidental features listed in parentheses. On the same horizontal plane with each is the more general group which most directly contrasts with it.

Although these characteristics are obvious in the case of some verbs, there are others which are on the borderline between two features or do not display a consistent actional character. Nevertheless, one can examine to see which of these features is predominant in a given context, and this will be an important element in deciding how the aspect-meaning should be interpreted in that text.

3. 2 The Effect of Compositional Elements on Aspectual Function

As mentioned above, the overall meaning of the aspects can be greatly influenced by other elements used in composition with the verb. Of particular importance in this regard are nominal phrases occurring as subject or object of the verb and adverbial phrases used to modify the verb.

STATES				
no change (unbounded) (durative)	Actions change (bounded or unbounded) (durative or non-durative) (prefaced or non-prefaced)			
	ACTIVITIES unbounded (durative)	Performances bounded (durative or non-durative) (prefaced or non-prefaced)		
		ACCOMPLISHMENTS durative (prefaced)	Achievements non-durative (prefaced or non-prefaced)	
			CLIMAXES prefaced	PUNCTUALS non-prefaced

FIG. 3.2. Summary of verb-classes

3. 2. 1 *Noun- or pronoun-phrases used as subject or object*

Variations in the subject- and object-phrases occurring with verbs can affect aspectual meaning in a number of ways. The most significant variations and how they normally influence the sense will be surveyed here.

3. 2. 1. 1 *Singular versus plural reference*

Whether the subject and object have singular or plural reference affects the aspectual sense primarily by applying the feature of 'number' to the verbal situation (state or action) itself: whether the verbal action or state is *single* or *multiple* has an important influence on the aspectual force.[74] As shown below, there is a natural association of the aorist 'viewpoint' with descriptions of *single* occurrences of whatever consistency, since it looks at an episode as a whole from the outside (with reference to beginning and end-point) without regard for internal make-up. On the other hand, the present 'viewpoint' is commonly associated with descriptions of occurrences which consist of multiple 'parts', since the present looks at an episode from within, giving attention to those multiple phases, without focus on the end-points which summarize the episode. The nature of the subject- and object-phrases plays a significant role in attaching 'number' to the verbal action.

1. *Singular subject and object.* When the subject and object are both singular in reference, the noun-phrase itself produces minimal variation in aspectual force. In these cases the action or state is usually single. Any reference to multiple occurrence must be produced by something outside the noun-phrase itself: by the combination of aspect with actional character (e.g. present aspect with PUNCTUAL verb; see section 3.1.2.4),

[74] As noted by Gustav Herbig, 'Aktionsart und Zeitstufe: Beiträge zur Funktionslehre des indogermanischen Verbums', *IF* 6 (1896), 219; Hans Jacobsthal, *Der Gebrauch der Tempora und Modi in den kretischen Dialektinschriften* (Strasburg: Trübner, 1907), 59; Felix Hartmann, 'Aorist und Imperfektum', *KZ* 49 (1919), 38–9; Jakob Wackernagel, *Vorlesungen über Syntax*, 2nd edn., 2 vols. (Basle: Emil Birkhäuser, 1926), i. 174; Arvid Svensson, *Zum Gebrauch der erzählenden Tempora im Griechischen* (Ph.D. thesis, University of Lund; Lund: H. Ohlsson, 1930), 119–20; SD, *Syntax*, pp. 278–9; BDF, *Grammar*, § 329 (rather vague reference); and Mateos, *Aspecto verbal*, pp. 33–6. Detailed discussion is given in Wolfgang Dressler, *Studien zur verbalen Pluralität: Iterativum, Distributivum, Durativum, Intensivum in der allgemeinen Grammatik, im Lateinischen und Hethitischen* (Vienna: Hermann Böhlaus, 1968), 51–6; and in Stork, *Aspectual Usage*, pp. 381–4.

by an adverbial modifier (e.g. πολλάκις, section 3.2.2), or by reference to non-specific action (section 3.3).

Apart from some other indicator, however, the action or state will be *single* when the subject and object are both singular in reference. In this book the term 'semelfactive' is used for such cases: an action or state 'done' *once* by or to a single individual. The different senses communicated by the two aspects with semelfactive occurrences should be mentioned here. The *aorist* will be the natural aspect to denote the single situation, unless time-reference (e.g. present or future in the indicative) precludes use of the aorist indicative. The aorist with all the active lexical types denotes the single occurrence of the action in its entirety, without regard for the character of the action itself. As noted above, the aorist of a stative verb usually assumes an ingressive sense (the act of entering the state), because the end-points of the state are in view.

Matt. 18: 30 ἔβαλεν αὐτὸν εἰς φυλακήν

Luke 9: 42 ἔρρηξεν αὐτὸν τὸ δαιμόνιον καὶ συνεσπάραξεν·
ἐπετίμησεν δὲ ὁ Ἰησοῦς τῷ πνεύματι τῷ ἀκαθάρτῳ καὶ ἰάσατο τὸν παῖδα καὶ ἀπέδωκεν αὐτὸν τῷ πατρὶ αὐτοῦ

Acts 13: 36 Δαυὶδ . . . ἐκοιμήθη

The *present* aspect, when used of a truly single situation, denotes the existence of a state or the continuing progress of an action without beginning or end in view.[75]

Matt. 3: 14 ὁ δὲ Ἰωάννης διεκώλυεν αὐτόν
8: 24 αὐτὸς δὲ ἐκάθευδεν

Mark 2: 16 ἰδόντες ὅτι ἐσθίει μετὰ τῶν ἁμαρτωλῶν καὶ τελωνῶν

---

[75] The only exception to this is the present with PUNCTUALS, for which the sense of 'continuing progress' is impossible in the nature of the case. With PUNCTUALS the present aspect, since it views the internal make-up of the action, defaults to an iterative reading: to have any internal make-up at all, it must be repeated action which is described (e.g. 'I am blinking because of the bright lights'; 'he was beating the drum, when we arrived'). However, no examples of this seem to exist in the NT. PUNCTUALS with present aspect occur, but not in this restricted circumstance (singular subject and object, specific reference).

5: 32 καὶ περιεβλέπετο ἰδεῖν τὴν τοῦτο ποιήσασαν
Luke 8: 42 αὐτὴ ἀπέθνῃσκεν
    22: 48 Ἰούδα, φιλήματι τὸν υἱὸν τοῦ ἀνθρώπου παραδίδως;
John 12: 2 ἡ Μάρθα διηκόνει

If the situation with singular subject and object is shown to be *multiple*[76] (by the addition of one of the features listed above) either the aorist or present may be used, and the difference between the two is closely related to the fundamental aspect-distinction developed earlier. The *present* views the situation from within, which means portraying the multiple occurrences as continuing, taking place over time, without end-points in view: Matt. 17: 15 πολλάκις γὰρ πίπτει εἰς τὸ πῦρ; 1 John 3: 8 ἀπ᾽ ἀρχῆς ὁ διάβολος ἁμαρτάνει. Thus, the present gives emphasis to the iterative nature of the occurrence. The *aorist* gives a summary or composite view of the multiple situations, with no emphasis on the repetition: Luke 17: 4 ἐὰν ἑπτάκις τῆς ἡμέρας ἁμαρτήσῃ εἰς σέ. The difference in the point of view one takes in regard to multiple situations is left up to the speaker's subjective choice in some cases. In others, it appears that some additional factor influences the choice of one or the other.[77]

2. *Plural subject or object.* When either subject or object is plural, the normal reference of the verb is to multiple occurrence, and the variation between present and aorist is similar to that just described for iteratives. The multiple situation with plural subject or object can fall into two different types, and the aspects denote their distinctive senses within each type.

The multiple occurrence may be a collective plurality, in which more than one individual 'acts' (or is acted upon), but they do it *together* rather than separately. In this type the

---

[76] The term 'iterative' will be used here for such a case—an action or state 'done' more than once by or to a single individual.

[77] For example, discourse-structure may influence the choice towards an aorist (to relate a foreground, sequenced event) or imperfect (for a background, simultaneous event). Cf. Lloyd, *Verb*, p. 114.

situation is almost single in reference, and so the aorist is the most likely aspect to express this collective sense. When the *aorist* is used, it refers to the 'multiple' occurrence in summary:

Matt. 26: 19 καὶ ἐποίησαν οἱ μαθηταὶ ὡς συνέταξεν αὐτοῖς ὁ Ἰησοῦς καὶ ἡτοίμασαν τὸ πάσχα

Acts 5: 40 καὶ προσκαλεσάμενοι τοὺς ἀποστόλους δείραντες παρήγγειλαν μὴ λαλεῖν ἐπὶ τῷ ὀνόματι τοῦ Ἰησοῦ καὶ ἀπέλυσαν

13: 13 οἱ περὶ Παῦλον ἦλθον εἰς Πέργην

20: 6 ἡμεῖς δὲ ἐξεπλεύσαμεν . . . καὶ ἤλθομεν πρὸς αὐτοὺς εἰς τὴν Τρῳάδα

(Many similar refs. in Acts to 'we/they came to _____': 13: 51, 14: 24, etc.)

If the *present* aspect is used of a collective occurrence, it denotes the progress of the multiple action or existence of the multiple state without regard for beginning or end. In such cases the lexical character of the verb tends to produce its normal effect in combination with aspect (e.g. 'incomplete' sense for bounded actions, 'continuing' sense for unbounded actions or STATES):

Matt. 8: 25 κύριε, σῶσον, ἀπολλύμεθα

25: 8 αἱ λαμπάδες ἡμῶν σβέννυνται

Luke 5: 18 ἐζήτουν αὐτὸν εἰσενεγκεῖν

Acts 5: 26 ἦγεν αὐτοὺς οὐ μετὰ βίας

21: 30 ἐπιλαβόμενοι τοῦ Παύλου εἷλκον αὐτὸν ἔξω τοῦ ἱεροῦ

Gal. 6: 12 οὗτοι ἀναγκάζουσιν ὑμᾶς περιτέμνεσθαι (conative: 'these men are trying to force you to be circumcised'; however, if the sense is distributive in this verse, the point could be different: 'these men are successfully forcing various ones of you to be circumcised')

More normally, however, the multiple occurrence has a distributive sense, in which *each* of the plural subjects or objects is involved with the occurrence individually, rather than together.[78] This type is clearly multiple in sense, and the aspects occur in more even proportion, with their distinctive meanings. The *aorist* sums up the distributive occurrences as a

---

[78] Cf. Dressler, *Studien zur verbalen Pluralität*, pp. 62–74.

whole, in a composite of the various occurrences viewed from the outside, and thus pays less attention to the individual parts which make up the total situation. The aorist is often used in this way out of narrative 'economy' as the simplest description of the occurrences, without emphasis on accomplishment, completion, or repetition. However, if the speaker/ writer emphasizes 'all' the occurrences, there may be a sense of accomplishment in view, since the individual events in series are viewed together as a process brought to completion. Some examples of distributive aorists are:

Mark 3: 10 πολλοὺς γὰρ ἐθεράπευσεν (simple narration)

12: 44 πάντες γὰρ ἐκ τοῦ περισσεύοντος αὐτοῖς ἔβαλον (simple narration)

Acts 8: 15 προσηύξαντο περὶ αὐτῶν ὅπως λάβωσιν πνεῦμα ἅγιον (simple reference to multiple receptions as a whole; cf. v. 17)

2 Tim. 3: 11 τοῖς διωγμοῖς, τοῖς παθήμασιν, οἷά μοι ἐγένετο (simple narration) ἐν Ἀντιοχείᾳ, ἐν Ἰκονίῳ, ἐν Λύστροις, οἵους διωγμοὺς ὑπήνεγκα (accomplishment) καὶ ἐκ πάντων με ἐρρύσατο (accomplishment) ὁ κύριος

The *present*, on the other hand, views the distributive occurrences from within, with greater attention paid to the repetition (i.e. individual occurrences) which makes up the total situation. However, the actional character of the individual acts is to some degree submerged in the description of the multiple occurrences in a distributive way.

Mark 6: 13 καὶ δαιμόνια πολλὰ ἐξέβαλλον, καὶ ἤλειφον ἐλαίῳ πολλοὺς ἀρρώστους καὶ ἐθεράπευον

12: 41 πολλοὶ πλούσιοι ἔβαλλον πολλά

Luke 4: 41 ἐξήρχετο δὲ καὶ δαιμόνια ἀπὸ πολλῶν

Acts 8: 17 τότε ἐπετίθεσαν τὰς χεῖρας ἐπ᾽ αὐτοὺς καὶ ἐλάμβανον πνεῦμα ἅγιον (either distributive emphasis on *each* receiving the Spirit, or descriptive narration of the reception with its outward effects being displayed: e.g. speaking in tongues)

Rev. 21: 24 οἱ βασιλεῖς τῆς γῆς φέρουσιν τὴν δόξαν αὐτῶν εἰς αὐτήν

Thus, singular or plural reference in the subject or object

can significantly affect aspectual function, but the basic senses for the aspects themselves can be seen in the different combinations.

3. 2. 1. 2 *Effected versus affected object*

Aspectual function can also be affected by variation in the sense-connection of the *object* to a verb in the active voice (or the *subject* with a passive verb). A specific object or subject which is effected or abolished (i.e. brought into existence or put out of existence) by the verbal action produces a bounded interpretation with some verbs which otherwise would be unbounded in their aspectual function. Affected objects, on the other hand, do not produce such variation in aspectual function.[79] The verb οἰκοδομέω with a specific object, for example, has a bounded sense (it is an ACCOMPLISHMENT) when it occurs with an effected object.[80]

Matt. 7: 24 (similar v. 26) ὅστις ᾠκοδόμησεν αὐτοῦ τὴν οἰκίαν ἐπὶ τὴν πέτραν

Acts 7: 47 Σολομὼν δὲ οἰκοδόμησεν αὐτῷ οἶκον

But with an affected object the verb is an ACTIVITY, with an unbounded sense.

1 Cor. 14: 4 ὁ λαλῶν γλώσσῃ ἑαυτὸν οἰκοδομεῖ· ὁ δὲ προφητεύων ἐκκλησίαν οἰκοδομεῖ
14: 17 ὁ ἕτερος οὐκ οἰκοδομεῖται

3. 2. 1. 3 *'Count'- versus 'mass'-nouns*

Aspectual function can also be affected by variation in the

---

[79] Cf. H. Jacobsohn, 'Aspektfragen', *IF* 51 (1933), 297–8. He distinguishes between 'Accusativus affectivus' and 'Accusativus effectivus' with a transitive verb and points out that the former is usually 'durative' in sense, while the latter produces a perfective meaning: 'In diesem Fall wird das Verb, verbunden mit diesem Objekt, perfektiv. Man kann sagen: der Accusativus effectivus macht das Verb perfektiv'.

[80] H. J. Verkuyl, *On the Compositional Nature of the Aspect* (FL Supplementary Series, 15, Dordrecht: D. Reidel Publishing Co., 1972), 85–96, adds a further qualification to this topic: in order to denote a bounded sense, the effected object must involve a 'specified quantity' of the entity being produced. Even with the sense of an effected object, the verbal phrase will be unbounded if the object is an unlimited plural (e.g. 'he makes chairs') or an unspecified 'mass'-noun ('he composed cello music').

semantic nature of the nouns occurring as subject or object: specifically the difference between 'count'- and 'mass'-nouns.[81] The important difference is that mass-nouns give an unbounded sense to expressions in which they occur, and thus preclude the use of the verb-phrase as a 'performance'. The word ὕδωρ as an object (unless a specified quantity[82] is implied, in which case it behaves as a count-phrase) gives a different sense compared with a count-noun as object:

Rev. 12: 15 καὶ ἔβαλεν ὁ ὄφις ἐκ τοῦ στόματος αὐτοῦ . . . ὕδωρ ὡς ποταμόν
(an arbitrary summary with an ACTIVITY expression)
16: 4 καὶ ὁ τρίτος ἐξέχεεν τὴν φιάλην αὐτοῦ εἰς τοὺς ποταμούς (a natural end-point with an ACCOMPLISHMENT-phrase)

This difference is closely related to the variation mentioned next.

3. 2. 1. 4 *Specific versus non-specific reference*

Whether the subject or object is specific in reference plays an important role in determining aspectual function. This distinction, however, is part of a larger difference between specific and general propositions as a whole: together with various elements (including subject- and object-phrases) which reflect specific or general reference, it will be treated later in this chapter (3.3).

3. 2. 2 *Adverbial phrases*

It is obvious that adverbial phrases would be a prime influence on the aspectual function of the verbs which they

---

[81] Cf. Mourelatos, 'Events, Processes, and States', pp. 424–5: 'Nouns such as "squirrel", "equation", and "snowflake" are count terms. Such terms have plural forms that involve no switch in meaning from the singular form; they take cardinal numerals . . . they can be used with the adjectives "many", "several", "few", "each", and "every". Nouns such as "wine", "snow", and "hunger" are mass terms. They generally do not have plural forms, or if they do there is a meaning shift: wines are *types* of wine. . . . Adjectives that go naturally with mass terms are: "much", "little", "too much", "too little", "enough", and the like.' Greek does not share the exact range of distinctions, but possesses some features of this variation.

[82] Verkuyl, *Compositional Nature*, pp. 60–73.

modify. Some adverbial phrases, however, do not affect the aspectual sense, even though they modify the verb in other ways. The phrases which do play a part in aspectual function will be surveyed here.

3. 2. 2. 1 *Directional and extent-phrases with movement-verbs*

Verbs denoting movement are bounded (i.e. ACCOMPLISH-MENTS) if used with a phrase denoting *source* (e.g. ἀπό, ἐκ, ἐκεῖθεν), *destination* (e.g. πρός, εἰς, ἐπί [+acc.], ἄχρι, ἕως, ἐκεῖ, ὧδε; a dative or ἔξω in this sense), or *extent* (διά with a specific object in the genitive; an accusative of extent). These phrases add a limit to verbs like ἔρχομαι, πορεύομαι, ἄγω, φέρω, and others, which are otherwise unbounded ACTIVITIES.[83]

Matt. 19: 15 ἐπορεύθη ἐκεῖθεν (bounded action viewed in summary)

Acts 18: 1 ἦλθεν εἰς Κόρινθον (bounded, summary)
    22: 5 εἰς Δαμασκὸν ἐπορευόμην (bounded, viewed in progress)

John 19: 13 ὁ οὖν Πιλᾶτος . . . ἤγαγεν ἔξω τὸν Ἰησοῦν (bounded, summary)

Acts 9: 17 ἐν τῇ ὁδῷ ᾗ ἤρχου (unbounded, in progress)

There are other adverbial phrases used with verbs of motion which do not affect the normal actional character of the verb, and thus have no impact on aspectual function. These include phrases of association (datives; phrases with σύν, μετά, etc.), of sphere or general location (datives; phrases with ἐν, διά [+gen.] with unbounded object, παρά [+acc.]), and other non-bounded adverbial ideas. Movement-verbs with these adjuncts function as unbounded ACTIVITIES, with character-istics appropriate to that type (durative; not 'complete' or 'incomplete'):

Matt. 12: 1 ἐπορεύθη ὁ Ἰησοῦς τοῖς σάββασιν διὰ τῶν σπορίμων
    15: 29 ὁ Ἰησοῦς ἦλθεν παρὰ τὴν θάλασσαν τῆς Γαλιλαίας

Luke 7: 6 ὁ δὲ Ἰησοῦς ἐπορεύετο σὺν αὐτοῖς

Acts 11: 12 ἦλθον δὲ σὺν ἐμοὶ καὶ οἱ ἓξ ἀδελφοὶ οὗτοι

---

[83] Cf. ibid. 41-6, 93-7; and Declerck, 'Bounded/Unbounded', pp. 785-8.

3. 2. 2. 2 *Durational temporal phrases*

Temporal phrases indicating 'how long' the situation occurs can affect aspectual function. With STATES and ACTIVITIES (which are naturally durative) and ACCOMPLISHMENTS (when they focus on the process leading up to the completion), the normal aspectual sense appears describing the action or state itself. In these cases the *present* denotes the action or state viewed from within and is clearly 'durative' in sense, as many older grammars emphasized, while the *aorist* indicates a summary of the extended action or state viewed from without. The choice of aspects is a subjective one here since either could be used without affecting the sense except in regard to the viewpoint from which the occurrence is portrayed.

Luke 15: 29 τοσαῦτα ἔτη δουλεύω σοι

Acts 9: 24 παρετηροῦντο δὲ καὶ τὰς πύλας ἡμέρας τε καὶ νυκτός

Rom. 1: 9 ὡς ἀδιαλείπτως μνείαν ὑμῶν ποιοῦμαι

Matt. 20: 12 οὗτοι οἱ ἔσχατοι μίαν ὥραν ἐποίησαν

John 1: 39 (cf. 4: 40) παρ' αὐτῷ ἔμειναν τὴν ἡμέραν ἐκείνην
    2: 20 τεσσεράκοντα καὶ ἓξ ἔτεσιν οἰκοδομήθη ὁ ναὸς οὗτος

On the other hand, with verbs focusing on a point of action (CLIMAXES, PUNCTUALS, and ACCOMPLISHMENTS which focus on the conclusion), there is a shift from the normal sense since duration is not compatible with a single-point-occurrence. Usually the meaning is *repetition* of the point-occurrence or continuance of a *resulting state*, regardless of the aspect. The choice of aspect, here also, is a more subjective one, reflecting the speaker's view of the durative occurrence from inside or from outside.

Acts 13: 31 ὃς ὤφθη ἐπὶ ἡμέρας πλείους
    16: 18 τοῦτο δὲ ἐποίει ἐπὶ πολλὰς ἡμέρας[84]

---

[84] This example shows that the 'point' action (here crying out a brief description of Paul and his company) need not be instantaneous in the strict sense; it is sufficient for the action to be relatively brief, i.e. short enough to be done more than once in the time predicated for it by the durational phrase.

Matt. 15: 28 (cf. 9: 22) καὶ ἰάθη ἡ θυγάτηρ αὐτῆς ἀπὸ τῆς ὥρας ἐκείνης

27: 8 ἐκλήθη . . . ἀγρὸς αἵματος ἕως τῆς σήμερον

Luke 4: 25 ἐκλείσθη ὁ οὐρανὸς ἐπὶ ἔτη τρία καὶ μῆνας ἕξ

Acts 18: 11 ἐκάθισεν δὲ ἐνιαυτὸν καὶ μῆνας ἕξ

This difference can be seen most clearly in Rev. 20: 2b and 20: 4, in which the same durational modifier occurs with verbs of different types, with predictable results: ἔδησεν αὐτὸν χίλια ἔτη (duration not of the action, but of the resulting state) . . . καὶ ἐβασίλευσαν μετὰ τοῦ Χριστοῦ χίλια ἔτη (duration of the action/state itself).

3. 2. 2. 3 *Phrases denoting repetition and habituality*

Adverbials which indicate repeated or customary occurrence also influence the overall meaning of the verbal expression and affect the function of the aspects. Multiple occurrence is a sense which both aspects can accommodate as an implicit meaning,[85] and the use of explicit phrases to denote repetition and habituality is easily tolerated by both aspects. However, it is more common with the present aspect.

The adverbs of repetition particularly in view here are adverbs of cardinal frequency, such as δίς, τρίς, πεντάκις, ἑπτάκις, and the related πολλάκις.[86] Adverbials of habituality are ἀεί, διὰ παντός, and πάντοτε. The *aorist* aspect with such expressions reflects a summary of all the occurrences, while the *present* gives more attention to the repetition by focusing on the internal feature of multiple occurrence.

Matt. 17: 15 πολλάκις γὰρ πίπτει εἰς τὸ πῦρ

Mark 9: 22 καὶ πολλάκις καὶ εἰς πῦρ αὐτὸν ἔβαλεν καὶ εἰς ὕδατα

Luke 17: 4 καὶ ἐὰν ἑπτάκις τῆς ἡμέρας ἁμαρτήσῃ εἰς σὲ καὶ ἑπτάκις ἐπιστρέψῃ πρὸς σέ

18: 12 νηστεύω δὶς τοῦ σαββάτου

---

[85] As discussed in 3.2.1.1.

[86] The adverbs περισσῶς and περισσοτέρως may indicate frequency, but they more normally denote degree: 'all the more intensely'.

Acts 7: 51 ὑμεῖς ἀεὶ τῷ πνεύματι τῷ ἁγίῳ ἀντιπίπτετε

2 Cor. 4: 11 ἀεὶ γὰρ ἡμεῖς . . . εἰς θάνατον παραδιδόμεθα
    8: 22 ὃν ἐδοκιμάσαμεν ἐν πολλοῖς πολλάκις σπουδαῖον
        ὄντα
    11: 24–5 ὑπὸ Ἰουδαίων πεντάκις τεσσεράκοντα παρὰ μίαν ἔλαβον, τρὶς
        ἐρραβδίσθην . . . τρὶς ἐναυάγησα

Phil. 3: 18 πολλοὶ γὰρ περιπατοῦσιν οὓς πολλάκις ἔλεγον ὑμῖν
    4: 16 καὶ ἅπαξ καὶ δὶς εἰς τὴν χρείαν μοι ἐπέμψατε

Heb. 13: 15 ἀναφέρωμεν θυσίαν αἰνέσεως διὰ παντὸς τῷ θεῷ

Also common are expressions with distributive κατά. These expressions, apparently because they refer almost always to indefinite rather than specific repetition, occur predominantly with *present* aspect: of the forty-nine NT instances of distributive κατά listed by Bauer's *Lexicon*,[87] forty-two occur with present aspect, only four with aorist, and three with no verb expressed. These presents highlight the repetition, while the aorists view all the occurrences as a whole.

Matt. 26: 55 καθ' ἡμέραν ἐν τῷ ἱερῷ ἐκαθεζόμην διδάσκων

Mark 15: 6 κατὰ δὲ ἑορτὴν ἀπέλυεν αὐτοῖς ἕνα δέσμιον

Luke 2: 41 καὶ ἐπορεύοντο οἱ γονεῖς αὐτοῦ κατ' ἔτος εἰς Ἰερουσαλὴμ τῇ
    ἑορτῇ τοῦ πάσχα
    8: 1 αὐτὸς διώδευεν κατὰ πόλιν καὶ κώμην κηρύσσων καὶ
        εὐαγγελιζόμενος

Acts 3: 2 ὃν ἐτίθουν καθ' ἡμέραν πρὸς τὴν θύραν τοῦ ἱεροῦ

Mark 6: 40 καὶ ἀνέπεσαν πρασιαὶ πρασιαὶ κατὰ ἑκατὸν καὶ κατὰ
    πεντήκοντα

Acts 15: 36 ἐπισκεψώμεθα τοὺς ἀδελφοὺς κατὰ πόλιν πᾶσαν

Titus 1: 5 ἵνα τὰ λείποντα ἐπιδιορθώσῃ καὶ καταστήσῃς κατὰ πόλιν
    πρεσβυτέρους

3. 2. 2. 4 *Negatives*

That negatives have an effect on aspectual function has long been observed, but there is little agreement concerning the kind of influence they exert. An illustration of this is the

---

[87] BAGD, *Lexicon*, p. 406.

treatment given by Hettrich. He cites eight works from 1907–53 which comment on the use of negatives with the present and aorist aspects, and then gives his estimate that the present stem is far more frequent in negated clauses than the aorist. This opinion is supported by statistical data from his study of temporal and causal clauses in Herodotus: the ratio of present to aorist in *positive* clauses is 0.88 to 1.0 (1,211 to 1,380), while in *negative* clauses it is 4.86 to 1.0 (102 to 21).[88] From this he argues that negative clauses behave differently from positive ones in regard to aspect-usage and confesses that his observations about the aspects in general do not apply to negative clauses.[89] However, he offers no explanation of why negative clauses are exceptional or how they should be interpreted.

Hettrich's presentation suggests two main issues which must be treated in regard to aspect-usage in negated sentences: first, is there any predominance of one aspect over the other in frequency? and second, what effect does the negative have on aspect-function?

In regard to frequency, Hettrich's data from one type of clause in Herodotus do not appear to be representative of wider Greek usage. Blass–Debrunner–Funk state the opposite estimate (that the aorist is more common),[90] and evidence of actual usage from the NT is mixed.[91] Rijksbaron suggests that different verb-types occur with different frequency in negative sentences compared to positive ones,[92] and this seems correct.

---

[88] Heinrich Hettrich, *Kontext und Aspekt in der altgriechischen Prosa Herodots* (Göttingen: Vandenhoeck and Ruprecht, 1976), 45–6.

[89] Ibid. 51.

[90] BDF, *Grammar*, § 327: 'The aor. is the rule with negatives because usually the action as a whole is negated . . . ; but the imperf. also makes sense'. It should be added that this statement is made in regard to the relative frequency of aorist and imperfect indicative, a different sample from aorist stem vs. present stem as a whole.

[91] For example, the frequency of aspects with the basic negative οὐ, οὐκ, οὐχ in Acts is 44 presents vs. 22 aorists; but within the past indicative there are 10 imperfects vs. the 22 aorists. The other basic negative μή reflects the following ratio in Acts: 29 presents to 22 aorists. See also the discussion above.

[92] A. Rijksbaron, Review of H. Hettrich, *Kontext und Aspekt in der altgriechischen Prosa Herodots'*, in *Lingua*, 48 (1979), 252 n. 24.

CLIMAXES and PUNCTUALS, when negated, occur more frequently in the *aorist:* for example, εὑρίσκω in the NT favours the aorist 17 to 11 over the present; the count for δέχομαι is 9 to 3; and for λαμβάνω the ratio is 16 to 12 in favour of aorist (including the exceptional ratio of no aorist to 8 presents in the Gospel and Epistles of John). On the other hand, STATES seem to occur more frequently in the *present* when negated: for θέλω the present predominates 37 to 9 and δύναμαι favours the present 118 to 8 (though for ἰσχύω the count favours aorist 11 to 9). In all these cases it is perhaps true that similar ratios would be found for positive sentences, and in general it appears that no broadly applicable statement can be made about the relative frequency of the aspects in negative sentences.

The more important question which this suggests is the issue of how the negative affects aspect-function. One common proposal found in traditional grammars is that the *imperfect* in particular picks up a different nuance when negated. Smyth, for example, describes an 'imperfect of resistance or refusal' as follows: 'With a negative, the imperfect often denotes resistance or refusal (*would not* or *could not*). The aorist with a negative denotes unrestricted denial of a fact'.[93] Examples often cited are οὐκ ἔπειθον/οὐκ ἐπείθοντο ('I could not persuade'/ 'they would not obey'), οὐκ ἐδέχεσθε ('you would not accept'), and οὐκ ἤθελεν ('he refused'). The negated aorist of these verbs is thought to be more factual rather than modal, denoting simple non-occurrence.

In evaluation of this proposal, several points must be made. First, it is true that the imperfect at times adopts a non-factual modal force (possibility, obligation, desire, etc.) and that it does this more frequently than the aorist indicative.[94] However, this cannot account as adequately as other factors

---

[93] Smyth, *Grammar*, § 1896. Similar descriptions are found in Gildersleeve, *Syntax*, § 216; C. W. Peppler, 'Durative and Aoristic', *AJP* 54 (1933), 50–1; SD, *Syntax*, p. 279; and Stephen Wallace, 'Figure and Ground: The Interrelationships of Linguistic Categories', in *Tense-Aspect* (1982), 203–4.

[94] Cf. sect. 4.2.3.

for the difference in meaning suggested here. Second, it is true that negation reflects other modal nuances beyond a factual statement of non-occurrence. But the aorist also occurs with non-factual nuances of refusal, inability, unwillingness, and so forth, although not as frequently as the imperfect.[95] These meanings are the products of the lexical sense of the verb and the broader context, in addition to the aspect-usage. Finally, the meanings suggested above illustrate the fact that negatives of some verbs occur as periphrases for missing or rarely used counterparts. Thus, the negative of παύομαι can mean 'continue'; of δύναμαι and ἰσχύω 'be unable, fail'; of θέλω 'dislike, refuse'; and of πείθομαι 'deny, reject'. These meanings are not due to aspect-usage, but to the lexical meaning of the verb and its structural position in the lexical stock of the language.

It is true, however, that the imperfect with the negative occurs more commonly than the aorist with the sense of inability, refusal, resistance, and the like. But the explanation of this seems to lie in a distinction between the aorist and imperfect which is broader than negated sentences alone. In negative as well as positive sentences, the aorist vs. present/ imperfect contrast is often one of 'single vs. multiple' or 'specific vs. general'. This accounts in many cases for the meanings in negative sentences noted above: the aorist is more factual because a single, specific occurrence is negated, while the imperfect is more 'modal' because it denotes repeated resistance, continuing inability, or general unwillingness to carry out the action:[96]

Matt. 27: 34 γευσάμενος οὐκ ἠθέλησεν ποιεῖν
Mark 6: 26 οὐκ ἠθέλησεν ἀθετῆσαι αὐτήν

---

[95] See aorists of δέχομαι and εὑρίσκω: Matt. 26: 60; Luke 7: 9, 9: 53, 18: 17; 2 Thess. 2: 10; and Heb. 12: 17.

[96] This is suggested by Svensson, *Zum Gebrauch der erzählenden Tempora*, pp. 27, 103–7; Lloyd, *Verb*, p. 159; Rijksbaron, Review of Hettrich, pp. 236–8; and Brian Newton, 'Habitual Aspect in Ancient and Modern Greek', *Byzantine and Modern Greek Studies*, 5 (1979), 36–41. The general vs. specific difference will be developed more fully in sect. 3.3.

Matt. 2: 18 οὐκ ἤθελεν παρακληθῆναι

Acts 7: 11 οὐχ ηὕρισκον χορτάσματα οἱ πατέρες ἡμῶν

However, if the aorist refers to general or repeated non-occurrence, it too can assume something of the idea of resistance, unwillingness, or inability:

Matt. 23: 37 (~Luke 13: 34) ποσάκις ἠθέλησα ἐπισυναγαγεῖν τὰ τέκνα σου . . . καὶ οὐκ ἠθελήσατε

Luke 7: 9 οὐδὲ ἐν τῷ Ἰσραὴλ τοσαύτην πίστιν εὗρον

Apart from this use of the imperfect and aorist, the effect of the negative on aspectual function is negligible. The negative seems to be most common with STATES and with CLIMAXES. It is rather infrequent with ACTIVITIES, ACCOMPLISHMENTS, and PUNCTUALS. In all of these verb-types the negated verb usually displays the same aspectual function as the positive. STATES predicate the continuing existence or lack of existence of some condition. CLIMAXES state that an act occurred or did not occur on a particular occasion or during a broader, indefinite period. If the negated verb refers to a broader period of non-occurrence (at times '. . . despite repeated attempts'), the 'non-CLIMAX' begins to take on the characteristics of a STATE, just as any habitual or general proposition does (e.g. Matt. 26: 55 καθ' ἡμέραν ἐν τῷ ἱερῷ ἐκαθεζόμην διδάσκων καὶ οὐκ ἐκρατήσατέ με; 1 Cor. 13: 8 ἡ ἀγάπη οὐδέποτε πίπτει). But this is true of positive as well as negative statements, so the negative does not significantly change the aspect-usage.[97]

3. 2. 3 'Aspectual' verbs

A final effect of compositional elements on aspectual function is the use of verbs[98] which in their *lexical* sense duplicate some

---

[97] This is the general conclusion of Stork, *Aspectual Usage*, pp. 384–7, based on his detailed statistical comparison of negative and positive aspectual usage in infinitive constructions in Herodotus.

[98] Nouns and other parts of speech may display similar meanings, but are not nearly as frequent as verbs in producing the effect discussed here.

of the secondary functions of the aspects. These are sometimes called aspectual verbs, though in the terms discussed in Chapter 1 it is better to label them 'aktionsartlich', since they pertain more to procedural character than to viewpoint-aspect. Thus, they produce analytical parallels to some of the combinatory senses of the aspects: e.g. ingressive, durative, conclusive, conative, or intensive nuances. These will be mentioned only briefly, since they do not affect the meanings of the aspects themeselves, but instead provide explicit means of paraphrasing some of the secondary senses of the aspects.

Thus, if one desires to express an *ingressive* meaning, one may do so explicitly by using ἄρχομαι or a compound (very common in Mark and Luke). Likewise, verbal paraphrases may express *duration* (μένω+compounds) *conclusion* or *accomplishment* (παύομαι, τελέω+compounds, τελειόω), *attempt* (ζητέω, πειράζω), or *intensity* (σπουδάζω, προσκαρτερέω, ἀγωνίζομαι).[99]

3. 3 The Effect of General versus Specific Reference on Aspectual Function

It was shown earlier that the basic aspect-distinction of present vs. aorist sometimes appears in usage as a distinction of *multiple vs. single* occurrence. The point to be covered in this section is that this distinction is often extended to become a distinction of *general vs. specific* occurrence, i.e. situations repeated at various unspecified occasions vs. situations occurring on a particular occasion.[100] A more detailed description

[99] Only some of the clearer examples are cited. These and other words of this sort are treated admirably in § 68 ('Aspect') in Johannes P. Louw and Eugene A. Nida (eds.), *Greek–English Lexicon of the New Testament Based on Semantic Domains*, 2 vols. (New York: United Bible Societies, 1988). I am indebted to Prof. Louw for allowing me to consult this section in a pre-publication copy.

[100] The most detailed treatment of this distinction for ancient Greek aspect-usage appears in Stork, *Aspectual Usage*, pp. 51–88, 368–71, 392–5, which came to my attention after this section was written. Stork demonstrates how important this feature is in influencing aspectual function. Other references to this may be found in Macauley, 'Aspect in English', pp. 67–90; Lloyd, *Verb*, pp. 113–16; Yurij S. Maslov, 'An Outline of Contrastive Aspectology', in id. (ed.), *Contrastive Studies in Verbal Aspect*,

of this difference and its effect on aspectual function will now be surveyed.

3. 3. 1 *Specific reference in propositions*

Propositions with specific reference are those which represent situations (i.e. actions or states) as occurring on a particular occasion. The situation may be multiple or single, but if multiple the occurrences must be limited and known, not open-ended or indefinite. The main feature is that specific utterances are limited in scope or frame of reference: they describe occurrences in a narrow range of time, not broad, general occurrences.

A number of common indicators of specific propositions can be set forth. Many of these involve the nature of the nominal phrases which occur as subject or object of the verb.[101] For example, the following features often occur in specific utterances: phrases which contain a proper name, a noun with individualizing article,[102] a personal or demonstrative pronoun referring to a specific antecedent, or some indefinite element (e.g. anarthrous noun, the indefinite pronoun τὶς, or the numeral εἷς) which is specific rather than non-specific in reference: meaning 'a certain one/certain ones'.[103] The pre-

trans. and annotated by James Forsyth in collaboration with Josephine Forsyth (Heidelberg: Julius Groos, 1985), 17–18; and BDF, *Grammar*, §§ 329, 335. Östen Dahl, 'On Generics', in E. L. Keenan (ed.), *Formal Semantics of Natural Language* (London: Cambridge University Press, 1975), 99–111, discusses generic tense more extensively, but his treatment is more philosophical than linguistic and thus not directly helpful for analysis of aspect-usage. John M. Lawler, 'Generic to a Fault', in *Papers from the Eighth Regional Meeting, Chicago Linguistics Society* (Chicago: Chicago Linguistics Society, 1972), 247–58, cites problems in treating generic presents in English but offers no solutions.

[101] As noted by Marja Leinonen, 'Specificness and Non-Specificness in Russian Aspect', in *Aspectology* (1979), 35–9.

[102] Cf. BDF, *Grammar*, § 252. An individualizing article, as opposed to the generic article, is one which refers to a particular item or items.

[103] Cf. BAGD, *Lexicon*, pp. 230–2, 819–20; and Lyons, *Semantics*, pp. 187–92. Distinguishing non-specific vs. specific indefinites is very difficult, and a decision cannot be based on the narrow indefinite phrase alone. See Östen Dahl, 'Some Notes on Indefinites', *Lg.* 46 (1970), 33–41.

sence of these features does not always indicate a specific interpretation, but such elements are commonly present in specific utterances.

The use of the aspects in propositions with specific reference requires no special treatment, since particular focus does not change the function of the aspects in the way that general reference does. Sentences with specific reference provide opportunity for normal interaction between aspect and actional character, producing more transparent differences between the aspects than is possible in general utterances. Meanings traditionally seen in the aspects, such as progression, duration, incompletion, accomplishment, and similar values, appear more clearly in specific propositions.[104] Most of the examples cited so far in this chapter are illustrations of aspect-usage with *specific* reference.

3. 3. 2 *General or non-specific reference in propositions*

Propositions with general reference represent situations as occurring on various unspecified occasions. The individual situations themselves may be of any actional character (stative, punctual, progressive, repeated, etc.), but the general proposition refers to the multiple occurrence of an unspecified number of such situations. The general proposition is open-ended or unlimited as to when and how many times these situations occur. The scope or frame of reference is wider and sometimes extends to 'timeless' or universal occurrences.

General propositions can also be recognized by explicit indicators. These often involve the nature of the subject- or object-phrase occurring with the verb, as indicated by features such as these:

1. Anarthrous count-noun (especially the noun ἄνθρωπος),

---

[104] In fact the entire taxonomy of verb-types presented earlier in this chapter is of little use in regard to general propositions. As noted in that discussion, meaningful combinations of aspect and such actional features appear primarily in specific utterances. Cf. Mourelatos, 'Events, Processes, and States', p. 421; and Smith, 'Aspectual Choice', p. 481.

the indefinite pronoun (τὶς), or the numeral εἷς (especially the negative variants οὐδείς, μηδείς) with the sense of 'anyone, someone' (non-specific indefinites)

Mark 2: 21–2 οὐδεὶς ἐπίβλημα ῥάκους ἀγνάφου ἐπιράπτει ἐπί ἱμάτιον παλαιόν . . . καὶ οὐδεὶς βάλλει οἶνον νέον εἰς ἀσκοὺς παλαιούς

Rom. 3: 28 (cf. Gal. 2: 16, Jas. 2: 24) λογιζόμεθα γὰρ δικαιοῦσθαι πίστει ἄνθρωπον χωρὶς ἔργων νόμου

1 Cor. 7: 18 περιτετμημένος τις ἐκλήθη, μὴ ἐπισπάσθων· ἐν ἀκροβυστίᾳ κέκληταί τις, μὴ περιτεμνέσθω

11: 28 δοκιμαζέτω δὲ ἄνθρωπος ἑαυτὸν καὶ οὕτως ἐκ τοῦ ἄρτου ἐσθιέτω καὶ ἐκ τοῦ ποτηρίου πινέτω

2. Noun with generic article[105]

Matt. 12: 35 ὁ ἀγαθὸς ἄνθρωπος . . . ἐκβάλλει ἀγαθά, καὶ ὁ πονηρὸς ἄνθρωπος . . . ἐκβάλλει πονηρά

15: 11 (cf. 15: 18) οὐ τὸ εἰσερχόμενον εἰς τὸ στόμα κοινοῖ τὸν ἄνθρωπον, ἀλλὰ τὸ ἐκπορευόμενον ἐκ τοῦ στόματος τοῦτο κοινοῖ τὸν ἄνθρωπον

2 Tim. 2: 6 τὸν κοπιῶντα γεωργὸν δεῖ πρῶτον τῶν καρπῶν μεταλαμβάνειν

3. Personal pronoun (or pronoun suffix) referring to a non-specific antecedent

Luke 17: 28 ἐν ταῖς ἡμέραις Λώτ· ἤσθιον, ἔπινον, ἠγόραζον, ἐπώλουν, ἐφύτευον, ᾠκοδόμουν

John 15: 6 συνάγουσιν αὐτὰ καὶ εἰς τὸ πῦρ βάλλουσιν

Rom. 14: 8 (cf. generalizing οὐδείς in v. 7) ἐάν τε ἀποθνήσκωμεν, τῷ κυρίῳ ἀποθνήσκομεν

Jas. 3: 3 εἰ δὲ τῶν ἵππων τοὺς χαλινοὺς εἰς τὰ στόματα βάλλομεν

4. Relative pronoun referring to a non-specific antecedent, especially with ἄν added ('whoever', 'he who', etc.)[106]

---

[105] Cf. BDF, *Grammar*, § 252.

[106] In these cases the verb of the relative clause is usually aorist (reflecting a single event which makes up the distributive general reference), while the main verb is present (reflecting the multiple occurrences). However, there are exceptions in which the relative clause also contains a present verb, as in Mark 9: 37b, cited above; there is

Mark 9: 37 ὃς ἂν ἓν τῶν τοιούτων παιδίων δέξηται ἐπὶ τῷ ὀνόματί μυ, ἐμὲ δέχεται· καὶ ὃς ἂν ἐμὲ δέχηται, οὐκ ἐμὲ δέχεται ἀλλὰ τὸν ἀποστείλαντά με

1 Cor. 12: 8 ᾧ μὲν γὰρ τοῦ πνεύματος δίδοται λόγος σοφίας

5. Adjective πᾶς with articular participle or anarthrous singular noun

Matt. 7: 17 οὕτως πᾶν δένδρον ἀγαθὸν καρποὺς καλοὺς ποιεῖ, τὸ δὲ σαπρὸν δένδρον καρποὺς πονηροὺς ποιεῖ

Matt. 7: 8 (~Luke 11: 10) πᾶς γὰρ ὁ αἰτῶν λαμβάνει, καὶ ὁ ζητῶν εὑρίσκει

Acts 13: 39 ἐν τούτῳ πᾶς ὁ πιστεύων δικαιοῦται

Heb. 3: 4 πᾶς γὰρ οἶκος κατασκευάζεται ὑπό τινός

6. Articular participle as substantive with sense 'the one who (ever) does'

Matt. 10: 40 ὁ δεχόμενος ὑμᾶς ἐμὲ δέχεται, καὶ ὁ ἐμὲ δεχόμενος δέχεται τὸν ἀποστείλαντά με

John 3: 21 ὁ δὲ ποιῶν τὴν ἀλήθειαν ἔρχεται πρὸς τὸ φῶς

3: 36 ὁ πιστεύων εἰς τὸν υἱὸν ἔχει ζωὴν αἰώνιον

It will be noticed that singular subjects often occur in these general statements. These are 'representative' or generic singulars since they make a distributive reference to a number of occurrences of the given situation.[107]

Other general utterances are shown only by broader contextual features. Sometimes the nature of the argument advanced in the larger paragraph or in the sentence itself indicates a general reference (e.g. Mark 6: 56, John 1: 1–14, 1 Thess. 3: 4, Heb. 11: 32–40). In other instances periodic summaries of general events are inserted between narratives of specific occurrences, as one finds regularly in Acts: the 'summaries of church growth' sections (e.g. 2: 41–7, 4: 32–5, 5: 12–16). In

---

an aorist variant reading at this point with considerable manuscript support (δέξηται A C D W θ ƒ 1 ƒ 13 𝔐), but it seems inferior on internal grounds.

[107] Mateos, *Aspecto verbal*, p. 34.

many texts the main indicator of general reference is *aspect*-combinations with actional features not normally appropriate in specific utterances (e.g. Acts 5: 36–7; 18: 8).

The demands of general reference obscure many of the major distinctions which, in specific utterances, the aspects are able to produce (in combination with actional character and other features). The differences of duration, progression, incompletion, accomplishment, instantaneous occurrence, and so on are often lost in the description of multiple, non-specific occurrences of the action or state. The present aspect is the most common in general utterances, and the indefinite, multiple occurrences which make up the general action are highlighted. Thus, one cannot normally stress duration (in the narrow sense), progression, or incompletion, when dealing with general utterances using the present aspect.

Acts 13: 39 ἐν τούτῳ πᾶς ὁ πιστεύων δικαιοῦται (present aspect of this verb with *specific* reference would denote 'continuing but not yet fulfilled process' but not with this general reference)

18: 8 πολλοὶ τῶν Κορινθίων ἀκούοντες ἐπίστευον καὶ ἐβαπτίζοντο (both distributive repetition, not individually progressive or 'continuous')

Rom. 14: 8 ἐάν τε ἀποθνήσκωμεν, τῷ κυρίῳ ἀποθνήσκομεν (not incomplete process 'we are dying', but distributive occurrences 'we die').

1 Cor. 11: 28 δοκιμαζέτω δὲ ἄνθρωπος ἑαυτὸν καὶ οὕτως ἐκ τοῦ ἄρτου ἐσθιέτω καὶ ἐκ τοῦ ποτηρίου πινέτω (multiple sense of 'whenever one partakes . . .', not progressive or continuous occurrence)

Heb. 3: 4 πᾶς γὰρ οἶκος κατασκευάζεται ὑπό τινός, ὁ δὲ πάντα κατασκευάσας θεός (not incomplete process ['is being built'] but distributive reference to the entire task of 'building')

The aorist also occurs in general utterances, but less frequently, and when it does so it gives a summary expression to the various occurrences. In these cases one cannot insist on the meaning (i.e. the combinatory sense of aspect with actional character) which might prevail if the utterance were specific. STATES, however, do normally still appear with an ingressive sense, with the multiple occurrence showing up with distributive meaning.

Matt. 28: 15 καὶ διεφημίσθη ὁ λόγος οὗτος παρὰ Ἰουδαίοις μέχρι τῆς σήμερον (not a *single* 'accomplishment', as a specific statement would denote)

Acts 1: 21 ἐν παντὶ χρόνῳ ᾧ εἰσῆλθεν καὶ ἐξῆλθεν ἐφ᾽ ἡμᾶς ὁ κύριος Ἰησοῦς (not merely a single occurrence of these 'climaxes')

1 Thess. 2: 9 νυκτὸς καὶ ἡμέρας ἐργαζόμενοι . . . ἐκηρύξαμεν εἰς ὑμᾶς τὸ εὐαγγέλιον τοῦ θεοῦ (various occasions of preaching)

1 Cor. 15: 6 τινὲς δὲ ἐκοιμήθησαν (distributive ingressive)

The fact that the aorist can occur in general utterances is the reason that Stagg is right to criticize the conclusions of some interpreters, who argue from aorist-usage alone that some text refers to a specific event.[108] For example, the aorist (οὐ) κατέλαβεν in John 1: 5 need not refer to a single, specific occasion when the darkness failed to overcome the light (e.g. the Passion?). Given the general nature of the prologue in which it occurs, it is more likely that the aorist sums up various unspecified failures.

The distinction of general vs. specific is of special importance in the use of present and aorist in commands and prohibitions as developed in Chapter 5.

3. 4 The Effect of Tense-Reference on Aspectual Function

Another influence on the meaning of the aspects is the time-value of the verb which comes into play in the indicative forms, and to some degree in others. There are several ways in which the temporal meaning affects aspectual function.[109]

---

[108] Frank Stagg, 'The Abused Aorist', *JBL* 91 (1972), 223–8.

[109] The influence at times goes the other way (i.e. aspect-meaning affects the time-value); these will be described in the chapters on aspect-use in the indicative (ch. 4) and participle (ch. 6).

3. 4. 1 *Relative time-values*

Mention was made in connection with the general definition of aspect[110] that the aspects in Greek have a common association with certain relative time-values, as a secondary effect of their aspectual meaning. The basic pattern is that the aorist is used when situations occur in a sequence (since it views each in summary), while the present aspect is used for a situation which is simultaneous with another (since it focuses on the internal features and leaves out the end-point). This use of aspects to denote temporal sequence occurs in dependent clauses as well as in main clauses when narrative sequence is to be shown.

In dependent clauses, including temporal clauses as well as other types of subordinate clause, this temporal sequencing can affect the choice of aspects. Thus, present aspect at times denotes occurrence *simultaneous* with the situation in the main clause, without any necessary emphasis on the customary, incomplete, or durative nature of the dependent occurrence.[111]

Luke 14: 12–13 ὅταν ποιῇς ἄριστον ἢ δεῖπνον, φώνει τοὺς φίλους σου
24: 32 οὐχὶ ἡ καρδία ἡμῶν καιομένη ἦν [ἐν ἡμῖν] ὡς ἐλάλει ἡμῖν ἐν τῇ ὁδῷ διήνοιγεν ἡμῖν τὰς γραφάς;
John 5: 23 ἵνα πάντες τιμῶσι τὸν υἱὸν καθὼς τιμῶσι τὸν πατέρα
Acts 10: 17 ὡς δὲ ἐν ἑαυτῷ διηπόρει ὁ Πέτρος . . . οἱ ἄνδρες . . . ἐπέστησαν ἐπὶ τὸν πυλῶνα
13: 25 ὡς δὲ ἐπλήρου Ἰωάννης τὸν δρόμον, ἔλεγεν
22: 20 καὶ ὅτε ἐξεχύννετο τὸ αἷμα Στεφάνου . . . καὶ αὐτὸς ἤμην ἐφεστὼς καὶ συνευδοκῶν καὶ φυλάσσων
1 Thess. 5: 3 ὅταν λέγωσιν . . . τότε . . . ἐφέσταται ὄλεθρος

The aorist in dependent clauses can denote *antecedent* occurrence, even though the occurrence may not otherwise be

[110] See sect. 1.1.3 and 1.4.3, and the literature cited there.
[111] This is frequent for the aspect of participles, which will be covered in sect. 6.2.

presented in summary or with stress on accomplishment or momentary occurrence:

Matt. 21: 34 ὅτε δὲ ἤγγισεν ὁ καιρός . . . ἀπέστειλεν . . .
  24: 32–3 ὅταν ἤδη . . . γένηται ἀπαλὸς καὶ τὰ φύλλα ἐκφύῃ, γινώσκετε ὅτι

Luke 1: 41 ἐγένετο ὡς ἤκουσεν τὸν ἀσπασμὸν τῆς Μαρίας . . . ἐσκίρτησεν τὸ βρέφος

John 19: 30 ὅτε οὖν ἔλαβεν τὸ ὄξος ὁ Ἰησοῦς εἶπεν . . .

1 Cor. 1: 6 καθὼς τὸ μαρτύριον τοῦ Χριστοῦ ἐβεβαιώθη ἐν ὑμῖν

Even between independent clauses the choice of aspects may reflect a narrative sequence in which aorist aspect denotes situations occurring one after another, regardless of their actional character, and present aspect denotes situations which are simultaneous to another occurrence, without emphasis on duration or incompletion:

John 11: 1–44 (aorists and historical presents give the main sequence of events, while imperfects [vv. 2, 5, 18, 20b, 38b] tell of circumstances which are contemporaneous)

Acts 10: 44–8 ἐπέπεσεν . . . καὶ ἐξέστησαν . . . ἤκουον γάρ . . . τότε ἀπεκρίθη . . . προσέταξεν δέ . . . τότε ἠρώτησαν

(See also Acts 7: 20–5, 1 Cor. 3: 6.)

3. 4. 2 Performative use of present indicative

Another common way in which temporal meaning affects the aspectual function is the 'performative' use of the present indicative. A performative action is one which is accomplished in the very act of speaking:[112] it is not one which is about to happen or in process of happening or which has just occurred;

---

[112] Cf. J. L. Austin, *How to Do Things with Words* (Cambridge, Mass.: Harvard University Press, 1962), 6: in the case of performatives 'to utter the sentence (in, of course, the appropriate circumstances) is not to *describe* my doing of [the act] or to state that I am doing it: it is to do it'. Description of the performative use of language and its philosophical implications originated in large measure with Austin and has been developed by many other writers. For contemporary refinements, see John Geoffrey Partridge, *Semantic, Pragmatic and Syntactic Correlates: An Analysis of Performative Verbs Based on English Data* (Tübingen: Gunter Narr, 1982).

it is an action *identical* with and thus simultaneous with the act of speaking. An excellent early description of this linguistic usage was given by Koschmieder (speaking of the Hebrew perfect):

tritt ein solches Perfectum, für das man im Deutschen das Präsens verwendet, dann auf, wenn die Handlung, von der in der betr. Form gesprochen wird, eben im Aussprechen dieser Form besteht, und man im Deutschen das Wörtchen *hiermit* hinzufügen kann. D. h. also: *ich segne dich (hiermit)* spricht nicht nur von der Handlung des Segnens, sondern ist gleichzeitig diese Handlung. Im Gegensatz hierzu sind die meisten Präsentia nur Berichte von einer Handlung, also z. B. *ich schreibe eben einen Brief* 'ist' nicht das Schreiben, sondern berichtet nur von ihm, *ich sitze am Tisch* 'ist' nicht das Sitzen; dagegen *ich bitte (hiermit) um die Fahrkarten* 'ist' eben diese Bitte. . . . Wenn nun die Handlung, von der gesprochen wird, eben im Aussprechen der betr. Form besteht, so kann es sich ganz offenbar nur um Verba dicendi natürlich im weitesten Sinne des Wortes handeln, d. h. um solche Verba, die eine durch Sprechen voll-ziehbare Handlung bezeichnen, oder auch deren Symbolisierung ausdrücken.[113]

However, Koschmieder related this only to the perfective or aoristic aspect (illustrated with examples of the Hebrew perfect), and did not note a similar meaning for the imperfective aspect in the Greek indicative present.[114]

This use of the present has been observed in earlier treatments of aspect, but the point not clearly made is the reason that the *present* is used in such cases. It is the contention of this book that the performative use of the present indicative is due to an emphasis on the present (primary or deictic)[115] time-value: there is such stress on the action occurring at

---

[113] Erwin Koschmieder, 'Zu den Grundfragen der Aspekttheorie', *IF* 53 (1935), 287–8. He gives this use the label 'Koinzidenzfall'. Earlier mention of this was made in his 'Durchkreuzung von Aspekt- und Tempus-System im Präsens', *Zeitschrift für Slavische Philologie*, 7 (1930), 352–8.

[114] There is a use of the NT Greek *aorist* with this sense, seemingly under the influence of the Hebrew perfect usage cited by Koschmieder. This is discussed in sect. 4.3.6.

[115] See sect. 1.3.2 and Lyons, *Semantics*, pp. 636–7, 677–8.

exactly the moment of speaking that the 'internal viewpoint' of the present is compressed and a possible durative or continuing sense is thus reduced. The present in this case does not denote 'the present moment and a range of time on either side of it' as it usually does; instead, the occurrence is pressed into the time of 'precisely now'. It is the combination with present-tense meaning in the indicative which affects the present aspect in this way.

Some verbs, because of their lexical sense, commonly occur as performatives when in the present: ὁρκίζω/ἐνορκίζω, ἀφίημι, παρατίθημαι (as 'commit'), συνίστημι (as 'commend'), ἐπικαλέομαι (as 'appeal'), and such. Others occur as performatives only rarely. The sense of the present performative is not an action 'taking place' but one which is 'done' at the moment of speaking:

Mark 2: 5, 9 (~Matt. 9: 2, 5) ἀφίενταί σου αἱ ἁμαρτίαι

Luke 17: 4 ἐάν . . . ἐπιστρέψῃ πρός σε λέγων· μετανοῶ, ἀφήσεις αὐτῷ
    23: 46 εἰς χεῖράς σου παρατίθημαι τὸ πνεῦμά μου

Acts 9: 34 Αἰνέα, ἰαταί σε Ἰησοῦς Χριστός
    20: 32 καὶ τὰ νῦν παρατίθημαι ὑμᾶς τῷ θεῷ
    25: 11 Καίσαρα ἐπικαλοῦμαι

Rom. 16: 1 συνίστημι δὲ ὑμῖν Φοίβην

1 Thess. 5: 26 ἐνορκίζω ὑμᾶς . . . ἀναγνωσθῆναι τὴν ἐπιστολήν

Closely related to the performative present is the use of the present indicative to describe acts of *speaking* narrowly focused on the present moment (e.g. 'I tell you *now* . . .'). These are not strict performatives (since the 'act' is performed in the brief utterance which follows the introductory words), but the temporal reason for the use is the same, since the emphasis on present time compresses the viewpoint of the present and thus reduces any possible durative or continuing sense. These presents denote not a durative, customary, incomplete, or futuristic 'saying', but speech done almost identically with the time of referring to it.[116]

[116] Verkuyl, *Compositional Nature*, pp. 62–6, discusses such uses of verbs like 'hear',

Acts 16: 18 παραγγέλλω σοι . . . ἐξελθεῖν ἀπ᾽ αὐτῆς
   17: 23 τοῦτο ἐγὼ καταγγέλλω ὑμῖν
   24: 4 παρακαλῶ ἀκοῦσαί σε ἡμῶν

1 Cor. 12: 3, 15: 1 γνωρίζω ὑμῖν

This use of the present is often listed in grammars of NT Greek as the 'aoristic present', and most make it clear that this is limited to the *indicative* present, citing as a reason that the indicative aorist (which fits the aspect better) is normally a *past* tense. But the performative nuance is not made clear, and the emphasis on the present moment is not felt strongly enough. The argument of this book is that this use is attributable not only to the *non-past* temporal value (thus excluding the aorist), but also to the stress on *exact simultaneity* with the time of speaking.[117]

3. 5 The Effect of Discourse Features on Aspectual Function

One final influence on the function of the aspects is the effect of discourse-structuring. Discourse-structure is the use of various features (conjunctions, articles, personal-pronoun reference, verbal mood, etc.) to give coherence and understandable 'flow' to a narrative or other literary unit. In general terms, it involves the influence of the larger context, including the paragraph level and higher, on a particular text. This was discussed in greater detail in Chapter 1, which can be consulted for further background on this concept and its role in aspect-usage.[118] There are four major influences of discourse-features on aspectual function which will be described here. The first two of these were discussed earlier and will be treated only briefly here, under a single heading.

'say', and 'play [an instrument]', and labels them 'performative'. The preference in this book will be to regard these as similar to, but not strictly, performatives. However, the point being made here would not change if these are seen as performatives, since the sense of temporal coincidence is virtually identical.

[117] See the further treatment of this is sect. 4.1.2.
[118] See sect. 1.4 and literature cited there.

3. 5. 1 *Narrative prominence and sequence*

As noted in Sections 1.4.2–3, the aspects have a secondary function at the discourse level to reflect *prominence* or *sequence* in narrative. These are separate functions, but they are often used together. As a means of showing prominence, the aorist can be used to narrate the main or 'foreground' events, while the imperfect or present is used to record subsidiary or 'background' ones.[119] This is almost always true in conjunction with other meanings for the aspects, such as temporal sequencing, general vs. specific differences, and the normal combination of aspect-meaning with actional character (i.e. stative or durative uses of the imperfect or present, and ingressive, punctual, or accomplishment uses of the aorist). But despite this qualification it is valuable to be aware of the possible influence of narrative prominence on aspectual choice.

Illustrations of this use (mixed here and there with other types of aspect functions) include: Mark 5: 1–20 (cf. parallel in Matt. 8 and Luke 8, in which Luke has the same effect but Matt. only the bare story, omitting most of the imperfects); Acts 7: 20–6, 8: 26–40; and Rev. 9: 1–11.

Closely related is the use of the aspects to show the sequence of events in a narrative. Since this was discussed in Chapter 1, as well as in section 3.4.1, it will not be taken up again here. But it should be noted that narrative-sequencing is one sort of discourse role played by the aspects which can affect aspectual function.

3. 5. 2 *Inceptive use of aspects*

Another influence from the larger context on the meaning of the aspects is the inceptive sense produced by 'narrative succession'.[120] This involves the close collocation of two verbs

---

[119] Cf. MT, *Syntax*, p. 66: 'the aorist advances the bare story and the imperfect supplies the picture's details, when the two tenses are woven together in narrative'.
[120] This is the phrase used by Mateos, *Aspecto verbal*, pp. 36–7, in discussing the idiom described here.

denoting sequenced situations such that the first indicates the
beginning-point of the second. An inceptive sense is commonly true of STATES with aorist aspect, but the narrative
succession described here can produce an inceptive sense for
present or aorist aspect, and this may occur with active verbs.
The only restriction seems to be that the situation must have
some duration (a STATE, ACTIVITY, or ACCOMPLISHMENT; or
some sort of repeated occurrence); otherwise the beginning-
point could not be noted without referring to the entire
situation.

Matt. 4: 11 ἄγγελοι προῆλθον καὶ διηκόνουν αὐτῷ

Mark 1: 35 ἀναστὰς ἐξῆλθεν καὶ ἀπῆλθεν εἰς ἔρημον τόπον κἀκεῖ
προσηύχετο

Mark 6: 41 (~Luke 9: 16) λαβών . . . ἀναβλέψας . . . εὐλόγησεν καὶ
κατέκλασεν τοὺς ἄρτους καὶ ἐδίδου τοῖς μαθηταῖς

Luke 5: 3 ἐμβάς . . . ἠρώτησεν . . . καθίσας δὲ ἐκ τοῦ πλοίου ἐδίδασκεν
τοὺς ὄχλους (cf. Mark 4: 2 ἐδίδασκεν and Matt. 13: 3 ἐλάλησεν)
19: 41 ἰδὼν τὴν πόλιν ἔκλαυσεν ἐπ' αὐτήν

Acts 18: 19 κατήντησαν . . . κατέλιπεν . . . αὐτὸς δὲ εἰσελθὼν εἰς τὴν
συναγωγὴν διελέξατο τοῖς Ἰουδαίοις

3. 5. 3 Conjunction reduction

A third function for the aspects which is affected by discourse
considerations is the possible use of one or more aspects in
'conjunction reduction'. Conjunction reduction is the linguistic feature which operates to avoid overstatement or repetition
of elements of meaning which are supplied by a parallel
construction. At a simple level it involves things like omission
of a verb if it would be the same as that of a conjoined clause:
e.g. 'John likes swimming and Bill sailing'.[121] The latter
clause is assumed to carry the sense of the former. This is
thought to operate also at the level of grammatical meaning in
areas like modal and aspectual usage. The most extensive
treatment of this is given by Kiparsky, who, to speak of his

[121] See the explanation of reduction in Paul Kiparsky, 'Tense and Mood in
Indo-European Syntax', FL 4 (1968), 33–5. This illustration is his.

aspectual suggestions only, argues that the historical present in Greek is a type of conjunction reduction, in which repeated occurrences of past tenses are 'reduced' by the use of the present in conjoined structures.[122] In this view, followed also by Reynolds,[123] the historical present is a 'zero tense', used merely to carry on the sense of the preceding past-tense–aspect form, with no separate meaning of its own. This view of the historical present is disputed by Thomas and others,[124] and there seems good reason to call it into question, as shown in section 4.1.8 below.

Louw has proposed another situation in which conjunction reduction may provide help in analysing a puzzling usage: the alternation of aorists and perfects in close proximity. Citing 1 John 1: 1 ὃ ἀκηκόαμεν, ὃ ἑωράκαμεν ... ὃ ἐθεασάμεθα καὶ αἱ χεῖρες ἡμῶν ἐψηλάφησαν ... and 4: 9–14 ἀπέσταλκεν ... ἠγαπήκαμεν ... ἠγάπησεν ... ἀπείστειλεν ... ἠγάπησεν ... ἀπέσταλκεν, he writes:

The aorist . . . serves not to over-emphasize the issue. It functions stylistically as reduction which means that semantically the intension is to carry the force of the perfect, though to continue with perfect tenses in the surface structure would be an over-statement. Exegetically no distinction in meaning should be made between the perfects and aorists in I Jh. 1: 1. They all have the semantic value of the perfect tense. . . . The force of these tenses [aorists in 4: 9–14] are that of the perfects, the aorists are reduction forms. To seek for any distinction of meaning between the perfects and aorists in this passage would distort the stylistic effect.[125]

This is certainly an option worth considering in these texts, but it seems marginally more likely that the author of 1 John

---

[122] Ibid. 30–57.

[123] Stephen M. Reynolds, 'The Zero Tense in Greek: A Critical Note', *Westminster Theological Journal*, 33 (1969), 68–72.

[124] Werner Thomas, *Historisches Präsens oder Konjunktionsreduktion? Zum Problem des Tempuswechsels in der Erzählung* (Wiesbaden: Franz Steiner, 1974), 72–88; and K. L. McKay, 'Further Remarks on the "Historical" Present and Other Phenomena', *FL* 11 (1974), 247–51. See literature cited in sect. 4.1.8.

[125] J. P. Louw, 'Verbal Aspect in the First Letter of John', *Neotestamentica*, 9 (1975), 101–2.

intends some difference in sense, however slight, in alternating aspects here. He is not averse to repetition in other ways, even to the point of what some may call overstatement, so one wonders whether this would cause him to shift away from the perfect in a series in which that sense is his desired meaning.

In summary, proposed instances of the effect of conjunction reduction on aspectual usage are not strongly persuasive, although specific research to discover other examples has not been carried out. Perhaps this suggestion will prove fruitful in analysing some texts, and it is worth recording here as a possible option.

3. 6 Conclusion: The Use of these Features in Interpretation of Aspectual Function

An attempt has been made in this chapter to survey the linguistic features which are most important in influencing the function of verbal aspect in NT Greek. It can be seen from this survey that aspect is a category of language which intersects in usage with a bewildering variety of lexical, contextual, and discourse features. As Lyons has pointed out. 'Few parts of a language-system illustrate better than its aspect-system does the validity of the structuralist slogan: *Tout se tient* ("Everything hangs together" . . .).'[126] Despite the intersection of so many elements, however, it is possible to sort out the combinations and discern a fairly predictable pattern of effects which particular features have when combined with particular aspects. This chapter has presented the most important of these patterns.

This welter of combinations can present problems, however, because it is easy to attach one of the 'combinatory senses' to the aspect itself and expect to find that sense in all occurrences of the aspect.[127] As Bache has argued, the very

---

[126] Lyons, *Semantics*, p. 714.

[127] See warnings against this in Dee Ann Holisky, 'Aspect Theory and Georgian Aspect', in *Tense and Aspect* (1981), 131–2; and D. Crystal, 'Specification and English Tenses', *JL* 2 (1966), 4–6.

semantic complexity of aspectual usage suggests that one must unpack several levels of meaning in order to give an adequate account of it. He offers an approach operating at a *definition* level ('comprising the BASIC meanings of systems [e.g. the aspect-system], that is, the meanings that pertain uniquely and pervasively to substitutional forms or constructions in a one-to-one relationship') and at a *function* level ('At this level we find composite meanings or variant meanings deriving from distinctive intersection of basic meanings from different systems').[128]

This approach has been followed in Chapters 2 and 3, where a *definition* of the aspects was stated in terms of the 'viewpoint which the speaker takes concerning an occurrence', whether internal or external. Somewhat separate from this are meanings like duration, completion, repetition, and so forth, which were treated as *functions* of the aspects in combination with lexical and contextual features. It is true that some of the clearest contrasts of the aspects in actual usage are these 'combinatory variants': durative vs. punctual, incomplete vs. complete, stative vs. ingressive, repeated vs. single occurrence, and so forth. Such meanings are often stated as the basic definitions of the aspects by traditional grammars of NT Greek. The argument of this book is that such meanings must not be given as *definitions* of the aspects themselves but should be clearly articulated as their secondary *functions* in combination with other elements. It may seem a poor exchange to trade the clear, simple distinctions offered by some of the traditional grammars for a vague definition in terms of 'internal vs. external viewpoint' and a confusing array of secondary distinctions, but this approach is better supported by the linguistic evidence.

---

[128] Carl Bache, 'The Semantics of Grammatical Categories: A Dialectical Approach', *JL* 21 (1985), 61–3 (quotations from p. 63). These points are presented also in his *Verbal Aspect: A General Theory and its Application to Present-Day English* (Odense: Odense University Press, 1985), 145–52. Maslov, 'An Outline of Contrastive Aspectology', pp. 30–1, also analyses aspect at two levels: the primary aspectual meanings are at one level and particular applications of those 'depending on the context' are at another.

What is recommended for the interpreter of the NT is an understanding of the aspects as differences in the speaker's viewpoint concerning the occurrence, a general awareness of this range of other features which can affect aspect-function, and a sensitivity in looking for such features in texts where the use of one of the aspects may be important to interpretation. In many ways this is no different from the procedure to be followed in any area of exegesis: applying linguistic and historical sensitivity, along with a generous dose of common sense, to a broad array of contextual factors in order to construe the sense. What is to be avoided in any interpretive task is an atomistic approach to the text and its linguistic elements, and this is certainly true in regard to verbal aspect in NT Greek.

II

SPECIFIC AREAS OF
ASPECT-USAGE

4

THE ASPECTS IN
THE INDICATIVE MOOD

THIS chapter makes a transition from the treatment of general issues to a discussion of how verbal aspect is used in more specific ways in NT Greek. The present chapter will explore the use of the aspects in the indicative mood, while the subsequent chapters will cover aspect-usage in the other forms.

The distinctive feature of aspectual usage in the indicative is the intersection in the same forms of *aspect*-value with *time*- or tense-meanings. The deictic time-values of past, present, and future, though distinct from the meanings of the aspects themselves, do interact with the aspects in the indicative, and the interplay of these two systems of meaning must be explored here.

The format followed in this chapter will be a survey of the main uses of the aspects in the individual tenses of the indicative, with an explanation of the characteristics of each use and citation of illustrations for each type.[1] This survey will be interrupted by several excursuses examining topics which concern more than one tense at a time.

4. 1 Uses of the Present Indicative

The present indicative combines the aspect-value of 'internal viewpoint concerning an occurrence' with the tense-meaning

---

[1] Linguistic usage does not fit neatly into discrete classes. Some indicatives in the texts are on the borderline between these uses and should not be forced artificially into one or the other. What these categories provide is a survey of recognizable combinations of aspect, tense, and other features. Their service to the interpreter is that they provide a list of possible meanings (and contextual characteristics of such meanings) to be considered when one is interpreting an indicative verb in a particular passage. These also correlate in most respects with syntactical categories and nomenclature of a more traditional sort.

of 'occurrence simultaneous with the time of speaking' (or, less frequently, simultaneous with some other reference-point indicated in the utterance).[2] Specific ways in which these two meanings work out in actual usage and alterations which they undergo in context will be discussed below.

By way of overview, it can be said that the uses of the present indicative fall into three groups: the uses which describe a *specific* occurrence and thus have a rather narrow focus or scope (progressive and instantaneous); the uses which denote a *general* occurrence and have a broader scope of the situation in view (customary, gnomic, and 'past action still in progress'); and *special* uses (conative, futuristic, historical, and perfective). These will be taken up in sequence.

4. 1. 1 *Progressive or descriptive or specific present*

This use of the present involves a *specific* situation (either action or state) viewed *as it is going on*, either for the sake of vivid description in narrative or to denote close simultaneity with another situation. For example:

Mark 4: 38 οὐ μέλει σοι ὅτι ἀπολλύμεθα;
Acts 3: 12 τί θαυμάζετε ἐπὶ τούτῳ ἢ ἡμῖν τί ἀτενίζετε . . .;
  14: 15 ἄνδρες, τί ταῦτα ποιεῖτε;
Rom. 9: 1 ἀλήθειαν λέγω ἐν Χριστῷ, οὐ ψεύδομαι

The aspectual viewpoint of the present is reflected in this

---

[2] Some have argued that the aspectual force of the ·present (i.e. as found in non-indicative forms) is neutralized or does not appear in the present *indicative*. Cf. Martin Sánchez Ruipérez, *Estructura del sistema de aspectos y tiempos del verbo griego antiguo: Análisis funcional sincrónico* (Salamanca: Consejo Superior de Investigaciones Científicas, 1954), 101–15; and id., 'The Neutralization of Morphological Oppositions as Illustrated by the Neutral Aspect of the Present Indicative in Classical Greek', *Word*, 9 (1953), 241–52. See also Carroll D. Osburn, 'The Present Indicative in Matthew 19: 9', *Restoration Quarterly*, 24 (1981), 193–203. The evidence usually cited for this is those present indicatives which cannot be durative (e.g. 'aoristic' and historical presents). However, the use can be better explained within an aspectual approach to the present indicative (sects. 4.1.2 and 4.1.8), and this view in general errs in looking for the procedural characteristic of 'duration' instead of 'internal viewpoint' as the aspect-value of the present·indicative.

use by the close focus on the internal process or state without reference to the beginning or end-point of the situation. The occurrence is usually durative, since the actional constraints of viewing a situation 'as it goes on' require an appreciable temporal extension. Thus, the verb-types which usually occur in this use are the three durative types: STATES, ACTIVITIES, and ACCOMPLISHMENTS (with emphasis on the continuing process, not on failure to reach the terminus). CLIMAXES may also occur if the emphasis is on the prefaced process rather than on the instantaneous point of transition. However, the primary feature of this use is the immediate and specific nature of the reference to the occurrence 'as it is taking place' or 'as it is existing' at a particular point.

Many grammars refer to a descriptive or progressive use of the present indicative,[3] but what is not frequently stressed is the specific and immediate quality of the reference. However, Gildersleeve does refer to this use as the 'specific' present ('of that which is going on now'),[4] and Mandilaras and Schwyzer–Debrunner touch on its immediacy of reference[5] Thus, in contrast to the uses with general reference to be covered later, the descriptive present is used of what *is occurring* now, not of what *does occur* more generally in present time. This close description of what is going on can reflect a vivid narration of events—as though the reader were an eyewitness to the action/state described.

Matt. 25: 8 αἱ λαμπάδες ἡμῶν σβέννυνται
    28: 5 (+parallels) οἶδα γὰρ ὅτι Ἰησοῦν τὸν ἐσταυρωμένον ζητεῖτε

Mark 4: 38 (+parallels) οὐ μέλει σοι ὅτι ἀπολλύμεθα;
    12: 15 (~Matt. 22: 18) ὁ δὲ εἰδὼς αὐτῶν τὴν ὑπόκρισιν εἶπεν αὐτοῖς· τί με πειράζετε;
    14: 60 (~Matt. 26: 62) τί οὗτοί σου καταμαρτυροῦσιν

Acts 3: 12 τί θαυμάζετε ἐπὶ τούτῳ ἢ ἡμῖν τί ἀτενίζετε . . .;
    8: 30 ἆρά γε γινώσκεις ἃ ἀναγινώσκεις;

---

[3] Cf. Burton, *MT*, § 8; and BW, Syntax, pp. 76–7.
[4] Gildersleeve, *Syntax*, § 189.
[5] Mandilaras, *Verb*, pp. 98–9; and SD, *Syntax*, p. 270.

14: 15 ἄνδρες, τί ταῦτα ποιεῖτε;
17: 20 ξενίζοντα γάρ τινα εἰσφέρεις εἰς τὰς ἀκοὰς ὑμῶν
21: 13 τί ποιεῖτε κλαίοντες καὶ συνθρύπτοντές μου τὴν καρδίαν;
21: 31 ὅλη συγχύννεται Ἱερουσαλήμ

Rom. 9: 1 ἀλήθειαν λέγω ἐν Χριστῷ, οὐ ψεύδομαι

On other occasions this use appears to indicate that an occurrence is closely simultaneous with another event.

Mark 2: 19 ὅσον χρόνον ἔχουσιν τὸ νυμφίον μετ' αὐτῶν οὐ δύνανται νηστεύειν
John 5: 7 ἐν ᾧ δὲ ἔρχομαι ἐγώ, ἄλλος πρὸ ἐμοῦ καταβαίνει
Acts 9: 11 ἀναστὰς πορεύθητι . . . καὶ ζήτησον . . . Σαῦλον . . . ἰδοὺ γὰρ προσεύχεαι

When the descriptive present is used with a STATIVE verb, the reference is just as clearly to a *specific* entity in existence in the *immediate* focus of the utterance. However, such verbs are usually not phrased in the English 'progressive form', whereas active verbs in this use are normally rendered into English with the progressive. This difference in English translation idiom should not lead one to think that the STATIVE verb expresses a major difference in meaning: it is still a specific situation viewed closely as it is 'in existence', and it is just as descriptive and durative as an active verb in this use.

Acts 3: 12 τί θαυμάζετε ἐπὶ τούτῳ . . .;
3: 16 τοῦτον ὃν θεωρεῖτε καὶ οἴδατε
8: 30 ἆρά γε γινώσκεις ἃ ἀναγινώσκεις;
17: 20 βουλόμεθα οὖν γνῶναι τίνα θέλει ταῦτα εἶναι
19: 40 καὶ γὰρ κινδυνεύομεν ἐγκαλεῖσθαι στάσεως τῆς σήμερον

Gal. 1: 6 θαυμάζω ὅτι οὕτως ταχέως μετατίθεσθε ἀπὸ τοῦ καλέσοντος ὑμᾶς
(focusing on his frame of mind as he writes, not his general response)

It is true, however, that STATES frequently indicate a condition more generally true and are thus 'customary' presents. These will be treated below.

4. 1. 2 *Instantaneous present*

Also focusing on a specific occurrence is the instantaneous present, but the sense here is not of an action 'taking place' but one which is 'done' at the moment of speaking. This present use falls into two closely related types: the *performative* present, and the use of the present to describe acts of *speaking* narrowly focused on the present moment.

As described in section 3.4.2, a 'performative' action is one which is 'done' in the very act of speaking. It is not one which is about to happen or in process of happening or which has just occurred, but rather an action *identical* with and thus simultaneous with the act of speaking. It has something of the idea of 'I *hereby* do . . .', in that the act is accomplished in the utterance itself.[6] As argued in 3.4.2, the performative use of the present indicative is due to an emphasis on the *present* time-value: there is such stress on the action occurring at exactly the moment of speaking that the 'internal viewpoint' of the present is compressed and any durative sense is thus reduced. The present in this case does not denote the present moment and a range of time on either side of it as it usually does; instead, the occurrence is pressed into the time of 'precisely now'. It is the combination with present-tense meaning in the indicative which affects the present aspect in this way.

Some verbs commonly occur as performatives because of their lexical sense (cf. section 3.4.2): ὁρκίζω/ἐνορκίζω, ἀφίημι, παρατίθημαι (as 'commit'), συνίστημι (as 'commend'), ἐπικαλέομαι (as 'appeal'), and so on. Others occur as performatives only rarely. Verbs from all of the *active* actional classes (listed in Chapter 3) occur without difficulty, but STATES do not appear often. When a STATE does appear, it shifts in sense

---

[6] For a clear statement of the performative nature of this see Burton, *MT*, § 13; Abel, *Grammaire*, p. 250; and Mandilaras, *Verb*, p. 94. See also Albrecht Klose, *Der Indikativ des Präsens bei Homer, Herodot, und Thukydides* (Ph.D. thesis, University of Erlangen-Nuremberg, Regensburg: Haas, 1968), 248–53, who follows Koschmieder closely in this (cf. literature cited in sect. 3.4.2).

to its ingressive counterpart (thus becoming an active verb), since the sense is pressed into something 'done in a moment'. Some illustrations are:

Matt. 26: 63 ἐξορκίζω σε κατὰ τοῦ θεοῦ τοῦ ζῶντος ἵνα ἡμῖν εἴπῃς

Mark 2: 5, 9 (~Matt. 9: 2, 5) ἀφίενταί σου αἱ ἁμαρτίαι

Luke 17: 4 ἐὰν . . . ἐπιστρέψῃ πρός σε λέγων· μετανοῶ, ἀφήσεις αὐτῷ
   23: 46 εἰς χεῖράς σου παρατίθημαι τὸ πνεῦμά μου

John 11: 41 πάτερ, εὐχαριστῶ σοι ὅτι ἤκουσάς μου

Acts 9: 34 Αἰνέα, ἰαταί σε Ἰησοῦς Χριστός
   20: 32 καὶ τὰ νῦν παρατίθημαι ὑμᾶς τῷ θεῷ
   23: 9 οὐδὲν κακὸν εὑρίσκομεν ἐν τῷ ἀνθρώπῳ τούτῳ
   25: 11 Καίσαρα ἐπικαλοῦμαι
   26: 1 ἐπιτρέπεταί σοι περὶ σεαυτοῦ λέγειν
   26: 17 ἐκ τῶν ἐθνῶν εἰς οὓς ἐγὼ ἀποστέλλω σε (this is the commission, not a futuristic reference)

Rom. 16: 1 συνίστημι δὲ ὑμῖν Φοίβην

1 Thess. 5: 26 ἐνορκίζω ὑμᾶς . . . ἀναγνωσθῆναι τὴν ἐπιστολήν

It is likely that this use would have been common in the spoken language, and it tends to occur in written texts at places where spoken usage is approximated (dialogue, personal epistolary remarks, etc.). As Mandilaras points out concerning the non-literary papyri, the instantaneous present 'occurs in a variety of agreements such as contracts, deeds, engagements, sales, leases, receipts and the like, serving, in particular, to express a statement which constitutes the basis of the agreement'.[7] Examples are 'we register as our property . . .', 'Heracleides receives in marriage . . .', 'we agree to all the terms . . .', and so on. A number of specific instances from papyrus texts are given, listed according to the verbs which commonly occur in this use.[8]

The other type of instantaneous present is the present

---

[7] Mandilaras, Verb, p. 94.
[8] Ibid. The verbs which he lists are: ἀναφέρω, ἀπογράφομαι, ἀποδέχομαι, γνωρίζω, ἐπιδέχομαι, ἐπιδίδωμι, ἐπιτείνω, ἐπιτρέπω, εὐδοκέω, λαμβάνω, μαρτυρέω, ὀμνύω, ὁμολογέω, παραιτέομαι, συγχωρέω, and συμφωνέω.

indicative used to describe acts of *speaking* narrowly focused on the present moment (e.g. 'I tell you *now* . . .').These are not strict performatives (since the 'act' is performed in the brief utterance which follows the introductory words), but the temporal reason for the use is the same, since the emphasis on present time compresses the viewpoint of the present. These presents denote not a progressive, customary, incomplete, or futuristic 'saying', but speech done almost identically with the time of referring to it. However, in order to fit this use, the sense must be specific and focused on the present moment (e.g. 'I *hereby* make known'; 'he *now* tells you'), rather than a progressive or customary reference. The instantaneous at times has the character of a *pronouncement*, formal or informal.

Acts 5: 38 καὶ τὰ νῦν λέγω ὑμῖν, ἀπόστητε ἀπὸ τῶν ἀνθρώπων τούτων
8: 34 δέομαί σου, περὶ τίνος ὁ προφήτης λέγει τοῦτο;
10: 29 πυνθάνομαι οὖν τίνι λόγῳ μετεπέμψασθέ με;
16: 18 παραγγέλλω σοι . . . ἐξελθεῖν ἀπ' αὐτῆς
20: 26 διότι μαρτύρομαι ὑμῖν ἐν τῇ σήμερον ἡμέρᾳ ὅτι . . .
21: 11 τάδε λέγει τὸ πνεῦμα τὸ ἅγιον . . .
24: 14 ὁμολογῶ δὲ τοῦτό σοι ὅτι . . .
27: 22 καὶ τὰ νῦν παραινῶ ὑμᾶς εὐθυμεῖν
(See also 15: 19, 21: 39, 24: 4, 26: 3, 27: 34.)

There are, of course, unclear cases, on the border between instantaneous and progressive meanings. Both are specific, and the issue is whether a speaker states what he 'hereby does' or describes what he 'is now doing'. Examples which seem to be *progressive* in sense (for comparison with the instantaneous cases given above) occur in several of the speeches in Acts:

Acts 13: 32 ἡμεῖς ὑμᾶς εὐαγγελιζόμεθα τὴν πρὸς τοὺς πατέρας ἐπαγγελίαν
13: 38 διὰ τούτου ὑμῖν ἄφεσις ἁμαρτιῶν καταγγέλλεται
17: 3 Ἰησοῦς ὃν ἐγὼ καταγγέλλω ὑμῖν (also 17: 23)
24: 10 εὐθύμως τὰ περὶ ἐμαυτοῦ ἀπολογοῦμαι
26: 25 ἀληθείας καὶ σωφροσύνης ῥήματα ἀποφθέγγομαι
26: 26 πρὸς ὃν καὶ παρρησιαζόμενος λαλῶ

The instantaneous use of the present is listed in grammars of NT Greek as the 'aoristic' or simple present, and the grammars normally point out that this is limited to the *indicative* present, since the indicative aorist (which fits the aspect better) is normally a *past* tense.[9] It seems important, however, to give more emphasis to the performative nuance and the focus on the present moment which creates this use. The instantaneous meaning is attributable not only to the *not-past* temporal value, but also to the stress on *exact simultaneity* with the time of speaking. Outside of the indicative, the aorist is used for such instantaneous occurrences, since the temporal value of simultaneity does not interfere.

It should be noted also that the use of the simple form in English translation does not necessarily reflect instantaneous or 'non-linear' action. The English simple present can be instantaneous, but it may be used also of customary or general *actions* (e.g. 'I walk for my health's sake') and of any sort of *stative* reference ('we know', 'they wish', etc.), all of which are durative rather than instantaneous occurrences.[10]

Both of these uses of the present focus on a specific occurrence. The present indicative can also be used to describe general or multiple occurrences. There are three related uses in which the present has this broader reference, and these are now taken up.

4. 1. 3 *Customary or iterative present*

As Schwyzer–Debrunner point out, what is labelled 'present' in linguistic matters is not limited to a single moment of time: '. . . der Ausdruck Gegenwart so gut wie griech. νῦν, lat. nunc, nhd. "jetzt" nicht auf einen Punkt beschränkt werden darf,

---

[9] BDF, *Grammar*, § 320; BW, *Syntax*, p. 81; Burton, *MT*, § 13; Robertson, *Grammar*, pp. 865–6; Mandilaras, *Verb*, pp. 94–6; and MT, *Syntax*, p. 64.

[10] The discussions of this use in the grammars are not entirely clear on this point. Cf. Moule, *Idiom Book*, p. 7; MT, *Syntax*, pp. 60, 64; R. T. France, 'The Exegesis of Greek Tenses in the New Testament', *Notes on Translation*, 46 (1972), 4–5; and Osburn, 'Present Indicative in Matt. 19: 9', pp. 193–6. In this connection it should be noted that this category is based on Greek linguistic features and is not merely a matter of English translation-equivalence (i.e. corresponding to the simple form rather than the '-ing' form in English), as suggested by HS, *Grammatik*, p. 317.

sondern die größere oder kleinere Zeitspanne bezeichnet, die der Sprechende und der Hörende als Gegenwart empfinden'.[11] In contrast to the two uses already covered in which the 'now' is narrowly focused, the present indicative in this use denotes a broader time-frame, still regarded as the 'now'. Thus, the *temporal* location is still 'present' or 'simultaneous with the time of speaking/writing'. In regard to the *aspectual* meaning in such cases, there is a similar adjustment in application. The internal viewpoint of the present aspect pictures not a specific occurrence seen as it is taking place, but the continuance of a process or state in a broader time-frame or, more commonly, the repeated occurrence of an action or state over a stretch of time.[12] This combination of temporal and aspectual meaning in *broader* reference is what constitutes the customary or iterative present. It denotes not a situation which *is occurring* in the immediate environment, but one which *does occur* in a wider time-frame.[13] At times this broader reference is indicated by adverbs or by plural nouns as subject or object, but frequently it is shown only by contextual factors of a vaguer sort (the nature of the predication in that circumstance, knowledge of the non-literary context of the utterance, etc.).

Matt. 17: 15 πολλάκις γὰρ πίπτει εἰς τὸ πῦρ

[11] SD, *Syntax*, p. 270. The distinction of narrow vs. broad scope or of particular vs. general reference is suggested also by Moorhouse, *Syntax*, p. 182; and Rijksbaron, *SSV*, p. 5. This is developed more fully by C. W. Peppler, 'Durative and Aoristic', *AJP* 54 (1933), 47–9; Klose, *Der Indikativ des Präsens*, pp. 80–96; Lloyd, *Verb*, pp. 57–69; and Antony Galton, *The Logic of Aspect: An Axiomatic Approach* (Oxford: Clarendon Press, 1984), 85–129.

[12] Several grammars list this category under the label 'iterative' or 'repeated'. See Smyth, *Grammar*, § 1876; Robertson, *Grammar*, p. 880; Abel, *Grammaire*, p. 250 ('fréquentatif'); Mandilaras, *Verb*, pp. 107–8; BW, *Syntax*, pp. 77–8; and HS, *Grammatik*, p. 317. But even though this is the most common sense, the general or customary present need not be iterative. If the lexical character of the verb is stative or denotes a process which can be extended at length, the sense is that of unbroken continuation, as seen in John 1: 38; Acts 15: 11, 26: 7; and 1 John 2: 8 above.

[13] This use and the gnomic or proverbial present (to be covered next) are alike in possessing a wider reference to the occurrence. The distinction in meaning between these uses will be clarified in the next section.

Luke 3: 16 ἐγὼ μὲν ὕδατι βαπτίζω ὑμᾶς

Luke 18: 12 νηστεύω δὶς τοῦ σαββάτου, ἀποδεκατῶ πάντα ὅσα κτῶμαι

John 1: 38 διδάσκαλε, ποῦ μένεις;

3: 2 οὐδεὶς γὰρ δύναται ταῦτα τὰ σημεῖα ποιεῖν ἃ σὺ ποιεῖς

3: 26 ἴδε οὗτος βαπτίζει καὶ πάντες ἔρχονται πρὸς αὐτόν

Acts 7: 51 ὑμεῖς ἀεὶ τῷ πνεύματι τῷ ἁγίῳ ἀντιπίπτετε

15: 11 διὰ τῆς χάριτος τοῦ κυρίου Ἰησοῦ πιστεύομεν σωθῆναι

17: 28 ἐν αὐτῷ γὰρ ζῶμεν καὶ κινούμεθα καὶ ἐσμέν

19: 13 (cf. 21: 21) ὁρκίζω ὑμᾶς τὸν Ἰησοῦν ὃν Παῦλος κηρύσσει

23: 8 Σαδδουκαῖοι μὲν γὰρ λέγουσιν μὴ εἶναι ἀνάστασιν μήτε ἄγγελον μήτε πνεῦμα, Φαρισαῖοι δὲ ὁμολογοῦσιν τὰ ἀμφότερα

(See also these examples from Acts: 10: 43, 15: 15, 15: 36, 17: 23, 17: 30, 19: 27, 20: 23, 24: 3, 24: 14, 24: 16, 26: 7, 27: 23, 28: 22.)

Rom. 1: 9 ὡς ἀδιαλείπτως μνείαν ὑμῶν ποιοῦμαι

1 Cor. 1: 23 ἡμεῖς δὲ κηρύσσομεν Χριστὸν ἐσταυρωμένον

9: 26–7 . . . τρέχω . . . πυκτεύω . . . ὑπωπιάζω μου τὸ σῶμα καὶ δουλαγωγῶ . . .

11: 26 ὁσάκις γὰρ ἐὰν ἐσθίητε . . . καὶ . . . πίνητε, τὸν θάνατον τοῦ κυρίου καταγγέλλετε ἄχρι οὗ ἔλθῃ

1 John 2: 8 ἡ σκοτία παράγεται καὶ τὸ φῶς τὸ ἀληθινὸν ἤδη φαίνει

At the same time it must be said that the customary use is on a fluid continuum with the progressive present, and the difference between narrow and broad reference is at times difficult to establish. Examples which lie on the borderline between the two uses can be found:

Acts 9: 4–5 (also 22: 7–8, 26: 14–15) Σαοὺλ Σαούλ, τί με διώκεις; . . . ἐγώ εἰμι Ἰησοῦς ὃν σὺ διώκεις (he did this customarily, but is the *focus* here on the immediate activity of journeying to Damascus for the purpose of persecution?)

25: 11 εἰ δὲ οὐδέν ἐστιν ὧν οὗτοι κατηγοροῦσίν μου (charges 'being pressed right now' or charges 'they have been bringing' over the longer period! Similar examples in 26: 2, 7)

26: 24–5 μαίνῃ, Παῦλε . . . οὐ μαίνομαι (immediate frame of mind or general condition?)

The problem cases should not obscure the fact that many instances are clear-cut and that the difference between specific, progressive reference and general, customary reference is often important to the sense of a passage.

Acts 26: 31 οὐδὲν θανάτου ἢ δεσμῶν ἄξιόν [τι] πράσσει ὁ ἄνθρωπος οὗτος (a verdict about his customary conduct, not just his behaviour at the hearing)

1 Cor. 2: 6–7 σοφίαν δὲ λαλοῦμεν ἐν τοῖς τελείοις . . . ἀλλὰ λαλοῦμεν θεοῦ σοφίαν ἐν μυστηρίῳ (not what he does in this passage, but his ministry practice)

One further topic of significance in regard to the customary present is the sense of habitual or *characteristic* occurrence which is attributed to it. Before this is taken up, however, it will be helpful to discuss the next use of the present.

4. 1. 4 *Gnomic present*

Closely related to the customary present is the use of the present to express timeless, universal occurrences: the gnomic or proverbial present.[14] As the name implies, this use of the present occurs in proverbial statements or general maxims about what occurs at *all* times. Some examples are:

John 3: 8 τὸ πνεῦμα ὅπου θέλει πνεῖ

Acts 7: 48 οὐχ ὁ ὕψιστος ἐν χειροποιήτοις κατοικεῖ
　17: 24–5 ὁ θεός . . . οὐκ ἐν χειροποιήτοις ναοῖς κατοικεῖ οὐδὲ ὑπὸ χειρῶν ἀνθρωπίνων θεραπεύεται
　26: 8 τί ἄπιστον κρίνεται παρ' ὑμῖν εἰ ὁ θεὸς νεκροὺς ἐγείρει;

1 Cor. 2: 10 τὸ γὰρ πνεῦμα πάντα ἐραυνᾷ, καὶ τὰ βάθη τοῦ θεοῦ

2 Cor. 9: 7 ἱλαρὸν γὰρ δότην ἀγαπᾷ ὁ θεός

Jas. 1: 13–15 ὁ γὰρ θεὸς ἀπείραστός ἐστιν κακῶν, πειράζει δὲ αὐτὸς οὐδένα . . . εἶτα ἡ ἐπιθυμία συλλαβοῦσα τίκτει ἁμαρτίαν, ἡ δὲ ἁμαρτία ἀποτελεσθεῖσα ἀποκύει θάνατον

1 John 3: 20 ὁ θεὸς . . . γινώσκει πάντα
　4: 7–8 ἡ ἀγάπη ἐκ τοῦ θεοῦ ἐστιν . . . ὁ θεὸς ἀγάπη ἐστίν

---

[14] Cf. SD, *Syntax*, p. 270: 'Zeitlos (tempusindifferent) steht der Ind. Präs. in *Feststellungen*, die an keine Zeit gebunden sind . . . so bes. in *Sentenzen* und *Sprichwörtern*'. Abel, *Grammaire*, p. 250, speaks of the present used in 'une maxime générale, vraie dans tous les temps'.

4: 17b–18 φόβος οὐκ ἔστιν ἐν τῇ ἀγάπῃ ἀλλ᾽ ἡ τελεία ἀγάπη ἔξω βάλλει τὸν φόβον, ὅτι ὁ φόβος κόλασιν ἔχει

Similar to these is the use of the present in generic or indefinite statements, which relate what occurs generally or at *any* time. These also have a proverbial character and fit the gnomic category, but in a slightly different way from those cited above:[15]

Matt. 6: 24 οὐδεὶς δύναται δυσὶ κυρίοις δουλεύειν

7: 17 οὕτως πᾶν δένδρον ἀγαθὸν καρποὺς καλοὺς ποιεῖ, τὸ δὲ σαπρὸν δένδρον καρποὺς πονηροὺς ποιεῖ

10: 40 ὁ δεχόμενος ὑμᾶς ἐμὲ δέχεται, καὶ ὁ ἐμὲ δεχόμενος δέχεται τὸν ἀποστείλαντά με.

12: 35 ὁ ἀγαθὸς ἄνθρωπος . . . ἐκβάλλει ἀγαθά, καὶ ὁ πονηρὸς ἄνθρωπος . . . ἐκβάλλει πονηρά

15: 11 (cf. 15: 18) οὐ τὸ εἰσερχόμενον εἰς τὸ στόμα κοινοῖ τὸν ἄνθρωπον, ἀλλὰ τὸ ἐκπορευόμενον ἐκ τοῦ στόματος τοῦτο κοινοῖ τὸν ἄνθρωπον

19: 9 ὃς ἂν ἀπολύσῃ τὴν γυναῖκα αὐτοῦ μὴ ἐπὶ πορνείᾳ καὶ γαμήσῃ ἄλλην μοιχᾶται[16]

Mark 2: 21–2 οὐδεὶς ἐπίβλημα ῥάκους ἀγνάφου ἐπιράπτει ἐπὶ ἱμάτιον παλαιόν . . . καὶ οὐδεὶς βάλλει οἶνον νέον εἰς ἀσκοὺς παλαιούς

Luke 11: 10 (~Matt. 7: 8) πᾶς γὰρ ὁ αἰτῶν λαμβάνει, καὶ ὁ ζητῶν εὑρίσκει

John 2: 10 πᾶς ἄνθρωπος πρῶτον τὸν καλὸν οἶνον τίθησιν

3: 21 ὁ δὲ ποιῶν τὴν ἀλήθειαν ἔρχεται πρὸς τὸ φῶς

3: 36 ὁ πιστεύων εἰς τὸν υἱὸν ἔχει ζωὴν αἰώνιον

Acts 13: 39 ἐν τούτῳ πᾶς ὁ πιστεύων δικαιοῦται

1 Cor. 12: 8 ᾧ μὲν γὰρ διὰ τοῦ πνεύματος δίδοται λόγος σοφίας

Heb. 3: 4 πᾶς γὰρ οἶκος κατασκευάζεται ὑπό τινός, ὁ δὲ πάντα κατασκευάσας θεός

Antoniadis observes quite correctly that a number of gnomic presents appear in didactic passages of the Synoptic Gospels

[15] Lyons, *Semantics*, pp. 680–2, gives a useful discussion of *gnomic* and *generic* statements, in which he notes the overlap in meaning between the two.

[16] Osburn, 'Present Indicative in Matt. 19: 9', pp. 196–203, is correct in arguing for this sense of the present here as opposed to the meaning 'continue to commit adultery'.

in the form of comparisons and illustrations from everyday occurrence, used as teaching-aids.[17] Some of the examples which she cites are:

Luke 3: 9 (~Matt. 3: 10) πᾶν οὖν δένδρον μὴ ποιοῦν καρπὸν καλὸν ἐκκόπτεται καὶ εἰς πῦρ βάλλεται

Luke 9: 58 (~Matt. 8: 20) οἱ ἀλώπεκες φωλεοὺς ἔχουσιν καὶ τὰ πετεινὰ . . . κατασκηνώσεις

Luke 12: 24, 27–8 (~Matt. 6: 26, 28–30) κατανοήσατε τοὺς κόρακας ὅτι οὐ σπείρουσιν οὐδὲ θερίζουσιν, οἷς οὐκ ἔστιν ταμεῖον οὐδὲ ἀποθήκη, καὶ ὁ θεὸς τρέφει αὐτοὺς . . . κατανοήσατε τὰ κρίνα πῶς αὐξάνειν· οὐ κοπιᾷ οὐδὲ νήθει

(See also Luke 5: 34–9, 6: 39, 6: 44–5, 11: 17–44.)

The gnomic present can be viewed as the final step on the continuum which moves from very narrow reference (instantaneous present), to narrow reference (descriptive present), over to wider reference (customary present), and finally to widest reference (gnomic present). Thus, the gnomic present is similar to the customary present in that they both express generalized continuing or repeated occurrence (this is the aspect-meaning), but the gnomic use is even *more* general and indefinite, even *less* focused on particular people and restricted circumstances.[18] This means that gnomic presents normally exhibit characteristics of absolute or monadic statements (speaking of God, sun, sea, wind, and the like) or of indefinite or generic statements (e.g. anarthrous nouns with indefinite reference, generic articles, indefinite pronouns, οὐδείς/μηδείς, πας with articular participle, etc.; for further details, see the

---

[17] Sophie Antoniadis, *L'Évangile de Luc: Esquisse de grammaire et de style* (Paris: Les Belles Lettres, 1930), 246.

[18] The customary sense and the gnomic sense could be treated together in one category of 'general present' (as done by Burton, *MT*, § 12). This has the virtue of not multiplying categories or cutting the senses too finely. But there seems to be a difference worth distinguishing, and a long tradition of NT grammars has separated the customary sense from the gnomic sense as done here. See Robertson, *Grammar*, pp. 866, 880; Abel, *Grammaire*, p. 250; DM, *Grammar*, pp. 183–4; Mandilaras, *Verb*, pp. 107–10; BW, *Syntax*, pp. 77–80; and HS, *Grammatik*, p. 317. Cf. Smyth, *Grammar*, §§ 1876–7.

list in section 3.3.2). They relate multiple occurrences true not only of the 'now' but of all time or any time. The customary present, on the other hand, tends to occur with nouns or pronouns referring to particular people or things, and it describes their repeated or continuing actions in the broad frame of time viewed as 'now'. The customary present includes a broad scope of occurrence within its view, but it does have certain limits; the gnomic, however, widens the scope so that there are no limits (see Fig. 4.1).

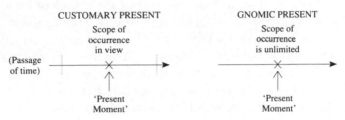

FIG. 4.1. Scope of customary present and gnomic present

Mandilaras reports that the gnomic present is infrequent in the non-literary papyri, but he can cite eight instances of it. His suggestion to explain this infrequency seems plausible: 'The gnomic present is not common in papyri, perhaps because of the nature of their subject matter (public documents, private affairs), and where it occurs, it is found to be in letters or papers of a didactic character'.[19] This reflects the range of its occurrence in the NT as well, since it tends to be rare in narrative and informal dialogue (e.g. only four cases in Acts), but more common in didactic material.

This is now the place to return to the discussion postponed at the end of the previous section—the habitual or characteristic meaning which is attributed to the customary present. As reflected in the term 'customary', it is common in many languages for the general or customary present (in contrast to the specific or progressive use) to be used of occurrences which are regular, usual, normal, habitual, or characteristic. But

---

[19] Mandilaras, *Verb*, p. 110.

distinctions are sometimes made concerning what may be regarded as 'characteristic' of a person or thing. In a certain sense, any action or state done or existed in by a subject could be seen as characteristic of that subject, though perhaps only in a temporary way: 'he is dancing wildly', 'she is ill right now', or 'I just struck the ball' would be 'characteristic', of the subjects, but only in a transitory sense. Actions or states which occur over a wider time-frame are more readily seen as permanent characteristics, though there is still a sliding scale in such matters: actions true of someone for a week or a month could be regarded as not characteristic of him in some still wider time-frame, or they could be seen as contingent rather than essential properties.[20] However, the more frequently an act occurs or the longer a state or process continues, the more likely it is to be regarded as genuinely characteristic of the subject. Thus, something which is frequent, normal, or regular in occurrence is usually taken as characteristic. It is in this sense that the Greek customary or iterative present is associated with ideas of habitual or characteristic occurrence, and examples exist in which this is certainly the sense.

Luke 4: 36 ἐν ἐξουσίᾳ καὶ δυνάμει ἐπιτάσσει τοῖς ἀκαθάρτοις πνεύμασιν
7: 5 ἄξιός ἐστιν ᾧ παρέξῃ τοῦτο· ἀγαπᾷ γὰρ τὸ ἔθνος ἡμῶν
18: 12 νηστεύω δὶς τοῦ σαββάτου, ἀποδεκατῶ πάντα ὅσα κτῶμαι

John 3: 2 οὐδεὶς γὰρ δύναται ταῦτα τὰ σημεῖα ποιεῖν ἃ σὺ ποιεῖς

Acts 7: 51 ὑμεῖς ἀεὶ τῷ ἁγίῳ ἀντιπίπτετε
23: 8 Σαδδουκαῖοι μὲν γὰρ λέγουσιν μὴ εἶναι ἀνάστασιν μήτε ἄγγελον μήτε πνεῦμα, Φαρισαῖοι δὲ ὁμολογοῦσιν τὰ ἀμφότερα

Some of these different senses in which 'characteristic' may be understood have surfaced (without elaboration) in discussions of an interpretive problem in 1 John 3: 4–10, for which the habitual meaning of the present may provide a solution. These verses include strong statements about the one who abides in Jesus Christ (3: 6 πᾶς ὁ ἐν αὐτῷ μένων οὐχ ἁμαρτάνει·

---

[20] Cf. Comrie, *Aspect*, pp. 103–6, and Lyons, *Semantics*, p. 717, for further treatment of permanent or essential conditions vs. transitory or contingent ones and the linguistic reflections of these in some languages.

πᾶς ὁ ἁμαρτάνων οὐχ ἑώρακεν αὐτὸν οὐδὲ ἔγνωκεν αὐτόν) and the one who is born of God (3: 9 πᾶς ὁ γεγεννημένος ἐκ τοῦ θεοῦ ἁμαρτίαν οὐ ποιεῖ, ὅτι σπέρμα αὐτοῦ ἐν αὐτῷ μένει, καὶ οὐ δύναται ἁμαρτάνειν, ὅτι ἐκ τοῦ θεοῦ γεγέννηται). These seem to speak of sinless perfection for the Christian, yet the epistle earlier denies such a thing in equally strong terms (1: 8–10) and gives reassurance to the apparently Christian readers in case they do in fact sin (2: 1 τεκνία μου, ταῦτα γράφω ὑμῖν ἵνα μὴ ἁμάρτητε. καὶ ἐάν τις ἁμάρτῃ, παράκλητον ἔχομεν πρὸς τὸν πατέρα Ἰησοῦν Χριστὸν δίκαιον).

One solution to this problem is to note the difference in the tenses used to refer to the Christian's sin in 2: 1 (aorists) vs. 3: 4–10 (presents), and to trace a distinction in meaning along the line of 'occasional vs. habitual' sin or 'committing a single sin vs. being characterized by sin as a ruling principle'. Zerwick's phrasing of it is: 'commit sin in the concrete, commit some sin or other' as opposed to 'be a sinner, as a characteristic <state>' or 'be—habitually—a sinner'. The point of 3: 9, accòrding to Zerwick, is to say that the Christian 'cannot continue the sinful life that was his before his regeneration'.[21] Turner follows Zerwick by arguing that ἁμαρτάνειν is stative in meaning (to be a sinner), while ἁμαρτεῖν is ingressive (to begin to be a sinner, as 'only an initial step along a certain road'): 'The apostle affirms that a Christian believer can never be a sinner. He will start to be one, will take the first (aoristic) step by committing this or that sin, but he stops short of the condition of being "a sinner". . . . Sin will not have dominion over him.'[22] This solution to the problem is followed in some form by other grammatical works[23] as well as by several commentators.[24]

---

[21] Zerwick, *Biblical Greek*, p. 82. As he mentions, this seems to be Paul's point in Rom. 6.

[22] Nigel Turner, *Grammatical Insights into the Greek New Testament* (Edinburgh: T. and T. Clark, 1965), 151. He suggests this idea more briefly in MT, *Syntax*, p. 72.

[23] DM, *Grammar*, p. 195; France, 'Greek Tenses', p. 9; and Robertson, *Grammar*, pp. 880, 890.

[24] A. E. Brooke, *A Critical and Exegetical Commentary on the Johannine Epistles* (ICC; Edinburgh: T. and T. Clark, 1912), 90; John R. W. Stott, *The Epistles of John* (Grand

Others, however, take the view that 1 John 3 speaks more absolutely and, in a context of opposing morally indifferent gnostics, it traces a sharp contrast between the gnostic and the Christian. Kubo has argued for this interpretation, based on his understanding of the contextual contrast:

To say in this context that the author means only that the Christian does not habitually sin is appreciably to weaken his point. . . . The heretic who defines sin as ignorance and not as lawlessness can sin, but the Christian who recognizes sin as lawlessness and that Jesus came to destroy sin and its instigator, the devil, cannot sin. The sharp antithesis is intentional and any qualifications or reservations at this point would undermine the argument.[25]

According to this approach, the reconciliation of 3: 4–10 with 2: 1–2 is not entirely clear, but Kubo phrases it as a difference between the 'idealistic' in 3: 4–10 and the 'realistic' in 2: 1–2.[26] The main point is that chapter 3 speaks in absolute terms and should not be qualified by 1: 5–2: 2.

Apart from contextual reasons for the absolute view, some have expressed doubt that the tenses alone can be relied upon to convey the sense required for the 'habitual' approach. Dodd, for example, questions 'whether the reader could be expected to grasp so subtle a doctrine simply upon the basis of a precise distinction of tenses without further guidance'.[27] Hodges has moved on from this to state: 'It cannot be shown anywhere in the New Testament that the present tense can bear this kind of meaning [i.e. habitual] *without the assistance of other words'*.[28] These are the *grammatical* points at issue, and

---

Rapids, Mich.: Wm. B. Eerdmans Publishing Co., 1964), 126–7; and A. N. Wilder, 'The First, Second, and Third Epistles of John', *The Interpreter's Bible* (New York: Abingdon, 1957), 227.

[25] Sakae Kubo, 'I John 3: 9: Absolute or Habitual?', *Andrews University Seminary Studies*, 7 (1969), 50. See also C. H. Dodd. *The Johannine Epistles* (New York: Harper and Row, 1946), 78–81.

[26] Kubo, 'I John 3: 9', pp. 50, 56. He does not put it this way, but one could see it also as polemical (3: 4–10) vs. pastoral (2: 1–2).

[27] Dodd, *Johannine Epistles*, p. 79.

[28] Zane C. Hodges, '1 John', in *The Bible Knowledge Commentary*, New Testament edn. (Wheaton, Ill.: Victor Books, 1983), 894 (emphasis is his).

leaving aside the theological and other exegetical arguments surrounding this interpretive problem, it is the grammatical evidence which will be touched upon here.

Hodges' contention that the present tense cannot without assistance be habitual has in its favour the fact that many of the clearest habitual presents are in fact reinforced by words or phrases which strengthen the sense:

Matt. 17: 15 πολλάκις γὰρ πίπτει εἰς τὸ πῦρ

Luke 18: 12 νηστεύω δὶς τοῦ σαββάτου

Acts 7: 51 ὑμεῖς ἀεὶ τῷ πνεύματι τῷ ἁγίῳ ἀντιπίπτετε
    17: 30 τὰ νῦν παραγγέλλει τοῖς ἀνθρώποις πάντας πανταχοῦ μετανοεῖν
    20: 23 τὸ πνεῦμα τὸ ἅγιον κατὰ πόλιν διαμαρτύρεταί μοι
    24: 3 πάντη τε καὶ πανταχοῦ ἀποδεχόμεθα
    28: 22 περὶ μὲν γὰρ τῆς αἱρέσεως ταύτης γνωστὸν ἡμῖν ἐστιν ὅτι πανταχοῦ ἀντιλέγεται

However, his basic point seems simply not true. There are numerous presents in the NT denoting a custom or habit *without* other explicit indicators. The sense of the context indicates the customary or habitual nature of the occurrence.

Luke 11: 39 ὑμεῖς οἱ Φαρισαῖοι τὸ ἔξωθεν τοῦ ποτηρίου . . . καθαρίζετε

John 3: 26 ἴδε οὗτος βαπτίζει καὶ πάντες ἔρχονται πρὸς αὐτόν

Acts 19: 13 ὁρκίζω ὑμᾶς τὸν Ἰησοῦν ὃν Παῦλος κηρύσσει
    20: 24 οὐδενὸς λόγου ποιοῦμαι τὴν ψυχὴν τιμίαν ἐμαυτῷ
    21: 21 κατηχήθησαν δὲ περὶ σοῦ ὅτι ἀποστασίαν διδάσκεις ἀπὸ Μωϋσέως
    24: 14 (also 17: 23, 27: 23) οὕτως λατρεύω τῷ πατρῴῳ θεῷ

1 John 1: 7 τὸ αἷμα Ἰησοῦ τοῦ υἱοῦ αὐτοῦ καθαρίζει ἡμᾶς ἀπὸ πάσης ἁμαρτίας
    2: 27 τὸ αὐτοῦ χρῖσμα διδάσκει ὑμᾶς περὶ πάντων

3 John 3 καθὼς σὺ ἐν ἀληθείᾳ περιπατεῖς
    9–10 Διοτρέφης οὐκ ἐπιδέχεται ἡμᾶς. διὰ τοῦτο, ἐὰν ἔλθω, ὑπομνήσω αὐτοῦ τὰ ἔργα ἃ ποιεῖ λόγοις πονηροῖς φλυαρῶν ἡμᾶς, καὶ μὴ ἀρκούμενος ἐπὶ τούτοις οὔτε αὐτὸς ἐπιδέχεται τοὺς ἀδελφοὺς καὶ τοὺς βουλομένους κωλύει καὶ ἐκ τῆς ἐκκλησίας ἐκβάλλει.

(See also these texts cited earlier: Luke 4: 36, 7: 5, 18: 12; John 3: 2; Acts 7: 51, 23: 8.)

Thus, the habitual interpretation of 1 John 3: 4–10 is certainly *possible*, based on NT usage. It is nevertheless true that this text, of all passages, seems an opportune place for reinforcing the habitual sense, if that is in fact the point. Yet there is little or no further indication of habitual meaning.[29] Compared with other NT usage, it does appear that the present by itself is quite a subtle way of communicating such a vital link in one's argument, as Dodd noted. This does not make the habitual sense impossible, but it makes it seem less likely.

The feature which seems stronger than these points against the habitual interpretation is the *generic* nature of the predication throughout the passage. Bearing in mind the differences traced above between *customary* (or habitual) presents and *gnomic* (or generic) presents, one can see that the statements of 1 John 3: 4–10 are clearly gnomic or generic: they contain repeated uses of πᾶς with articular participle in the sense of 'whoever . . .' rather than pronouns referring to particular people. Note the parallels with the following generics, and the contrasts with the customary presents cited above.

Matt. 7: 17 οὕτως πᾶν δένδρον ἀγαθὸν καρποὺς καλοὺς ποιεῖ, τὸ δὲ σαπρὸν δένδρον καρποὺς πονηροὺς ποιεῖ
    12: 35 ὁ ἀγαθὸς ἄνθρωπος . . . ἐκβάλλει ἀγαθά, καὶ ὁ πονηρὸς ἄνθρωπος . . . ἐκβάλλει πονηρά

Luke 11: 10 (~Matt. 7: 8)· πᾶς γὰρ ὁ αἰτῶν λαμβάνει, καὶ ὁ ζητῶν εὑρίσκει

John 2: 10 πᾶς ἄνθρωπος πρῶτον τὸν καλὸν οἶνον τίθησιν
    3: 21 ὁ δὲ ποιῶν τὴν ἀλήθειαν ἔρχεται πρὸς τὸ φῶς
    3: 36 ὁ πιστεύων εἰς τὸν υἱὸν ἔχει ζωὴν αἰώνιον

1 Cor. 12: 8 ᾧ μὲν γὰρ διὰ τοῦ πνεύματος δίδοται λόγος σοφίας

(See other texts cited earlier: Matt. 6: 24, 10: 40, 15: 11, 15: 18; Mark 2: 21–2; Heb. 3: 4.)

It should be observed from these examples that generics are

---

[29] The periphrasis of ἁμαρτάνειν with ποιεῖν τὴν ἁμαρτίαν in 3: 4, 8 and the parallel description in 3: 8 of the devil who sinned ἀπ᾽ ἀρχῆς may be a hint towards the idea of 'continuance in sin as a rule of life', but it seems rather weak. The former of these is suggested by J. P. Louw, 'Verbal Aspect in the First Letter of John', *Neotestamentica*, 9 (1975), 102.

usually multiple in a distributive sense: the plurality which is predicated consists of each one of a group doing an act a single time, rather than repeatedly. Thus, the sense of a generic utterance is usually an *absolute* statement of what each one does once, and not a statement of the individual's customary or habitual activity. This is true particularly when the present verb is a *bounded* action (an ACCOMPLISHMENT, CLIMAX, or PUNCTUAL), rather than an unbounded STATE or ACTIVITY. In regard to 1 John 3, it is important to analyse the actional character of ἁμαρτάνειν and ποιεῖν τὴν ἁμαρτίαν. These verbal expressions seem most likely to be bounded actions (to commit sin), rather than ACTIVITIES or STATES. Again the possibility of a habitual sense cannot be ruled out entirely (cf. Matt. 7: 17, John 3: 36), but it seems less likely. On purely grammatical grounds, therefore, the absolute interpretation of 1 John 3: 4–10 is to be preferred.

4. 1. 5 *Present of Past Action still in Progress*

Far more specialized than the customary or gnomic presents but sharing the same broad frame of reference is the use of the present indicative to denote a situation which began in the past and continues in the present. This is more specialized because it always includes an *adverbial phrase* or other time-indication with the present verb to signal the past-time meaning.[30] However, it is otherwise like the customary or gnomic in sense.

Luke 13: 7 ἰδοὺ τρία ἔτη ἀφ᾽ οὗ ἔρχομαι ζητῶν καρπόν . . . καὶ οὐχ εὑρίσκω
    15: 29 ἰδοὺ τοσαῦτα ἔτη δουλεύω σοι

John 5: 6 γνοὺς ὅτι πολὺν ἤδη χρόνον ἔχει
    14: 9 τοσούτῳ χρόνῳ μεθ᾽ ὑμῶν εἰμι καὶ οὐκ ἔγνωκάς με

---

[30] It is suggested in BW, *Syntax*, p. 77, that an adverbial expression is not needed to constitute this sense, but the examples which they cite for this (2 Cor. 12: 9 ἀρκεῖ σοι ἡ χάρις μου, ἡ γὰρ δύναμις ἐν ἀσθενείᾳ τελεῖται) are better understood as gnomic presents, and the customary or gnomic categories serve quite well for any instances which, without adverbial addition, refer to actions which include a portion of past occurrence along with the present.

15: 27 ἀπ' ἀρχῆς μετ' ἐμοῦ ἐστε

Acts 15: 21 Μωϋσῆς γὰρ ἐκ γενεῶν ἀρχαίων κατὰ πόλιν τοὺς κηρύσσοντας αὐτὸν ἔχει ἐν ταῖς συναγωγαῖς κατὰ πᾶν σάββατον ἀναγινωσκόμενος
27: 33 τεσσαρεσκαιδεκάτην σήμερον ἡμέραν προσδοκῶντες ἄσιτοι διατελεῖτε μηθὲν προσλαβόμενοι (the only two occurrences in Acts)

2 Pet. 3: 4 ἀφ' ἧς γὰρ οἱ πατέρες ἐκοιμήθησαν, πάντα οὕτως διαμένει ἀπ' ἀρχῆς κτίσεως

1 John 3: 8 ἀπ' ἀρχῆς ὁ διάβολος ἁμαρτάνει

This category is typical of the present indicative in denoting a *present* action or state which is *viewed from within*, and thus as continuing or repeated. It is unlike the other uses in that it *explicitly* includes a period of the past during which the situation continued as well. This would be unremarkable, except for the problem of translating this Greek present into English.[31] Because of the past-time indication, the idiomatic translation is an English present perfect, and not a simple or progressive present (cf. the RSV translation of the examples cited above). There seems to be no shorthand term which serves well to label this category; several grammars suggest the title 'progressive',[32] but this term is better kept for the more specific category discussed first in this chapter. Gildersleeve creatively calls this the 'Present of Unity of Time',[33] and McKay uses the phrase 'extension from past'.[34] But most grammars are content to use some form of the lengthy description 'past action still in progress' without a shorthand title,[35] and this seems the most accurate approach.

[31] For example, these Greek presents are easily translated into German as presents. This perhaps explains why this category does not appear in German NT grammars. There is a reference in BDR, *Grammatik*, § 322 (3), to some NT examples cited above, but only to deny that they are examples of 'perfective present'.

[32] Robertson, *Grammar*, p. 879; and Mandilaras, *Verb*, pp. 96–7. BW, *Syntax*, p. 77, cite the term 'progressive' as possible, but choose the label 'durative', which seems no improvement.

[33] Gildersleeve, *Syntax*, § 202.

[34] K. L. McKay, *Greek Grammar for Students: A Concise Grammar of Classical Attic with Special Reference to Aspect in the Verb* (Canberra: Department of Classics, The Australian National University, 1974), 142.

[35] Burton, *MT*, § 17; Abel, *Grammaire*, p. 251; SD, *Syntax*, pp. 273–4; Moorhouse, *Syntax*, p. 182.

There are four other uses of the present which do not fit so easily into the 'specific vs. general' framework followed in these first five uses. These later uses apply the aspectual-cum-temporal meaning of the present indicative in more specialized ways, without regard to narrow or broad reference.

4. 1. 6 *Conative present*

The present is used at times of an action (specific or general) which is *attempted* or *intended* but *not accomplished*. This is a rather infrequent use of the present, but it is a natural application of the aspectual sense. The present aspect views the action from within, without reference to beginning or end-point, and thus it can be used with verbs of a certain lexical type or in particular contexts to denote an action which is continuing or intended, but which does not reach its termination.[36] The sense of incompletion is a natural concomitant of the 'internal viewpoint'. However, the incomplete sense is only actualized in certain circumstances which emphasize the absence of termination.

One set of circumstances is the use of a present verb of the ACCOMPLISHMENT or CLIMAX type (verbs which lexically imply a natural end-point or termination to the action) in a context implying effort, difficulty, or resistance to the action. This combination with the present indicative describes the action as actually *in process*, but not brought to its termination.[37] Even though the action is shown to have started, the sense is not inchoative (emphasizing the beginning of the

---

[36] As Moorhouse, *Syntax*, p. 182, states, the main characteristic of the conative is that 'the absence of termination in the action is stressed'. Cf. KG, *Satzlehre*, p. 140; Burton, *MT*, § 11; BDF, *Grammar*, § 319; Abel, *Grammaire*, p. 252; Moule, *Idiom Book*, p. 8; MT, *Syntax*, p. 63; Robertson, *Grammar*, p. 880; and Mayser, *Grammatik*, p. 134.

[37] Burton, *MT*, § 11, and Mandilaras, *Verb*, p. 106, both note that the lexical sense of the verb is important to the conative meaning. However, the conative sense is not *always* valid for ACCOMPLISHMENTS and CLIMAXES in the present. They may occur in some other application of the present, but when the context suggests resistance the sense of incompletion comes to the fore.

occurrence) but progressive;[38] the point is that the process, though under way, is not completed.

Acts 26: 28 ἐν ὀλίγῳ με πείθεις Χριστιανὸν ποιῆσαι

Rom. 2: 4 τὸ χρηστὸν τοῦ θεοῦ εἰς μετάνοιάν σε ἄγει

1 Cor. 7: 28 θλῖψιν δὲ τῇ σαρκὶ ἕξουσιν οἱ τοιοῦτοι, ἐγὼ δὲ ὑμῶν φείδομαι

Gal. 5: 4 κατηργήθητε ἀπὸ Χριστοῦ, οἵτινες ἐν νόμῳ δικαιοῦσθε

6: 12 ὅσοι θέλουσιν εὐπροσωπῆσαι ἐν σαρκί, οὗτοι ἀναγκάζουσιν ὑμᾶς περιτέμνεσθαι

There is, however, a different sort of 'incomplete' present which the grammars also label as conative: it is used of actions which have not actually started, but are *intended, contemplated,* or *desired.*[39] These are much like futuristic presents,[40] but are better seen as conative because of the strong sense of incompletion which is expressed in them. However, the stress on lack of termination in these cases is due to a different combination of circumstances from those present in the other type of conative described above. In these cases the intention or desire to do an act is, by easy association, seen as part of the process of doing the act itself, but to *intend* or *contemplate* is not to *do* or *accomplish*, and if the context shows that the action itself is not under way the overall sense is one of incompletion, similar to the other type of conative (action actually in process but not accomplished). Verbs of all types of *active* actional characteristics (not just ACCOMPLISHMENTS and CLIMAXES as above) could occur in this sort of conative expression, but STATES do not seem to occur.

John 10: 32 διὰ ποῖον αὐτῶν ἔργον ἐμὲ λιθάζετε;

[38] MT, *Syntax*, p. 63, and Robertson, *Grammar*, p. 880, link the conative with an inchoative sense, but the illustrations they cite (Mark 4: 17, 11: 23) do not fit this nuance, and the examples normally cited for the conative stress not the *beginning* only, but the incomplete *process*.

[39] The label 'tendential' rather than conative is used for this whole category in BW, *Syntax*, pp. 78–9, and DM, *Grammar*, p. 186, which tends to highlight this sort of meaning over the idea of attempt; but they as well as the grammars cited above include examples from both types distinguished here.

[40] Mandilaras, *Verb*, pp. 106–7, notes the similarity between conative and futuristic presents.

13: 6 κύριε, σύ μου νίπτεις τοὺς πόδας;
13: 27 ὃ ποιεῖς ποίησον τάχιον

4. 1. 7 *Futuristic present*

The Greek present indicative is also used to record an occurrence to be done not in the present but in the *future*, relative to the time of speaking. Sometimes the future reference is shown by explicit adverbial modifiers, but at other times it is merely implicit in the larger context or sense of the verbal statement. Thus, the tense-meaning is not what is normally expected for the present indicative, and in many (but not all) cases the idiomatic English translation will be a future verb.

But how is it that the present indicative comes to be used of future occurrences? Most explain this use as a rhetorical application of the present time-value for the sake of *vividness* and *certainty* in portraying a future occurrence 'as though present'.[41] This explanation makes good sense for some of the cases of futuristic presents, but a better rationale for it is needed in regard to others. This highlights the fact that futuristic presents are of different types, even though they share the common feature of future-time reference. In order to understand the futuristic sense clearly, it is necessary to distinguish these different types.[42]

One kind of construction normally listed as a futuristic present involves the statement of a *process going on in the present* with its (stated or implied) *termination to be reached only in the*

[41] Burton, *MT*, § 15; Ludwig Radermacher, *Neutestamentliche Grammatik: Das Griechisch des Neuen Testaments im Zusammenhang mit der Volkssprache*, 2nd edn. (Tübingen: J. C. B. Mohr, 1925), 152; BDF, *Grammar*, § 323; SD, *Syntax*, p. 273; and BW, *Syntax*, pp. 80–1.
[42] Different kinds of futuristic presents are noted by KG, *Satzlehre*, pp. 137–40; Jakob Wackernagel, *Vorlesungen über Syntax*, 2nd edn., 2 vols., (Basle: Emil Birkhäuser, 1926), 158–62; Klose, *Der Indikativ des Präsens*, pp. 159–78; BDF, *Grammar*, § 323; Mandilaras, *Verb*, pp. 102–5; and Gottfried Steyer, *Handbuch für das Studium des neutestamentlichen Griechisch*, ii. *Satzlehre* (Berlin: Evangelische Verlagsanstalt, 1968), 56, and their ideas will be noted in the paragraphs below.

future. Since the termination is not reached until some future moment, the action itself is regarded as future, even though the process leading up to the terminus is already taking place in the present.[43] It can be seen that this type of futuristic present is not due to a rhetorical transfer of time-reference ('future event as though present'), but to the aspect-value of the present. This is similar to the conative use, in that the aspectual function in context is that of *incomplete* action in the present (an action going on but not yet done); it is different from the conative, however, since one envisages the termination actually being reached at a point in the future. This construction occurs only with verbs of the ACCOMPLISHMENT or CLIMAX type (or ACTIVITY verbs with terminus added by an adjunct phrase). Verbs of movement are the most common among these types.

Matt. 26: 45 ὁ υἱὸς τοῦ ἀνθρώπου παραδίδοται εἰς χεῖρας ἁμαρτωλῶν (vv. 46–7 show the action going on but not 'finished' until a point in the future)

Mark 10: 33 (~Matt. 20: 18) ἰδοὺ ἀναβαίνομεν εἰς Ἱεροσόλυμα [followed by 8 futures] (previous verse shows them under way: ἦσαν . . . ἀναβαίνοντες εἰς Ἱεροσόλυμα)

Luke 12: 54 ὅταν ἴδετε [τὴν] νεφέλην ἀνατέλλουσαν ἐπὶ δυσμῶν, εὐθέως λέγετε ὅτι ὄμβρος ἔρχεται (cf. future in the parallel, v. 55)
22: 22 ὁ υἱὸς μὲν τοῦ ἀνθρώπου κατὰ τὸ ὡρισμένον πορεύεται

John 8: 14 οἶδα πόθεν ἦλθον καὶ ποῦ ὑπάγω· ὑμεῖς δὲ οὐκ οἴδατε πόθεν ἔρχομαι ἢ ποῦ ὑπάγω

Acts 20: 22 καὶ νῦν ἰδοὺ δεδεμένος ἐγὼ τῷ πνεύματι πορεύομαι εἰς Ἱερουσαλήμ

The vividness and certainty sometimes attributed to futuristic presents is not so clearly valid for these. They are vivid only to the degree that the process is viewed in narrow focus 'as it is going on', but in many instances the focus is broad and lively description is lost. The sense of certainty is also dependent

---

[43] This futuristic sense is distinguished and this explanation given in Wackernagel, *Vorlesungen über Syntax*, pp. 160–1; BDF, *Grammar*, § 323 (3); and Mandilaras, *Verb.* p. 103.

upon factors other than the use of the present: the process which is already under way is assumed to run to its terminus, but this is no more assured than a future tense would be.

A second kind of futuristic is similar to this, but only the *intention, pledge,* or *expectation* to act is present: both the process and its termination are future (or, if non-durative, the entire act is future). The present is used here by extension from the type described above, inasmuch as the act is regarded as already under way, even if only in intention.[44] This too is similar to the conative use since there also an intention to act is sometimes viewed as the initial stage of the action itself (see John 10: 32).

Matt. 26: 18 ὁ καιρός μου ἐγγύς ἐστιν, πρὸς σὲ ποιῶ τὸ πάσχα μετὰ τῶν μαθητῶν μου

Luke 3: 16 ἔρχεται δὲ ὁ ἰσχυρότερός μου
14: 19 ζεύγη βοῶν ἠγόρασα πέντε καὶ πορεύομαι δοκιμάσαι αὐτά
19: 8 εἴ τινός τι ἐσυκοφάντησα ἀποδίδωμι τετραπλοῦν
24: 49 καὶ [ἰδοὺ] ἐγὼ ἀποστέλλω τὴν ἐπαγγελίαν τοῦ πατρός μου ἐφ᾽ ὑμᾶς

John 7: 8 ἐγὼ οὐκ ἀναβαίνω εἰς τὴν ἑορτὴν ταύτην
11: 11 πορεύομαι ἵνα ἐξυπνίσω αὐτόν
14: 2–4 πορεύομαι ἑτοιμάσαι τόπον ὑμῖν . . . πάλιν ἔρχομαι καὶ παραλήμψομαι ὑμᾶς πρὸς ἐμαυτόν . . . καὶ ὅπου [ἐγὼ] ὑπάγω οἴδατε τὴν ὁδόν
14: 12 ἐγὼ πρὸς τὸν πατέρα πορεύομαι (also 14: 18, 28)
20: 17 ἀναβαίνω πρὸς τὸν πατέρα μου καὶ πατέρα ὑμῶν
21: 3 ὑπάγω ἁλιεύειν . . . ἐρχόμεθα καὶ ἡμεῖς σὺν σοί

1 Cor. 16: 5 ἐλεύσομαι δὲ πρὸς ὑμᾶς ὅταν Μακεδονίαν διέλθω· Μακεδονίαν γὰρ διέρχομαι

2 Cor. 13: 1 τρίτον τοῦτο ἔρχομαι πρὸς ὑμᾶς

---

[44] This type and its connection with the first type are best explained by Mandilaras, *Verb.* p. 103: 'In particular, the futuristic present is found . . . with verbs of motion which are often determinative in meaning: they denote a process leading to a definite "term" or result (thus "come" implies "arrive"). Consequently the present of such a verb, when denoting the action as now in progress, also implies the "term" as to be realized in the future ("he is coming" = "he is now on his way and will arrive"): hence, by extension, it can be used even when the action is not yet in

This second kind of futuristic present sometimes involves a sense of imminent occurrence, since the event anticipated may be not the *termination* of a process (usually extended in duration), as in the first type, but the *beginning* of the act or process itself, which could occur immediately (e.g. Luke 3: 16; John 14: 12, 28; 20: 17). Thus, the sense of 'to be about to . . .' or 'to be on the verge of . . .' can appear alongside this idea of intention or expectation. However, the sense of vivid description or certainty of occurrence is not clear in this type, which is also the case with the first type given above.[45]

A third kind of futuristic present is related to the gnomic or generic use in that the present is used as though to state a general principle (denoting an occurrence which may take place at *any* time), but with the context focusing on a particular outworking of this principle at a point in the future.[46]

Matt. 2: 4 ἐπυνθάνετο παρ' αὐτῶν ποῦ ὁ χριστὸς γεννᾶται

18: 12–13 οὐχὶ ἀφήσει τὰ ἐνενήκοντα ἐννέα ἐπὶ τὰ ὄρη καὶ πορευθεὶς ζητεῖ τὸ πλανώμενον; καὶ ἐὰν γένηται εὑρεῖν αὐτό, ἀμὴν λέγω ὑμῖν ὅτι χαίρει ἐπ' αὐτῷ μᾶλλον ἢ ἐπὶ τοῖς ἐνενήκοντα ἐννέα τοῖς μὴ πεπλανημένοις

24: 43 εἰ ᾔδει ὁ οἰκοδεσπότης ποίᾳ φυλακῇ ὁ κλέπτης ἔρχεται

Luke 3: 9 (~Matt. 3: 10) πᾶν οὖν δένδρον μὴ ποιοῦν καρπὸν καλὸν ἐκκόπτεται καὶ εἰς πῦρ βάλλεται

John 3: 18 ὁ πιστεύων εἰς αὐτὸν οὐ κρίνεται

4: 35 οὐχ ὑμεῖς λέγετε ὅτι ἔτι τετράμηνός ἐστιν καὶ ὁ θερισμὸς ἔρχεται;

10: 15, 18 καὶ τὴν ψυχὴν μου τίθημι ὑπὲρ τῶν προβάτων . . . οὐδεὶς αἴρει

progress, but only intended or expected ("he is coming" = "he intends or is expected to come, arrive").

[45] A sense of certainty is present in some of the instances, but this is due to the assumed trustworthiness of the speaker (see John 14: 2–4, 12, 28 in contrast to Luke 19: 8), who states his intention to act in a certain way, and not to the futuristic present itself.

[46] In some of these examples (e.g. Matt. 18: 2–3; 2 Cor. 5: 1) a conditional clause occurs to give the sentence its indefinite reference to a future event of a 'whenever' sort. Futuristic presents in apodoses are noted by Mandilaras, *Verb*, pp. 104–5. BDF, *Grammar*, § 323 (2), cite some of these examples, but do not give the description of them offered here.

αὐτὴν ἀπ' ἐμοῦ, ἀλλ' ἐγὼ τίθημι αὐτὴν ἀπ' ἐμαυτοῦ (cf. v. 11, where a similar phrase is simply gnomic)

1 Cor. 15: 32 φάγωμεν καὶ πίωμεν, αὔριον γὰρ ἀποθνήσκομεν

2 Cor. 5: 1 οἴδαμεν γὰρ ὅτι ἐὰν ἡ ἐπίγειος ἡμῶν οἰκία τοῦ σκήνους καταλυθῇ, οἰκοδομὴν ἐκ θεοῦ ἔχομεν

The final kind of futuristic present is the use of the present in prophetic or oracular pronouncements, giving a vision of a future occurrence as if it were occurring already.[47] This is a rhetorical application of the normal meaning of the present indicative (an action occurring at the time of speaking) to describe a future event as though it were present. Here at last one finds examples which reflect vividness and confident assertion about the future occurrence, as many grammars have noted.[48] However, it will be noted that the features characteristic of the kinds of futuristic presents listed earlier are not in any way necessary here (e.g. verbs of movement, action either in progress or imminent, generic action envisaged in its future occurrence).

Matt. 26: 2 οἴδατε ὅτι μετὰ δύο ἡμέρας τὸ πάσχα γίνεται, καὶ ὁ υἱὸς τοῦ ἀνθρώπου παραδίδοται εἰς τὸ σταυρωθῆναι

27: 63 ἐκεῖνος ὁ πλάνος εἶπεν ἔτι ζῶν· μετὰ τρεῖς ἡμέρας ἐγείρομαι

Mark 9: 31 ἐδίδασκεν γὰρ τοὺς μαθητὰς αὐτοῦ καὶ ἔλεγεν αὐτοῖς ὅτι ὁ υἱὸς τοῦ ἀνθρώπου παραδίδοται εἰς χεῖρας ἀνθρώπων, καὶ ἀποκτενοῦσιν αὐτόν, καὶ ἀποκτενθεὶς μετὰ τρεῖς ἡμέρας ἀναστήσεται

Luke 12: 20 ἄφρων, ταύτῃ τῇ νυκτὶ τὴν ψυχήν σου ἀπαιτοῦσιν ἀπὸ σοῦ

John 21: 23 ἐξῆλθεν οὖν οὗτος ὁ λόγος εἰς τοὺς ἀδελφοὺς ὅτι ὁ μαθητὴς ἐκεῖνος οὐκ ἀποθνήσκει· οὐκ εἶπεν δὲ αὐτῷ ὁ Ἰησοῦς ὅτι οὐκ ἀποθνήσκει

Rev. 9: 6 καὶ ἐν ταῖς ἡμέραις ἐκείναις ζητήσουσιν οἱ ἄνθρωποι τὸν θάνατον καὶ οὐ μὴ εὑρήσουσιν αὐτόν, καὶ ἐπιθυμήσουσιν ἀποθανεῖν καὶ φεύγει ὁ

---

[47] Cf. Gildersleeve, *Syntax*, § 194, who explains this use as 'the present as a vision of the future'. See also Wackernagel, *Vorlesungen über Syntax*, pp. 161-2; BDF, *Grammar*, § 323 (1); Mandilaras, *Verb*, p. 105; and Steyer, *Satzlehre*, p. 56.

[48] Burton, *MT*, § 15; Moulton, *Proleg.*, p. 120; Robertson, *Grammar*, pp. 869–70; Radermacher, *Grammatik*, p. 152; BDF, *Grammar*, § 323; SD, *Syntax*, p. 273; and BW, *Syntax*, pp. 80–1.

θάνατος ἀπ' αὐτῶν (variant readings shift from future to present for most of the verbs of this verse, but this seems the best text)

4. 1. 8 *Historical present*

The rhetorical force of the fourth type of futuristic present (picturing a non-present event as though present) is thought to be the key element *mutatis mutandis* in the next major use of the present: the historical present. The commonly accepted explanation of the Greek historical present (as for similar presents in other languages) is that the present is used to bring a past occurence into immediate view, portraying the event as though it occurs before the reader's eyes.[49] Although the historical present appears in different specific patterns of usage through ancient Greek literature, it does appear that *vivid or dramatic narration* of past events is the common characteristic of the use.[50]

To be more specific, the historical present as a vivid narrative tense is usually divided into two main types, with different applications of the rhetorical effect. Schwyzer–Debrunner, for example, offer these two divisions:

> Das *expressive* praesens pro praeterito (auch dramatisches Präsens genannt) hebt entscheidende und neue Momente der Ereignisse heraus und belebt dadurch die Darstellung; der Sprecher und der Hörer sehen in warmer Anteilnahme die Geschehnisse gleichsam vor Augen, wie auf einer Bühne. . . .
> Das praesens pro praeterito erscheint aber auch *inexpressiv* (andere Bezeichnungen dafür sind registrierend, notizenhaft, praesens annalisticum oder tabulare). Es ist nicht nur bei Historikern, sondern auch in der Tragödie neben dem erstgenannten Gebrauche, von

---

[49] Cf. KG, *Satzlehre*, pp. 132–4; Gildersleeve, *Syntax*, §§ 199–201; Stahl, *Syntax*, pp. 90–2; Wackernagel, *Vorlesungen über Syntax*, pp. 162–4; Smyth, *Grammar*, §§ 1883–4; SD, *Syntax*, pp. 271–3; Klose, *Der Indikativ des Präsens*, pp. 223–46; Burton, *MT*, § 14; BDF, *Grammar*, § 323; Radermacher, *Grammatik*, p. 155; MT, *Syntax*, pp. 60–2; and Robertson, *Grammar*, pp. 866–8.

[50] There is an alternative approach which denies the 'vivid' theory entirely, and many who hold to the 'vivid' approach suggest adjustments to it. These points will be surveyed here in due course.

dem es sich nicht immer scharf abhebt, häufig; es gibt ein trockenes Faktum, das durch den Zusammenhang zeitlich bestimmt wird. . . . Die gleiche Ausdrucksweise boten alte chronikartige Aufzeichnungen nach Art der römischen Fasten, in denen das Datum gegeben war. . . . An die Chronisten schlossen sich die Historiker und die Tragödie an.[51]

The effect of the 'expressive' type, then, is to give vivid *description* by, as it were, transferring the past event into the present. Most historical presents in ancient Greek fit this sort, occurring as a single present amidst a series of aorists and imperfects or in a series of presents understood from context to describe past events. On the other hand, the 'annalistic' type uses the present not as vivid description but as immediate *note-taking* or chronicling of facts, as though recording the event on the scene. It communicates an air of immediacy and nearness to the occurrence, but it does not have the lively, dramatic force of the expressive type. It is used most commonly to relate facts such as births, deaths, marriages, royal accessions, key military victories, and so on.[52]

What is it about the present indicative which produces these meanings? It is the argument of this book that, in both types of historical present, the key feature which prompts the use of the present is the *temporal* transfer, not some sort of *aspectual* effect.[53] Some have argued that the historical present

---

[51] SD, *Syntax*, pp. 271–2. See similar divisions in Smyth, *Grammar*, §§ 1883–4; Mayser, *Grammatik*, pp. 131–2 (who adds a further division, 'in Traumberichten', which seems to add nothing to the 'expressive' type); and Gildersleeve, *Syntax*, §§ 199–201.

[52] Examples often cited are: Xenophon, *Anab.* 1. 1. 1 Δαρείου καὶ Παρυσάτιδος γίγνονται παῖδες δύο ('two sons were born of Darius and Parysatis'); Hdt. 1. 106 Κυαξάρης μὲν . . . τελευτᾷ, ἐκδέχεται δὲ Ἀστυάγης . . . τὴν βασιληίην ('Cyaxares died and Astyages succeeded to the throne'). Wackernagel, *Vorlesungen über Syntax*, pp. 164–5, feels that this is really a use of the 'timeless' present, and Kurt von Fritz, 'The So-Called Historical Present in Early Greek', *Word*, 5 (1949), 190–201, extends this to cover all uses of the historical present, but the explanation given above connecting the event with *present* time seems more consistent with actual occurrences.

[53] Stahl, *Syntax*, p. 90, follows this approach in explaining the historical present: 'Indem dieses [historical present] vergangene Ereignisse in die Gegenwart rückt, bringt es sie der Anschauung und Betrachtung näher und veranlaßt dadurch eine besondere Beachtung derselben. Es liegt in der Natur der Sache, daß das nicht

gains its vividness from the aspectual force of viewing action as it is going on,[54] and this is plausible in comparison with the 'descriptive' presents discussed first in this section: viewing an occurrence as it takes place does give a lively, dramatic effect. However, as most acknowledge, the historical present appears more frequently as a substitute for the *aorist* in recording an event in simple, not progressive, narration.[55] It occasionally occurs in places where an imperfect seemingly would be used, but this simply illustrates its aspectually neutral meaning.[56] The point of the historical present is not how the occurrence is viewed, but that it occurs (rhetorically) 'now'. It is presentation of a clearly past occurrence as though it were simultaneous with the writer/reader which produces the vivid or immediate effect. In this regard it is similar to the instantaneous present, in that the *temporal* meaning predominates and neutralizes the *aspectual* force. An illustrative parallel to this is the use of the English simple present in narrating events exactly simultaneous with the time of speaking, as for example in narrating a sporting event or a demonstration of some kind. Leech describes this use and gives the following examples: 'Napier *passes* the ball to Attwater, who *heads* it straight into the goal! | Walker *swings* a right at the West Indian—he *ducks* and it *glances* harmlessly off his shoulder. . . . | Look, I *take* this card from the pack and *place* it under the handkerchief—so. |

---

allgemeine Vorgänge sein können, sondern nur einzelne Ereignisse, die nicht nebensächlicher Natur sind, sondern als bedeutsam erscheinen, wobei nicht so sehr das dauernde Moment ihres Verlaufes als ihr wirksames Eintreten hervorgehoben wird'. Cf. Jesse L. Rose, *The Durative and Aoristic Tenses in Thucydides* (Language Dissertation 35, supp. to *Lg*; Baltimore: Linguistic Society of America, 1942). 27–8.

[54] For example, Mandilaras, *Verb*, p. 108, feels that it derives its vivid effect 'by means of stressing the continuous verbal aspect'.

[55] Cf. Sd, *Syntax*, p. 271; and BDF, *Grammar*, § 321. Hermann Koller, 'Praesens historicum und erzählendes Imperfekt: Beitrag zur Aktionsart der Praesensstammzeiten im Lateinischen und Griechischen', *Museum Helveticum*, 8 (1951), 63–99, argues that the historical present is consistently *inceptive*, but this is not so common as a *constative* (i.e. simple, summary) meaning.

[56] Moorhouse, *Syntax*, pp. 184–6, also suggests that the historical present is aspectually neutral, and cites texts from Sophocles in which it varies between aorist and imperfect in narrative equivalent.

Now I *put* the cake-mixture into this bowl and *add* a drop of vanilla essence'.[57] This sort of vivid, immediate narration is, at least originally, the force of the Greek historical present: a past event portrayed as though just occurring.

In contrast to this approach, the major alternative explanation of the historical present is the suggestion that it is a 'zero tense', which has no tense/aspect on its own but takes its force from the verbs with which it is conjoined in the context (i.e. past tenses). This view was advanced first by Kiparsky, who points to weaknesses in the other approach and speaks of 'the impossibility of adequately characterizing the so-called historical present on a semantic basis alone. Rather, a syntactic solution is called for'.[58] He explains his solution as follows:

It is beginning to look as if the historical present in early Indo-European is a present tense only in its superficial form. It functions syntactically as a past tense, as shown by sequence of tenses, it is semantically indistinguishable from the past tenses, and it alternates with these in conjoined structures.

Everything points to its being an underlying past tense, and its conversion into the present tense in the surface structure must be governed by a syntactic rule, evidently some form of conjunction reduction, which optionally reduces repeated occurrences of the same tense to the present.[59]

Thus, the sequence in Greek of '. . . Past . . . and . . . Past . . .' is changed to '. . . Past . . . and . . . zero . . .' and, Kiparsky

---

[57] Geoffrey N. Leech, *Meaning and the English Verb* (London: Longman, 1971), 2–3. He notes that most events of this sort do not take place precisely at the moment of speaking: 'it is subjective rather than objective simultaneity that is conveyed'.

[58] Paul Kiparsky, 'Tense and Mood in Indo-European Syntax', *FL* 4 (1968), 33. His view is anticipated to some degree by Karl Theodor Rodemeyer, *Das Präsens historicum bei Herodot und Thukydides* (Basle: Werner Riehm, 1889), who argues that the historical present simply indicates that the event described occurred at the time already given in the context; and more recently by Harald Weinrich, *Tempus: Besprochene und erzählte Welt* (Stuttgart: W. Kohlhammer, 1964), who posits zero tenses in the verb, but in a somewhat different sense.

[59] 'Tense and Mood in Indo-European Syntax', pp. 33–4. He adds in a footnote: 'I am using the term conjunction reduction rather loosely for all the various rules that factor out shared constituents in coordinate structures'. See sect. 3.5.2 for an explanation of conjunction reduction.

argues, 'since it is the present which is the zero tense, the reduced structure . . . Past . . . and . . . zero . . . is realized morphologically as . . . Past . . . and . . . Present . . .'.[60] According to this approach, the historical present does not possess heightened vividness or emphasis, but is merely a duplicate of the simple past. Others who follow Kiparsky's lead in this are Levin, Reynolds, and to some degree Osburn (the latter two apply the view to NT usage).[61]

Kiparsky's approach has, of course, not gone unchallenged. The main difficulty is that the pattern of 'past—and—present' which Kiparsky cites is not as common as (1) patterns of numerous pasts with a single or only a few presents inserted in the middle, or (2) numerous presents in uninterrupted series with or without a past at the beginning to set the temporal value.[62] Others have attacked the evidence he cites from older IE languages.[63]

Compared to this 'zero-tense' theory, the 'vivid' approach does a superior job of explaining the meaning of the present in the range of actual texts in which it occurs in ancient Greek. The present does appear to possess some degree of heightened vividness or narrative emphasis in a wide variety of literature.[64] However, this approach needs to be modified in two

---

[60] Ibid. 35.

[61] Saul Levin, 'Remarks on the "Historical" Present and Comparable Phenomena of Syntax', *FL* 5 (1969), 386–90; Stephen M. Reynolds, 'The Zero Tense in Greek: A Critical Note', *Westminster Theological Journal*, 33 (1969), 68–72; and Carroll D. Osburn, 'The Historical Present in Mark as a Text Critical Criterion', *Biblica*, 64 (1983), 486–500.

[62] K. L. McKay, 'Further Remarks on the "Historical" Present and other Phenomena', *FL* 11 (1974), 247–51; Nimrod Barri, 'The Greek Historical Present in a Double Verbal System', *Linguistics*, 204 (1978), 43–56; and Nessa Wolfson, 'The Conversational Historical Present Alternation', *Lg.* 55 (1979), 169. This is the critique of Rodemeyer's approach (similar to Kiparsky's) given by Karl Eriksson, *Das Praesens Historicum in der nachclassischen griechischen Historiographie* (Ph.D. thesis, University of Lund; Lund: H. Ohlsson, 1943), 11–12.

[63] For this as well as the most extensive overall critique of Kiparsky's approach, see Werner Thomas, *Historisches Präsens oder Konjunktionsreduktion? Zum Problem des Tempuswechsels in der Erzählung* (Wiesbaden: Franz Steiner, 1974), 1–88, esp. 72–88.

[64] See e.g. the arguments to this effect in Saara Lilja, *On the Style of the Earliest Greek Prose* (Helsinki: Societas Scientiarum Fennica, 1968), 109–19; Mandilaras, *Verb*, p. 109; and Moorhouse, *Syntax*, pp. 184–7.

directions, which will now be discussed in connection with applying the theory to NT usage.

One adjustment to the vivid approach is the observation that this portrayal often works its way out by *drawing attention to crucial events* or *highlighting new scenes or actors* in the narrative. This was suggested by Thackeray in regard to Septuagint usage (specifically in Samuel–Kings),[65] is mentioned by standard grammars and other treatments,[66] and has been developed at length by more recent writers, who describe this as part of the discourse-function of the historical present.[67] This sort of use shows up most clearly in the NT in Mark, where the historical present is used quite frequently—approximately 150 times, of which 72 are λέγει/λέγουσιν.[68] The use of the historical present with verbs of speaking like λέγει/λέγουσιν, φησίν, and so on appears to be a stereotyped idiom

---

[65] H. St. John Thackeray, *The Septuagint and Jewish Worship: A Study in Origins*, 2nd edn. (The Schweich Lectures; London: Oxford University Press, 1923), 20–2. Speaking of the dramatic type of historical present (not the annalistic), he says (p. 21): 'The tense as a rule is, I believe, "dramatic" in the sense that *it serves to introduce new scenes in the drama.* It heralds the arrival of a new character or a change of locality or marks a turning-point in the march of events. ... The main function is thus, I maintain, to introduce a date, a new scene, a new character, occasionally a new speaker; in other words a fresh paragraph in the narrative'. Later he adds (p. 22): 'I can only remark in passing that the presents in St. Mark (λέγει excluded) are used in a precisely similar way to introduce new scenes and characters . . . [they are] a feature which to the observant reader serves to divide the . . . Gospel into rough paragraphs'.

[66] Cf. SD, *Syntax*, p. 271; BDF, *Grammar*, § 321; Rijksbaron, *SSV*, pp. 22–5; Arvid Svensson, *Zum Gebrauch der erzählenden Tempora im Griechischen* (Ph.D. thesis, University of Lund; Lund: H. Ohlsson, 1930), 100–2; Eriksson, *Das Praesens Historicum*, pp. 8–11, 113; Fritz, 'Historical Present in Early Greek', 196, 199; and Lilja, *On the Style of the Earliest Greek Prose*, pp. 109–12, 116–17.

[67] Randy Buth, 'Mark's Use of the Historical Present', *Notes on Translation*, 65 (1977), 7–13; Stephen H. Levinsohn, 'Preliminary Observations on the Use of the Historical Present in Mark', *Notes on Translation*, 65 (1977), 13–28; Ralph Enos, 'The Use of the Historical Present in the Gospel According to St. Mark', *Journal of the Linguistic Association of the Southwest*, 3 (1981), 281–98; Osburn, 'Historical Present in Mark', pp. 495–500; and Ronald Lowell Shive, 'The Use of the Historical Present and its Theological Significance' (Th.M. thesis, Dallas Theological Seminary, 1982), 46–9, 76–95.

[68] John C. Hawkins, *Horae Synopticae: Contributions to the Study of the Synoptic Problem*, 2nd edn. (Oxford: Clarendon Press, 1909), 144–8.

without any sense of vividness or a discourse function,[69] but the other occurrences of the historical present display a clear pattern of discourse-structuring functions, such as to highlight the beginning of a paragraph, to introduce new participants into an existing paragraph, to show participants moving to new locations, or to portray key events in lively fashion (see examples cited below). In all of this the underlying point of the tense appears to be vivid narration, but the secondary development of that—highlighting new scenes or participants—comes to the fore more frequently. More specifically, the historical present (non-λέγει) occurs with the following discourse-functions in Mark.[70]

1. to begin a paragraph (usually indicating a new scene and new participants as well as a new unit of narrative)—1: 12, 2: 15, 2: 18, 3: 13 (bis), 3: 20 (bis), 3: 31, 4: 36 (after λέγει), 5: 35, 6: 30, 7: 1, 8: 22 (ter), 9: 2 (bis), 10: 1 (bis), 10: 35, 10: 46, 11: 1, 11: 15, 11: 27 (bis), 12: 13, 12: 18, 14: 17, 14: 32, 14: 43, 14: 66;

2. to introduce new participants in an existing paragraph or setting—1: 40, 2: 3, 4: 37, 14: 53;

3. to show participants moving to new locations within a paragraph—5: 15, 5: 38 (bis), 5: 40 (bis), 6: 1, 11: 7, 14: 33, 14: 37, 14: 41, 16: 2;

4. to begin a *specific* unit after a sentence introducing the *general* section in which it falls (Buth calls the sentence preceding the historical present 'a macro-episodic introductory sentence'[71])—4: 1, 5: 22–3, 6: 7, 7: 32.[72]

---

[69] Cf. BDF, *Grammar*, § 321: 'Λέγει, φησίν and the like appear to be especially vernacular (occasionally in Plut.) in the reporting of a conversation (λέγει chiefly in Mt, Mk, Jn, φησίν especially in Lk)'. So MT, *Syntax*, p. 61. An alternative view of the historical present with λέγει is offered by Levinsohn, 'Preliminary Observations on the Use of the Historical Present in Mark', pp. 15–16. He feels that it is used to denote the 'direction' which subsequent action or dialogue will take, but this is not borne out in NT usage.

[70] This is based on Buth's article, 'Mark's Use of the Historical Present,' pp. 7–13, but takes his work a bit further. The main deficiency in his analysis is a tendency to break the narrative up into too many small paragraphs based on the occurrence of historical presents. It seems better to see the tense doing other scene-changing duties within existing paragraphs.

There are only two types of exceptions in Mark to these discourse-functions: verbs with meanings like λέγει which occur in a stereotyped use (7: 5 ἐπερωτῶσιν, 8: 6 παραγγέλλει, 10: 49 φωνοῦσιν), and verbs which seem to occur with vivid narrative force (2: 4, 4: 38, 6: 48, 11: 4, 14: 13, 14: 51, 15: 16-27, 16: 4).[73] In the second type of exception the more basic sense reasserts itself, but it is possible in some of these to see a type of discourse-function as well as vivid narration—the use to highlight key events. This is true especially of Mark 15: 16–27, where nine historical presents occur in the account of the crucifixion; this may be 'a climax-marker' in the Gospel, as Buth notes.[74]

While these discourse-functions for the historical present seem valid in Mark, it is evident that not all paragraph-beginnings or changes within paragraphs are highlighted by the historical present. It is not clear how the present differs from other features used to structure the narrative.

Apart from the discourse use of the historical present, there is a second adjustment to the vivid approach which has been suggested. This is the observation that in some writers or with

[71] Ibid. 13; cf. 8, 9, 10.

[72] These discourse-functions for the historical present often leave concluding statements to the aorist, as the normal narrative tense. Thus, it seems unlikely that the thesis of F. C. Synge is correct in 'A Matter of Tenses: Fingerprints of an Annotator in Mark', *Exp. T.* 88 (1976), 168–71. He argues that such aorists are the work of a pre-Markan annotator who added (unnecessary) details to an original present-tense narrative. But shift to the aorist is part of structuring the discourse, not the sign of a different writer.

[73] In his brief treatment of the historical present in Mark, Doudna includes only these two types in his comments: John Charles Doudna, *The Greek of the Gospel of Mark* (Philadelphia: Society of Biblical Literature, 1961), 40–2.

[74] 'Mark's Use of the Historical Present', p. 13. Levinsohn, 'Preliminary Observations on the Use of the Historical Present in Mark', pp. 26–7, while observing something of the same discourse-functions which Buth notes, goes on to argue that Mark uses the historical present to give prominence to the crucial themes of his Gospel. This does not seem correct, since it can be shown that several themes which appear prominent on other grounds (e.g. discipleship) are not highlighted by historical presents. Osburn details this objection to Levinsohn in 'Historical Present in Mark', p. 496 n. 30.

some verbs the historical present is dulled to a *standard narrative tense which loses its original vivid force*. This is essentially the point mentioned already about verbs of speaking, which make up so many of the historical presents in the NT.[75] However, it seems to be true also about chains of historical presents in some writers, as Lilja notes about the repeated use in one of the early Greek historians:

If an author uses, as Pherecydes of Athens does, the narrative present throughout the story, or at least in all main sentences, that form lacks special significance from the stylistic point of view. In such cases the repeated use of the present tense might be explained as the author's individual predilection, perhaps originally conscious, but gradually becoming a habit. Perhaps we should explain the occurrence of several historic presents in succession as one present mechanically bringing along the others . . .[76]

This may be true of chains of historical presents in John, perhaps under the influence of his frequent use of λέγει (etc.) in such a way. It is certainly true of the seven historical presents in 2: 1–10 (only one non-λέγει use: φωνεῖ in v. 9); it seems to be true also of the fourteen in 4: 1–38 (all λέγει, but for ἔρχεται in vv. 5, 7); and perhaps this is the explanation for the fifteen in 1: 29–51 (4 non-λέγει), for which Blass posited a discourse-function.[77] More debatable are the chains of historical presents in 13: 1–30 (strings of non-λέγει examples in vv. 4–6, 24–6), 20: 1–29 (cf. vv. 1–2, 5–6), 21: 1–14 (cf. v. 13). It is possible in these cases to argue that the historical presents emphasize crucial events or give vivid portrayal of events, but

---

[75] For example, in John verbs of speaking make up 78% of the total historical presents (127 of 162, as corrected from the list of John J. O'Rourke, 'The Historical Present in the Gospel of John', *JBL* 93 [1974], 585–90). In Mark the proportion is 48% (72 of 151), in Matthew 73% (68 of 93), in Luke 73% (8 of 11), and in Acts 85% (11 of 13), according to the count of Hawkins, *Horae Synopticae*, pp. 144–9.

[76] Lilja, *On the Style of the Earliest Greek Prose*, p. 117; see also p. 109.

[77] Cf. BDF, *Grammar*, § 321: 'thus the circumstances, or all that is secondary, are given in a past tense; on the other hand the main action is likely to be represented by the present, while the concluding events are again put into the aor. because here a historical present would not be natural'. Verses from John 1: 29–43 are cited as illustrations of this.

in each passage they are mixed with verses and paragraphs in which narration of events which seem equally significant is given in past tenses (e.g. 13: 7, 12, 21; 20: 3–4, 7–8, 19–23; 21: 6–8). It seems that the choice of tenses in some of these cases is due to a combination of a kind of 'linguistic momentum' (use of one historical present prompts several in series) and an idiomatic predilection to use the historical present more commonly with some verbs. For example, among the 162 instances in John several verbs predominate: λέγω (122 times), ἔρχομαι (13), βλέπω (5), θεωρέω (4), εὑρίσκω (4).[78]

The preceding discussion covers the historical present in Mark and John, who use it more frequently by far than other NT writers. A few comments are needed now on its usage (and relative non-usage) in the other major narrative books of the NT: Matthew and Luke–Acts. Before discussing these details, however, a few notes about the historical present in ancient Greek in general will be useful as background.

The historical present is not used in Homer or Pindar (with only a few exceptions), but this is usually explained as a matter of stylistic choice.[79] It is used freely by historians, dramatists, and orators of the classical period but in different ways.[80]

---

[78] Cf. O'Rourke, 'Historical Present in the Gospel of John', pp. 585–6. Henry St. John Thackeray, 'The Greek Translators of the Four Books of Kings', *JTS* 8 (1906), 273–4, reports that verbs of seeing, coming, and sending are often found in the historical present in the LXX, but not verbs of saying.

[79] Gildersleeve, *Syntax*, § 200; SD, *Syntax*, p. 271. Fritz, 'Historical Present in Early Greek', p. 195, argues that it does not occur in Homer because 'the Greek language of that early period . . . did not permit an event of the past and of definite extension in time to be expressed by the so-called present tense'. Lilja, *On the Style of the Earliest Greek Prose*, pp. 102–3, notes: 'Actually there are some historic presents in Homer, sufficiently many to prove that FRITZ is wrong, and few enough to corroborate the view that the avoidance of them was due to stylistic reasons'. Lilja suggests that Homeric style seeks to give the impression of 'very distant, truly prehistoric times', and thus avoids the immediacy of the historical present.

[80] For example, in Sophocles historical presents usually occur singly within a series of aorists and imperfects, but they appear 'at specially dramatic moments', according to Moorhouse, *Syntax*, pp. 184–6. On the other hand, historical presents can be found in long, unbroken series either introduced or followed by a past tense verb, e.g. in a number of early historians studied by Lilja, *On the Style of the Earliest Greek Prose*,

In Hellenistic Greek there is also a varied picture. According to Eriksson, the historical present died out in standard literary Koine ('die normalen Schriftprosen der Koine'), such as that of Polybius and Diodorus. It continued to be used readily, however, in the vernacular Koine, as for example in the NT and the Septuagint. In addition, it was revived in works influenced by classical style ('die Kunstprosa der Klassizisten'), where it was used in imitation of the classic historians. In this category Eriksson includes writers such as Dionysius of Halicarnassus, Herodian, and Nicolaus of Damascus.[81]

This sketch of the pattern of usage is correct, but the reasons for it are not entirely clear. The historical present occurs only infrequently in Polybius and Diodorus,[82] and it is usually said that these writers avoided it as unliterary.[83] An advance on this is the idea that they rejected it as a feature of style too 'popular' and novelistic and thus not suitable for their ideas of objective historical narration.[84]

---

pp. 107–19; in Thuc. 7. 43. 3–4 and Hdt. 1. 106. 3–107. 1, cited by McKay, 'Further Remarks on the "Historical" Present', p. 247; and in a number of other passages of Thucydides cited by Rose, *Durative and Aoristic Tenses in Thucydides*, pp. 27–30. See the summary of how the historical present is used in classical writers in Eriksson, *Das Praesens Historicum*, pp. 21–4. He observes (pp. 8–11) the use of the historical present in Xenophon, Thucydides, and Herodotus to introduce important points in the narrative, as described earlier in this section.

[81] Eriksson, *Das Praesens Historicum*, pp. 25–8, 112–13. He makes a distinction between writers who are strongly Atticizing (e.g. Arrian) and others who are influenced to a lesser degree. It is writers of the latter group who are described above.

[82] Jules-Albert de Foucault, *Recherches sur la langue et le style de Polybe* (Paris: Les Belles Lettres, 1972), 127–8, notes that it is rather infrequent in Polybius (only 56 in the first five books, e.g. 19 in 120 pages of text for the first book), but he offers no explanation for this. Eriksson, *Das Praesens Historicum*, also notes the infrequent occurrence in Polybius (pp. 29–38) and Diodorus (pp. 25–6), but he attributes it not so much to the individual choice of the writer but to the larger stylistic development of literary Koine.

[83] For a summary of this and its implications for the style and sources of the Gospels and Acts see G. D. Kilpatrick, 'The Historic Present in the Gospels and Acts', *ZNW* 68 (1977), 258–62.

[84] For example, Jonas Palm, *Über Sprache und Stil des Diodorus von Sizilien* (Lund: C. W. K. Gleerup, 1955), 83–4, attributes its absence in Diodorus to a preference for a less emotional, more literary style as opposed to the oral, spoken character of e.g. the

Among writers with no aspirations to literary style (i.e. most vernacular Koine writers), the historical present appears often, limited only by the genre of literature. So it appears readily in the Septuagint,[85] in the papyri,[86] and in books like Mark and John.

Finally, the historical present occurs frequently among Koine writers influenced by classical style. For example, in Josephus it is common, apparently for this reason.[87] As already mentioned, Eriksson includes Dionysius of Halicarnassus, Herodian, and Nicolaus of Damascus in this category.[88] Perhaps Plutarch and Dio Chrysostom can also be cited.[89] According to Eriksson, the historical present in these writers follows two characteristics: (1) a tendency towards stereotyped use with some verbs and expressions; and (2) usage to emphasize important events and appeal to the feeling

---

Anabasis and vernacular Koine writers, where the historical present is common. This is the explanation given also by Eriksson, *Das Praesens Historicum*, p. 114, for the infrequency of usage in Dio Cassius: in imitation of Thucydides, he specifically rejected the style of 'popular romance' found in some historical writers of his time.

[85] According to the count given in Hawkins, *Horae Synopticae*, pp. 213–14, the historical present occurs 337 times in the LXX, but these come predominantly from a few books: 1 Kingdoms (151), 2 Kingdoms (32), 3 Kingdoms (47), Job (25), and Exodus (24); compared with 58 in the remaining 17 books in which it occurs at all. Of course, LXX Greek differs in stylistic level from book to book, and many books are not narrative in genre.

[86] The historical present does not appear often in the papyri, but this is due to the nature of most papyrus documents of the Hellenistic period (e.g. bills, receipts, personal letters, public documents), in which narrative itself is little used. However, examples are not lacking, and both Mayser, *Grammatik*, p. 131, and Mandilaras, *Verb*, p. 109, cite particularly its use in petitions about criminal acts, in which the plaintiff records the decisive events and chief points of complaint in the present, to give the most vivid portrayal of the deeds done against him and thus increase his chance of gaining redress for the damages suffered.

[87] Eriksson, *Das Praesens Historicum*, pp. 76–82, 113. He reports that Josephus uses the historical present an average of 188 times per 100 pages of text in the *Antiquities* and 175 times per 100 pages in the *Jewish War*. This is comparable to an average of 165 per 100 pages in Xenophon. Eriksson's view is that Josephus was influenced both by classicizing writers of his own time and by exposure to the classical writers themselves. Kilpatrick, 'Historic Present', p. 261, also cites Josephus as Atticizing in his use of the historical present.

[88] Eriksson, *Das Praesens Historicum*, pp. 25–8, 39–69, 113–14.

[89] Kilpatrick, 'Historic Present', p. 261.

or fantasies of the readers, in order to give a more lively novelistic style to the narrative. In his opinion, the latter feature explains why some later writers choose or reject the historical present, depending on whether they prefer this narrative style or think it unsuitable.[90]

The point of this variety is that the historical present appears to be available through a broad period of ancient Greek, but its use by a particular writer can be greatly influenced by individual style or by changing opinions of its acceptability. The use of the historical present in Matthew and Luke–Acts must be seen in this light. In comparison to Mark and John, Matthew uses the historical present rather infrequently (93 times; 68 are verbs of speaking) and Luke–Acts uses it extremely infrequently (Luke: 11 times; 8 verbs of speaking; Acts: 13 times; 11 verbs of speaking).[91] This difference in frequency is essentially a matter of individual style, as discussed above. In regard to the historical present, Matthew seems to be neutral, neither favouring it nor rigorously avoiding it, while Luke clearly goes out of his way to avoid it.[92] In numerous parallels where Mark has historical presents, Matthew and Luke have aorists. Compared to Mark, Matthew exhibits a parallel historical present twenty-one times and Luke only once (8: 49). Matthew, of course, uses the historical present an additional seventy-two times (of which fifteen are in parables, a use not found in Mark), while Luke displays only ten others (five in parables) in his Gospel and only thirteen in all of Acts. In terms of frequency, then, Matthew is somewhere between Mark and Luke, while Luke almost never uses the historical present. So it is clear that Luke, like some other Hellenistic writers, avoids the historical

---

[90] Eriksson, *Das Praesens Historicum*, pp. 112–14.

[91] Hawkins, *Horae Synopticae*, pp. 143–9.

[92] This point is made on the basis of frequency alone, apart from any theory of Synoptic dependency. As E. P. Sanders, *The Tendencies of the Synoptic Tradition* (Cambridge: at the University Press, 1969), 253–4, points out, use or non-use of the historical present cannot by itself be used to determine priority of sources. If Matthew and Luke did use Mark (as I prefer to see it), the argument here is strengthened.

present, and perhaps this is because he regarded it as unsuitable for the kind of objective historical account which he attempts to give (Luke 1: 1–4).[93] There is no evidence that the greater frequency of the historical present in Mark and John and the lesser use in Matthew and Luke has anything to do with Aramaic influence, as some have argued.[94]

When the historical present does occur in Matthew and Luke–Acts, it has either the stereotyped sense of simple narrative (usually verbs of speaking) or some sort of vivid sense—either in dramatic narration of an event (e.g. Matt. 13: 44 [ter], Luke 16: 23, Acts 10: 11) or in emphasis on an important event or a shift in the narrative (Matt. 4: 5, 8 [bis]).[95] Some of Mark's use to denote new units of the narrative appear in Matthew (e.g. 2: 13, 3: 1, 3: 13, all independently of Mark), but not as systematically.

4. 1. 9 *Perfective present*

There is one more category of present usage which is relatively minor in importance, the present used with 'perfective' meaning. Only a limited number of verbs appear in this use, but they do reflect a meaning which is like the aspect-value of the perfect tense in Greek: they denote a present state or condition and imply the occurrence of an action which produced that condition. Except for the latter feature, one might simply dismiss the whole category as examples of the STATIVE lexical class. As a matter of fact the verbs which occur in this category are very close in sense to STATES, and some verbs listed by the

[93] Cf. Kilpatrick, 'Historic Present', pp. 259–62; MT, *Syntax*, pp. 60–1; and Robertson, *Grammar*, p. 868.

[94] Matthew Black, *An Aramaic Approach to the Gospels and Acts*, 3rd edn. (Oxford: Clarendon Press, 1967), 130; and Ernest Cadman Colwell, *The Greek of the Fourth Gospel: A Study of its Aramaisms in the Light of Hellenistic Greek* (Chicago: University of Chicago Press, 1931), 64–7. Cf. Thackeray, *The Septuagint and Jewish Worship*, pp. 20–1; and Sanders, *Tendencies of the Synoptic Tradition*, pp. 253–4.

[95] Cf. Wolfgang Schenk, 'Das Präsens historicum als makrosyntaktisches Gliederungssignal im Matthäusevangelium', *NTS* 22 (1976), 464–75, who argues that the historical present occurs with a discourse-function in Matt. to emphasize the chief point in a pericope.

grammars as perfective presents should be regarded as merely STATIVE.[96] However, there are verbs which imply an action as well as the condition which was produced by it, and such a sense is distinctive enough and overlaps with the perfect tense sufficiently to warrant classification into a separate category of present usage.[97] The verbs which legitimately seem to fit the perfective use are ἥκω, ἀπέχω, ἀκούω, and πάρειμι. The latter three occur as perfectives only sometimes, while ἥκω is almost always perfective.[98] Some examples are:

Matt. 6: 2 (also 6: 5, 16) ἀπέχουσιν τὸν μισθὸν αὐτῶν

Luke 15: 27 ὁ ἀδελφός σου ἥκει

16: 2 τί τοῦτο ἀκούω περὶ σοῦ; (cf. Luke 9: 9, customary use of same verb)

John 8: 42 ἐγὼ γὰρ ἐκ τοῦ θεοῦ ἐξῆλθον καὶ ἥκω

Acts 10: 21 τίς ἡ αἰτία δι' ἣν πάρεστε;

17: 6 οἱ τὴν οἰκουμένην ἀναστατώσαντες οὗτοι καὶ ἐνθάδε πάρεισιν

1 Cor. 11: 18 ἀκούω σχίσματα ἐν ὑμῖν ὑπάρχειν

Phil. 4: 18 ἀπέχω δὲ πάντα καὶ περισσεύω

2 Thess. 3: 11 ἀκούομεν γάρ τινας περιπατοῦντας ἐν ὑμῖν ἀτάκτως

1 John 5: 20 οἴδαμεν δὲ ὅτι ὁ υἱὸς τοῦ θεοῦ ἥκει καὶ δέδωκεν ὑμῖν διάνοιαν

4. 2 Uses of the Imperfect Indicative

The imperfect indicative is much like the present indicative in that it takes the basic aspect-value of the present ('internal viewpoint on an occurrence') and displays many of the same particular applications of this aspect. The major difference, of course, is that the imperfect moves this aspect-value into the past-time frame, since it indicates *past* tense (i.e. occurrence

---

[96] E.g. ἀδικέω, νικάω.

[97] The perfective present is listed by a number of grammars, most of which limit it to a small range of verbs such as that given above. See KG, *Satzlehre*, pp. 135–7; SD, *Syntax*, pp. 274–5; Klose, *Der Indikativ des Präsens*, pp. 182–223; BDF, *Grammar*, § 322; Robertson, *Grammar*, p. 881; Abel, *Grammaire*, p. 251; Mayser, *Grammatik*, pp. 132–3; MT, *Syntax*, p. 62; Mandilaras, *Verb*, pp. 99–102; and HS, *Grammatik*, p. 319.

[98] See BAGD, *Lexicon*, pp. 32–3, 84–5, 344, 624.

antecedent to the time of speaking). The meanings which result from the combination of past tense and internal viewpoint will be detailed below. The three major uses of the imperfect, however, are virtually identical in aspect-value to the corresponding categories of the present, so these will be treated more briefly, assuming the foundation of the discussion given above.

4. 2. 1 *Progressive or descriptive imperfect*

The aspectual function displayed in the progressive or descriptive imperfect is identical to the corresponding use of the present indicative (see 4.1.1): it has a narrow frame of reference, and thus it portrays a *specific* situation (action or state) viewed *as it is going on*.[99] The difference from the progressive present, of course, is the temporal shift: the imperfect views the situation as it goes on in *past* time. The aspectual viewpoint of the present is reflected in this use by the close focus on the internal process or state without reference to the beginning or end-point of the situation. The combination of these features produces either vivid narration of a situation in the past[100] or the presentation of an occurrence in close simultaneity with another situation in the past.[101] The characteristic of this use, in contrast to the next use of the imperfect, is the immediate and specific nature of the reference to the situation 'as it is taking place' or 'as it is existing' at a particular point in the past. It portrays what *was*

---

[99] See the comment of Willam W. Goodwin, *Syntax of the Moods and Tenses of the Greek Verb* (Boston: Ginn and Co., 1890), § 35, on this use of the imperfect: 'if it refers to a single action (as it very frequently does), it represents it in its progress'.

[100] Many have noted the descriptive effect of the imperfect: KG, *Satzlehre*, p. 143; Gildersleeve, *Syntax*, § 207; Stahl, *Syntax*, pp. 96–8; Jean Humbert, *Syntaxe grecque*, 3rd edn. (Paris: Klincksieck, 1960), 139–40; BDF, *Grammar*, § 327; and Moorhouse, *Syntax*, pp. 189–90 ('a graphic use, that of the "eye-witness", with vivid presentation of the event'). However, it seems to be vivid primarily when the imperfect refers to a *specific* situation, since the customary imperfect (sect. 4.2.2) does not produce this effect.

[101] Cf. Abel, *Grammaire*, p. 253; Mayser, *Grammatik*, p. 135; and BW, *Syntax*, p. 83.

occurring at that point, not what *did occur* in a broader frame of time.

Matt. 26: 58 ὁ δὲ Πέτρος ἠκολούθει αὐτῷ ἀπὸ μακρόθεν ἕως τῆς αὐλῆς τοῦ ἀρχιερέως καὶ εἰσελθὼν ἔσω ἐκάθητο μετὰ τῶν ὑπηρετῶν ἰδεῖν τὸ τέλος

Mark 12: 41 ἐθεώρει πῶς ὁ ὄχλος βάλλει χαλκὸν εἰς τὸ γαζοφυλάκιον, καὶ πολλοὶ πλούσιοι ἔβαλλον πολλά

Luke 1: 62 ἐνένευον δὲ τῷ πατρὶ αὐτοῦ
18: 11, 13 ὁ Φαρισαῖος . . . προσηύχετο . . . ὁ δὲ τελώνης . . . ἔτυπτεν τὸ στῆθος

Acts 16: 13–14 ἐλαλοῦμεν ταῖς συνελθούσαις γυναιξίν. καί τις γυνὴ ὀνόματι Λυδία . . . ἤκουεν

Like the progressive present, this use of the imperfect involves an occurrence which is durative, since the actional constraints of viewing a situation 'as it goes on' require an appreciable temporal extension. Thus, the verb-types which usually occur in this use are the three durative types, STATES, ACTIVITIES, and ACCOMPLISHMENTS (with emphasis on the continuing process, not on failure to reach the terminus). CLIMAXES may also occur if the emphasis is on the prefaced process rather than on the instantaneous point of transition. Even PUNCTUALS can occur, when they relate multiple occurrences viewed together as taking place in close sequence. However, it must be nòted that the durative sense comes from the lexical character of the verb or from other contextual features, and not directly from the imperfect itself: the aspect-value of the imperfect should not be identified as durative.

Active verbs in this use are normally translated into English with the 'past progressive form', which communicates well the sense of 'action viewed as it is taking place in the past'. When a Greek STATIVE verb occurs in this use, however, English idiom does not readily permit a progressive form to be used, even though it is parallel to the active in its specific reference: that is, it describes a *specific* condition in existence at the point in the past which is in focus. This difference in English translation idiom does not reflect a difference in Greek aspectual force.

Matt. 25: 5 ἐνύσταξαν πᾶσαι καὶ ἐκάθευδον
26: 63 ὁ δὲ Ἰησοῦς ἐσιώπα
Luke 8: 23 καὶ κατέβη λαῖλαψ ἀνέμου . . . καὶ ἐκινδύνευον
Acts 15: 37–8 Βαρναβᾶς δὲ ἐβούλετο . . . Παῦλος δὲ ἠξίου . . .

The nature of this use of the imperfect often puts it in clear contrast to the aorists which may occur in a text around it. By focusing on a specific occurrence as it takes place, progressive imperfects contrast with aorists in two major ways. The contrast at times is one of *descriptive vs. factual* narration: the imperfect highlights the manner of the occurrence while the aorist merely relates the fact of it.[102] This distinction can show up in contrasting paragraphs or larger sections each containing predominantly aorists or imperfects, or as a mixture of aorists and imperfects within the same paragraph. In these larger units, strings of imperfects give a tone of vivid, lively description (which as a consequence seems to move more slowly),[103] while aorists give a straightforward recounting which moves along more rapidly.[104]

Mark 9: 20 καὶ ἤνεγκαν αὐτὸν πρὸς αὐτόν. καὶ ἰδὼν αὐτὸν τὸ πνεῦμα εὐθὺς συνεσπάραξεν αὐτόν, καὶ πεσὼν ἐπὶ τῆς γῆς ἐκυλίετο ἀφρίζων (or inceptive?)

Acts 3: 1–5 five imperfects (one customary) with one aorist in this narrative give a picturesque quality to the section, in contrast to 2: 1–4, in which the narrative is carried rapidly along by six aorists with three imperfects (first two give background information and the last is simultaneous to the final aorist)

8: 28 ἦν τε ὑποστρέφων καὶ καθήμενος ἐπὶ τοῦ ἅρματος αὐτοῦ καὶ ἀνεγίνωσκεν τὸν προφήτην Ἠσαίαν (two periphrastic imperfects in the verse give the same descriptive force)

8: 38–40a seven aorists give the basic narration with one imperfect

---

[102] Cf. Robertson, *Grammar*, p. 883; and MT, *Syntax*, p. 66.

[103] The events related, however, must be *specific*. If the reference is to general occurrence, the imperfect in such strings has a different effect. See next section.

[104] This point about *pace* of the narrative is made by W. B. Sedgwick, 'The Use of the Imperfect in Herodotus', *CQ*, NS 7 (1957), 116–17, and is developed by W. F. Bakker, 'A Remark on the Use of the Imperfect and the Aorist in Herodotus', *Mnemosyne*, 4th ser. 21 (1968), 26–7.

presenting more vivid description, aided by a manner participle: ἐπορεύετο . . . χαίρων (cf. 5: 40–1)

On the other hand, the contrast of progressive imperfects with aorists may involve the temporal feature of *simultaneous vs. sequential* occurrence. The imperfect can be used of particular situations which were going on at the same time as another event, while an aorist usually involves an occurrence which took place in its entirety before the next situation narrated and thus sets up a sequence of events.[105] This 'simultaneous' imperfect can appear in paragraphs with a mixture of aorists and imperfects or in a section of predominantly imperfects, all of which are understood to take place at more or less the same time.

Matt. 8: 24 καὶ ἰδοὺ σεισμὸς μέγας ἐγένετο ἐν τῇ θαλάσσῃ, ὥστε τὸ πλοῖον καλύπτεσθαι ὑπὸ τῶν κυμάτων, αὐτὸς δὲ ἐκάθευδεν

Luke 7: 6 ὁ δὲ Ἰησοῦς ἐπορεύετο σὺν αὐτοῖς . . . δὲ . . . ἔπεμψεν φίλους ὁ ἑκατοντάρχης . . .

10: 30 ἄνθρωπός τις κατέβαινεν ἀπὸ Ἰερουσαλὴμ εἰς Ἰεριχὼ καί λῃσταῖς περιέπεσεν

Acts 2: 12–13 ἐξίσταντο δὲ πάντες καὶ διηπόρουν, ἄλλος πρὸς ἄλλον λέγοντες· τί θέλει τοῦτο εἶναι; ἕτεροι δὲ διαχλευάζοντες ἔλεγον ὅτι γλεύκους μεμεστωμένοι εἰσίν

12: 15–16 οἱ δὲ πρὸς αὐτὴν εἶπαν· μαίνῃ. ἡ δὲ διισχυρίζετο οὕτως ἔχειν. οἱ δὲ ἔλεγον· ὁ ἄγγελός ἐστιν αὐτοῦ. ὁ δὲ Πέτρος ἐπέμενεν κρούων

Another group of verbs which often appear in the imperfect with progressive sense are verbs of asking or commanding and verbs of speaking. These have a more specialized sense, however, and they will be treated in the later excursus on aorist vs. imperfect used with such verbs (4.4).

4. 2. 2 *Customary or iterative imperfect*

The other major use of the imperfect is the customary or iterative, which, in comparison with the progressive, broadens

---

[105] Radermacher, *Grammatik*, p. 156, mentions this briefly. More recently, this is argued in Rijksbaron, *SSV*, pp. 12–16, and Heinrich Hettrich, *Kontext und Aspekt in der*

out the focus and holds a wider frame of the situation in view, as the customary present does. It refers not to what *was going on* or *was in existence* in the past, but to what *did take place or exist*.[106] The situation in view will be an ACTIVITY or STATE which continues without interruption over a broad range of time, or (more frequently) it will be an action or state which occurs repeatedly in a wide time-frame. The iterative sense is more likely with CLIMAXES and PUNCTUALS, since their instantaneous character can hardly fit into a broad time-frame unless repetition of the event is denoted. Some illustrations of this use are:

Luke 2: 51 καὶ ἡ μήτηρ αὐτοῦ διετήρει πάντα τὰ ῥήματα ἐν τῇ καρδίᾳ αὐτῆς
      8: 29 πολλοῖς γὰρ χρόνοις συνηρπάκει αὐτὸν καὶ ἐδεσμεύετο ἁλύσεσιν καὶ πέδαις φυλασσόμενος καὶ διαρρήσσων τὰ δεσμὰ ἠλαύνετο ὑπὸ τοῦ δαιμονίου εἰς τὰς ἐρήμους
      17: 27 ἤσθιον, ἔπινον, ἐγάμουν, ἐγαμίζοντο, ἄχρι . . .
      21: 37–8 ἦν δὲ τὰς ἡμέρας ἐν τῷ ἱερῷ διδάσκων, τὰς δὲ νύκτας ἐξερχόμενος ηὐλίζετο εἰς τὸ ὄρος τὸ καλούμενον Ἐλαιῶν· καὶ πᾶς ὁ λαὸς ὤρθριζεν πρὸς αὐτὸν ἐν τῷ ἱερῷ ἀκούειν αὐτοῦ
      24: 21 ἡμεῖς δὲ ἠλπίζομεν ὅτι αὐτὸς ἐστιν ὁ μέλλων λυτροῦσθαι τὸν Ἰσραήλ

John 3: 22 ἐκεῖ διέτριβεν μετ' αὐτῶν καὶ ἐβάπτιζεν.
      11: 36 ἴδε πῶς ἐφίλει αὐτόν

Acts 6: 7 καὶ ὁ λόγος τοῦ θεοῦ ηὔξανεν καὶ ἐπληθύνετο ὁ ἀριθμὸς τῶν μαθητῶν ἐν Ἰερουσαλήμ σφόδρα, πολύς τε ὄχλος τῶν ἱερέων ὑπήκουον τῇ πίστει

---

altgriechischen Prosa Herodots (Göttingen: Vandenhoeck and Ruprecht, 1976), 12–24, 94–7. They emphasize this event-sequencing function for the imperfect and aorist, and it is valid in its place. However, this is not the primary value of these, as they have argued. See sect. 1.1.3 and 1.4.3.

[106] Grammars often list this category as 'iterative/habitual', but they emphasize the repetition of the occurrence more than the customary or general sense. As a result, they usually include a mixture of habitual imperfects (suggesting translations like 'used to do', 'was accustomed to do') along with some very specific iteratives: e.g. Mark 12: 41 ἔβαλλον, Matt. 27: 30 ἔτυπτον. Cf. BDF, *Grammar*, § 325; Robertson, *Grammar*, p. 884; and MT, *Syntax*, p. 67. In contrast to this approach, it seems better to highlight the difference of narrow vs. broad reference, and separate the uses as done here.

8: 3 Σαῦλος δὲ ἐλυμαίνετο τὴν ἐκκλησίαν κατὰ τοὺς οἴκους εἰσπορευόμενος, σύρων τε ἄνδρας καὶ γυναῖκας παρεδίδου εἰς φυλακήν

18: 3–4 καὶ διὰ τὸ ὁμότεχνον εἶναι ἔμενεν παρ' αὐτοῖς, καὶ ἠργάζετο . . . διελέγετο δὲ ἐν τῇ συναγωγῇ κατὰ πᾶν σάββατον ἔπειθέν τε Ἰουδαίους καὶ Ἕλληνας

18: 8 πολλοὶ τῶν Κορινθίων ἀκούοντες ἐπίστευον καὶ ἐβαπτίζοντο

Rom. 6: 17 ἦτε δοῦλοι τῆς ἁμαρτίας ὑπηκούσατε δὲ ἐκ καρδίας

1 Cor. 6: 11 καὶ ταῦτά τινες ἦτε· ἀλλὰ ἀπελούσασθε (last three illustrate the use of the imperfect—usually customary—to contrast *past* with *present*)

Just like the customary present, the imperfect can be used for situations which are habitual or characteristic of a person or thing. The more an act is repeated or the longer a state or process continues, the more likely it is to be regarded as genuinely characteristic of the subject. Thus, something which is frequent, normal, or regular in occurrence is usually taken as characteristic. Sometimes this is reinforced by adverbs noting the regularity.

Matt. 26: 55 καθ' ἡμέραν ἐν τῷ ἱερῷ ἐκαθεζόμην διδάσκων καὶ οὐκ ἐκρατήσατέ με

Mark 15: 6 κατὰ δὲ ἑορτὴν ἀπέλυεν αὐτοῖς ἕνα δέσμιον

Luke 2: 41 καὶ ἐπορεύοντο οἱ γονεῖς αὐτοῦ κατ' ἔτος εἰς Ἰερουσαλὴμ τῇ ἑορτῇ

6: 23 κατὰ τὰ αὐτὰ γὰρ ἐποίουν τοῖς προφήταις οἱ πατέρες αὐτῶν

John 5: 18 οὐ μόνον ἔλυεν τὸ σάββατον, ἀλλὰ καὶ πατέρα ἴδιον ἔλεγεν τὸν Θεόν

21: 18 ὅτε ἦς νεώτερος, ἐζώννυες σεαυτὸν καὶ περιεπάτεις ὅπου ἤθελες

Acts 3: 2 ὃν ἐτίθουν καθ' ἡμέραν πρὸς τὴν θύραν τοῦ ἱεροῦ

16: 18 τοῦτο δὲ ἐποίει ἐπὶ πολλὰς ἡμέρας

Just as for the corresponding present uses, the difference between narrow and broad reference (in the progressive and customary imperfects) is at times difficult to establish, and borderline cases can be found. However, many instances are clear-cut, and the difference between specific reference and general reference with the imperfect can be a useful insight into a text under study.

Matt. 3: 4–6 αὐτὸς δὲ Ἰωάννης εἶχεν τὸ ἔνδυμα αὐτοῦ ἀπὸ τριχῶν καμήλου. . . τότε ἐξεπορεύετο πρὸς αὐτὸν Ἱεροσόλυμα καὶ πᾶσα ἡ Ἰουδαία καὶ πᾶσα ἡ περίχωρος τοῦ Ἰορδάνου, καὶ ἐβαπτίζοντο ἐν τῷ Ἰορδάνῃ ποταμῷ ὑπ' αὐτοῦ (Could 5–6 be descriptive, vivid narration? The repetition of πᾶς makes it more likely to be general background, with a shift in vv. 7 ff. to a specific account of a typical occasion of his ministry)

Mark 4: 33 καὶ τοιαύταις παραβολαῖς πολλαῖς ἐλάλει αὐτοῖς τὸν λόγον καθὼς ἠδύναντο ἀκούειν· χωρὶς δὲ παραβολῆς οὐκ ἐλάλει αὐτοῖς, κατ' ἰδίαν δὲ τοῖς ἰδίοις μαθηταῖς ἐπέλυεν πάντα (almost certainly a general summary of Jesus' teaching-method at this time, but in the light of Mark's frequent descriptive use of imperfects, could this be a vivid narration of events in a narrower frame?)

15: 3 καὶ κατηγόρουν αὐτοῦ οἱ ἀρχιερεῖς πολλά (descriptive of a period of intense accusations or a summary of their testimony?)

Luke 15: 16 καὶ ἐπεθύμει χορτασθῆναι ἐκ τῶν κερατίων ὧν ἤσθιον οἱ χοῖροι, καὶ οὐδεὶς ἐδίδου αὐτῷ (last verb is customary, but could the first two be descriptive of the occasion when, in great need, he 'came to himself' and decided to return home?)

What is more clear-cut in some passages is the difference between a customary imperfect and an aorist which relates a particular occurrence in the past. This is another important difference between imperfect and aorist in narrative, and it can combine with other features to reflect two types of distinctions. One is the difference between *specific* and *generalized* narrative. This difference appears when entire paragraphs or larger sections contain mainly aorists or imperfects, and not in places where there is a mixture of aorists and imperfects within the same unit. The point to be noted here is that aorists in series often relate specific, usually single, occurrences,[107] while customary imperfects relate generalized, usually multiple, occurrences. In contrast to specific imperfects which highlight the manner of the action in a vivid way (as noted in

---

[107] While this is common, aorists are, of course, not always specific in reference. The aorist is sometimes used of generalized, multiple, or broad-based occurrences which are summed up and reported in their entirety, without the emphasis on the internal make-up (i.e. the repetition) which the imperfect displays.

section 4. 2. 1), this type of imperfect tends to be less vivid than the aorist, since it is so general that it produces a somewhat remote tone in the narrative. One gets the impression that a great deal takes place in the general time-frame which is narrated, but the narrative is less direct and immediate than with aorists. Strings of imperfects such as this occur at a number of places in the book of Acts, where Luke records 'summaries of church growth' (2: 41–7, 4: 32–5, 5: 12–16, in addition to briefer 'summaries'). It occurs also in the Gospels and elsewhere with similar generalized meanings, as shown below.

Acts 5: 1–11 (22 aorists, 2 imperfects, 1 future: particular account of Ananias and Sapphira in contrast to 5: 12–16 with 6 imperfects denoting general events occurring at that time)

Mark 6: 55b–6 (Shift in 6: 55 from specific narrative with mainly aorist verbs to generalized summary with 5 customary imperfects, and 2 occurrences of ἄν to supplement the generalized sense)

Gal. 1: 13–14 (3 customary imperfects in contrast to 1: 15–21 with aorists denoting specific events)

The second type of contrast between customary imperfect and aorist is the difference of *foreground* events vs. *background* circumstances. Here the imperfect usually occurs singly in a series of aorists, and it relates parenthetical or explanatory information supplementing the main narrative given by the aorists.[108] This is noted by some writers as a discourse-function for the two tenses, in that the alternation of tenses is a means by which a writer can structure a larger discourse and indicate the relative prominence of the situations being described.[109]

Mark 5: 1–20 (main narrative carried by aorists and historical presents, with imperfect filling in background details)

---

[108] Cf. Smyth, *Grammar*, § 1899; McKay, *Greek Grammar for Students*, pp. 142–3. Abel, *Grammaire*, p. 254, mentions that parenthetical notes about geography (e.g. John 4: 6, 11: 18) are usually imperfect.
[109] Cf. 1.4.2 and the literature cited there.

Acts 6: 1 ἐγένετο γογγυσμός . . . ὅτι παρεθεωροῦντο ἐν τῇ διακονίᾳ τῇ καθημερινῇ αἱ χῆραι αὐτῶν

7: 20–5 (9 aorists carry the basic narrative; 4 imperfects give background)

10: 44–8 (one imperfect in v. 46: explanatory in the midst of 6 aorists which tell the basic story)

11: 29–30 τῶν δὲ μαθητῶν, καθὼς εὐπορεῖτό τις, ὥρισαν ἕκαστος αὐτῶν εἰς διακονίαν πέμψαι τοῖς κατοικοῦσιν ἐν τῇ Ἰουδαίᾳ ἀδελφοῖς· ὃ καὶ ἐποίησαν

1 Cor. 3: 6 ἐγὼ ἐφύτευσα, Ἀπολλῶς ἐπότισεν, ἀλλὰ ὁ θεὸς ηὔξανεν

10: 2–4 καὶ πάντες εἰς τὸν Μωϋσῆν ἐβαπτίσθησαν ἐν τῇ νεφέλῃ καὶ ἐν τῇ θαλάσσῃ καὶ πάντες τὸ αὐτὸ πνευματικὸν βρῶμα ἔφαγον καὶ πάντες τὸ αὐτὸ πνευματικὸν ἔπιον πόμα· ἔπινον γὰρ ἐκ πνευματικῆς ἀκολουθούσης πέτρας, ἡ πέτρα δὲ ἦν ὁ Χριστός

The further point to be noted concerning the customary imperfect is that, like the customary present, it falls short of a gnomic or generic sense. In other words, though the customary imperfect denotes a *wide* scope of occurrence at a point in the past and it is broad in comparison with the narrow reference of the progressive, it always possesses some limits to the frame of reference. It is not used of *unlimited*, universal occurrence in past time, like some sort of 'past gnomic'.[110] On this point the imperfect is unlike the present in that it does not move this further step on the continuum to a totally general, unlimited reference, such as is characteristic of the gnomic present.

4. 2. 3 *Conative imperfect*

In a way similar to the present, the imperfect can be used of actions which are *attempted* or *intended* but *not accomplished*. One difference between the two is that this 'conative' sense is far more frequent for the imperfect than for the present, in comparison with the other uses for each tense.[111]

---

[110] See the distinction between customary and gnomic presents given in sect. 4.1.4.

[111] Greater frequency for the conative imperfect is noted by BDF, *Grammar*, § 319; and Robertson, *Grammar*, p. 880. Perhaps it is more common with the imperfect

The conative meaning derives naturally from the aspect-value of the imperfect, since the aspect views the action from within, without reference to beginning or end-point, and thus it can denote the sense of 'incompletion' under certain circumstances which emphasize the lack of completion. These circumstances are virtually identical to those stated earlier for the conative present, but the details will be repeated here.

One set of circumstances is the use of a verb of the ACCOMPLISHMENT or CLIMAX type (verbs which lexically imply a natural end-point or termination to the action) in a context implying difficulty, resistance, or interruption of the action. This combination with the imperfect indicative describes the action as actually *in process* in the past, but not brought to its termination in the frame of time which is in view.[112] The point here is that the action is under way and an attempt is being made to succeed in it, but the effort is not consummated—the process is not brought to its conclusion. There may be a sense, however, that the termination is imminent: it is impending or just about to come.

Matt. 3: 14–15 ὁ δὲ Ἰωάννης διεκώλυεν αὐτόν . . . τότε ἀφίησιν αὐτόν

Mark 15: 23 καὶ ἐδίδουν αὐτῷ ἐσμυρνισμένον οἶνον· ὃς δὲ οὐκ ἔλαβεν

Luke 9: 49 εἴδομέν τινα . . . ἐκβάλλοντα δαιμόνια καὶ ἐκωλύομεν αὐτόν

Acts 7: 26 συνήλλασσεν αὐτοὺς εἰς εἰρήνην

Heb. 11: 17 τὸν μονογενῆ προσέφερεν, ὁ τὰς ἐπαγγελίας ἀναδεξάμενος

The conative imperfect can also be used of actions which were not actually begun, but were *intended, contemplated,* or *desired* in the scope of past time which is in view. Here the construction can involve verbs of all the *active* lexical types, not just ACCOMPLISHMENTS and CLIMAXES (but STATIVES do not occur). In these cases the intention or desire to do an act

because the contrast with the summary aorist (denoting accomplishment) is more direct than for the present, which differs from the aorist in tense-reference as well and thus is not so directly in contrast aspectually.

[112] Rijksbaron, *SSV,* pp. 16–17, gives a very clear articulation of this type of conative, but he does not include the second type described above.

is, by easy association, seen as part of the process of doing the
act itself, but to *intend* or *contemplate* is not to *do* or *accomplish*,
and if the context shows that the action itself is not under way
the overall sense is likewise one of incompletion.[113] Here also
there may be a sense of impending or imminent occurrence:
the intended event is on the verge of happening, but has not
begun.

Luke 1: 59 ἐκάλουν αὐτὸ ἐπὶ τῷ ὀνόματι τοῦ πατρὸς αὐτοῦ Ζαχαρίαν

Acts 25: 22 ἐβουλόμην καὶ αὐτὸς τοῦ ἀνθρώπου ἀκοῦσαι

Rom. 9: 3 ηὐχόμην γὰρ ἀνάθεμα εἶναι αὐτὸς ἐγὼ ἀπὸ τοῦ Χριστοῦ ὑπὲρ τῶν
ἀδελφῶν μου

Gal. 4: 20 ἤθελον δὲ παρεῖναι πρὸς ὑμᾶς ἄρτι

Included in the list above are examples of another idiom
with the imperfect which seems to fit under this category of
conative use, the so-called 'desiderative' imperfect.[114] This
occurs with verbs of *desiring* or *wishing* and has the sense of 'to
be on the verge of wanting', 'to contemplate the desire, but fail
to bring oneself actually to the point of wishing'. The use
borders also on a modal function for the tense, in that there is
a rhetorical shift in the time-reference: a present situation is
portrayed as though past, in order to make it more *remote* and
thus reduce the force of the statement. Burton explains the
temporal shift as follows: 'Failure to realize the desire, or the
perception that it cannot be realized, or reluctance to express
a positive and deliberate choice may lead the speaker to use
the Imperfect rather than the Present.'[115] Thus, the reference
with these imperfects of verbs of desiring is actually present,
although it is designed to avoid a definite statement about

[113] Stahl, *Syntax*, pp. 100–3, includes in his discussion of the conative imperfect
both types of conatives listed here: actions begun but not fulfilled, and actions
intended or impending but not yet begun.

[114] Cf. Burton, *MT*,§ 33; Robertson, *Grammar*, pp. 885–6; Moule, *Idiom Book*, p. 9;
Mandilaras, *Verb*, pp. 134–6; and BW, *Syntax*, pp. 85–6.

[115] Burton, *MT*, § 33. A similar explanation is given in William Douglas
Chamberlain, *An Exegetical Grammar of the Greek New Testament* (New York: Macmillan,
1941), 75.

one's immediate wishes. The English translation can be a modal phrase (e.g. Acts 25: 22 'I could wish to hear . . .', 'I should like to hear . . .') or a similar diffident past in English idiom ('I wanted to hear . . .', or 'I was almost wishing to hear . . .').[116]

A similar 'unreal' use of the imperfect to refer actually to a present situation occurs in contrary-to-fact conditions and with verbs of propriety, obligation, or necessity. The past 'incomplete' sense of the imperfect indicative is used to make the statement *modally* more remote, and it approaches the meaning of the subjunctive: not describing what *is* or *was*, but what *could have* or *ought to have been*.[117]

4. 2. 4 *Inceptive imperfect*

This use is called by Moorhouse the imperfect 'of consecutive action' and he describes it as 'the use denoting consecutive action (entering upon the next action, in a sequence, which is further on in the line)'.[118] Mateos also attributes the inceptive sense for the imperfect to 'la sucesión narrativa'.[119] The point of their description is that the inceptive sense for the imperfect ('began to . . .') is an effect of the context. The context in these instances involves the close collocation of two verbs denoting sequenced situations such that the first indicates the beginning-point of the second (see section 3.5.2 for further discussion).[120]

---

[116] The use of a past tense in English and French for diffident or polite statements about the present is discussed in Leech, *Meaning and the English Verb*, p. 11; and Stephen Wallace, 'Figure and Ground: The Interrelationships of Linguistic Categories', in *Tense-Aspect* (1982), 202–3.

[117] Cf. Robertson, *Grammar*, pp. 885–7; BDF, *Grammar*, §§ 358–60. Cf. further discussion in K. L. McKay, 'Repeated Action, the Potential and Reality in Ancient Greek', *Antichthon*, 15 (1981), 36–46.

[118] Moorhouse, *Syntax*, p. 191.

[119] Mateos, *Aspecto verbal*, pp. 36–7.

[120] Most Greek grammars do not include a separate category for this sense. Some include it under the conative use (e.g. Robertson, *Grammar*, p. 885; BDR, *Grammatik*, § 326), and some deny its validity altogether (e.g. SD, *Syntax*, p. 277). But it is different enough from the conative, and the inceptive meaning produced in combination with the context seems worthy of separate notice.

Matt. 4: 11 ἄγγελοι προσῆλθον καὶ διηκόνουν αὐτῷ

Mark 1: 35 ἀναστὰς ἐξῆλθεν καὶ ἀνῆλθεν εἰς ἔρημον τόπον κἀκεῖ προσηύχετο

14: 72 καὶ ἐπιβαλὼν ἔκλαιεν

Mark 6: 41 (~Luke 9: 16) λαβών . . . ἀναβλέψας . . . εὐλόγησεν καὶ κατέκλασεν τοὺς ἄρτους καὶ ἐδίδου τοῖς μαθηταῖς

Luke 5: 3 ἐμβάς . . . ἠρώτησεν . . . καθίσας δὲ ἐκ τοῦ πλοίου ἐδίδασκεν τοὺς ὄχλους (many instances of inceptive sense with this verb occur in the NT)

5: 6 συνέκλεισαν πλῆθος ἰχθύων πολύ, διερρήσσετο δὲ τὰ δίκτυα αὐτῶν

13: 13 καὶ παραχρῆμα ἀνωρθώθη καὶ ἐδόξαζεν τὸν Θεόν

Acts 3: 8 ἐξαλλόμενος ἔστη καὶ περιεπάτει καὶ εἰσῆλθεν σὺν αὐτοῖς εἰς τὸ ἱερόν

7: 54 ἀκούοντες δὲ ταῦτα διεπρίοντο ταῖς καρδίαις αὐτῶν καὶ ἔβρυχον τοὺς ὀδόντας ἐπ' αὐτόν

1. 2. 5 *Excursus: frequency of the imperfect in the New Testament*

In conclusion to this treatment of the imperfect in the NT, it should be noted that two books, Matthew and Mark, display exceptional patterns of imperfect usage relative to the other NT works. The idiosyncrasies of these two are opposite, as can be seen from frequency-counts of imperfects used in the Gospels and Acts (and in a few other books for comparison). The data are shown in Table 4.1.

The first point to be observed from these figures is the relatively *low* occurrence of imperfects in Matthew, even taking into account the higher proportion of discourse material within the narrative. The predominant narrative tense in Matthew is clearly the aorist, and in a number of instances where either imperfect or aorist could occur, an aorist is chosen.[121] Leaving behind this difference in frequency (which is similar to the sample of papyri cited by Mandilaras), it must

---

[121] For a listing of changes to aorist from Mark's imperfect see W. C. Allen, *A Critical and Exegetical Commentary of the Gospel according to St. Matthew*, 3rd edn. (ICC; Edinburgh: T. and T. Clark, 1912), pp. xx–xxii.

TABLE 4. 1. *Frequency of Imperfect Indicative*

Book	Imperfect indicatives			Aorist indicatives	
	No.[a]	% of all verbs[b]	% of imp. + aor. indic.	% of all verbs[b]	% of imp. + aor. indic.
Matt.	79	3	13	21	87
Mark	222	11	37	19	63
Luke	252	8	26	23	74
John	151	7	21	22	79
Acts	314	10	29	25	71
Homer, *Odyssey*		17	44	22	56
Herodotus, book 1		13	50	13	50
Sophocles, *Oedipus Tyrannus*[c]		7	44	9	56
Xenophon, *Anabasis*		19	61	12	39
Polybius, book 1		12	48	13	52
2 Maccabees		9	33	18	66

For non-literary papyri in the Hellenistic period Mandilaras reports the following frequency in 456 papyrus texts examined by him: 161 imperfect indicatives to 1,186 aorist indicatives (a ratio of 12 to 88).[b]

[a] According to the count of Hawkins, *Horae Synopticae*, p. 51, excluding the imperfects of εἰμί and the occurrences of ἔφη.

[b] The % columns are taken from the figures given by L. Schlachter, 'Statistiche Untersuchungen über den Gebrauch der Tempora und Modi bei einzelnen griechischen Schriftstellern', *IF* 22 (1907), 229 (with % of imperfect and aorist indicatives in Mark corrected according to my count).

[c] Excluding the chorus.

[d] Mandilaras, *Verb*, p. 130 n. 2.

be said that, in regard to the *meanings* of these tenses, Matthew displays no discernible differences from the rest of the NT. He apparently chose, whether deliberately or unconsciously, not to utilize the descriptive or customary notions of the imperfect as frequently as the other NT writers have done.[122]

The second point to note from these statistics is the relatively high frequency of imperfects in Mark, compared with other NT writers. This book displays a high proportion of

[122] Turner, in MT, *Style*, p. 40, observes on other grounds a difference between Matt. and Mark which seems to explain this pattern of tense-choice: 'Matthew will often avoid the vividly and descriptively colourful in Mark, and will seek a more commonplace expression . . . he is certainly less dramatically picturesque'.

imperfects both as a percentage of all forms (despite frequent use of historical presents) and in comparison with aorist indicatives. Others have noticed the frequent use of imperfects and have concluded that Mark misuses the imperfect.[123] It should be noted that compared with earlier Greek, Mark's ratio of aorists and imperfects is more in line than the other NT writers. A more likely position based on study of actual examples throughout his Gospel is that Mark uses the imperfect quite competently and his greater frequency of imperfects is due to his desire to portray events in vivid fashion.[124]

The 'periphrastic imperfect' (imperfect of εἰμί with a present participle) occurs frequently in the NT, with similar meanings to those described above. These are discussed in section 4.7.

4. 3 Uses of the Aorist Indicative

The aorist indicative clearly displays the aspectual meaning set forth for the aorist forms in Chapter 2: that of 'external viewpoint concerning an occurrence as a whole, including beginning and end-point, without reference to its internal make-up'. To this it adds, with a few exceptions to be explained below, the temporal meaning of *past* occurrence: an action or state seen as antecedent to the time of speaking/ writing. The first three of the categories listed below are the more common uses, while the other four involve relatively rare combinations of these two values with other features.

4. 3. 1 *Constative or complexive aorist*

This is by far the most common use of the aorist indicative, and it is the one which displays the most direct application of

---

[123] C. H. Turner, *The Gospel According to St. Mark: Introduction and Commentary*, repr. from C. Gore, H. L. Goudge, and A. Guillaume (eds.), *A New Commentary on Holy Scripture* (London: SPCK, 1931), 77, comments 'Mark quite habitually uses the imperfect where he ought to have used another tense'. It must be admitted that his opinion is based not on statistics, but on careful study of Markan style.

[124] This is the opinion of Cecil Emden, 'St. Mark's Use of the Imperfect Tense',

the basic aspectual value. Here the aorist indicative makes a summary reference to a past action or state as a whole without emphasis on any of the actional features which may be involved in the internal constituency of the occurrence. There is no focus on the beginning or the end of the situation exclusively, but rather on the whole occurrence viewed as a single entity regardless of its make-up.[125] Because of this simple reference to a past situation without further qualification, the aorist indicative is the most common[126] and most 'economical' narrative tense: it relates an occurrence as a whole without further description, whatever its particular actional character.

Because of this simple portrayal of the ocurrence, an aorist is flexible in sense, and the combinations of meanings in which it occurs are clearly dependent upon the lexical character of the verb and other features of the context. The grammars usually point out in a helpful way that the constative aorist may appear in at least three different actional combinations.[127]

1. The aorist may relate an *instantaneous* or momentary occurrence: this sense is produced when verbs with instantaneous lexical character (i.e. CLIMAXES or PUNCTUALS; cf. section 3.1.2.4) occur in the aorist and refer to a specific instance of the action.[128] Although the aorist fits such cases

Exp. T. 65 (1953–4), 146–9; H. B. Swete, *The Gospel According to St. Mark*, 3rd edn. (London: Macmillan, 1909), pp. xlix–l; and Vincent Taylor, *The Gospel According to St. Mark*, 2nd edn. (London: Macmillan and Co., 1966), 180, 253, 271, 297, 460.

[125] KG, *Satzlehre*, p. 155; Burton, *MT*, § 38; Robertson, *Grammar*, pp. 830–4: Mayser, *Grammatik*, p. 143; MT, *Syntax*, p. 72; Abel. *Grammaire*, p. 255; and BW, *Syntax*, p. 90.

[126] See the statistics given in sect. 4.2.5.

[127] Burton, *MT*, § 39; Robertson, *Grammar*, pp. 830–4; DM. *Grammar*, p. 196; and HS, *Grammatik*, pp. 307–9, 324–6. For the last two of these see Zerwick, *Biblical Greek*, p. 83 ('the global aorist'), and BDF, *Grammar*, § 332.

[128] The aorist indicative with CLIMAXES may give a consummative sense (cf. sect. 4.3.3) if the context indicates that the act is done despite difficulty or resistance. More frequently, however, it focuses on the instantaneous climax or moment of transition only and gives a simple report that the action is done, similar to aorist with the PUNCTUALS.

naturally, this is by no means its only or even predominant use. In contrast to the aorist, the imperfect could hardly be used in these cases since it would give a different sense—with PUNCTUALS an iterative meaning and with CLIMAXES a focus on the prefaced process leading towards but not yet reaching the climax

Matt. 7: 27 ἔπνευσαν οἱ ἄνεμοι καὶ προσέκοψαν τῇ οἰκίᾳ ἐκείνῃ καὶ ἔπεσεν
    8: 3 καὶ ἐκτείνας τὴν χεῖραν ἥψατο αὐτοῦ
    25: 10 εἰσῆλθον . . . καὶ ἐκλείσθη ἡ θύρα

Mark 12: 42–4 μία χήρα πτωχὴ ἔβαλεν λεπτὰ δύο . . . ἡ χήρα αὕτη ἡ πτωχὴ πλεῖον πάντων ἔβαλεν . . . αὕτη δέ . . . ἔβαλεν ὅλον τὸν βίον αὐτῆς
    15: 38 (+ parallels) καὶ τὸ καταπέτασμα τοῦ ναοῦ ἐσχίσθη εἰς δύο

Luke 22: 50 ἐπάταξεν εἰς τις ἐξ αὐτῶν τοῦ ἀρχιερέως τὸν δοῦλον

Acts 5: 5 ἀκούων δὲ ὁ Ἀνανίας τοὺς λόγους τούτους πεσὼν ἐξέψυξεν
    8: 39 πνεῦμα κυρίου ἥρπασεν τὸν Φίλιππον
    9: 40 ἡ δὲ ἤνοιξεν τοὺς ὀφθαλμοὺς αὐτῆς, καὶ ἰδοῦσα τὸν Πέτρον ἀνεκάθισεν
    12: 23 παραχρῆμα δὲ ἐπάταξεν αὐτὸν ἄγγελος κυρίου

Rev. 5: 5 ἐνίκησεν ὁ λέων ὁ ἐκ τῆς φυλῆς Ἰούδα

2. The aorist may relate an *extended* action or state: this sense results when verbs with durative lexical character (i.e. STATES, ACTIVITIES, or ACCOMPLISHMENTS; cf. sections 3.1.2.1–3 are used. Adverbial indicators of the duration may or may not occur but the durative sense remains, since this is implicit in the verb itself. The aorist again merely records the whole occurrence in summary without regard for the internal character of the situation. In instances such as these the imperfect is a viable option for the speaker, since it would merely change the focus and emphasis, but not the basic sense: this is a place where the speaker's subjective choice and narrative style are free to operate.[129]

---

[129] The aorist records the situation simply and sums it up, without paying attention to the duration. It may do this for the sake of narrative sequence in a series of aorists presenting one situation after another without need to pause over any of them. The imperfect places some emphasis on the internal character of the situation,

Matt. 12: 1 ἐπορεύθη ὁ Ἰησοῦς . . . διὰ τῶν σπορίμων
20: 12 οὗτοι οἱ ἔσχατοι μίαν ὥραν ἐποίησαν
25: 35–6, 42–3 ἐπείνασα. . . ἐδίψησα. . . ἠσθένησα

Luke 9: 36 καὶ αὐτοὶ ἐσίγησαν
20: 19 ἐζήτησαν . . . ἐπιβαλεῖν ἐπ' αὐτόν

John 1: 14 ἐσκήνωσεν ἐν ἡμῖν, καὶ ἐθεασάμεθα τὴν δόξαν αὐτοῦ
1: 39 (cf. 4: 40) παρ' αὐτῷ, ἔμειναν τὴν ἡμέραν ἐκείνην
2: 20 τεσσεράκοντα καὶ ἓξ ἔτεσιν οἰκοδομήθη ὁ ναὸς οὗτος

Acts 3: 17 κατὰ ἄγνοιαν ἐπράξατε
11: 12 ἦλθον δὲ σὺν ἐμοὶ καὶ οἱ ἓξ ἀδελφοὶ οὗτοι
13: 18 ὡς τεσσερακονταετῆ χρόνον ἐτροποφόρησεν αὐτοὺς ἐν τῇ ἐρήμῳ
17: 15 οἱ δὲ καθιστάνοντες τὸν Παῦλον ἤγαγον ἕως Ἀθηνῶν
18: 11 ἐκάθισεν δὲ ἐνιαυτὸν καὶ μῆνας ἓξ διδάσκων ἐν αὐτοῖς τὸν λόγον
26: 5 κατὰ τὴν ἀκριβεστάτην αἵρεσιν . . . ἔζησα Φαρισαῖος
28: 30 ἐνέμεινεν δὲ διετίαν ὅλην ἐν ἰδίῳ μισθώματι

Rom. 5: 14 ἐβασίλευσεν ὁ θάνατος ἀπὸ Ἀδὰμ μέχρι Μωϋσέως
15: 3 καὶ γὰρ ὁ Χριστὸς οὐχ ἑαυτῷ ἤρεσεν

Heb. 11: 23 πίστει Μωϋσῆς γεννηθεὶς ἐκρύβη τρίμηνον ὑπὸ τῶν πατέρων αὐτοῦ

Rev. 20: 4 καὶ ἐβασίλευσαν μετὰ τοῦ Χριστοῦ χίλια ἔτη

3. The aorist may relate a *series* of repeated actions or states: this sense can appear with any lexical type, but the reference is to multiple rather than single actions or states. Adverbial modifiers, plural-noun adjuncts, or broader features of the context show that an aorist is used in a particular text to refer to *multiple* occurrences. The multiple situations may be either iterative (one individual repeating the action or state) or distributive (each one of a group involved with the occurrence once or more). The aorist in either case indicates a summary or composite of the repeated situations. This is another place where the imperfect could be used, according to the subjective choice of the speaker.[130]

either for the sake of more picturesque description or to denote simultaneity with other occurrences.

[130] The aorist sums up the multiple occurrences as a whole, in a composite of the various situations viewed from the outside, and thus pays less attention to the

Mark 3: 10 πολλοὺς γὰρ ἐθεράπευσεν
   9: 22 πολλάκις καὶ εἰς πῦρ αὐτὸν ἔβαλεν καὶ εἰς ὕδατα
   12: 23 (+ parallels) οἱ ἑπτὰ ἔσχον αὐτὴν γυναῖκα
   12: 44 πάντες γὰρ ἐκ τοῦ περισσεύοντος αὐτοῖς ἔβαλον

John 18: 2 πολλάκις συνήχθη ᾿Ιησοῦς ἐκεῖ μετὰ τῶν μαθητῶν αὐτοῦ (also
   18: 20)

Acts 9: 42 ἐπίστευσαν πολλοὶ ἐπὶ τὸν κύριον
   10: 41 ἡμῖν, οἵτινες συνεφάγομεν καὶ συνεπίομεν αὐτῷ
   13: 31 ὃς ὤφθη ἐπὶ ἡμέρας πλείους τοῖς συναναβᾶσιν αὐτῷ

Rom. 1: 21 διότι γνόντες τὸν θεὸν οὐχ ὡς θεὸν ἐδόξασαν ἢ ηὐχαρίστησαν
   3: 23 πάντες γὰρ ἥμαρτον

2 Cor. 8: 22 ὃν ἐδοκιμάσαμεν ἐν πολλοῖς πολλάκις σπουδαῖον ὄντα
   11: 24-5 ὑπὸ ᾿Ιουδαίων πεντάκις τεσσεράκοντα παρὰ μίαν ἔλαβον, τρὶς
   ἐρραβδίσθην. . . τρὶς ἐναυάγησα

Phil. 4: 16 καὶ ἅπαξ καὶ δὶς εἰς τὴν χρείαν μοι ἐπέμψατε

2 Tim. 3: 11 τοῖς παθήμασιν, οἷά μοι ἐγένετο ἐν ᾿Αντιοχείᾳ, ἐν ᾿Ικονίῳ

Heb. 11: 13 κατὰ πίστιν ἀπέθανον οὗτοι πάντες
   11: 33–9 (16 aorists, denoting multiple actions in a general
   account)

Thus, the constative aorist can be used of situations which are either durative or instantaneous, either single or multiple. In each case the sense is dependent on the lexical character of the verb and other features, not on the use or non-use of the aorist.[131]

Another observation to keep in mind for interpretation is the difference of general vs. specific reference (see section 3.3).

individual parts which make up the whole. The aorist is often used in this way out of narrative 'economy' as the simplest description of the occurrences, without emphasis on the repetition. The imperfect gives more attention to the repetition by focusing on the internal feature of multiple occurrence. See the application of this to several passages in Sophocles by Moorhouse, *Syntax*, pp. 193–4.

[131] P. V. Pistorius, 'Some Remarks on the Aorist Aspect in the Greek New Testament', *Acta Classica*, 10 (1967), 33–9, correctly shows that other features of the sentence affect the sense of the aorist greatly, but he is unsuccessful in his argument that there is no constative or complexive use of the aorist. The range of examples listed here shows that the aorist must be broader than the ingressive and effective sense (in which he attempts to place all such instances) can account for.

The aorist is more commonly specific in scope,[132] but not always; the frame of reference must be determined from other factors, not from the use of aorist indicative. For example, these uses should probably be taken as general references to past occurrences, usually repeated, and do not refer to specific occasions just because the aorist is used:[133]

Acts 10: 37 μετὰ τὸ βάπτισμα ὃ ἐκήρυξεν Ἰωάννης
  11: 18 ἄρα καὶ τοῖς ἔθνεσιν ὁ θεὸς τὴν μετάνοιαν εἰς ζωὴν ἔδωκεν
  15: 12 ὅσα ἐποίησεν ὁ Θεὸς σημεῖα καὶ τέρατα ἐν τοῖς ἔθνεσιν δι' αὐτῶν

Phil. 2: 22 σὺν ἐμοὶ ἐδούλευσεν εἰς τὸ εὐαγγέλιον

1 Thess. 2: 9 νυκτὸς καὶ ἡμέρας ἐργαζόμενοι . . . ἐκηρύξαμεν εἰς ὑμᾶς τὸ εὐαγγέλιον
  2: 14 ὑμεῖς γὰρ μιμηταὶ ἐγενήθητε . . . ὅτι τὰ αὐτὰ ἐπάθετε

Related to this is the fact that the constative use includes aorist verbs denoting 'recent past' and 'indefinite past' occurrences. These are distinct senses but they are united by the fact that they are translated into English with the 'present perfect' tense, the forms with *have/has* as auxiliary.[134] Unfortunately, this seems to have led some grammarians to surmise that the aorist in these cases displays some sort of Greek 'perfective' meaning.[135] These are simply uses of the constative aorist in more particular circumstances, still denoting the occurrence as a whole at some point in the past.[136]

Matt. 9: 18 ἡ θυγάτηρ μου ἄρτι ἐτελεύτησεν
  26: 65 ἴδε νῦν ἠκούσατε τὴν βλασφημίαν

---

[132] Cf. Peppler, 'Durative and Aoristic', pp. 47–9, and Felix Hartmann, 'Aorist und Imperfektum im Griechischen', *Neue Jahrbücher für das klassische Altertum*, 43 (1919), 334, who note that the aorist can be seen in some texts to present a 'specific vs. general' contrast with the imperfect, but this must be confirmed by other factors beyond the tense-contrast alone.

[133] Frank Stagg, 'The Abused Aorist', *JBL* 91 (1972), 223–8, cites a number of NT examples in which this is at issue and surveys the treatment given the aorist by commentators on these texts.

[134] Cf. Leech, *Meaning and the English Verb*, pp. 32–3, 36–8.

[135] See BW, *Syntax*, p. 91; and DM, *Grammar*, pp. 196–7.

[136] An excellent discussion of these two types of constative aorists is given in Moulton, *Proleg.*, pp. 135–41, esp. 140. Treatment of possible overlap in sense between aorist and perfect in the NT will be given in sect. 4.5.4.

Mark 12: 26 οὐκ ἀνέγνωτε ἐν τῇ βίβλῳ Μωϋσέως

Luke 1: 1 ἐπειδήπερ πολλοὶ ἐπεχείρησαν ἀνατάξασθαι διήγησιν

In regard to the constative use of the aorist, it is certainly true, as Stagg has posited for all aorist uses, that the absence of the aorist is more significant for interpretation than its presence.[137] By using the constative aorist the speaker or writer narrates an action or state in summary as something which occurred, without further description. When he departs from this basic narrative tense to another form, this is worthy of more note, since some sort of emphasis or additional point beyond basic predication is made.

4. 3. 2 Ingressive aorist

A second major use of the aorist indicative applies the aspect-value of the aorist in a different way from the constative. In general terms this use highlights the *beginning-point of an action* or the *entrance into a state* rather than viewing the action or state in its entirety as the constative does. But the explanation for this sense must be undertaken in connection with further specification of the circumstances under which it appears. The ingressive use of the aorist comes to the fore in two well-defined situations.

1. The most common ingressive use appears when a STATIVE verb (see section 3. 1. 2) is used in the aorist.[138] In these cases the STATE makes a shift in sense and becomes a type of *active* verb, because of the aorist's focus on the beginning and end-point of the situation. This focus on the *terminal points* of the situation normally produces the shift to an ingressive, active sense—the 'event' of entering the state.[139]

---

[137] 'The Abased Aorist', p. 231

[138] Goodwin, *Moods and Tenses*, § 55; Burton, *MT*, § 41; KG, *Satzlehre*, pp. 155–6;, Moulton, *Proleg.*, p. 130; MT, *Syntax*, pp. 71–2; Mayser, *Grammatik*, pp. 141–2; Nunn, *Short Syntax*, p. 69; and Zerwick, *Biblical Greek*, pp. 81–2.

[139] See the treatment of this effect of summary aspect on English statives in Carlota S. Smith, 'A Theory of Aspectual Choice', *Lg* 59 (1983), 483–91.

Matt. 2: 16 τότε Ἡρῴδης ἰδὼν ὅτι ἐνεπαίχθη ὑπὸ τῶν μάγων ἐθυμώθη λίαν

22: 7 ὁ δὲ βασιλεὺς ὠργίσθη καί . . . ἀπώλεσεν τοὺς φονεῖς ἐκείνους

Luke 20: 19 ἐφοβήθησαν τὸν λαόν (as result of the parable just told)

20: 26 θαυμάσαντες ἐπὶ τῇ ἀποκρίσει αὐτοῦ ἐσίγησαν

John 1: 10 ὁ κόσμος αὐτὸν οὐκ ἔγνω[140]

4: 52 ἐπύθετο οὖν τὴν ὥραν παρ' αὐτῶν ἐν ᾗ κομψότερον ἔσχεν

Acts 7: 60 καὶ τοῦτο εἰπὼν ἐκοιμήθη

11: 18 ἀκούσαντες δὲ ταῦτα ἡσύχασαν καὶ ἐδόξασαν τὸν Θεὸν

Rom. 14: 9 εἰς τοῦτο γὰρ Χριστὸς ἀπέθανεν καὶ ἔζησεν[141]

1 Cor. 4: 8 ἤδη ἐπλουτήσατε, χωρὶς ἡμῶν ἐβασιλεύσατε

2 Cor. 7: 9 νῦν χαίρω, οὐχ ὅτι ἐλυπήθητε ἀλλ' ὅτι ἐλυπήθητε εἰς μετάνοιαν

8: 9 δὶ ὑμᾶς ἐπτώχευσεν πλούσιος ὤν

On the other hand, it is possible for the aorist indicative of a stative verb to have a *constative* sense and take a summary view of the entire situation, denoting the past existence of the subject in the state, or a summary of repeated past states.

Mark 12: 23 (+ parallels) οἱ ἑπτὰ ἔσχον αὐτὴν γυναῖκα

Luke 9: 36 καὶ αὐτοὶ ἐσίγησαν καὶ οὐδενὶ ἀπήγγειλαν

Acts 26: 5 κατὰ τὴν ἀκριβεστάτην αἵρεσιν . . . ἔζησα Φαρισαῖος

28: 30 ἐνέμεινεν δὲ διετίαν ὅλην ἐν ἰδίῳ μισθώματι

2. Less frequently, the aorist indicative of an active verb (especially of the durative types ACTIVITIES and ACCOMPLISHMENTS) picks up an ingressive sense due to *narrative sequence* (see sections 3.5.2 and 4.2.4 for full discussion). Here the close association of two verbs denoting sequenced events

---

[140] See the discussion of the effect of different aspects on verbs of knowing in the NT in K. L. McKay, 'On the Perfect and Other Aspects in New Testament Greek', *Nov. T.* 23 (1981), 307–9; and Richard J. Erickson, 'Oida and Ginōskō and Verbal Aspect in Pauline Usage', *Westminster Theological Journal*, 44 (1982), 110–22.

[141] The STATIVE verb ζάω occurs in the NT 8 times in the aorist indicative, 7 of which have the ingressive sense 'came to life' (Luke 15: 24, 32; Rom. 14: 9; Rev. 2: 8, 13: 14, 20: 4, 5), while one (Acts 26: 5) has the past stative idea (i.e. constative). In contrast, ζάω occurs 29 times in the present or imperfect indicative, all of which have a stative sense (e.g. Rom. 7: 9 ἐγὼ δὲ ἔζων χωρὶς νόμου ποτέ).

in the narrative shows that the first indicates the beginning-point of the second.

Luke 19: 41 ἰδὼν τὴν πόλιν ἔκλαυσεν ἐπ' αὐτήν

Acts 16: 10 ὡς δὲ τὸ ὅραμα εἶδεν, εὐθέως ἐζητήσαμεν ἐξελθεῖν εἰς Μακεδονίαν

  18: 19 κατήντησαν . . . κατέλιπεν . . . αὐτὸς δὲ εἰσελθὼν εἰς τὴν συναγωγὴν διελέξατο τοῖς Ἰουδαίοις

  18: 27 ὃς παραγενόμενος συνεβάλετο πολὺ τοῖς πεπιστευκόσιν

With most active verbs, however, the aorist indicative denotes not merely the beginning of the action, even when other events immediately precede it, but the whole action from beginning to end. This is especially true with instantaneous verbs, for which it is unlikely that a speaker would distinguish between beginning-point and entire occurrence: for example, it seems unlikely that βαλεῖν means 'let fly' as Moulton posits, or that at John 1: 11–12 παρέλαβον . . . ἔλαβον the verbs have an ingressive sense.[142] The constative sense is preferable also for verbs of motion in cases where the verb itself actually means 'depart, set off' or where in a close sequence the verb in fact relates an entire journey as the next event; in both cases the whole act is denoted, not just the beginning-point (e.g. Acts 13: 4, 13; 14: 24–6; 20: 13–15).

4. 3. 3 *Consummative or effective aorist*

The third major use of the aorist indicative is in one sense the opposite of the ingressive use, since it emphasizes the end-point of the action instead of the beginning-point. However, this consummative use appears in significantly different circumstances and is not just an easy shift of focus to the other end of the occurrence. The places where the consummative sense occurs are these two:

1. Use of the aorist with a verb of the ACCOMPLISHMENT or CLIMAX type (verbs which lexically imply a natural end-point

---

[142] Moulton, *Proleg.*, p. 109; and Robertson, *Grammar*, p. 834.

264   SPECIFIC AREAS OF ASPECT-USAGE

or termination to the action) in a context implying difficulty or resistance to the action.[143]

Matt. 25: 16–22 ἐκέρδησεν ἄλλα πέντε . . . ἐκέρδησεν ἄλλα δύο . . . ἄλλα πέντε τάλαντα ἐκέρδησα . . . ἄλλα δύο τάλαντα ἐκέρδησα.

27: 20 οἱ δὲ ἀρχιερεῖς καὶ οἱ πρεσβύτεροι ἔπεισαν τοὺς ὄχλους

Acts 5: 39 (cf. 17: 4) ἐπείσθησαν δὲ αὐτῷ

7: 36 οὗτος ἐξήγαγεν αὐτούς

12: 11 ἐξείλατό με ἐκ χειρὸς Ἡρῴδου

27: 43 βουλόμενος διασῶσαι τὸν Παῦλον ἐκώλυσεν αὐτοὺς τοῦ βουλήματος

Rom. 1: 13 πολλάκις προεθέμην ἐλθεῖν πρὸς ὑμᾶς, καὶ ἐκωλύθην ἄχρι τοῦ δεῦρο

2 Cor. 12: 11 γέγονα ἄφρων, ὑμεῖς με ἠναγκάσατε

Phil. 4: 11 ἐγὼ γὰρ ἔμαθον ἐν οἷς εἰμι αὐτάρκης εἶναι

1 Thess. 2: 18 διότι ἠθελήσαμεν ἐλθεῖν πρὸς ὑμᾶς. . . καὶ ἐνέκοψεν ἡμᾶς ὁ σατανᾶς

Rev. 5: 5 ἐνίκησεν ὁ λέων ὁ ἐκ τῆς φυλῆς Ἰούδα

2. Use of the aorist with a verb of the ACTIVITY type, or a PUNCTUAL verb (with reference to multiple occurrences), but including in either case some adverbial or nominal adjunct which adds a *limit* to the action (see sections 3.2.1–2). These verbal expressions come to have, in effect, the same sense which the ACCOMPLISHMENT or CLIMAX types bear simply as part of their lexical meaning.

Acts 28: 14 καὶ οὕτως εἰς τὴν Ῥώμην ἤλθαμεν

2 Tim. 3: 11 οἵους διωγμοὺς ὑπήνεγκα καὶ ἐκ πάντων με ἐρρύσατο ὁ κύριος

Heb. 11: 7 (cf. 9: 2) κατεσκεύασεν κιβωτόν

In both cases listed above the aorist is the reverse of one of the types of conative present and imperfect, and the difference

[143] A note about the lexical character of verbs occurring with consummative sense, somewhat along the line of this one, is given in Burton, *MT*, § 35, 42; KG, *Satzlehre*, p. 154; Mayser, *Grammatik*, pp. 142–3; DM, *Grammar*, pp. 196–7; MT, *Syntax*, p. 72; and BW, *Syntax*, p. 91. A clearer statement of the point is given by Zerwick, *Biblical Greek*, p. 82: 'the aorist of verbs indicating action directed to some end may express the actual attainment of that end'.

between the aspects is clearly illustrated. If a process must reach a termination before it is thought to be 'truly done' (as the expressions listed above must), then an aspect which views the action from within, ignoring the end-points—as the present and imperfect do—can denote an incomplete sense: the action is not yet 'done'. In contrast, an aspect which takes an external view of the action and sees both end-points—as the aorist does—can denote the completion of the action: the termination is reached. However, in both cases the conative or consummative sense is not automatic, and must be emphasized by a contextual tone of difficulty or resistance, since the completion or lack of it could be a minor point otherwise.[144]

4. 3. 4 *Gnomic aorist*

This is a use of the aorist well attested in classical Greek, and found but not frequent in the NT.[145] In this use the aorist expresses a general or proverbial truth, a maxim about occurrences which take place not only in the past but in the present and future as well. It is difficult to decide what motivates this use, although several theories have been advanced.[146] The most plausible is the rationale advanced by Gildersleeve (and others), who explains that the gnomic aorist is like the generic article: a single specific instance is taken as typical of all such occurrences and thus gives expression to the general truth.[147] An illustration of how this works is provided

---

[144] The aorist in the NT, especially the consummative use, is sometimes said to reflect a meaning much like the Greek perfect. This possible overlap in meaning will be covered in the treatment of the perfect tense (sect. 4.5.).

[145] Some in fact deny its presence in the NT: cf. Radermacher, *Grammatik*, p. 152; and WL, *Grammatik*, pp. 260–1. Moule, *Idiom Book*, pp. 12–13, resists the gnomic use for NT examples. But the gnomic sense is a better explanation for some of the instances to be cited here than the interpretations offered as alternatives, and the NT examples are quite parallel with accepted gnomic instances in earlier Greek. Wackernagel, *Vorlesungen über Syntax*, p. 178, cites NT examples in his discussion of ancient Greek gnomic aorists.

[146] Cf. Humbert, *Syntaxe*, pp. 145–6; Wackernagel, *Vorlesungen über Syntax*, pp. 178–81; and SD, *Syntax*, pp. 283–6.

[147] Gildersleeve, *Syntax*, § 255; Goodwin, *Moods and Tenses*, § 155; Smyth, *Grammar*,

in the closely related category of the 'aorist used in similes', which occurs in earlier Greek, especially in poetry: here a concrete example is used to give the point of comparison which is proverbially valid. Gildersleeve cites Demosthenes 25. 95: δεῖ δὴ πάντας, ὥσπερ οἱ ἰατροί, ὅταν καρκίνον . . . ἴδωσιν, ἀπέκαυσαν ἢ ὅλως ἀπέκοψαν, οὕτω τοῦτο τὸ θηρίον ὑμᾶς ἐξορίσαι 'just as physicians, when they detect a cancer . . . *cauterize* it or *cut* it off completely, so all of you must banish this savage creature'.[148] The gnomic aorist does the same thing without the explicit comparision of a simile: it phrases a statement which is proverbially true by referring, as it were, to a representative instance from which the general truth is abstracted. Some examples are:

Luke 7: 35 καὶ ἐδικαιώθη ἡ σοφία ἀπὸ πάντων τῶν τέκνων αὐτῆς

Jas. 1: 11 ἀνέτειλεν γὰρ ὁ ἥλιος σὺν τῷ καύσωνι καὶ ἐξήρανεν τὸν χόρτον καὶ τὸ ἄνθος αὐτοῦ ἐξέπεσεν καὶ ἡ εὐπρέπεια τοῦ προσώπου αὐτοῦ ἀπώλετο· οὕτως καὶ ὁ πλούσιος ἐν ταῖς πορείαις αὐτοῦ μαρανθήσεται (see simile in 1: 10 to introduce this)

1: 24 κατενόησεν γὰρ ἑαυτὸν καὶ ἀπελήλυθεν καὶ εὐθέως ἐπελάθετο ὁποῖος ἦν (see simile in 1: 23 as introduction)

1 Pet. 1: 24 διότι πᾶσα σὰρξ ὡς χόρτος καὶ πᾶσα δόξα αὐτῆς ὡς ἄνθος χόρτου· ἐξηράνθη ὁ χόρτος καὶ τὸ ἄνθος ἐξέπεσεν (simile in v. 24a)

The characteristics of this use are that (1) it refers in context not to a single occurrence in the past but to universal occurrences of the event; and (2) it displays other features of proverbial statement, such as nouns with generic articles, indefinite noun or pronoun reference, and so on.

The gnomic aorist is similar to the gnomic present on both of these counts (universal reference, generic adjuncts) and makes *essentially* the same point. There is a difference between them in two areas. One is the route used in order to arrive at this proverbial sense: the present looks at multiple occurrences

§ 1931; Zerwick, *Biblical Greek*, p. 84; this view is discussed in the works cited in the previous note.

[148] Gildersleeve, *Syntax*, § 256. See this category in Smyth, *Grammar*, § 1935; SD, *Syntax*, pp. 284–5.

of the event and abstracts to a general principle, while the
aorist points to a single instance as typical of many. The
second difference is the resulting meaning: the aorist tends to
occur with verbs of instantaneous meaning and thus state a
more vivid, sudden occurrence. The present seems to occur
more frequently with verbs of durative meaning, and pays
more attention to the extension in time.[149] However, the basic
sense communicated by the two is the same: they relate an
action which occurs not just in past or present but 'always'. It
is for this reason that Moule's objections to several examples
listed above are not to the point, although they express a valid
observation about the gnomic use. He argues that 1 Pet. 1: 21,
Jas. 1: 11, and perhaps Jas. 1: 24 display not the gnomic use
but a sense of 'the suddenness and completeness' of the
action.[150] This observation seems correct, but such a nuance is
consonant with the gnomic aorist and does not lead away
from it.

Although this is a natural Greek idiom, it is very infrequent
in the Hellenistic papyri,[151] as could be expected in material of
that sort. It is possible that the few occurrences of the gnomic
aorist in the NT may be influenced by the Semitic idiom
which parallels it. In Hebrew the perfect (suffixed) conjuga-
tion, which expresses an aspect-value similar to the Greek
aorist and is often used for past tense, can be used to state
general or gnomic truths.[152] This gnomic perfect in Hebrew is
rendered into Greek in several ways by the Septuagint translators. At times the present tense is used, with obvious

---

[149] For this distinction see Goodwin, *Moods and Tenses*, § 157; Robertson, *Grammar*,
p. 836; Abel, *Grammaire*, p. 256; and Chamberlain, *Exegetical Grammar*, pp. 77–8.

[150] Moule, *Idiom Book*, pp. 12–13. He appears correct in calling Matt. 13: 44, 46, 48
'true Narrative (as opposed to generalizing Gnomic) Aorists'.

[151] Mandilaras, *Verb*, p. 169.

[152] S. R. Driver, *A Treatise on the Use of the Tenses in Hebrew and Some Other Syntactical
Questions*, 2nd edn. (Oxford: at the Clarendon Press, 1881), 20; and E. Kautzsch (ed.),
Gesenius' Hebrew Grammar, trans. and rev. by A. E. Cowley, 2nd English edn. (Oxford:
at the Clarendon Press, 1910), 312. The same idiom occurs in biblical Aramaic: cf.
Hans Bauer and Pontus Leander, *Grammatik des Biblisch-Aramäischen* (Halle:
Niemeyer, 1927), 278.

appropriateness (e.g. Ps. 10: 3 [=9: 24]; Prov. 22: 12–13). Sometimes the future is used, focusing on instances of the action which are yet to take place (Gen. 49: 11; Prov. 1: 7, 14: 19). However, a frequent translation of this Hebrew idiom is the Greek aorist (Ps. 1: 1; 9: 11; 14 [13]: 1–5; 49 [48]: 13, 21; 84 [83]: 4; 102: 3–11 [101: 4–12]; Isa. 1: 3; 40: 7; Jer. 8: 7).

Several NT texts have been cited as products of this sort of Semitic influence—the Greek aorist used according to the pattern of the Hebrew 'perfect of general truths'. For example, 1 Pet. 1: 24 (ἐξηράνθη, ἐξέπεσεν) and Jas. 1: 11 (ἐξήρανεν, ἐξέπεσεν) are obviously modelled after the Septuagint of Isa. 40: 7, the former as a quotation and the latter as an allusion. This pattern appears to draw the first and fourth verbs of Jas. 1: 11 (ἀνέτειλεν, ἀπώλετο) over to the gnomic aorist as well. Black suggests that the Semitic perfect of general truths has influenced Matthew's use of the aorist ὡμοιώθη to introduce 'parables of the kingdom' (13: 24, 18: 23, 22: 2; the first two in pericopes peculiar to him; the last with Lucan parallel in which Luke avoids the expression).[153] This does have some precedent in the Septuagint (ὡμοιώθη for perfect of דָּמָה : Ps. 49 [48]: 13, 21; 102 [101]: 7; 143 [144]: 4), and the expression appears to be equivalent to the more common phrase ὁμοίαν ἐστιν (eight times in Matt., three of these with parallels in Luke). However, this use of the aorist reflects not a gnomic use but a *present stative* idea (also reflecting a Semitic idiom, to be discussed below): the scope of the statement is not likely to be universal, but rather what it has come to be like and presently '*is* like'. Finally, several suggest that the aorists of Luke 1: 51–5 are expressions of gnomic truths and reflect Hebrew perfects of that type.[154] It is certain that the phrasing is similar

---

[153] Black, *Aramaic Approach*, p. 129. He also cites (p. 260) the aorists of Luke 11: 52, which are paralleled in Matt. by present verbs and are preceded in Luke itself by a series of customary presents (11: 39–48). The aorists in Luke are somewhat odd, but perhaps he uses them (at the end of the discourse rather than in the middle as in Matt.) as the climactic charge against the Jewish authorities, and the aorists summarize as their worst offence what they have done to obstruct the way to God. These seem to be constative rather than gnomic.

[154] Zerwick, *Biblical Greek*, pp. 84–5; and BDF, *Grammar*, § 333.

to the song of Hannah in 1 Sam. 2 (cf. 2: 4–5, where five Hebrew perfects are rendered by five aorists in the Septuagint). It is a difficult question whether these aorists in Luke are statements of general truth or 'statements of confidence' which anticipate God's full accomplishment yet to come of that which he has now begun.[155] The latter idea seems better and it also is a type of Semitism, which will be treated in the next section.[156]

4. 3. 5 *Proleptic or futuristic aorist*

Another unusual and rather infrequent use of the aorist indicative is the proleptic or futuristic sense, which involves a rhetorical transfer of viewpoint, envisaging an event yet future as though it had already occurred. This use can be divided into two types, one more consistent in its pattern than the other.

The first type of proleptic aorist involves the aorist verb occurring in the apodosis of a sentence which contains a future *condition* (an 'if-clause' referring to the future, either explicit or implicit). The speaker/writer thus looks at the occurrence from a future viewpoint—when the condition has been fulfilled—and this change of viewpoint influences him towards the aorist indicative, though from the normal reference-point the action is still future. This 'aorist after a future condition' is noted by a number of grammars of ancient Greek.[157] Examples of this type are:

1. With an explicit condition (εἰ or ἐάν clause):

Matt. 12: 26 εἰ ὁ σατανᾶς τὸν σατανᾶν ἐκβάλλει, ἐφ' ἑαυτὸν ἐμερίσθη
18: 15 ἐάν σου ἀκούσῃ, ἐκέρδησας τὸν ἀδελφόν σου

---

[155] G. B. Caird, *The Gospel of Luke* (The Pelican New Testament Commentaries; London: Penguin Books, 1963), 55; and I. Howard Marshall, *The Gospel of Luke: A Commentary of the Greek Text* (Exeter: Paternoster Press, 1978), 83–4.

[156] Brief comments on the gnomic aorist used under the influence of the Semitic perfect are given in Klaus Beyer, *Semitische Syntax im Neuen Testament,* i. *Satzlehre,* p. 1 (Göttingen: Vandenhoeck and Ruprecht, 1962), 88–9; and HS, *Grammatik,* p. 327.

[157] BDF, *Grammar,* § 333 (2); MT, *Syntax,* p. 74; Zerwick, *Biblical Greek,* pp. 84–5; Wackernagel, *Vorlesungen über Syntax,* pp. 176–7; and SD, *Syntax,* pp. 282–3.

John 15: 6 ἐὰν μή τις μένῃ ἐν ἐμοί, ἐβλήθη ἔξω ὡς τὸ κλῆμα καὶ ἐξηράνθη καὶ συνάγουσιν αὐτὰ καὶ εἰς τὸ πῦρ βάλλουσιν καὶ καίεται (it is possible that these aorists should be taken as *gnomic*, in parallel with the presents which follow; but it seems that the ἐάν clause sets the tone and gives the first part of the verse a futuristc sense)

1 Cor. 7: 28 ἐὰν δὲ καὶ γαμήσῃς, οὐχ ἥμαρτες, καὶ ἐὰν γήμῃ ἡ παρθένος, οὐχ ἥμαρτεν

Jas. 2: 2–4 [ἐάν clause vv. 2–3] οὐ διεκρίθητε ἐν ἑαυτοῖς καὶ ἐγένεσθε κριταὶ διαλογισμῶν πονηρῶν;

2. With an implied condition (participle, relative clause, or ἵνα clause):

Matt. 5: 28 πᾶς ὁ βλέπων γυναῖκα πρὸς τὸ ἐπιθυμῆσαι αὐτὴν ἤδη ἐμοίχευσεν αὐτὴν ἐν τῇ καρδίᾳ αὐτοῦ

John 15: 8 ἐν τούτῳ ἐδοξάσθη ὁ πατήρ μου, ἵνα καρπὸν πολὺν φέρητε καὶ γένησθε ἐμοὶ μαθηταί

Gal. 5: 4 κατηργήθητε ἀπὸ-Χριστοῦ, οἵτινες ἐν νόμῳ δικαιοῦσθε, τῆς χάριτος ἐξεπέσατε

Heb. 4: 10 ὁ γὰρ εἰσελθὼν εἰς τὴν κατάπαυσιν αὐτοῦ καὶ αὐτὸς κατέπαυσεν ἀπὸ τῶν ἔργων αὐτοῦ ὥσπερ ἀπὸ τῶν ἰδίων ὁ θεός

1 Pet. 3: 6 ὡς Σάρρα ὑπήκουσεν τῷ Ἀβραὰμ κύριον αὐτὸν καλοῦσα, ἧς ἐγενήθητε τέκνα ἀγαθοποιοῦσαι καὶ μὴ φοβούμεναι μηδεμίαν πτόησιν

The second type of futuristic aorist is more difficult to describe in specific terms. It involves the use of the aorist in a statement which by context seems to point to the future, and the aorist is used to portray a future occurrence *as if it were already done*. The aorist gives a vivid picture of the occurrence or emphasizes its certainty or imminence. This use is not reflected so clearly in NT grammars, but it is cited by classical grammars and by commentators struggling with the NT texts presented below.[158] It is seen more clearly in the light of

---

[158] Very clear in William Webster, *The Syntax and Synonyms of the Greek Testament* (London: Rivingtons, 1864), 91; only alluded to in Robertson, *Grammar*, pp. 846–7. Cf. Goodwin, *Moods and Tenses*, § 61; Smyth, *Grammar*, § 1934; and Gildersleeve, *Syntax*, § 263. For commentators see the following discussion.

similar uses of the Hebrew perfect which may have influenced the NT writers.

There are three uses of the Hebrew 'perfect with future sense' which have some sort of parallel (and may have an influence) in the NT use of the futuristic aorist. One type is the 'perfect of confidence or certainty', in which, as Davidson explains it, 'Actions depending on a resolution of the will of the speaker (or of others whose mind is known), or which appear inevitable from circumstances, or which are confidently expected, are conceived and described as having taken place'.[159] A second use is the Hebrew prophetic perfect, which occurs in the midst of imperfects in descriptions of future events. This occurs most commonly in prophetic literature and is thought to reflect the prophet's imagined or visionary glimpse of the future as though already accomplished. A third use involves an event viewed as complete in reference to another future event: the *futurum exactum* (like an English future perfect).[160]

In the Septuagint these 'futuristic' Hebrew perfects are translated in various ways: frequently the Greek future is used, especially in instances of *futurum exactum*. In a few cases the Greek present or perfect appears, usually to describe an imminent state or condition of the subject or to denote his resolved state of mind to carry out a certain action. But quite often a Greek aorist is used, and one must inquire what the translators had in mind when they used this tense. Sometimes it seems that the Hebrew perfects were understood as true past tenses, especially those in which the sense of 'I have decided to

---

[159] A. B. Davidson, *Hebrew Syntax*, 3rd edn. (Edinburgh: T. and T. Clark, 1901), 61.

[160] For discussion of these three types see Driver, *Use of the Tenses in Hebrew*, pp. 19–22; Davidson, *Syntax*, pp. 61–2; Gesenius–Kautzsch–Cowley, *Hebrew Grammar*, pp. 312–13; Paul Joüon, *Grammaire de l'hébreu biblique* (Rome: Pontifical Biblical Institute, 1923), 298–9; and Ronald J. Williams, *Hebrew Syntax: An Outline*, 2nd edn. (Toronto: University of Toronto Press, 1976), 30. The prophetic perfect occurs at least once in biblical Aramaic (Dan. 7: 27, translated by aorists in LXX and Theodotion); for this see Hermann L. Strack, *Grammatik des Biblisch-Aramäischen*, 6th edn. (Munich: C. H. Beck, 1921), 26.

do' may be seen (e.g. Deut. 8: 10 ἔδωκεν; 2 Sam. 14: 21 ἐποίησα, 24: 23 ἔδωκεν). At times the aorist appears for the *futurum exactum* and may be used consciously to reflect 'what will be past' in a way comparable to the Hebrew perfect's use (e.g. 1 Kings 8: 47; Ezek. 29: 13). At other places the simple future sense is almost certainly grasped, since the aorist intermingles with futures in a way similar to Hebrew prophetic perfects with imperfects. In these it is possibly the case that the translator intended the Greek aorist to express (perhaps too literally) a similar idiom to that of the Hebrew perfect: an expected or prophesied event presented as though it were already accomplished. These texts illustrate futuristic uses:

Gen. 17: 20 (after Abraham's prayer for Ishmael) 'I have heard you; behold, I *will bless* him [εὐλόγησα]'—followed by four Greek futures

Ps. 20 (19): 7 'The Lord *will help* [ἔσωσεν] his anointed; he will answer him [Gk. fut.] from . . . heaven'
    36 (35): 13 'There the evil-doers *will lie prostrate* [ἔπεσον], they *will be thrust down* [ἐξώσθησαν]'—as a conclusion to what began as a lament over the *present* prosperity of the wicked.

Isa. 5: 13–14 'My people *will go* into exile; they *will die* of hunger and thirst' (ἐγενήθη twice)
    9: 6 'A child *will be born* . . . a son *will be given* . . . government *will rest* on his shoulder . . .' (ἐγεννήθη, ἐδόθη, ἐγενήθη)
    11: 9 'The earth *shall be full* of the knowledge of the Lord' (ἐνεπλήσθη)—in a chapter dominated by LXX futures

Jer. 4: 29 'Every city *will flee* . . . they *will enter* caves . . . they *will go up* into the rocks . . . every city *will be forsaken*' (ἀνεχώρησεν, εἰσέδυσαν, ἀνέβησαν, ἐγκατελείφθη)

Hos. 10: 7, 15 'He *will cut off* Samaria's king . . . the king of Israel *shall be cut off*' (ἀπέρριψεν, ἀπερρίφη)—in context of Greek futures

Amos 5: 2 'The virgin of Israel *will lie fallen* . . . *will be forsaken*' (ἔπεσεν, ἔσφαλεν)—a vision of Israel's future 'funeral' if obedience does not come

It is possible that some of these may be cases of 'mechanical renderings': places in which the context was not clear and the translator simply resorted to the common equation of 'Greek aorist for Hebrew perfect'.[161] However, it seems certain that, whether the translators always understood the sense or not, these forms would be read by many as futuristic: the Greek aorist indicative used to some degree under Hebrew influence to portray a future occurrence as if already done.

When one turns to the NT with this background in mind, one encounters several uses of the Greek aorist which resemble these Hebrew and Septuagint cases. Discussion of these NT examples has often raised the question of Semitic influence, but it must be remembered that the idiom occurs also in non-Semitized Greek. This is not a *non-Greek* idiom, although it perhaps occurs more frequently or seems more natural to the NT writers and readers because of the Hebrew and Septuagint background.[162] Examples of this type of futuristic aorist are:

Mark 11: 24 πάντα ὅσα προσεύχεσθε καὶ αἰτεῖσθε, πιστεύετε ὅτι ἐλάβετε, καὶ ἔσται ὑμῖν .

13: 20 καὶ εἰ μὴ ἐκολόβωσεν κύριος τὰς ἡμέρας, οὐκ ἂν ἐσώθη πᾶσα σάρξ· ἀλλὰ διὰ τοὺς ἐκλεκτοὺς οὓς ἐξελέξατο ἐκολόβωσεν τὰς ἡμέρας (Matt. 24: 22 uses future)

Luke 1: 51–4 (7 aorists, fulfilled in some sense in Mary's experience, but in a still larger sense future).

John 13: 31 νῦν ἐδοξάσθη ὁ υἱὸς τοῦ ἀνθρώπου καὶ ὁ θεὸς ἐδοξάσθη ἐν αὐτῷ

Rom. 8: 30 οὓς δὲ προώρισεν, τούτους καὶ ἐκάλεσεν καὶ οὓς ἐκάλεσεν, τούτους καὶ ἐδικαίωσεν οὓς δὲ ἐδικαίωσεν, τούτους καὶ ἐδόξασεν

1 Thess. 2: 16 ἔφθασεν δὲ ἐπ' αὐτοὺς ἡ ὀργὴ εἰς τέλος

Jude 14 προεφήτευσεν . . . Ἑνὼχ λέγων· ἰδοὺ ἦλθεν κύριος ἐν ἁγίαις μυριάσιν αὐτοῦ

---

[161] See the comments on this method as practised by the translators of Isaiah in R. R. Ottley, *The Book of Isaiah According to the Septuagint (Codex Alexandrinus)*, i. *Introduction and Translation*, 2nd edn. (Cambridge: at the University Press, 1909), 43–4.

[162] It must be remembered in addition that this sort of influence need not be limited to texts where a Semitic original or Semitic sources may be posited. The influence may be more indirect and affect the language of 1st-cent. Jews in more pervasive ways.

Rev. 10: 7 καὶ ἐτελέσθη τὸ μυστήριον τοῦ θεοῦ
   11: 2 μὴ αὐτὴν [τὴν αὐλὴν] μετρήσῃς, ὅτι ἐδόθη τοῖς ἔθνεσιν. καὶ τὴν
       πόλιν τὴν ἁγίαν πατήσουσιν μῆνας τεσσεράκοντα καὶ δύο
   14: 8 ἔπεσεν ἔπεσεν Βαβυλὼν ἡ μεγάλη
   15: 1 ἐν αὐταῖς ἐτελέσθη ὁ θυμὸς τοῦ θεοῦ

These display varying degrees of the three senses discussed
above for the Septuagint aorists and Hebrew perfects lying
behind them. Several are like the prophetic perfect: a vivid,
certain vision of a future occurrence as though already fulfilled
(Jude 14; Rev. 10: 7, 14: 8, 15: 1; perhaps Mark 13: 20).[163]
Others fit the sense of the perfect of confidence: occurrences
which have not yet started or, having started, have not been
completed but which the circumstances show to be inevitable
or for some other reason are viewed as certain (Luke 1: 51–5;
John 13: 31; perhaps 1 Thess. 2: 16).[164] Closely related to this
is the aorist of 'divine decree' which views a future event as
certain because of God's predestination of it in eternity past or
else portrays a course of action just determined in the councils
of heaven but not yet worked out on earth: the aorist refers to
the future working out, but it is seen as certain in the light of
God's decree (e.g. Rom. 8: 30; Rev. 11: 2; perhaps Mark 11:
24, 13: 20; 1 Thess. 2: 16).[165]

[163] This sense and several of these examples are discussed by Angelo Lancellotti,
Sintassi ebraica nel greco dell'Apocalisse, i. *Uso delle forme verbali* (Collectio Assisiensis, 1,
Assisi: Porziuncola, 1964), 48–53; and Steven Thompson, *The Apocalypse and Semitic
Syntax* (Cambridge: Cambridge University Press, 1985), 38–42. See also Mussies,
Morphology, pp. 337–40, who acknowledges such a meaning for Rev. 14: 8 but tends to
discount the prophetic sense in other places cited by Lancellotti. Mussies' point,
which seems valid, is that many aorists occur in Revelation not within a series of
futures (as the Hebrew perfect tends to do), but in groups, and that this is due to a
shift in viewpoint for entire pericopes. Thus, he argues that many such aorists are not
futuristic, but past tenses reflecting the time of the *vision*, not of the events predicted.
This certainly seems true for texts like 19: 17 ff.; 20: 1 ff.; 21: 1 ff.; and some of the
other visions.
   [164] Cf. G. B. Caird, 'The Glory of God in the Fourth Gospel: An Exercise in
Biblical Semantics', *NTS* 15 (1969), 266; id., *Gospel of Luke*, p. 55; and Marshall,
Gospel of Luke, pp. 83–4. Reginald H. Fuller, *The Mission and Achievement of Jesus: An
Examination of the Presuppositions of New Testament Theology* (London: SCM Press, 1954),
26, suggests this sense for the aorist in 1 Thess. 2: 16.
   [165] Cf. Lancellotti's category 'L'aoristo di "predestinazione" ' in *Sintassi ebraica nel*

4. 3. 6 *Dramatic aorist or aorist of present state*

Another use of the aorist indicative in which the past-time value is not so evident is the 'dramatic' aorist, common in classical drama. In this use an aorist of a verb of *emotion* or *understanding* appears in dialogue, expressing a state of feeling or of comprehension reached either in the immediate past or exactly contemporary with the utterance.[166] The verb is usually in the first person and, as Moorhouse says, it is normally used for 'a sudden feeling, or act of comprehension, especially as expressed in quick repartee'.[167] Examples commonly cited are: ἐδεξάμην (I welcome), ἥσθην (I am pleased), ἐγέλασα (I must laugh), ἐπήνεσα (I approve), συνῆκα (I understand), ἔδοξα (I think). All agree that such aorists should be translated into English (German, French, etc.) as present verbs. It is difficult to decide whether the aorist is used in this way because the access of emotion or comprehension is thought of as having *just occurred* (and thus *past* even though immediately past) or as an instantaneous occurrence in the exact present (and thus the *aspect*-value of the aorist is thought to overshadow the temporal meaning). The former explanation seems marginally better, since the present indicative can serve for the latter idea (cf. section 4.1.2) and since the aorist does not in itself express 'instantaneous' aspect. It is true, however, that with STATIVE verbs, such as those of emotion and understanding, the aorist usually denotes the *moment* of entrance into the state, and so an instantaneous sense is likely for the combination dealt with here.

---

greco dell'Apocalisse, pp. 50–1. He describes it as follows: 'esprime la divina disposizione reguardante un evento futuro'. A similar idea is advanced by Ernest Best, *A Commentary on the First and Second Epistle to the Thessalonians* (London: Adam and Charles Black, 1972), 119, regarding the aorist in 1 Thess. 2: 16 and a parallel use of the verb in Theodotion's Daniel 4: 24; and by C. E. B. Cranfield, *A Critical and Exegetical Commentary on the Epistle to the Romans*, i. *Introduction and Commentary on Romans I–VIII* (Edinburgh: T. and T. Clark, 1975), 433, concerning Rom. 8: 30.

[166] KG, *Satzlehre*, pp. 163–5; Gildersleeve, *Syntax*, § 262; Smyth, *Grammar*, § 1937; Humbert, *Syntaxe*, pp. 144–5; SD, *Syntax*, pp. 281–2; Moorhouse, *Syntax*, pp. 195–6; and Rijksbaron, *SSV*, pp. 28–9.

[167] Moorhouse, *Syntax*, p. 195.

This classical use of the aorist is mentioned by several NT grammars,[168] but examples of this are rare in the NT and in the papyri.[169] The one instance which fits the character of the classical dramatic aorist as described above is found in Luke 16: 4 ἔγνων τί ποιήσω 'I know what I shall do!' Several other examples are cited which do not have these characteristics, but which share the *present*-time value seen in the dramatic aorist. These, however, possess a present meaning for a different reason—they are Greek aorists influenced by the Semitic *stative perfect*. This influence on the NT aorist must now be discussed.

The Hebrew stative perfect is the use of the perfect with verbs denoting a state or condition in which the perfect *implies* the past action which produced this state but *emphasizes* the present condition which results from that completed action.[170] The difficulty with such perfects is that they are best rendered, in Greek and in English, by the *present* tense (e.g. יָדַע 'he knows'), or in some cases by the Greek or English *perfect* ('he has come to know'). But this is a contextually determined meaning, because the same form יָדַע could mean 'he knew' (cf. Gen. 28: 16 לֹא יָדַעְתִּי I did not know it). Apart from stative perfect, most perfects in Hebrew are equivalent to past tenses, usually aorists, in Greek, and the Septuagint reflects a common 'Greek aorist for Hebrew perfect' correlation. Mistranslation or mechanical translation occurs when a stative perfect with present meaning is translated into Greek as an

---

[168] Cf. Nunn, *Short Syntax of NT*, p. 70, and HS, *Grammatik*, pp. 327–8 (both very clear); and Zerwick, *Biblical Greek*, pp. 84–5 (clear statement of dramatic use, but confused with the proleptic). In three grammars the dramatic use is mentioned but confused with aorists of acts *just completed* or completed in the *indefinite* past: see Robertson, *Grammar*, pp. 841–2; DM, *Grammar*, pp. 198–9, and BW, *Syntax*, p. 93.

[169] Mayser, *Grammatik*, pp. 144–5, cites five examples which are not parallel. Mandilaras, *Verb*, pp. 168–9, uses the term 'dramatic' to refer to vivid futuristic aorists, and does not cite examples which follow the classical pattern.

[170] Driver, *Use of the Tenses in Hebrew*, pp. 18–19; Gesenius–Kautzsch–Cowley, *Hebrew Grammar*, p. 311; Joüon, *Grammaire de l'hébreu biblique* pp. 294–6; Carl Brockelmann, *Hebräische Syntax* (Neukirchen: Verlag der Buchhandlung des Erziehungsvereins, 1956), 40. The same idiom appears in biblical Aramaic: Bauer–Leander, *Grammatik des Biblisch-Aramäischen*, p. 279.

aorist. Examples of probable mistranslations or mechanical translations of Hebrew stative perfects by aorists in the Septuagint are shown in Table 4.2.

TABLE 4. 2. *Septuagint Mistranslations of Hebrew Stative Perfects*

Verse (MT)	RSV	Septuagint
Gen. 21: 26 (cf. 22: 12)	I do not know	ἔγνων
Num. 11: 5	we remember	ἐμνήσθημεν
1 Sam. 2: 1	I rejoice	εὐφράνθην
Psalm 5: 6	you hate evil doers	ἐμίσησας
7: 2	in thee I take refuge	ἤλπισα
92: 6	how great are thy works	ἐμεγαλύνθη
	thy thoughts are deep	ἐβαθύνθησαν
104: 24	how manifold are thy works	ἐμεγαλύνθη
	the earth is full	ἐπληρώθη
130: 5	I hope in his word	ἤλπισεν
Isaiah 1: 3	Israel does not know	ἔγνω
	my people does not understand	συνῆκεν
2: 6	thy people are full	ἐνεπλήσθη
3: 16	they are haughty	ὑψώθησαν
33: 9	the land mourns	ἐπένθησεν

It is obvious from the examples in the table that the Hebrew stative perfect was not always clearly understood or rendered idiomatically by the Greek translators. The Greek aorist, while it preserves a portion of the original meaning (the completed action which produced the state), essentially falls short of the sense of the Hebrew. A Greek present or perhaps a Greek perfect tense conveys more of the intended sense to the Greek reader (cf. Gen. 27: 2 זָקַנְתִּי I am old, LXX γεγήρακα; also Judges 14: 16), and these do occur in the Septuagint. But the aorist also occurs quite commonly.[171] Whether a first-century Jew might have been aware of the correspondence between stative perfect and Greek aorist in his Greek Bible is difficult to answer. It is probable that some sense of 'past act

---

[171] Thompson, *The Apocalyse and Semitic Syntax*, p. 37, reports that of the 95 Hebrew stative perfects listed by Driver and Gesenius–Kautzsch–Cowley, 45 are translated in the LXX with the aorist, with only 21 presents and 7 perfects.

with its present consequences' would be the meaning understood from the aorist used in the sort of contexts shown above, since this is the sort of intuitive interpretation which the stative perfect requires from the Hebrew reader.

Are there Greek aorists in the NT which should be understood as stative presents following this Hebrew pattern? Here are the most likely prospects for such an understanding.

Matthew 23: 2 ἐκάθισαν. A present meaning 'sit' seems clear in this verse (cf. RSV, NEB). The meanings which are more typical of the aorist seem inadequate: a timeless or gnomic sense,[172] a summary of the whole period of scribal ascendancy viewed from the Evangelist's later time,[173] an indefinite time in the past when each rabbi takes his position of authority.[174] Rather, it is better to regard this as a non-idiomatic Greek expression for the present meaning of the Semitic stative perfect: 'they sit on Moses' seat'.[175]

Mark 1: 11 (~*Matt. 3: 17, Luke 3: 22*) εὐδόκησα.[176] Here again several meanings from idiomatic Greek have been suggested,[177] but a stative meaning from Semitic idiom is preferred: 'I am well pleased'. In this saying the Semitic influence appears to come from the language of the Septuagint, drawn from various texts which speak of God's dealings with his chosen nation and Messiah (Gen. 22: 2; Ps. 2: 7; Isa. 42: 1, 43: 10, 44: 2, 62: 4 in Vaticanus' original hand). Thus the stative perfects of the OT (e.g. Isa. 42: 1 רָצְתָה and 62: 4 חָפֵץ) are likely to have influenced this Greek wording via the Septuagint, resulting in a Semitic use of the aorist.[178]

Luke 1: 47 ἠγαλλίασεν. This aorist occurs in parallelism with

---

[172] Robertson, *Grammar*, p. 837.

[173] Allen, *Matthew*, p. 244.

[174] MH, *Accidence*, p. 458.

[175] J. Wellhausen, *Einleitung in die drei ersten Evangelien* (Berlin: Georg Reimer, 1905), 25; Black, *Aramaic Approach*, p. 128; and BDR, *Grammatik*, § 333 (1b).

[176] Matt. 17: 5 and Luke 12: 32 are similar.

[177] For suggestions along Greek lines see MH, *Accidence*, p. 458, and Taylor, *Mark*, pp. 161–2. A lengthy discussion which stays totally within the bounds of idiomatic Greek (but is not convincing) is found in Burton, *MT*, § 55.

[178] Black, *Aramaic Approach*, p. 128; MT, *Style*, p. 16; and Taylor, *Mark*, p. 64.

a present (μεγαλύνει) and in a section of Luke where Semitic influence is felt to be strong. The translations consistently make this an English present: 'my spirit rejoices' (RSV, NEB, NIV). Black suggests that this is an instance of the aorist used like the Semitic stative perfect.[179] Zerwick notes another possible avenue of Semitic influence: that the aorist after the present verb is 'a servile version of a Hebrew inverted future (form *wayyiktol*) which, though it commonly refers to the past, can itself take a present value after a participle with that value'.[180] A variation on this which can be illustrated from Septuagint translation of Hebrew tenses is the possible use of an imperfect consecutive (i.e. 'inverted future') after a stative perfect:[181] this is the sequence of Hebrew tenses in Psalm 16: 9 (perfect שָׂמַח and imperfect וַיָּגֶל) and 97: 8 (perfect שָׂמְעָה and imperfects וַתַּגֵלְנָה , וַתִּשְׂמַח), where aorists of ἀγαλλιάω occur in the Septuagint translation. It seems that either of these Semitic influences is possible.[182]

Antoniadis appears to stay within the bounds of the classical Greek dramatic aorist in suggesting that the aorist here is used in place of the present in order to express the *depth of feeling* more clearly.[183] This does not seem as likely for this passage as the explanation based on Semitic influence. Plummer explains the aorist in strictly Greek terms as a type of recent or indefinite past, something to be translated into English as a perfect tense;[184] but it can hardly have a past meaning in this verse. Fitzmyer makes it a 'timeless' aorist,[185]

---

[179] Black, *Aramaic Approach*, p. 129.

[180] Zerwick, *Biblical Greek*, p. 85.

[181] Cf. Gesenius–Kautzsch–Cowley, *Hebrew Grammar*, p. 329 (§ 111 r).

[182] Buth does not think either of these Semitic explanations is likely, but posits a type of Semitic influence based on Hebrew poetic style. See Randall Buth, 'Hebrew Poetic Tenses and the Magnificat', *Journal for the Study of the New Testament*, 21 (1984), 78–80.

[183] Antoniadis, *L'Évangile de Luc*, p. 255.

[184] A. Plummer, *A Critical and Exegetical Commentary on the Gospel according to S. Luke*, 4th edn. (ICC; Edinburgh: T. and T. Clark, 1904), 31–2.

[185] Joseph Fitzmyer, *The Gospel according to Luke (I–IX)*, (The Anchor Bible, 28; Garden City, NY: Doubleday, 1981), 366. In this view he is following the suggestion

but this does not fit the features of the gnomic or other category as seen in other Greek literature, and a use based on Semitic influence provides a better explanation of the sense of the aorist here.

Matthew 13: 24, 18: 23, 22: 2 ὡμοιώθη. Black sees these aorists as equivalent to a Semitic perfect of general truth,[186] and this is certainly a possible use in the NT, as shown above. However, the sense of this introduction to parables about the kingdom appears not to state what the kingdom 'is like' in some gnomic or proverbial sense (this is the pattern of the Septuagint aorists used to translate corresponding perfects in Hebrew: ὡμοιώθη for perfect of דָּמָה : Ps. 49 [48]: 13, 21; 102 [101]: 7; 143 [144]: 4). Instead, it tells the hearers what the kingdom 'is like' in the present. A present stative meaning is better,[187] although the distinction is a narrow one. The verb ὡμοιώθη appears in the Septuagint several times with a present stative meaning as the translation for a Hebrew perfect (Cant. 7: 7 [8]; Hos. 4: 6; Zeph. 1: 11).[188] Taken this way, the aorist expression is synonymous with the more common present phrase ὁμοία ἐστίν.[189]

Several other aorists which Black mentions in his list of 'Aorist for the Semitic Perfect'[190] are better taken as simply aorists of *recent past* or *indefinite past* events, both types being

of BDF, *Grammar*, § 333 (2). BDR, *Grammatik*, § 333 (1b), identifies this aorist (correctly in my view) not as 'timeless', but as *stative* in meaning.

[186] Black, *Aramaic Approach*, p. 129.

[187] Cf. BDR, *Grammatik*, § 333 (1b).

[188] The last two of these are mistranslations of the verb דָּמָה 'to destroy', but the grammatical correlation is the same as for דָּמָה ('to be like, resemble').

[189] D. A. Carson, 'The Ὅμοιος Word-Group as Introduction to Some Matthean Parables', *NTS* 31 (1985), 277–82, argues that the aorist bears the sense 'has become like', but he does not say whether this is different from the present phrase. The Semitic background indicates that the past-tense meaning need not be insisted upon; the aorist verb seems to be equivalent to the present verb with adjective. It seems that Carson is correct to hold that both are different in sense from the future ὁμοιωθήσεται used with some parables.

[190] Black, *Aramaic Approach*, pp. 128–9, 194. All but the last of these are cited in MT, *Style*, pp. 16, 33, as aorists influenced by the Hebrew stative perfect, but a past constative sense is preferred.

quite idiomatic Greek. Gnomic or stative present meanings do not appear valid in these texts (see below):

Matt. 6: 12 ἀφήκαμεν 'as we have forgiven'[191]
   10: 25 ἐπεκάλεσαν 'if they have called'
   14: 31 τί ἐδίστασας; 'why did you doubt?'

Mark 1: 8 ἐβάπτισα 'I have baptized'

John 11: 14 ἀπέθανεν 'he has died'

In summary, the aorist occurs infrequently in the NT with a present stative meaning, but this is usually attributable more to Semitic influence than to the use of the classical 'dramatic' aorist.

4. 3. 7 *Epistolary aorist*

The epistolary aorist is quite straightforward, though foreign to English idiom. This is a use of the aorist indicative in letters, with its normal aspectual and temporal meaning, but with a shift in viewpoint: the writer puts himself in the place of his readers and from that perspective views the writing of the letter (and certain items of business closely related to the letter) as *past*, though from his actual viewpoint these things are *present*.[192] English, which takes the position of the writer, must translate such aorists as presents. This use of the aorist occurs, though infrequently, in classical Greek and is well attested in the Hellenistic papyri.[193] In the NT, the most

---

[191] Paul Joüon, *L'Évangile de Notre Seigneur Jésus-Christ: Traduction et commentaire*, 2nd edn. (Paris: G. Beauchesne, 1930), 35, suggests a performative meaning for this example, under the influence of the Aramaic perfect: '*Comme nous remettons* en ce moment même; l'action est déjà accomplie au moment où l'on parle. C'est la valeur de l'aoriste ἀφήκαμεν, qui répond à un parfait araméen'. This would be similar to the Greek dramatic aorist as explained at the beginning of this section, but such a sense does not fit Matt. 6: 12 as well as the constative past rendering.

[192] Cf. Burton, *MT*, § 44; MT, *Syntax*, pp. 72–3; Moule, *Idiom Book*, p. 12; Robertson, *Grammar*, pp. 845–6; and BDR, *Grammatik*, § 334 (this treatment is superior to that found in BDF, *Grammar*).

[193] SD, *Syntax*, p. 281; Gildersleeve, *Syntax*, §§ 297–8 (not frequently attested in classical era, since few genuine letters are preserved); Mayser, *Grammatik*, pp. 143–4 (who notes that the perfect can be used this way as well); and Mandilaras, *Verb*, pp. 136, 166–8 (who notes that the imperfect can also have an epistolary use).

commonly occurring epistolary aorist is the form ἔπεμψα/-αμεν and compounds (Acts 23: 30; 2 Cor. 8: 18, 22; 9: 3; Eph. 6: 22; Phil. 2: 28; Col. 4: 8; Philem. 12). Ironically, epistolary use of the form ἔγραψα is disputed: it seems likely in Gal. 6: 11 and Philem. 19 (and perhaps 1 Cor. 5: 11),[194] but other instances involve some sort of normal aorist sense of 'past from the viewpoint of the writer'. Blass–Debrunner–Rehkopf divide these uses of ἔγραψα into three groups: reference to the letter just being finished (Rom. 15: 5; 1 Pet. 5: 12), reference to some part of the present letter (1 Cor. 9: 15; Philem. 21; etc.), and reference to an earlier letter (1 Cor. 5: 9; 2 Cor. 2: 3–4, 9; 7: 12; 3 John 9). A few other verbs occur in the epistolary aorist referring to affairs closely related to the sending of a letter: 2 Cor. 8: 17 ἐξῆλθεν, 2 Cor. 9: 5 ἀναγκαῖον ἡγησάμην . . . παρακαλέσαι, and Phil. 2: 25 ἀναγκαῖον ἡγησάμην . . . πέμψαι.[195] An epistolary use may be part of the explanation for the aorists in 1 John 2: 12–14 (three aorists [ἔγραψα] in parallel with three presents [γράφω]), but the significance of the phrasing in these verses is not greatly clarified by a grammatical 'solution' of any sort.[196]

4. 4 Excursus: Aorist and Imperfect Indicative with

Verbs of Sending, Commanding, Asking, and Speaking

Two groups of verbs are thought to require special treatment in regard to the usage of the aorist and imperfect indicative:

---

[194] Cf. BDR, *Grammatik*, § 334, for the first two examples. The example in 1 Cor. 5: 11 may refer to a previous letter (as 5: 9) or to what is just being written. On Gal. 6: 11 and 1 Cor. 5: 11 see Moule, *Idiom Book*, p. 12.

[195] Mayser, *Grammatik*, p. 144, and Mandilaras, *Verb*, pp. 167–8, cite several similar examples, especially with the expression ἀναγκαῖον ἡγησάμην (four Oxyrhynchus occurrences in Mandilaras, p. 167). Adolf Deissmann, *Light from the Ancient East: The New Testament Illustrated by Recently Discovered Texts of the Graeco-Roman World*, trans. Lionel R. M. Strachan (London: Hodder and Stoughton, 1927), 176, cites two epistolary aorists in P.Oxy. 115, a letter of sympathy from the 2nd cent. AD: ἐλυπήθην, ἔκλαυσα 'I am sorry, I weep over the departed'.

[196] Cf. Moule, *Idiom Book*, p. 12.

(1) verbs of sending, commanding, and asking; and (2) verbs of speaking.

The first group was singled out for special treatment by Blass in a study published a century ago, and many grammars have followed his lead. In an essay on aorist and imperfect in Demosthenes, Blass cited the following rule:

Es giebt eine Anzahl Verba, Handlungen bezeichnend, die ihr Ziel und ihre Vollendung in dem Thun eines Andern haben, und diese Verba können in weitem Umfange als imperfecta behandelt, d.h. statt in den Aorist ins Imperfektum gesetzt werden, sobald diese Unvollständigkeit und diese Beziehung zu dem ergänzenden Thun eines Andern hervorgehoben werden soll. Dahin gehören κελεύειν, ἀξιοῦν, παρακελεύεσθαι, ἐρωτᾶν, λέγειν, πέμπειν, ἀποστέλλειν u.s.w.[197]

Observations of this sort, especially concerning the imperfect, are cited by a number of grammars, both for Hellenistic Greek usage[198] and for classical.[199] Thus, one would expect to find the imperfect used when the response of another is uncertain or not forthcoming (i.e. when the command or request is essentially *unfulfilled* as far as the focus of the utterance is concerned). In contrast, the aorist is expected when the order is carried out, or is assumed to be carried out, by the one addressed, and thus the action of requesting is *completed*.

This is perhaps the explanation for the frequency of the imperfect with such verbs in classical usage, but it does not

---

[197] Friedrich Blass, 'Demosthenische Studien, III: Aorist und Imperfekt', *Rheinisches Museum für Philologie*, 44 (1889), 410–11. It should be recalled from the treatment in sect. 2.1.2 that Blass was a strong proponent of the view that the aorist denotes *completed* action.

[198] BDF, *Grammar*, § 328; MT, *Syntax* pp. 64–5; Zerwick, *Biblical Greek*, p. 91; Abel, *Grammaire*, pp. 252–3; Mayser, *Grammatik*, p. 135; Mandilaras, *Verb*, pp. 133–4.

[199] Svensson, *Zum Gebrauch der erzählenden Tempora*, pp. 1–77, takes this as one of his main topics and investigates the usage in portions of Herodotus, Thucydides, and Xenophon. He concludes that Blass is essentially correct. See also: KG, *Satzlehre*, pp. 143–5; Stahl, *Syntax*, pp. 97–100; SD, *Syntax*, pp. 277–8; N. E. Collinge, 'Some Reflexions on Comparative Historical Syntax', *AL* 12 (1960), 83–4; Sedgwick, 'The Use of the Imperfect in Herodotus', p. 117; Moorhouse, *Syntax*, pp. 191–2; and Rijksbaron, *SSV*, pp. 18–20. Wackernagel, *Vorlesungen über Syntax*, p. 183, notes the preference for the imperfect with some of these verbs, but does not feel that a clear reason for this can be given.

appear true to actual usage in the NT. In the case of many of the verbs in this category, the imperfect either does not occur in the NT or occurs infrequently compared with the aorist. With other verbs, the imperfect appears commonly enough, but the choice of imperfect or aorist does not seem to be related to the *fulfilment* (or even expectation of fulfilment) of the command or request by another. Note the count of occurrences of aorist indicative vs. imperfects in the NT shown in Table 4.3.

TABLE 4. 3. *Aorist vs. Imperfect in NT Verbs of Sending, Commanding, and Asking*

Verb	Aorist uses	Imperfect uses
ἀποστέλλω	66	none
πέμπω	15 (some epistolary)	none
κελεύω	17	1 (Acts 16: 22)[a]
παραγγέλλω	11	1 (2 Thess. 3: 10)[b]
προστάσσω	6	none
αἰτέω	12	2 (Luke 23: 25, Acts 12: 20)[c]
ἐρωτάω	14	14
ἐπερωτάω	23	20[d]
παρακαλέω	19	18[b]
πυνθάνομαι	1	7

[a] There is certainly no failure to comply with this command, and even if another verb is added to denote compliance (cited by BDF, *Grammar*, § 328, as partial explanation for the imperfect), this order can hardly be regarded as unfulfilled (cf. Acts 25: 6, where another verb relates the compliance after an aorist; and 21: 34, where the command is not carried out until repeated at 22: 24, but aorist is still used). The imperfect here may be attributable to the plural subject; all the aorists are singular.

[b] The imperfect in this verse is customary/iterative in sense. There is an imperfect occurring as a variant at Luke 8: 29, but the aorist is the preferred reading.

[c] Luke 23: 25 is iterative in sense; Acts 12: 20 may be an example of the imperfect used to narrate a tentative, hesitant request. See discussion of this in the following pages.

[d] The large proportion of these imperfects occur in Mark, in keeping with his preference for this tense in narrative. The statistics are as follows: Matt—7 aor./no impf.; Mark—6 aor./15 impf.; Luke—8 aor./5 impf. (none paralleled in Mark.); John—1 aor./no impf.; Acts—1 aor./no impf.

[e] In the Gospels and Acts the count is 12 aor./18 impf.

Only with the last four verbs in the table (ἐρωτάω, ἐπερωτάω, παρακαλέω, πυνθάνομαι) does Blass's rule appear in any way likely, and with these it seems to be valid only in a few cases. With παρακαλέω, for example, some of the imperfect uses could be construed as denoting unsuccessful commands (e.g. Matt. 18: 29; Mark 5: 18; Luke 15: 28; Acts 21: 12), but some of them relate commands which were actually fulfilled (e.g. Matt. 8: 31, 14: 36; Mark 5: 23; Luke 7: 4, 8: 41). In addition, a few of the aorists are also unsuccessful, contrary to the rule's prediction (e.g. 1 Cor. 16: 12; 2 Cor. 12: 8). Many of the imperfects seem to be used to give descriptive vividness to the narrative (Luke 15: 28; Acts 2: 40, 13: 42, 15: 32, 19: 31, 27: 33) and at least one is used to denote customary action (Acts 11: 33). Displaying a similar lack of conformity to this rule are the verbs ἐρωτάω and ἐπερωτάω, and while πυνθάνομαι certainly has an idiomatic preference for the imperfect, this does not seem to be connected in any way with the response of those to whom the request is made. A different explanation is needed for the variation between aorist and imperfect with these verbs. For this purpose, they should be joined with the second major group listed above (verbs of speaking), since the pattern of variation in aspect-usage is similar.

In regard to aorist and imperfect usage with verbs of speaking as well as with the related ideas of commanding, asking, instructing, and the like, the most important observation to be made is that they are almost always used in situations where the *subjective* choice of the speaker/writer is free to operate. As discussed in section 3.2.2.2, past occurrences with an appreciable duration (as speech almost always is) can be narrated with either tense, since there are no objective criteria to force the expression into one aspect or the other.[200] Thus, the speaker is free to select aorist or imperfect with, in many cases, only subtle differences in meaning between the two. At times it is not possible to discern clearly why one tense is chosen over the other, apart from the general aspectual difference: the aorist views the occurrence in its

---

[200] For further discussion see Carl Bache, 'Aspect and Aktionsart: Towards a Semantic Distinction', *JL* 18 (1982), 67–8.

entirety without emphasis on the internal make-up, while the imperfect gives attention to the internal details of the occurrence without regard for the end-points.[201] However, a few broad patterns of more specific distinctions can be suggested, which may explain the variation in many cases. Some of these are differences between the two tenses in narrative which are valid for all verbs, as suggested earlier in this chapter.

One difference is the distinction of *simple* vs. *descriptive* narration, which may appear simply as a difference in the vividness of portrayal used by a writer in narrating a dialogue or a single utterance. This is particularly true of those uses of the imperfect which vividly picture the give-and-take of dialogue, in contrast to the simple narration provided by the aorist. Alternatively, the descriptive difference can work its way out as a distinction between simple reference to the *fact* that an utterance has been made vs. emphasis on the *content* of what is said. As it is put in Blass–Debrunner–Funk, 'the aorist serves for a simple reference to an utterance previously made . . . the imperfect for the delineation of the content of a speech'.[202] It may be recalled that Mark tends to use the descriptive imperfect more than the other Gospels, and it can be observed that this pattern holds good for verbs of speaking.

Mark 2: 24–7 οἱ Φαρισαῖοι ἔλεγον αὐτῷ . . . καὶ λέγει αὐτοῖς . . . καὶ ἔλεγεν αὐτοῖς

3: 21b–3 ἔλεγον γὰρ ὅτι ἐξέστη. καὶ οἱ γραμματεῖς . . . ἔλεγον ὅτι Βεελζεβοὺλ ἔχει καὶ ὅτι ἐν τῷ ἄρχοντι τῶν δαιμονίων ἐκβάλλει τὰ δαιμόνια. καὶ προσκαλεσάμενος αὐτοὺς ἐν παραβολαῖς ἔλεγεν αὐτοῖς

Luke 6: 11 αὐτοὶ δὲ ἐπλήσθησαν ἀνοίας καὶ διελάλουν πρὸς ἀλλήλους τί ἂν ποιήσαιεν τῷ Ἰησοῦ

---

[201] This is the view of McKay, *Greek Grammar for Students*, p. 216. It seems that this general distinction can be maintained even with the very subtle interchange in some texts between εἶπον and ἔλεγον, which many despair of distinguishing. Cf. Burton, *MT*, § 57 and MT, *Syntax* p. 64, who state that no difference can be found between these two.

[202] BDF, *Grammar*, § 329. See similar distinction stated in Zerwick, *Biblical Greek*, p. 91. BDF also suggest that the *length* of the recorded utterance may influence the choice, with longer discourses tending to follow an imperfect. This is not true for Acts (cf. 2: 14, 7: 2, 10: 34, 13: 16, 15: 13, 17: 22, 20: 18) and it seems unlikely to be valid elsewhere except in rare cases.

12: 54 ἔλεγεν δὲ καὶ τοῖς ὄχλοις (after nine aorists)

John 5: 10, 19 ἔλεγον οὖν οἱ Ἰουδαῖοι τῷ τεθεραπευμένῳ . . . ἀπεκρίνατο οὖν ὁ Ἰησοῦς καὶ ἔλεγεν αὐτοῖς

8: 21–8 εἶπεν οὖν πάλιν αὐτοῖς . . . ἔλεγον οὖν οἱ Ἰουδαῖοι . . . καὶ ἔλεγεν αὐτοῖς . . . ἔλεγον οὖν αὐτῷ . . . εἶπεν οὖν [αὐτοῖς] ὁ Ἰησοῦς

Acts 16: 17 αὕτη κατακολουθοῦσα τῷ Παύλῳ καὶ ἡμῖν ἔκραζεν λέγουσα (this verb often in impf., perhaps because it is often part of vivid description)

17: 32 ἀκούσαντες δὲ ἀνάστασιν νεκρῶν οἱ μὲν ἐχλεύαζον, οἱ δὲ εἶπαν

19: 6 ἦλθε τὸ πνεῦμα τὸ ἅγιον ἐπ᾽ αὐτούς, ἐλάλουν τε γλώσσαις καὶ ἐπροφήτευον

28: 17 συνελθόντων δὲ αὐτῶν ἔλεγεν πρὸς αὐτούς (ἔλεγεν/-ον is rarely descriptive in Acts; usually refers to multiple utterances, as shown below)

(See also Mark 4: 21–30; 6: 21–9; Luke 9: 23; 10: 2; 15: 11; 19: 11; 21: 10; 21: 29.)

Another difference which appears commonly is the combined distinction of *single* vs. *multiple* occurrence and *specific* vs. *general* occurrence. It is not always possible to separate these two features, and they are so closely related that they may be stated together.[203] The point here is that an utterance by one individual is more likely to be reported with an aorist verb, while an utterance made by more than one (especially unspecified individuals) is more likely to be reported with an imperfect. Working often in parallel with this, and sometimes at odds with it, is the similar distinction that utterances on *specific* occasions (even with plural subject) may be put in the aorist, but *general* references to utterances made on various occasions are more likely to be phrased with imperfect. This occurs more frequently in Luke–Acts and less frequently in Mark, compared with the previous distinction.

Mark 4: 33 καὶ τοιαύταις παραβολαῖς πολλαῖς ἐλάλει αὐτοῖς τὸν λόγον καθὼς ἠδύναντο ἀκούειν

---

[203] Note how they are combined in BDF, *Grammar*, § 329: the aorist occurs 'especially for a specific pronouncement of an individual. . . . Statements of an unspecified number of individuals are . . . usually indicated by the imperfect'.

4: 41 καὶ ἐφοβήθησαν φόβον μέγαν καὶ ἔλεγον πρὸς ἀλλήλους

Luke 22: 64 καὶ περικαλύψαντες αὐτὸν ἐπηρώτων λέγοντες· προφήτευσον, τίς ἐστιν ὁ παίσας σε;

John 4: 42 τῇ τε γυναικὶ ἔλεγον ὅτι
  5: 18 ἐζήτουν αὐτὸν οἱ Ἰουδαῖοι ἀποκτεῖναι, ὅτι . . . πατέρα ἴδιον ἔλεγεν τὸν θεόν (customary occurrence)
  7: 12 καὶ γογγυσμὸς περὶ αὐτοῦ ἦν πολὺς ἐν τοῖς ὄχλοις· οἱ μὲν ἔλεγον ὅτι ἀγαθός ἐστιν, ἄλλοι [δὲ] ἔλεγον· οὔ, ἀλλὰ πλανᾷ τὸν ὄχλον (imperfects used like these in 7: 25, 40–1; 9: 9, 16; 10: 20–1; 12: 29)

Acts 2: 13–14 ἕτεροι δὲ διαχλευάζοντες ἔλεγον ὅτι γλεύκους μεμεστωμένοι εἰσίν. σταθεὶς δὲ ὁ Πέτρος σὺν τοῖς ἕνδεκα ἐπῆρεν τὴν φωνὴν αὐτοῦ καὶ ἀπεφθέγξατο αὐτοῖς.
  9: 17, 21 ἀπῆλθεν δὲ Ἀνανίας καὶ εἰσῆλθεν . . . καὶ . . . εἶπεν . . . ἐξίσταντο δὲ πάντες οἱ ἀκούοντες καὶ ἔλεγον
  16: 22 οἱ στρατηγοὶ περιρήξαντες αὐτῶν τὰ ἱμάτια ἐκέλευον ῥαβδίζειν
(Also Mark 6: 14–16, 18; Luke 9: 11; John 19: 3; Acts 8: 5, 40; 11: 16, 20; 13: 45; 17: 17–18; 28: 4, 6.)

Another more widespread distinction which appears also with verbs of speaking is the difference of *sequenced* vs. *simultaneous* occurrence. The aorist records events, including utterances, in sequence occurring *in toto* one after another, but the imperfect can be inserted to denote conversation going on at the same time as some event.[204]

Mark 2: 2 καὶ συνήχθησαν πολλοὶ ὥστε μηκέτι χωρεῖν μηδὲ τὰ πρὸς τὴν θύραν, καὶ ἐλάλει αὐτοῖς τὸν λόγον
  4: 2 καὶ ἐδίδασκεν αὐτοὺς ἐν παραβολαῖς πολλὰ καὶ ἔλεγεν αὐτοῖς ἐν τῇ διδαχῇ αὐτοῦ

Luke 24: 32 οὐχὶ ἡ καρδία ἡμῶν καιομένη ἦν [ἐν ἡμῖν] ὡς ἐλάλει ἡμῖν ἐν τῇ ὁδῷ, ὡς διήνοιγεν ἡμῖν τὰς γραφάς;

John 2: 21 ἐκεῖνος δὲ ἔλεγεν περὶ τοῦ ναοῦ τοῦ σώματος αὐτοῦ (a pattern peculiar to John, but similar to these 'simultaneous' uses; imperfect in explanatory clauses with the sense of 'in saying this, what he meant was . . .'; also in John 6: 6, 6: 71, 8: 27, 12: 33; aorist in 7: 39)

Acts 5: 3, 8 εἶπεν δὲ ὁ Πέτρος . . . ἀπεκρίθη δὲ πρὸς αὐτὴν Πέτρος . . . ἡ δὲ

---

[204] Noted by Mateos, *Aspecto verbal*, p. 107.

εἶπεν (aorists in a paragraph of sequenced events: 22 aorists, 2 imperfects, 1 future)

12: 14b–16a εἰσδραμοῦσα δὲ ἀπήγγειλεν ἑστάναι τὸν Πέτρον πρὸ τοῦ πυλῶνος. οἱ δὲ πρὸς αὐτὴν εἶπαν· μαίνῃ. ἡ δὲ διισχυρίζετο οὕτως ἔχειν. οἱ δὲ ἔλεγον· ὁ ἄγγελός ἐστιν αὐτοῦ. ὁ δὲ Πέτρος ἐπέμενεν κρούων (very picturesque: the two aorists are sequenced; then the three imperfects record repeated occurrences taking place all at the same time in the confusion of the situation)

(See also Mark 5: 8, 28; Acts 10: 44–8—present participles record the simultaneous events, aorist indicatives the sequenced ones.)

Turner suggests another difference which may explain the preference for the imperfect displayed by the verb πυνθάνομαι and others: the imperfect may highlight a *tentative* or hesitant request, while the aorist can be more *forceful* and demanding.[205]

Mark 9: 16, 21, 28 καὶ ἐπηρώτησαν αὐτοὺς ... καὶ ἐπηρώτησεν τὸν πατέρα αὐτοῦ ... οἱ μαθηταὶ αὐτοῦ κατ᾽ ἰδίαν ἐπηρώτων αὐτόν

12: 18, 28 Σαδδουκαῖοι . . . ἐπηρώτων αὐτὸν . . . εἷς τῶν γραμματέων ἀκούσας αὐτῶν συζητούντων, ἰδὼν ὅτι καλῶς ἀπεκρίθη αὐτοῖς ἐπηρώτησεν αὐτόν (false hesitancy as a guise, and then guileless confidence?)

Luke 8: 9 ἐπηρώτων δὲ αὐτὸν οἱ μαθηταὶ αὐτοῦ τίς αὕτη εἴη ἡ παραβολή (similar in the parallel Mark 4: 10)

18: 36 ἀκούσας δὲ ὄχλου διαπορευομένου ἐπυνθάνετο τί εἴη τοῦτο

Acts 1: 6 οἱ μὲν οὖν συνελθόντες ἠρώτων αὐτὸν λέγοντες· κύριε, εἰ ἐν τῷ χρόνῳ τούτῳ ἀποκαθιστάνεις τὴν βασιλείαν τῷ Ἰσραήλ;

(This pattern does not seem to occur in John.)

Another proposal which has merit was suggested by Joüon. He observed that verbs of asking or speaking in certain passages in the Letter of Aristeas fell into a predictable pattern of aspect-usage depending on the order of verbs: the *first* verb in the account of a dialogue appeared in the aorist, while *second* or later verbs occurred in the imperfect with the sense 'he

---

continued to ask/say'. Joüon discovered passages in the Gospels in which the same pattern seems to occur.[206] For example, the pattern εἶπεν ... ἔλεγεν occurs with this sense in Mark 7: 6, 9; 8: 34 with 9: 1; Luke 5: 34, 36; 13: 2, 6; 14: 5, 7; 17: 37 with 18: 1; John 6: 61, 65; 8: 13, 19 (plural). The pattern ἐπηρώτησεν ... ἐπηρώτα appears in Mark 14: 60–1 and 15: 2, 4.

Finally, it seems likely that an observation given in Blass–Debrunner–Funk is valid in some cases: the concluding statement in a dialogue may be expected to occur in the aorist rather than the imperfect.[207] See the following texts for illustrations: Mark 5: 28–34, 5: 43, 7: 29, 9: 29; Luke 3: 14, 23: 43; John 8: 28. See also Matt. 8: 13, 12: 49, 13: 52, 21: 27; however, since the aorist is so common in Matthew, these may be just the normal narrative form.

In summary, it must be emphasized that no single specific pattern of variation can be found to govern the use of aorist and imperfect with *verba dicendi* and related concepts. However, several kinds of subtle, sometimes conflicting, distinctions can be stated which explain the variation in many passages. All of these are based ultimately on the more general aspect-distinction, which can be maintained even in the face of quite free interchange between tenses of these verbs in some passages.

4. 5 Uses of the Perfect Indicative

The perfect indicative displays the general meaning of the perfect which is set forth in section 2.3 and adds to it a tense-value, as one expects of all the indicative forms. The general meaning of the perfect involves three elements which combine to produce the basic sense: there is an Aktionsart-feature of *stative* situation, an internal tense-feature of *anteriority*, and an aspect-feature of summary viewpoint concerning

---

[206] Paul Joüon, 'Imparfaits de "continuation" dans la Lettre d'Aristée et dans les Évangiles', *Recherches de science religieuse*, 28 (1938), 93–6.
[207] BDF, *Grammar*, § 329.

an occurrence. Put together, these result in a sense usually described as denoting 'a condition resulting from an anterior occurrence'. In the indicative forms the temporal element which is added is the correlation of the condition or result with the time of speaking: in other words, the result of the occurrence is seen to be 'present' or simultaneous with the time of speaking. These elements of meaning combine in different ways with other contextual features to produce several distinguishable uses.

4. 5. 1 *Perfect of resulting state* [208]

This is the normal use and it is the most direct application of the threefold meaning of the perfect: the three elements of meaning which make up its basic sense are all apparent. While the emphasis in this use falls on the *state* or condition existing at the time of speaking, there is also a clear implication of the *anterior occurrence* which produced it.[209]

For interpreting the specific sense of a perfect verb, the most important feature to note is the lexical character of the verb itself. The primary distinction in this regard is the difference between STATIVE and active verbs.[210] Among the four types of active verbs (described in Chapter 3) only minor differences in the nuance of the perfect can be cited; the reader is referred to that chapter for details.

1. The perfect indicative of 'resulting state' with a STATIVE verb describes an existing condition of the subject and implies the action which produced it (or the act of entrance which led into that condition), with the emphasis usually on the condi-

---

[208] There is no standard nomenclature for these categories, and the grammars reflect confusion over what various labels denote, especially the terms 'intensive' and 'extensive'. The titles used here are chosen in an attempt to be as transparent as possible concerning the sense of the categories.

[209] Cf. Burton, *MT*, § 74 (he unfortunately calls this the 'Perfect of Completed Action', a phrase which I feel serves better for the other major use, given below); Moorhouse, *Syntax*, pp. 197–8; and McKay, 'On the Perfect', p. 296.

[210] Cf. Ruipérez, *Estructura*, pp. 45–65; McKay, 'On the Perfect', pp. 296–7; and Moorhouse, *Syntax*, p. 199.

tion rather than on the action. Thus, the perfect indicatives of these verbs contrast to some degree with the corresponding present and aorist, which refer only to the continuing state or to the beginning of it, respectively.[211] In a sense, the perfect with STATES combines the meaning of the aorist and the present together in one form, denoting the ingressive sense of the aorist and the stative meaning of the present.[212] This use occurs with various types of STATES, but especially with verbs of emotion, perception, cognition, and mental state.

John 5: 42 ἀλλὰ ἔγνωκα ὑμᾶς ὅτι τὴν ἀγάπην τοῦ θεοῦ οὐκ ἔχετε ἐν ἑαυτοῖς
   11: 11–12 Λάζαρος . . . κεκοίμηται . . . κύριε, εἰ κεκοίμηται σωθήσεται
   11: 27 πιστεύεις τοῦτο; . . . ναὶ κύριε, ἐγὼ πεπίστευκα ὅτι σὺ εἶ ὁ χριστός
   15: 24 νῦν δὲ καὶ ἑωράκασιν καὶ μεμισήκασιν καὶ ἐμὲ καὶ τὸν πατέρα μου
   17: 7 νῦν ἔγνωκαν ὅτι πάντα . . . παρὰ σοῦ εἰσιν

Rom. 5: 2 δι' οὗ καὶ τὴν προσαγωγὴν ἐσχήκαμεν [τῇ πίστει] εἰς τὴν χάριν ταύτην

2 Cor. 1: 10 (cf. John 5: 45; 1 Tim. 4: 10, 5: 5) ἠλπίκαμεν [ὅτι] καὶ ἔτι ῥύσεται
   11: 21 κατὰ ἀτιμίαν λέγω, ὡς ὅτι ἡμεῖς ἠσθενήκαμεν

1 Tim. 6: 4 [εἴ τις ἑτεροδιδασκαλεῖ . . .] τετύφωται, μηδὲν ἐπιστάμενος

1 John 4: 14 ἡμεῖς τεθεάμεθα καὶ μαρτυροῦμεν ὅτι . . .

Rev. 3: 17 πλούσιός εἰμι καὶ πεπλούτηκα καὶ οὐδὲν χρείαν ἔχω (parallel clauses repeating essentially the same idea for emphasis)

Since the present and perfect indicatives of stative verbs display similar meanings (both denoting continuing condition of the subject), it is natural to inquire what difference there is, if any, between these tenses. Some grammarians have detected a strengthened or *intensive* meaning for the perfect compared to the present.[213] For example, πεπίστευκα would thus express a

---

[211] Thus, as McKay, 'On the Perfect', pp. 299–303, esp. 299, says about ἔγνωκα, it has a stative meaning but differs from the present and from the stative οἶδα 'in having an inbuilt reference to the event of acquisition of knowledge'.

[212] In this way it is true for these verbs (but *not* for actives) that the perfect combines the meanings of the present and aorist, as stated by BDF, *Grammar*, § 340; Abel, *Grammaire*, p. 257; and MT, *Syntax*, p. 82.

[213] Cf. Gildersleeve, *Syntax*, §§ 229–32; Smyth, *Grammar*, § 1947; Wackernagel,

present faith, but stronger than πιστεύω, ἤλπικα a firmer hope than ἐλπίζω, and τεθέαμαι more vivid sight than θεάομαι. However, this suggested difference of meaning does not fit the evidence of actual NT usage. Perfects of STATIVE verbs consistently reflect the sense described above: a present condition resulting from a past act of entering that state.[214] This sense is intensive or strengthened only in that it adds the implication of the act which produced the state, a feature not included by the present.[215]

2. The perfect indicative of 'resulting state' with an *active* verb describes a present condition or state of affairs produced by the action of the verb. There is debate over whether the 'state' denoted by the perfect pertains to the *subject* or *object* of the verb. It is clear that the state of the *subject* is at least more frequently in view, and McKay argues that NT perfects always refer to the condition of the subject and not that of the object.[216]

The question of perfects which are concerned with the state

Vorlesungen über Syntax, pp. 166–7; Rijksbaron, *SSV*, p. 36 ('expresses the highest degree of that state'); and Burton, *MT*, § 77. It is suggested that different classes of verbs occur with this sense, but most are STATIVE: verbs of emotion, appearance, and sight are most frequently cited. One group is not stative—verbs of sound (of which John 1: 15 κέκραγεν is an idiomatic example). Several other grammars infelicitously use the term 'intensive' as the label for the whole category of 'perfect of resulting state'. See DM, *Grammar*, p. 202; BW, *Syntax*, p. 95.

[214] This can be seen most clearly by comparing the perfect and present uses of ὁράω, γινώσκω, πιστεύω, ἔχω, and θεάομαι. These are the stative verbs which have the most frequent perfect usage in the NT. Edwin A. Abbott, *Johannine Grammar* (London: Adam and Charles Black, 1906), 345, suggests that the perfect of πιστεύω in John possesses the meaning of 'having a perfect [i.e. complete, full-orbed] belief', but this simply cannot be made to fit the evidence of usage. Steyer, *Satzlehre*, p. 60, likewise holds that 2 Tim. 1: 12 οἶδα ᾧ πεπίστευκα, as an example of the intensive perfect, means: 'ich weiß, an wen ich glaube (wem mein ganzer Glaube gehört)'. The context may imply this strengthened meaning, but it is not due to the tense-use alone, to judge from usage of the perfect with other stative verbs in the NT.

[215] This is the conclusion regarding the 'intensive' perfect reached by Moorhouse, *Syntax*, pp. 198–9, and McKay, 'On the Perfect', pp. 297, 311–12.

[216] McKay, 'On the Perfect', pp. 311–14. He has produced a series of articles advancing this thesis for other bodies of ancient Greek usage. The most comprehensive of these is K. L. McKay. 'The Use of the Ancient Greek Perfect down to the Second Century A.D.', *BICS* 12 (1965), 1–21. See the Bibliography for others.

of the *object* was raised by Wackernagel and later by Chantraine both of whom trace a process of development in which the ancient Greek perfect moved from intransitive usage with an exclusive focus on the condition of the subject in Homeric Greek to the growth of a transitive active perfect with focus on the state of the object in late classical and Hellenistic Greek.[217]

To investigate this question in NT usage, one notices first of all that there are a number of *intransitive* perfects and *passives* which clearly have the state of the *subject* in view. There appear to be no exceptions to this, even when an agent or other noun-adjunct occurs with the verb. These examples should be cited to put the whole discussion in perspective, but they are somewhat beside the point, since no one disputes the sense of them.[218] The particular condition of the subject varies, of course, depending on the lexical sense of the verb.

Matt. 2: 20 τεθνήκασιν γὰρ οἱ ζητοῦντες τὴν ψυχὴν τοῦ παιδίου
    4: 4, 6, 7 γέγραπται . . . γέγραπται . . . γέγραπται (66 times in passive in NT)
    8: 6 ὁ παῖς μου βέβληται ἐν τῇ οἰκίᾳ παραλυτικός

Mark 1: 15 πεπλήρωται ὁ καιρὸς καὶ ἤγγικεν ἡ βασιλεία τοῦ θεοῦ[219]

Luke 5: 23 ἀφέωνταί σοι αἱ ἁμαρτίαι σου

John 5: 24 (cf. 1 John 3: 14) μεταβέβηκεν ἐκ τοῦ θανάτου εἰς τὴν ζωήν
    19: 28 ὅτι ἤδη πάντα τετέλεσται

Acts 8: 14 ἀκούσαντες . . . ὅτι δέδεκται ἡ Σαμάρεια τὸν λόγον τοῦ θεοῦ
    10: 45 ἐξέστησαν . . . ὅτι καὶ ἐπὶ τὰ ἔθνη ἡ δωρεὰ τοῦ ἁγίου πνεύματος ἐκκέχυται

---

[217] Jacob Wackernagel, 'Studien zum griechischen Perfectum', *Programm zur akademischen Preisverteilung* (1984), 3–24, repr. in *Kleine Schriften* (Göttingen: Vandenhoeck and Ruprecht, [1953]), 1000–21; and Pierre Chantraine, *Histoire du parfait grec* (Paris: H. Champion, 1927). Wackernagel labels this perfect the 'Resultativperfektum', a term easily confused with the larger use of the perfect to denote an existing result. A. Debrunner in a review of Chantraine in *IF* 46 (1928), 290, suggests a better label: 'Objektsresultativum'.

[218] The debate centres on transitive active perfects, to be treated below.

[219] The latter perfect here seems to mean 'has drawn near' or 'is at hand', rather than 'has arrived', but such a difference is more lexical than aspectual. See the discussion of this in: J. Y. Campbell, 'The Kingdom of God has Come', *Exp. T.* 48 (1936–7), 91–4; C. H. Dodd, 'The Kingdom of God has Come', ibid. 138–42; and J. M. Creed, 'The Kingdom of God has Come', ibid. 184–5.

Rom. 3: 21 (cf. 2 Cor. 5: 11) νυνὶ δὲ χωρὶς νόμου δικαιοσύνη θεοῦ πεφανέρωται
  4: 14 (cf. Gal. 5: 11) εἰ γὰρ οἱ ἐκ νόμου κληρονόμοι, κεκένωται ἡ πίστις καὶ κατήργηται ἡ ἐπαγγελία

1 Cor. 1: 13 μεμέρισται ὁ Χριστός;
  7: 27 δέδεσαι γυναικί, μὴ ζήτει λύσιν· λέλυσαι . . . μὴ ζήτει γυναῖκα

2 Cor. 7: 4 πεπλήρωμαι τῇ παρακλήσει, ὑπερπερισσεύομαι τῇ χαρᾷ
  9: 2 Ἀχαία παρεσκεύασται ἀπὸ πέρυσι

Col. 1: 16 τὰ πάντα δι' αὐτοῦ καὶ εἰς αὐτὸν ἔκτισται

Heb. 2: 18 ἐν ᾧ γὰρ πέπονθεν αὐτὸς πειρασθείς, δύναται τοῖς πειραζομένοις βοηθῆσαι (state of subject shown in 18b)
  12: 2 ἐν δεξιᾷ τε τοῦ θρόνου τοῦ θεοῦ κεκάθικεν

1 John 2: 29 (cf. 4: 7, 5: 1) πᾶς ὁ ποιῶν τὴν δικαιοσύνην ἐξ αὐτοῦ γεγέννηται

In the case of *transitive active* perfects, the pattern is not so uniform. These may still be concerned with a state true of the *subject*, especially in denoting the 'responsibility' on the part of the subject for having done the action (whether for credit or for blame) or in emphasizing his authority to act in such a way.[220] But there are clear cases which emphasize a condition of the *object* (i.e. the 'goal' of the action rather than the agent), reflecting how it has been effected or affected by the action of the verb.

Matt. 22: 4 τὸ ἄριστόν μου ἡτοίμακα . . . καὶ πάντα ἕτοιμα (result emphasized by adjective in the following clause)

Mark 7: 37 καὶ ὑπερπερισσῶς ἐξεπλήσσοντο λέγοντες· καλῶς πάντα πεποίηκεν (credit to the subject; similar use Mark 5: 19, Luke 1: 25)

John 4: 38 ἄλλοι κεκωπιάκασιν (to their credit: μισθόν, v. 36)
  5: 36 τὰ γὰρ ἔργα ἃ δέδωκέν μου ὁ πατὴρ ἵνα τελειώσω αὐτά, αὐτὰ τὰ ἔργα ἃ ποιῶ μαρτυρεῖ περὶ ἐμοῦ ὅτι ὁ πατήρ με ἀπέσταλκεν (here the authority of the Father in giving and sending is stressed, but see 7: 19, 22, which seem to highlight the condition of the

---

[220] This is one of the valuable insights provided by McKay in his study of perfect usage. See e.g. 'On the Perfect', pp. 296–7, 311–14.

recipients; perhaps the 'condition' to be noted here in 5: 36 encompasses both subject and object, as in 1 John 4: 14, as noted below)

11: 34 ποῦ τεθείκατε αὐτόν; (surely his location is in view, not their responsibility etc.)

15: 3 ἤδη ὑμεῖς καθαροί ἐστε διὰ τὸν λόγον ὃν λελάληκα ὑμῖν (state of subject or of indirect object? Seemingly the latter)

16: 6 ἀλλ' ὅτι ταῦτα λελάληκα ὑμῖν ἡ λύπη πεπλήρωκεν ὑμῶν τὴν καρδίαν (state of 'object affected' in both cases)

17: 6 τὸν λόγον σου τετήρηκαν (to their credit; here the meaning of the verb suggests 'action up to the time of speaking', but this is unusual for the perfect)

17: 14 ἐγὼ δέδωκα αὐτοῖς τὸν λόγον σου καὶ ὁ κόσμος ἐμίσησεν αὐτούς (condition of the recipients; but perfect of δίδωμι occurs 11 times in this prayer, usually stressing the authority of the subject to act)

Acts 5: 28 (cf. Luke 4: 21; Rom. 1: 29, 13: 8) πεπληρώκατε τὴν Ἰερουσαλὴμ τῆς διδαχῆς ὑμῶν (their responsibility for the act is in view)

21: 28 κεκοίνωκεν τὸν ἅγιον τόπον τοῦτον (state of the subject for having done this deed: his guilt is proclaimed)

25: 11 εἰ . . . ἀδικῶ καὶ ἄξιον θανάτου πέπραχά τι (present responsibility for the past act is in view)

1 Cor. 7: 15, 17 ἐν δὲ εἰρήνῃ κέκληκεν ὑμᾶς ὁ θεός . . . εἰ μὴ ἑκάστῳ ὡς ἐμέρισεν ὁ κύριος, ἕκαστον ὡς κέκληκεν ὁ θεός, οὕτως περιπατείτω (both seem to focus on condition of object)

Heb. 8: 13 ἐν τῷ λέγειν καινὴν πεπαλαίωκεν τὴν πρώτην (state of object)

11: 28 πίστει πεποίηκε τὸ πάσχα καὶ τὴν πρόσχυσιν τοῦ αἵματος (the dative in this context seems to point to a focus on the subject who is credited with doing this, rather than on the objects 'performed')

1 John 4: 13 ἐν τούτῳ γινώσκομεν ὅτι ἐν αὐτῷ μένομεν καὶ αὐτὸς ἐν ἡμῖν, ὅτι ἐκ τοῦ πνεύματος αὐτοῦ δέδωκεν ἡμῖν (state of indirect object)

4: 14 ὁ πατὴρ ἀπέσταλκεν τὸν υἱὸν σωτῆρα τοῦ κόσμου (state of object is important here but perhaps this is the counterpart to e.g. John 5: 43 ἐγὼ ἐλήλυθα ἐν τῷ ὀνόματι τοῦ πατρός μου, in which there is focus both on the 'originating authority' and on the resulting status of 'the one who comes/is sent')

One further point concerning this use of the perfect is to

note that it is used in the Gospel and Epistles of John more frequently than in any other NT books. This seems to be due to a desire to dwell on the continuing *effects* of the events of Jesus' life recorded in the Gospel and reflected upon in the Epistles.[221] This is related to the observable fact that perfect indicatives are more characteristic of a reflective and discursive style in which the significance of events is dwelt upon, and they occur less in straightforward narrative.[222]

4. 5. 2 *Perfect of completed action*

In contrast to the use just described, the perfect may place emphasis on the *completion* (or actual occurrence) of the action, with any result of the occurrence referred to only secondarily.[223] This is simply a case of one of the features of its basic sense coming to the fore in certain contexts: here the aspectual element stands out, the sense (shared with the aorist) of viewing the action in *summary*. To see the action 'as a whole' can give the effect of highlighting the *completion* of it, while leaving the resulting condition in the background. Alternatively, one could say that the accomplishment of the action is so emphasized that the resulting state is merely the vague condition of 'the occurrence having actually taken place on a particular occasion or, more generally, at least once in the past'. This is similar in many respects to the use of the perfect which Comrie calls the 'experiential perfect'. This use 'indicates that a given situation [i.e. action or state] has held at

---

[221] This point is developed most clearly by Morton S. Enslin, 'The Perfect Tense in the Fourth Gospel', *JBL* 55 (1936), 121–31, esp. 126–31. See also MT, *Syntax*, p. 83.

[222] Cf. Basil Lanneau Gildersleeve, 'Stahl's Syntax of the Greek Verb, Second Article: Tenses', *AJP* 29 (1908), 396.

[223] This use is absent from the major grammars, but it appears in some intermediate grammars under the label 'consummative' perfect. See DM, *Grammar*, pp. 202–3; BW, *Syntax*, pp. 95–6; and Philip R. Williams, *Grammar Notes on the Noun and the Verb and Certain Other Items*, rev. (Tacoma: Northwest Baptist Seminary Press, 1976), 32. Abel. *Grammaire*, p. 258, also describes this use very clearly ('Le parfait désigne alors *l'action passée* de préférence à l'état résultant de cette action'), but does not give it a specific label.

least once during some time in the past leading up to the present'.[224] The point is that the action has *actually* occurred: it *has* taken place at least once, or it did occur on the particular occasion under discussion. With a negative this use of the perfect emphasizes that the occurrence has never taken place or did not occur on a specific occasion.

Emphasis on completion of the action appears commonly when the perfect verb occurs in the active voice with transitives, especially with verbs of the ACCOMPLISHMENT or CLIMAX types.[225] It seems appropriate also in a context which implies resistance to the action or difficulty in performing it. In this way the perfect is similar to, though not identical with, the use of the consummative aorist. It is not identical in that this use of the perfect does still imply a resulting state (though it is not emphasized), while the aorist itself does not.

Mark 5: 34 (+parallels) θυγάτηρ, ἡ πίστις σου σέσωκέν σε

John 1: 18 θεὸν οὐδεὶς ἑώρακεν πώποτε
   1: 41 εὑρήκαμεν τὸν Μεσσίαν
   13: 12 γινώσκετε τί πεποίηκα ὑμῖν;
   16: 33 (cf. 1 John 2: 13–14) ἀλλὰ θαρσεῖτε, ἐγὼ νενίκηκα τὸν κόσμον

Acts 17: 28 ὡς καί τινες τῶν καθ' ὑμᾶς ποιητῶν εἰρήκασιν

1 Cor. 5: 3 ἐγὼ μὲν γάρ . . . ἤδη κέκρικα . . . τὸν οὕτως τοῦτο κατεργασάμενον

Col 2: 14 καὶ αὐτὸ ἦρκεν ἐκ τοῦ μέσου προσηλώσας αὐτὸ τῷ σταυρῷ

2 Tim. 4: 7 τὸν καλὸν ἀγῶνα ἠγώνισμαι, τὸν δρόμον τετέλεκα, τὴν πίστιν τετήρηκα

Heb. 1: 13 πρὸς τίνα δὲ τῶν ἀγγέλων εἴρηκέν ποτε . . .;
   4: 4 εἴρηκεν γάρ που περὶ τῆς ἑβδόμης οὕτως
   7: 13b ἀφ' ἧς οὐδεὶς προσέσχηκεν τῷ θυσιαστηρίῳ
   10: 14 μιᾷ γὰρ προσφορᾷ τετελείωκεν εἰς τὸ διηνεκὲς τοὺς ἁγιαζομένους

1 John 1: 10 ἐὰν εἴπωμεν ὅτι οὐχ ἡμαρτήκαμεν

---

[224] Comrie, *Aspect*, pp. 58–9.
[225] Mateos, *Aspecto verbal*, pp. 121–2.

4. 5. 3 *Perfect with purely present meaning*

A third use of the perfect occurs with a limited number of verbs, in which the tense has acquired a *present stative* meaning with no implication of a prior action which produced the state. This is like the first use in emphasizing a present state, but unlike it in lacking the sense of antecedent occurrence.[226] Of the verbs which are commonly thought to possess this sense, three occur frequently in the NT: οἶδα, ἕστηκα, and πέποιθα/ πέπεισμαι.[227] Other verbs with this use occur less frequently: ἀνέῳγεν (1 Cor. 16: 9; 2 Cor. 6: 11), ἔοικεν (Jas. 1: 6, 23), and μέμνησθε (1 Cor. 11: 2).[228] Examples of the first three are:

Luke 8: 20 ἡ μήτηρ σου καὶ οἱ ἀδελφοί σου ἑστήκασιν ἔξω ἰδεῖν θέλοντές σε

John 16: 30 νῦν οἴδαμεν ὅτι οἶδας πάντα καὶ οὐ χρείαν ἔχεις

21: 15, 16, 17 ναὶ κύριε, σὺ οἶδας ὅτι φιλῶ σε . . . ναὶ κύριε, σὺ οἶδας ὅτι φιλῶ σε . . . κύριε, πάντα σὺ οἶδας, σὺ γινώσκεις ὅτι φιλῶ σε

Acts 1: 11 ἄνδρες Γαλιλαῖοι, τί ἑστήκατε [ἐμ]βλέποντες εἰς τὸν οὐρανόν;

Rom. 14: 14 οἶδα καὶ πέπεισμαι ἐν κυρίῳ Ἰησοῦ ὅτι . . .

Gal. 5: 10 ἐγὼ πέποιθα εἰς ὑμᾶς ἐν κυρίῳ ὅτι . . .

Heb. 10: 11 καὶ πᾶς μὲν ἱερεὺς ἕστηκεν καθ' ἡμέραν λειτουργῶν

4. 5. 4 *Perfect with aoristic sense*

A fourth category of the perfect, over which there is dispute, is the use of the tense as an equivalent to the aorist: that is, as a simple narrative tense to report past occurrences without

---

[226] Cf. Burton, *MT*, § 75; BDF, *Grammar*, § 341; and Robertson, *Grammar*, pp. 881, 894.

[227] These three verbs account for 28% of all perfect indicatives in the NT. According to Leslie W. Sloat, 'New Testament Verb Forms', in John H. Skilton (ed.), *The New Testament Student at Work*, (Nutley, NJ: Presbyterian and Reformed Publishing Co., 1975), 211, there are 834 perfect indicatives in the NT (601 active, 231 middle-passive). My count for these verbs is as follows: οἶδα (208), ἕστηκα (17), and πέποιθα/πέπεισμαι (12).

[228] Perhaps others can be included. HS, *Grammatik*, p. 329, list these verbs in addition: τέθνηκα, κέκλημαι, ἀπόλωλα, κέκτημαι. My preference is to see these as 'perfects of resulting state' (sect. 4.5.1): i.e. they include some nuance of 'completed action' as well as the sense of 'present state'.

attention paid to their present consequences. It is certain that the perfect suffered this confusion with the aorist in late Koine and Byzantine Greek,[229] and the path towards this is made easier by the fact that the true perfect shares with the aorist the feature of denoting a past occurrence in summary. But the question remains whether this aoristic use of the perfect appears in the NT.

Mandilaras suggests three criteria which may be used to indicate that a perfect is used in an aoristic sense: (1) when it is co-ordinated with an aorist, (2) 'when the context denotes no relationship of the past action to present time', and (3) when the perfect is accompanied by an adverbial modifier highlighting the past-time reference.[230] He goes on to evaluate these criteria, and his comments will serve as a starting-point for the assessment given here.

Mandilaras notes that the first criterion 'is not always valid', since an author may use two tenses side by side and yet preserve the distinctive sense of each.[231] This is certainly correct, and what remains is a guideline which *may* be of use but cannot be totally reliable, as illustrated by these examples:

Matt. 13: 46 εὑρὼν δὲ ἕνα πολύτιμον μαργαρίτην ἀπελθὼν πέπρακεν πάντα ὅσα εἶχεν καὶ ἠγόρασεν αὐτόν (seems equivalent)

John 12: 40 τετύφλωκεν αὐτῶν τοὺς ὀφθαλμοὺς καὶ ἐπώρωσεν αὐτῶν τὴν καρδίαν (distinctive)

Acts 21: 28 ἔτι τε καὶ Ἕλληνας εἰσήγαγεν εἰς τὸ ἱερὸν καὶ κεκοίνωκεν τὸν ἅγιον τόπον τοῦτον (distinctive)

---

[229] Chantraine, *Parfait*, pp. 243–5; and Mandilaras, *Verb*, p. 221.

[230] Mandilaras, *Verb*, pp. 225–6. These three are the main criteria and they are used by other grammarians as well. Chantraine, *Parfait*, pp. 235–7, utilizes two other features of usage in his treatment of aoristic perfects in the NT: the interchange of aorist and perfect in Synoptic parallels and the confusion of the two in manuscript variants at numerous points in the textual tradition. But these cannot be taken as valid. Variation (of all sorts) in Synoptic accounts is usually taken to show different purposes or stylistic idiosyncrasies among the evangelists, not as an indication that the variations mean the same thing. The second criterion demonstrates perhaps confusion of tenses by the copyists, but not directly by the writers of the NT.

[231] *Verb*, p. 225. Cf. Robertson, *Grammar*, p. 90, for the same point. Or the aorist may carry on the force of the perfect in conjunction reduction, as suggested by Louw, 'Verbal Aspect in the First Letter of John', pp. 101–2. See sect. 3.5.2 for discussion.

1 Cor. 15: 3b–5a Χριστὸς ἀπέθανεν ὑπὲρ τῶν ἁμαρτιῶν ἡμῶν κατὰ τὰς γραφὰς καὶ ὅτι ἐτάφη καὶ ὅτι ἐγήγερται τῇ ἡμέρα τῇ τρίτῃ κατὰ τὰς γραφὰς καὶ ὅτι ὤφθη (distinctive)

2 Cor. 11: 25 τρὶς ἐρραβδίσθην, ἅπαξ ἐλιθάσθην, τρὶς ἐναυάγησα, νυχθήμερον ἐν τῷ βυθῷ πεποίηκα (equivalent)

Rev. 5: 7 καὶ ἦλθεν καὶ εἴληφεν ἐκ τῆς δεξιᾶς τοῦ καθημένου (equivalent)

(See also Luke 4: 18; John 18: 20; 2 Cor. 2: 13; Rev. 8: 5.)

Mandilaras states that the second criterion 'is often uncertain because the context alone may mislead us'.[232] It is true that context is difficult to judge in a matter such as this, but the second criterion is nevertheless the primary focus of this issue: is the perfect used as a simple past tense without concern for present consequences, or does the writer seem to have some sort of present result of the action in mind as he chooses the perfect? The previous set of examples and their accompanying comments may be consulted as illustrations of this point as well.

Mandilaras settles on the third criterion as the best indicator of aoristic use of the perfect: 'the perfect tends to become a mere preterite when a definite point of time in the past is stated or otherwise implied'.[233] While this feature may be of some value, Mandilaras's confidence in it seems to go too far. Where it may be valid is (in aid of the second criterion) in indicating an exclusive focus on the past occurrence and an absence of any reference to present consequences. But one must be careful to investigate whether, even while noting the time of the past event, the writer desires to include an allusion to its continuing present result.[234] This is certainly the case in 1 Cor. 15: 4. Here Paul locates the past act of resurrection 'on the third day', but his emphasis in the entire passage as well as

---

[232] Verb, pp. 225–6.

[233] Ibid. 226.

[234] McKay includes several illuminating examples of this in his discussion of perfects in papyrus texts which Mandilaras has labelled 'aoristic'. See K. L. McKay, 'On the Perfect and Other Aspects in the Greek Non-Literary Papyri', BICS 27 (1980), 31–2.

in this verse is upon the present significance of this past act, first for Christ and then for the Corinthians. Verses 12–19 use this perfect five times to argue the point that if Christ 'has not been raised' various unacceptable conclusions about the present must be drawn. Along the way there is a clear reference (aorist verbs, v. 15) to the past act alone apart from implications in the verb itself about the present. Then in verse 20 the perfect occurs again to underscore the present focus: νυνὶ δὲ Χριστὸς ἐγήγερται ἐκ νεκρῶν ἀπαρχὴ τῶν κεκοιμημένων.[235]

In fact all three of these criteria may be useful if applied with discernment, and the ultimate focus of the question falls on the second criterion: whether the perfect in context seems to allude to present results of the past occurrence or not. While it is often difficult to decide, this is the point at issue.

There are several occurrences of the perfect in the NT which the grammars generally agree should be labelled aoristic,[236] and they seem to be correct in this. These are:

Matt. 13: 46 εὑρὼν δὲ ἕνα πολύτιμον μαργαρίτην ἀπελθὼν πέπρακεν πάντα ὅσα εἶχεν καὶ ἠγόρασεν αὐτόν

Acts 7: 35 τοῦτον ὁ θεὸς [καὶ] ἄρχοντα καὶ λυτρωτὴν ἀπέσταλκεν σὺν χειρὶ ἀγγέλου τοῦ ὀφθέντος αὐτῷ ἐν τῇ βάτῳ

2 Cor. 2: 13 οὐκ ἔσχηκα ἄνεσιν τῷ πνεύματί μου
    11: 25 τρὶς ἐρραβδίσθην, ἅπαξ ἐλιθάσθην, τρὶς ἐναυάγησα, νυχθήμερον ἐν τῷ βυθῷ πεποίηκα

---

[235] The other note to be added to this discussion is that one must not confuse Greek idiom with English on this point. English perfects cannot be accompanied by time-references to the 'past' (i.e. a time which cannot be included in the broad 'now' of the time of speaking); the time-feature is central to the meaning of the English perfect. But the Greek perfect has no such restriction, and one must not confuse *translation* problems with confusion of actual *Greek* idiom. See sect. 2.3.3 for elaboration and illustration of this.

[236] Cf. Burton, *MT*, §§ 80–8; BDF, *Grammar*, § 343; Moulton, *Proleg.*, pp. 141–6; MT, *Syntax*, pp. 68–71; Moule, *Idiom Book*, p. 14; and Douglas S. Sharp, *Epictetus and the New Testament* (London: Charles H. Kelly, 1914), 86–7, who cites similar examples from Epictetus. Robertson, *Grammar*, pp. 899–902, counters that many of these have the sense of a 'dramatic historical perfect' which rhetorically emphasizes the suddenness of the occurrence. This, however, comes as a result of the aoristic sense and does not exclude it.

Rev. 5: 7 καὶ ἦλθεν καὶ εἴληφεν ἐκ τῆς δεξιᾶς τοῦ καθημένου ἐπὶ τοῦ θρόνου
7: 14 καὶ εἴρηκα αὐτῷ . . . καὶ εἶπέν μοι
8: 5 καὶ εἴληφεν ὁ ἄγγελος τὸν λιβανωτὸν καὶ ἐγέμισεν αὐτὸν ἐκ τοῦ πυρὸς
τοῦ θυσιαστηρίου καὶ ἔβαλεν εἰς τὴν γῆν, καὶ ἐγένοντο βρονταί
19: 3 καὶ δεύτερον εἴρηκαν (note aorists in parallel with this)

Some have noted that the aoristic sense for the perfect may be due in part to confusion in morphology.[237] For example, perfect actives could be confused with the 'alpha' endings of the first aorist, especially with the third plural -αν for -ασι(ν), and perfects with indistinct reduplication such as εἴληφα and εἴρηκα could be misread for aorists. Alternatively, idiomatic frequency of some perfects in Hellenistic Greek may have led to their over-extension.[238]

It must be emphasized in conclusion that the aoristic use of the perfect is rather rare in the NT.[239] Even when perfects are used in close connection with aorists, they normally preserve a distinctive sense in that they refer not only to a past occurrence but also to some present result of the action. There are, of course, many cases where either aorist or perfect could be used, and it is up to the writer's subjective choice whether he includes in the verb itself a reference to the continuing result or is content to refer to the past occurrence alone.[240]

---

[237] For details see BDF, *Grammar*, § 343; Moulton, *Proleg.*, p. 145; and Basil G. Mandilaras, *Studies in the Greek Language* (Athens: Hellenic Ministry of Culture and Sciences, 1972), 12–14.

[238] Cf. Mandilaras, *Studies*, pp. 19–20, and *Verb*, p. 218, where it is noted that the same verbs occur repeatedly in the perfect in various bodies of Hellenistic papyri: these include ἀπέσταλκα, γέγονα, γέγραφα, δέδωκα, εἴληφα, εἴρηκα, ἐνήνοχα, ἔστηκα, ἔσχηκα, πέπρακα, τέθεικα, and οἶδα. Note that several of these are suspected of aoristic use in the NT. My count shows that a similar frequency of use appears in the NT, though in most cases these perfects have true perfect sense. The most frequently occurring perfects in the NT are from these verbs: οἶδα (208+1 compound), γράφω (68+1), γίνομαι (46), δίδωμι (34+1), ὁράω (32), γινώσκω (19), λέγω (17), ἵστημι (17+6), ἔρχομαι (17+8), λαλέω (14), ἀποστέλλω (12), πείθω (12), πιστεύω (10), πληρόω (10), μαρτυρέω (9), ἐγείρω (9), σώζω (8), ἀκούω (8), λαμβάνω (7), and τηρέω (7).

[239] See the similar warning in J. P. Louw, 'Die semantiese waarde van die perfektum in hellenistiese grieks', *Acta Classica*, 10 (1967), 29–31.

[240] See Burton, *MT* §§ 86–8, for elaboration of this point.

4. 5. 5 *Other uses of the perfect*

Three other rare uses of the perfect will be treated here in brief fashion.[241] The first is the *gnomic* or empiric perfect, used in statements of general, proverbial occurrence. The basic sense of the perfect is preserved in this use, but the 'existing result of an antecedent occurrence' is not limited to a particular time or occasion; instead, it refers to a generic situation which could be true on numerous occasions.[242]

John 3: 18 ὁ δὲ μὴ πιστεύων ἤδη κέκριται
    5: 24 ὁ τὸν λόγον μου ἀκούων καὶ πιστεύων τῷ πέμψαντί με ἔχει ζωὴν αἰώνιον καὶ εἰς κρίσιν οὐκ ἔρχεται, ἀλλὰ μεταβέβηκεν ἐκ τοῦ θανάτου εἰς τὴν ζωήν

1 Cor. 7: 39 γυνὴ δέδεται ἐφ' ὅσον χρόνον ζῇ ὁ ἀνὴρ αὐτῆς

Jas. 1: 24 κατενόησεν γὰρ ἑαυτὸν καὶ ἀπελήλυθεν καὶ εὐθέως ἐπελάθετο ὁποῖος ἦν

Close to this in sense is the *proleptic* perfect. Like the parallel use of the aorist, the proleptic perfect occurs after a conditional element of some kind which throws the entire statement into the future.[243] The sense of the perfect is again reflected, but the 'result of the antecedent occurrence' is foreseen to be valid not now but in the future, when the condition is fulfilled.

John 20: 23 ἄν τινων ἀφῆτε τὰς ἁμαρτίας ἀφέωνται αὐτοῖς, ἄν τινων κρατῆτε κεκράτηνται

---

[241] Two uses beyond these are sometimes cited. One is the *epistolary* use, which occurs in classical Greek and in the Hellenistic papyri but does not happen to occur in the NT. This has the same origin as the epistolary aorist discussed earlier, since it takes the viewpoint of the reader and locates the sense of the perfect in that time rather than in the time of the writer. For this see Mandilaras, *Verb*, pp. 227–8, and Goodwin, *Moods and Tenses*, § 50. The other use is the *dramatic* perfect, which is thought to emphasize the suddenness of an occurrence, as in the English 'before you know it, he *has done* it'. This use is described in Robertson, *Grammar*, pp. 896–7; DM, *Grammar*, p. 204; and BW, *Syntax*, pp. 96–7. This is undoubtedly a possible application of the perfect tense, but it does not seem to warrant a separate category. All of the examples cited fit quite well into the aoristic perfect or the perfect of completed action.

[242] Cf. BDF, *Grammar*, § 344; Robertson, *Grammar*, p. 897; Smyth, *Grammar*, § 1948; and Moorhouse, *Syntax*, p. 200.

[243] Cf. Burton, *MT*, § 50; BDF, *Grammar*, § 344; and Moorhouse, *Syntax*, p. 201.

Rom. 13: 8 ὁ γὰρ ἀγαπῶν τὸν ἕτερον νόμον πεπλήρωκεν
14: 23 ὁ δὲ διακρινόμενης ἐὰν φάγῃ κατακέκριται

Jas. 2: 10 ὅστις γὰρ ὅλον τὸν νόμον τηρήσῃ πταίσῃ δὲ ἐν ἑνί, γέγονεν πάντων ἔνοχος

1 John 2: 5 ὅς δ᾽ ἂν τηρῇ αὐτοῦ τὸν λόγον, ἀληθῶς ἐν τούτῳ ἡ ἀγάπη τοῦ θεοῦ τετελείωται

The *perfect of allegory* is named thus by Moule, who shows that the basic sense of the perfect appears here as well. This perfect is used 'when the O.T. is being expounded' and evidences a 'type of Christian interpretation [which] viewed the O.T. narrative as "contemporary", and could therefore say "such-and-such an incident *has happened*". It is, in fact, a logical extension of the Greek Perfect used of a past but still relevant event'.[244]

Gal. 3: 18 τῷ δὲ Ἀβραὰμ δι᾽ ἐπαγγελίας κεχάρισται ὁ θεός
4: 23 ἀλλ᾽ ὁ μὲν ἐκ τῆς παιδίσκης κατὰ σάρκα γεγέννηται

Heb. 7: 6 ὁ δὲ μὴ γενεαλογούμενος ἐξ αὐτῶν δεδεκάτωκεν Ἀβραὰμ καὶ τὸν ἔχοντα τὰς ἐπαγγελίας εὐλόγηκεν
7: 9 ὡς ἔπος εἰπεῖν, δι᾽ Ἀβραὰμ καὶ Λευὶ ὁ δεκάτας λαμβάνων δεδεκάτωται[245]
8: 5 καθὼς κεχρημάτισται Μωϋσῆς μέλλων ἐπιτελεῖν τὴν σκηνήν
11: 17 πίστει προσενήνοχεν Ἀβραὰμ τὸν Ἰσαάκ
11: 28 πίστει πεποίηκεν τὸ πάσχα

The perfect occurs in a periphrastic form on numerous occasions in the NT, and the meaning of these constructions is treated in section 4.7.

4. 6 Uses of the Pluperfect Indicative

The pluperfect indicative can be briefly treated, since it is rather infrequent and its meaning is so similar to the perfect indicative. The sense of the pluperfect is simply that of the

---

[244] Moule, *Idiom Book*, pp. 14–15. A similar explanation is given by BDF, *Grammar*, § 342 (5), and Moulton, *Proleg.*, pp. 142–4.

[245] Heb. 7: 13, 14, which are sometimes put in this category, do not fit here, as noted by Moule, *Idiom Book*, p. 15.

perfect (with three fold meaning as presented earlier) removed one step into past time: its general use is to denote a *past* 'condition resulting from an anterior occurrence' instead of a present one, as the perfect does.[246] The 'pastness' of the condition is reckoned from the reference-point of the time of speaking, as is normal for the indicative. There are variations on this general sense in particular situations, but these are much like the variations displayed by the perfect. The particular uses are as follows.

4. 6. 1 *Pluperfect of resulting state*

This use is the most basic in that it expresses the threefold meaning of the perfect and locates it in past time. The focus here is upon a *state* which existed in the past, with implication of a prior occurrence which produced it.[247] This is sometimes best translated as an English pluperfect and at other times as a past stative.

Mark 15: 7 ἦν δὲ ὁ λεγόμενος Βαραββᾶς μετὰ τῶν στασιαστῶν δεδεμένος οἵτινες ἐν τῇ στάσει φόνον πεποιήκεισαν

15: 10 ἐγίνωσκεν γὰρ ὅτι διὰ φθόνον παραδεδώκεισαν αὐτὸν οἱ ἀρχιερεῖς (emphasis on their responsibility for this deed)

Luke 4: 29 ἤγαγον αὐτὸν ἕως ὀφρύος τοῦ ὄρους ἐφ' οὗ ἡ πόλις ᾠκοδόμητο αὐτῶν

16: 20 πτωχὸς δέ τις ὀνόματι Λάζαρος ἐβέβλητο πρὸς τὸν πυλῶνα αὐτοῦ

19: 15 τοὺς δούλους τούτους οἷς δεδώκει τὸ ἀργύριον (focus on the condition of the indirect object?)

John 6: 17 καὶ σκοτία ἤδη ἐγεγόνει

11: 44 ἡ ὄψις αὐτοῦ σουδαρίῳ περιεδέδετο

Acts 14: 23 παρέθεντο αὐτοὺς τῷ κυρίῳ εἰς ὃν πεπιστεύκεισαν

17: 23 εὗρον καὶ βωμὸν ἐν ᾧ ἐπεγέγραπτο Ἀγνώστῳ θεῷ

19: 32 οἱ πλείους οὐκ ᾔδεισαν τίνος ἕνεκα συνεληλύθεισαν

This use of the pluperfect often occurs in *explanatory* clauses

---

[246] Cf. Moulton, *Proleg.*, p. 148; MT, *Syntax*, p. 86; Zerwick, *Biblical Greek* p. 98; Moorhouse, *Syntax*, p. 201; and McKay, 'On the Perfect', pp. 322–3.

[247] Burton, *MT*, § 89; BDF, *Grammar*, § 347 (1); BW, *Syntax*, pp. 98–9; Mandilaras, *Verb*, pp. 235–7; and Smyth, *Grammar*, § 1952.

(introduced by δέ, γάρ, or by relative pronouns) which, like the similar use of the imperfect, fill in background information to illuminate an account of sequential events narrated mostly by means of the aorist. The past 'state consequent on an action' provides explanation of the foreground narrative.

Matt. 7: 25 καὶ σκοτία ἤδη ἐγεγόνει (also v.l. in Luke 6: 48, but apparently due to harmonization with this parallel)

Mark 14: 44 δεδώκει δὲ ὁ παραδιδοὺς αὐτὸν σύσσημον αὐτοῖς

Luke 8: 29 πολλοῖς γὰρ χρόνοις συνηρπάκει αὐτόν
16: 20 πτωχὸς δέ τις ὀνόματι Λάζαρος ἐβέβλητο πρὸς τὸν πυλῶνα αὐτοῦ

John 4: 8 οἱ γὰρ μαθηταὶ αὐτοῦ ἀπεληλύθεισαν εἰς τὴν πόλιν
9: 22 ἤδη γὰρ συνετέθειντο οἱ Ἰουδαῖοι ἵνα
11: 19 πολλοὶ δὲ ἐκ τῶν Ἰουδαίων ἐληλύθεισαν πρὸς τὴν Μάρθαν καὶ Μαριὰμ ἵνα παραμυθήσωνται αὐτὰς περὶ τοῦ ἀδελφοῦ
11: 30 οὔπω δὲ ἐληλύθει ὁ Ἰησοῦς εἰς τὴν κώμην
11: 57 δεδώκεισαν δὲ οἱ ἀρχιερεῖς καὶ οἱ Φαρισαῖοι ἐντολάς

4. 6. 2 *Pluperfect of completed action*

This use of the pluperfect highlights the antecedent past occurrence while still implying the past state consequent upon it, similar to the perfect use with which it is parallel. It occurs almost always with transitive active pluperfects and emphasizes the actual occurrence of the action in an antecedent past time (or, with negative, the non-occurrence).[248]

Luke 8: 2 Μαρία . . . ἀφ᾽ ἧς δαιμόνια ἑπτὰ ἐξεληλύθει
8: 38 ὁ ἀνὴρ ἀφ᾽ οὗ ἐξεληλύθει τὰ δαιμόνια (these two uses *imply* the resulting absence of demons, but *emphasize* the actual departure)

John 6: 17 καὶ οὔπω ἐληλύθει πρὸς αὐτοὺς ὁ Ἰησοῦς
7: 30 οὔπω ἐληλύθει ἡ ὥρα αὐτοῦ (similar use 8: 20)

Acts 4: 22 ὁ ἄνθρωπος ἐφ᾽ ὃν γεγόνει τὸ σημεῖον τοῦτο τῆς ἰάσεως
20: 38 ὀδυνώμενοι μάλιστα ἐπὶ τῷ λόγῳ ᾧ εἰρήκει (similar John 11: 13)

With this emphasis the pluperfect sometimes approaches

---

[248] BDF, *Grammar*, § 347 (3); DM, *Grammar*, p. 206; and BW, *Syntax*, p. 99.

the use of the Latin (and English etc.) pluperfect in denoting mainly an *anterior past occurrence*, relative to other past events.[249] The Greek pluperfect does not primarily denote this and is not frequently used with this emphasis,[250] in contrast to the Latin pluperfect, but this is the sense which sometimes results.

Luke 22: 13 ἀπελθόντες δὲ εὗρον καθὼς εἰρήκει αὐτοῖς καὶ ἡτοίμασαν τὸ πάσχα

Acts 8: 27 ὃς ἐληλύθει προσκυνήσων εἰς Ἱερουσαλήμ

9: 21 καὶ ὧδε εἰς τοῦτο ἐληλύθει ἵνα δεδεμένους αὐτοὺς ἀγάγῃ ἐπὶ τοὺς ἀρχιερεῖς (emphasizing the past occurrence, because the state resulting from it was no longer in effect at the time of the events narrated)[251]

4. 6. 3 *Pluperfect with past stative meaning*

As a third major use, there are pluperfects which occur with simply *past stative* meaning, implying no antecedent action. These come from the same limited number of verbs which display a purely present stative meaning in the perfect forms, but they actually constitute the largest number of pluperfects occurring in the NT. The four verbs are: οἶδα (32 pluperfects in NT), ἵστημι (14), εἴωθα (2), πείθω (1), and παρίστημι (1). Some examples of these are:

Matt. 12: 46 ἰδοὺ ἡ μήτηρ καὶ οἱ ἀδελφοὶ αὐτοῦ εἱστήκεισαν ἔξω (cf. 13: 2)

27: 15 κατὰ δὲ ἑορτὴν εἰώθει ὁ ἡγεμὼν ἀπολύειν ἕνα τῷ ὄχλῳ δέσμιον ὃν ἤθελον (cf. Mark 10: 1)

Luke 6: 8 αὐτὸς δὲ ᾔδει τοὺς διαλογισμοὺς αὐτῶν, εἶπεν δὲ τῷ ἀνδρὶ τῷ ξηρὰν ἔχοντι τὴν χεῖρα

11: 22 τὴν πανοπλίαν αὐτοῦ αἴρει ἐφ' ᾗ ἐπεποίθει

John 1: 31, 33 κἀγὼ οὐκ ᾔδειν αὐτόν (plupf. of οἶδα another 13 times in John)

1: 35 τῇ ἐπαύριον πάλιν εἱστήκει ὁ Ἰωάννης (another 6 times in John)

---

[249] Cf. Abel, *Grammaire*, p. 259; and Rijksbaron, *SSV*, pp. 36–7.
[250] As rightly noted by BDF, *Grammar*, § 347; and Moulton, *Proleg.*, p. 148.
[251] Cf. BDF, *Grammar*, § 347 (3).

Acts 1: 10 καὶ ἰδοὺ ἄνδρες δύο παρειστήκεισαν αὐτοῖς

Rom. 7: 7 τήν τε γὰρ ἐπιθυμίαν οὐκ ᾔδειν εἰ μὴ ὁ νόμος ἔλεγεν (only occurrence of ᾔδειν etc. outside of Gospels and Acts)

Finally, the pluperfect occurs a few times in the NT in counterfactual conditional sentences, either in protasis or apodosis. In these cases the pluperfects can be regarded as displaying one of the three senses just presented, but in addition they serve to express an 'unreal' situation. In most of these the reference is to an unreal condition in regard to the *past* (e.g. 'if A *had* been true, B *would have* followed'), but in John 8: 19c at least the reference is apparently to a present unreal situation (as confirmed by the preceding clause): οὔτε ἐμὲ οἴδατε οὔτε τὸν πατέρα μου· εἰ ἐμὲ ᾔδειτε, καὶ τὸν πατέρα μου ἂν ᾔδειτε. The other occurrences are: Matt. 12: 7; 24: 43 (~Luke 12: 39); John 4: 10; Acts 26: 32; and 1 John 2: 19.

The pluperfect also occurs in a periphrastic form in the NT, and the meaning of these constructions will be treated in the section 4.7.

The simple *future perfect* was rare in all periods of ancient Greek, and none of these forms occurs in the NT.[252] A few instances of periphrastic future perfects do appear in the NT, and these will be discussed also in the next section.

4. 7 Excursus: Periphrastic Constructions

In this section several constructions with the Greek participle which occur as equivalents or near-equivalents of indicative forms will be treated.[253] These periphrastic constructions occur also as substitutes for subjunctives, imperatives, optatives, and for infinitives and participles, but their main use is in parallel to indicatives, and for this reason the major

---

[252] Burton, *MT*, §§ 93–4; Smyth, *Grammar*, §§ 1955–8; Robertson, *Grammar*, pp. 906–7; and Moorhouse, *Syntax*, p. 202.

[253] Periphrasis with μέλλω and the infinitive will not be covered here, since these occur as substitutes for *temporal* (i.e. future tense) or *modal* categories (i.e. intention or anticipation) rather than directly for aspectual usage in the indicative.

treatment of them is undertaken here. The other periphrastic uses will be covered in the next two chapters, in connection with treating the forms to which they are parallel.

Periphrasis with the participle consists essentially of a *participle* used in connection with *another verb-form* (in this chapter an indicative) in such a way that the two function together as a unit, as a verb-phrase which is equivalent or nearly equivalent to a simple (or 'monolectic') verb. In the NT the participle in a periphrastic construction is either present or perfect in aspect,[254] and the related indicative verb is almost always a form of εἰμί,[255] either present, imperfect, or future in tense.

Aerts has detailed three types of periphrasis which may be usefully distinguished. The first of these is 'substitute' periphrasis, in which the periphrastic combination is equivalent (or virtually equivalent) in meaning to an available monolectic form. The second is 'suppletive' periphrasis, where the periphrastic expression fills in for a monolectic form which is no longer extant. Finally, there is 'expressive' periphrasis, when the periphrastic phrase provides a sense which a parallel monolectic form does not possess.[256] Examples of each of these types of periphrasis in the NT will be cited below.

---

[254] The aorist participle occurs in periphrasis with εἰμί very rarely. In the NT this appears only at Luke 23: 19; 2 Cor. 5: 19; (and as a v.l. at John 18: 30). The sense of these is similar to the pluperfect. Cf. Willem Johan Aerts, *Periphrastica: An Investigation into the Use of* εἶναι *and* ἔχειν *as Auxiliaries or Pseudo-Auxiliaries in Greek from Homer up to the Present Day* (Amsterdam: Adolf M. Hakkert, 1965), 76–90; Paul F. Regard, *La Phrase nominale dans la langue du Nouveau Testament* (Paris: Ernest Leroux, 1919), 151–2; and Gudmund Björck, ῏Ην διδάσκων: *Die periphrastischen Konstruktionen im Griechischen* (Uppsala: Almqvist and Wiksell, 1940), 74–85. For the aorist participle with ἔχω see the next note.

[255] A few instances of periphrasis with γίνομαι do occur in the NT, and they have the sense of 'coming to be in a process or state'. These uses (not all indicative) are: Mark 9: 3; 2; Cor. 6: 14; Col. 1: 18; Heb. 5: 12; Rev. 3: 2, 16: 10 (Mark 9: 7 is not periphrastic). Some of these may be adjectival. Periphrasis with ἔχω and the aorist participle occurs in classical Greek but not in the NT. Finally, expressions with ἔχω, an object, and a supplementary participle do occur in the NT, but these are not regarded as 'periphrasis' in the sense discussed here. See Aerts, *Periphrastica*, pp. 161–7.

[256] Ibid. 3.

It must also be stated that not all expressions containing a
form of εἰμί and a participle can be put into the periphrastic
category as described here. There are expressions in the NT
which look similar, but bear a different sense from the
periphrastic phrases, and there is very little beyond appropriateness in the context to serve as a basis for deciding between
the options. Two of these similar expressions are: (1) independent εἰμί denoting existence, location, or a quality, with the
participle as a separate modifier of some sort (e.g. Mark 4: 38
καὶ αὐτὸς ἦν ἐν τῇ πρύμνῃ ἐπὶ τὸ προσκεφάλαιον καθεύδων 'he was in
the stern, sleeping . . .'; cf. also Mark 1: 13; Jas. 1: 17); and (2)
equative εἰμί with the participle functioning as a predicate
adjective or substantive (e.g. Jas. 3: 15 οὐκ ἔστιν αὕτη ἡ σοφία
ἄνωθεν κατερχομένη ἀλλὰ ἐπίγειος, ψυχική, δαιμονιώδης 'this
wisdom is not the kind from above, but is earthly, natural,
demonic'; cf. Tit. 3: 3).[257] It is at times difficult to judge
whether a given phrase is periphrastic in the sense intended
here, and some problem cases will be touched upon briefly in
what follows. Periphrasis with present participles will be
covered first and then periphrasis with perfect participles.

4. 7. 1 *Periphrasis using present participles*

This is the most common sort of periphrastic expression in the
NT. Here one is dealing with mostly 'substitute periphrasis',
since the indicative forms to which these are parallel are all
extant and the periphrastics are more or less equivalent to
them in sense. The future periphrastics, however, are generally 'expressive periphrasis', since they communicate a different
sense from the monolectic future.[258]

The NT use of these periphrastics is considerably different
from the classical use, because in the earlier era εἰμί plus the

---

[257] These types of 'pseudo-periphrasis' are discussed in Aerts, *Periphrastica*,
pp. 9–17, 53; Björck, Ἦν διδάσκων, pp. 13–15, 49–50; and Lars Hartman, *Testimonium
Linguae* (Coniectanea Neotestamentica, 19; Lund: C. W. K. Gleerup, 1963), 12–13.

[258] Cf. Burton, *MT*, §§ 20, 34, 71; BDF, *Grammar*, § 353; Moule, *Idiom Book*,
pp. 16–18; and MT, *Syntax*, pp. 87–8.

present participle carried only a static, adjective-like meaning. It perhaps developed from the model of the periphrastic with perfect participles, in which the stative sense would be more natural: for example, in Homer periphrasis with present participle does not occur and with perfect participle it appears in a limited range of intransitive and stative verbs. In Hellenistic Greek, and especially in biblical Greek, the present periphrastic developed a progressive sense to go along with the more static meaning.[259]

4. 7. 1. 1 Present periphrastic

This periphrastic construction is infrequent in all of ancient Greek as well as in the NT. It consists of the present tense of εἰμί with a present participle (either active or middle-passive in voice). The usage perhaps developed by analogy from the imperfect periphrastic pattern, which is far more frequent. While the present periphrastic is parallel in structure to the English progressive present, it is by no means as frequent and does not relate to the simple form of the present in the way that the English expression does.

Instances of this construction are subject to much dispute, and many examples cited by grammars must be relegated to one of the constructions with independent or equative εἰμί.[260] However, the following cases seem to reflect the present periphrastic sense. These are parallel in meaning to the uses of the monolectic present. displaying usually a progressive or customary sense with little difference from the simple present.

Matt. 1: 23 ὅ ἐστιν μεθερμηνευόμενον (same phrase in Mark 5: 41; 15: 22, 34; John 1: 41 [note parallel simple indicative in 1: 42 ἑρμηνεύεται]; and Acts 4: 36)
27: 33 Γολγοθᾶ, ὅ ἐστιν Κρανίου Τόπος λεγόμενος

---

[259] Cf. Aerts, *Periphrastica*, pp. 7–17, 26; Moorhouse, *Syntax*, p. 204; and Smyth, *Grammar*, §§ 1857, 1961.

[260] These examples and the ones assigned to another sense (see next list) are discussed by Regard, *La Phrase nominale*, pp. 117–22; Aerts, *Periphrastica*, pp. 69–72; and some of them by Björck, Ἦν διδάσκων, pp. 14–15, 49, 51.

Luke 6: 43 οὐ γάρ ἐστιν δένδρον καλὸν ποιοῦν καρπὸν σαπρόν, οὐδὲ πάλιν δένδρον σαπρὸν ποιοῦν καρπὸν καλόν

Acts 5: 25 ἰδοὺ οἱ ἄνδρες οὓς ἔθεσθε ἐν τῇ φυλακῇ εἰσὶν ἐν τῷ ἱερῷ ἑστῶτες καὶ διδάσκοντες τὸν λαόν

2 Cor. 9: 12 ὅτι ἡ διακονία τῆς λειτουργίας ταύτης οὐ μόνον ἐστὶν προσαναπληροῦσα τὰ ὑστερήματα τῶν ἁγίων, ἀλλὰ καὶ περισσεύουσα διὰ πολλῶν εὐχαριστιῶν τῷ θεῷ

Gal. 4: 24 ἅτινά ἐστιν ἀλληγορούμενα

Col. 1: 6 καθὼς καὶ ἐν παντὶ τῷ κόσμῳ ἐστὶν καρποφορούμενον καὶ αὐξανόμενον
3: 1 οὗ ὁ Χριστός ἐστιν ἐν δεξιᾷ τοῦ θεοῦ καθήμενος

Rev. 1: 18 ἰδοὺ ζῶν εἰμι εἰς τοὺς αἰῶνας τῶν αἰώνων

Other examples which are sometimes cited here seem better taken as cases of independent εἰμί with the participle serving as a separate adjectival or adverbial element. The following may be compared with the periphrastics listed above, and it will be noted that at times the decision between these senses is difficult.

Acts 14: 15 ἡμεῖς ὁμοιοπαθεῖς ἐσμεν ὑμῖν ἄνθρωποι εὐαγγελιζόμενοι ὑμᾶς ἀπὸ τούτων τῶν ματαίων ἐπιστρέφειν ἐπὶ θεὸν ζῶντα
21: 23 εἰσὶν ἡμῖν ἄνδρες τέσσαρες εὐχὴν ἔχοντες ἐφ' ἑαυτῶν

Rom. 13: 6 λειτουργοὶ γὰρ θεοῦ εἰσιν εἰς αὐτὸ τοῦτο προσκαρτεροῦντες

1 Cor. 8: 5 καὶ γὰρ εἴπερ εἰσὶν λεγόμενοι θεοί

2 Cor. 2: 17 οὐ γάρ ἐσμεν ὡς οἱ πολλοὶ καπηλεύοντες τὸν λόγον τοῦ θεοῦ

Jas. 1: 17 πᾶσα δόσις ἀγαθὴ καὶ πᾶν δώρημα τέλειον ἄνωθέν ἐστιν καταβαῖνον ἀπὸ τοῦ πατρὸς τῶν φώτων

(See also Mark 4: 38; John 5: 2; Acts 1: 12; 2 Cor. 10: 11; Col. 2: 5; 1 Tim. 5: 24; Jas. 3: 15.)

4. 7. 1. 2 *Imperfect periphrastic*

The most common periphrastic construction in the NT consists of the imperfect of εἰμί with a present participle (either active or middle-passive in voice).[261] These are essentially

---

[261] The count of these varies depending on how many of the possibilities are considered to reflect an independent εἰμί of some kind, but in my judgement there are

parallel in meaning to the monolectic imperfect, with the present participle serving to add the 'present' aspectual element to the expression. There are some instances in which the imperfect periphrastic seems to carry a stronger emphasis on the imperfective sense (i.e. stressing a progressive or customary meaning more than the simple imperfect would), but for the most part it is equivalent in meaning to the monolectic imperfect.

The uses of the imperfect periphrastic fall into the two primary meanings of the simple imperfect, the progressive and the customary. These are distinct in the same way as the categories of the imperfect (cf. sections 4.2.1–2), reflecting a *narrow* vs. a *broad* focus on the occurrence being related.

Some examples of the *progressive* use are given below. One can notice how they provide a descriptive narration of a particular occurrence 'as it is going on' or denote something which was in process at the time of another occurrence, with greater stress on the aspectual meaning in some cases.

Mark 5: 11 (+parallels) ἦν δὲ ἐκεῖ πρὸς τῷ ὄρει ἀγέλη χοίρων μεγάλη βοσκομένη

9: 4 καὶ ὤφθη αὐτοῖς Ἠλίας σὺν Μωϋσεῖ καὶ ἦσαν συλλαλοῦντες τῷ Ἰησοῦ

15: 40 ἦσαν δὲ καὶ γυναῖκες ἀπὸ μακρόθεν θεωροῦσαι (parallel to Matt. 27: 55)

Luke 1: 21–2 καὶ ἦν ὁ λαὸς προσδοκῶν τὸν Ζαχαρίαν καὶ ἐθαύμαζον ... καὶ αὐτὸς ἦν διανεύων αὐτοῖς καὶ διέμενεν κωφός (parallel imperfects in each verse)

4: 31 καὶ ἦν διδάσκων αὐτοὺς ἐν τοῖς σάββασιν (similar in 5: 17, 13: 10)

John 18: 18 ψῦχος ἦν, καὶ ἐθερμαίνοντο· ἦν δὲ καὶ ὁ Πέτρος μετ' αὐτῶν ἑστὼς καὶ θερμαινόμενος (similar in 18: 25 and Mark 14: 54; note parallel imperfect 18: 18)

Acts 1: 10 ὡς ἀτενίζοντες ἦσαν εἰς τὸν οὐρανὸν (similar Luke 4: 20)

8: 28 ἦν τε ὑποστρέφων καὶ καθήμενος ἐπὶ τοῦ ἅρματος αὐτοῦ καὶ

89 imperfect periphrastics in the NT, with a few of these containing multiple participles after one occurrence of εἰμί. See Regard, *La Phrase nominale*, pp. 123–34; MH, *Accidence*, pp. 451–2; and MT, *Syntax*, p. 88, for lists of occurrences.

ἀνεγίνωσκεν τὸν προφήτην Ἡσαίαν (parallel imperfect)

10: 30 ἤμην τὴν ἐνάτην προσευχόμενος ἐν τῷ οἴκῳ μου (only a slight difference between this periphrastic and the independent expression in 11: 5; it is possible that 11: 5 is also periphrastic)

16: 9 ἀνὴρ Μακεδών τις ἦν ἑστὼς καὶ παρακαλῶν αὐτὸν καὶ λέγων

(Also Luke 11: 14; 24: 32; John 13: 23; Acts 8: 1; 12: 6.)

The *customary*, general, or iterative sense is also common. Here the imperfect periphrastic denotes a generalized multiple occurrence or one which is characteristic of a broad period.

Matt. 7: 29 ἦν γὰρ διδάσκων αὐτοὺς ὡς ἐξουσίαν ἔχων καὶ οὐχ ὡς οἱ γραμματεῖς αὐτῶν (similar uses in Mark 1: 22; Luke 19: 47, 21: 37)

24: 38 ὡς γὰρ ἦσαν ἐν ταῖς ἡμέραις [ἐκείναις] ταῖς πρὸ τοῦ κατακλυσμοῦ τρώγοντες καὶ πίνοντες, γαμοῦντες καὶ γαμίζοντες (parallel to imperfects in Luke 17: 28)

Mark 10: 22(~Matt. 19: 22) ἦν γὰρ ἔχων κτήματα πολλά

Luke 2: 51 καὶ ἦν ὑποτασσόμενος αὐτοῖς. καὶ ἡ μήτηρ αὐτοῦ διετήρει πάντα τὰ ῥήματα ἐν τῇ καρδίᾳ αὐτῆς

4: 44 καὶ ἦν κηρύσσων εἰς τὰς συναγωγάς τῆς Ἰουδαίας

5: 16 αὐτὸς δὲ ἦν ὑποχωρῶν ἐν ταῖς ἐρήμοις καὶ προσευχόμενος (similar in 13: 10)

John 3: 23 ἦν δὲ καὶ ὁ Ἰωάννης βαπτίζων ἐν Αἰνὼν ἐγγὺς τοῦ Σαλείμ, ὅτι ὕδατα πολλὰ ἦν ἐκεῖ, καὶ παραγίνοντο καὶ ἐβαπτίζοντο (also 1: 28, 10: 40)

Acts 1: 14 οὗτοι πάντες ἦσαν προσκαρτεροῦντες ὁμοθυμαδὸν τῇ προσευχῇ (similar 2: 42)

9: 28 καὶ ἦν μετ᾽ αὐτῶν εἰσπορευόμενος καὶ ἐκπορευόμενος εἰς Ἰερουσαλήμ, παρρησιαζόμενος ἐν τῷ ὀνόματι τοῦ κυρίου (3 imperfects follow in v. 29)

18: 7 οὗ ἡ οἰκία ἦν συνομοροῦσα τῇ συναγωγῇ

Phil. 2: 26 ἐπειδὴ ἐπιποθῶν ἦν πάντας ἡμᾶς καὶ ἀδημονῶν

1 Pet. 2: 25 ἦτε γὰρ ὡς πρόβατα πλανώμενοι

(Also Mark 1: 6; 5: 5; 15: 43; Luke 6: 12; 13: 11; John 18: 30; Acts 8: 13; 9: 9; 22: 19; Gal. 1: 22–3.)

It can be noted that this periphrastic construction occurs more commonly in some NT books than in others. The actual count of occurrences is: Matt. (6), Mark (15), Luke (28), John (10), Acts (25), 2 Cor. (1), Gal. (2), Phil. (1), and 1 Pet. (1).[262] This level of frequency in the Gospels and Acts has led some to suspect Semitic influence, since these books might be expected to reflect a Semitic background more clearly than the epistles.[263] Why Revelation reflects so little of this usage is difficult to explain according to this line of thought.

A clearer line of evidence for Semitic influence comes from the combination of (1) greater frequency of periphrasis with the present participle in biblical Greek compared to extrabiblical usage, especially using the present and future of εἰμί;[264] and (2) the close parallels found in the periphrastic constructions of the Semitic languages. These parallels are found in biblical Hebrew as well as in later (Mishnaic) Hebrew and in Aramaic. Especially common in these Semitic languages is the phrase using the perfect of היה and an active participle to express repeated action in the past.[265] Only rarely, however, are periphrastic constructions in the NT due to 'translation Semitisms'. More frequently they should be regarded as 'Septuagintisms', or as the influence of the general background of 'Jewish Greek' spoken by people who were bilingual or trilingual and who tended to choose Greek constructions which had parallels in their Semitic tongue(s).[266] Overall, the frequent occurrence of periphrasis

---

[262] Excluded from these numbers are the following instances sometimes cited, which seem to contain independent uses of εἰμί instead of periphrastics: Mark 1: 13, 3: 1, 4: 38, 14: 49; Luke 2: 8, 3: 23, 4: 33, 24: 53; John 5: 5; Acts 11: 5, 21: 9; Eph. 2: 12; Tit. 3: 3. For discussion of differences among the Synoptic Gospels on this idiom, see Hartman, *Testimonium Linguae*, pp. 23–7, 36, 45.

[263] So BDF, *Grammar*, § 353.

[264] Cf. Mayser, *Grammatik*, pp. 223–5; and Aerts, *Periphrastica*, pp. 56, 59.

[265] Cf. Gesenius–Kautzsch–Cowley, *Hebrew Grammar*, § 116r; Driver, *Use of the Tenses*, § 135 (5); M. H. Segal, *A Grammar of Mishnaic Hebrew* (Oxford: at the Clarendon Press, 1927), § 324; Bauer–Leander, *Grammatik des Biblisch-Aramäischen*, § 81 p–q; W. B. Stevenson, *Grammar of Palestinian Jewish Aramaic*, 2nd edn., with an Appendix on the Numerals by J. A. Emerton (Oxford: at the Clarendon Press, 1962), § 22; and T. W. Thacker, 'Compound Tenses Containing the Verb "Be" in Semitic and Egyptian', in D. Winton Thomas and W. D. McHardy (eds.), *Hebrew and Semitic Studies Presented to Godfrey Rolles Driver* (Oxford: at the Clarendon Press, 1963), 161–2.

[266] See these three types of Semitic influence surveyed by BDF, *Grammar*, § 4; and

using the present participle is certainly a feature of Semitic influence on the language of the NT.[267]

4. 7. 1. 3 *Future Periphrastic*

The future of εἰμί with a present participle occurs almost exclusively in biblical Greek: it appears in the Septuagint infrequently (apparently under the influence of the (rare) Hebrew use of the *imperfect* of היה with an active participle),[268] but certainly enough to influence the NT writers. Perhaps the analogy of the perfect of היה with active participle also exerted an influence towards developing the pattern into other time-frames besides the past. It is not common in the NT either, but these examples seem to be valid:

Matt. 10: 22 καὶ ἔσεσθε μισούμενοι ὑπὸ πάντων διὰ τὸ ὄνομά μου (also Matt. 24: 9; Mark 13: 13; Luke 21: 17)

Mark 13: 25 καὶ οἱ ἀστέρες ἔσονται ἐκ τοῦ οὐρανοῦ πίπτοντες (quotation from Isa. 34: 4, changing from monolectic future)

Luke 1: 20 καὶ ἰδοὺ ἔσῃ σιωπῶν καὶ μὴ δυνάμενος λαλῆσαι
    5: 10 ἀπὸ τοῦ νῦν ἀνθρώπους ἔσῃ ζωγρῶν
   21: 24 καὶ Ἰερουσαλὴμ ἔσται πατουμένη ὑπὸ ἐθνῶν

the discussion of bilingualism and its possible influence in Moisés Silva, 'Bilingualism and the Character of Palestinian Greek', *Biblica*, 61 (1980), 198–219.

[267] Mussies, *Morphology*, pp. 304–6; Lars Rydbeck, 'Bemerkungen zu Periphrasen mit εἶναι und Präsens Partizip bei Herodot und in der Koine', *Glotta*, 47 (1969), 196–8; Aerts, *Periphrastica*, pp. 56–75 (stressing the influence of the LXX); David Tabachovitz, *Die Septuaginta und das neue Testament: Stilstudien* (Lund: C. W. K. Gleerup, 1956), 41–7; BDF, *Grammar*, § 353; MH, *Accidence*, pp. 451–2; MT, *Style*, pp. 20, 34, 52, 72, 89, 118, 137. Ch. Rabin, 'Hebrew and Aramaic in the First Century', in S. Safrai and M. Stern (eds.), *Compendia Rerum Iudaicarum ad Novum Testamentum*, sect. 1, vol. ii. *The Jewish People in the First Century* (Philadelphia: Fortress Press, 1976), 1020–4, suggests that in some ways the influence may have gone the other way in Palestine: Greek may have influenced Aramaic and Mishnaic Hebrew towards greater expression of time in the verb-system.

[268] Cg. Gesenius–Kautzsch–Cowley, *Hebrew Grammar*, § 116r; Thacker, 'Compound Tenses', p. 162. For LXX use see Aerts, *Periphrastica*, pp. 59, 68; and F. C. Conybeare and St. George Stock, *Selections from the Septuagint* (Boston: Ginn and Co., 1905), 68.

22: 69 ἀπὸ τοῦ νῦν δὲ ἔσται ὁ υἱὸς τοῦ ἀνθρώπου καθήμενος ἐκ δεξιῶν τῆς δυνάμεως τοῦ θεοῦ

Acts 6: 4 ἐσόμεθα προσκαρτεροῦντες (v.l. in D only)

1 Cor. 14: 9 ἔσεσθε γὰρ εἰς ἀέρα λαλοῦντες

The sense of these ranges from a future stative sense for the lexically STATIVE verbs and the passives (Matt. 10: 22 etc.; Luke 1: 20, 21: 24, 22: 69) to a progressive or iterative sense for the actives (Mark 13: 25; Luke 5: 10; 1 Cor. 14: 9). It is the latter sense which is 'expressive' periphrasis, since the monolectic future indicative does not on its own denote such an aspect-value.

A few others are sometimes cited as future periphrastics, but they display an independent use of εἰμί with the participle functioning as a modifier, e.g. Luke 17: 35 (parallel in Matt. 24: 40 aids the independent interpretation, but this could be periphrastic), Acts 13: 11, Jude 18.[269]

4. 7. 2 Periphrastic using perfect participles

The use of perfect participles in periphrasis with a form of εἰμί is an idiom which is found more commonly in classical Greek than the constructions with present participles, and it is an idiom which carries over more of the same meaning from the earlier usage into the NT. This form of periphrasis from Homer onward was essentially stative in sense, and the stative meaning is predominant in NT usage as well.[270]

4. 7. 2. 1 Perfect periphrastic

Under this heading fall those phrases which use a *present* form of εἰμί with the perfect participle. These are parallel in sense to

---

[269] For discussion of these see Bjӧrck, Ἦν διδάσκων, pp. 86–8; Regard, *La Phrase nominale*, pp. 134–7; and Aerts, *Periphrastica*, pp. 59–68.

[270] Aerts, *Periphrastica*, pp. 36–51, 91–6; Smyth, *Grammar*, §§ 599–601; and Moorhouse, *Syntax*, pp. 205–6. For NT use see Burton, *MT*, §§ 84, 91, 94; BDF, *Grammar*, § 352; Moule, *Idiom Book*, pp. 18–19; and MT, *Syntax*, pp. 88–9. See Regard, *La Phrase nominale*, pp. 138–51, for lists of NT occurrences.

the monolectic perfect and display something of its range of uses. Perfect periphrastics contain far more middle-passive participles than active ones (the ratio is 31 to 6), and as a result they predominantly reflect the stative sense common to passive perfects in general.

Thus, most perfect periphrastics in the NT display the sense of the perfect of resulting state, focusing on a condition with an implication of the occurrence which produced it (see section 4.5.1). Some examples of this are:

John 2: 17 γεγραμμένον ἐστιν (also 6: 31, 6: 45, 10: 34, 12: 14)
  20: 30–1 ἄλλα σημεῖα ... ἃ οὐκ ἔστιν γεγραμμένα ἐν τῷ βιβλίῳ τούτῳ· ταῦτα δὲ γέγραπται ἵνα (note parallel with monolectic perfect)

Acts 2: 13 ἔλεγον ὅτι γλεύκους μεμεστωμένοι εἰσίν
  25: 14 ἀνήρ τίς ἐστιν καταλελειμμένος ὑπὸ Φήλικος δέσμιος

1 Cor. 4: 8 ἤδη κεκορεσμένοι ἐστέ
  5: 2 καὶ ὑμεῖς πεφυσιωμένοι ἐστέ

2 Cor. 4: 3 εἰ δὲ καὶ ἔστιν κεκαλυμμένον τὸ εὐαγγέλιον ἡμῶν, ἐν τοῖς ἀπολλυμένοις ἐστὶν κεκαλυμμένον

Eph. 2: 5, 8 (τῇ γὰρ) χάριτί ἐστε σεσωσμένοι

Heb. 7: 20 οἱ μὲν γὰρ χωρὶς ὁρκωμοσίας εἰσὶν ἱερεῖς γεγονότες (similar 7: 23)
  10: 10 ἡγιασμένοι ἐσμὲν διὰ τῆς προσφορᾶς τοῦ σώματος Ἰ. Χ. ἐφάπαξ

2 Pet. 3: 7 οἱ δὲ νῦν οὐρανοὶ καὶ ἡ γῆ . . . τεθησαυρισμένοι εἰσὶν πυρί

1 John 4: 12 ἡ ἀγάπη αὐτοῦ ἐν ἡμῖν τετελειωμένην ἐστίν (monolectic perfect in 2: 5)

Much less common is the use of the perfect periphrastic to highlight the actual occurrence of an event with only the implication of its consequent state; this is parallel to the perfect of completed action (section 4.5.2). There are two texts which seem to have this sense:

John 3: 21 ἵνα φανερωθῇ αὐτοῦ τὰ ἔργα ὅτι ἐν θεῷ ἐστιν εἰργασμένα

Acts 26: 26 οὐ γάρ ἐστιν ἐν γωνίᾳ πεπραγμένον τοῦτο

Finally, there are periphrastic expressions using a perfect participle of one of the small number of verbs which display a purely present meaning in the indicative, and they impart this sense also to the periphrastic phrase (cf. section 4.5.3). Here there is no implication in the verb of an antecedent occurrence as the origin of the condition in view.

Luke 20: 6 πεπεισμένος γάρ ἐστιν ᾿Ιωάννην προφήτην εἶναι

Acts 5: 25 ἰδοὺ οἱ ἄνδρες οὓς ἔθεσθε ἐν τῇ φυλακῇ εἰσὶν ἐν τῷ ἱερῷ ἑστῶτες
    καὶ διδάσκοντες τὸν λαόν
    25: 10 ἐπὶ τοῦ βήματος Καίσαρος ἑστώς εἰμι

It should be noted that some of the perfect periphrastics described in this section constitute what Aerts labelled 'suppletive' periphrasis, since they serve for monolectic forms which no longer occur. This is true for all middle-passive third-person plural forms of verbs whose bases end in a consonant. Such verbs began to lose these monolectic forms in the late classical period, and the periphrastic construction filled the gap.[271]

4. 7. 2. 2 *Pluperfect periphrastic*

This form of periphrasis uses an imperfect of εἰμί with a perfect participle, and the meaning is almost identical to the pluperfect tense. The normal use is to denote a state which existed in the past, with implication of a prior occurrence which produced it. Here also the most common voice-form is the middle-passive (the ratio over actives is 38 to 14), and a stative, almost adjectival sense predominates. But some implication of the occurrence which produced the past state is normally to be found even in these expressions.

Most frequently, then, the pluperfect periphrastic displays a sense like the pluperfect of resulting state (section 4.6.1), and highlights a past condition with some reference to the occurrence which produced it.

Mark 15: 26 καὶ ἦν ἡ ἐπιγραφὴ τῆς αἰτίας αὐτοῦ ἐπιγεγραμμένη· ὁ

---

[271] See Aerts, *Periphrastica*, p. 41; MH, *Accidence*, p. 223; and Mussies, *Morphology*, pp. 302–3, for further details.

βασιλεὺς τῶν Ἰουδαίων (cf. Acts 17: 23 ἐπεγέγραπτο)

Luke 1: 7 ἀμφότεροι προβεβηκότες ἐν ταῖς ἡμέραις αὐτῶν ἦσαν
4: 17 ἀναπτύξας τὸ βιβλίον εὗρεν τὸν τόπον οὗ ἦν γεγραμμένον (also
John 12: 16; 19: 19, 20)
5: 18 φέροντες ἐπί κλίνης ἄνθρωπον ὃς ἦν παραλελυμένος (cf. Acts 9: 33)
15: 24 οὗτος ὁ υἱός μου νεκρὸς ἦν καὶ ἀνέζησεν. ἦν ἀπολωλὼς καὶ εὑρέθη

Acts 22: 29 ἐπιγνοὺς ὅτι Ῥωμαῖός ἐστιν καὶ ὅτι αὐτὸν ἦν δεδεκώς

Gal. 4: 3 οὕτως καὶ ἡμεῖς, ὅτε ἦμεν νήπιοι, ὑπὸ τὰ στοιχεῖα τοῦ κόσμου
ἤμεθα δεδουλωμένοι

Sometimes this periphrastic emphasizes the completion of the occurrence in the past and the past state fades into the background (cf. section 4.6.2). It is used to highlight the actual occurrence (or lack of it), viewed from the reference-point of a time in the past.

Luke 8: 2 καὶ γυναῖκές τινες αἳ ἦσαν τεθεραπευμέναι ἀπὸ πνευμάτων
πονηρῶν καὶ ἀσθενειῶν
23: 53 ἔθηκεν αὐτὸν ἐν μνήματι λαξευτῷ οὗ οὐκ ἦν οὐδεὶς οὔπω κείμενος

Acts 8: 16 οὐδέπω γὰρ ἦν ἐπ' οὐδενὶ αὐτῶν ἐπιπεπτωκός

Pluperfect periphrastics of both sorts appear in explanatory clauses introduced by δέ, γάρ, or by relative pronouns, and provide background information for the main events of the narrative.

Luke 4: 16 καὶ ἦλθεν εἰς Ναζαρά, οὗ ἦν τεθραμμένος

John 3: 24 οὔπω γὰρ ἦν βεβλημένος εἰς τὴν φυλακὴν ὁ Ἰωάννης

Acts 19: 32 ἦν γὰρ ἡ ἐκκλησία συγκεχυμένη
20: 13 οὕτως γὰρ διατεταγμένος ἦν μέλλων αὐτὸς πεζεύειν
21: 29 ἦσαν γὰρ προεωρακότες Τρόφιμον τὸν Ἐφέσιον ἐν τῇ πόλει σὺν
αὐτῷ

Finally, these periphrastics can also occur with emphasis on the anteriority of the occurrence (a 'previous past'), as noted for the monolectic pluperfect.[272]

Luke 2: 26 καὶ ἦν αὐτῷ κεχρηματισμένον ὑπὸ τοῦ πνεύματος τοῦ ἁγίου μὴ

---

[272] Aerts, *Periphrastica*, p. 91.

ἰδεῖν θάνατον πρὶν [ἢ] ἂν ἴδῃ τὸν χριστὸν κυρίου

5: 17 Φαρισαῖοι καὶ νομοδιδάσκαλοι οἳ ἦσαν ἐληλυθότες ἐκ πάσης κώμης τῆς Γαλιλαίας καὶ Ἰουδαίας καὶ Ἰερουσαλήμ (cf. 23: 5)

Acts 14: 26 κἀκεῖθεν ἀπέπλευσαν εἰς Ἀντιόχειαν, ὅθεν ἦσαν παραδεδομένοι τῇ χάριτι τοῦ θεοῦ εἰς τὸ ἔργον ὃ ἐπλήρωσαν

Verbs with a purely present meaning in the perfect occur in the pluperfect periphrastic and display a past stative meaning without reference to an antecedent occurrence (cf. section 4.6.3).

Luke 5: 1 αὐτὸς ἦν ἑστὼς παρὰ τὴν λίμνην Γεννησαρέτ

John 18: 18 ψῦχος ἦν, καὶ ἐθερμαίνοντο· ἦν δὲ καὶ ὁ Πέτρος μετ᾽ αὐτῶν ἑστὼς καὶ θερμαινόμενος (similar in 18: 25)

Acts 16: 9 ἀνὴρ Μακεδών τις ἦν ἑστὼς καὶ παρακαλῶν αὐτὸν καὶ λέγων
22: 20 καὶ αὐτὸς ἤμην ἐφεστὼς καὶ συνευδοκῶν καὶ φυλάσσων τὰ ἱμάτια

4. 7. 2. 3 Future perfect periphrastic

In the NT this periphrastic substitutes entirely for the monolectic future perfect forms which were fading from usage. Even the periphrastics are rare (6 uses), since the future perfect is a specialized sense. These denote the basic sense of the perfect (a condition produced by an antecedent occurrence) moved into future time.

Matt. 16: 19 ὃ ἐὰν δήσῃς, ἐπὶ τῆς γῆς ἔσται δεδεμένον ἐν τοῖς οὐρανοῖς, καὶ ὃ ἐὰν λύσῃς ἐπὶ τῆς γῆς ἔσται λελυμένον ἐν τοῖς οὐρανοῖς
18: 18 ὅσα ἐὰν δήσητε ἐπὶ τῆς γῆς ἔσται δεδεμένα ἐν οὐρανῷ, καὶ ὅσα ἐὰν λύσητε ἐπὶ τῆς γῆς ἔσται λελυμένα ἐν οὐρανῷ

Luke 12: 52–3a ἔσονται γὰρ ἀπὸ τοῦ νῦν πέντε ἐν ἑνὶ οἴκῳ διαμεμερισμένοι, τρεῖς ἐπὶ δυσὶν καὶ δύο ἐπὶ τρισίν, διαμερισθήσονται πατὴρ ἐπὶ υἱῷ

Heb. 2: 13 ἐγὼ ἔσομαι πεποιθὼς ἐπ᾽ αὐτῷ (quoting Isa. 8: 17 LXX; this example has a simple stative meaning like the other perfects of πείθω)

The two texts in Matthew have engendered some discussion over the sense of the future perfect in Greek. The grammar does not require that these denote the sense of action 'already determined' in heaven *before* Peter and the apostolic company act.[273] Instead, in bolstering the position of leaders in the Christian community, these verses emphasize the *permanence* of their actions: whatever they decide will be confirmed in heaven.[274]

4. 8 Conclusion

This chapter has surveyed the use of verbal aspect in the indicative mood in the NT. These are the most frequently occurring verbal forms, and they illustrate the complex interaction of the aspects with a wide variety of other linguistic and contextual features in producing meaning. However, one can still detect the basic sense of the aspects as 'differing viewpoints concerning an occurrence', operating in combination with other features to produce specific contextual meanings. In the indicative, the tense-meaning (the sense of temporal relationship to some reference-point) is almost always a major consideration in the overall sense. There are some indicatives which occur in timeless uses or in times other than the normal ones (e.g. gnomic tenses, historical and futuristic presents, proleptic aorists and perfects, etc.), but for the most part time-connection is a primary feature of the overall meaning. Even with this important temporal feature, it has been shown here that the aspectual meaning is also central to the meanings of indicative verbs. Only rarely does the tense-meaning supersede or dim the aspectual force (e.g. with instantaneous and perhaps historical presents). Both time and aspect, in combination with other features of lexical and

---

[273] As argued by Wilber T. Dayton, 'John 20: 23; Matthew 16: 19 and 18: 18 in the Light of the Greek Perfect Tenses', *The Asbury Seminarian*, 2 (1947), 74–89; J. R. Mantey, 'The Mistranslation of the Perfect Tense in John 20: 23, Matthew 16: 19, and Matthew 18: 18', *JBL* 48 (1939), 243–9; and Turner, *Grammatical Insights*, pp. 80–2.

[274] Cf. Smyth, *Grammar*, §§ 1955–6; and F. F. Bruce, *The English Bible: A History of Translations from the Earliest English Versions to the New English Bible*, rev. edn. (New York: Oxford University Press, 1970), 180–1.

contextual meaning, are important for the interpreter to consider in deciding the sense of an indicative verb in the NT.

In the next two chapters the aspects will be examined in regard to their usage in forms of the verb in which time is less significant or not significant at all: in the subjunctive, imperative, and optative moods and in the participle and infinitive.

5

THE ASPECTS IN COMMANDS AND PROHIBITIONS

THE purpose of this chapter is to describe the meanings which the aspects display in commands and prohibitions in the NT. This includes usage in the imperative, as well as in parallel idioms using the subjunctive (hortatory and prohibitory uses).[1] A section at the end of the chapter will treat aspect-usage in indirect commands (i.e. infinitive or ἵνα clause with subjunctive after a verb of commanding) and in other constructions which express commands (participles and infinitives used independently).

5. 1 General Principle for the Meaning of the Aspects in Commands and Prohibitions

There is general agreement among the grammarians, and this is validated by studies of NT texts, that the basic meaning of the present and the aorist in commands and prohibitions is not *temporal* but *aspectual*.[2] The 'primary tense' values (i.e. past, present, and future) so important in the tenses of the indicative are not seen at all in the aspects of commands and prohibitions.[3] Indeed, due to the nature of such predication,

[1] Use of the future to express a command will not be covered here, since it is a development of the *tense*-meaning rather than an aspectual matter. For this use see KG, *Satzlehre*, pp. 173–6; SD, *Syntax*, p. 291; Burton, *MT*, §§ 67–8; BDF, *Grammar*, § 362; Mayser, *Grammatik*, pp. 212–13; MT, *Syntax*, p. 86; and Mandilaras, *Verb*, pp. 188–90.

[2] Moulton, *Proleg.*, pp. 122–6, 173–4; BDF, *Grammar*, § 335; SD, *Syntax*, pp. 339–44; Mandilaras, *Verb*, pp. 296–300; and Moorhouse, *Syntax*, pp. 217–22.

[3] Some have explained the meaning of the present and aorist commands in terms of 'secondary tense' or temporal meanings relative to other occurrences in the context. For this view see Rijksbaron, *SSV*, pp. 43–7. These meanings (where they occur) are

commands and prohibitions refer to occurrences which are future (or present and future), relative to the time of speaking. The meanings of the present and aorist in these forms centre instead on the basic aspectual distinction developed in Chapter 2: in their invariant meanings they are 'viewpoint aspects' which picture the occurrence either from an internal perspective, focusing on the course or internal details of the occurrence but with no focus on the end-points (*present*), or from an external perspective, seeing the occurrence as a whole from beginning to end without focus on the internal details which may be involved (*aorist*).[4] In this area of usage the choices are almost completely limited to present and aorist. The perfect occurs so infrequently in commands and prohibitions in the NT that it was apparently not an idiomatic option.[5]

Just as it does in the indicative, this basic aspectual distinction combines with other linguistic features to produce secondary functions of the aspects in commands and prohibitions as well. Thus, it is possible to find distinctions between present and aorist such as: stative/ingressive, descriptive/simple, simultaneous/sequenced, durative/momentary, conative/consummative, multiple/single, and general/particular. Some of these will be illustrated later. However, one secondary distinction appears to have assumed a greater frequency of usage than in the indicative forms—the difference between *general* and *specific* occurrence (or, as a rough equivalent, the distinction of multiple vs. single occurrence). This will be developed in the major portion of the chapter.

---

better seen as occasional secondary functions of the aspectual values, rather than as the essential or central meanings of the forms (as discussed in sect. 1.1.3).

[4] Cf. K. L. McKay, 'Aspect in Imperatival Constructions in New Testament Greek', *Nov. T.* 27 (1985), 203–4, which articulates the aspectual distinction in terms of viewpoint, as is done here: 'The difference between the aorist and imperfective aspects is that the former represents an activity as a total action, in its entirety without dwelling on its internal details; while the latter represents an activity as a process going on, with the focus on its progress or development'.

[5] The perfect imperatives in the NT are: πεφίμωσο in Mark 4: 39, ἔρρωσθε in Acts 15: 29 (a stereotyped greeting; occurs in singular as v.l. in 23: 30), and ἴστε (which can be indicative or imperative) in Eph. 5: 5, Heb. 12: 17, and Jas. 1: 19.

5. 2 The Distinction of General Precept versus Specific Command

The 'general vs. specific' distinction as the pattern of present vs. aorist usage in commands and prohibitions was suggested by Blass in 1896 and is reflected in other grammars since that time. As Blass–Debrunner–Funk state it: 'The result of this distinction [between present and aorist aspects] is that in general precepts (also to an individual) concerning attitudes and conduct there is a preference for the present, in commands related to conduct in specific cases (much less frequent in the NT) for the aorist.'[6]

This distinction appears to be a genuinely helpful guide to NT usage. In the sections which follow, its validity will be examined more closely and exceptions which occur will be evaluated.

5. 2. 1 *Explanation and general validation of this distinction*

Before going further, it is important to clarify the distinction drawn between 'general precepts' and 'commands related to conduct in specific cases' (here labelled 'specific commands'). Although these are not described further by Blass–Debrunner–Funk, the difference between the two seems fairly obvious. To put such an intuitive distinction in written form is a little more difficult, but the following descriptions may serve well enough for the present purpose:

General precept: a moral regulation which is broadly applicable; a rule for conduct to be applied in multiple situations; a command or prohibition to be followed by an individual or a group not only in the immediate situation in which it is given,

---

[6] BDF, *Grammar*, § 335. For similar suggestions in other grammars see Zerwick, *Biblical Greek*, p. 79; Moule, *Idiom Book*, p. 135; and MT, *Syntax*, p. 74. In the more recent German edition of Blass–Debrunner the same distinction is given, with the following addition: 'In einer Anzahl von Fällen ist dieser Unterschied jedoch aufgegeben. Es stand bisweilen im persönlich Belieben des Schriftstellers, zwischen der schärferen Befehlsform des Aor. und der milderen des Präs. zu wählen' (BDR, *Grammatik*, § 335).

but also in subsequent (repeated or continuing) circumstances in which the precept is appropriate.

Specific command: an order or request for action to be done in a particular instance. The speaker commands or prohibits some attitude or action, but does so only in reference to the immediate circumstances and hearers involved: he does not intend to regulate conduct in broader terms.[7]

Clear examples are perhaps more valuable than definitions in such cases. General precepts would include things like:

Luke 6: 27–8 Love your enemies, do good to those who hate you, bless those who curse you, pray for those who mistreat you
    6: 31 Treat others as you want them to treat you

Specific commands would include these (in their contexts):

Luke 5: 4 Put out into the deep water and let down your nets for a catch
    6: 8, 10 Arise and come forward. . . . Stretch out your hand[8]

---

[7] These definitions are my own, but it may be helpful to compare them with several relevant distinctions made by Nicholas Rescher in *The Logic of Commands* (London: Routledge and Kegan Paul, 1966), 21–3. (In the following, the first member in each pair corresponds to 'specific command' and the second to 'general precept' as used above.) Rescher writes:

An important characteristic of any command revolves about its execution-timing.

Here we must distinguish between:

(i) *Do-it-now commands*. Certain commands require that something be done (or realized) at once. For example: 'Close the window!'

(ii) *Do-it-always commands* or *standing orders*. Certain commands require that something be 'done' constantly and always, strange though this may seem, because it is rather strained to speak of *doing* here. For example: 'Don't inflict needless pain!!' 'Keep to the path of righteousness!!'

Another important component or possible component of a command is the setting of conditions specifying the occasion for its execution.

Here we shall distinguish primarily between:

(i) *One-shot conditional commands* or *when-next commands*. These have the type-paradigm. 'The next time that such and such a condition is satisfied, do so-and-so!'
. . .

(ii) *Conditional standing orders (commands)* or *whenever-commands*. These have the paradigm: 'Whenever such and such a condition is satisfied, do so-and-so!!'

[8] The verb 'arise' occurs here in the *present*, despite the specific nature of the command. This is an exception to the pattern and is discussed in sect. 5.3.1.1.

These descriptions are not precise enough to cover all questions which may be raised; instead they are intended to mark out clear areas at either end of a spectrum of usage. There are admittedly a number of examples which fall in a grey area between the two, and some of these cases will be discussed later.

As noted in the statement quoted from Blass–Debrunner–Funk, this guideline of 'general vs. specific' is a subsidiary distinction, based on the primary *aspectual* difference between present and aorist commands. The general validity of this secondary distinction appears to be due to the natural and plausible connection between the aspectual values of present and aorist and the normal difference which a speaker would envisage between a general precept and a specific command. A specific command normally calls for action viewed as a single whole, for action to be done in its entirety on that occasion, and the aorist is natural for this. A general precept, on the other hand, has multiple applications and pictures the action in its multiplicity rather than totality, and so the 'internal' focus of the present comes into play. In bare summary, this guideline focuses the distinction of aspects on to that of 'single vs. multiple': the aorist is used of action to be done once and the present is used of action to be done more than once or which is to be characteristic of the hearer.[9]

The general validity of this rule is reflected in the patterns of usage which one finds in the individual books of the NT. Those books which are predominantly *didactic* in nature (epistles) could be expected to contain mainly 'general precepts' rather than 'specific commands', and those which are predominantly *narrative* in content (Gospels and Acts) should reflect the opposite pattern.[10] With some exceptions, this expected pattern is confirmed by actual frequency-counts

---

[9] See sect. 3.3 for further discussion of the general vs. specific distinction and its effect on aspectual function.

[10] Obviously the epistles contain some narration (and specific commands) and the Gospels and Acts contain much which is didactic (with its general precepts), but it is the predominant content which is in view here.

TABLE 5. 1. *Frequency of Present and Aorist in NT Commands and Prohibitions*[a]

Book	Presents		Aorists	
	No.	%	No.	%
Matt.	117	38	189	62
Mark	78	50	77	49 [+1 perf.]
Luke	127	42	176	58
John	60	44	75	56
Acts	38	30	89	70
Rom.	35	54	30	46
1 Cor.	88	84	17	16
2 Cor.	12	52	11	48
Gal.	20	83	4	17
Eph.	34	85	6	15
Phil.	23	88	3	12
Col.	22	69	10	31
1 Thess.	23	96	1	4
2 Thess.	7	78	2	22
1 Tim.	41	93	3	7
2 Tim.	16	47	18	53
Titus	11	79	3	21
Philem.	2	50	2	50
Heb.	33	75	11	25
Jas.	29	54	25	46
1 Pet.	10	28	27	72
2 Pet.	4	57	3	43
1 John	10	83	2	17
2 John	3	100	0	—
3 John	2	100	0	—
Jude	3	60	2	40
Rev.	29	30	67	70
TOTAL	877	51	853	49

[a] This list is based on my own count, using the Greek text of the UBS, 3rd edn., and Nestle–Aland, 26th edn. The following forms are omitted, since they are used as stereotyped exclamations or greetings rather than as true imperatives: ἰδού (all 198 uses omitted), ἴδε (all 28 exclamatory uses omitted; 12 imperative uses are included), δεῦρο/δεῦτε (all 21 uses omitted), χαῖρε/χαίρετε (all 6 greeting-uses omitted; 13 uses as imperatives 'rejoice' are included), and ἄγε (the two exclamatory uses in Jas. 4: 13, 5: 1 are omitted).

from NT books. Table 5.1 shows the frequency of present and aorist tenses in commands and prohibitions (including pro- hibitory and hortatory subjunctives) in the NT.

The broad pattern of usage is the fact which should be

noted from the table at this point. Some predictable types of exceptions do occur and these must be taken into account later; but for now it should be observed that in those books where narrative predominates (and thus where one would expect more specific commands) the aorist tense is used more frequently than the present. This is clearly true in Acts, Matthew, and Luke. On the other hand, in those books which are mainly didactic (where general precepts would be more common), the present tense occurs more frequently than the aorist. See especially some letters among the Pauline corpus (1 Thess., 1 Cor., Gal., Phil., Eph., and 1 Tim.), but also Heb. and 1 John.[11]

Of course, within each book there can be a mixture of narrative and didactic material (and of general precepts and specific commands), which means that one cannot look at the data in broad terms only. In the Gospels, for example, the discourses of Jesus abound in general precepts, and this increases the proportion of present-tense commands in those books. In some of the epistles specific greetings and requests at the end of the letter account for a large portion of the aorist commands which are indicated in Table 5.1. Thus, one must take these differences into account and look more closely at the individual commands in order to gain a more accurate estimate of the patterns of usage. What seems to be required to evaluate this guideline properly is to examine the *context* of individual commands and seek to distinguish general precepts from specific commands by broader criteria, and then to determine how the use of the aspects corresponds with those distinctions. An analysis of some NT books using this approach produces the data shown in Table 5.2.[12]

It can be seen from this table that most of the books studied

---

[11] Notable exceptions to this pattern are immediately obvious. Mark, for example, has slightly more presents than aorists, in contrast to the other Gospels and Acts, where the aorist is predominant. Among the epistles, 1 Pet., 2 Tim., and Jas. seem to be exceptions to the pattern. Comment will be made later concerning these exceptions.

[12] The distinction of general vs. specific commands is not clear in some individual

TABLE 5. 2. *Occurrence of Present vs. Aorist in General and Specific Commands in Some NT Books*

Book	General Precepts			Specific Commands		
	Total	Pres.	Aor.	Total	Pres.	Aor.
Luke	124	84	40	179	43	136
Acts	9	8	1	118	30	88
Rom.	48	35	13	17	0	17
1 Cor.	97	87	10	8	1	7
2 Cor.	9	8	1	14	4	10
Gal.	18	18	0	5	1	4
Eph.	37	32	5	3	2	1
Phil.	24	22	2	2	1	1
Col.	28	22	6	4	0	4
1 Thess.	23	23	0	1	0	1
2 Thess.	9	7	2	0	—	—
1 Tim.	44	41	3	0	—	—
2 Tim.	29	14	15	5	2	3
Titus	11	11	0	3	0	3
Jas.	48	27	21	6	2	4
1 Pet.	36	10	26	1	0	1

follow this guideline quite closely: that is, for general precepts the present tense is normal, while for specific commands the aorist tends to occur. However, percentages in support of this rule are not as high in some books as expected. Again, in this case the broad statistics alone are not sufficient to show the full validity of the rule, since the tally is influenced in some cases by idiosyncrasies of usage which produce exceptional data. These exceptions fall into patterns which will be discussed in the next section, but before they are treated some illustrations of the validity of the general vs. specific pattern should be cited.

5. 2. 2 *Illustrations of this distinction in positive commands*

In regard to positive commands, the point of this guideline is that present aspect should normally be understood as *customary*

cases, but the broad patterns of the data would not be altered by differing analyses of the problem cases. For examples of how some NT commands have been classified here see the illustrations cited in this and subsequent sections.

or *multiple* in sense, rather than progressive or descriptive in a narrow scope: it does not mean 'keep on doing', 'be constantly doing', but 'make it your habit to do', or 'respond in this way whenever it is called for'. The following examples should be noted:

Matt. 6: 9 οὕτως οὖν προσεύχεσθε ὑμεῖς· Πάτερ ἡμῶν
 7: 12 πάντα οὖν ὅσα ἐὰν θέλητε ἵνα ποιῶσιν ὑμῖν οἱ ἄνθρωποι, οὕτως καὶ ὑμεῖς ποιεῖτε αὐτοῖς
 10: 23 ὅταν δὲ διώκωσιν ὑμᾶς ἐν τῇ πόλει ταύτῃ, φεύγετε εἰς τὴν ἑτέραν
 19: 12 ὁ δυνάμενος χωρεῖν χωρείτω

Mark 9: 7 οὗτός ἐστιν ὁ υἱός μου ὁ ἀγαπητός, ἀκούετε αὐτοῦ (cf. Mark 7: 14 ἀκούσατε in specific command)
 11: 25 ὅταν στήκητε προσευχόμενοι, ἀφίετε εἴ τι ἔχετε κατά τινος

Luke 6: 35 πλὴν ἀγαπᾶτε τοὺς ἐχθροὺς ὑμῶν καὶ ἀγαθοποιεῖτε καὶ δανίζετε μηδὲν ἀπελπίζοντες
 9: 60 σὺ δὲ ἀπελθὼν διάγγελλε τὴν βασιλείαν τοῦ θεοῦ
 11: 9 αἰτεῖτε καὶ δοθήσεται ὑμῖν, ζητεῖτε καὶ εὑρήσετε, κρούετε καὶ ἀνοιγήσεται ὑμῖν (parallel in Matt. 7: 7; does not necessarily mean 'keep on asking', etc., even with the parable of the friend at midnight preceding; seems better as 'if you ask at any time, it will be given you', etc.[13])
 22: 19 τοῦτο ποιεῖτε εἰς τὴν ἐμὴν ἀνάμνησιν

John 21: 15–17 βόσκε τὰ ἀρνία μου ... ποίμαινε τὰ πρόβατά μου ... βόσκε τὰ πρόβατά μου

Rom. 12: 14 εὐλογεῖτε τοὺς διώκοντας [ὑμᾶς], εὐλογεῖτε καὶ μὴ καταρᾶσθε
 14: 5 ἕκαστος ἐν τῷ ἰδίῳ νοΐ πληροφορείσθω
 15: 7 διὸ προσλαμβάνεσθε ἀλλήλους, καθὼς καὶ ὁ Χριστὸς προσελάβετο ὑμᾶς εἰς δόξαν τοῦ θεοῦ (also 14: 1)

1 Cor. 11: 28 δοκιμαζέτω δὲ ἄνθρωπος ἑαυτὸν καὶ οὕτως ἐκ τοῦ ἄρτου ἐσθιέτω καὶ ἐκ τοῦ ποτηρίου πινέτω
 14: 29 προφῆται δὲ δύο ἢ τρεῖς λαλείτωσαν καὶ οἱ ἄλλοι διακρινέτωσαν

Gal. 6: 1 ἀδελφοί, ἐὰν καὶ προλημφθῇ ἄνθρωπος ἔν τινι παραπτώματι, ὑμεῖς οἱ πνευματικοὶ καταρτίζετε τὸν τοιοῦτον ἐν πνεύματι πραΰτητος (not 'be restoring', 'constantly restore')
 6: 10 ἄρα οὖν ὡς καιρὸν ἔχομεν, ἐργαζώμεθα τὸ ἀγαθὸν πρὸς πάντας

---

[13] See the arguments toward this interpretation in I. Howard Marshall, *The Gospel of Luke: A Commentary on the Greek Text* (Exeter: Paternoster Press, 1978), 462–8.

1 Thess. 5: 14 νουθετεῖτε τοὺς ἀτάκτους, παραμυθεῖσθε τοὺς ὀλιγοψύχους, ἀντέχεσθε τῶν ἀσθενῶν, μακροθυμεῖτε πρὸς πάντας

Heb. 3: 13 ἀλλὰ παρακαλεῖτε ἑαυτοὺς καθ᾽ ἑκάστην ἡμέραν
4: 16 προσερχώμεθα οὖν μετὰ παρρησίας τῷ θρόνῳ τῆς χάριτος, ἵνα λάβωμεν ἔλεος καὶ χάριν εὕρωμεν εἰς εὔκαιρον βοήθειαν (also 10: 22)
12: 1 δι᾽ ὑπομονῆς τρέχωμεν τὸν προκείμενον ἡμῖν ἀγῶνα (see 13: 1–25, containing 14 present general precepts and one aorist specific command)

Jas. 2: 12 οὕτως λαλεῖτε καὶ οὕτως ποιεῖτε ὡς διὰ νόμου ἐλευθερίας μέλλοντες κρίνεσθαι

On the other hand, an aorist command is normally used to call for a single specific action in a particular situation, without regard for the other combinatory distinctions between the aspects (e.g. momentary vs. durative, consummative vs. conative, ingressive vs. stative, etc.). The force of the aorist is to command the whole occurrence on that specific occasion (or at the future occasion indicated), and the command is not intended to govern behaviour more broadly. Some illustrations of specific commands using the aorist are:

Matt. 13: 30 συλλέξατε πρῶτον τὰ ζιζάνια καὶ δήσατε αὐτὰ εἰς δέσμας πρὸς τὸ κατακαῦσαι αὐτά, τὸν δὲ σῖτον ἀναγάγετε εἰ τὴν ἀποθήκην μου
18: 26 πεσὼν οὖν ὁ δοῦλος προσεκύνει αὐτῷ λέγων· μακροθύμησον ἐπ᾽ ἐμοί, καὶ πάντα ἀποδώσω σοι (cf. pres. in 1 Thess. 5: 14 above)

Mark 4: 35 καὶ λέγει αὐτοῖς ἐν ἐκείνῃ τῇ ἡμέρᾳ ὀψίας γενομένης· διέλθωμεν εἰς τὸ πέραν
6: 31 δεῦτε ὑμεῖς αὐτοὶ κατ᾽ ἰδίαν εἰς ἔρημον τόπον καὶ ἀναπαύσασθε ὀλίγον
9: 5 ῥαββί, καλόν ἐστιν ἡμᾶς ὧδε εἶναι, καὶ ποιήσωμεν τρεῖς σκηνάς
14: 34 μείνατε ὧδε καὶ γρηγορεῖτε

Luke 2: 15 διέλθωμεν δὴ ἕως Βηθλέεμ καὶ ἴδωμεν τὸ ῥῆμα τοῦτο τὸ γεγονός
7: 22 πορευθέντες ἀπαγγείλατε Ἰωάννῃ ἃ εἴδετε καὶ ἠκούσατε (pres. in 9: 60)
13: 24–5 ἀγωνίζεσθε εἰσελθεῖν διὰ τῆς στενῆς θύρας ... κύριε ἄνοιξον ἡμῖν (general then specific command)
22: 10 ἀκολουθήσατε αὐτῷ εἰς τὴν οἰκίαν εἰς ἣν εἰσπορεύεται

John 2: 5, 7–8 ὅ τι ἂν λέγῃ ὑμῖν ποιήσατε ... γεμίσατε τὰς ὑδρίας ὕδατος

. . . ἀντλήσατε νῦν καὶ φέρετε τῷ ἀρχιτρικλίνῳ (see sect. 5.3.1.1 for idiomatic use of present of φέρω)

4: 31 ἐν τῷ μεταξὺ ἠρώτων αὐτὸν οἱ μαθηταὶ λέγοντες· ῥαββί, φάγε

6: 10 εἶπεν ὁ Ἰησοῦς· ποιήσατε τοὺς ἀνθρώπους ἀναπεσεῖν. ἦν δὲ χόρτος πολὺς ἐν τῷ τόπῳ

9: 7 ὕπαγε νίψαι εἰς τὴν κολυμβήθραν τοῦ Σιλωάμ (see sect. 5.3.1.1 for idiomatic use of present of ὑπάγω)

Acts 2: 22 ἄνδρες Ἰσραηλῖται, ἀκούσατε τοὺς λόγους τούτους (also 13: 16, 15: 13, 22: 1)

9: 11 ἀναστὰς πορεύθητι ἐπὶ τὴν ῥύμην τὴν καλουμένην Εὐθεῖαν καὶ ζήτησον ἐν οἰκίᾳ Ἰούδα Σαῦλον ὀνόματι Ταρσέα

1 Cor. 5: 13 ἐξάρατε τὸν πονηρὸν ἐξ ὑμῶν αὐτῶν (Deut. 17: 7 quoted in reference to the sinning man of v. 1)

16: 11 προπέμψατε δὲ αὐτὸν ἐν εἰρήνῃ

Col. 4: 10 ἐὰν ἔλθῃ πρὸς ὑμᾶς, δέξασθε αὐτόν (cf. pres. in general precept; 1 Cor. 11: 33 ἀλλήλους ἐκδέχεσθε)

4: 16 ὅταν ἀναγνωσθῇ παρ' ὑμῖν ἡ ἐπιστολή, ποιήσατε ἵνα καὶ ἐν τῇ Λαοδικέων ἐκκλησίᾳ ἀναγνωσθῇ, καὶ τὴν ἐκ Λαοδικείας ἵνα καὶ ὑμεῖς ἀναγνῶτε

4: 17 καὶ εἴπατε Ἀρχίππῳ· βλέπε τὴν διακονίαν ἣν παρέλαβες ἐν κυρίῳ, ἵνα αὐτὴν πληροῖς

5. 2. 3 *Illustrations of this distinction in prohibitions*

It is the contention of this book that the general vs. specific pattern is applicable to *prohibitions* (negative commands) as well as to positive commands. This is important to emphasize, since it runs counter to the commonly cited rule for the present and aorist in prohibitions. What is usually said is that the present aspect is used to forbid action which is already under-way (e.g. 'Stop doing'), whereas the aorist warns against action which has not yet begun ('Do not start do do').[14] Valid instances of this rule are easy to find in the NT

[14] Two articles by Headlam served to popularize this rule, and Moulton, *Proleg.*, pp. 122–6, picked up the rule from him and applied it to NT Greek. See W. Headlam, 'Some Passages of Aeschylus and Others', *CR* 17 (1903), 294–5, and 'Greek Prohibitions', ibid. 19 (1905), 30–6. Henry Jackson, 'Prohibitions in Greek', ibid. 18 (1904), 262–3, responded in agreement with Headlam's rule and cited the amusing

(e.g. Rev. 5: 4–5 ἔκλαιον πολὺ ... καὶ εἷς ἐκ τῶν πρεσβυτέρων λέγει μοι· μὴ κλαῖε and Matt. 17: 9 καταβαινόντων αὐτῶν ἐκ τοῦ ὄρους ἐνετείλατο αὐτοῖς ὁ Ἰησοῦς λέγων· μηδενὶ εἴπητε τὸ ὅραμα). Moulton adopts this guideline and uses it as evidence of moral lapses in the early Church in the light of prohibitions such as μὴ μεθύσκεσθε (Eph. 5: 18) and μὴ ψεύδεσθε (Col. 4: 9).[15] Such sins probably did continue to be problematic, but surely in the face of Paul's penchant for present imperatives (see Tables 5.1 and 5.2) one must be careful in applying this rule to his use of the present prohibition.[16] Many of his uses almost certainly mean 'make it your habit not to do', rather than 'stop doing'. The same is true of most books in the NT.

In a thesis examining aspectual usage in NT prohibitions, Louw investigated, among other issues, the validity of the traditional rule for present and aorist prohibitions (the 'stop vs. don't start' distinction), and concluded that it is not a reliable guide to actual usage. In an article summarizing the thesis, Louw states the conclusion succinctly:

The various contexts in which prohibitions occur enable us to distinguish three main groups of negative commands: (a) The action to which the prohibition refers is taking place, lasting or frequently repeating. (b) The prohibition is directed to an action which may possibly take place at some future time, i.e. the action is to be present. (c) The command simply forbids an action irrespective of the qualifications observed under (a) or (b). In this case the

story from Modern Greek usage which Moulton repeats; Jackson writes (p. 263): 'Davidson told me that, when he was learning modern Greek, he had been puzzled about the distinction until he heard a Greek friend use the present imperative to a dog who was barking. This gave him the clue'. Two other writers replied to Headlam's work expressing disagreement, or at least scepticism, about the rule's validity: see H. Darnley Naylor, 'Prohibitions in Greek', CR 19 (1905), 26–30, and 'More Prohibitions in Greek', ibid. 20 (1906), 348; and R. C. Seaton, 'Prohibition in Greek', ibid. 20 (1906), 438. Others who support this distinction are: Robertson, Grammar, pp. 851–4; MT, Syntax, pp. 74–8; William Heidt, 'Translating New Testament Imperatives', Catholic Biblical Quarterly, 13 (1951), 255–6; and Andrew P. Fernando, 'Translation of Questions and Prohibitions in Greek', BT 27 (1976), 140–1.

[15] Moulton, Proleg, p. 126.
[16] Ibid. 125 acknowledges Paul's common use of the present in prohibitions, and does not insist that the meaning must be 'Stop doing' in all cases.

prohibition is simply regarded as a regulation, a moral precept applicable to all time, to any person or circumstance. This we naturally find in literature of a pulpit style.

For each of these, both present imperative and aorist subjunctive can be used. . . .

The *context* has to point out whether a particular action is occurring, still lies in the future, or is thought of (e.g. in the case of a moral precept) as applicable to any time or circumstance.[17]

I believe that Louw is correct in this conclusion. More specifically, when studying prohibitions it seems important to examine the nature of the command in each instance, to discover from contextual features whether the prohibition is general or specific in scope. In *specific commands*, prohibitions appear to follow the traditional rule fairly well, with the present almost always bearing the sense of 'stop doing [this action presently occurring]' (cf. section 5.3.2.1 for explanation of this progressive use of the present) and the aorist meaning 'do not do [this imminent act]'. However, *general precepts* do not fit this pattern: the present prohibition usually means 'make it your practice not to do', and the aorist usually adds an urgency to the prohibition and forbids the whole act ever to occur: 'never do' (like the aorist use described in section 5.3.1.2.2.(*d*)). Some illustrations of this follow:

Prohibitory specific commands

Matt. 1: 20 Ἰωσὴφ υἱὸς Δαυίδ, μὴ φοβηθῇς παραλαβεῖν Μαρίαν τὴν γυναῖκά σου

5: 17 μὴ νομίσητε ὅτι ἦλθον καταλῦσαι τὸν νόμον ἢ τοὺς προφήτας

Mark 8: 26 καὶ ἀπέστειλεν αὐτὸν εἰς οἶκον αὐτοῦ λέγων· μηδὲ εἰς τὴν κώμην εἰσέλθῃς

Luke 8: 28 δέομαί σου, μή με βασανίσῃς

John 3: 7 μὴ θαυμάσῃς ὅτι εἶπόν σοι· δεῖ ὑμᾶς γεννηθῆναι ἄνωθεν (clearly not 'do not start to marvel')

19: 24 μὴ σχίσωμεν αὐτόν, ἀλλὰ λάχωμεν περὶ αὐτοῦ τίνος ἔσται

---

[17] J. P. Louw, 'On Greek Prohibitions', *Acta Classica*, 2 (1959), 57 (emphasis mine). Cf. the thesis itself, Johannes Petrus Louw, 'Prohibitions in the Greek New Testament: A Study of the Construction of μή with the Present Imperative and the Aorist Subjunctive' (D. Litt. thesis, University of Pretoria, 1958), 169–73.

Acts 16: 28 μηδὲν πράξῃς σεαυτῷ κακόν, ἅπαντες γάρ ἐσμεν ἐνθάδε
   23: 21 σὺ οὖν μὴ πεισθῇς· ἐνεδρεύουσιν γὰρ αὐτὸν ἐξ αὐτῶν ἄνδρες πλείους
       τεσσεράκοντα οἵτινες ἀνεθεμάτισαν ἑαυτούς
Rev. 10: 4 σφράγισον ἃ ἐλάλησαν αἱ ἑπτὰ βρονταί, καὶ μὴ αὐτὰ γράψῃς

Luke 2: 9–10 ἐφοβήθησαν φόβον μέγαν καὶ εἶπεν αὐτοῖς ὁ ἄγγελος· μὴ
       φοβεῖσθε
    7: 6 κύριε, μὴ σκύλλου, οὐ γὰρ ἱκανός εἰμι ἵνα ὑπὸ τὴν στέγην μου
       εἰσέλθῃς
John 6: 43 μὴ γογγύζετε μετ' ἀλλήλων
   20: 17 λέγει αὐτῇ Ἰησοῦς· μή μου ἅπτου, οὔπω γὰρ ἀναβέβηκα πρὸς τὸν
       πατέρα
Acts 20: 10 μὴ θορυβεῖσθε, ἡ γὰρ ψυχὴ αὐτοῦ ἐν αὐτῷ ἐστιν

Prohibitory General Precepts

Matt. 9: 30 καὶ ἠνεῴχθησαν αὐτῶν οἱ ὀφθαλμοὶ καὶ ἐνεβριμήθη αὐτοῖς ὁ
       Ἰησοῦς λέγων· ὁρᾶτε μηδεὶς γινωσκέτω
    19: 6 ὃ οὖν ὁ θεὸς συνέζευξεν ἄνθρωπος μὴ χωριζέτω

Mark 13: 21 καὶ τότε ἐάν τις ὑμῖν εἴπῃ· ἴδε ὧδε ὁ Χριστός, ἴδε ἐκεῖ, μὴ
       πιστεύετε

Luke 10: 7 καὶ ὑμεῖς μὴ ζητεῖτε τί φάγητε καὶ τί πίητε καὶ μὴ
       μετεωρίζεσθε
    12: 29 καὶ ὑμεῖς μὴ ζητεῖτε τί φάγητε καὶ τί πίητε καὶ μὴ μετεωρίζεσθε
    21: 21 τότε οἱ ἐν τῇ Ἰουδαίᾳ φευγέτωσαν εἰς τὰ ὄρη καὶ οἱ ἐν μέσῳ αὐτῆς
       ἐκχωρείτωσαν καὶ οἱ ἐν ταῖς χώραις μὴ εἰσερχέσθωσαν εἰς αὐτήν

John 2: 16 μὴ ποιεῖτε τὸν οἶκον τοῦ πατρός μου οἶκον ἐμπορίου
    5: 14 ἴδε ὑγιὴς γέγονας, μηκέτι ἁμάρτανε, ἵνα μὴ χεῖρόν σοί τι γένηται
    7: 24 μὴ κρίνετε κατ' ὄψιν, ἀλλὰ τὴν δικαίαν κρίσιν κρίνετε
(v.l. has ingressive aorist for the positive command)
    10: 37 εἰ οὐ ποιῶ τὰ ἔργα τοῦ πατρός μου, μὴ πιστεύετέ μοι

Rom. 12: 14 εὐλογεῖτε τοὺς διώκοντας [ὑμᾶς], εὐλογεῖτε καὶ μὴ καταρᾶσθε
    13: 8 μηδενὶ μηδὲν ὀφείλετε εἰ μὴ τὸ ἀλλήλους ἀγαπᾶν
    14: 20 μὴ ἕνεκεν βρώματος κατάλυε τὸ ἔργον τοῦ θεοῦ

1 Cor. 7: 18 περιτετμημένος τις ἐκλήθη, μὴ ἐπισπάσθω· ἐν ἀκροβυστίᾳ
       κέκληταί τις, μὴ περιτεμνέσθω
    10: 7–10 μηδὲ εἰδωλολάτραι γίνεσθε . . . μηδὲ πορνεύωμεν . . . μηδὲ
       ἐκπειράζωμεν τὸν Χριστόν . . . μηδὲ γογγύζετε

14: 39 ὥστε, ἀδελφοί [μου], ζηλοῦτε τὸ προφητεύειν καὶ τὸ λαλεῖν μὴ κωλύετε γλώσσαις

Eph. 4: 26 ὁ ἥλιος μὴ ἐπιδυέτω ἐπὶ [τῷ] παροργισμῷ ὑμῶν
    6: 4 καὶ οἱ πατέρες, μὴ παροργίζετε τὰ τέκνα ὑμῶν ἀλλὰ ἐκτρέφετε αὐτὰ ἐν παιδείᾳ καὶ νουθεσίᾳ κυρίου

1 Tim. 4: 12, 14 μηδείς σου τῆς νεότητος καταφρονείτω . . . μὴ ἀμέλει τοῦ ἐν σοὶ χαρίσματος
    5: 22 χεῖρας ταχέως μηδενὶ ἐπιτίθει μηδὲ κοινώνει ἁμαρτίαις ἀλλοτρίαις

1 John 4: 1 ἀγαπητοί, μὴ παντὶ πνεύματι πιστεύετε ἀλλὰ δοκιμάζετε τὰ πνεύματα εἰ ἐκ τοῦ θεοῦ ἐστιν

2 John 10 εἴ τις ἔρχεται πρὸς ὑμᾶς καὶ ταύτην τὴν διδαχὴν οὐ φέρει, μὴ λαμβάνετε αὐτὸν εἰς οἰκίαν καὶ χαίρειν αὐτῷ μὴ λέγετε

Luke 3: 14 μηδένα διασείσητε μηδὲ συκοφαντήσητε καὶ ἀρκεῖσθε τοῖς ὀψωνίοις ὑμῶν
    12: 4–5 μὴ φοβηθῆτε ἀπὸ τῶν ἀποκτεινόντων τὸ σῶμα καὶ μετὰ ταῦτα μὴ ἐχόντων περισσότερόν τι ποιῆσαι φοβήθητε τὸν μετὰ τὸ ἀποκτεῖναι ἔχοντα ἐξουσίαν ἐμβαλεῖν εἰς τὴν γέενναν. ναὶ λέγω ὑμῖν, τοῦτον φοβήθητε (positive aorist commands here are also urgent; perhaps the prohibition is less urgent when repeated as μὴ φοβεῖσθε in v. 7)
    18: 20 τὰς ἐντολὰς οἶδας· μὴ μοιχεύσῃς, μὴ φονεύσῃς, μὴ κλέψῃς, μὴ ψευδομαρτυρήσῃς (similar in Mark 10: 10, future indicatives in Matt. 19: 18, LXX Exod. 20: 13–16 and Deut. 5: 17–20)

Acts 18: 9 εἶπεν δὲ ὁ κύριος ἐν νυκτὶ δι᾽ ὁράματος τῷ Παύλῳ· μὴ φοβοῦ, ἀλλὰ λάλει καὶ μὴ σιωπήσῃς

1 Cor. 16: 11 μή τις οὖν αὐτὸν ἐξουθενήσῃ

1 Tim. 5: 1 πρεσβυτέρῳ μὴ ἐπιπλήξῃς ἀλλὰ παρακάλει ὡς πατέρα

2 Tim. 1: 8 μὴ οὖν ἐπαισχυνθῇς τὸ μαρτύριον τοῦ κυρίου ἡμῶν μηδὲ ἐμὲ τὸν δέσμιον αὐτοῦ

To summarize the argument to this point, study of commands and prohibitions in the NT shows that the *basic* distinction between present and aorist is the aspectual one traced earlier in this book. However, the most frequent *secondary function* of these aspects involves the general or specific scope of the command. Thus, general precepts usually occur in the present and specific commands usually occur in the aorist. Conversely, the present is most commonly used

because the occurrence is intended to be done customarily or
as a normal practice, and the aorist is often used because the
desired response is a single act to be done at once or at a future
time specified by the speaker.

5. 3 Exceptions to the General versus Specific Distinction

Although the distinction between general precepts and specific commands is a pattern which explains many instances of
present and aorist commands and prohibitions in the NT,
there are exceptions to this pattern, as acknowledged in connection with Tables 5.1 and 5.2 above. Examination of these
exceptions reveals that most of them fall into three areas: (1)
some verbs are used idiomatically in one aspect rather than
the other, regardless of the general or specific scope of the
command; (2) at times the general–specific pattern is super-
seded by the more basic aspectual distinction in one of its
other combinatory contrasts; (3) some books of the NT do not
follow the general–specific pattern. These exceptions will now
be explored in detail.

5. 3. 1 *Individual verbs which are exceptional*

The largest group of exceptions to the general vs. specific
pattern involves the idiomatic use of individual verbs in one
aspect or the other regardless of the general or specific nature
of the command.[18] For most of these verbs this idiomatic use
appears to be related at least originally to the aspectual
character of the verb's lexical meaning and how that character
is usually associated with the typical combinatory senses of
the aspects. Thus, actions which are normally regarded as
durative or stative (i.e. STATES and ACTIVITIES; cf. sections

---

[18] Stereotyped use of some verbs in the imperative has been observed, usually in
regard to the present, by a number of writers: Georges Cuendet, *L'Impératif dans le texte
grec et dans les versions gotique, arménienne et vieux slave des Évangiles* (Paris: Guethner,
1924), 50; MT, *Syntax*, p. 75; Mandilaras, *Verb*, p. 301.

3.1.2.1–2) can become fixed as presents, while actions viewed as essentially momentary or consummative (i.e. CLIMAXES, PUNCTUALS, and ACCOMPLISHMENTS; cf. 3.1.2.3–4) can become stereotyped as aorists. For most of these verbs, however, this connection seems to be a 'dead' one; that is, the original motivation for using present or aorist is lost and the tenses are used out of idiomatic.habit rather than to express the particular combinatory meaning which lies behind it.

5. 3. 1. 1 *Verbs which idiomatically appear in the present aspect in specific commands*

1. *Verbs of motion.* This is the largest group of verbs which occur in the present tense in specific commands. The reason for this tense appears to be the continuing or extended nature of 'coming', 'going', and the like, even in a specific instance. At least, this is almost certainly the original reason for it, but the subsequent force of the idiom seems to overshadow any conscious choice on the part of the speaker at a later stage.

It is important to realize that there is no necessity to use the present with such verbs; the aorist could be used to stress the *beginning* of the motion ('start to walk', especially where the hearer is not walking when spoken to) or to stress the *end* of the motion (especially when the destination is stated: 'go to your house'), or to command the total action without regard for its extended nature. By way of comparison, there are other actions which are extended or durative in nature, yet which normally occur in the *aorist* tense in specific commands (general precepts usually take the present aspect with these verbs): for example, ἀκούσατε used to command listening to an extended utterance; ποιήσατε in the sense of 'make [an object]' or 'do [an extended action]'; and various *compounds* of motion-verbs which bring the end of the movement into focus (go in, out, near, away, up, down).

However, although one could plausibly use the aorist tense of these verbs of motion, in actual usage they occur consistently in the *present* tense regardless of the general or specific nature of the command. The procedural character of the action has somehow influenced the usage to such an extent that the present has become idiomatically fixed, and the rule of 'general vs. specific' does not override this idiom. Specific verbs which fit this group are now listed.

πορεύου, πορεύεσθε. Almost all of the uses of this verb in the NT are specific in nature, yet as an imperative this verb occurs twenty-three times in the present and only four times in the aorist (Matt. 8: 9~Luke 7: 8; Acts 9: 11, 28: 26). There is one prohibitory (aorist) subjunctive (Luke 21: 8—a general precept). The aorists are used perhaps for greater forcefulness, but the variation in aspect is difficult to explain. Of the twenty-three presents, only one need be taken as a general precept (Matt. 10: 6, a mission charge). Perhaps the expression πορεύου εἰς εἰρήνην (Luke 7: 50, 8: 48; Acts 16: 36) should be seen as a general precept to an individual, but it seems to be rather a specific command: 'depart in peace'. In the other instances of the present no customary action is called for, but rather the action of 'proceeding' in a single instance. For example:

Matt. 2: 20 ἐγερθεὶς παράλαβε τὸ παιδίον καὶ τὴν μητέρα αὐτοῦ καὶ πορεύου εἰς γῆν Ἰσραήλ
21: 2 πορεύεσθε εἰς τὴν κώμην τὴν κατέναντι ὑμῶν, καὶ εὐθέως εὑρήσετε ὄνον

Luke 5: 24 ἔγειρε καὶ ἄρας τὸ κλινίδιόν σου πορεύου εἰς τὸν οἶκόν σου

As others have observed,[19] Mark avoids this verb entirely in its simple form (unless one counts three participles in 16: 10–15), using ὑπάγω instead in most parallels where Matthew and Luke have πορεύομαι (28 uses in Matt.; 50 in Luke).[20]

[19] Cf. C. H. Turner, 'Marcan Usage: Notes, Critical and Exegetical, on the Second Gospel', *JTS* 29 (1927–8), 288–9.

[20] In the LXX the aorist imperative of πορεύομαι is more frequent than in the NT, but the present still predominates. In the first 12 books of the LXX (Genesis to 4 Kingdoms) the figures for commands and prohibitions (by my count) are 29 aorists and 55 presents, but 12 of the aorists are the hortatory subjunctive πορευθῶμεν, whose present counterpart does not occur at all in that material (thus a fixed idiom of the aorist?). It is difficult to see a difference in meaning in these books between πορεύου (32 times) and πορευθῆτι (9 times). Both are normally specific commands.

ὕπαγε, ὑπάγετε. This verb does not take an aorist form of any kind in the NT. It occurs twice in John (where it is a favourite word) as an imperfect, and all other occurrences are presents (seventy-eight uses). In the imperative form there are twenty-five uses of the singular and fourteen of the plural (thirty of the thirty-nine imperatives occur in Matthew and Mark). Luke uses the imperative only twice (ὑπάγετε 10: 3, 19: 30) and other forms only three times. He seems not to like the word at all, preferring to use πορεύομαι, περιπατέω, ὑποστρέφω, or a compound of ἔρχομαι or to omit the phrase with ὑπάγω altogether.[21]

Although a few of these imperatives of ὑπάγω could be general precepts, the overwhelming majority of them seem to be specific commands ('go away'), and the usage makes it evident that the present is used as a fixed idiom rather than because of a conscious preference for it by the writer. The other factor which certainly influences this idiom is the difference of transitive vs. intransitive meaning: the present root of the simple verb (ἀγ-) is capable of both transitive ('lead') and intransitive meaning ('go'), but the aorist root of the simple verb (ἀγαγ-) seems to have only the transitive sense in NT usage (see treatment of ἄγωμεν below). Changes in transitiveness are not uncommon in Hellenistic Greek, but in ὑπάγω at least the influence towards aorist aspect with the intransitive meaning 'go' seemed never to be strong enough.[22]

περιπάτει, περιπατεῖτε. Here is another verb with a marked tendency to occur in the present aspect (present and imperfect forms) rather than in the aorist, as shown in Table 5.3. In both the Gospels and Acts, where the meaning is normally literal ('to walk'), and in the other books, where the meaning is usually metaphorical ('to live'), the usage is similar, show-

---

[21] Cf. Hubert Pernot, Études sur la langue des Évangiles (Paris: Les Belles Lettres, 1927), 20, and Turner, 'Marcan Usage', pp. 287–8.

[22] This verb is seldom used in the LXX (7 times): twice in the transitive sense (aorist indicative and participle), once in the present indicative (intransitive), and four times in the present imperative use seen above: ὕπαγε (in ℵ text of Tobit 8: 21, 10: 12, 10: 13, 12: 5, all specific commands).

TABLE 5. 3. *Aspect Usage with* περιπατέω *in NT*

	Indicative	Imperative	Subjunctive	Participle	Infinitive
Frequency in Gospels and Acts:					
Present	4	8	2	15	5
Aorist	2		1 (or fut. indic.?)		
Imperfect	9				
Frequency in other NT books:					
Present	10	6	6	11	5
Aorist	4		3		2
Future	2				

ing a predominance of present aspect. All six of the imperatives outside of the Gospels and Acts are in the Pauline corpus (Eph.—2; Col.—2; Rom.—1; Gal.—1) and all are general precepts with a metaphorical sense. Also used in this way is one of the imperatives from John (12: 35). But the other seven imperatives in the Gospels and Acts appear to be specific commands, influenced to the present by the overall pattern of this verb. These uses all occur in healing stories, where an ingressive aorist would be appropriate ('arise and begin to walk'). But instead the present is used:

Matt. 9: 5(+parallels) ἔγειρε καὶ περιπάτει

John 5: 8 (similar vv. 11, 12) ἔγειρε ἆρον τὸν κράβαττόν σου καὶ περιπάτει

Acts 3: 6 ἐν τῷ ὀνόματι Ἰησοῦ Χριστοῦ τοῦ Ναζωραίου [ἔγειρε καὶ] περιπάτει

It seems hardly likely that the present is used to present a general precept in these cases, although some idea of the continuative nature of 'walking' is almost certainly involved in the choice of present tense.

ἔρχου, ἔρχεσθε. Evidence for the simple form of this verb is mixed. Though the use of its imperative in the whole NT favours the present strongly (15 pres., 5 aor.), the specific distribution of the uses reveals a different story. In the three

Gospels in which this imperative occurs the usage is mixed: Matthew (1 pres., 3 aor.), Luke (2 pres., 1 aor.), and John (4 pres., 1 aor.). In contrast, Revelation has eight present imperatives and no aorists. Here the form ἔρχου seems fixed and idiomatic (occurs seven times; ἐρχέσθω is used in 22: 17). Elsewhere the count is seven presents to five aorists, but the usage is unpredictable. Two of the aorists occur in prayer (Matt. 6: 10~Luke 11: 2), where aorists seem obligatory, but these are probably specific requests anyway. One of the aorists is in the mission charge in Matthew (10: 13) and appears to be a general precept. The other two aorists are clearly specific commands (Matt. 14: 29, John 4: 16). But of the seven presents, six appear to be specific commands (Matt. 8: 9~Luke 7: 8; Luke 14: 17; John 1: 39, 1: 46, 11: 34). Only John 7: 37 seems to be a general precept, but some question could be raised about that as well. Thus, ἔρχομαι in NT usage departs from the general/specific rule in a way similar to other verbs of motion.[23]

ἀκολούθει, ἀκολουθείτω. At first glance this verb seems to fit this group quite well: it also has a predominance of present forms in the imperative (16 pres., 2 aor.). However, in this case the imperative normally occurs as a general precept (in invitations to discipleship): fifteen of sixteen presents are used in this way. The three specific commands are the two aorists (Mark 14: 13~Luke 22: 10, instructions for preparing the Last Supper) and one present: Acts 12: 8, in the angel's words to Peter. Here the present probably reflects the maze-like journey to be described in 12: 9–10 ('out of the cell . . . he continued to follow [*imperfect*]. . . . Past the first and second guard . . . through the iron gate leading to the city . . . along a certain street . . .' before the angel left Peter). The preference

---

[23] In the LXX the usage is closer to the general vs. specific pattern: commands with ἔρχομαι occur predominantly in the aorist (30 aorists, 6 presents), and most of the presents have some. nuance of customary action or general precept. A few of the aorists have the same flavour, but most of them occur as specific commands for action to be done at once. The command ἔρχου, so characteristic of the Apocalypse, occurs only once in the LXX (Cant. 4: 16), so this is not an idiom derived from LXX usage.

for aorist in specific commands is here upset by the extended nature of the action, which the angel's command reflects (see discussion of this type of exception in section 5.3.2 below). Thus, ἀκολουθέω is not actually an exception to the general vs. specific rule, and is included for comment here because it is a motion-verb commonly used in the imperative in the NT.

ἄγωμεν. This intransitive use of ἄγω in the hortatory subjunctive occurs seven times in the NT, with no correspond- ing aorist uses. The transitive sense ('lead', 'bring') occurs in commands in Matt. 21: 2~Luke 19: 30 and Luke 19: 27 (aorists, specific commands), and in 2 Tim. 4: 11 (also a specific command, but present). Of the seven uses of ἄγωμεν, six appear to be specific commands, and in three of these the durative nature of the action does not seem to be in view at all (John 11: 7, 15, 16). These uses, plus 2 Tim. 4: 11, constitute clear exceptions to the general/specific rule, apparently due to the idiomatic use of motion-verbs in the present. The other three occurrences of ἄγωμεν, while specific commands, have a sense of 'let us go out from here', with no goal or specific destination in view: Matt. 26: 4~Mark 14: 42 (in Geth- semane) and John 14: 31 (in the Upper Room?). This 'open-ended' meaning may give livelier motivation for the use of the present in these cases.[24] In its other occurrence, ἄγωμεν should be regarded as a general precept: Mark 1: 38, the departure from Capernaum to preach in other towns.

As mentioned under the treatment of ὕπαγε above, the reason for the present in these cases seems to be the exclusive- ly transitive meaning of the aorist root ἀγαγ- and the fact that it seems to resist the encroaching intransitive meaning, while in Hellenistic Greek the present ἀγ- does not. Compounds of ἄγω in the NT all reflect this pattern of transitive and

---

[24] BDF, *Grammar*, § 336, states that one of the ways in which the durative force of the present is manifested in the imperative is thus: 'The action hangs in the balance; no definite goal is envisaged. . . . Often ὕπαγε and πορεύου'. This seems to be relevant in these three instances of ἄγωμεν. However, in many other cases of motion-verbs a definite goal can be stated and the present still occurs, seemingly because of the stereotyped pattern of using the present.

intransitive usage.[25] One possible exception to this is ἐπανάγω, which occurs in the aorist form ἐπαναγαγών at Matt. 21: 18 with intransitive meaning ('returning'). But the present ἐπανάγων is better attested and should be taken as original. Also, in Luke 5: 3 (ἐπαναγαγεῖν) and 5: 4 (ἐπανάγαγε) the use could be intransitive ('move out into the deep water'), but should probably be regarded as transitive with an ellipsis of the clearly understood object: 'put out [sc. the boat] into the deep water'.

φέρε, φέρετε. This verb also occurs in a stereotyped predominance of present aspect in NT commands.[26] This is perhaps related to the idiom traced here for the other verbs of motion. It is possible, on the other hand, that the usage is influenced by an idiomatic desire to avoid the suppleted aorist imperative ἐνέγκατε.[27] In the imperative mood the present form is used nine times (all in specific commands), while the aorist occurs just once in the NT (John 21: 10). There is, in addition, one occurrence of the present subjunctive φερώμεθα in an exhortation (Heb. 6: 1), but this seems to be a general precept, and the present is appropriate for the process of maturing which is in view there. However, the nine present imperatives occur in utterances which seem to call for aorist aspect: they involve specific commands, and many have a goal or destination stated, which in the indicative mood tends to produce aorist usage (viewing the whole act of 'bringing' or 'leading' in summary). The present imperatives are as follows:

Matt. 14: 18 φέρετέ μοι ὧδε αὐτούς (sc. loaves and fish; a specific, single act)

---

[25] Cf. MT, *Syntax*, p. 51.

[26] Mark's preference for φέρω over ἄγω and the interchange of these two verbs as an issue in Synoptic criticism do not affect the question of aspectual usage with φέρω. A recent discussion of these issues is Joseph A. Fitzmyer, 'The Use of *Agein* and *Pherein* in the Synoptic Gospels' in Eugene Howard Barth and Ronald Edwin Cocroft (eds.), *Festschrift to Honor F. Wilbur Gingrich* (Leiden: E. J. Brill, 1972), 147–60.

[27] On this point cf. BDF, *Grammar*, § 336 (3): 'φέρε, φέρετε "bring" is a special case (always pres. impera. in the simple verb except for John 21: 10 ἐνέγκατε); pres. impera. is used for the aor. as in class., since this verb has no aor. stem'.

Mark 9: 19 (~Matt. 17: 17) φέρετε αὐτὸν [epileptic boy] πρός με (Luke
9: 41 has προσάγαγε)

Mark 11: 2 λύσατε αὐτὸν [colt] καὶ φέρετε (specific command; Matt.
and Luke have ἀγάγετε)
12: 15 φέρετέ μοι δηνάριον ἵνα ἴδω. οἱ δὲ ἤνεγαν (a single act; Matt.
and Luke have (ἐπι)δείξατε)

Luke 15: 22–3; in a series of 6 specific commands 5 are aorists and 1
is φέρετε

John 2: 8 ἀντλήσατε νῦν καὶ φέρετε τῷ ἀρχιτρικλίνῳ. οἱ δὲ ἤνεγκαν
20: 27 φέρε τὸν δάκτυλόν σου. . . . φέρε τὴν χεῖρά σου

Concerning Mark 11: 2, Swete says 'the aorist and present
imperatives are both appropriate',[28] and Taylor writes: 'The
distinction of tenses in λύσατε and φέρετε is noteworthy'.[29] In
the light of the usage of φέρω, it seems better to say that these
two imperatives are virtually equivalent in grammatical
aspect and the use of φέρετε does not reflect a durative or
extended meaning.

2. *Other verbs.* There are several other verbs which consistently occur in the present tense in specific commands, whose
use in this tense seems to be a virtually fixed idiom rather than
a free choice by the speaker between two equally possible
tenses.

ἔγειρε, ἐγείρεσθε (ἐγείρου in textual variants). This verb
differs from the verbs of motion listed above in that it is
difficult to understand why its present became established as a
predominant usage: 'arise' or 'get up' is not a distinctly linear
or extended action like 'walk' or 'proceed'. Nevertheless, the
present imperative of ἐγείρω occurs sixteen times in the NT,
while the aorist occurs just twice (Matt. 17: 7, Luke 7: 14 both
specific commands). Though the aorist imperatives and the
present plural imperatives are passive in form (ἐγέρθητι,
ἐγέρθητε, ἐγείρεσθε), they are intransitive and thus equal in

[28] Henry Barclay Swete, *The Gospel According to St. Mark*, 3rd edn. (London:
Macmillan and Co., 1909), 247.
[29] Vincent Taylor, *The Gospel According to Mark*, 2nd edn. (London: Macmillan and
Co., 1966), 454.

'voice' to the present active ἔγειρε, which is likewise intransitive. They all mean 'arise', without any sense of 'be raised' for the passives, or transitive 'raise up [object]' for the active. In addition, the two aspects in commands display little difference in meaning. The occurrences of the present in the NT, all in apparently specific commands, are these:

Mark 1: 9–11~Matt. 9: 5–6~Luke 5: 23–4 (2 occurrences each):
    healing of the paralytic

Mark 3: 3~Luke 6: 8: healing of man with withered hand

Mark 5: 41~Luke 8: 54: healing of Jairus' daughter

Mark 10: 49: healing of Bartimaeus

Mark 14: 42~Matt. 26: 46: exit from Gethsemane

John 5: 8: healing of the lame man
    14: 31: exit from the Upper Room?

Eph. 5: 14: citation of a hymn?

In the Septuagint the *aorist* of this verb is predominant in commands and prohibitions: it is used four times with intransitive sense ('arise') and four times with transitive meaning ('raise up'). The present occurs twice, both plural: ἐγείρεσθε in Ps. 126 (127): 2 (some manuscripts have infinitive ἐγείρεσθαι) and ἐγειρέσθωσαν in Joel 3 (4)a: 12. The more frequently used compound ἐξεγείρω occurs with intransitive meaning about a dozen times each in aorist and present commands (ἐξεγέρθητι, -θητε vs. ἐξεγείρου). However, the present active form ἔγειρε, so common in the NT, does not occur in either verb in the Septuagint.

θάρσει, θαρσεῖτε. Though 'have courage' could be seen as a command for a customary state of mind, it usually seems to have the contextual nuance of 'take courage', 'cheer up', with an ingressive idea involved (i.e. 'don't be fearful any longer, start to think positively about your situation'). Since the aorist never occurs in the NT and all the NT presents are imperative, it seems more likely that we are dealing with an idiomatic usage, almost an exclamation. Therefore, again, the use of the present should not be stressed by the interpreter. The singular occurs four times (Matt. 9: 2, 9: 22; Mark 10: 49; Acts 23: 11) and the plural three times (Matt. 14: 27~Mark 6: 50, John 16: 33), with the last occurrence listed in each group perhaps being a general precept.

In the Septuagint this verb (θαρσέω, θαρρέω) occurs as an imperative in twenty-nine of thirty-one occurrences, and twenty-seven of the imperatives are presents. The two aorist imperatives do not seem to differ in meaning from the presents, and both occur, strangely, in contexts where they are accompanied by present imperatives of θαρσέω in the near context: Judith 11: 1 θάρσησον (with presents in 11: 3 and 7: 30), and Baruch 4: 27 θαρρήσατε/θαρσήσατε (with presents in 4: 5, 21, 30).

αἶρε. This imperative form occurs three times in the NT (all in Luke–Acts). These are Luke 23: 18; Acts 21: 36, 22: 22, where αἶρε means 'away (with him)', 'kill (him)'. This use is paralleled by John 19: 15 ἆρον, where the aorist seems more in keeping with the specific nature of the command. The variation of aorist and present in these expressions is difficult to explain, since it seems hardly likely for the present to have a progressive force. One might argue that αἶρε is an idiomatically fixed form, but there is little evidence of either present or aorist imperative with this sense outside the NT. Neither occurs in the Septuagint or Josephus. Deissmann lists one occurrence of the aorist (ἆρρον=ἆρον) with this meaning in a papyrus letter of the second or third century AD.[30] Philo, *In Flaccum* 144, has the present infinitive αἴρειν used in an imperatival sense, and it occurs in a similar setting to the NT instances—an assembled mob calling for the death of someone standing before them. The text reads ἀνεβόων, οἱ μὲν ἀτιμοῦν, οἱ δὲ φυγαδεύειν, οἱ δ᾽ αἴρειν, which Colson renders '[the audience] . . . shouted out some for disfranchisement, some for banishment, some for death'.[31] The present imperative with this

---

[30] Adolf Deissmann, *Light from the Ancient East: The New Testament Illustrated by Recently Discovered Texts of the Graeco-Roman World*, trans. Lionel R. M. Strachan (London: Hodder and Stoughton, 1910), 188.

[31] *Philo*, trans. F. H. Colson vol. ix (The Loeb Classical Library; Cambridge, Mass.: Harvard University Press, 1941), 381.

meaning occurs three times in the *Martyrdom of Polycarp* (3. 2, 9. 2 *bis*), in which the cry of αἶρε τοὺς ἀθέους by the pagan crowd against Christians would parallel the NT occurrences. But how much does the NT wording influence this later account? Wilcox suggests a more specialized origin for the wording in Luke–Acts, and his idea seems correct. He argues that Luke is influenced by the Septuagint of Isa. 53: 8, which is quoted in Acts 8: 33: ὅτι αἴρεται ἀπὸ τῆς γῆς ἡ ζωὴ αὐτοῦ. This phrasing is reflected in Acts 22: 22 αἶρε ἀπὸ τῆς γῆς τὸν τοιοῦτον, with the shift to imperative and active to fit the setting. Thus the other two instances of αἶρε, though briefer, may reflect this influence indirectly. In the case of Luke 23: 18 the influence would be more appropriate (αἶρε τοῦτον, of Jesus). Wilcox's conclusion gives his view of how this influence might have operated: 'it seems once again that the source of a special term is to be sought not so much in a kind of generalized drawing on LXX terminology and idiom, as in a marked influence of certain special sections of it: notably "testimonia"-passages and others known independently to have had a prominent place in the life of the early Church'.[32]

There are two other verbs or groups of verbs which deserve comment in this section:

(*a*) *Verbs of speaking* (λέγω, εἶπον, λαλέω, etc.). These usually follow the general vs. specific guideline quite closely. However, there are puzzling exceptions (e.g. Matt. 10: 27, Luke 10: 5 vs. 10: 10, Acts 5: 20, 13: 15, 22: 27), which make one wonder what other influences come to bear on these verbs. Comparing the pattern of usage in the *indicative* of verbs of speaking (see section 4.4), one is led to think that the aspect-choice in commands and prohibitions is similarly rather flexible and subjective, and follows no rule consistently beyond the basic aspect-difference. Apparently these offer the speaker a more open choice than do other verbs between viewing the utterance as a whole (aorist) or seeing it in its

[32] Max Wilcox, *The Semitisms of Acts* (Oxford: at the Clarendon Press, 1965), 66–7.

progress or repetition (present). At times this results in commands which do not follow the general/specific pattern.

(*b*) γινώσκω. This verb does not follow the general vs. specific rule at all. Four aorists are used in commands, all seemingly in general precepts (Matt. 6: 3, Luke 21: 20?, Phil. 4: 5, Heb. 8: 11), and twelve presents occur, of which four are general (Matt. 24: 33~Mark 13: 29~Luke 21: 31, John 15: 18) but eight are specific commands (Matt. 9: 30, Matt. 24: 43~Luke 12: 39, Luke 10: 11, Acts 2: 36, Gal. 3: 7, 2 Tim. 3: 1, Jas. 5: 20). The distinction of general vs. specific is a difficult one with a verb such as 'know', but the use of aspects nevertheless seems erratic. At any rate, it does appear that some other factors influence the usage of this verb. Theoretically it seems that the lexical distinction of 'recognize', 'come to know' (ingressive aorist) vs. 'be aware', 'keep in mind' (stative present) ought to be helpful in explaining the usage, but this does not seem satisfactory for commands and prohibitions. One might suspect that metonymic extension operates on occasion: 'know' being put for 'act in keeping with this knowledge'. But this helps in only a few cases. The pattern for this verb is elusive.

In this section various verbs have been mentioned which depart from the general vs. specific guideline by occurring consistently in the present tense in specific commands. These departures appear to be due to idiosyncrasies of usage on the part of the particular verbs rather than to a lack of validity for the guideline itself. It would be well, in summary, to reiterate the number of instances in which this guideline is valid. In Luke, for example, there are 179 commands which, according to context, seem to be *specific* commands; this total is made up of 136 aorists and 43 presents. But of these 43 specific commands which occur in the present tense, 19 are instances of verbs which have been treated in this section and 14 are prohibitions (all of which carry the sense of 'stop doing [this action presently occurring]', as described in section 5.2.3). This leaves only ten examples not accounted for. These are as follows, with brief explanatory comments:

Luke 8: 39 ὑπόστρεφε: parallels ὕπαγε of Mark 5: 19, which has perhaps influenced the use of the present here. This verb is usually aorist in the NT, but this is the only imperative form of either tense.

8: 39 διηγοῦ: perhaps this should be regarded as a general precept, 'make it your practice to tell of God's work in your healing'. If a *specific* report is intended, as seems more likely, the present reflects the extended action of telling 'the things God has done' for him. In otherwise similar phrasing Mark 5: 19 has ἀπάγγειλον.

14: 18–19 ἔχε με παρητημένον (bis): here the idea is probably 'consider me excused' (a specific command, but stative) rather than 'get me excused' (specific; ingressive). Marshall suggests: 'The formula . . . may be a Latinism (Martial 2: 79 "*Excusatum habeas me rogo*", but is found in the papyri'.[33]

17: 8 διακόνει: here the present appears to be used, even of a specific single act, because the details of the occurrence are emphasized: 'serve me throughout the meal in the various duties of such table-service'.

22: 40, 46 προσεύχεσθε (bis): here also the extended nature of the desired action is underlined: on that specific occasion the disciples should 'be (engaged in) praying' so as not to yield to temptation.

22: 51 ἐᾶτε: this seems a strange phrasing from any viewpoint. RSV has 'No more of this'. Perhaps there is an extended sense instead, 'allow them to continue with the arrest'. This is the only imperative of ἐάω and the only *present* use in the NT (among 6 aorists, 3 imperfects, and 1 future), but the three imperfects all occur in Luke–Acts, with an extended sense (Luke 4: 41; Acts 19: 30, 27: 40).

23: 21 σταύρου, σταύρου αὐτόν: also unusual, especially in comparison with the other gospel accounts:

Matt. 27: 22–3 σταυρωθήτω . . . σταυρωθήτω

Mark 15: 13–14 σταύρωσον αὐτόν . . . σταύρωσον αὐτόν

John 19: 6 σταύρωσον, σταύρωσον . . . σταυρώσατε

19: 15 σταύρωσον αὐτόν

Also, one could note the aorist infinitive (σταυρωθῆναι) used in Luke 23: 23, 24: 7. The aorist imperatives seem to be the more

---

[33] Marshall, *Luke*, p. 589.

natural usage in such contexts, and Luke's presents are something of a puzzle. Could they be an intimation of the drawn-out ordeal of such an execution? Perhaps they are used because of some less obvious reason.

It should be noted that several of these have the present aspect in order to emphasize the extension or the details of the occurrence. This underlines the point that the 'general vs. specific' distinction is a subsidiary difference and that the underlying cause for choosing aorist or present is the aspectual value. Thus, on occasion the general specific guideline is upset when the more basic aspectual distinction asserts itself. This type of exception to the pattern will be discussed in section 5.3.2.

5. 3. 1. 2 *Verbs which idiomatically appear in the aorist aspect in general precepts*

In contrast to the group of verbs discussed above there are some verbs which defy the general vs. specific guideline in the opposite way. The following verbs predominantly occur in the aorist tense in commands, even in general precepts where one expects the present tense.

1. δίδωμι and its compounds. δίδωμι is used frequently in commands and prohibitions, and the aorist tense is predominant in these: thirty-two aorists and four presents occur in the NT. Of the compound verbs, three are used in commands in the NT: ἀποδίδωμι (5 aor., 1 pres.), διαδίδωμι (1 aor.), and μεταδίδωμι (1 aor.). If these figures are combined, it will be seen that the aorist is clearly the normal form used in commands: thirty-nine aorists vs. 5 presents. Of course, many of these aorists (twenty-six) occur in *specific* commands, and *all* of the presents occur in general precepts. However, this leaves thirteen uses of the aorist in commands which seem to be general precepts. It will be helpful to list these in two groups:

(*a*) Commands giving a general principle for all, but in a *distributive* sense (each individual is to do the action *once*):

Matt. 5: 31 δότω αὐτῇ ἀποστάσιον (Deut. 24: 1 LXX)

Luke 3: 11 ὁ ἔχων δύο χιτῶνας μεταδότω τῷ μὴ ἔχοντι
11: 41 τὰ ἐνόντα δότε ἐλεημοσύνην (or does this fit below?)
12: 33 πωλήσατε . . . καὶ δότε ἐλεημοσύνην

The distributive sense has almost certainly influenced the writer/speaker towards aorist usage in these commands, and one can see the logic of such a choice. For the present in such cases see 1 Cor. 7: 12, 13, 15, 18.

(b) Commands giving a general precept with an *iterative* sense (each individual is to do the action whenever it is called for by circumstances appropriate to the command):

Matt. 5: 42 τῷ αἰτοῦντί σε δός (a 'whenever' type of command)
   7: 6 μὴ δῶτε τὸ ἅγιον τοῖς κυσίν (i.e. 'never give')
   10: 8 δωρεὰν δότε (preceded by 6 present imperatives as general precepts)
Matt. 22: 21 (+parallels) ἀπόδοτε τὰ καίσαρος καίσαρι
John 6: 34 πάντοτε δὸς ἡμῖν τὸν ἄρτον τοῦτον
Rom. 12: 19 δότε τόπον τῇ ὀργῇ (the wrath may be single, but surely the 'giving way' is multiple)
   13: 7 ἀπόδοτε πᾶσιν τὰς ὀφειλάς

With most verbs this type of command is normally expressed by the present tense, to reflect the repetitive nature of the occurrence called for. It seems that the aorist came to be used with δίδωμι originally because of the sense of consummative or instantaneous action inherent in its lexical character: 'to give' was thought of not as 'to offer' or 'to be presenting' (i.e. conative) but as actually 'to hand over'. Thus, it seems, the aorist developed as the normal pattern of aspect usage. In the NT, however, such motivation for the use has become stereotyped: the aorist forms are used for the most part from idiomatic habit rather than to stress the consummative or instantaneous sense appropriate to that tense.

In the Lucan and Pauline writings more than others the aorist pattern is broken and a *present* imperative is used when an iterative or other customary sense is appropriate for δίδωμι. The five present imperatives in the NT are as follows (all general precepts):

Luke 6: 30 παντὶ αἰτοῦντί σε δίδου (*contra* Matt. 5: 42 δός; Luke has παντί, which Matthew does not have, but would that have altered Matthew's usage? He has 11 aorist and no present commands with δίδωμι)

  6: 38 δίδοτε καὶ δοθήσεται ὑμῖν

  11: 3 τὸν ἄρτον ἡμῶν τὸν ἐπιούσιον δίδου ἡμῖν τὸ καθ' ἡμέραν (Matt. 6: 11 is worded differently—a specific command for bread 'today')

1 Cor. 7: 3 ἀποδιδότω (of marital obligation)

Eph. 4: 27 μηδὲ δίδοτε τόπον τῷ διαβόλῳ (by improper anger against someone in the church)

2. ἀσπάζομαι. This verb also occurs predominantly in the aorist tense in commands and prohibitions. In the NT there are twenty-seven aorists and one present command of ἀσπάζομαι. The aorist commands fall into three groups:

(*a*) Commands which are clearly specific (using proper names of those to be greeted):

Rom. 16: 3–15 (15 uses of ἀσπάζομαι)
Col. 4: 15 . . . the brethren in Laodicea and Nympha and the church in her house
2 Tim. 4: 19 . . . Prisca and Aquilla

(*b*) Commands which are also specific but which use generic titles for those to be greeted:

Phil. 4: 21 . . . every saint in Christ Jesus
Tit. 3: 15 . . . those who love us in faith
Heb. 13: 24 . . . all your leaders and all saints

The single present command in the NT fits this group, and perhaps the addition of a clear distributive phrase influences the writer towards the present: 3 John 15 ἀσπάζου τοὺς φίλους κατ' ὄνομα.

(*c*) Commands which are phrased more generally:

Rom. 16: 16 . . . one another with a holy kiss
1 Cor. 16: 20 . . . one another with a holy kiss
2 Cor. 13: 12 . . . one another with a holy kiss

1 Thess. 5: 26 . . . all the brethren with a holy kiss
1 Pet. 5: 14 . . . one another with a kiss of love

Are these to be taken as general precepts ('always greet one another in this way') or specific commands ('give everyone an affectionate greeting for me', i.e. on this occasion)? Even though the general term ἀλλήλους is used and these commands sometimes occur after other general precepts (e.g. 2 Cor. 13: 12, 1 Thess. 5: 26), these should perhaps be regarded as specific commands and viewed as typical of other particular details which occur in epistolary conclusions. But the use of the aorist tense here cannot be irrefutable evidence in favour of this decision, since it is so predominant with this verb.[34]

(d) Commands which seem to be general precepts:

Matt. 10: 12 εἰσερχόμενοι δὲ εἰς τὴν οἰκίαν ἀσπάσασθε αὐτήν

Luke 10: 4 μηδένα κατὰ τὴν ὁδὸν ἀσπάσησθε

Both of these occur in mission charges with various *present* commands and they seem to be general precepts with repetitive application in view. But they are phrased in terms of a single generic instance when they are to be applied. Thus, the aorist is certainly appropriate, since a single act is the focus of the immediate sentence in which it occurs. But it must be kept in mind that similar phrasing more often occurs with *present* imperatives, since the multiple sense of the general precept is in view (cf. Luke 6: 30 δίδου, Luke 10: 5 λέγεται, Gal. 6: 1 καταρτίζεσθε, 2 Thess. 3: 14 σημειοῦσθε). The aorist is used here because of an idiomatic preference with this verb rather than by conscious choice.

3. ἀποτίθημι, ἐνδύω, *and other verbs used in the 'old life–new life' motif in Pauline literature*. These verbs occur in contexts which are theologically more significant than some of the previous

---

[34] The aorist ἀσπάσασθε after a string of five present commands in 2 Cor. 13: 12 is puzzling to Moule, *Idiom Book*, p. 21 and to MT, *Syntax*, p. 75; but the idiomatic pattern of usage with this verb puts the aorist in perspective, even if the pattern itself is not entirely explainable.

verb-groups discussed here. Yet some of the same principles apply to this group and will help in analysing the Pauline use of the aorist in these contexts.

This group of commands constitutes the largest group of exceptions in Pauline usage to the normal pattern of *present* commands expressing general precepts. As one can see from the data given in Tables 5.1 and 5.2, the present tense is used for commands in Pauline material in overwhelming proportions compared to the aorist. Especially common are commands for normal Christian behaviour: exhortations to practise as a habit conduct and attitudes which are appropriate for the Christian and to avoid as a habit various deeds which are not fitting. Long sections of material in the Pauline corpus are given over to such moral instruction, abounding in present-tense commands: e.g. Rom. 12: 14–21 (8 pres., 1 aor.), 1 Cor. 10 (13 pres., 1 aor.), 1 Cor. 14 (21 pres., no aor.), and Eph. 4: 25–6: 9 (32 pres., 2 aor.); or, to consider entire epistles with commands scattered throughout: Gal. (20 pres.; 4 aor., all in OT quotations), Phil. (23 pres., 2 aor.), 1 Thess. (23 pres. 1 aor.—ἀσπάσασθε in 5: 26). In 1 Tim. the count is 41 pres. and 3 aor.

In the midst of this high frequency of present commands for habitual attitudes and customary actions one encounters several *aorist* commands which seem as though they too should be expressed by the present tense. Note the following, which also deal with behaviour which is fitting or not fitting for the Christian:

(Rom. 6: 4 ἵνα . . . ἡμεῖς ἐν καινότητι ζωῆς περιπατήσωμεν)[35]
  6: 13 παραστήσατε ἑαυτοὺς τῷ θεῷ ὡσεὶ ἐκ νεκρῶν ζῶντας
  6: 19 οὕτως νῦν παραστήσατε τὰ μέλη ὑμῶν δοῦλα τῇ δικαιοσύνῃ εἰς ἁγιασμόν
    (12: 1 παρακαλῶ οὖν ὑμᾶς . . . παραστῆσαι τὰ σώματα ὑμῶν θυσία ζῶσαν)
  13: 12 ἀποθώμεθα οὖν τὰ ἔργα τοῦ σκότους, ἐνδυσώμεθα [δὲ] τὰ ὅπλα τοῦ φωτός

---

[35] Parentheses here indicate an infinitive, participle, or ἵνα clause used with imperatival force. See sect. 5.4.2 for further treatment of such indirect commands.

13: 13 ὡς ἐν ἡμέρᾳ εὐσχημόνως περιπατήσωμεν
13: 14 ἐνδύσασθε τὸν κύριον Ἰησοῦν Χριστὸν καὶ τῆς σαρκὸς πρόνοιαν μὴ ποιεῖσθε εἰς ἐπιθυμίας

2 Cor. 7: 1 καθαρίσωμεν ἑαυτοὺς ἀπὸ παντὸς μολυσμοῦ σαρκὸς καὶ πνεύματος

(Eph. 4: 1 παρακαλῶ οὖν ὑμᾶς . . . ἀξίως περιπατῆσαι τῆς κλήσεως ἧς ἐκλήθητε)
(4: 22, 24 ἀποθέσθαι ὑμᾶς κατὰ τὴν προτέραν ἀναστροφὴν τὸν παλαιὸν ἄνθρωπον . . . καὶ ἐνδύσασθαι τὸν καινὸν ἄνθρωπον τὸν κατὰ θεὸν κτισθέντα ἐν δικαιοσύνῃ καὶ ὁσιότητι τῆς ἀληθείας)
4: 31 ἀρθήτω ἀφ᾽ ὑμῶν (of various evil deeds)

Col. 3: 5 νεκρώσατε οὖν τὰ μέλη τὰ ἐπὶ τῆς γῆς (various evil deeds listed)
3: 8 νυνὶ δὲ ἀπόθεσθε καὶ ὑμεῖς τὰ πάντα (various evil deeds listed)
(3: 9–10 μὴ ψεύδεσθε εἰς ἀλλήλους, ἀπεκδυσάμενοι τὸν παλαιὸν ἄνθρωπον σὺν ταῖς πράξεσιν αὐτοῦ καὶ ἐνδυσάμενοι τὸν νέον τὸν ἀνακαινούμενον εἰς ἐπίγνωσιν κατ᾽ εἰκόνα τοῦ κτίσαντος αὐτόν) (these participles are perhaps not imperatival but are reasons for the other imperatives.)
3: 12 ἐνδύσασθε οὖν, ὡς ἐκλεκτοὶ τοῦ θεοῦ ἅγιοι καὶ ἠγαπημένοι (various godly activities listed)

In interpreting these texts one cannot avoid the question of aspectual usage: why is the aorist aspect used with these commands, against the marked Pauline tendency to prefer the present? Is it plausible that these texts call for a specific, 'once-for-all' act, never to be repeated?[36] In the Pauline view of things, can all sorts of ungodly deeds be put away and features of Christian conduct be adopted in a single act? The evidence of instructions to Christians throughout the Pauline epistles suggests that this would be the wrong explanation of these commands. These aorists are better accounted for by a combination of two influences on Pauline language, one theological and the other linguistic in nature.[37]

---

[36] Randy L. Maddox, 'The Use of the Aorist Tense in Holiness Exegesis', *Wesleyan Theological Journal*, 16 (1981), 106–18, argues against this interpretation of the aorist in such texts, but suggests that the aorist's stress on completeness (in constative or effective uses) supports the Wesleyan understanding of them.

[37] It will be seen that the reasons for aorist usage here involve idiomatic uses of

The theological influence is the Pauline idea that when a person comes to be 'in Christ', he is a new person: 'old things have passed away; behold new things have come' (2 Cor. 5: 17). When a person becomes a Christian, he is so identified with Christ that his 'old man' (all that he was before conversion) is, as it were, crucified and buried with Christ so that the old life is ended and done away with. Instead the Christian is identified with Christ's resurrection, so that he is now a 'new man', raised to a new life with a new power over the old enslavements to sin and darkness. This is developed primarily in Rom. 6: 1–11 but it also shows up in passages such as Gal. 2: 19–20, 5: 24, 6: 14–15; 1 Cor. 6: 11, 2 Cor. 5: 14–17; Eph. 5: 8; and Col. 2: 11–15, 3: 1–4. Pauline teaching is that when a person comes to be in Christ there is a definite break with the old life and the beginning of a new one.

However, what is equally clear from Paul's teaching is that this transformation is not immediately realized in the Christian's practical experience. This change in the person must be continually acted upon and transferred from the realm of the potential to the actual. The Christian must be progressively putting to death the deeds of the old life (Rom. 8: 13), must be more and more transformed (Rom. 12: 2, 2 Cor. 3: 18) and renewed (Eph. 4: 23), and must be always working out in practice the deliverance which Christ has given (Phil. 2: 12). There are all sorts of wicked deeds to be eliminated and godly behaviour to be adopted (1 Cor. 6; Gal. 5: 16–26, Eph. 4: 25–32, Col. 3: 5–17, etc.), and even the best of Christians has further to go in this regard (Phil. 3: 12–15). But the great strength and attractiveness of Paul's moral code is that all these practical changes in behaviour have a genuine and God-given basis; they are not changes which men must attempt in their own moral power, constantly working themselves up to do the impossible. There is a true emancipation

---

some verbs, but also ingressive aspect-function and incorporation of catechetical phrases. These latter two factors will be discussed in more detail later in the chapter.

from the old enslavements and a new power in the Spirit to live as God desires (Rom. 8: 1–8).

It is because of this factual basis of the Christian's new life in Christ that Paul is influenced to call upon Christians to make a definite *practical* break with the past and to begin to live *in practice* as new people. It seems that this ingressive idea is the motivation for several of the Pauline aorists listed earlier. But such commands are not merely for the new convert, nor are they intended to reflect a single 'new beginning', never to need repeating. Instead the Christian must be progressively leaving behind aspects of the 'old life' and reaching out anew for the things which alone are worthy of his new life in Christ. The ingressive aorists simply remind him of the *changes* which must be made in practice.[38] In this ingressive sense the following commands are appropriate for the Christian at whatever stage in his Christian experience, and it is a reflection of Paul's theological framework that he uses aorist rather than present in them:

(Rom. 6: 4 ἵνα . . . ἡμεῖς ἐν καινότητι ζωῆς περιπατήσωμεν)

Rom. 6: 13 παραστήσατε ἑαυτοὺς τῷ θεῷ ὡσεὶ ἐκ νεκρῶν ζῶντας

  6: 19 οὕτως νῦν παραστήσατε τὰ μέλη ὑμῶν δοῦλα τῇ δικαιοσύνῃ εἰς ἁγιασμόν

  (12: 1 παρακαλῶ οὖν ὑμᾶς . . . παραστῆσαι τὰ σώματα ὑμῶν θυσίαν ζῶσαν)

  13: 13 ὡς ἐν ἡμέρᾳ εὐσχημόνως περιπατήσωμεν

2 Cor. 7: 1 καθαρίσωμεν ἑαυτοὺς ἀπὸ παντὸς μολυσμοῦ σαρκὸς καὶ πνεύματος

(Eph. 4: 1 παρακαλῶ οὖν ὑμᾶς . . . ἀξίως περιπατῆσαι τῆς κλήσεως ἧς ἐκλήθητε)

  4: 31 ἀρθήτω ἀφ' ὑμῶν

Col. 3: 5 νεκρώσατε οὖν τὰ μέλη τὰ ἐπὶ τῆς γῆς (various evil deeds listed)

---

[38] Cf. BDF, *Grammar*, § 337: 'The aorist imperative (subjunctive) can (1) express the coming about of conduct which contrasts with prior conduct; in this case it is ingressive. . . . Thus R 13: 13 περιπατήσωμεν with reference to the commencement of this way of life; cf. vv. 12, 14. Περιπατεῖν (and στοιχεῖν) appears in admonitions usually in the pres. . . . but where the new life of the Christian, corresponding to the divine call which creates a new beginning, is meant, the aor. is used'.

There is another influence, however, which comes into play alongside this theological one in the case of some of the examples listed. This is the 'clothing' imagery and the linguistic pattern which is found with it in the verbs ἀποτίθημι, ἐνδύω, and several related verbs. Verbs of 'putting on' and 'putting off' clothing exhibit a remarkable tendency to occur in the *aorist* tense in biblical Greek.[39] It is not clear exactly why this should be so, since the *process* of 'dressing' or 'disrobing' could conceivably be pictured in a continuative way. But in usage these ideas are uniformly regarded not as ACTIVITIES but as ACCOMPLISHMENTS, not as processes, but as events. A count

TABLE 5. 4. *Use of Tense-Aspect with Verbs of 'Clothing' in NT and Septuagint*

	NT	Septuagint
ἀποτίθημι	9 aor.	13 aor., 5 fut.
ἐνδύω	24 aor., 5 perf.	52 aor., 23 perf., 3 plpf., 34 fut., 1 pres. (indic.)
ἐκδύω	5 aor.	22 aor., 8 fut., 1 pres.
ἀπεκδύομαι	2 aor.	none
ἐπενδύομαι	2 aor.	none
ἐνδιδύσκω	1 pres., 1 impf.	3 pres., 3 impf.[a]

[a] This reversal of the pattern with ἐνδιδύσκω is perhaps due to its unusual formation, with reduplication and suffix -σκω.

of the tense-distribution for all occurrences of this group of verbs in biblical literature is given in Table 5.4. The pattern of preference for the aorist shown in this count reflects an idiomatic linguistic influence on the Pauline choice of aspect with these verbs. Even such fixed patterns can be broken if there is sufficient reason to do so, but it appears that the combination of the Pauline theological conception of the new life with this linguistic idiom gave little cause to choose the present aspect with these verbs of 'clothing'. The fact that *in*

[39] My research on this point was aided by the work of one of my students, Alan Tomlinson, 'The Relationship between Aspect and Lexical Aspectual Meaning' (Th.M. thesis, Dallas Theological Seminary, 1979).

practical terms un-Christian behaviour and attitudes are not 'put off' in a single act and that godly conduct is not attained immediately by a single, unrepeated act of 'putting on' does not prevent use of the aorist in the following texts.[40]

Rom. 13: 12 ἀποθώμεθα οὖν τὰ ἔργα τοῦ σκότους, ἐνδυσώμεθα [δὲ] τὰ ὅπλα τοῦ φωτός

13: 14 ἐνδύσασθε τὸν κύριον Ἰησοῦν Χριστὸν καὶ τῆς σαρκὸς πρόνοιαν μὴ ποιεῖσθε εἰς ἐπιθυμίας

(Eph. 4: 22, 24 ἀποθέσθαι ὑμᾶς κατὰ τὴν προτέραν ἀναστροφὴν τὸν παλαιὸν ἄνθρωπον . . . καὶ ἐνδύσασθαι τὸν καινὸν ἄνθρωπον τὸν κατὰ θεὸν κτισθέντα ἐν δικαιοσύνῃ καὶ ὁσιότητι τῆς ἀληθείας) (in these last two verses the 'old man' and the 'new man' are metonymies for the *deeds* of the old life and new life)

Col. 3: 8 νυνὶ δὲ ἀπόθεσθε καὶ ὑμεῖς τὰ πάντα

(3: 9–10 μὴ ψεύδεσθε εἰς ἀλλήλους, ἀπεκδυσάμενοι τὸν παλαιὸν ἄνθρωπον σὺν ταῖς πράξεσιν αὐτοῦ καὶ ἐνδυσάμενοι τὸν νέον τὸν ἀνακαινούμενον εἰς ἐπίγνωστιν κατ' εἰκόνα τοῦ κτίσαντος αὐτόν)

3: 12 ἐνδύσασθε οὖν, ὡς ἐκλεκτοὶ τοῦ θεοῦ ἅγιοι καὶ ἠγαπημένοι[41]

It seems that these are to be regarded as a summary of all that the Christian is called on to do by his new life in Christ: the process and repeated efforts which lead to a transformed daily walk are all incorporated into the imagery of 'putting off the old life with its deeds' and 'putting on the new life' of righteousness and Christ-likeness.

In this section several groups of verbs have been discussed which consistently depart from the general vs. specific guide-line by occurring in the aorist tense in general precepts. These departures are due to idiosyncrasies of these particular verbs, and do not disprove the rule itself.

The exceptions discussed in this section account for a

---

[40] The use of the aspects here is influenced more by the *vehicle* of the metaphor than by the *tenor* of it. Cf. G. B. Caird, *The Language and Imagery of the Bible* (London: Duckworth, 1980), 152–5.

[41] Three imperatives in Eph. 6 are probably influenced by this idiom as well, though they are not so clearly related to the 'old life–new life' motif: Eph. 6: 11 ἐνδύσασθε, 6: 13 ἀναλάβετε, and 6: 17 δέξασθε, all used of 'putting on' armour in one way or another.

significant number of the instances in which aorist verbs are used in general precepts, at least in the Pauline corpus. For example, these account for four of the five instances in Ephesians, and for three of the six instances in Colossians, the other three being the slogan-prohibitions of 2: 21. Of the thirteen instances in Romans, eight are dealt with in this section. For Romans this leaves five cases unaccounted for: one seems to be a slogan quoted by Paul (3: 8 ποιήσωμεν), three are OT quotations (10: 6 μὴ εἴπῃς, 15: 10–11 εὐφράνθητε, ἐπαινεσάτωσαν), and the other is 14: 13 κρίνατε. Perhaps this is not to be taken as a general precept but a 'do-it-now' specific appeal to his readers: 'decide (now) never to put a hindrance in your brother's way'.

The broad pattern of usage in the NT reveals the validity of the guideline under scrutiny: in general precepts the present usually occurs, while specific commands tend to be expressed by the aorist. Some exceptions are explained by idiomatic usage of individual verbs, as seen in this section. Another type of exception will now be treated.

5. 3. 2 *Instances where the aspect distinction supersedes*

As mentioned earlier, the general vs. specific rule is super-seded in some individual instances by the more basic aspec-tual distinction of 'internal' vs. 'external' viewpoint, or by one of the secondary distinctions produced when the aspects combine with other features (e.g. stative vs. ingressive, de-scriptive vs. simple, simultaneous vs. antecedent, durative vs. momentary, conative vs. consummative). These differ from the previous category of exceptions in that the usage has not become stereotyped but occurs in particular cases. In these, the speaker chooses one aspect over the other to highlight a desired aspectual value regardless of the general or specific nature of the command. Many of these cases are more forceful because of the departure from the normal general/specific pattern for commands and prohibitions.

5. 3. 2. 1 *Present aspect in specific commands*

The present can occur in specific commands in order to highlight an 'internal' perspective concerning the occurrence, rather than following the aorist's summary presentation of the single specific occurrence, which would be normal. Usually the internal viewpoint of the present aspect appears in combination with other features as one of the secondary functions expressed by the present.

For example, sometimes the present is used with its *progressive* or *descriptive* sense, emphasizing the process or the various details constituting the specific occurrence which is commanded or forbidden.

Matt. 11: 15 ὁ ἔχων ὦτα ἀκουέτω ('pay careful attention'; also 13: 9, 13: 43)
   21: 28 τέκνον, ὕπαγε σήμερον ἐργάζου ἐν τῷ ἀμπελῶνι
   26: 38 μείνατε ὧδε καὶ γρηγορεῖτε μετ' ἐμοῦ

Mark 4: 3 ἀκούετε. ἰδοὺ ἐξῆλθεν ὁ σπείρων (cf. normal aor. in Mark 7: 14 ἀκούσατέ μου πάντες)

Luke 17: 8 ἑτοίμασον τί δειπνήσω καὶ περιζωσάμενος διακόνει μοι ἕως φάγω
   22: 46 τί καθεύδετε; ἀναστάντες προσεύχεσθε, ἵνα μὴ εἰσέλθητε εἰς πειρασμόν (similar in v. 40 and Matt. 26: 41)

Acts 12: 8 ἀκολούθει μοι
   19: 38 εἰ μὲν οὖν Δημήτριος καὶ οἱ σὺν αὐτῷ τεχνῖται ἔχουσι πρός τινα λόγον . . . ἐγκαλείτωσαν ἀλλήλοις (also 25: 5; perhaps conative: 'try to bring charges')
   21: 28 κράζοντες· ἄνδρες Ἰσραηλῖται, βοηθεῖτε

In other cases the function of the present is to command an occurrence as *simultaneous* to some other event. This sense is common with specific prohibitions, in which the sense is 'stop this occurrence which is taking place right now' (other illustrations in section 5.2.3).

Mark 16: 6 μὴ ἐκθαμβεῖσθε· Ἰησοῦν ζητεῖτε τὸν Ναζαρηνὸν τὸν ἐσταυρωμένον· ἠγέρθη, οὐκ ἔστιν ὧδε

Luke 5: 10 μὴ φοβοῦ· ἀπὸ τοῦ νῦν ἀνθρώπους ἔσῃ ζωγρῶν

7: 13 ἰδὼν αὐτὴν ὁ κύριος ἐσπλαγχνίσθη ἐπ' αὐτῇ καὶ εἶπεν αὐτῇ· μὴ κλαῖε

11: 7 μή μοι κόπους πάρεχε· ἤδη ἡ θύρα κέκλεισται καὶ τὰ παιδία μου μετ'. ἐμοῦ εἰς τὴν κοίτην εἰσίν

John 4: 21 λέγει αὐτῇ ὁ Ἰησοῦς· πίστευέ μοι, γύναι, ὅτι ἔρχεται ὥρα (i.e. 'believe me as I tell you this')

In some instances a *conative* sense can be discerned, since the specific command envisages not the entire occurrence carried out to its end, but endeavour or engagement in the activity.[42] Perhaps these have this sense:

Matt. 2: 13 ἐγερθεὶς παράλαβε τὸ παιδίον καὶ τὴν μητέρα αὐτοῦ καὶ φεῦγε εἰς Αἴγυπτον καὶ ἴσθι ἐκεῖ ἕως ἂν εἴπω σοι

Mark 9: 39 μὴ κωλύετε αὐτόν. οὐδεὶς γάρ ἐστιν ὃς ποιήσει δύναμιν ἐπὶ τῷ ὀνόματί μου καὶ δυνήσεται ταχὺ κακολογῆσαί με

12: 7 οὗτός ἐστιν ὁ κληρονόμος· δεῦτε ἀποκτείνωμεν αὐτόν, καὶ ἡμῶν ἔσται ἡ κληρονομία

Luke 18: 16 ἄφετε τὰ παιδία ἔρχεσθαι πρός με καὶ μὴ κωλύετε αὐτά

John 19: 21 μὴ γράφε· ὁ βασιλεὺς τῶν Ἰουδαίων (a difficult use to explain, since the writing is actually complete; perhaps the chief priests are appealing to Pilate as though the notice were not finally done—'do not think to write this, but write that'. Pilate's response to them shows that he regards it as settled: ὃ γέγραφα, γέγραφα)

Acts 5: 20 σταθέντες λαλεῖτε ἐν τῷ ἱερῷ τῷ λαῷ πάντα τὰ ῥήματα τῆς ζωῆς ταύτης

Philem. 22 ἅμα δὲ καὶ ἑτοίμαζέ μοι ξενίαν

5. 3. 2. 2 *Aorist aspect in general precepts*

Conversely, the aorist can be used in general precepts to give an external or summary view of the occurrence commanded. This is used in place of the multiple or customary sense which the present provides in such instances. The aorist in general

---

[42] See the suggestions along this line by McKay, 'Aspect in Imperatival Constructions', pp. 210-11.

precepts appears usually to bring out one of the secondary functions of the summary aspect, as shown below.[43]

1. One context in which the summary aspect seems to assert itself in general precepts is in the case of *distributive* commands: each individual is to do the action once, or the action is to be done once in each setting described by the speaker. These are general precepts in a collective way, since the action commanded will occur in multiple instances, and most distributive general precepts appear in the present for this reason. But the aorist is used on occasion, apparently under the influence of the sense of *single* occurrence for each individual or each occasion. Some examples of this are:

Matt. 10: 11 εἰς ἣν δ᾽ ἂν πόλιν ἢ κώμην εἰσέλθητε, ἐξετάσατε τίς ἐν αὐτῇ ἄξιός ἐστιν· κἀκεῖ μείνατε ἕως ἂν ἐξέλθητε (parallels at Mark 6: 10/ Luke 9: 4 have μένετε)

Luke 9: 23 ἀρνησάσθω ἑαυτὸν καὶ ἀράτω τὸν σταυρὸν αὐτοῦ καθ᾽ ἡμέραν καὶ ἀκολουθείτω μοι (the second imperative, ἀράτω, is also general, but it is distributive in a different sense, with the specification καθ᾽ ἡμέραν)

12: 11 ὅταν δὲ εἰσφέρωσιν ὑμᾶς ἐπὶ τὰς συναγωγὰς ... μὴ μεριμνήσητε πῶς ἢ τί ἀπολογήσησθε ἢ τί εἴπητε (v. 11a describes a particular future occasion; cf. v. 22, where the more general phrasing seems to prompt the present μὴ μεριμνᾶτε. Perhaps a similar thing occurs in Matt. 6: 25, 34, where the more particular verse has aorist: v. 34 μὴ οὖν μεριμνήσητε εἰς τὴν αὔριον)

12: 33 πωλήσατε τὰ ὑπάρχοντα ὑμῶν καὶ δότε ἐλεημοσύνην

17: 3 ἐὰν ἁμάρτῃ ὁ ἀδελφός σου ἐπιτίμησον αὐτῷ, καὶ ἐὰν μετανοήσῃ ἄφες αὐτῷ

22: 36 νῦν ὁ ἔχων βαλλάντιον ἀράτω, ὁμοίως καὶ πήραν, καὶ ὁ μὴ ἔχων πωλησάτω τὸ ἱμάτιον αὐτοῦ καὶ ἀγορασάτω μάχαιραν (note how these last two verses differ in scope from the specific commands in 18: 22 to the rich young ruler: πώλησον ... διάδος)

1 Cor. 7: 21 δοῦλος ἐκλήθης, μή σοι μελέτω· ἀλλ᾽ εἰ καὶ δύνασαι ἐλεύθερος γενέσθαι, μᾶλλον χρῆσαι (this seems to be the place for Paul's cryptic command to the slave who is 'able to become free'. In

---

[43] These functions are suggested but not developed in detail by Walter C. Barrett, 'The Use of Tense in the Imperative Mood in First Corinthians' (Th.M. thesis, Dallas Theological Seminary, 1973), 56–9.

the light of Paul's preference for present aspect, the shift to aorist here supports the interpretation 'use the opportunity to become free'. The sense 'use your slavery' would almost certainly be *present* aspect in Paul. The aorist in this case focuses on the single act of becoming free—single for each individual but a distributive plural in overall sense)[44]

It is obvious that the aorist is a plausible choice in these cases, but it is worth recalling that even this type of general precept more commonly occurs in the present aspect (cf. John 7: 37; 1 Cor. 7: 12, 13, 15, 18; Gal. 6: 1).

2. A frequent secondary function for the aorist which appears in general precepts, displacing the general/specific distinction, is the *ingressive* sense. This is commonly true with STATIVE verbs, but it can occur in any context in which there is an emphasis on the beginning of the occurrence or on a change from some previous conduct. This has been illustrated already in the treatment of Pauline commands relating to the 'new life' motif, where it combines at times with the lexical idiosyncrasies of some verbs (section 5.3.1.2). These aorists used in general precepts seem to be ingressive as well:

1 Cor. 3: 18 εἴ τις δοκεῖ σοφὸς εἶναι ἐν ὑμῖν ἐν τῷ αἰῶνι τούτῳ, μωρὸς γενέσθω, ἵνα γένηται σοφός

7: 9 εἰ δὲ οὐκ ἐγκρατεύονται, γαμησάτωσαν

7: 11 ἐὰν δὲ καὶ χωρισθῇ, μενέτω ἄγαμος ἢ τῷ ἀνδρὶ καταλλαγήτω

15: 34 ἐκνήψατε δικαίως καὶ μὴ ἁμαρτάνετε

Phil. 4: 5 τὸ ἐπιεικὲς ὑμῶν γνωσθήτω πᾶσιν ἀνθρώποις

2 Thess. 3: 13 ὑμεῖς δέ, ἀδελφοί, μὴ ἐγκακήσητε καλοποιοῦντες

2 Tim. 1: 8 μὴ οὖν ἐπαισχυνθῇς τὸ μαρτύριον τοῦ κυρίου ἡμῶν

Jude 17 ὑμεῖς δέ, ἀγαπητοί, μνήσθητε τῶν ῥημάτων τῶν προειρημένων ὑπὸ τῶν ἀποστόλων τοῦ κυρίου ἡμῶν Ἰησοῦ Χριστοῦ (cf. Heb. 13: 3 μιμνήσκεσθε 'keep in mind')

3. It is also common to find the *consummative* sense for the

---

[44] Cf. Nigel Turner, *Grammatical Insights into the Greek New Testament* (Edinburgh: T. and T. Clark, 1965), 103; and Moule, *Idiom Book*, p. 21. See Margaret E. Thrall, *Greek Particles in the New Testament: Linguistic and Exegetical Studies* (Grand Rapids: Wm. B. Eerdmans, 1962), 78–82, for discussion of evidence related to εἰ καί at the beginning of the sentence. Her conclusion is that the use of the particles supports the freedom view.

aorist in general precepts. In these the aorist is used to emphasize the accomplishment or fulfilment of an effort: a command not merely to work at or attempt the action, as the present may imply, but to do it successfully or actually. The focus is on the end-point of the action even though the command is a general precept. Some examples are:

Matt. 3: 8 ποιήσατε οὖν καρπὸν ἄξιον τῆς μετανοίας

19: 17 εἰ δὲ θέλεις εἰς τὴν ζωὴν εἰσελθεῖν, τήρησον τὰς ἐντολάς (v.l. has present)

28: 19 πορευθέντες οὖν μαθητεύσατε πάντα τὰ ἔθνη

Luke 16: 9 ἑαυτοῖς ποιήσατε φίλους ἐκ τοῦ μαμωνᾶ τῆς ἀδικίας

1 Cor. 11: 6 εἰ γὰρ οὐ κατακαλύπτεται γυνή, καὶ κειράσθω[45]

Phil. 2: 2 πληρώσατέ μου τὴν χαρὰν

1 Tim. 6: 20 ὦ Τιμόθεε, τὴν παραθήκην φύλαξον

2 Tim. 1: 14 τὴν παραθήκην φύλαξον διὰ πνεύματος ἁγίου

4: 5 ἔργον ποίησον εὐαγγελιστοῦ, τὴν διακονίαν σου πληροφόρησον

Heb. 12: 12 διὸ τὰς παρειμένας χεῖρας καὶ τὰ παραλελυμένα γόνατα ἀνορθώσατε

1 John 5: 21 τεκνία, φυλάξατε ἑαυτὰ ἀπὸ τῶν εἰδώλων

4. Another possibility is the *constative* sense, in which the aorist is used to command an occurrence as a whole or in summary (without regard for internal details of process, repetition, etc.). The significance of this sense when used in a general precept is to underline the *urgency* of the command calling for some customary or general occurrence. Since the aorist is more normally used in pointed specific commands for

---

[45] In a monograph containing a very useful survey of aspectology, William J. Martin has argued that the aorist here displays a sense of limited duration. He paraphrases (pp. 238–9): ' "For if a woman is not 'covered' (has not long hair) then let her remain cropped (for the time being; κειράσθω, aorist imperative with cessative force, referring to a particular situation), but since it is a shame for a woman to be cropped or shorn let her become 'covered' "—(i.e. let her hair grow again; κατακαλυπτέσθω, present imperative for a non-terminative, inchoative action)'. Though his survey is quite good, this suggestion is not supported by usage in other texts and is unlikely to reflect the sense of this verse; see William J. Martin, 'I Corinthians 11: 2–16: An Interpretation', in W. Ward Gasque and Ralph P. Martin (eds.), *Apostolic History and the Gospel*, (Grand Rapids: Wm. B. Eerdmans, 1970), 234–9.

actions 'to be done now', it carries with it a more forceful rhetorical effect than the present; for example, 'Shut that door' is more insistent in tone than 'Help those in need', despite the fact that the latter is far more important and far more difficult to carry out. Thus, it seems that the constative aorist is used in some general precepts in the NT in order to heighten the urgency of the command,[46] even though the desired action is a thing to be done not only (or perhaps not at all) in the immediate circumstance but as a customary practice:

John 15: 4, 9 μείνατε ἐν ἐμοί ... μείνατε ἐν τῇ ἀγάπῃ τῇ ἐμῇ (μένετε in 1 John 2: 28)

1 Cor. 6: 20 ἠγοράσθητε γὰρ τιμῆς· δοξάσατε δὴ τὸν θεὸν ἐν τῷ σώματι ὑμῶν

2 Thess. 2: 3 μή τις ὑμᾶς ἐξαπατήσῃ κατὰ μηδένα τρόπον

1 Tim. 5: 1 πρεσβυτέρῳ μὴ ἐπιπλήξῃς

2 Tim. 2: 2–3 ταῦτα παράθου πιστοῖς ἀνθρώποις . . . συγκακοπάθησον ὡς καλὸς στρατιώτης Χριστοῦ Ἰησοῦ

4: 2 κήρυξον τὸν λόγον, παρακάλεσον, ἐν πάσῃ μακροθυμίᾳ καὶ διδαχῇ (note of urgency is emphasized by 4: 1, 3–4, 6)

Jas. 5: 7–8 μακροθυμήσατε οὖν, ἀδελφοί, ἕως τῆς παρουσίας τοῦ κυρίου . . . μακροθυμήσατε καὶ ὑμεῖς, στηρίξατε τὰς καρδίας ὑμῶν, ὅτι ἡ παρουσία τοῦ κυρίου ἤγγικεν

1 Pet. 5: 2 ποιμάνατε τὸ ἐν ὑμῖν ποίμνιον τοῦ θεοῦ

5. 3. 3 Individual books which are exceptional

A third area of exceptions to the general vs. specific guideline for commands and prohibitions involves several books of the NT which do not follow this pattern. At an initial examination, five books seem to be exceptional: 2 Timothy, James, 1 Peter, and perhaps 2 Peter and Jude. The latter two epistles

---

[46] That the aorist is more forceful than the present in commands is the conclusion of most grammarians, although they do not usually give any rationale for this. Rehkopf includes this opinion in the recent edition of BDR, *Grammatik*, § 335. But it is also given as far back as WL, *Grammatik* (1867), pp. 294–5, and in numerous grammars in between.

seem to belong here, but the small number of imperatives used in them (seven in 2 Pet. and five in Jude) makes it more difficult to be sure of the pattern of usage.

These epistles diverge from the normal pattern primarily in regard to *general* precepts. They contain few specific commands, but most of the these follow the rule and take the aorist aspect (4 of 6 specific commands in Jas., the single one in 1 Pet., and 3 of 5 in 2 Tim.;[47] 2 Pet. and Jude do not contain any specific commands). However, with general precepts there is either a free variation between present and aorist or a preference for the aorist rather than the present. The count of *general precepts* in these epistles (repeated from Table 5.2) is given in a different format in Table 5.5. It can be seen from this count that these books particularly depart from the normal pattern in their use of *aorist* imperatives in general precepts of the sort expressed consistently by the *present* aspect elsewhere in the NT.[48] Several suggestions have been offered to explain the use of the aorist in these books.

TABLE 5. 5. *General Precepts in 2 Timothy, James, 1 and 2 Peter, and Jude*

	Total	Presents (normal)	Aorists (exceptional)
2 Timothy	29	14	15
James	48	27	21
1 Peter	36	10	26
2 Peter	7	4	3
Jude	5	3	2

Several commentators on 1 Peter offer the ingressive meaning as an explanation of the frequent aorist commands in that epistle: the aorist has the sense of 'begin to . . .' or 'change

[47] See 2 Tim. 4: 9, 19, 21; Jas. 2: 3, 5, 18, 5: 10; 1 Pet. 5: 14.

[48] Several commentators have observed that the pattern of aspect-usage with imperatives in 1 Pet. is different from other NT writings. See Charles Bigg, *A Critical and Exegetical Commentary on the Epistles of St. Peter and St. Jude* (ICC; Edinburgh: T. and T. Clark, 1901), 116; and Edward Gordon Selwyn, *The First Epistle of St. Peter* (London: Macmillan and Co., 1946), 171–2. See also MT, *Syntax*, p. 174; Robertson, *Grammar*, p. 856; Zerwick, *Biblical Greek*, p. 79; and MT, *Style*, p. 128.

your conduct to . . .'. This is not commonly suggested for the aorists in the other epistles. The ingressive meaning for the aorist was developed in section 5.3.2.2 as an instance of the more basic aspectual meaning superseding the general/specific distinction. The argument advanced here is simply that these books may be exceptional in having a larger proportion of ingressive aorists.

This ingressive meaning for the aorists in 1 Peter is often linked to a view of the epistle as addressed primarily to newly converted Christians. Further along the same line is the hypothesis that it is composed of two parts which were originally separate: a baptismal homily addressed to those about to be baptized (1: 3–4: 11) and a sermon or epistle addressed more broadly to the whole Church. Beare takes the latter view in his commentary, although he argues that the same writer composed both parts, inserting his earlier baptismal discourse into this 'epistle to persecuted Christians' (1: 1–2, 4: 12–5: 14).[49] Because of this view, Beare consistently explains the aorist imperatives in the earlier portion as ingressive commands to new Christians. For example, on ἀγαπήσατε in 1: 22, he writes:

> The use of the aorist should be noted as supporting the interpretation that this is an injunction to newly-converted Christians. Otherwise the present would be more appropriate, as an exhortation to continue loving one another; the aorist (ingressive, cf. ἐλπίσατε in v. 13) has rather the force of inculcating the adoption of a new attitude, the necessary consequence of their admission to the Christian brotherhood.[50]

The ingressive aorist is a quite plausible interpetation of the

---

[49] Francis Wright Beare, *The First Epistle of Peter*, 3rd edn. (Oxford: Blackwell, 1970), 25–8, 220–6. This view of the epistle is usually traced to R. Perdelwitz, *Die Mysterienreligion und das Problem des ersten Petrusbriefes* (Gießen: Alfred Töpelmann, 1911), and was subsequently advanced by B. H. Streeter, *The Primitive Church* (London: Macmillan and Co. 1929), 122–4, and H. Windisch, *Die katholischen Briefe*, 2nd edn. (Tübingen: J. C. B. Mohr, 1930). Further development of this view may be traced in Beare or in Ernest Best, *1 Peter* (New Century Bible; London: Oliphants, 1971), 20–7. Best argues against this two-source hypothesis.

[50] Beare, *1 Peter*, pp. 110–11.

aorists in the early part of 1 Peter, whether one follows the hypothesis of an original baptismal setting for the verses or not. Moule suggests, for example, that the baptismal motif was common among early Christian writers and was used by them in exhortations to godly living addressed to older Christians as well as new converts, and not necessarily in connection with baptismal rites.[51] There are clear references in chapters 1 and 2 to the new birth, the change from the old life, and so forth, which make an ingressive sense quite plausible for several of the aorists in those chapters (cf. 1: 15, 1: 22, 2: 2).

Selwyn alludes to a type of ingressive meaning for aorists in 2: 13 and 2: 17, which does not seem so plausible: concerning ὑποτάγητε in 2: 13, he writes: 'The aorist [points] less to the continual course of submission [as Paul might have it] than to the act of decision by which this policy of submission is adopted. What is inculcated, in that case, is an act of faith rather than a rule of conduct'.[52] This is possible, but not as likely as a suggestion to be given later.

It is also difficult to see the ingressive meaning with the aorist imperatives which occur in chapter 5. Beare sticks to this opinion even for the aorist in 5: 2 ποιμάνετε: 'The aorist may be taken as ingressive—"take up the task of shepherding". The itinerant ministry of apostles, prophets, teachers, and evangelists would be hampered by the activity of the persecutors, with the consequence that wider responsibilities would fall upon the local officials'.[53] But surely the ministry of the πρεσβύτεροι would have been commonly seen as 'shepherding the flock' (cf. Acts 20), and this would not be a task they would take up only in the absence of itinerant ministers. Spicq also consistently adopts an ingressive sense for the aorists in 1 Peter, and in 5: 2 he sees a slightly more plausible nuance than the interpretation of Beare. His view is that the aorist is a call

[51] C. F. D. Moule, 'The Nature and Purpose of 1 Peter', *NTS* 3 (1956–7), 1–11.

[52] Selwyn, *1 Peter*, p. 172.

[53] Beare, *1 Peter*, p. 199. He does not attribute this aorist to the baptismal influence of the early section.

for *renewed fervour* in shepherding, necessitated by the persecutions which have come upon the Church.[54] See the further discussion of this verse in a later section.

It is possible that the ingressive sense is the best interpretation of several aorists in 2 Timothy and James (2 Tim. 1: 8, 1: 14, 2: 3; Jas. 4: 8–10), but the next suggestion is more commonly cited by commentators on those epistles.

A second explanation for the use of the aorist in these books is that the aorist carries a more urgent and authoritative force than the present imperative. This is another use for the aorist developed in section 5.3.2.2 as an appearance of the more basic aspectual meaning without regard for the general/specific distinction.

Kelly adopts this idea frequently for the aorists in 1 Peter (cf. 1: 13: 'The imperative is aorist (*elpisate*), the tense striking a more urgent, insistent note than the present would'[55]). Beare refers to this explanation at 1 Pet. 5: 8,[56] and Selwyn alludes to this sense at 1: 13 and 2: 2.[57] Among older writers, Hort adopts this interpretation for 1 Pet. 2: 17,[58] and Mayor sees this urgent force for the aorist in many of the occurrences in James, 2 Peter, and Jude.[59] Abbott refers to this sense as 'the authoritative imperative' and cites 2 Tim. 1: 8, 1: 14, 2: 3, 2: 15 as examples.[60]

This second explanation for the aorist commands in 2

---

[54] Ceslas Spicq, *Les Épîtres de Saint Pierre* (Sources Bibliques; Paris: Lecoffre, 1966), 165–6.

[55] J. N. D. Kelly, *A Commentary on the Epistles of Peter and of Jude* (London: Adam and Charles Black, 1969), 66.

[56] Beare, *1 Peter*, p. 204.

[57] Selwyn, *1 Peter*, pp. 140, 156.

[58] F. J. A. Hort, *The First Epistles of St. Peter: I. 1–II. 17* (London: Macmillan and Co., 1898), 146.

[59] Joseph B. Mayor, *The Epistle of St. James*, 3rd edn., with *Further Studies in the Epistle of St. James* (London: Macmillan and Co., 1913), pp. ccxxx, 33; id., *The Epistle of St. Jude and the Second Epistle of St. Peter* (London: Macmillan and Co., 1907), pp. xliii–xliv.

[60] Edwin A. Abbott, note to Mayor, *James*, p. 33. He discusses this further in his *Johannine Grammar* (London: Adam and Charles Black, 1906), 318–19, where he gives John 15: 4, 9 and 20: 10–12 as examples.

Timothy and James seems to be a promising suggestion. Such an interpretation is supported by contextual features of urgency and the like in several passages (e.g. 2 Tim. 4: 2, 5, and Jas. 4: 8, 5: 1, and 5: 7, 8). This does not seem as likely for the aorists in 1 Peter, though perhaps those in chapter 5 (5: 2, 5, 6, 8, 9, 12) could be seen in this light.

A third suggestion is that the aorists in these epistles are to be interpreted in a consummative or conclusive sense: as commands for 'conduct up to a final point',[61] for action to be done over an interval of time and completed or brought to its appropriate end. Thus, the aorist denotes the total action but with special emphasis on carrying it to its final point.

This explanation appears to originate with Blass and it seems fairly certain that others who adopt this view have taken it from his treatment. It was Blass's distinctive view of the aorist in general that it focuses on the end-point of an action, and he developed this concept in regard to aorist imperatives in the first edition of his *Grammatik* (1896). He cites the following examples, with explanatory comments like 'up to the end', 'until the coming of Christ': Jas. 5: 7–8; 2 Tim. 1: 14, 4: 2, 4: 5; 1 Pet. 1: 17, 5: 2.[62] This treatment has been preserved through the various editions under Debrunner and in the English translations by Thackeray and Funk.[63] Rehkopf, in the fourteenth edition, has preserved the basic point but omitted many of Blass's examples and further comments.[64] Blass's work has influenced several towards this view in their exegesis of these epistles.

Thus, Moffatt says of the aorist imperative in 1 Pet. 5: 2: 'here, as in i.13, 17, 22, referring to a specific period, the

---

[61] Friedrich Blass, *Grammar of New Testament Greek*, trans. Henry St. John Thackeray, 2nd edn. (London: Macmillan and Co., 1905), 195.

[62] Friedrich Blass, *Grammatik des neutestamentlichen Griechisch* (Göttingen: Vandenhoeck and Ruprecht, 1896), 190–2.

[63] See the 4th edn. (1913) and 7th edn. (1943), by Debrunner. Also Blass–Thackeray (cited above), and BDF, *Grammar*, § 337 (2).

[64] BDR, *Grammatik*, § 337 (2).

interval before the end'.[65] A clear statement of this position is given by Hillard in reference to 2 Tim. 4: 2:

> As the actions implied are to be continued and repeated, we might have expected *Present* Imperatives. But the proper force of the Aorist is to signify the completion and conclusion of an action as a whole, and this is exactly what is emphasized here, as if the writer were saying, 'Preach the word right up to the coming of our Lord'. Cf. τὴν καλὴν παραθήκην φύλαξον in i.14.[66]

What evaluation should be given for this explanation of the aorists in these epistles? It seems that it can be allowed as a possible interpretation, but it should be given a somewhat different sense and the range of instances should be limited. According to the earlier discussion of lexical character and how it combines with aspect (section 3.1), one expects the aorist to assume a conclusive sense like this (focus on action done to the *end*-point) only with verbs of a particular lexical type: ACCOMPLISHMENTS. The primary characteristic to note here is that the verb denotes a *process* which extends over time but is also such that the action is not 'truly' done unless a certain *goal* or end-point is reached (see section 3.1.2.3). That is, the verb portrays a process leading up to a goal, and with such a verb the aoristic aspect usually points to the accomplishment of the process (the goal is reached or the action is 'done' *successfully*), while the continuative aspect usually points to the process only, with the goal not reached as yet (effort being exerted or action going on, but not consummated).

In this sense, the aorist in these epistles may express the writer's wish that the desired action be not simply attempted or engaged in, but that it be 'done successfully'. Of the examples listed by Blass, some clearly do not fit this sense (Jas. 5: 7–8; 2 Tim. 4: 2, 4: 5a; 1 Pet. 1: 17). But others may

---

[65] James Moffatt. *The General Epistles* (Moffatt New Testament Commentary; London: Hodder and Stoughton, 1928), 162. Mention of Blass is made by J. Howard B. Masterman, *The First Epistle of S. Peter (Greek Text)* (London: Macmillan and Co., 1900), 109–10, but he does not develop the point.

[66] A. E. Hillard, *The Pastoral Epistles of St. Paul* (London: Rivingtons, 1919), 101.

well carry this meaning: 2 Tim. 1: 14 φύλαξον; 4: 5 ποίησον and πληροφόρησον; 1 Pet. 5: 2 ποιμάνατε (perhaps; but aorist as enforcing the *urgency* of this seems better).

Understood in this way, the consummative sense is another use for the aorist developed in section 5.3.2.2 as an appearance of the more basic aspectual meaning without regard for the general/specific distinction.

A fourth suggestion to explain the significance of the aorist in these epistles is that some of these imperatives are stock expressions current in the early Church which the writers of the epistles incorporate without any conscious choice of aspect. Best gives some general comments along this line in regard to 1 Peter:

The way in which these quotations [OT] are used shows us that the writer can make formal quotations but more often incorporates O.T. material without informing us; if we did not possess the O.T. we should never have been aware of his extensive use of it. It is therefore probable that if there was other material to hand he would also use this without telling us; since this other material, e.g., catechisms, hymns, creeds, would not have the authority of the O.T. in the eyes of the church he would never make formal quotations from it. . . . The frequent use of the O.T. by our author shows us the way his mind works—through the compilation of material ready to hand rather than through his own words; this again suggests that he will be predisposed to use material in circulation in the church.[67]

Hints for seeing 1 Peter in this way were provided by Carrington in his *Primitive Christian Catechism* (1940).[68] He compared instructions given in various epistles and found parallels in theme, phraseology, and order of treatment, of a

---

[67] Best, *1 Peter*, pp. 28–9. Cf. his comments on 4: 1, p. 150.

[68] Philip Carrington, *The Primitive Christian Catechism: A Study in the Epistles* (Cambridge: at the University Press, 1940), esp. 22–57. Other valuable works on this topic are Selwyn, 'Essay II: On the Inter-Relation of I Peter and Other NT Epistles', pp. 365–466 in his *1 Peter;* C. H. Dodd, *Gospel and Law: The Relation of Faith and Ethics in Early Christianity* (Cambridge: at the University Press, 1951), 19–21; and A. M. Hunter, *Paul and his Predecessors*, new rev. edn. (London: SCM Press, 1961), 52–7, 128–31.

sort which he was led to explain not by dependence of one epistle upon the other but by dependence in each epistle on a general catechetical tradition in the early Church. Working from parallels in Ephesians, Colossians, James, and 1 Peter, Carrington delineates 'Four Points' in the tradition which are reflected in these epistles: putting off all evil, submitting oneself, watching and praying, and resisting the Devil or standing firm. These are found in the same order and with little variation in wording between the four epistles.[69] He proceeded to examine the Greek vocabulary used in these parallels and discovered that the keywords were not used commonly in the NT but occurred for the most part in these parallels only. Thus, some sort of dependence on a body of fairly fixed instruction seems inescapable.[70]

What Carrington and others did not cite is the use of the aorist imperative in much of this material. In the parallels which reflect the 'Four Points' (Eph. 4: 25, 5: 21, 6: 11–14, 6: 18; Col. 3: 8, 3: 18, 4: 2, 4: 12; Jas. 1: 21, 4: 7; 1 Pet. 2: 1, 2: 13, 4: 1, 4: 7, 5: 5, 5: 8–9) there are only two present imperatives and two present participles (all Pauline). In contrast, there are thirteen imperatives, three participles, two infinitives, and one subjunctive which occur in the *aorist* in these parallels. Why this catechetical material is characterized by aorist commands is not clear: perhaps an ingressive sense is used to underline the change of behaviour expected of catechumens; perhaps aorists heightened the urgency of the instructions. Regardless of the reason for the aorist in the catechetical tradition, these epistles have adopted the aspect-choice with little alteration. They have duplicated the stock expressions which were common for such instruction, rather than making a totally free choice of wording and grammar.

---

[69] Carrington, *Catechism*, pp. 30–44. It should be noticed that one of the points (putting off all evil) was examined earlier in this book as an example or a verb-group which uses the aorist in a stereotyped way.

[70] Ibid. 46–57. Selwyn, *1 Peter*, pp. 386–8, also examined these parallels in detail and structured the material into six divisions.

Looking beyond Carrington's 'Four Points' to examine other texts in James and 1 Peter, one finds other commands which are perhaps derived from similar traditional material. Carrington himself suggests this broader search in an earlier chapter on parallels between these two epistles.[71] Of particular interest here are the parallels between Jas. 4: 7–10 and 1 Pet. 5: 5–12: both passages contain a series of terse, aphoristic commands (all aorist: 10 in Jas., 7 in 1 Pet.), which are not arranged in any clear logical sequence. Some of the commands in both passages relate to the 'Four Points', but there are others as well. This seems to be a point in both epistles where their dependence on common didactic tradition shows through, and this perhaps explains the use of the aorist imperative in these sections.

A similar kind of dependence appears to operate in the case of OT citations in these epistles: the aspect is drawn from the prior source with little or no alteration. Note, for example, the string of eight aorist imperatives in 1 Pet. 3: 10–15, all of which are derived from Septuagint wording, the latter three of these (3: 14–15) are not as obvious as the first five (3: 10–11)). In James the OT quotations are less frequent and more obvious (2: 11 bis).

In summary, these epistles depart from the general/specific pattern of usage in using the aorist more frequently for general precepts than is found in the rest of the NT. Many of the exceptional uses are due to one of the secondary functions of the aspect coming to the fore: an ingressive, consummative, or urgent sense is chosen despite the general nature of the command (the sort of exception treated in section 5.3.2.2). A few are due to the influence of catechetical or OT material which used aorist commands (perhaps originally ingressive, consummative, or urgent).

---

[71] *Catechism*, pp. 22–9.

5. 4 Other Issues Involving Aspectual Usage in Commands and Prohibitions

5. 4. 1 *Relative forcefulness of the aspects in commands and the predominance of the aorist in prayers*

Two issues must be discussed together in this section: the relative forcefulness (or dramatic effect) of the two aspects and the predominance of the aorist aspect in prayers to the deity. The latter issue was raised by Mozley, who reported that in a survey of Septuagint and NT Greek he discovered only five Septuagint examples and one NT example (Luke 11: 3 δίδου) of the *present* aspect used in requests uttered to God, compared to an apparently large number of *aorist* imperatives in such prayers (Mozley cites no figures for these).[72] Other studies have been published on this phenomenon since Mozley's day, and they have shown that the predominance of the aorist holds true for all of the ancient Greek language, from Homeric to patristic usage.[73] However, each study seems to advance a different reason to explain this usage and there is no consensus or clearly superior viewpoint which has carried the day.[74]

The question of 'dramatic force' in the present and aorist commands is related to the use of the aspects in prayer, because several authors have tried to explain the predomin-

[72] F. W. Mozley, 'Notes on the Biblical Use of the Present and Aorist Imperative', *JTS* 4 (1903), 279–82. In the NT there are actually 2 present imperatives used in prayer, as compared with 35 aorists according to my count. See the specific texts mentioned at the end of this section.

[73] See E. Kieckers, 'Zum Gebrauch des Imperativus Aoristi und Praesentis', *IF* 24 (1909), 10–17: L. A. Post, 'Dramatic Uses of the Greek Imperative', *AJP* 59 (1938), 31–59; SD, *Syntax*, p. 341; and Moorhouse, *Syntax*, pp. 218–19.

[74] The most recent study of this question, and the best survey of previous work, is Willem Frederik Bakker, *The Greek Imperative: An Investigation into the Aspectual Differences between the Present and Aorist Imperatives in Greek Prayer from Homer up to the Present Day* (Amsterdam: Adolf M. Hakkert, 1966), esp. 11–17. Bakker's conclusion about the aspects is not convincing: he holds that they are distinct in regard to whether the speaker sees (thus the present) or does not see (aorist) a *connection* between the action commanded and the existing situation (pp. 19–66). This view is based on a temporal approach to the aspects, which is evaluated in sect. 1.1.3 above.

ance of the aorist on this basis. Kretschmer, for example, suggested that the aorist in prayer was more reverential or respectful, while the stronger present would be impolite and impudent.[75] Post, writing about a broader topic than aspect in prayer, comes to similar conclusions: that the aorist gives a softer request, while the present expresses a harsher or impatient command. In this connection he writes: 'The present emphasizes details and difficulties. The aorist ignores or belittles them'.[76]

It seems likely, in fact, that the present is more forceful in *specific* commands where it is unexpected and thus assumes a more peremptory tone. On the other hand, in *general* precepts the aorist appears to carry greater urgency, as argued in section 5.3.2.2. Because of its common use in specific commands ('do this now!'), the insistent force of the aorist may be utilized for rhetorical effect in commands which actually refer to customary or continuing action. Thus, the forcefulness of the aspects is due in both cases to use of the 'unexpected' form: departure from the normal pattern of general vs. specific makes the command insistent and urgent.

Turner's explanation for the predominance of the aorist in prayer seems the most plausible for NT usage: 'Requests to the deity are regularly aorist, for they aim to gain a hearing for specific matters rather than to bind continually'.[77] In NT

[75] P. Kretschmer, 'Literaturbericht für das Jahr 1909', *Glotta*, 3 (1912), 342. Cf. the similar idea expressed by Martin, 'I Cor. 11: 2–16: An Interpretation', pp. 237–8; and by Judy Glaze, 'The Septuagintal Use of the Third Person Imperative' (M.A. thesis, Harding Graduate School of Religion, 1979), 56–9. Moulton, *Proleg.*, p. 173, advances the idea that even in prayer the aorist is urgent and direct.

[76] Post, 'Dramatic Uses of the Greek Imperative', pp. 38–40.

[77] MT, *Syntax*, p. 75. This is the view favoured by Mozley, 'Biblical Use of the Present and Aorist Imperatives', pp. 279–80. According to a notice by Paul Kretschmer in *Glotta*, 18 (1930), 240, W. Beschewliew in a monograph of 1927 shows that the present imperative is used in prayers more frequently than others have admitted (300 instances cited) and that the difference between the aspects in prayers is the same as for the other moods: 'd. h. Aor., wenn es sich um einen einzelnen konkreten Fall handelt, Präs. bei generellem, iterativem, durativem oder imperfektivem Charakter der erbetenen Zustände oder Handlungen' (quotation is from Kretschmer's summary). The work by Beschewliew is 'Der Gebrauch des Imperati-

usage most requests in prayer are concerned with specific occurrence rather than customary or general action, and the aorist is the most natural in such requests (e.g. Matt. 6: 9–13/Luke 11: 2–4; Matt. 26: 39, 42/Mark 14: 36/Luke 22: 42; Luke 18: 13, 23: 34; John 17: 1, 5, 11, 17; Acts 1: 24, 4: 29, 7: 60) Also, the two imperatives in prayer which have the present are in fact general requests:

Luke 11: 3 τὸν ἄρτον ἡμῶν τὸν ἐπιούσιον δίδου ἡμῖν τὸ καθ᾽ ἡμέραν (Matt. 6: 11 is phrased in specific terms: τὸν ἄρτον ἡμῶν τὸν ἐπιούσιον δὸς ἡμῖν σήμερον. Note how the adverbial expression in each helps to show the general or specific reference)

22: 42 εἰ βούλει παρένεγκε τοῦτο τὸ ποτήριον ἀπ᾽ ἐμοῦ· πλὴν μὴ τὸ θέλημά μου ἀλλὰ τὸ σὸν γινέσθω (this is more questionable, but it seems general; Matt. 26: 42 maintains the specific focus: εἰ οὐ δύναται τοῦτο παρελθεῖν ἐὰν μὴ αὐτὸ πίω, γενηθήτω τὸ θέλημά σου)

In the normal (specific) request seen in the NT, the aorist is not more forceful than the present: both assume a milder tone in a context of 'inferior to superior' utterance, and relative forcefulness is not the factor which has influenced the predominance of aorist in prayer.

5. 4. 2 *Use of the aspects in indirect commands*

Commands and prohibitions in the NT are quite frequently given in indirect form rather than as direct imperatives or as hortatory/prohibitory subjunctives. These commands and prohibitions in reported speech have the same range of modal forces as the direct forms (e.g. demand, instruction, appeal, request). At times their indirect form is merely a stylistic variation rather than a reflection of true 'reported speech', especially when the introductory verb is in the first person: e.g. Matt. 5: 34–6 ἐγὼ δὲ λέγω ὑμῖν μὴ ὀμόσαι ὅλως· μήτε ἐν τῷ οὐρανῷ . . . μήτε ἐν τῇ γῇ . . . μήτε ἐν τῇ κεφαλῇ σου ὀμόσῃς and 1 Thess. 5: 12–13 ἐρωτῶμεν δὲ ὑμᾶς, ἀδελφοί, εἰδέναι τοὺς κοπιῶντας

vus Aoristi und Praesentis im altgriechischen Gebet', *Annuaire de l'Université de Sofia*, 23 (1927), 27–59, which I have not seen.

ἐν ὑμῖν . . . καὶ ἡγεῖσθαι αὐτοὺς ὑπερεκπερισσοῦ ἐν ἀγάπῃ διὰ τὸ ἔργον αὐτῶν. εἰρηνεύετε ἐν ἑαυτοῖς (shift from infinitive to imperative, but the sense of command is no different). Thus, it is important to analyse the use of aspect in such forms as part of the larger question of aspect-usage in commands and prohibitions.[78]

Such an analysis shows that the patterns of usage traced in this chapter for direct commands are found also in indirect commands: the *aspectual* distinction is the primary difference between present and aorist forms and the most frequent secondary distinction is the general vs. specific difference. Note these examples of *general precepts* using the present infinitive or subjunctive in indirect commands:

Mark 6: 8 καὶ παρήγγειλεν αὐτοῖς ἵνα μηδὲν αἴρωσιν εἰς ὁδόν
　　6: 12 καὶ ἐξελθόντες ἐκήρυξαν ἵνα μετανοῶσιν

John 13: 34 ἐντολὴν καινὴν δίδωμι ὑμῖν, ἵνα ἀγαπᾶτε ἀλλήλους, καθὼς ἠγάπησα ὑμᾶς ἵνα καὶ ὑμεῖς ἀγαπᾶτε ἀλλήλους
　　15: 12, 17 αὕτη ἐστὶν ἡ ἐντολὴ ἡ ἐμή, ἵνα ἀγαπᾶτε ἀλλήλους καθὼς ἠγάπησα ὑμᾶς . . . ταῦτα ἐντέλλομαι ὑμῖν, ἵνα ἀγαπᾶτε ἀλλήλους
　　(also in 2 John 5)

Acts 4: 18 καὶ καλέσαντες αὐτοὺς παρήγγειλαν τὸ καθόλου μὴ φθέγγεσθαι μηδὲ διδάσκειν ἐπὶ τῷ ὀνόματι τοῦ Ἰησοῦ
　　26: 20 ἀπήγγελλον μετανοεῖν καὶ ἐπιστρέφειν ἐπὶ τὸν θεόν

Rom. 2: 21–2 ὁ κηρύσσων μὴ κλέπτειν κλέπτεις; ὁ λέγων μὴ μοιχεύειν μοιχεύεις;
　　12: 3 λέγω γὰρ διὰ τῆς χάριτος τῆς δοθείσης μοι παντὶ τῷ ὄντι ἐν ὑμῖν μὴ ὑπερφρονεῖν παρ' ὃ δεῖ φρονεῖν ἀλλὰ φρονεῖν εἰς τὸ σωφρονεῖν

1 Cor. 1: 10 παρακαλῶ δὲ ὑμᾶς, ἀδελφοί . . . ἵνα τὸ αὐτὸ λέγητε πάντες καὶ μὴ ᾖ ἐν ὑμῖν σχίσματα, ἦτε δὲ κατηρτισμένοι ἐν τῷ αὐτῷ νοῒ καὶ ἐν τῇ αὐτῇ γνώμῃ
　　5: 9, 11 ἔγραψα ὑμῖν ἐν τῇ ἐπιστολῇ μὴ συναναμίγνυσθαι πόρνοις . . . νῦν δὲ ἔγραψα ὑμῖν μὴ συναναμίγνυσθαι ἐάν τις ἀδελφὸς ὀνομαζόμενος ἢ πόρνος . . . τῷ τοιούτῳ μηδὲ συνεσθίειν

---

[78] These are not usually covered in such discussions, but see Moulton, *Proleg.*, pp. 176–84; Stork, *Aspectual Usage*, pp. 178–80; and McKay, 'Aspect in Imperatival Constructions', pp. 222–6.

1 Thess. 4: 1 λοιπὸν οὖν, ἀδελφοί, ἐρωτῶμεν ὑμᾶς καὶ παρακαλοῦμεν ἐν κυρίῳ Ἰησοῦ, ἵνα . . . περισσεύητε μᾶλλον

4: 10–11 παρακαλοῦμεν δὲ ὑμᾶς, ἀδελφοί, περισσεύειν μᾶλλον καὶ φιλοτιμεῖσθαι

2 Thess. 3: 12 τοῖς δὲ τοιούτοις παραγγέλλομεν καὶ παρακαλοῦμεν ἐν κυρίῳ Ἰησοῦ Χριστῷ, ἵνα μετὰ ἡσυχίας ἐργαζόμενοι τὸν ἑαυτῶν ἄρτον ἐσθίωσιν

1 Tim. 2: 1 παρακαλῶ οὖν πρῶτον πάντων ποιεῖσθαι δεήσεις . . . ὑπὲρ πάντων ἀνθρώπων

6: 17–18 τοῖς πλουσίοις ἐν τῷ νῦν αἰῶνι παράγγελλε μὴ ὑψηλοφρονεῖν μηδὲ ἠλπικέναι ἐπὶ πλούτου ἀδηλότητι . . . ἀγαθοεργεῖν, πλουτεῖν ἐν ἔργοις καλοῖς, εὐμεταδότους εἶναι (perfect infinitives in indirect commands appear to have their normal range of perfect meaning; here the perfect is *stative* in focus)

Specific commands using the aorist infinitive or subjunctive in indirect form are very common:

Matt. 8: 34 ἰδόντες αὐτὸν παρεκάλεσαν ὅπως μεταβῇ ἀπὸ τῶν ὁρίων αὐτῶν

18: 25 ἐκέλευσεν αὐτὸν ὁ κύριος πραθῆναι . . . καὶ ἀποδοθῆναι

26: 63 ἐξορκίζω σε κατὰ τοῦ θεοῦ τοῦ ζῶντος ἵνα ἡμῖν εἴπῃς εἰ σὺ εἶ ὁ Χριστὸς ὁ υἱὸς τοῦ θεοῦ

Mark 6: 27 εὐθὺς ἀποστείλας ὁ βασιλεὺς σπεκουλάτορα ἐπέταξεν ἐνέγκαι τὴν κεφαλὴν αὐτοῦ

6: 39 ἐπέταξεν αὐτοῖς ἀνακλῖναι πάντας συμπόσια συμπόσια ἐπὶ τῷ χλωρῷ χόρτῳ

7: 26 ἠρώτα αὐτὸν ἵνα τὸ δαιμόνιον ἐκβάλῃ ἐκ τῆς θυγατρὸς αὐτῆς

10: 48 καὶ ἐπετίμων αὐτῷ πολλοὶ ἵνα σιωπήσῃ

14: 35 προσηύχετο ἵνα εἰ δυνατόν ἐστιν παρέλθῃ ἀπ᾽ αὐτοῦ ἡ ὥρα

Luke 10: 40 εἰπὲ οὖν αὐτῇ ἵνα μοι συναντιλάβηται

11: 37 ἐρωτᾷ αὐτὸν Φαρισαῖος ὅπως ἀριστήσῃ παρ᾽ αὐτῷ

12: 13 διδάσκαλε, εἰπὲ τῷ ἀδελφῷ μου μερίσασθαι μετ᾽ ἐμοῦ τὴν κληρονομίαν

John 4: 47 ἠρώτα ἵνα καταβῇ καὶ ἰάσηται αὐτοῦ τὸν υἱόν

19: 31 ἠρώτησαν τὸν Πιλᾶτον ἵνα κατεαγῶσιν αὐτῶν τὰ σκέλη καὶ ἀρθῶσιν

Acts 10: 22 ἐχρηματίσθη ὑπὸ ἀγγέλου ἁγίου μεταπέμψασθαί σε εἰς τὸν οἶκον αὐτοῦ καὶ ἀκοῦσαι ῥήματα παρὰ σοῦ

16: 18 παραγγέλλω σοι ἐν ὀνόματι Ἰησοῦ Χριστοῦ ἐξελθεῖν ἀπ᾽ αὐτῆς

26: 3 διὸ δέομαι μακροθύμως ἀκοῦσαί μου
27: 34 διὸ παρακαλῶ ὑμᾶς μεταβαλεῖν τροφῆς

2 Cor. 2: 8 διὸ παρακαλῶ ὑμᾶς κυρῶσαι εἰς αὐτὸν ἀγάπην
12: 8 ὑπὲρ τούτου τρὶς τὸν κύριον παρεκάλεσα ἵνα ἀποστῇ ἀπ' ἐμοῦ

Exceptions to the general/specific pattern occur in much the same way as for direct commands, either because the verb is stereotyped in aspect or because the speaker chooses to highlight one of the other secondary functions of the aspects:

Matt. 5: 34 ἐγὼ δὲ λέγω ὑμῖν μὴ ὀμόσαι ὅλως (aor. as more urgent, peremptory)

Mark 12: 19 (~Luke 20: 28) Μωυσῆς ἔγραψεν ἡμῖν . . . ἵνα λάβῃ ὁ ἀδελφὸς αὐτοῦ τὴν γυναῖκα καὶ ἐξαναστήσῃ σπέρμα τῷ ἀδελφῷ αὐτοῦ (distributive aor.)

Acts 21: 4 ἔλεγον διὰ τοῦ πνεύματος μὴ ἐπιβαίνειν εἰς Ἱεροσόλυμα (pres. in specific prohibition: 'stop doing')
21: 34 ἐκέλευσεν ἄγεσθαι αὐτὸν εἰς τὴν παρεμβολήν (pres. idiomatic with motion-verb)

Rom. 12: 1 παρακαλῶ οὖν ὑμᾶς, ἀδελφοί, διὰ τῶν οἰκτιρμῶν τοῦ θεοῦ παραστῆσαι τὰ σώματα ὑμῶν θυσίαν ζῶσαν ἁγίαν (ingressive in old life/new life motif)

Eph. 1: 17 ἵνα ὁ θεὸς τοῦ κυρίου ἡμῶν Ἰησοῦ Χριστοῦ, ὁ πατὴρ τῆς δόξης, δώῃ ὑμῖν πνεῦμα σοφίας καὶ ἀποκαλύψεως (aor. idiomatic with δίδωμι; also in 3: 16, 6: 19)
4: 1 παρακαλῶ οὖν ὑμᾶς ἐγὼ ὁ δέσμιος ἐν κυρίῳ ἀξίως περιπατῆσαι τῆς κλήσεως ἧς ἐκλήθητε (like Rom. 12: 1)

2 Thess. 3: 1–2 προσεύχεσθε, ἀδελφοί, περὶ ἡμῶν . . . ἵνα ῥυσθῶμεν ἀπὸ τῶν ἀτόπων καὶ πονηρῶν ἀνθρώπων (consummative aor.)

5. 4. 3 Use of the aspects in imperatival infinitives and participles

Apparently as an extension of their use in indirect commands, *infinitives* appear on occasion (by ellipsis of the introductory verb) as independent verbs expressing commands: the so-called imperatival infinitive.[79] The only clear examples of this

---

[79] Cf. Smyth, *Grammar*, § 2013; SD, *Syntax*, pp. 380–2; and BDF, *Grammar*, § 389.

in the NT are Rom. 12: 15 χαίρειν μετὰ χαιρόντων, κλαίειν μετὰ κλαιόντων and Phil. 3: 16 πλὴν εἰς ὃ ἐφθάσαμεν, τῷ αὐτῷ στοιχεῖν. These three infinitives appear to use the present aspect to denote general precepts, in keeping with the pattern traced above. Other examples are sometimes cited, but they are either indirect commands (to be attached to some main verb in the near context) or cases of the stereotyped greeting χαίρειν.[80]

Occurring more frequently in the NT as an independent imperatival verb is the Greek *participle*. These appear most clearly in two passages: Rom. 12: 9–19 (17 participles) and 1 Pet. 2: 18; 3: 1, 7, 9; 4: 10 (7 participles). This type of participle is a development from the use as an adverbial adjunct with imperatives: when an adverbial participle attaches to an imperative, it may take on the modal force of the main verb and thus bear an imperatival sense as a *dependent* verb.[81] For example, the first participle in Matt. 28: 19 is part of the command: 'Therefore go and make disciples' (πορευ-θέντες οὖν μαθητεύσατε).[82] Instances of this are common (Matt. 2: 8; Luke 17: 19, 22: 46; Eph. 5: 18–21; Phil. 1: 27–8, 2: 2–4, 2: 14–16; Col. 3: 12–13, 3: 22; 2 Tim. 4: 11).

An intermediate step along the way from this towards the independent imperatival participle can be seen in instances where a participle is dependent in this adverbial way on an imperative-like verb, but only by 'lax agreement'. In these the participle is construed as dependent upon another verb, but it appears in nominative plural form (since that is most common in adverbial use), even though there is nothing in the main clause with that form. Some instances of this are:

---

[80] Cf. MT, *Syntax*, p. 78.

[81] This seems more likely than an ellipsis of the imperative ἐστέ, as argued by Moulton, *Proleg.*, p. 180, since periphrastic expressions of that sort are quite rare and since εἰμί is almost never omitted in instances of indicative periphrasis. Instances of adjectives which have an imperatival meaning (e.g. Rom. 12: 9–11; 1 Pet. 2: 16, 3: 8, 3: 15, 4: 9) are more difficult, but they can be accounted for by ellipsis of an adverbial participle of εἰμί rather than by supplying ἐστέ

[82] The best discussion of this use of the participle is Cleon L. Rogers, 'The Great Commission', *Bibliotheca Sacra*, 130 (1973), 258–67.

Eph. 4: 1–3 παρακαλῶ οὖν ὑμᾶς ἐγὼ ὁ δέσμιος ἐν κυρίῳ ἀξίως περιπατῆσαι τῆς κλήσεως ἧς ἐκλήθητε, μετὰ πάσης ταπεινοφροσύνης καὶ πραΰτητος, μετὰ μακροθυμίας, ἀνεχόμενοι ἀλλήλων ἐν ἀγάπῃ, σπουδάζοντες τηρεῖν τὴν ἑνότητα τοῦ πνεύματος ἐν τῷ συνδέσμῳ τῆς εἰρήνης

Col. 3: 16–17 ὁ λόγος τοῦ Χριστοῦ ἐνοικείτω ἐν ὑμῖν πλουσίως, ἐν πάσῃ σοφίᾳ διδάσκοντες καὶ νουθετοῦντες ἑαυτούς, ψαλμοῖς ὕμνοις ᾠδαῖς πνευματικαῖς ἐν τῇ χάριτι ᾄδοντες ἐν ταῖς καρδίαις ὑμῶν τῷ θεῷ· καὶ πᾶν ὅ τι ἐὰν ποιῆτε ἐν λόγῳ ἢ ἐν ἔργῳ, πάντα ἐν ὀνόματι κυρίου Ἰησοῦ, εὐχαριστοῦντες τῷ θεῷ πατρὶ δι' αὐτοῦ

(See also 1 Pet. 2: 11–12, 2: 15–16.)

This kind of use constitutes the *Greek* linguistic background for the imperatival participle as an independent verb-form. There is a clear path of usage from the adverbial connection with an imperative, through the lax construction described above, and finally over to the fully independent use of the participle with an imperative meaning. This independent use can be clearly seen in Rom. 12: 9–19 and 1 Pet. 2: 18; 3: 1, 7, 9; 4: 10. Some illustrations from these texts are given below:

Rom. 12: 12–13 τῇ ἐλπίδι χαίροντες, τῇ θλίψει ὑπομένοντες, τῇ προσευχῇ προσκαρτεροῦντες, ταῖς χρείαις τῶν ἁγίων κοινωνοῦντες, τὴν φιλοξενίαν διώκοντες

1 Pet. 2: 18 οἱ οἰκέται ὑποτασσόμενοι ἐν παντὶ φόβῳ τοῖς δεσπόταις

3: 7 οἱ ἄνδρες ὁμοίως, συνοικοῦντες κατὰ γνῶσιν ὡς ἀσθενεστέρῳ σκεύει τῷ γυναικείῳ, ἀπονέμοντες τιμήν

4: 10 ἕκαστος καθὼς ἔλαβεν χάρισμα εἰς ἑαυτοὺς αὐτὸ διακονοῦντες ὡς καλοὶ οἰκονόμοι ποικίλης χάριτος θεοῦ

The frequency of this Greek construction in the NT is quite surprising, however, and the concentration of these participles and others similar to them in the *Haustafeln* sections of the epistles suggests that other influences may be important in accounting for it. The argument of Daube and Davies is that these participles are reflections of an analogous use of the Hebrew participle in early Mishnaic writings. The Mishnaic Hebrew participle was used in moral codes to record 'the correct practice' expected of the community. As Daube points out, this imperatival participle was always expressive of a general precept, never of a specific command, because of the habitual or customary sense of the participle in the Hebrew construction.[83] This corresponds exactly with the sort of commands expressed by the imperatival participle in Rom. 12 and in 1 Pet. 2–4. Whether or not these passages are dependent in any direct way on sources written in Hebrew, it seems likely that this Semitic construction exerted at least a general influence in smoothing the way for a rare Greek usage[84] to appear more commonly in early Christian moral codes written in Greek.

5. 5 Conclusion

This chapter has analysed the meanings of the present and aorist in commands and prohibitions in the NT. The aspects in these uses display the distinction developed earlier in this book: the present pictures an occurrence from an internal perspective, focusing on the course or internal details of the occurrence but with no focus on the end-points, while the aorist views it from an external perspective, seeing the occurrence as a whole from beginning to end without focus on the internal details which may be involved. This basic aspectual distinction combines to some degree with other linguistic features to produce secondary functions of the aspects, as seen in the indicative. However, the secondary distinction which is most important in commands and prohibitions is the difference between general and specific—here between general precepts and specific commands, as developed above.

---

[83] David Daube. 'Appended Note: Participle and Imperative in I Peter', in Selwyn, *1 Peter*, pp. 387–8, 467–88, esp. 470; Daube, *The New Testament and Rabbinic Judaism* (London: Athlone Press, 1956), 90–7; and W. D. Davies, *Paul and Rabbinic Judaism: Some Rabbinic Elements in Pauline Theology*, 4th edn. (Philadelphia: Fortress Press, 1980), 130–2, 329. Philip Kanjuparambil, 'Imperatival Participles in Romans 12: 9–21', *JBL* 102 (1983), 285–8, provides additional support for Daube's view with evidence from Qumran *Manual of Discipline*, 5. 1–7.

[84] H. G. Meecham, 'The Use of the Participle for the Imperative in the New Testament', *Exp. T.* 58 (1947), 207–8, and A. P. Salom, 'The Imperatival Use of the Participle in the New Testament', *Australian Biblical Review*, 11 (1963), 41–9, have established that the imperatival participle was a legitimate but rare use in papyrus texts from around the 1st cent.

6

THE ASPECTS IN THE OTHER NON-INDICATIVE FORMS OF THE VERB

THE purpose of this chapter is to describe the meanings which the aspects display in the large number of non-indicative forms not covered in the preceding chapter on commands and prohibitions. This will include aspect-usage in the participle, infinitive, optative, and subjunctive (excluding uses in direct and indirect commands, treated in Chapter 5).

Except for the participle, these non-indicative forms of the verb stand together in that the 'tense-aspects' (i.e. present, aorist, perfect) display no *time*-value: they indicate nothing about the temporal relation of the action to a reference-point. Instead, the meanings of the aspects in the infinitive, subjunctive, and optative are the *aspectual* ones.[1] The participle is exceptional, because in many of its uses the 'tense-aspects' display a predictable pattern of *temporal* relations (relative to the action of the main verb) alongside the aspectual differences. These generalizations will be elaborated in the course of this chapter.

Because the participle is different in its meaning, it will be taken up separately, after the other forms are treated. The infinitive, subjunctive, and optative will be discussed together since the function of the aspects is similar in these forms. Exceptional patterns of aspect-function with some uses of these forms will be mentioned after the normal functions are presented.

---

[1] Cf. Burton, *MT*, §§ 95–114; Smyth, *Grammar*, §§ 1859–65; and SD, *Syntax*, pp. 294–5.

6. 1   Aspectual Usage in the Infinitive, Subjunctive, and Optative

6. 1. 1   *General principle for the meaning of the aspects in the infinitive, subjunctive, and optative*

The meaning of the present, aorist, and perfect forms in the infinitive, subjunctive, and optative follow the basic distinctions in aspectual significance and function which were set forth in Chapters 1–3. More specifically, the *primary* aspect-distinction in these forms is the contrast between present and aorist, in which the basic significance is that of 'viewpoint' aspect: the present focuses on the internal make-up of the occurrence without regard for end-points, while the aorist views the occurrence as a whole from beginning to end without regard for internal details. The general meaning of the perfect, on the other hand, is the sense presented in Chapter 2—a state produced by an anterior occurrence. In all three cases the general significance undergoes modification produced by its combination with other linguistic features, as shown in Chapter 3. These other features affect the aspectual function in many of the same ways as can be seen in the indicative, producing similar combinatory meaning (e.g. ingressive vs. consummative sense, general vs. specific reference, single vs. multiple occurrence). These will now be presented.

6. 1. 2   *Normal combinatory functions of the aspects in the infinitive, subjunctive, and optative*

6. 1. 2. 1   *Normal functions of the present aspect*

In general terms the *present* aspect in the infinitive, subjunctive, and optative views the occurrence from the inside, focusing on its internal make-up without regard for its beginning or end. Combined with other linguistic features, this produces several types of normal aspectual function.[2]

---

[2] Burton's general summary in *MT*, § 96, states that the present outside the indicative is either 'in progress' or 'repeated'.

For example, the present may denote a *progressive* (or descriptive) sense, viewing a specific occurrence with emphasis on its internal details, either for the sake of vivid description or to denote simultaneity with another occurrence.[3] This may involve STATIVE verbs as well as various types of actives.

Matt. 5: 23 ἐὰν οὖν προσφέρῃς τὸ δῶρόν σου ἐπὶ τὸ θυσιαστήριον κἀκεῖ μνησθῇς

27: 12 καὶ ἐν τῷ κατηγορεῖσθαι αὐτὸν ὑπὸ τῶν ἀρχιερέων καὶ πρεσβυτέρων οὐδὲν ἀπεκρίνατο

27: 14 καὶ οὐκ ἀπεκρίθη αὐτῷ πρὸς οὐδὲ ἓν ῥῆμα, ὥστε θαυμάζειν τὸν ἡγεμόνα λίαν

Mark 2: 12 καὶ ἠγέρθη καὶ εὐθὺς ἄρας τὸν κράβαττον ἐξῆλθεν ἔμπροσθεν πάντων, ὥστε ἐξίστασθαι πάντας καὶ δοξάζειν τὸν θεόν

2: 15 καὶ γίνεται κατακεῖσθαι αὐτὸν ἐν τῇ οἰκίᾳ αὐτοῦ, καὶ πολλοὶ . . . συνανέκειντο

10: 14 ἄφετε τὰ παιδία ἔρχεσθαι πρός με (seems specific, but could be general, customary)

13: 11 καὶ ὅταν ἄγωσιν ὑμᾶς παραδιδόντες, μὴ προμεριμνᾶτε τί λαλήσητε

15: 8 καὶ ἀναβὰς ὁ ὄχλος ἤρξατο αἰτεῖσθαι καθὼς ἐποίει αὐτοῖς

Luke 11: 21 ὅταν ὁ ἰσχυρὸς καθωπλισμένος φυλάσσῃ τὴν ἑαυτοῦ αὐλήν, ἐν εἰρήνῃ ἐστὶν τὰ ὑπάρχοντά αὐτοῦ

23: 26 ἐπέθηκαν αὐτῷ τὸν σταυρὸν φέρειν ὄπισθεν τοῦ Ἰησοῦ

Acts 4: 2 διαπονούμενοι διὰ τὸ διδάσκειν αὐτοὺς τὸν λαὸν καὶ καταγγέλλειν ἐν τῷ Ἰησοῦ τὴν ἀνάστασιν τὴν ἐκ νεκρῶν

17: 18 τινες ἔλεγον· τί ἂν θέλοι ὁ σπερμολόγος οὗτος λέγειν;

25: 20 ἔλεγον εἰ βούλοιτο πορεύεσθαι εἰς Ἱεροσόλυμα

1 Cor. 14: 14, 16, 23 ἐὰν προσεύχωμαι γλώσσῃ . . . ἐὰν εὐλογῇς πνεύματι . . . ἐὰν οὖν συνέλθῃ ἡ ἐκκλησία ὅλη ἐπὶ τὸ αὐτὸ καὶ πάντες λαλῶσιν γλώσσαις

1 Thess. 5: 3 ὅταν λέγωσιν εἰρήνη καὶ ἀσφάλεια, τότε αἰφνίδιος αὐτοῖς ἐφίσταται ὄλεθρος

It is also common to find present infinitives, subjunctives, and optatives with a *customary* or gnomic sense, taking a

---

[3] Cf. Zerwick, *Biblical Greek*, p. 93, who suggests that the present is used to show simultaneous occurrence with some other action.

broader scope of the occurrence into view. This occurrence may be an activity which continues in some way over a period of time or it may involve multiple repetitions of the occurrence (perhaps in a distributive sense: each individual in a plurality does the action once). Another very common use of the customary sense is the present aspect with STATIVE verbs. This is the aspect which must be used if one wishes to refer to the state or condition itself, since the aorist almost always yields an *ingressive* sense and thus shifts the reference to the entrance into the condition.[4]

Mark 3: 14 καὶ ἐποίησεν δώδεκα ... ἵνα ὦσιν μετ' αὐτοῦ καὶ ἵνα ἀποστέλλη αὐτοὺς κηρύσσειν

11: 28 τίς σοι ἔδωκεν τὴν ἐξουσίαν ταύτην ἵνα ταῦτα ποιῇς;

12: 33 καὶ τὸ ἀγαπᾶν αὐτὸν ἐξ ὅλης τῆς καρδίας ... καὶ τὸ ἀγαπᾶν τὸν πλησίον ὡς ἑαυτόν

Luke 6: 33 ἐὰν ἀγαθοποιῆτε τοὺς ἀγαθοποιοῦντες ὑμᾶς, ποία ὑμῖν χάρις ἐστίν;

13: 14 ἐξ ἡμέραι εἰσὶν ἐν αἷς δεῖ ἐργάζεσθαι

18: 15 προσέφερον δὲ αὐτῷ καὶ τὰ βρέφη ἵνα αὐτῶν ἅπτηται

John 4: 24 πνεῦμα ὁ θεός, καὶ τοὺς προσκυνοῦντας αὐτὸν ἐν πνεύματι καὶ ἀληθείᾳ δεῖ προσκυνεῖν

11: 9–10 ἐάν τις περιπατῇ ἐν τῇ ἡμέρᾳ ... ἐὰν δέ τις περιπατῇ ἐν τῇ νυκτί

13: 17 εἰ ταῦτα οἴδατε, μακάριοί ἐστε ἐὰν ποιῆτε αὐτά

Acts 8: 19 ἵνα ᾧ ἐὰν ἐπιθῶ τὰς χεῖρας λαμβάνῃ πνεῦμα ἅγιον (distributive)

17: 11 ἀνακρίνοντες τὰς γραφὰς εἰ ἔχοι ταῦτα οὕτως

Rom. 1: 24 διὸ παρέδωκεν αὐτοὺς ὁ θεὸς ἐν ταῖς ἐπιθυμίαις τῶν καρδιῶν αὐτῶν εἰς ἀκαθαρσίαν τοῦ ἀτιμάζεσθαι τὰ σώματα αὐτῶν ἐν αὐτοῖς

1 Cor. 11: 25 τοῦτο ποιεῖτε, ὁσάκις ἐὰν πίνητε, εἰς τὴν ἐμὴν ἀνάμνησιν

14: 39 ζηλοῦτε τὸ προφητεύειν καὶ τὸ λαλεῖν μὴ κωλύετε γλώσσαις

Gal. 4: 18 καλὸν δὲ ζηλοῦσθαι ἐν καλῷ πάντοτε

5: 2 ἐὰν περιτέμνησθε, Χριστὸς ὑμᾶς οὐδὲν ὠφελήσει (clearly distributive; present infinitive in 6: 12 is the same)

2 Thess. 3: 9 ἀλλ' ἵνα ἑαυτοὺς τύπον δῶμεν ὑμῖν εἰς τὸ μιμεῖσθαι ἡμᾶς

---

[4] On the predominance of ingressive sense for the aorist of stative verbs outside of the indicative, see Mateos, *Aspecto verbal*, pp. 59–61.

Heb. 5: 1 πᾶς γὰρ ἀρχιερεὺς ... καθίσταται τὰ πρὸς τὸν θεόν, ἵνα προσφέρῃ δῶρά τε καὶ θυσίας ἁμαρτιῶν (cf. 9: 25; similar 7: 27, 8: 3)

13: 18 καλὴν συνείδησιν ἔχομεν, ἐν πᾶσιν καλῶς θέλοντες ἀναστρέφεσθαι

1 Pet. 2: 15 ὅτι οὕτως ἐστὶν τὸ θέλημα τοῦ θεοῦ ἀγαθοποιοῦντας φιμοῦν τὴν τῶν ἀφρόνων ἀνθρώπων ἀγνωσίαν

2 Pet. 2: 9 οἶδεν κύριος εὐσεβεῖς ἐκ πειρασμοῦ ῥύεσθαι, ἀδίκους δὲ εἰς ἡμέραν κρίσεως κολαζομένους τηρεῖν

It is also possible to discover a *conative* sense for the present in these forms, highlighting a process which has not been brought to completion but is on the verge of completion or is attempted. This occurs with verbs of the ACCOMPLISHMENT and CLIMAX types (cf. 3.1.2.3 and 3.1.2.4), as well as with other types of active verbs if the context denotes difficulty or resistance to the action.

Mark 4: 37 καὶ γίνεται λαῖλαψ ἀνέμου μεγάλη καὶ τὰ κύματα ἐπέβαλλεν εἰς τὸ πλοῖον, ὥστε ἤδη γεμίζεσθαι τὸ πλοῖον

Luke 5: 7 ἔπλησαν ἀμφότερα τὰ πλοῖα ὥστε βυθίζεσθαι αὐτά

Col. 4: 17 καὶ εἴπατε Ἀρχίππῳ· βλέπε τὴν διακονίαν ἣν παρέλαβες ἐν κυρίῳ, ἵνα αὐτὴν πληροῖς

6. 1. 2. 2 *Normal functions of the aorist aspect*

The aorist infinitive, subjunctive, and optative in their general meaning present the occurrence in summary, viewed as a whole without regard for its internal details of occurrence. This produces several common types of aspectual function when combined with lexical meaning and other contextual features.[5] The *ingressive* sense is common with verbs of the STATIVE lexical type and less common with active verbs occurring in constructions which for some reason emphasize the point of transition which begins an activity or process.

Matt. 19: 16 διδάσκαλε, τί ἀγαθὸν ποιήσω ἵνα σχῶ ζωὴν αἰώνιον;

Mark 8: 38 ὃς γὰρ ἐὰν ἐπαισχυνθῇ με καὶ τοὺς ἐμοὺς λόγους ἐν τῇ γενεᾷ ταύτῃ

[5] See the summary given in Burton, *MT*, § 98.

Luke 15: 32 εὐφρανθῆναι δὲ καὶ χαρῆναι ἔδει

19: 15 εἶπεν φωνηθῆναι αὐτῷ τοὺς δούλους τούτους οἷς δεδώκει τὸ ἀργύριον, ἵνα γνοῖ τί διεπραγματεύσαντο

John 9: 36 τίς ἐστιν, κύριε, ἵνα πιστεύσω εἰς αὐτόν;

10: 38 τοῖς ἔργοις πιστεύετε, ἵνα γνῶτε καὶ γινώσκητε ὅτι ἐν ἐμοὶ ὁ πατὴρ κἀγὼ ἐν τῷ πατρί (note the difference between aor. and pres. with this STATIVE verb)

Acts 15: 13 μετὰ δὲ τὸ σιγῆσαι αὐτοὺς ἀπεκρίθη Ἰάκωβος

Rom. 6: 4 ἵνα . . . οὕτως καὶ ἡμεῖς ἐν καινότητι ζωῆς περιπατήσωμεν (emphasis on the change of behaviour)

1 Cor. 4: 8 καὶ ὄφελόν γε ἐβασιλεύσατε, ἵνα καὶ ἡμεῖς ὑμῖν συμβασιλεύσωμεν

7: 9 κρεῖττον γάρ ἐστιν γαμῆσαι ἢ πυροῦσθαι (the aorist here focuses on 'getting married' in contrast to the present γαμεῖν 'to be in a married state', a variant reading in ℵ* A C* P 33 81 etc.)

2 Cor. 1: 15 καὶ ταύτῃ τῇ πεποιθήσει ἐβουλόμην πρότερον πρὸς ὑμᾶς ἐλθεῖν, ἵνα δευτέραν χάριν σχῆτε

8: 9 δι' ὑμᾶς ἐπτώχευσεν πλούσιος ὤν, ἵνα ὑμεῖς τῇ ἐκείνου πτωχείᾳ πλουτήσητε

Jas. 4: 4 ὃς ἐὰν οὖν βουληθῇ φίλος εἶναι τοῦ κόσμου, ἐχθρὸς τοῦ θεοῦ καθίσταται

Rev. 11: 6 ἐξουσίαν ἔχουσιν ἐπὶ τῶν ὑδάτων στρέφειν αὐτὰ εἰς αἷμα καὶ πατάξαι τὴν γῆν ἐν πάσῃ πληγῇ ὁσάκις ἐὰν θελήσωσιν

The aorist can occur also with a *consummative* sense, emphasizing the accomplishment of an effort or the conclusion of a process for which there is resistance or difficulty. This is more common with verbs of the ACCOMPLISHMENT and CLIMAX types but may occur with other types, and it is the opposite of the conative present.

Matt. 1: 22 τοῦτο δὲ ὅλον γέγονεν ἵνα πληρωθῇ τὸ ῥηθὲν ὑπὸ κυρίου διὰ τοῦ προφήτου (cf. 2: 15, 4: 14, 12: 17, 21: 4, 26: 56)

5: 17 οὐκ ἦλθον καταλῦσαι ἀλλὰ πληρῶσαι

8: 2 (+parallels) κύριε, ἐὰν θέλῃς δύνασαί με καθαρίσαι

Acts 17: 27 ζητεῖν τὸν θεόν, εἰ ἄρα γε ψηλαφήσειαν αὐτὸν καὶ εὕροιεν

23: 24 κτήνη τε παραστῆσαι ἵνα ἐπιβιβάσαντες τὸν Παῦλον διασώσωσι πρὸς Φήλικα τὸν ἡγεμόνα

1 Cor. 4: 6 ἵνα ἐν ἡμῖν μάθητε τὸ μὴ ὑπὲρ ἃ γέγραπται

Phil. 3: 21 κατὰ τὴν ἐνέργειαν τοῦ δύνασθαι αὐτὸν καὶ ὑποτάξαι αὐτῷ τὰ πάντα

2 Tim. 1: 12 δυνατός ἐστιν τὴν παραθήκην μου φυλάξαι εἰς ἐκείνην τὴν ἡμέραν

1 Pet. 3: 18 καὶ Χριστὸς ἅπαξ περὶ ἁμαρτιῶν ἔπαθεν . . . ἵνα ὑμᾶς προσαγάγῃ τῷ θεῷ

The most common sense for the aorist in these forms, however, is the *constative* use, which is closest to the basic 'summary' meaning of the aorist. Here the occurrence, of whatever internal constituency, is simply viewed in its entirety without regard for duration, repetition, or other Aktionsart features and with no emphasis on beginning or end-point alone. The occurrence in these cases is often a single specific act, and the aorist is the simplest way to make reference to it. On the other hand, there are a number of cases in which the occurrence is multiple, repeated, or generalized and the aorist sums up the various parts in simple reference without emphasis on such details.

Matt. 1: 19 ἐβουλήθη λάθρᾳ ἀπολῦσαι αὐτήν
    7: 5 τότε διαβλέψεις ἐκβαλεῖν τὸ κάρφος ἐκ τοῦ ὀφθαλμοῦ τοῦ ἀδελφοῦ σου
  26: 16 ἐζήτει εὐκαιρίαν ἵνα αὐτὸν παραδῷ

Mark 1: 38 ἄγωμεν ἀλλαχοῦ εἰς τὰς ἐχομένας κωμοπόλεις, ἵνα καὶ ἐκεῖ κηρύξω
  15: 20 ἐξάγουσιν αὐτὸν ἵνα σταυρώσωσιν αὐτόν

Luke 4: 43 ταῖς ἑτέραις πόλεσιν εὐαγγελίσασθαί με δεῖ τὴν βασιλείαν τοῦ θεοῦ
  6: 11 αὐτοὶ δὲ ἐπλήσθησαν ἀνοίας καὶ διελάλουν πρὸς ἀλλήλους τί ἂν ποιήσαιεν τῷ Ἰησοῦ
  6: 34 καὶ ἐὰν δανίσητε παρ' ὧν ἐλπίζετε λαβεῖν, ποία ὑμῖν χάρις [ἐστίν];
  11: 50 ἵνα ἐκζητηθῇ τὸ αἷμα πάντων τῶν προφητῶν τὸ ἐκκεχυμένον ἀπὸ καταβολῆς κόσμου ἀπὸ τῆς γενεᾶς ταύτης

John 1: 7 οὗτος ἦλθεν εἰς μαρτυρίαν ἵνα μαρτυρήσῃ περὶ τοῦ φωτός
  3: 17 ἵνα σωθῇ ὁ κόσμος δι' αὐτοῦ

Acts 15: 37 Βαρναβᾶς δὲ ἐβούλετο συμπαραλαβεῖν καὶ τὸν Ἰωάννην τὸν καλούμενον Μᾶρκον (it is likely that the constative aorist here is intentionally in contrast with παραλαμβάνειν of v. 38, perhaps portraying Paul as envisaging more of the details of the continuing journey with one who had shown himself unreliable)

26: 9 ἐγὼ μὲν οὖν ἔδοξα ἐμαυτῷ πρὸς τὸ ὄνομα ᾽Ιησοῦ τοῦ Ναζωραίου δεῖν πολλὰ ἐναντία πρᾶξαι

Rom. 11: 32 συνέκλεισεν γὰρ ὁ θεὸς τοὺς πάντας εἰς ἀπείθειαν, ἵνα τοὺς πάντας ἐλεήσῃ

14: 21 καλὸν τὸ μὴ φαγεῖν κρέα μηδὲ πιεῖν οἶνον μηδὲ ἐν ᾧ ὁ ἀδελφός σου προσκόπτει (cf. BDF, *Grammar*, § 338: aorist used of a specific instance of refraining, not general abstention)

(Also Matt. 20: 28/Mark 10: 45, Mark 14: 5, Luke 5: 18, 18: 13, 19: 10, John 3: 7, 2 Tim. 2: 2, 1 Pet. 2: 5.)

6. 1. 2. 3 *Normal functions of the perfect forms*

The perfect is very infrequent in these non-indicative forms of the verb, occurring in the NT only forty-six times in the infinitive, only in periphrastic form in the subjunctive (except for the subjunctive of οἶδα, which occurs ten times), and not at all in the optative.[6] When the perfect does occur, it preserves its basic sense of 'aspect-Aktionsart-tense' in denoting a state or condition resulting from an anterior occurrence. The perfect infinitive or periphrastic subjunctive often emphasizes the *resulting state* and only implies the anterior occurrence. With the forms of οἶδα or ἵστημι, of course,-the perfect denotes only a stative meaning without prior action implied (e.g. Luke 20: 7, 22: 34, Acts 12: 14, 1 Cor. 2: 12, 10: 2, 13: 2, Eph. 1: 18)

Luke 24: 23 ἦλθον λέγουσαι καὶ ὀπτασίαν ἀγγέλων ἑωρακέναι

John 3: 27 οὐ δύναται ἄνθρωπος λαμβάνειν οὐδὲ ἓν ἐὰν μὴ ᾖ δεδομένον αὐτῷ ἐκ τοῦ οὐρανοῦ (periphrastic perfect subjunctive)

12: 18 διὰ τοῦτο ὑπήντησεν αὐτῷ ὁ ὄχλος, ὅτι ἤκουσαν τοῦτο αὐτὸν πεποιηκέναι τὸ σημεῖον

---

[6] These figures are taken from Leslie W. Sloat, 'New Testament Verb Forms', in John H. Skilton (ed.), *The New Testament Student at Work* (Nutley, NJ: Presbyterian and Reformed Publishing Co., 1975), 211–12, with adjustments based on personal study. The infrequent occurrence of non-indicative perfect forms is discussed by K. L. McKay, 'On the Perfect and Other Aspects in New Testament Greek', *Nov. T.* 23 (1981), 324–5 (NT uses); id., 'On the Perfect and Other Aspects in the Greek Non-Literary Papyri', *BICS* 27 (1980), 36; and Mayser, *Grammatik*, pp. 185–92 (usage in Hellenistic papyri).

Acts 14: 19 λιθάσαντες τὸν Παῦλον ἔσυρον ἔξω τῆς πόλεως νομίζοντες
αὐτὸν τεθνηκέναι

16: 27 ἤμελλεν ἑαυτὸν ἀναιρεῖν νομίζων ἐκπεφευγέναι τοὺς δεσμίους

25: 25 ἐγὼ δὲ κατελαβόμην μηδὲν ἄξιον αὐτὸν θανάτου πεπραχέναι

26: 32 ἀπολελύσθαι ἐδύνατο ὁ ἄνθρωπος οὗτος

1 Cor. 8: 2 εἴ τις δοκεῖ ἐγνωκέναι τι, οὔπω ἔγνω καθὼς δεῖ γνῶναι

2 Cor. 5: 11 ἐλπίζω δὲ καὶ ἐν ταῖς συνειδήσεσιν ὑμῶν πεφανερῶσθαι

11: 5 λογίζομαι γὰρ μηδὲν ὑστερηκέναι τῶν ὑπερλίαν ἀποστόλων

Jas. 5: 15 κἂν ἁμαρτίας ἦ πεποιηκώς, ἀφεθήσεται αὐτῷ (periphrastic pf.
subjunc.)

Less commonly, the perfect in these forms highlights the
actual *completion* of the action with less attention paid to its
result.

Mark 5: 4 διὰ τὸ αὐτὸν πολλάκις πέδαις καὶ ἁλύσεσιν δεδέσθαι καὶ
διεσπάσθαι ὑπ' αὐτοῦ τὰς ἁλύσεις καὶ τὰς πέδας συντετρῖφθαι

Luke 12: 58 ὡς γὰρ ὑπάγεις μετὰ τοῦ ἀντιδίκου σου ἐπ' ἄρχοντα ἐν τῇ ὁδῷ
δὸς ἐργασίαν ἀπηλλάχθαι ἀπ' αὐτοῦ

14: 8 ὅταν κληθῇς ὑπό τινος εἰς γάμους, μὴ κατακλιθῇς εἰς τὴν
πρωτοκλισίαν, μήποτε ἐντιμότερός σου ᾖ κεκλημένος ὑπ' αὐτοῦ

Acts 27: 9 διὰ τὸ καὶ τὴν νηστείαν ἤδη παρεληλυθέναι

Rom. 15: 19 ὥστε με ἀπὸ Ἰερουσαλὴμ καὶ κύκλῳ μέχρι τοῦ Ἰλλυρικοῦ
πεπληρωκέναι τὸ εὐαγγέλιον τοῦ Χριστοῦ

Heb. 10: 15 μαρτυρεῖ δὲ ἡμῖν καὶ τὸ πνεῦμα τὸ ἅγιον· μετὰ γὰρ τὸ εἰρηκέναι

6. 1. 3 *Idiosyncrasies of aspect-usage in the infinitive, subjunctive, and optative*

6. 1. 3. 1 *Unusual aspect-usage in the infinitive*

Table 6.1 shows the occurrence of present, aorist, and perfect
infinitives in various major categories of infinitive usage in the
NT. It will be noted that the general pattern of frequency in
these uses favours aorist over present, with perfect infinitives a
very rare third choice. The relative frequency of the aspects in
NT infinitive usage is: present 991 occurrences (43%), aorist
1,245 (54%), and perfect 46 (2%).[7] There are, however,

---

[7] Cf. Sloat, 'NT Verb Forms', pp. 211–12. In addition, he counts 5 future

TABLE 6. 1. *Aspect-Frequency in Some Uses of NT Infinitive*[a]

	Present	Aorist	Perfect
1. Complementary infinive with:			
δύναμαι*	57	154	2
θέλω	48	80	2
δεῖ	45	75	
μέλλω*	84	7	
βούλομαι	14	25	
ἔξεστιν	7	22	
ἐξουσία	9	16	
ὀφείλω*	19	6	
ἰσχύω	2	15	
σπουδάζω	3	8	
δυνατός	3	7	
ἐάω	4	3	
2. Indirect discourse (reported statement)*			
	93	32	23
3. Introduced by prepositions			
εἰς	32	37	2
ἐν*	44	12	
διά*	24	1	7
μετά*		14	1
πρός	3	8	
πρό	1	8	
4. Purpose infinitive:			
simple anarthrous infin.*	34	184	1
infin. with τοῦ	12	23	
5. Result infinitive			
after ὥστε*	40	23	1
simple infinitive	1	8	
infin. with τοῦ	5	1	
6. After πρίν (ἤ)		11	

[a] This count is based on data obtained by James L. Boyer in a Gramcord computer search of NT infinitive uses and recorded in his unpublished 'Supplemental Manual of Information: Infinitive Verbs' (Winona Lake, Ind.: Grace Theological Seminary, n.d.). His discussion of these categories is given in 'The Classification of Infinitives: A Statistical Study', *Grace Theological Journal*, 6 (1985), 3–27. Asterisks denote the more common categories in which the aspect-frequency is markedly different from the normal ratio of present and aorist usage in the infinitive.

infinitives in the NT, which occur in Acts 11: 28, 23: 30, 24: 15, 27: 10 (all ἔσεσθαι), and Heb. 3: 18 (the future appears in variant readings at John 21: 25 and Acts 26: 7). The count for the NT given in Clyde W. Votaw, *The Use of the Infinitive in Biblical Greek* (Chicago: published by the author, 1896), 49, 59, is: aorist 1,214, present 1,025, perfect 31, and future 6. (These differences between the two counts are to some degree marked differences from this ratio in some categories of usage; the more common unusual patterns are indicated by asterisks in Table 6.1.

Several of the idiosyncrasies shown by the asterisks appear to be beyond explanation—at least there is no obvious reason to explain the predominance of aorist or present in some of these uses. For example, the marked predominance of *aorist* infinitives after δύναμαι and in the simple infinitive of purpose is difficult to account for, except to fall back in a general way upon aspect-distinctions: one assumes that in these uses it is normally not important to focus on the internal make-up of the occurrence, and instead the writer/speaker refers to the infinitive action in summary without describing its internal details.[8] On the other side, the reason for the frequency of *present* over aorist infinitives after ὀφείλω, διά, and ὥστε is not clear. The striking predominance of present infinitives with μέλλω can perhaps be traced to its frequent use as a periphrasis for the future tense, but it is not obvious why that should affect the aspect-choice in this way.[9]

A few of the unusual patterns are perhaps more explicable.

due to textual variations.) For comparison, Votaw's count of infinitives in the LXX (including Apocrypha) produced the following figures: aorist 4,270, present 2,302, perfect 56, and future 68 (of which 54 are in the Apocrypha).

[8] Stork, *Aspectual Usage*, pp. 325–47, cites a roughly similar frequency-ratio for infinitives of the first type (with δύναμαι; his group includes other constructions with similar meaning). His explanation of the preference for the aorist is that such constructions are more likely to focus on the *effectuation* or *actualization* of a specific act or event, which prompts the aorist usage.

[9] The future ἔσεσθαι occurs 3 times with μέλλω (Acts 11: 28, 24: 15, 27: 10). The present and future were equally common in classical usage after μέλλω, but use of the future infinitive in general was greatly reduced in later Greek. The aorist does occur in classical usage, but it is rare. See BDF, *Grammar*, §§ 338, 350; BAGD, *Lexicon*, pp. 500–1; Moorhouse, *Syntax*, p. 209; and Stahl, *Syntax*, pp. 195–6. Mayser, *Grammatik*, p. 166, however, reports that the aorist is most common in papyri, the present occurring only in more vernacular usage and the future sporadically in official documents. Stork, *Aspectual Usage*, pp. 109–32, 372–3, finds a similar predominance of present infinitive with μέλλω. His explanation is that this construction emphasizes the initial phase of the action described by the infinitive with no stress on its termination, and thus the present is preferred to the aorist.

For example, the relative-time function of the aspects (i.e. the tendency of the present to reflect simultaneous occurrence and of the aorist to show sequenced or antecedent occurrence as a secondary function of the aspect-value) certainly affects aspect-choice in the temporal constructions with ἐν and μετά. Thus, the sequenced occurrence indicated by the construction with μετά ('after A, then B') leads to the idiomatic avoidance of the present infinitive. In the phrase with ἐν plus an infinitive the present is the expected form, producing the simultaneous

TABLE 6. 2. *Aspect-Frequency in Some Uses of NT Subjunctive*[a]

	Present	Aorist	Perfect
1. Purpose or result clauses with:			
ἵνα	154	424	14[b]
μή*	2	30	1
ὅπως*	4	37	
2. Substantive or epexegetic clauses with:			
ἵνα	60	154	1
μή*	2	22	
ὅπως*		14	
3. Temporal clauses with:			
ὅταν	37	85	
ἕως*		50	
ἄχρι(ς) or μέχρι(ς)		14	
ὁσάκις	3	1	
other connectives	3	9	
4. Indefinite relative clauses*			
(Gospels and Acts)	25	82	
(Epistles and Rev.)	19	11	
5. Conditional clauses*	114	211	6[c]
6. Emphatic denial with οὐ μή*		85	
7. Deliberative questions*	5	97	

[a] This count is based on data obtained by James L. Boyer in a Gramcord computer search of NT subjunctives and recorded in his unpublished 'Supplemental Manual of Information: Subjunctive Verbs' (Winona Lake, Ind.: Grace Theological Seminary, n.d.). His discussion of these categories (without treatment of aspect-usage) is given in 'The Classification of Subjunctives: A Statistical Study', *Grace Theological Journal*, 7 (1986), 3–19. Asterisks denote the more common categories in which the aspect-frequency is markedly different from the normal ratio of present and aorist usage in the subjunctive.
[b] 7 of οἶδα, 7 periphrastics.
[c] 3 of οἶδα, 3 periphrastics.

sense 'while . . .' (i.e. 'at the time when A was occurring, B took place'; e.g. Luke 1: 8, 21; 2: 43; 5: 1; 8: 5, 42), and the aorist, which is less common, normally produces a slightly different sense: 'when . . .' ('at the time when A occurred, B took place'; e.g. Luke 2: 27; 3: 21; 11: 37; 19: 15).[10]

A second case is not so easy: the predominance of present infinitives in indirect discourse (i.e. reported statement, introduced by verbs of saying, thinking, etc.). This is weakened somewhat by the fact that fifty of the ninety-three presents are the form εἶναι, for which no aorist counterpart was available. On the other side the count for aorists is skewed a bit by the predominance of aorists occurring as indirect statement after the verb ἐλπίζω (no presents, 12 aorists, and 1 perfect); thus, twelve of the thirty-two aorists in this construction come from an idiomatic use with one verb. So one is left with a comparatively small number of aorists in this construction. This seems attributable to the rise of the parallel construction with ὅτι and the indicative, which more clearly preserves the sense of a direct statement using the aorist aspect.[11] The instances in the NT of aorist infinitives in indirect discourse display a *future* or *potential present* sense, rather than an indirect statement about the past (e.g. Luke 22: 5; John 21: 25; Acts 10: 43, 15: 11; Rom. 14: 2, 15: 24). The aorist infinitive was used in earlier Greek to preserve an aorist indicative of the direct statement,[12] but in the NT this is apparently taken over completely by ὅτι clauses.[13] However, this change has not eliminated *perfect* infinitives from indirect discourse use:[14] they

[10] For a similar explanation see: Burton, *MT*, § 109; Zerwick, *Biblical Greek*, pp. 134–5; and MT, *Syntax*, p. 145.

[11] Concerning this shift in constructions see BDF, *Grammar*, §§ 396–7.

[12] Smyth, *Grammar*, §§ 1867, 1871; and Moorhouse, *Syntax*, pp. 207–9. As Burton argues in *MT*, §§ 110–14, it seems that the tense of the indirect discourse infinitive simply preserves the *aspect* which occurred (or would occur) in direct speech, and does not express as its primary meaning any relative time-value (in reference to the time of the main verb), as many grammars state.

[13] Burton, *MT*, § 114 notes: 'There is apparently no instance in the New Testament of the Aorist Infinitive in indirect discourse representing the Aorist Indicative of the direct form'. He does not suggest an explanation for this absence.

[14] NT examples are Luke 10: 36, 20: 7, 22: 34, 24: 23; John 12: 18, 12: 29; Acts 12:

occur far more frequently in this use than in any other, and they appear to preserve the sense of the perfect indicative in direct speech.[15]

Stork's extensive study, including detailed statistical comparisons, of the 'dynamic' infinitive in Herodotus should be consulted for further information on aspectual usage in the ancient Greek infinitive.[16]

6. 1. 3. 2 *Unusual aspect-usage in the subjunctive*

The data in Table 6.2 show the occurrence of present, aorist, and perfect subjunctives in several important categories of usage in the NT. The general pattern of usage in the subjunctive very strongly favours the aorist over the present, and the perfect is extremely rare. The actual count of all subjunctives in the NT is (including hortatory and prohibitory uses and indirect commands): present 455 occurrences (24.7%), aorist 1,376 (74.7%), and perfect 10 (0.5%).[17] The more common categories of usage which display marked differences from this ratio are highlighted by asterisks in Table 6.2.

Several of these idiosyncrasies require further comment. Two of the uses display a higher incidence of *present* aspect than the normal pattern (though aorists are still more numerous than presents): conditional clauses and indefinite relative clauses. One might expect that the explanation of this lies in the generic nature of these constructions (i.e. that they normally involve indefinite reference), since general or indefinite reference tends to be linked with presents or imperfects in the

14, 14: 19, 16: 27, 25: 25, 27: 13: Rom. 4: 1, 15: 8; 1 Cor. 8: 2, 10: 12; 2 Cor. 11: 5; Phil. 3: 4; 2 Tim. 1: 8; Heb. 4: 1, 11: 5.

[15] More specifically, they denote the normal range of emphases focusing on some features of 'a resulting state produced by an anterior occurrence'. This means that action anterior to the time of the main verb is often implied when a perfect infinitive occurs in indirect discourse, as MT, *Syntax*, p. 85, points out.

[16] See Stork, *Aspectual Usage*, aspecially his summary, pp. 360–95. The category of 'dynamic' infinitive includes all the uses except the infinitive in indirect discourse.

[17] Cf. Sloat, 'NT Verb Forms', pp. 211–12. His figure for perfect subjunctives is 9, which I have raised by one based on personal count (all 10 are forms of οἶδα).

indicative and imperative, while the aorist of those forms is linked with specific reference.[18] However, study of actual examples belies this hypothesis. In some cases these presents reflect distributive or customary-iterative meaning (e.g. Luke 9: 5, 10: 5; John 5: 19; 1 Cor. 11: 25, 27; Col. 3: 17, 23; 1 John 3: 22, 5: 15), but this does not explain most of the instances of the present, and aorists also occur with distributive or multiple senses (e.g. Matt. 5: 19, 5: 46–7, 12: 32, 23: 3; Mark 6: 10, 6: 23, among many others). Instead, a large number of presents are due to the *stative vs. ingressive* contrast which exists for the present and aorist when STATES are used in the subjunctive. In other words, a large proportion of the present subjunctives in these uses display a stative sense, for which the aorist either does not exist or (with its ingressive meaning) would not be suitable.[19] This is apparently a coincidental feature, since there is no certain connection between stative predication and these uses of the subjunctive. Presumably any other subjunctive occurrence with STATES would also tend to occur in the present, unless the ingressive idea is acceptable in its context.

Other idioms reflect a higher than average incidence of *aorist* usage: ὅπως and μή clauses, ἕως clauses, emphatic denial, and deliberative questions. The sense of the temporal connection with ἕως ('until', excluding a simultaneous occurrence of the subordinate action) explains the aorist usage with such

---

[18] MT, *Syntax*, p. 114, suggests that in conditional clauses with ἐάν the present is used with a 'general and iterative sense' while the aorist portrays 'a definite event as occurring only once in the future, and conceived as taking place before the time of the action of the main verb'. There is sometimes a difference of general or specific reference, but it is not reliable as a general distinction, as shown above. Turner's statement (p. 107) that in indefinite relative clauses 'The use of pres. or aor. subj. bears little or no relation to the *Aktionsart*' must be disputed. It is easier to trace a pattern of aspect-distinctions than he implies, despite the occasional difficulties, and this approach is superior to the differences in relative time which he suggests in its place.

[19] Of the 44 present subjunctives in relative clauses with ἄν or ἐάν, 25 are STATIVE verbs (e.g. εἰμί, θέλω, ἔχω, βούλομαι). Aorists of STATIVE verbs with ingressive sense do occur, but they are not so common: Mark 8: 38; Jas. 4: 4. Similar statistics could be cited for conditional clauses.

clauses. It is difficult to explain why the aorist subjunctive predominates in the others. The parallel construction with ἵνα does not display the degree of preference for the aorist which ὅπως and μή clauses do, yet the general sense seems no different. The total absence from the NT of present subjunctive in emphatic denial with οὐ μή is not shared by ancient Greek in general: the present does occur in classical usage, though it is still rare.[20] The nature of the deliberative or dubitative question in itself does not seem to limit the likelihood of present-aspect functions.[21] Yet even if no explanation is forthcoming, the idiomatic pattern is clear: aorist usage predominates in these constructions, and one should not expect the normal range of variation between present and aorist which is found elsewhere.[22]

6. 1. 3. 3 Unusual aspect-usage in the optative

The optative is quite rare in the NT, and many occurrences come in stereotyped phrases, which cannot be relied upon to reflect living idiom in regard to aspect-function. The actual count of all optatives in the NT is: present 23 occurrences (35%) and aorist 43 (65%).[23] The ratio of aspect-usage in individual uses of the optative is shown in Table 6.3.

---

[20] Useful discussion of this idiom in general is given by BDF, *Grammar*, § 365; Moulton, *Proleg.*, pp. 188–92; and MT, *Syntax*, pp. 95–7. Rijksbaron, *SSV*, p. 48, suggests that the aorist is more emphatic with the negative and that it is pointless to focus on the *course* of the action, as the present does, in an expression which negates the action entirely. This explanation is certainly plausible. Moulton, *Proleg.*, p. 189, records a similar suggestion.

[21] Cf. BDF, *Grammar*, § 366; MT, *Syntax*, pp. 98–9; and Moorhouse, *Syntax*, pp. 223–4. The aorist was most frequent in earlier Greek as well, but not to the same extent. According to Ashton Waugh McWhorter, 'A Study of the So-Called Deliberative Type of Question (τί ποιήσω;)', *Transactions and Proceedings of the American Philological Association*, 41 (1910), 159, the count of tenses in deliberative questions in several early dramatists is as follows: *Aeschylus*: pres. subj. 15; aor. subj. 35; fut. indic. 7 (aor. or fut. 8); *Sophocles*: pres. subj. 11; aor. subj. 26; fut. indic. 13 (aor. or fut. 19); *Euripides*: pres. subj. 38; aor. subj. 114; fut. indic. 76 (aor. or fut. 63).

[22] Even with verbs which consistently occur in present aspect these constructions elicit aorist usage: e.g. οὐ μή θεωρήσῃ in John 8: 51 one of only 4 aorists of this verb in NT, compared to 52 presents.

[23] Cf. Sloat, 'NT Verb Forms', p. 212. His count for aorist optatives is 44, which I

It can be seen that these figures are distorted by the stereotyped use of μὴ γένοιτο and by the liberal occurrence of

TABLE 6. 3. *Aspect-Frequency in Some Uses of NT Optative*

	Present	Aorist
1. Voluntative optative	1 (εἴη Acts 8: 20)	36 (15 μὴ γένοιτο)
2. Conditional clauses (with εἰ)	6 (1 εἴη)	4
3. Potential optative (with ἄν):		
–in direct speech	2	1
–in indirect speech[a]	6 (4 εἴη)	2
4 Oblique optative	8 (6 εἴη)	

[a] These could be regarded as oblique optatives, but they occur with ἄν and seem to preserve a potential optative of direct speech rather than substituting for indicative or subjunctive. See BDF, *Grammar*, § 386 (1).

εἴη without a clear aorist counterpart. Two other observations can be made. The first is that all but one of the occurrences of present aspect is the result of *stative* meaning, which excludes the aorist from likelihood. Present optatives in the NT involve a small range of verbs: εἰμί (12 uses), θέλω (4), δύναμαι (3), ἔχω (2), βούλομαι (1), and πάσχω (1). Except for the last one, these are STATES; an aorist would not be appropriate since an ingressive meaning would result. The only present optative which is not stative is πάσχοιτε in 1 Pet. 3: 14, which is consistent with the author's custom of using πάσχω more frequently in the present aspect throughout the epistle, perhaps to emphasize the details of undergoing persecution in a somewhat descriptive portrayal as opposed to the summary reference which the aorist yields.[24]

have reduced by one based on personal count. MT, *Syntax*, pp. 119–33, contains a very helpful treatment of the NT optative, which I have relied upon for examples and explanation of usage.

[24] The present of πάσχω occurs 7 other times in 1 Pet., while the aorist occurs 5 times, 3 times of Christ's suffering and twice of the Christian's suffering (4: 1, 5: 10—both aorist participles, in which a temporal meaning affects the choice: the suffering is considered after it has ceased).

The other observation about aspectual function in the optative concerns the predominance of *aorist* aspect in the voluntative use. After discounting the occurrences of μὴ γένοιτο, one still has twenty-one instances of aorist optative used in wishes, compared with one present (εἴη in Acts 8: 20). This frequency may be of a piece with the frequency of aorist imperatives in prayers to the deity (as discussed in Chapter 5): fifteen of these optatives are clearly used in wishes or prayers directed to God (Luke 1: 38; Rom. 15: 5, 13; 1 Thess. 3: 11–12, 5: 23; 2 Thess. 2: 17; 3: 5, 16; 2 Tim. 1: 16, 18; 4: 16; Heb. 13: 21). Three others are in epistolary greeting which are likely to be prayers (1 Pet. 1: 2; 2 Pet. 1: 2; and Jude 2), and two are curses which invoke God's disfavour (Mark 11: 14 and Jude 9). Only one is a request directed towards an individual apart from prayer (Philem. 20).

6. 2 Aspectual Usage in the Participle

Because the participle displays a pattern of usage somewhat different from the other non-indicative forms, it is treated separately here.

6. 2. 1 *General principle for the meaning of the aspects in the participle*

How to describe the meaning of the aspects in the participle has puzzled grammarians since the time of Curtius, who first noted the predominance of aspect meanings, as opposed to tense-meanings, in the Greek verb. The difficulty centres around two features difficult to reconcile.[25] The first is the fact that tense-meanings are not expected for the present and aorist outside of the indicative. This is in keeping with the essentially non-temporal usage displayed in the infinitive,

---

[25] The problems of balancing these two factors are evidenced in explanations given in these grammars: Burton, *MT*, §§ 118, 132, 143; Moulton, *Proleg.*, pp. 126–7; Robertson, *Grammar*, pp. 858–64, 891–2; BDF, *Grammar*, § 339; Zerwick, *Biblical Greek*, pp. 85–90; Moule, *Idiom Book*, pp. 99–103; and MT, *Syntax*, p. 79.

subjunctive, and optative as contrasted with the temporal-cum-aspectual character of present and aorist in the indicative. The second is the evidence of actual usage, showing that the present and aorist participles do reflect a consistent pattern of temporal meanings relative to the action of their main or leading verb. The action of a present participle is almost always *simultaneous* with the main verbal action and that of an aorist participle is almost always *antecedent* to it.[26]

The reconciliation of these two factors which is most consistent with what has been seen about the aspects throughout this book is an explanation which sees both *temporal* and *aspectual* values for the aspects in the participle, but which regards the temporal meanings as secondary to the aspectual ones. The participles of the present and aorist, since they share the same stems and morphology with the present and aorist of the other forms (indicative and non-indicative), can be expected to display the same aspectual values for their *primary* or essential element of meaning, and the evidence of usage bears this out. However, the aspects in the participle, as in the other forms, have a *secondary* function of showing relative time-values, due to the common and logical association of present aspect with simultaneous occurrence and of aorist aspect with antecedent occurrence. This relative time-value ('secondary tense') as a function of the aspects is distinct from the temporal meaning of the indicative forms (i.e. so-called 'primary tense': past, present, and future). See the discussion of these topics in sections 1.1.3, 1.4.3, and 3.4.1. For some reason such secondary temporal functions are more commonly seen in the participle than in the other non-indicative forms.

Thus, a general statement of the meanings of the present,

---

[26] There are exceptions, of course, but the general pattern is clear. For example, in his study of participles in Acts, Williams concluded that of 594 instances of present participles, 518 (87%) reflect simultaneous occurrence, and of 588 aorists, 540 (92%) display antecedent occurrence: Charles Bray Williams, *The Participle in the Book of Acts* (Chicago: University of Chicago Press, 1909), 34–5. A similar pattern is seen in the Apostolic Fathers, as shown by Henry B. Robison, *Syntax of the Participle in the Apostolic Fathers* (Chicago: University of Chicago Press, 1913), 11–22.

aorist, and perfect should focus primarily on the *aspectual* values of these forms: their essential meanings are the aspectual ones described earlier in this book. However, it must be noted that these values often display, as a secondary function, a *temporal* meaning in relation to some reference-point, usually the action of the main verb. Details of this will now be set forth for the individual aspects.

6. 2. 2   *Normal functions of the present aspect in the participle*

The primary meaning of the present 'tense' in the participle is the aspectual one discussed earlier: it focuses on the internal make-up of the occurrence and views it in its course (or in its repetition or its continuing existence, etc., whatever the specific make-up may be), without regard for the beginning or end-point. This 'viewpoint aspect', or particular focus on the occurrence, is the consistent element of meaning which can be seen in the various combinatory functions which are produced by interaction with other features of meaning. It can easily be seen how this aspect-meaning will normally result in the participial occurrence being seen as 'going on' in some way at the time of another occurrence. The simultaneous temporal meaning for the present participle is very consistent, and this is the value which the grammars tend to emphasize. However, most of the grammars also note that some instances do occur which violate the pattern of simultaneous occurrence: some present participles denote occurrences antecedent or subsequent to the main verb, while others describe occurrences so general that one cannot limit them to any single time-frame.[27] What remains consistent in all of these instances is the aspectual sense stated above: some occurrence is viewed in its extension (whether as in progress or as customary or repeated), despite the fact that the occurrence is before or after

---

[27] See the discussions given in Burton, *MT*, §§ 119–22; Robison, *Participle in the Apostolic Fathers*, pp. 11–16: Williams, *Participle in Acts*, pp. 34–5; BDF, *Grammar*, 339; Rob, *Grammar*, pp. 891–2; and MT, *Syntax*, pp. 80–1

the main verb or is true more universally. This demonstrates that the aspect-value should be regarded as primary and the temporal one as secondary. Examples of these will be cited below.

Since aspect is primary in the present participle, it is important to analyse and describe its variation in usage along aspectual lines rather than temporal ones, as the grammars generally do. When viewed aspectually the present participle displays the same range of combinatory functions as the present in other forms of the verb: progressive, customary, conative meanings and so on.

The present participle may be *progressive* in function, denoting a specific occurrence viewed as it is taking place and thus emphasizing either the simultaneity of the participial occurrence with the main verbal occurrence or portraying it with greater vividness in description. This function is more frequent in the adverbial uses of the participle, but it can appear even in a distinctly adjectival or substantival use. It is especially common in cases of the supplementary participle after verbs of perception or cognition.[28]

Matt. 3: 16 εἶδεν [τὸ] πνεῦμα [τοῦ] θεοῦ καταβαῖνον ὡσεὶ περιστερὰν [καὶ] ἐρχόμενον ἐπ᾽ αὐτόν
   24: 3 καθημένου δὲ αὐτοῦ ἐπὶ τοῦ Ὄρους τῶν Ἐλαιῶν προσῆλθον αὐτῷ οἱ μαθηταί

Mark 1: 16 καὶ παράγων παρὰ τὴν θάλασσαν τῆς Γαλιλαίας εἶδεν Σίμωνα καὶ Ἀνδρέαν τὸν ἀδελφὸν Σίμωνος ἀμφιβάλλοντας ἐν τῇ θαλάσσῃ
   1: 40 καὶ ἔρχεται πρὸς αὐτὸν λεπρὸς παρακαλῶν αὐτὸν [καὶ γονυπετῶν] καὶ λέγων αὐτῷ ὅτι ἐὰν θέλῃς δύνασαί με καθαρίσαι

Luke 2: 20 καὶ ὑπέστρεψαν οἱ ποιμένες δοξάζοντες καὶ αἰνοῦντες τὸν θεὸν ἐπὶ πᾶσιν οἷς ἤκουσαν καὶ εἶδον
   23: 10 εἱστήκεισαν δὲ οἱ ἀρχιερεῖς καὶ οἱ γραμματεῖς εὐτόνως κατηγοροῦντες αὐτοῦ
   23: 26 ὡς ἀπήγαγον αὐτόν, ἐπιλαβόμενοι Σίμωνά τινα Κυρηναῖον ἐρχόμενον ἀπ᾽ ἀγροῦ ἐπέθηκαν αὐτῷ τὸν σταυρὸν φέρειν ὄπισθεν τοῦ Ἰησοῦ

---

[28] See this use of the participle in BDF, *Grammar*, § 416.

John 6: 6 τοῦτο δὲ ἔλεγεν πειράζων αὐτόν, αὐτὸς γὰρ ᾔδει τί ἔμελλεν ποιεῖν
   7: 32 ἤκουσαν οἱ Φαρισαῖοι τοῦ ὄχλου γογγύζοντος περὶ αὐτοῦ ταῦτα
Acts 10: 10 παρασκευαζόντων δὲ αὐτῶν ἐγένετο ἐπ᾽ αὐτὸν ἔκστασις
   10: 44 ἔτι λαλοῦντος τοῦ Πέτρου τὰ ῥήματα ταῦτα ἐπέπεσεν τὸ πνεῦμα τὸ
       ἅγιον ἐπὶ πάντας τοὺς ἀκούοντας τὸν λόγον
   23: 18 ὁ δέσμιος Παῦλος προσκαλεσάμενός με ἠρώτησεν τοῦτον τὸν
       νεανίσκον ἀγαγεῖν πρὸς σέ, ἔχοντά τι λαλῆσαί σοι
Heb. 11: 21 πίστει Ἰακὼβ ἀποθνήσκων ἕκαστον τῶν υἱῶν Ἰωσὴφ
       εὐλόγησεν
(See also Matt. 4: 21, Mark 1: 10, Luke 1: 64, Acts 8: 39, 14: 19.)

Also very common is the *customary* sense for the present participle. This is the function which denotes a more general occurrence: either (1) something done on multiple occasions by a specific individual or individuals and perhaps customary of him or them, or (2) a generic, indefinite occurrence in which the multiple sense is perhaps distributive (each individual does the act only once). This use of the present participle is found more frequently in the adjective and substantive uses, but it can occur with one of the adverbial or supplementary uses. Examples of the first type are:

Matt. 2: 20 τεθνήκασιν γὰρ οἱ ζητοῦντες τὴν ψυχὴν τοῦ παιδίου
   23: 37 Ἰερουσαλὴμ Ἰερουσαλήμ, ἡ ἀποκτείνουσα τοὺς προφήτας καὶ
       λιθοβολοῦσα τοὺς ἀπεσταλμένους πρὸς αὐτήν
Mark 1: 14–15 ἦλθεν ὁ Ἰησοῦς εἰς τὴν Γαλιλαίαν κηρύσσων τὸ εὐαγγέλιον
       τοῦ θεοῦ καὶ λέγων
Luke 23: 5 οἱ δὲ ἐπίσχυον λέγοντες ὅτι ἀνασείει τὸν λαὸν διδάσκων καθ᾽
       ὅλης τῆς Ἰουδαίας
John 9: 25 εἰ ἁμαρτωλός ἐστιν οὐκ οἶδα· ἓν οἶδα, ὅτι τυφλὸς ὢν ἄρτι βλέπω
Acts 1: 12 τότε ὑπέστρεψαν εἰς Ἰερουσαλὴμ ἀπὸ ὄρους τοῦ καλουμένου
       Ἐλαιῶνος
   8: 4 οἱ μὲν οὖν διασπαρέντες διῆλθον εὐαγγελιζόμενοι τὸν λόγον
   15: 27 ἀπεστάλκαμεν οὖν Ἰούδαν καὶ Σιλᾶν, καὶ αὐτοὺς διὰ λόγου
       ἀπαγγέλλοντας τὰ αὐτά
   19: 9 ἀποστὰς ἀπ᾽ αὐτῶν ἀφώρισεν τοὺς μαθητὰς καθ᾽ ἡμέραν διαλε-
       γόμενος ἐν τῇ σχολῇ Τυράννου
1 Cor. 4: 12–13 καὶ κοπιῶμεν ἐργαζόμενοι ταῖς ἰδίαις χερσίν· λοιδορούμενοι

εὐλογοῦμεν, διωκόμενοι ἀνεχόμεθα, δυσφημούμενοι παρακαλοῦμεν

Gal. 1: 23 ὁ διώκων ἡμᾶς ποτε νῦν εὐαγγελίζεται τὴν πίστιν ἥν ποτε ἐπόρθει

1 Thess. 2: 4 οὕτως λαλοῦμεν, οὐχ ὡς ἀνθρώποις ἀρέσκοντες ἀλλὰ θεῷ τῷ δοκιμάζοντι τὰς καρδίας ἡμῶν

4: 8 τὸν θεὸν τὸν |καὶ| διδόντα τὸ πνεῦμα αὐτοῦ τὸ ἅγιον εἰς ὑμᾶς

2 Thess. 3: 11 ἀκούομεν γάρ τινας περιπατοῦντας ἐν ὑμῖν ἀτάκτως, μηδὲν ἐργαζομένους ἀλλὰ περιεργαζομένους

Jas. 4: 1 πόθεν πόλεμοι καὶ πόθεν μάχαι ἐν ὑμῖν; οὐκ ἐντεῦθεν, ἐκ τῶν ἡδονῶν ὑμῶν τῶν στρατευομένων ἐν τοῖς μέλωσιν ὑμῶν;

(See also Luke 16: 21, Acts 14: 22, 18: 23, 1 Thess. 1: 10, 2: 9, 2: 12, 5: 24.)

The second type of customary sense (generic, indefinite, perhaps distributive occurrence) occurs in the texts given below. It will be noted that this generic sense includes instances in which the indefinite individual is seen as engaged in the occurrence repeatedly or habitually (somewhat like the first type of customary except for the indefinite feature), but there are also generic uses in which the present is multiple in a distributive sense: an individual is envisaged as engaging in the occurrence only once.[29] The cases of distributive meaning could be phrased with an aorist participle, involving merely a shift in viewpoint from highlighting the collective-multiple occurrences or referring only to the single generic occurrence. However, even though the aorist is possible in such cases (cf. aorists in Mark 4: 18 and Luke 8: 12, 14, compared with present in Matt. 13: 19, 22), the present participle is far more frequent.

Matt. 5: 32 ἐγὼ δὲ λέγω ὑμῖν ὅτι πᾶς ὁ ἀπολύων τὴν γυναῖκα αὐτοῦ παρεκτὸς λόγου πορνείας ποιεῖ αὐτὴν μοιχευθῆναι

5: 42 τῷ αἰτοῦντί σε δός, καὶ τὸν θέλοντα ἀπὸ σοῦ δανίσασθαι μὴ ἀποστραφῇς

7: 14 στενὴ ἡ πύλη καὶ τεθλιμμένη ἡ ὁδὸς ἡ ἀπάγουσα εἰς τὴν ζωήν, καὶ ὀλίγοι εἰσὶν οἱ εὑρίσκοντες αὐτήν

---

[29] Illuminating discussion and illustrations of this are given in Burton, *MT*, §§ 123–4.

John 5: 24 ὁ τὸν λόγον μου ἀκούων καὶ πιστεύων τῷ πέμψαντί με ἔχει ζωὴν αἰώνιον

Acts 4: 34 ὅσοι γὰρ κτήτορες χωρίων ἢ οἰκιῶν ὑπῆρχον, πωλοῦντες ἔφερον τὰς τιμὰς τῶν πιπρασκομένων

Gal. 6: 6 κοινωνείτω δὲ ὁ κατηχούμενος τὸν λόγον τῷ κατηχοῦντι ἐν πᾶσιν ἀγαθοῖς

Eph. 4: 28 ὁ κλέπτων μηκέτι κλεπτέτω

1 Thess. 4: 8 τοιγαροῦν ὁ ἀθετῶν οὐκ ἄνθρωπον ἀθετεῖ ἀλλὰ τὸν θεόν

1 Tim. 6: 15 ὁ βασιλεὺς τῶν βασιλευόντων καὶ κύριος τῶν κυριευόντων

Heb. 7: 8 καὶ ὧδε μὲν δεκάτας ἀποθνῄσκοντες ἄνθρωποι λαμβάνουσιν (i.e. 'mortal'; contrast this with 11: 21 'Jacob, when dying . . .')
    10: 14 μιᾷ γὰρ προσφορᾷ τετελείωκεν εἰς τὸ διηνεκὲς τοὺς ἁγιαζομένους

1 John 2: 23 πᾶς ὁ ἀρνούμενος τὸν υἱὸν οὐδὲ τὸν πατέρα ἔχει· ὁ ὁμολογῶν τὸν υἱὸν καὶ τὸν πατέρα ἔχει

2 John 7, 9–11 ὅτι πολλοὶ πλάνοι ἐξῆλθον εἰς τὸν κόσμον, οἱ μὴ ὁμολογοῦντες Ἰησοῦν Χριστὸν . . . πᾶς ὁ προάγων καὶ μὴ μένων ἐν τῇ διδαχῇ . . . ὁ μένων ἐν τῇ διδαχῇ . . . ὁ λέγων αὐτῷ χαίρειν

Rev. 14: 13 μακάριοι οἱ νεκροὶ οἱ ἐν κυρίῳ ἀποθνῄσκοντες ἀπ' ἄρτι

Several other functions of the present aspect are seen in the present participle, but they are far less frequent than the two already listed. These include the conative sense, the futuristic sense, and the present participle used of a 'past action still in progress', each with characteristics similar to the functions of the present indicative by the same names (cf. sections 4.1.5–7).[30]

Conative

Matt. 23: 13 ὑμεῖς γὰρ οὐκ εἰσέρχεσθε, οὐδὲ τοὺς εἰσερχομένους ἀφίετε εἰσελθεῖν
    27: 40 ὁ καταλύων τὸν ναὸν καὶ ἐν τρισὶν ἡμέραις οἰκοδομῶν, σῶσον σεαυτόν, εἰ υἱὸς εἶ τοῦ θεοῦ

Acts 28: 23 οἷς ἐξετίθετο διαμαρτυρόμενος τὴν βασιλείαν τοῦ θεοῦ πείθων τε αὐτοὺς περὶ τοῦ Ἰησοῦ

1 Thess. 2: 16 κωλυόντων ὑμᾶς τοῖς ἔθνεσιν λαλῆσαι ἵνα σωθῶσιν

---

[30] These categories are cited by Burton, *MT*, §§ 128–31.

Heb. 11: 6 πιστεῦσαι γὰρ δεῖ τὸν προσερχόμενον τῷ θεῷ ὅτι ἔστιν

Futuristic

Mark 14: 24 καὶ εἶπεν αὐτοῖς, τοῦτό ἐστιν τὸ αἷμά μου τῆς διαθήκης τὸ ἐκχυννόμενον ὑπὲρ πολλῶν

Acts 3: 26 ὑμῖν πρῶτον ἀναστήσας ὁ θεὸς τὸν παῖδα αὐτοῦ ἀπέστειλεν αὐτὸν εὐλογοῦντα ὑμᾶς ἐν τῷ ἀποστρέφειν ἕκαστον ἀπὸ τῶν πονηριῶν ὑμῶν

1 Thess. 1: 10 Ἰησοῦν τὸν ῥυόμενον ἡμᾶς ἐκ τῆς ὀργῆς τῆς ἐρχομένης (this participle is very common with futuristic sense)

Past action still in progress

Matt. 9: 20 (similar in parallels) καὶ ἰδοὺ γυνὴ αἱμορροοῦσα δώδεκα ἔτη . . . ἥψατο τοῦ κρασπέδου τοῦ ἱματίου αὐτοῦ

John 5: 5 ἦν δέ τις ἄνθρωπος ἐκεῖ τριάκοντα [καὶ] ὀκτὼ ἔτη ἔχων ἐν τῇ ἀσθενείᾳ

Acts 24: 10 ἀπεκρίθη τε ὁ Παῦλος νεύσαντος αὐτῷ τοῦ ἡγεμόνος λέγειν, ἐκ πολλῶν ἐτῶν ὄντα σε κριτὴν τῷ ἔθνει τούτῳ ἐπιστάμενος εὐθύμως τὰ περὶ ἐμαυτοῦ ἀπολογοῦμαι

(Also Acts 3: 2, 9: 33, 26: 5.)

6. 2. 3 *Normal functions of the aorist aspect in the participle*

The aorist 'tense' of the participle has, likewise, an aspectual value as its basic meaning: it presents the occurrence as a whole from beginning to end without regard for its internal make-up. The aorist of the participle does not in itself denote a time-value, but such a 'summary aspect', since it takes in the whole occurrence including the end-point, most naturally yields a secondary sense of sequenced occurrence or occurrence antecedent to the verb to which it is related. This secondary function is not central to the aorist participle, however, as is demonstrated by the instances which relate an occurrence simultaneous with the main verb or even subsequent to it.[31] In these the aspect-value is retained, regardless

---

[31] See the discussion of the temporal relation of the aorist participle to its main verb in Burton, *MT*, §§ 139–41, 144, 146; Robison, *Participle in the Apostolic Fathers*, pp. 16–22; Williams, *Participle in Acts*, p. 35; BDF, *Grammar*, § 339; Robertson,

of the temporal connection. Illustrations of this will be given below.

A pattern of aspect-functions similar to those seen in the aorist of the other forms can be traced for the aorist participle: the main functions are the ingressive, consummative, and constative senses.

The *ingressive* meaning appears most often with participles of STATIVE verbs, denoting not the state itself but the act of entering that condition. This sense can be found in all types of participles, attributive as well as adverbial.

Matt. 14: 9 καὶ λυπηθεὶς ὁ βασιλεὺς διὰ τοὺς ὅρκους καὶ τοὺς συνανακειμένους ἐκέλευσεν δοθῆναι

Mark 1: 41 καὶ σπλαγχνισθείς ... ἥψατο καὶ λέγει αὐτῷ, θέλω, καθαρίσθητι

6: 38 ὁ δὲ λέγει αὐτοῖς, πόσους ἄρτους ἔχετε; ὑπάγετε ἴδετε. καὶ γνόντες λέγουσιν, πέντε, καὶ δύο ἰχθύας

Luke 14: 21 τότε ὀργισθεὶς ὁ οἰκοδεσπότης εἶπεν τῷ δούλῳ αὐτοῦ

John 20: 29 λέγει αὐτῷ ὁ Ἰησοῦς, ὅτι ἑώρακάς με πεπίστευκας; μακάριοι οἱ μὴ ἰδόντες καὶ πιστεύσαντες

Acts 9: 37 ἐγένετο δὲ ἐν ταῖς ἡμέραις ἐκείναις ἀσθενήσασαν αὐτὴν ἀποθανεῖν

Gal. 4: 9 νῦν δὲ γνόντες θεόν, μᾶλλον δὲ γνωσθέντες ὑπὸ θεοῦ

1 Thess. 4: 14 οὕτως καὶ ὁ θεὸς τοὺς κοιμηθέντας διὰ τοῦ Ἰησοῦ ἄξει σὺν αὐτῷ

Rev. 18: 15 οἱ ἔμποροι τούτων, οἱ πλουτήσαντες ἀπ᾽ αὐτῆς

The *consummative* meaning is seen most often with verbs of the ACCOMPLISHMENT or CLIMAX types, but it can be seen

---

Grammar, pp. 858–64; MT, *Syntax*, pp. 79–80; Zerwick, *Biblical Greek*, pp. 87–90; and Moule, *Idiom Book*, p. 100. The issue of subsequent occurrence as a possible meaning for the aorist participle is much discussed, but it seems in the light of examples like Acts 25: 13 that this must be seen as valid. This is the conclusion also of C. D. Chambers, 'On a Use of the Aorist Participle in Some Hellenistic Writers', *JTS* 23 (1922), 183–7; W. F. Howard, 'On the Futuristic Use of the Aorist Participle in Hellenistic', *JTS* 24 (1923), 403–6; and the grammars cited above. Other examples are presented in G. M. Lee, 'The Aorist Participle of Subsequent Action (Acts 16, 6)?', *Biblica*, 50 (1970), 235–6.

with any verb if the context stresses in some way the actual performance of an action in contrast to mere attempt.

Luke 9: 25 τί γὰρ ὠφελεῖται ἄνθρωπος κερδήσας τὸν κόσμον ὅλον ἑαυτὸν δὲ ἀπολέσας ἢ ζημιωθείς;

John 17: 4 ἐγώ σε ἐδόξασα ἐπὶ τῆς γῆς, τὸ ἔργον τελειώσας ὃ δέδωκάς μοι ἵνα ποιήσω

Acts 12: 20 ἦν δὲ θυμομαχῶν Τυρίοις καὶ Σιδωνίοις· ὁμοθυμαδὸν δὲ παρῆσαν πρὸς αὐτόν, καὶ πείσαντες Βλάστον τὸν ἐπὶ τοῦ κοιτῶνος τοῦ βασιλέως ἠτοῦντο εἰρήνην (also in 14: 19)

12: 25 Βαρναβᾶς δὲ καὶ Σαῦλος ὑπέστρεψαν εἰς Ἰερουσαλὴμ πληρώσαντες τὴν διακονίαν

Rom. 6: 18 ἐλευθερωθέντες δὲ ἀπὸ τῆς ἁμαρτίας ἐδουλώθητε τῇ δικαιοσύνῃ

Eph. 6: 13 ἵνα δυνηθῆτε ἀντιστῆναι ἐν τῇ ἡμέρᾳ τῇ πονηρᾷ καὶ ἅπαντα κατεργασάμενοι στῆναι

The most common meaning by far for the aorist participle is the *constative* sense, which presents an occurrence in its entirety without regard for the details of how it occurs: this can involve momentary or extended, single or multiple, specific or general occurrences, but the aorist just presents the occurrence as a whole without focus on such features.

Matt. 2: 11 καὶ ἐλθόντες εἰς τὴν οἰκίαν εἶδον τὸ παιδίον μετὰ Μαρίας τῆς μητρὸς αὐτοῦ, καὶ πεσόντες προσεκύνησαν αὐτῷ, καὶ ἀνοίξαντες τοὺς θησαυροὺς αὐτῶν προσήνεγκαν αὐτῷ δῶρα

4: 2 νηστεύσας ἡμέρας τεσσεράκοντα καὶ νύκτας τεσσεράκοντα ὕστερον ἐπείνασεν

27: 50 ὁ δὲ Ἰησοῦς πάλιν κράξας φωνῇ μεγάλῃ ἀφῆκεν τὸ πνεῦμα

Mark 1: 31 καὶ προσελθὼν ἤγειρεν αὐτὴν κρατήσας τῆς χειρός

Luke 10: 37 ὁ δὲ εἶπεν, ὁ ποιήσας τὸ ἔλεος μετ' αὐτοῦ. εἶπεν δὲ αὐτῷ ὁ Ἰησοῦς, πορεύου καὶ σὺ ποίει ὁμοίως

John 5: 29 καὶ ἐκπορεύσονται, οἱ τὰ ἀγαθὰ ποιήσαντες εἰς ἀνάστασιν ζωῆς, οἱ δὲ τὰ φαῦλα πράξαντες εἰς ἀνάστασιν κρίσεως

Acts 1: 21 δεῖ οὖν τῶν συνελθόντων ἡμῖν ἀνδρῶν ἐν παντὶ χρόνῳ ᾧ εἰσῆλθεν καὶ ἐξῆλθεν ἐφ' ἡμᾶς ὁ κύριος Ἰησοῦς

10: 39 ὃν καὶ ἀνεῖλαν κρεμάσαντες ἐπὶ ξύλου

12: 4 ὃν καὶ πιάσας ἔθετο εἰς φυλακήν, παραδοὺς τέσσαρσιν τετραδίοις στρατιωτῶν φυλάσσειν αὐτόν

1 Cor. 5: 2 ἵνα ἀρθῇ ἐκ μέσου ὑμῶν ὁ τὸ ἔργον τοῦτο πράξας

Eph. 1: 3 εὐλογητὸς ὁ θεὸς καὶ πατὴρ τοῦ κυρίου ἡμῶν Ἰησοῦ Χριστοῦ, ὁ εὐλογήσας ἡμᾶς ἐν πάσῃ εὐλογίᾳ πνευματικῇ ἐν τοῖς ἐπουρανίοις ἐν Χριστῷ

1 Thess. 2: 2 ἀλλὰ προπαθόντες καὶ ὑβρισθέντες καθὼς οἴδατε ἐν Φιλίπποις ἐπαρρησιασάμεθα ἐν τῷ θεῷ ἡμῶν λαλῆσαι πρὸς ὑμᾶς τὸ εὐαγγέλιον τοῦ θεοῦ ἐν πολλῷ ἀγῶνι

2 Thess. 2: 16 θεὸς ὁ πατὴρ ἡμῶν, ὁ ἀγαπήσας ἡμᾶς καὶ δοὺς παράκλησιν αἰωνίαν καὶ ἐλπίδα ἀγαθὴν ἐν χάριτι

Heb. 6: 10 οὐ γὰρ ἄδικος ὁ θεὸς ἐπιλαθέσθαι τοῦ ἔργου ὑμῶν καὶ τῆς ἀγάπης ἧς ἐνεδείξασθε εἰς τὸ ὄνομα αὐτοῦ, διακονήσαντες τοῖς ἁγίοις καὶ διακονοῦντες

10: 29 πόσῳ δοκεῖτε χείρονος ἀξιωθήσεται τιμωρίας ὁ τὸν υἱὸν τοῦ θεοῦ καταπατήσας, καὶ τὸ αἷμα τῆς διαθήκης κοινὸν ἡγησάμενος ἐν ᾧ ἡγιάσθη, καὶ τὸ πνεῦμα τῆς χάριτος ἐνυβρίσας;

(Also Matt. 26: 26, Luke 4: 20, Acts 3: 7, 8: 25, 9: 12, 1 Cor. 1: 4, 1 Thess. 1: 6, 5: 10, Heb. 11: 9, 1 Pet. 1: 10.)

6. 2. 4 *Normal functions of the perfect aspect in the participle*

The perfect participle is infrequent in comparison with the present and aorist, occurring in the NT only 670 times (the present occurs 3,652 and the aorist 2,267 times).[32] The perfect participle preserves the basic sense of the other perfect forms in denoting a state or condition resulting from an anterior occurrence. The normal functions of the basic sense are seen in the participle: it often emphasizes the *resulting state* and only implies the anterior occurrence. This sense comes through especially in instances of passive participles. With the forms of οἶδα or ἵστημι, only the stative meaning is denoted, without implying a prior action.[33]

[32] Sloat, 'NT Verb Forms', pp. 211–12.

[33] Owing to the nature of this basic sense, the perfect participle's normal temporal relation to the main verb is that the resulting state is contemporaneous with the main verbal occurrence, and the action which produced it is thus antecedent to the main verb. There are cases, however, in which the resulting state is seen as antecedent to the main verb: Mark 5: 15, John 11: 44, 1 Cor. 2: 7. For discussion of these matters see Burton, *MT*, §§ 154–6; Robertson, *Grammar*, pp. 909–10; and MT, *Syntax*, p. 85.

Matt. 5: 10 μακάριοι οἱ δεδιωγμένοι ἕνεκεν δικαιοσύνης, ὅτι αὐτῶν ἐστιν ἡ βασιλεία τῶν οὐρανῶν
  16: 28 εἰσίν τινες τῶν ὧδε ἐστώτων οἵτινες οὐ μὴ γεύσωνται θανάτου ἕως ἂν ἴδωσιν τὸν υἱὸν τοῦ ἀνθρώπου ἐρχόμενον ἐν τῇ βασιλείᾳ αὐτοῦ (purely stative meaning)

Mark 5: 15 θεωροῦσιν τὸν δαιμονιζόμενον ... τὸν ἐσχηκότα τὸν λεγιῶνα (a past state, relative to the main verb)
  16: 6 Ἰησοῦν ζητεῖτε τὸν Ναζαρηνὸν τὸν ἐσταυρωμένον· ἠγέρθη, οὐκ ἔστιν ὧδε (cf. 1 Cor. 2: 2)

Luke 14: 10 ἵνα ὅταν ἔλθῃ ὁ κεκληκώς σε ἐρεῖ σοι, φίλε, προσανάβηθι ἀνώτερον (slight difference from aorist in 14: 9 in stressing the authority of 'the one who invited' to place his guests in places of honour)
  16: 18 ὁ ἀπολελυμένην ἀπὸ ἀνδρὸς γαμῶν μοιχεύει
  18: 14 λέγω ὑμῖν, κατέβη οὗτος δεδικαιωμένος εἰς τὸν οἶκον αὐτοῦ παρ' ἐκεῖνον

John 1: 51 ὄψεσθε τὸν οὐρανὸν ἀνεῳγότα (purely stative meaning)
  3. 6 τὸ γεγεννημένον ἐκ τῆς σαρκὸς σάρξ ἐστιν, καὶ τὸ γεγεννημένον ἐκ τοῦ πνεύματος πνεῦμά ἐστιν (common in Johannine writings)
  8: 31 ἔλεγεν οὖν ὁ Ἰησοῦς πρὸς τοὺς πεπιστευκότας αὐτῷ Ἰουδαίους
  11: 44 ἐξῆλθεν ὁ τεθνηκὼς δεδεμένος τοὺς πόδας καὶ τὰς χεῖρας κειρίαις, καὶ ἡ ὄψις αὐτοῦ σουδαρίῳ περιεδέδετο (a past state and a present state, respectively, relative to the main verb)

Acts 16: 4 παρεδίδοσαν αὐτοῖς φυλάσσειν τὰ δόγματα τὰ κεκριμένα ὑπὸ τῶν ἀποστόλων καὶ πρεσβυτέρων τῶν ἐν Ἱεροσολύμοις
  16: 34 ἀναγαγών τε αὐτοὺς εἰς τὸν οἶκον παρέθηκεν τράπεζαν, καὶ ἠγαλλιάσατο πανοικεὶ πεπιστευκὼς τῷ θεῷ (used 6 times in Acts)

Rom. 6: 9 εἰδότες ὅτι Χριστὸς ἐγερθεὶς ἐκ νεκρῶν οὐκέτι ἀποθνήσκει (very common perfect participle; purely stative meaning)
  16: 25 κατὰ ἀποκάλυψιν μυστηρίου χρόνοις αἰωνίοις σεσιγημένου φανερωθέντος δὲ νῦν διά τε γραφῶν προφητικῶν (past state)

1 Cor. 15: 20 νυνὶ δὲ Χριστὸς ἐγήρεται ἐκ νεκρῶν, ἀπαρχὴ τῶν κεκοιμημένων (also Matt. 27: 52)

Eph. 4: 18–19 ἐσκοτωμένοι τῇ διανοίᾳ ὄντες, ἀπηλλοτριωμένοι τῆς ζωῆς τοῦ θεοῦ ... οἵτινες ἀπηλγηκότες ἑαυτοὺς παρέδωκαν τῇ ἀσελγείᾳ (first is one of two periphrastic perfect participles in NT; Col. 1: 21 is the other)

2 Tim. 1: 4 ἐπιποθῶν σε ἰδεῖν, μεμνημένος σου τῶν δακρύων (purely
    stative meaning for this verb)
    4: 8 οὐ μόνον δὲ ἐμοὶ ἀλλὰ καὶ πᾶσι τοῖς ἠγαπηκόσι τὴν ἐπιφάνειαν αὐτοῦ
    (state is their 'credit' for having done so)

Heb. 5: 14 τελείων δὲ ἐστιν ἡ στερεὰ τροφή, τῶν διὰ τὴν ἕξιν τὰ
    αἰσθητήρια γεγυμνασμένα ἐχόντων πρὸς διάκρισιν καλοῦ τε καὶ κακοῦ

1 John 4: 2 πᾶν πνεῦμα ὃ ὁμολογεῖ Ἰησοῦν Χριστὸν ἐν σαρκὶ ἐληλυθότα ἐκ
    τοῦ θεοῦ ἐστιν

Rev. 7: 4 καὶ ἤκουσα τὸν ἀριθμὸν τῶν ἐσφραγισμένων, ἑκατὸν τεσσεράκοντα
    τέσσαρες χιλιάδες, ἐσφραγισμένοι ἐκ πάσης φυλῆς υἱῶν Ἰσραήλ
    9: 15 καὶ ἐλύθησαν οἱ τέσσαρες ἄγγελοι οἱ ἡτοιμασμένοι εἰς τὴν ὥραν καὶ
    ἡμέραν καὶ μῆνα καὶ ἐνιαυτόν

(See also Matt. 10: 6, 12: 44, 18: 13, 25: 41; Luke 1: 42, 6: 40, 7: 25,
    16: 20, 19: 32; John 4: 6, 6: 13, 17: 13, 18: 21, 19: 33; Acts 15: 16,
    15: 26, 19: 16; Rom. 1: 29, 4: 19, 9: 2, 15: 14; 1 Cor. 2: 7, 7: 18; 2
    Cor. 12: 21; Eph. 1: 18, 3: 9, 3: 16–17, 6: 16; 2 Tim. 3: 8; Tit. 1:
    15; Heb. 9: 13, 10: 2; Rev. 4: 13, 6: 9, 9: 1, 18: 2, 21: 2, 21: 8.)

Less commonly, the perfect participle emphasizes the actual
completion of the action and only implies the result.

Matt. 25: 24 προσελθὼν δὲ καὶ ὁ τὸ ἓν τάλαντον εἰληφὼς εἶπεν (thought to
    be equivalent to 25: 16, 18, 20 ὁ . . . λαβών)
    26: 75 καὶ ἐμνήσθη ὁ Πέτρος τοῦ ῥήματος Ἰησοῦ εἰρηκότος ὅτι πρὶν
    ἀλέκτορα φωνῆσαι τρὶς ἀπαρνήσῃ με

Luke 8: 46 ὁ δὲ Ἰησοῦς εἶπεν, ἥψατό μού τις, ἐγὼ γὰρ ἔγνων δύναμιν
    ἐξεληλυθυῖαν ἀπ' ἐμοῦ

John 7: 15 ἐθαύμαζον οὖν οἱ Ἰουδαῖοι λέγοντες, πῶς οὗτος γράμματα οἶδεν
    μὴ μεμαθηκώς;
    12: 37 τοσαῦτα δὲ αὐτοῦ σημεῖα πεποιηκότος ἔμπροσθεν αὐτῶν οὐκ
    ἐπίστευον εἰς αὐτόν

Acts 3: 12 ἢ ἡμῖν τί ἀτενίζετε ὡς ἰδίᾳ δυνάμει ἢ εὐσεβείᾳ πεποιηκόσιν τοῦ
    περιπατεῖν αὐτόν;
    18: 2 καὶ εὑρών τινα Ἰουδαῖον ὀνόματι Ἀκύλαν, Ποντικὸν τῷ γένει,
    προσφάτως ἐληλυθότα ἀπὸ τῆς Ἰταλίας

Heb. 9: 6 τούτων δὲ οὕτως κατεσκευασμένων, εἰς μὲν τὴν πρώτην σκηνὴν
    διὰ παντὸς εἰσίασιν οἱ ἱερεῖς τὰς λατρείας ἐπιτελοῦντες

6. 3 Conclusion

This chapter has described the meanings displayed by the aspects in the infinitive, optative, subjunctive, and participle (excluding the uses in commands, treated in Chapter 5). It has been shown that the aspectual values for the present, aorist, and perfect presented earlier in this book are central to their meaning in these non-indicative forms of the verb as well. Some of the same secondary functions of the aspects which appear in the indicative in combination with other linguistic features (i.e. progressive, customary, conative, ingressive, consummative, constative uses) appear also in these forms. It has been argued also that temporal meanings for the aspects in these non-indicative forms is a secondary function: relative time-values occur from time to time (especially in the participle), but they are not central to the meaning.

CONCLUSION

THE primary argument of this book has been that understanding verbal aspect requires a grasp of both the basic meanings of the aspects themselves and their function in combination with other linguistic and contextual features. The semantic complexity of aspectual usage suggests that one must unpack several levels of meaning in order to give an adequate account of aspect. More particularly, it has been argued that aspect should be analysed both at a *definition* level and at a *function* level.

The *definition* of the aspects should be stated in terms of the 'viewpoint' which the speaker takes concerning an occurrence. Aspect reflects the focus or viewpoint of the speaker in regard to the occurrence (action or state) which the verb describes. It presents the speaker's way of viewing the occurrence and its make-up, the perspective from which it is regarded, or its portrayal apart from the (actual or perceived) nature of the occurrence itself. The two major aspects of NT Greek are the present and the aorist. The *present* reflects an internal viewpoint concerning the occurrence which focuses on its development or progress and sees the occurrence in regard to the details of its make-up, without beginning or end in view, while the *aorist* presents an external view of the occurrence in summary, from beginning to end, without regard for its internal make-up. The *perfect*, on the other hand, is a complex verbal category which, in one point of its basic meaning, shares the aspectual sense of the aorist. It combines three elements in its invariant meaning: the Aktionsart-feature of stative situation, the tense-feature of anteriority, and the aspect of summary viewpoint concerning the occurrence. In

purely aspectual terms the perfect is secondary to the primary
contrast of present and aorist.

Somewhat separate from the basic aspectual distinction are
meanings like duration, completion, repetition, and so forth,
which are *functions* of the aspects in combination with lexical
and contextual features. It is true that some of the clearest
contrasts of the aspects in actual usage are these combinatory
variants. Such meanings are often stated as the basic definitions of the aspects by traditional grammars of NT Greek. The
argument of this book is that these meanings must not be
given as *definitions* of the aspects themselves but should be
clearly articulated as their secondary *functions* in combination
with other elements.

Understood in this way, aspect has nothing inherently to do
with temporal sequence, with procedural characteristics of
actual situations or of verbs and verb-phrases, or with prominence in discourse. It is instead a matter of viewpoint or focus,
which is a rather subjective category, since a speaker may
choose to view or portray certain occurrences by one aspect or
another without regard to the nature of the occurrence itself.
However, fully subjective choices between aspects are not
common, since the nature of the occurrence or the procedural
character of the verb or verb-phrase can restrict the way an
occurrence is viewed by a speaker. In fact, aspect interacts so
closely with such features and is so significantly affected by
them that no analysis of aspect can be comprehensive without
taking into account these interactions. The book has analysed
ways in which aspect combines with various other features to
produce such secondary functions. These combinations fall
into various predictable patterns, although interpretation of
aspectual function is not thus rendered automatic. The interpreter must be sensitive to the sort of combinations which may
occur and then use that sensitivity within the normal
framework of contextual and historical considerations important to interpretation.

It is hoped that the book will have provided a stimulus for
further research in NT and Hellenistic Greek grammar, both

on the topic covered here and on other questions of grammar. The student of NT Greek is furnished with a number of grammatical reference-works providing a wealth of important information about usage and meaning, and these are indispensable. However, such work can never be considered finished, and fresh research is needed in numerous areas—if not to overturn accepted ideas and approaches, at least to improve and refine them. Apart from the value which it possesses on its own as a field of human inquiry, the study of NT and Hellenistic grammar should provide a linguistic base for interpreting the NT and other literature from its era in Greek. NT exegesis and theology are, of course, occupied with wider and more significant issues than grammatical ones, but responsible interpretation of the NT must make use of the best linguistic resources possible — in lexical, grammatical, and other areas. Seeking a better understanding of NT idiom and attempting to provide these linguistic resources are tasks which must never be regarded as complete.

BIBLIOGRAPHY

Abbott, Edwin A., *Johannine Grammar* (London: Adam and Charles Black, 1906).

Abel, F.-M., *Grammaire du grec biblique suivie d'un choix de papyrus*, 2nd edn. (Paris: J. Gabalda et Fils, 1927).

Ackrill, J. L., 'Aristotle's Distinction between Energeia and Kinesis', in Renford Bambrough (ed.), *New Essays on Plato and Aristotle* (London: Routledge and Kegan Paul, 1965), 121–41.

Adrados, F. R., 'Observaciones sobre el aspecto verbal', *Estudios clásicos*, 1 (1950), 11–25.

Aerts, Willem Johan, *Periphrastica: An Investigation into the Use of εἶναι and ἔχειν as Auxiliaries or Pseudo-Auxiliaries in Greek from Homer up to the Present Day* (Amsterdam: Adolf M. Hakkert, 1965).

Agrell, Sigurd, *Aspektänderung und Aktionsartbildung beim polnischen Zeitworte* (Lunds Universitets Årsskrift 4. 2; Lund: H. Ohlsson, 1908).

Allen, Hamilton Ford, *The Use of the Infinitive in Polybius Compared with the Use of the Infinitive in Biblical Greek* (Chicago: University of Chicago Press, 1907).

Allen, Robert L., *The Verb System of Present-Day American English* (The Hague: Mouton, 1966).

Allen, W. C., *A Critical and Exegetical Commentary on the Gospel According to St. Matthew*, 3rd edn. (ICC; Edinburgh: T. and T. Clark, 1912).

Anderson, John, *An Essay Concerning Aspect* (Janua Linguarum, Series Minor, 167; The Hague: Mouton, 1973).

Andersson, Sven-Gunnar, *Aktionalität im Deutschen: Eine Untersuchung unter Vergleich mit dem russischen Aspektsystem*, 2 vols. (Uppsala: Acta Universitatis Upsaliensis, 1972–8).

Antoniadis, Sophie, *L'Évangile de Luc: Esquisse de grammaire et de style* (Paris: Les Belles Lettres, 1930).

Armstrong, David, 'The Ancient Greek Aorist as the Aspect of Countable Action', in *Tense and Aspect* (1981), 1–12.

Aspectology, ed. Thore Pettersson (Stockholm: Almqvist and Wiksell, 1979).

Austin, J. L., *How to Do Things with Words* (Cambridge, Mass.: Harvard University Press, 1962).

Azzalino, Walther, 'Wesen und Wirken von Aktionsart und Aspekt', *Neuphilologische Zeitschrift*, 2 (1950), 105–10, 192–203.

Bache, Carl, 'Aspect and Aktionsart: Towards a Semantic Distinction', *JL* 18 (1982), 57–72.

—— 'The Semantics of Grammatical Categories: A Dialectical Approach', *JL* 21 (1985), 51–77.

—— *Verbal Aspect: A General Theory and its Application to Present Day English* (Odense: Odense University Press, 1985).

Bakker, W. F., *The Greek Imperative: An Investigation into the Aspectual Differences between the Present and Aorist Imperatives in Greek Prayer from Homer up to the Present Day* (Amsterdam: Adolf M. Hakkert, 1966).

—— 'A Remark on the Use of the Imperfect and Aorist in Herodotus', *Mnemosyne*, 4th ser. 21 (1968), 22–8.

Banerjee, Satya Ranjan, *Indo-European Tense and Apect in Greek and Sanskrit* (Calcutta: Sanskrit Book Depot, 1983).

Barrett, Walter C., 'The Use of Tense in the Imperative Mood in First Corinthians' (Th.M. thesis, Dallas Theological Seminary, 1973).

Barri, Nimrod, 'The Greek Historical Present in a Double Verbal System', *Linguistics*, 204 (1978), 43–56.

Bauer, Gero, 'The English "Perfect" Reconsidered', *JL* 6 (1970), 189–98.

Bauer, Hans, and Leander, Pontus, *Grammatik des Biblisch-Aramäischen* (Halle: Niemeyer, 1927).

Bauer, Walter, *A Greek–English Lexicon of the New Testament and Other Early Christian Literature*, trans. and adapted by William F. Arndt and F. Wilbur Gingrich, 2nd edn., rev. and augmented by F. Wilbur Gingrich and Frederick W. Danker (Chicago: University of Chicago Press, 1979).

Beare, Francis Wright, *The First Epistle of Peter*, 3rd edn. (Oxford: Blackwell, 1970).

Bernhardy, G., *Wissenschaftliche Syntax der griechischen Sprache* (Berlin: Duncker and Humbolt, 1829)

Beschewliew, W., 'Der Gebrauch des Imperativs Aoristi und

Praesentis im altgriechischen Gebet', *Annuaire de l'Université de Sofia*, 23 (1927), 27–59.

Best, Ernest, *1 Peter* (New Century Bible; London: Oliphants, 1971).

—— *A Commentary on the First and Second Epistle to the Thessalonians* (London: Adam and Charles Black, 1972).

Beyer, Klaus, *Semitische Syntax im Neuen Testament*, i. *Satzlehre*, pt. 1 (Göttingen: Vandenhoeck and Ruprecht, 1962).

Bigg, Charles, *A Critical and Exegetical Commentary on the Epistles of St. Peter and St. Jude* (ICC; Edinburgh: T. and T. Clark, 1901).

Björck, Gudmund, Ἦν διδάσκων: *Die periphrastischen Konstruktionen im Griechischen* (Uppsala: Almqvist and Wiksell, 1940).

Black, Matthew, *An Aramaic Approach to the Gospels and Acts*, 3rd edn. (Oxford: Clarendon Press, 1967).

Blass, Friedrich, 'Demosthenische Studien, III: Aorist und Imperfekt', *Rheinisches Museum für Philologie*, 44 (1889), 406–30.

—— *Grammatik des neutestamentlichen Griechisch* (Göttingen: Vandenhoeck and Ruprecht, 1896).

—— *Grammar of New Testament Greek*, trans. by Henry St. John Thackeray, 2nd edn. (London: Macmillan and Co., 1905).

—— and Debrunner, A., *Grammatik des neutestamentlichen Griechisch*, 4th edn. (Göttingen: Vandenhoeck and Ruprecht, 1913).

—— *Grammatik des neutestamentlichen Griechisch*, ed. Friedrich Rehkopf, 15th edn. (Göttingen: Vandenhoeck and Ruprecht, 1979).

—— *A Greek Grammar of the New Testament and Other Early Christian Literature*, trans. and rev. of the 9th–10th German edn., by Robert W. Funk (Chicago: University of Chicago Press, 1961).

Boel, G. de, 'Aspect, Aktionsart und Transitivität', *IF* 92 (1987), 33–57.

Bondarko, Aleksandr V., 'Stand und Perspektiven der Aspektologie in der UdSSR', in Wolfgang Girke and Helmut Jachnow (eds.), *Theoretische Linguistik in Osteuropa* (Tübingen: Niemeyer, 1976), 123–39.

Boyer, James L., 'The Classification of Infinitives: A Statistical Study', *Grace Theological Journal*, 6 (1985), 3–27.

—— 'Supplemental Manual of Information: Infinitive Verbs' (Winona Lake, Ind.: Grace Theological Seminary, n.d.).

—— 'The Classification of Subjunctives: A Statistical Study', *Grace Theological Journal*, 7 (1986), 3–19.

—— 'Supplemental Manual of Information: Subjunctive Verbs' (Winona Lake, Ind.: Grace Theological Seminary, n.d.).

Brockelmann, Carl, *Hebräische Syntax* (Neukirchen: Verlag der Buchhandlung des Erziehungsvereins, 1956).

Brooke, A. E., *A Critical and Exegetical Commentary on the Johannine Epistles* (ICC; Edinburgh: T. and T. Clark, 1912).

Brooks, James A., and Winbery, Carlton L., *Syntax of New Testament Greek* (Washington, DC: University Press of America, 1979).

Bruce, F. F., *The English Bible: A History of Translations from the Earliest English Versions to the New English Bible*, rev. edn. (New York: Oxford University Press, 1970).

Brugmann, Karl, *Kurze vergleichende Grammatik der indogermanischen Sprachen* (Strasburg: Karl J. Trübner, 1902–4).

Brunel, J., 'L'aspect et "l'ordre de procès" en grec', *BSL* 42 (1946), 43–75.

Bryan, W., 'The Preterite and Perfect Tense in Present-Day English', *JEGP* 35 (1936), 363–82.

Burton, Ernest De Witt, *Syntax of the Moods and Tenses in New Testament Greek*, 3rd edn. (Edinburgh: T. and T. Clark, 1898).

Buth, Randall, 'Mark's Use of the Historical Present', *Notes on Translation*, 65 (1977), 7–13.

—— 'Hebrew Poetic Tenses and the Magnificat', *Journal for the Study of the New Testament*, 21 (1984), 67–83.

Buttmann, Alex, *Grammatik des neutestamentlichen Sprachgebrauchs* (Berlin: Ferd. Dümmler, 1859).

Buttmann, Philipp, *Ausführliche griechische Sprachlehre*, 2 vols. (Berlin: in der Myliussischen Buchhandlung, 1819–27).

Bybee, Joan, *Morphology: A Study of the Relation between Meaning and Form* (Amsterdam and Philadelphia: John Benjamins, 1985).

Caird, G. B., *The Gospel of Luke* (The Pelican New Testament Commentaries; London: Penguin Books, 1963).

—— 'The Glory of God in the Fourth Gospel: An Exercise in Biblical Semantics', *NTS* 15 (1969), 265–77.

—— *The Language and Imagery of the Bible* (London: Duckworth, 1980).

Campbell, J. Y., 'The Kingdom of God has Come', *Exp. T.* 48 (1936–7), 91–4.

Carlson, Lauri, 'Aspect and Quantification', in *Tense and Aspect* (1981), 31–64.

Carrington, Philip, *The Primitive Christian Catechism: A Study in the Epistles* (Cambridge: at the University Press, 1940).

Carson, D. A., 'The Ὅμοιος Word-Group as Introduction to Some Matthean Parables', *NTS* 31 (1985), 277–82.

Chamberlain, William Douglas, *An Exegetical Grammar of the Greek New Testament* (New York: Macmillan, 1941).

Chambers, C. D., 'On a Use of the Aorist Participle in Some Hellenistic Writers', *JTS* 23 (1922), 183–7.

Chantraine, Pierre, *Histoire du parfait grec* (Paris: H. Champion, 1927).

Chatterjee, Ranjit, 'On Cross-Linguistic Categories and Related Problems', in *Tense-Aspect* (1982), 335–45.

Classen, Peter, 'On the Trichotomic Time Structure of the Tenses in German and English', *Linguistics*, 17 (1979), 795–823.

Collinge, N. E., Review of M. S. Ruipérez, *Estructura del sistema de aspectos y tiempos del verbo griego antiguo*, in *AL* 7 (1955), 60–2.

——— 'Some Reflexions on Comparative Historical Syntax', *AL* 12 (1960), 79–101.

Colson, F. H., trans., *Philo*, vol. ix (The Loeb Classical Library; Cambridge, Mass.: Harvard University Press, 1941).

Colwell, Ernest Cadman, *The Greek of the Fourth Gospel: A Study of its Aramaisms in the Light of Hellenistic Greek* (Chicago: University of Chicago Press, 1931).

Comrie, Bernard, *Aspect: An Introduction to the Study of Verbal Aspect and Related Problems* (Cambridge: Cambridge University Press, 1976).

——— 'Aspect and Voice: Some Reflections on Perfect and Passive', in *Tense and Aspect* (1981), 65–78.

Conybeare, F. C., and Stock, St. George, *Selections from the Septuagint* (Boston: Ginn and Co., 1905).

Cranfield, C. E. B., *A Critical and Exegetical Commentary on the Epistle to the Romans*, i. *Introduction and Commentary on Romans I–VIII* (Edinburgh: T. and T. Clark, 1975).

Creed, J. M., 'The Kingdom of God has Come', *Exp. T.* 48 (1936–7), 184–5.

Crisafulli, Virgil Santi, 'Aspect and Tense Distribution in Homeric Greek' (Ph.D. dissertation, University of North Carolina at Chapel Hill, 1968).

Crystal, D., 'Specification and English Tenses', *JL* 2 (1966), 1–34.

Cuendet, Georges, *L'Impératif dans le texte grec et dans les versions gotique, arménienne et vieux slave des Évangiles* (Paris: Geuthner, 1924).

Curtius, Georg, *Die Bildung der Tempora und Modi im Griechischen und*

Lateinischen sprachvergleichend dargestellt (Berlin: Wilhelm Besser, 1846).

Curtius, Georg, *Griechische Schulgrammatik,* 2nd edn. (Prague: F. Tempsky, 1855).

—— *Erläuterungen zu meiner griechischen Schulgrammatik* (Prague: F. Tempsky, 1863).

—— *Das Verbum der griechischen Sprache* (Leipzig: S. Hirzel, 1873).

Dahl, Östen, 'Some Notes on Indefinites', *Lg.* 46 (1970), 33–41.

—— 'On Generics', in E. L. Keenan (ed.), *Formal Semantics of Natural Language* (London: Cambridge University Press, 1975), 99–111.

—— 'On the Definition of the Telic/Atelic (Bounded/Nonbounded) Distinction', in *Tense and Aspect* (1981), 79–90.

—— *Tense and Aspect Systems* (Oxford: Basil Blackwell, 1985).

Dana, H. E., and Mantey, Julius R., *A Manual Grammar of the Greek New Testament* (New York: Macmillan, 1927).

Daube, David, *The New Testament and Rabbinic Judaism* (London: Athlone Press, 1956).

Davidson, A. B., *Hebrew Syntax,* 3rd edn. (Edinburgh: T. and T. Clark, 1901).

Davies, W. D., *Paul and Rabbinic Judaism: Some Rabbinic Elements in Pauline Theology,* 4th edn. (Philadelphia: Fortress Press, 1980).

Dayton, Wilber T., 'John 20: 23; Matthew 16: 19 and 18: 18 in the Light of the Greek Perfect Tenses', *The Asbury Seminarian,* 2 (1947), 74–89.

Debrunner, A., Review of P. Chantraine, *Histoire du parfait grec,* in *IF* 46 (1928), 287–90.

Declerck, Renaat, 'Aspect and the Bounded/Unbounded (Telic/Atelic) Distinction', *Linguistics,* 17 (1979), 761–94.

Deissmann, Adolf, *Light from the Ancient East: The New Testament Illustrated by Recently Discovered Texts of the Graeco-Roman World,* trans. Lionel R. M. Strachan (London: Hodder and Stoughton, 1910).

Delancey, Scott, 'Aspect, Transitivity and Viewpoint', in *Tense-Aspect* (1982), 167–83.

Delbrück, Berthold, *Die Grundlagen der griechischen Syntax* (Syntaktische Forschungen 4; Halle: Waisenhaus, 1879).

—— *Vergleichende Syntax der indogermanishen Sprachen,* pt. 2 (Strasburg: Karl J. Trübner, 1897).

Deutschbein, Max, 'Aspekte und Aktionsarten im Neuenglischen', *Neuphilologische Monatsschrift,* 10 (1939), 129–48, 190–201.

Dinneen, Francis P., *An Introduction to General Linguistics* (New York: Holt, Rinehart, and Winston, 1967).

Diver, William, 'The System of Relevance of the Homeric Verb', *Acta Linguistica Hafniensia*, 12 (1969), 45–68.

Dodd, C. H., 'The Kingdom of God has Come', *Exp. T.* 48 (1936–7), 138–42.

—— *The Johannine Epistles* (New York: Harper and Row, 1946).

—— *Gospel and Law: The Relation of Faith and Ethics in Early Christianity* (Cambridge: at the University Press, 1951).

Donovan, J., 'Greek Jussives', *CR* 9 (1895), 145–9, 289–93, 342–6, 444–7.

Doudna, John Charles, *The Greek of the Gospel of Mark* (Philadelphia: Society of Biblical Literature, 1961).

Dowty, David, *Studies in the Logic of Verb Aspect and Time Reference in English* (Studies in Linguistics, 1; Austin: Department of Linguistics, University of Texas, 1972).

Dressler, Wolfgang, *Studien zur verbalen Pluralität: Iterativum, Distributivum, Durativum, Intensivum in der allgemeinen Grammatik, im Lateinischen und Hethitischen* (Vienna: Hermann Böhlaus, 1968).

Driver, S. R., *A Treatise on the Use of the Tenses in Hebrew and Some Other Syntactical Questions*, 2nd edn. (Oxford: at the Clarendon Press, 1881).

Duțescu-Coliban, Taina, 'Towards a Definition of Aspect', *Revue roumaine de linguistique*, 26 (1981), 263–74.

Emden, Cecil, 'St. Mark's Use of the Imperfect Tense', *Exp. T.* 65 (1953–4), 146–9.

Enos, Ralph, 'The Use of the Historical Present in the Gospel According to St. Mark', *Journal of the Linguistic Association of the Southwest*, 3 (1981), 281–98.

Enslin, Morton S., 'The Perfect Tense in the Fourth Gospel', *JBL* 55 (1936), 121–31.

Erickson, Richard J., 'Oida and Ginōskō and Verbal Aspect in Pauline Usage', *Westminster Theological Journal*, 44 (1982), 110–22.

Eriksson, Karl, *Das Praesens Historicum in der nachclassischen griechischen Historiographie* (Ph.D. thesis, University of Lund; Lund: H. Ohlsson, 1943).

Fabricius-Hansen, Cathrine, *Transformative, intransformative und kursive Verben* (Linguistische Arbeiten, 26; Tübingen: Max Niemeyer, 1975).

Faddegon, B., 'The Categories of Tense; or Time, Manner of Action, and Aspect, as Expressed by the Verb', in *Donum Natalicium Schrijnen* (Nijmegen: N. V. Dekker and Van de Vegt, 1929), 116–29.

Fitzmyer, Joseph, 'The Use of *Agein* and *Pherein* in the Synoptic Gospels', in Eugene Howard Barth and Ronald Edwin Cocroft (eds.), *Festschrift to Honor F. Wilbur Gingrich* (Leiden: E. J. Brill, 1972), 147–60.

—— *The Gospel According to Luke (I–IX)* (The Anchor Bible, 28; Garden City, NY: Doubleday, 1981).

Fleischman, Suzanne, *The Future in Thought and Language: Diachronic Evidence from Romance* (Cambridge: Cambridge University Press, 1982).

Forsyth, James A., *A Grammar of Aspect: Usage and Meaning in the Russian Verb* (Cambridge: at the University Press, 1970).

Foucault, Jules-Albert de, *Recherches sur le langue et le style de Polybe* (Paris: Les Belles Lettres, 1972).

France, R. T., 'The Exegesis of Greek Tenses in the New Testament', *Notes on Translation*, 46 (1972), 3–12.

François, Jacques, 'Aktionsart, Aspekt und Zeitkonstitution', in Christoph Schwarze and Dieter Wunderlich (eds.), *Handbuch der Lexikologie* (Königstein: Athenäum, 1985), 229–49.

Friedrich, Paul, *On Aspect Theory and Homeric Aspect* (International Journal of American Linguistics, Memoir 28; Chicago: University of Chicago Press, 1974).

Fritz, Kurt von, 'The So-Called Historical Present in Early Greek', *Word*, 5 (1949), 186–201.

Fuller, Reginald H., *The Mission and Achievement of Jesus: An Examination of the Presuppositions of New Testament Theology* (London: SCM Press, 1954).

Funk, Robert W., *A Beginning–Intermediate Grammar of Hellenistic Greek*, 2nd edn., ii. *Syntax* (Missoula, Mont. Society of Biblical Literature, 1973).

Galton, Antony, *The Logic of Aspect: An Axiomatic Approach* (Oxford: Clarendon Press, 1984).

Galton, Herbert, *Aorist und Aspekt im Slavischen: Eine Studie zur funktionellen und historischen Syntax* (Wiesbaden: Harrassowitz, 1962).

—— 'A New Theory of the Slavic Verbal Aspect', *AL* 16 (1964), 133–44.

—— *The Main Functions of the Slavic Verbal Aspect* (Skopje: Macedonian Academy of Sciences and Arts, 1976).

Garey, J. B., 'Verbal Aspect in French', *Lg*. 33 (1957), 91–110.

Gildersleeve, Basil Lanneau, *Syntax of Classical Greek, from Homer to Demosthenes*, 2 vols. (New York: American Book Co., 1900–11).

—— 'Stahl's Syntax of the Greek Verb, Second Article: Tenses', *AJP* 29 (1908), 389–409.

Givón, T., *Syntax: A Functional-Typological Introduction*, i (Amsterdam and Philadelphia: John Benjamins, 1984).

Glaze, Judy, 'The Septuagintal Use of the Third Person Imperative' (MA thesis, Harding Graduate School of Religion, 1979).

Goedsche, C. R., 'Aspect versus *Aktionsart*', *JEGP* 39 (1940), 189–96.

Gonda, Jan, *The Aspectual Function of the Ṛgvedic Present and Aorist* (The Hague: Mouton, 1962).

Goodwin, William W., *Syntax of the Moods and Tenses of the Greek Verb* (Boston: Ginn and Co., 1890).

Green, Thomas Sheldon, *A Treatise on the Grammar of the New Testament*, new edn. (London: Samuel Bagster and Sons, 1862).

Guillaume, Gustave, *Temps et verbe: Théorie des aspects, des modes et des temps* (Paris: Champion, 1929; repr. by Champion, 1984).

—— *Langage et science du langage* (Quebec: Presses de l'Université Laval, 1964).

Hartman, Lars, *Testimonium Linguae* (Coniectanea Neotestamentica, 19; Lund: C. W. K. Gleerup, 1963).

Hartmann, Felix, 'Aorist und Imperfektum', *KZ* 48 (1918), 1–47; ibid. 49 (1919), 1–73.

—— 'Aorist und Imperfektum im Griechischen', *Neue Jahrbücher für das klassische Altertum*, 43 (1919), 316–39.

—— 'Zur Frage der Aspektbedeutung beim griechischen Futurum', *KZ* 62 (1934), 116–31.

Harweg, Roland, 'Aspekte als Zeitstufen und Zeitstufen als Aspekte', *Linguistics*, 181 (1976), 5–28.

Hawkins, John C., *Horae Synopticae: Contributions to the Study of the Synoptic Problem*, 2nd edn. (Oxford: Clarendon Press, 1909).

Headlam, W., 'Some Passages of Aeschylus and Others', *CR* 17 (1903), 286–95.

—— 'Greek Prohibitions', *CR* 19 (1905), 30–6.

Heath, Jeffrey, 'Aspectual "Skewing" in Two Australian Languages: Mara, Nunggubuyu', in *Tense and Aspect* (1981), 91–102.

Heidt, William, 'Translating New Testament Imperatives', *Catholic Biblical Quarterly*, 13 (1951), 253–6.

Heltoft, Lars, 'Information about Change', in *Aspectology* (1979), 141–2.

Hentze, C., 'Aktionsart und Zeitstufe der Infinitive in den Homerischen Gedichten', *IF* 22 (1907–8), 267–89.

Herbig, Gustav, 'Aktionsart und Zeitstufe: Beiträge zur Funktionslehre des indogermanischen Verbums', *IF* 6 (1896), 157–269.

Hermann, Eduard, 'Objektive und subjektive Aktionsart', *IF* 45 (1927), 207–28.

—— 'Aspekt und Aktionsart', *NGG* 5 (1933), 470–80.

—— 'Aspekt und Zeitrichtung', *IF* 54 (1936), 262–4.

—— 'Die altgriechischen Tempora: Ein strukturanalytischer Versuch', *NGG* 15 (1943), 583–649.

Hettrich, Heinrich, *Kontext und Aspekt in der altgriechischen Prosa Herodots* (Göttingen: Vandenhoeck and Ruprecht, 1976).

Hillard, A. E., *The Pastoral Epistles of St. Paul* (London: Rivingtons, 1919).

Hirtle, W. H., *The Simple and Progressive Forms: An Analytical Approach* (Quebec: Les Presses de l'Université Laval, 1967).

—— *Time, Aspect and the Verb* (Quebec: Les Presses de l'Université Laval, 1975).

Hjelmslev, Louis, *La Catégorie des cas*, pt. 1 (Acta Jutlandica, 7. 1; Copenhagen: C. A. Reitzel, 1935).

—— 'Essai d'une théorie des morphèmes', in *Actes du Quatrième Congrès International de Linguistes (1936)* (Copenhagen: Munksgaard, 1938), 140–51.

Hockett, Charles F., *A Course in Modern Linguistics* (New York: Macmillan, 1958).

Hodges, Zane C., '1 John' in *The Bible Knowledge Commentary*, New Testament edn. (Wheaton, Ill.: Victor Books, 1983), 881–904.

Hoepelman, Jakob, *Verb Classification and the Russian Verbal Aspect* (Tübingen: Gunter Narr, 1981).

Hoffmann, Ernst G., and von Siebenthal, Heinrich, *Griechische Grammatik zum Neuen Testament* (Riehen: Immanuel-Verlag, 1985).

Hofmann, Erich, 'Zu Aspekt und Aktionsart', in *Corolla Linguistica: F. Sommer Festschrift* (Wiesbaden: Otto Harrassowitz, 1955), 86–91.

Holenstein, Elmar, *Roman Jakobson's Approach to Language: Phenomenological Structuralism*, trans. by Catherine Schelbert and Tarcisius

Schelbert (Bloomington, Ind.: Indiana University Press, 1976).

Holisky, Dee Ann, 'Aspect Theory and Georgian Aspect', in *Tense and Aspect* (1981), 127–44.

Hollmann, Else, *Untersuchungen über Aspekt und Aktionsart, unter besonderer Berücksichtigung des Altenglischen* (Ph.D. thesis, University of Jena, 1935; Würzburg: Konrad Triltsch, 1937).

Holt, Jens, *Études d'aspect* (Acta Jutlandica, 15. 2; Copenhagen: Munksgaard, 1943).

Hopper, Paul J., 'Aspect and Foregrounding in Discourse', in T. Givón (ed.), *Syntax and Semantics*, xii. *Discourse and Syntax* (New York: Academic Press, 1979), 213–41.

—— 'Aspect between Discourse and Grammar: An Introductory Essay for the Volume', in *Tense-Aspect* (1982), 3–18.

—— and Thompson, Sandra A., 'Transitivity in Grammar and Discourse', *Lg.* 56 (1980), 251–99.

Hort, F. J. A., *The First Epistle of St. Peter: I. 1–II. 17* (London: Macmillan and Co., 1898).

Householder, Fred W., and Nagy, Gregory, *Greek: A Survey of Recent Work* (Janua Linguarum, Series Practica, 211; The Hague: Mouton, 1972).

Howard, W. F., 'On the Futuristic Use of the Aorist Participle in Hellenistic', *JTS* 24 (1923), 403–6.

Hultsch, Friedrich, 'Die erzählenden Zeitformen bei Polybios: Ein Beitrag zur Syntax der gemeingriechischen Sprache', *Abhandlungen der philologisch-historischen Classe der königlich Sächsischen Gesellschaft der Wissenschaften*, 13 (1893), 1–210, 347–467.

Humbert, Jean, *Syntaxe grecque*, 3rd edn. (Paris: Klincksieck, 1960).

Hunter, A. M., *Paul and his Predecessors*, new rev. edn. (London: SCM Press, 1961).

Jackson, Henry, 'Prohibitions in Greek', *CR* 18 (1904), 262–3.

Jacob, André, *Temps et langage* (Paris: Libraire Armand Colin, 1967).

Jacobsen, Wesley M., 'Lexical Aspect in Japanese', in David Testen, Veena Mishra, and Joseph Drago (eds.), *Papers from the Parasession on Lexical Semantics* (Chicago: Chicago Linguistic Society, 1984), 150–61.

Jacobsohn, Hermann, Review of J. Wackernagel, *Vorlesungen über Syntax*, in *Gnomon*, 2 (1926), 369–95.

—— 'Aspektfragen', *IF* 51 (1933), 292–318.

Jacobsthal, Hans, *Der Gebrauch der Tempora und Modi in den kretischen Dialektinschriften* (Strasburg: Trübner, 1907).

Jakobson, Roman, 'Zur Struktur des russischen Verbums', in *Charisteria Guilelmo Mathesia* (Prague: Cercle Linguistique de Prague, 1932), 74–83; repr. in Roman Jakobson, *Selected Writings*, ii. *Word and Language* (The Hague: Mouton, 1971), 3–15.

Jakobson, Roman, 'Observations sur le classement phonologiques des consonnes' (1939); repr. in Roman Jakobson, *Selected Writings*, i. *Phonological Studies* (The Hague: Mouton, 1962), 272–9.

—— *Shifters, Verbal Categories, and the Russian Verb* (Cambridge, Mass.: Harvard University Press. 1957), in Roman Jakobson, *Selected Writings*, ii *Word and Language* (The Hague: Mouton, 1971), 130–47.

—— *Main Trends in the Science of Language* (London: George Allen and Unwin, 1973).

Jespersen, Otto, *The Philosophy of Grammar* (London: George Allen and Unwin, 1924).

Jessen, M., 'A Semantic Study of Spatial and Temporal Expressions in English' (Ph.D. thesis, University of Edinburgh, 1974).

Johanson, Lars, *Aspekt im Türkischen* (Uppsala: Acta Universitatis Upsaliensis, 1971).

Johnson, Marion R., 'A Unified Temporal Theory of Tense and Aspect', in *Tense and Aspect* (1981), 145–75.

Joüon, Paul, *Grammaire de l'hébreu biblique* (Rome: Pontifical Biblical Institute, 1923).

—— *L'Évangile de Notre Seigneur Jésus-Christ: Traduction et commentaire*, 2nd edn. (Paris: G. Beauchesne, 1930).

—— 'Imparfaits de "continuation" dans la Lettre d'Aristée et dans les Évangiles', *Recherches de science religieuse*, 28 (1938), 93–6.

Kanjuparambil, Philip, 'Imperatival Participles in Romans 12: 9–21', *JBL* 102 (1983), 285–8.

Kautzsch, E., (ed.) *Gesenius' Hebrew Grammar*, trans. and rev. by A. E. Cowley, 2nd English edn. (Oxford: at the Clarendon Press, 1910).

Kelly, J. N. D., *A Commentary on the Epistles of Peter and of Jude* (London: Adam and Charles Black, 1969).

Kenny, Anthony, *Action, Emotion and Will* (London: Routledge and Kegan Paul, 1963).

Kieckers, E., 'Zum Gebrauch des Imperativus Aoristi und Praesentis', *IF* 24 (1909), 10–17.

Kilpatrick, G. D., 'The Historic Present in the Gospels and Acts', *ZNW* 68 (1977), 258–62.

Kiparsky, Paul, 'Tense and Mood in Indo-European Syntax', *FL* 4 (1968), 30–57.

Klein, Horst G., *Tempus, Aspekt, Aktionsart* (Tübingen: Max Niemeyer, 1974).

Klose, Albrecht, *Der Indikativ des Präsens bei Homer, Herodot, und Thukydides* (Ph.D. thesis, University of Erlangen-Nuremberg; Regensburg: Haas, 1968).

Kobliska, A., *Über das Verhältnis des Aorists zu den Formen des čechischen Verbums* (Königgräz, 1851).

Koller, Hermann, 'Praesens historicum und erzählendes Imperfekt: Beitrag zur Aktionsart der Praesensstammzeiten im Lateinischen und Griechischen', *Museum Helveticum*, 8 (1951), 63–99.

Koschmieder, Erwin, 'Studien zum slavischen Verbalaspekt', *KZ* 55 (1927), 280–304; ibid. 56 (1928), 78–95.

—— *Zeitbezug und Sprache: Ein Beitrag zur Aspekt- und Tempusfrage* (Leipzig: B. G. Teubner, 1929).

—— 'Durchkreuzung von Aspekt- und Tempus-System im Präsens', *Zeitschrift für slavische Philologie*, 7 (1930), 341–58.

—— 'Zu den Grundfragen der Aspekttheorie', *IF* 53 (1935), 280–300.

—— 'Aspekt und Zeit', in M. Braun and E. Koschmieder (eds.), *Slawistische Studien zum V. Internationalen Slawistenkongreß in Sofia 1963* (Göttingen: Vandenhoeck and Ruprecht, 1963), 1–22.

Kretschmer, P., 'Literaturbericht für das Jahr 1909', *Glotta*, 3 (1912), 340–3.

Kubo, Sakae, 'I John 3: 9: Absolute or Habitual?', *Andrews University Seminary Studies*, 7 (1969), 47–56.

Kuehne, C., 'Keeping the Aorist in its Place', *Journal of Theology*, 16 (1976), 2–10.

—— 'The Viewpoint of the Aorist', *Journal of Theology*, 18 (1978), 2–10.

—— 'Translating the Aorist Indicative', *Journal of Theology*, 18 (1978), 19–26.

Kühner, Raphael, and Gerth, Bernhard, *Ausführliche Grammatik der griechischen Sprache*, pt. 2. *Satzlehre*, i, 3rd edn. (1898; repr. edn. Hannover: Verlag Hahnsche Buchhandlung, 1976).

Lancellotti, Angelo, *Sintassi ebraica nel greco dell'Apocalisse*, i. *Uso delle forme verbali* (Collectio Assisiensis, 1; Assisi: Porziuncola, 1964).

Lawler, John, 'Generic to a Fault', in *Papers from the Eighth Regional*

Meeting, Chicago Linguistics Society (Chicago: Chicago Linguistics Society, 1972), 247–58.

Lee, G. M., 'The Aorist Participle of Subsequent Action (Acts 16, 6)?', *Biblica*, 50 (1970), 235–6.

Leech, Geoffrey N., *Meaning and the English Verb* (London: Longman, 1971).

Lehmann, Winfred P., *Descriptive Linguistics: An Introduction* (New York: Random House, 1972).

Leinonen, Marja, 'Specificness and Non-Specificness in Russian Aspect', in *Aspectology* (1979), 35–50.

Lepschy, Giulio C., *A Survey of Structural Linguistics* (London: Faber and Faber, 1970).

Levin, Saul, 'Remarks on the "Historical" Present and Comparable Phenomena of Syntax', *FL* 5 (1969), 386–90.

Levinsohn, Stephen H., 'Preliminary Observations on the Use of the Historical Present in Mark', *Notes on Translation*, 65 (1977), 13–28.

Lilja, Saara, *On the Style of the Earliest Greek Prose* (Helsinki: Societas Scientiarum Fennica, 1968).

Lindroth, Hjalmar, 'Zur Lehre von den Aktionsarten', *BGDSL* 31 (1905), 239–60.

Lloyd, Albert L., *Anatomy of the Verb: The Gothic Verb as a Model for a Unified Theory of Aspect, Actional Types, and Verbal Velocity* (Amsterdam: John Benjamins, 1979).

Louw, Johannes P., 'Prohibitions in the Greek New Testament: A Study of the Construction of μή with the Present Imperative and the Aorist Subjunctive' (D.Litt. thesis, University of Pretoria, 1958).

—— 'On Greek Prohibitions', *Acta Classica*, 2 (1959), 43–57.

—— 'Die semantiese waarde van die perfektum in hellenistiese grieks', *Acta Classica*, 10 (1967), 23–32.

—— 'Verbal Aspect in the First Letter of John', *Neotestamentica* 9 (1975), 87–97.

—— and Nida, Eugene A. (eds.), *Greek–English Lexicon of the New Testament Based on Semantic Domains*, 2 vols. (New York: United Bible Societies, 1988).

Lyons, John, *Introduction to Theoretical Linguistics* (Cambridge: at the University Press, 1968).

—— *Semantics* (Cambridge: Cambridge University Press, 1977).

Macauley, Ronald Kerr Steven, 'Aspect in English' (Ph.D. dissertation, University of California at Los Angeles, 1971).

McCoard, Robert W., *The English Perfect: Tense Choice and Pragmatic Inferences* (Amsterdam: North-Holland, 1978).

McFall, Leslie, *The Enigma of the Hebrew Verbal System: Solutions from Ewald to the Present Day* (Sheffield: Almond Press, 1982).

McKay, K. L. 'The Use of the Ancient Greek Perfect Down to the Second Century A.D.', *BICS* 12 (1965), 1–21.

—— 'Syntax in Exegesis', *Tyndale Bulletin*, 23 (1972), 39–57.

—— 'Further Remarks on the "Historical" Present and Other Phenomena', *FL* 11 (1974), 247–51.

—— *Greek Grammar for Students: A Concise Grammar of Classical Attic with Special Reference to Aspect in the Verb* (Canberra: Department of Classics, the Australian National University, 1974).

—— 'On the Perfect and Other Aspects in the Greek Non-Literary Papyri', *BICS* 27 (1980), 23–49.

—— 'On the Perfect and Other Aspects in New Testament Greek', *Nov. T.* 23 (1981), 289–329.

—— 'Repeated Action, the Potential and Reality in Ancient Greek', *Antichthon*, 15 (1981), 36–46.

—— 'Aspect in Imperatival Constructions in New Testament Greek', *Nov. T.* 27 (1985), 201–26.

—— 'Aspects of the Imperative in Ancient Greek', *Antichthon*, 20 (1986), 41–58.

MacLennan, L. Jenaro, *El problema del aspecto verbal* (Madrid: Editorial Gredos, 1962).

McWhorter, Ashton Waugh, 'A Study of the So-Called Deliberative Type of Question (τί ποιήσω;)', *Transactions and Proceedings of the American Philological Association*, 41 (1910), 157–67.

Maddox, Randy L., 'The Use of the Aorist Tense in Holiness Exegesis', *Wesleyan Theological Journal*, 16 (1981), 106–18.

Mahlow, G., Über den Futurgebrauch griechischer Praesentia', *KZ* 26 [NF 6] (1883), 570–603.

Majawicz, Alfred F., 'Understanding Aspect', *Lingua Posnaniensis*, 24 (1982), 29–61; ibid. 25 (1983), 17–40.

Mandilaras, Basil G., *Studies in the Greek Language* (Athens: Hellenic Ministry of Culture and Sciences, 1972).

—— *The Verb in the Greek Non-Literary Papyri* (Athens: Hellenic Ministry of Culture and Sciences, 1973).

Mantey, J. R., 'The Mistranslation of the Perfect Tense in John 20: 23, Matthew 16: 19, and Matthew 18: 18', *JBL* 48 (1939), 243–9.

Marshall, I. Howard, *The Gospel of Luke: A Commentary on the Greek Text* (Exeter: Paternoster Press, 1978).

Martin, Robert, *Temps et aspect: Essai sur l'emploi des temps narratifs en moyen français* (Paris: Klincksieck, 1971).

Martin, William J., 'I Corinthians 11: 2–16: An Interpretation', in W. Ward Gascque and Ralph P. Martin (eds.), *Apostolic History and the Gospel* (Grand Rapids: Wm. B. Eerdmans, 1970), 231–41.

Maslov, Yurij S., 'An Outline of Contrastive Aspectology', in id. (ed.) *Contrastive Studies in Verbal Aspect*, trans. and annotated by James Forsyth in collaboration with Josephine Forsyth (Heidelberg: Julius Groos, 1985), 1–44.

Masterman, J. Howard B., *The First Epistle of S. Peter (Greek Text)* (London: Macmillan and Co., 1900).

Mateos, Juan, *El aspecto verbal en el nuevo testamento* (Estudios de nuevo testamento, 1; Madrid: Ediciones Cristiandad, 1977).

Mayor, Joseph B., *The Epistle of St. Jude and the Second Epistle of St. Peter* (London: Macmillan and Co., 1907).

—— *The Epistle of St. James*, 3rd edn., with *Further Studies in the Epistle of St. James* (London: Macmillan and Co., 1913).

Mayser, Edwin, *Grammatik der griechischen Papyri aus der Ptolemäerzeit*, ii. *Satzlehre*, pt. 1 (Berlin: Walter de Gruyter and Co., 1926).

Mazon, André, 'La notion morphologique de l'aspect des verbes chez les grammariens russes', in *Mélanges offerts à Émile Picot*, 2 vols. (Paris: E. Rahir, 1913), i. 343–67.

Meecham, H. G., 'The Use of the Participle for the Imperative in the New Testament', *Exp. T.* 58 (1947), 207–8.

Meltzer, Hans, 'Vermeintliche Perfectivierung durch präpositionale Zusammensetzung im Griechischen', *IF* 12 (1901), 319–71.

—— 'Zur Lehre von den Aktionen bes. im Griechischen', *IF* 17 (1904–5), 187–277.

Mettinger, Tryggve N. D., 'The Hebrew Verb System: A Survey of Recent Research', *Annual of the Swedish Theological Institute*, 9 (1973), 65–84.

Miller, C. W. E., 'The Imperfect and the Aorist in Greek', *AJP* 16 (1895), 141–85.

Mitchell, T. F., 'The English Appearance of Aspect', in D. J. Allerton, Edward Carney, and David Holdcroft (eds.), *Function and Context in Linguistic Analysis: A Festschrift for William Haas* (Cambridge: Cambridge University Press, 1979), 159–84.

Moffatt, James, *The General Epistles* (Moffatt New Testament Commentary; London: Hodder and Stoughton, 1929).

Moorhouse, A. C., *The Syntax of Sophocles* (Leiden: E. J. Brill, 1982).

Moule, C. F. D., 'The Nature and Purpose of 1 Peter', *NTS* 3 (1956–7), 1–11.

—— *An Idiom Book of New Testament Greek*, 2nd edn. (Cambridge: at the University Press, 1959).

Moulton, James Hope, *A Grammar of New Testament Greek*, i. *Prolegomena*, 3rd edn. (Edinburgh: T. and T. Clark, 1908).

—— *A Grammar of New Testament Greek*, ii. *Accidence and Word Formation*, by Wilbert Francis Howard (Edinburgh: T. and T. Clark, 1929).

—— *A Grammar of New Testament Greek*, iii. *Syntax*, by Nigel Turner (Edinburgh: T. and T. Clark, 1963).

—— *A Grammar of New Testament Greek*, iv. *Style*, by Nigel Turner (Edinburgh: T. and T. Clark, 1976).

Mourelatos, A. P. D., 'Events, Processes, and States', *Linguistics and Philosophy*, 2 (1978), 415–34; repr. *Tense and Aspect* (1981), 191–212.

Mozley, F. W., 'Notes on the Biblical Use of the Present and Aorist Imperative', *JTS* 4 (1903), 279–82.

Mussies, G., *The Morphology of Koine Greek as Used in the Apocalypse of John: A Study in Bilingualism* (Leiden: E. J. Brill, 1971).

Mutzbauer, Carl, *Die Grundlagen der griechischen Tempuslehre und der homerische Tempusgebrauch* (Strasburg: Karl J. Trübner, 1893).

Naylor, H. Darnley, 'Prohibitions in Greek', *CR* 19 (1905), 26–30.

—— 'More Prohibitions in Greek', *CR* 20 (1906), 348.

Newton, Brian, 'Habitual Aspect in Ancient and Modern Greek', *Byzantine and Modern Greek Studies*, 5 (1979), 29–41.

Nordenfelt, Lennart, *Events, Actions, and Ordinary Language* (Lund: Doxa, 1977).

Nunn, H. P. V., *A Short Syntax of New Testament Greek*, 5th edn. (Cambridge: at the University Press, 1938).

O'Rourke, John J., 'The Historical Present in the Gospel of John', *JBL* 93 (1974), 585–90.

Osburn, Carroll D., 'The Present Indicative in Matthew 19: 9', *Restoration Quarterly*, 24 (1981), 193–203.

—— 'The Historical Present in Mark as a Text Critical Criterion', *Biblica*, 64 (1983), 486–500.

Østergaard, Frede, 'The Progressive Aspect in Danish', in *Aspect-*

ology (1979), 89–109.

Ottley, R. R., *The Book of Isaiah According to the Septuagint (Codex Alexandrinus)*, i. *Introduction and Translation*, 2nd edn. (Cambridge: at the University Press, 1909).

Palm, Jonas, *Über Sprache und Stil des Diodorus von Sizilien* (Lund: C. W. K. Gleerup, 1955).

Partridge, John Geoffrey, *Semantic, Pragmatic and Syntactic Correlates: An Analysis of Performative Verbs based on English Data* (Tübingen: Gunter Narr, 1982).

Pedersen, Holger, 'Vorschlag', *IF: Anzeiger*, 12 (1901), 152–3.

—— 'Zur Lehre von den Aktionsarten', *KZ* 37 (1904), 219–50.

Peppler, C. W., 'Durative and Aoristic', *AJP* 54 (1933), 47–53.

Perdelwitz, R., *Die Mysterienreligion und das Problem des ersten Petrusbriefes* (Gießen: Alfred Töpelmann, 1911).

Pernot, Hubert, *Études sur la langue des Évangiles* (Paris: Les Belles Lettres, 1927).

Pinkster, H., *On Latin Adverbs* (Amsterdam: North-Holland, 1972).

Pistorius, P. V., 'Some Remarks on the Aorist Aspect in the Greek New Testament', *Acta Classica*, 10 (1967), 33–9.

Platzack, Christer, *The Semantic Interpretation of Aspect and Aktionsarten: A Study of Internal Time Reference in Swedish* (Dordrecht: Foris Publications, 1979).

Plummer, A., *A Critical and Exegetical Commentary on the Gospel According to S. Luke*, 4th edn. (ICC; Edinburgh: T. and T. Clark, 1904).

Porzig, Walter, 'Zur Aktionsart indogermanischer Präsensbildungen', *IF* 45 (1927), 152–67.

Post, L. A., 'Dramatic Uses of the Greek Imperative', *AJP* 59 (1938), 31–59.

Potts, Timothy C., 'States Activities and Performances, I', *Proceedings of the Aristotelian Society*, supp. vol. 39 (1965), 65–84.

Poutsma, A., *Over de tempora van de imperativus en de conjunctivus hortativus-prohibitivus in het grieks* (Amsterdam: Uitgave van de Koninklijke Akademie van Wetenschappen, 1928).

Purdie, Eleanor, 'The Perfective "Aktionsart" in Polybius', *IF* 9 (1898), 63–153.

Rabin, Ch., 'Hebrew and Aramaic in the First Century', in S. Safrai and M. Stern (eds.), *Compendia Rerum Iudaicarum ad Novum Testamentum*, Sect. 1, vol. ii. *The Jewish People in the First Century* (Philadelphia: Fortress Press, 1976), 1007–39.

Radermacher, Ludwig, *Neutestamentliche Grammatik: Das Griechisch des Neuen Testaments im Zusammenhang mit der Volkssprache*, 2nd edn. (Tübingen: J. C. B. Mohr, 1925).

Raith, Josef, 'Aktionsart und Aspekt', in *Probleme der englischen Grammatik* (Munich: Manz, 1969) 45–53; repr. in Alfred Schopf (ed.), *Der englische Aspekt* (Darmstadt: Wissenschaftliche Buchgesellschaft, 1974), 61–73.

Regard, Paul F., *La Phrase nominale dans la langue du Nouveau Testament* (Paris: Ernest Leroux, 1919).

Reichenbach, Hans, *Elements of Symbolic Logic* (New York: Macmillan, 1947).

Renicke, Horst, 'Die Theorie der Aspekte und Aktionsarten', *BGDSL* 72 (1950), 150–93.

Rescher, Nicholas, *The Logic of Commands* (London: Routledge and Kegan Paul, 1966).

Reynolds, Stephen M., 'The Zero Tense in Greek: A Critical Note', *Westminster Theological Journal*, 33 (1969) 68–72.

Riemann, Othon, 'La question de l'aoriste grec', in *Mélanges Graux: Recueil de travaux d'érudition classique* (Paris: Librairie du Collège de France, 1884), 585–99.

Rijksbaron, A., 'Review of H. Hettrich, *Kontext und Aspekt in der altgriechischen Prosa Herodots*', in *Lingua*, 48 (1979), 223–57.

—— *The Syntax and Semantics of the Verb in Classical Greek: an Introduction* (Amsterdam: J. C. Gieben, 1984).

Robertson, A. T., *A Grammar of the Greek New Testament in the Light of Historical Research* (Nashville, Tenn.: Broadman Press, 1914).

Robins, R. H., *A Short History of Linguistics*, 2nd edn. (London: Longman, 1979).

Robison, Henry B., *Syntax of the Participle in the Apostolic Fathers* (Chicago: University of Chicago Press, 1913).

Rodemeyer, Karl Theodor, *Das Präsens historicum bei Herodot und Thukydides* (Basle: Werner Riehm, 1889).

Rodenbusch, E., 'Beiträge zur Geschichte der griechischen Aktionsarten', *IF* 21 (1907), 116–45.

—— 'Praesensstamm und Perfektive Aktionsart', *IF* 22 (1908), 402–8.

—— 'Präsentia in perfektischer Bedeutung', *IF* 28 (1911), 252–85.

Rogers, Cleon L., 'The Great Commission', *Bibliotheca Sacra*, 130 (1973), 258–67.

Rose, Jesse L., *The Durative and Aoristic Tenses in Thucydides* (Language

Dissertation 35, suppl. to *Lg.*; (Baltimore: Linguistic Society of America, 1942).

Rost, V. C. F., *Griechische Grammatik*, 3rd edn. (Göttingen: Vandenhoeck und Ruprecht, 1826).

Ruijgh, C. J., *Autour de 'τε épique': Études sur la syntaxe grecque* (Amsterdam: Adolf M. Hakkert, 1971).

—— 'L'emploi "inceptif" du thème du présent du verbe grec: Esquisse d'une théorie de valeurs temporelles des thèmes temporels', *Mnemosyne*, 4th ser. 38 (1985), 1–61.

Ruipérez, Martín Sánchez, 'The Neutralization of Morphological Oppositions as Illustrated by the Neutral Aspect of the Present Indicative in Classical Greek', *Word*, 9 (1953), 241–52.

—— *Estructura del sistema de aspectos y tiempos del verbo griego antiguo: Análisis funcional sincrónico* (Salamanca: Consejo Superior de Investigaciones Científicas, 1954); French trans: *Structure du système des temps du verbe en grec ancien*, trans. M. Menet and P. Serça (Paris: Les Belles Lettres, 1982).

Rundgren, Frithiof, *Das althebräische Verbum: Abriß der Aspektlehre* (Stockholm: Almqvist and Wiksell, 1961).

Ružić, Rajko Hariton, *The Aspects of the Verb in Serbo-Croatian* (Univ. of California Publications in Modern Philology, 25. 2; Berkeley: University of California Press, 1943).

Rydbeck, Lars, 'Bemerkungen zu Periphrasen mit εἶναι und Präsens Partizip bei Herodot und in der Koine', *Glotta*, 47 (1969), 186–200.

—— 'What Happened to New Testament Greek Grammar after Albert Debrunner?', *NTS* 21 (1975), 424–7.

Ryle, Gilbert, *The Concept of Mind* (London: Hutchinson and Co., 1949).

Salom, A. P., 'The Imperatival Use of the Participle in the New Testament', *Australian Biblical Review*, 11 (1963), 41–9.

Sanders, E. P., *The Tendencies of the Synoptic Tradition* (Cambridge: at the University Press, 1969).

Saussure, Ferdinand de, *Course in General Linguistics*, ed. Charles Bally and Albert Sechehaye in collaboration with Albert Reidlinger, trans. by Wade Baskin, rev. edn. (London: Peter Owen, 1974).

Schenk, Wolfgang, 'Das Präsens historicum als makrosyntaktisches Gliederungssignal im Matthäusevangelium', *NTS* 22 (1976), 464–75.

Schlachter, L., 'Statistische Untersuchungen über den Gebrauch der Tempora und Modi bei einzelnen griechischen Schriftstellern', *IF* 22 (1907), 202–42; ibid. 23 (1908), 165–204; ibid. 24 (1909), 189–21.

Schlachter, Wolfgang, 'Der Verbalaspekt als grammatische Kategorie', *Münchener Studien zur Sprachwissenschaft*, 13 (1959), 22–78; repr. in Björn Collinder, Hans Fromm, and Gerhard Ganschow (eds.), *Arbeiten zur strukturbezogenen Grammatik* (Munich: Wilhelm Fink, 1968), 150–86.

Schwyzer, Eduard, *Griechische Grammatik*, ii. *Syntax und syntaktische Stilistik*, ed. Albert Debrunner (Munich: C. H. Beck, 1950).

Seaton, R. C., 'Prohibition in Greek', *CR* 20 (1906), 438.

Sedgwick, W. B., 'Some Uses of the Imperfect in Greek', *CQ* 34 (1940), 118–22.

—— 'The Use of the Imperfect in Herodotus', *CQ*, NS 7 (1957), 113–17.

Segal, M. H., *A Grammar of Mishnaic Hebrew* (Oxford: at the Clarendon Press, 1927).

Seidel, Eugen, 'Zu den Funktionen des Verbalaspekts', *Travaux du Cercle Linguistique de Prague*, 6 (1936), 111–29.

Seiler, Hansjakob, *L'Aspect et le temps dans le verbe neo-grec* (Paris: Les Belles Lettres, 1952).

—— 'Zur Problematik des Verbalaspekts', *Cahiers Ferdinand de Saussure*, 26 (1969), 119–35.

Selwyn, Edward Gordon, *The First Epistle of St. Peter* (London: Macmillan and Co., 1946).

Sharp, Douglas S., *Epictetus and the New Testament* (London: Charles H. Kelly, 1914).

Shive, Ronald Lowell, 'The Use of the Historical Present and its Theological Significance' (Th.M. thesis, Dallas Theological Seminary, 1982).

Silva, Moisés, 'Bilingualism and the Character of Palestinian Greek', *Biblica*, 61 (1980), 198–219.

Sloat, Leslie W., 'New Testament Verb Forms', in John H. Skilton (ed.), *The New Testament Student at Work* (Nutley, NJ: Presbyterian and Reformed Publishing Co., 1975), 204–12.

Smith, Carlota S., 'A Theory of Aspectual Choice', *Lg.* 59 (1983), 479–501.

Smith, Charles R., 'Errant Aorist Interpreters', *Grace Theological Journal*, 2 (1980), 205–26.

Smyth, Herbert Weir, *Greek Grammar* (1910), rev. by Gordon M. Messing (Cambridge, Mass.: Harvard University Press, 1956).

Sørensen, H. M., 'Om definitionerne af verbets aspekter', in *Im Memoriam Kr. Sandfeld* (Copenhagen: Gyldendalske Boghandel Nordisk Forlag, 1943), 221–33.

Spicq, Ceslas, *Les Épîtres de Saint Pierre* (Sources Bibliques; Paris: Lecoffre, 1966).

Stagg, Frank, 'The Abused Aorist', *JBL* 91 (1972), 222–31.

Stahl, J. M., *Kritisch-historische Syntax des griechischen Verbums der klassischen Zeit* (Heidelberg: Carl Winter, 1907).

Stevenson, W. B., *Grammar of Palestinian Jewish Aramaic*, 2nd edn., with an Appendix on the Numerals by J. A. Emerton (Oxford: at the Clarendon Press, 1962).

Steyer, Gottfried, *Handbuch für das Studium des neutestamentlichen Griechisch*, ii. *Satzlehre* (Berlin: Evangelische Verlagsanstalt, 1968).

Stiebitz, F., 'Aspekt und Aktionsart', *Listy filologicke*, 55 (1928), 1–13.

Stork, Peter, *The Aspectual Usage of the Dynamic Infinitive in Herodotus* (Groningen: Bouma, 1982).

Stott, John R. W., *The Epistles of John* (Grand Rapids, Mich.: Wm. B. Eerdmans, 1964).

Strack, Hermann L., *Grammatik des Biblisch-Aramäischen*, 6th edn. (Munich: C. H. Beck, 1921).

Streeter, B. H., *The Primitive Church* (London: Macmillan and Co., 1929).

Streitberg, Wilhelm, 'Perfective und imperfective Actionsart im Germanischen', *BGDSL* 15 (1889), 70–177.

—— *Urgermanische Grammatik* (Heidelberg: Carl Winter, 1896).

Svensson, Arvid, *Zum Gebrauch der erzählenden Tempora im Griechischen* (Ph.D. thesis, University of Lund; Lund: H. Ohlsson. 1930).

Swete, Henry Barclay, *The Gospel According to St. Mark*, 3rd edn. (London: Macmillan and Co., 1909).

Synge, F. C., 'A Matter of Tenses: Fingerprints of an Annotator in Mark', *Exp. T.* 88 (1976), 168–71.

Szemerényi, Oswald, 'Review Article: Unorthodox Views of Tense and Aspect', *AL* 17 (1965), 161–71.

—— *Einführung in die vergleichende Sprachwissenschaft* (Darmstadt: Wissenschaftliche Buchgesellschaft, 1970).

Tabachovitz, David, *Die Septuaginta und das neue Testament: Stilstudien* (Lund: C. W. K. Gleerup, 1956).

Taylor, Barry, 'Tense and Continuity', *Linguistics and Philosophy*, 1 (1977), 199–220.

Taylor, C. C. W., 'States, Activities and Performances, II', *Proceedings of the Aristotelian Society*, Supp. vol. 39 (1965), 85–102.

Taylor, Vincent, *The Gospel According to St. Mark*, 2nd edn. (London: Macmillan and Co., 1966).

Tense and Aspect, vol. xiv of Philip J. Tedeschi and Annie Zaenen (eds.), *Syntax and Semantics* (New York: Academic Press, 1981).

Tense-Aspect: Between Semantics and Pragmatics, ed. Paul J. Hopper (Amsterdam and Philadelphia: John Benjamins, 1982).

Thacker, T. W., 'Compound Tenses Containing the Verb "Be" in Semitic and Egyptian', in D. Winton Thomas and W. D. McHardy (eds.), *Hebrew and Semitic Studies Presented to Godfrey Rolles Driver* (Oxford: at the Clarendon Press, 1963), 156–7.

Thackeray, Henry St. John, *The Septuagint and Jewish Worship: A Study in Origins*, 2nd edn. (The Schweich Lectures 1920; London: Oxford University Press, 1923).

Thelin, Nils B., *Towards a Theory of Aspect, Tense and Actionality in Slavic* (Uppsala: Acta Universitatis Upsaliensis, 1978).

Thomas, Werner, *Historisches Präsens oder Konjunktionsreduktion? Zum Problem des Tempuswechsels in der Erzählung* (Wiesbaden: Franz Steiner, 1974).

Thompson, Steven, *The Apocalypse and Semitic Syntax* (Cambridge: Cambridge University Press, 1985).

Thrall, Margaret E., *Greek Particles in the New Testament: Linguistic and Exegetical Studies* (Grand Rapids: Wm. B. Eerdmans, 1962).

Thurot, C., 'Observations sur la signification des radicaux temporaux en grec', *Mélanges de la Société de Linguistique de Paris*, 1 (1898), 111–25.

Timberlake, Alan, 'Invariance and the Syntax of Russian Aspect', in *Tense-Aspect* (1982), 305–31.

Tomlinson, Alan, 'The Relationship between between Aspect and Lexical Aspectual Meaning' (Th.M. thesis, Dallas Theological Seminary, 1979).

Turner, C. H., 'Marcan Usage: Notes, Critical and Exegetical, on the Second Gospel', *JTS* 29 (1927–8), 275–89.

—— *The Gospel According to St. Mark: Introduction and Commentary*; C. Gore, H. L. Goudge, and A. Guillaume (eds.), *A New Commentary on Holy Scripture* (London: SPCK, 1931).

Turner, Nigel, *Grammatical Insights into the Greek New Testament* (Edinburgh: T. and T. Clark, 1965).

Trubetzkoy, N. S., 'Die phonologischen Systeme', *Travaux du Cercle Linguistique de Prague*, 4 (1931), 96–116.

—— *Grundzüge der Phonologie* (Prague: Cercle Linguistique de Prague, 1939).

Vendler, Zeno, 'Verbs and Times', *Philosophical Review*, 66 (1957), 43–60; repr. in id., *Linguistics in Philosophy* (Ithaca, NY: Cornell University Press, 1967), 97–121.

Verkuyl, H. J., *On the Compositional Nature of the Aspects* (FL Supplementary Series, 15; Dordrecht: D. Reidel Publishing Co., 1972).

Votaw, Clyde W., *The Use of the Infinitive in Biblical Greek* (Chicago: published by the author, 1896).

Wackernagel, Jakob, 'Studien zum griechischen Perfectum', *Programm zur akademischen Preisverteilung* (1904), 3–24; repr. in *Kleine Schriften* (Göttingen: Vandenhoeck and Ruprecht, [1953]), 1000–21.

—— *Vorlesungen über Syntax*, 2nd edn., 2 vols. (Basle: Emil Birkhäuser, 1926).

Wallace, Stephen, 'Figure and Ground: The Interrelationships of Linguistic Categories', in *Tense-Aspect* (1982), 201–23.

Waugh, Linda R., *Roman Jakobson's Science of Language* (Lisse: Peter de Ridder Press, 1976).

—— and Monville-Burston, Monique, 'Aspect and Discourse Function: The French Simple Past in Newspaper Usage', *Lg*. 62 (1986), 846–77.

Webster, William, *The Syntax and Synonyms of the Greek Testament* (London: Rivingtons, 1864).

Weinrich, Harald, *Tempus: Besprochene und Erzählte Welt* (Stuttgart: Kohlhammer, 1964).

—— 'Tense and Time', *AL* NS 1 (1970), 31–41.

Wellhausen, J., *Einleitung in die drei ersten Evangelien* (Berlin: Georg Reimer, 1905).

Wijk, N. Van, '"Aspect" en "aktionsart"', *Die nieuwe taalgids*, 22 (1929) 225–39.

Wilcox, Max, *The Semitisms of Acts* (Oxford: at the Clarendon Press, 1965).

Wilder, A. N., 'The First, Second, and Third Epistles of John', *The Interpreter's Bible* (New York: Abingdon, 1957).

Williams, Charles Bray, *The Participle in the Book of Acts* (Chicago: University of Chicago Press, 1909).

Williams, Philip R., *Grammar Notes on the Noun and the Verb and Certain Other Items*, rev. (Tacoma: Northwest Baptist Seminary Press, 1976).

Williams, Ronald J., *Hebrew Syntax: An Outline*, 2nd edn. (Toronto: University of Toronto Press, 1976).

Windfuhr, Gernot L., 'A Spatial Model for Tense, Aspect, and Mood', *Folia Linguistica*, 19 (1985), 415–61.

Windisch, H., *Die katholischen Briefe*, 2nd edn. (Tübingen: J. C. B. Mohr, 1930).

Winer, G. B., *Grammatik des neutestamentlichen Sprachidioms*, 2nd edn. (Leipzig: F. C. W. Vogel, 1825).

—— *Grammatik des neutestamentlichen Sprachidioms*, 7th edn., ed. Gottlieb Lünemann (Leipzig: F. C. W. Vogel, 1867).

—— *A Treatise on the Grammar of New Testament Greek*, trans. with additions, by W. F. Moulton, 3rd edn. (Edinburgh: T. and T. Clark, 1882).

Wolfson, Nessa, 'The Conversational Historical Present Alternation', *Lg.* 55 (1979), 168–82.

Worthington, M. G., 'In Search of Linguistic Time', *Romance Philology*, 22 (1969), 515–30.

Zerwick, Maximilian, *Biblical Greek: Illustrated by Examples*, trans. and adapted by Joseph Smith (Rome: Scripta Pontificii Instituti Biblici, 1963).

Zuber, Beat, *Das Tempussystem des biblischen Hebräisch: Eine Untersuchung am Text* (Beiheft zur *ZAW* 164; Berlin: Walter de Gruyter, 1986).

Zydatiß, Wolfgang, ' "Continuative" and "Resultative" Perfects in English?', *Lingua*, 44 (1978), 339–62.

INDEX OF BIBLICAL PASSAGES

Matt. 1: 19   395
Matt. 1: 20   337
Matt. 1: 22   394
Matt. 1: 23   312
Matt. 2: 4   224
Matt. 2: 8   386
Matt. 2: 11   415
Matt. 2: 13   239, 366
Matt. 2: 15   394
Matt. 2: 16   262
Matt. 2: 18   178
Matt. 2: 20   160, 294,
   342, 410
Matt. 3: 1   239
Matt. 3: 4–6   247
Matt. 3: 7   247
Matt. 3: 8   153, 369
Matt. 3: 10   210
Matt. 3: 13   239
Matt. 3: 14   99, 165
Matt. 3: 14–15   250
Matt. 3: 16   409
Matt. 3: 17   278
Matt. 4: 2   410, 415
Matt. 4: 4   294
Matt. 4: 5   239
Matt. 4: 6, 7   294
Matt. 4: 8   239
Matt. 4: 11   192, 253
Matt. 4: 14   394
Matt. 5: 10   417
Matt. 5: 17   337, 394
Matt. 5: 19   403
Matt. 5: 23   391
Matt. 5: 28   270
Matt. 5: 31   354
Matt. 5: 32   411
Matt. 5: 34   385
Matt. 5: 34–6   382

Matt. 5: 42   355, 356,
   411
Matt. 5: 46–7   403
Matt. 6: 2   240
Matt. 6: 3   352
Matt. 6: 5   240
Matt. 6: 9   333
Matt. 6: 9–13   382
Matt. 6: 10   345
Matt. 6: 11   356, 382
Matt. 6: 12   281
Matt. 6: 16   240
Matt. 6: 24   209, 216
Matt. 6: 25   367
Matt. 6: 26   210
Matt. 6: 28–30   210
Matt. 6: 34   367
Matt. 7: 5   395
Matt. 7: 6   355
Matt. 7: 7   333
Matt. 7: 8   183, 209, 216
Matt. 7: 12   333
Matt. 7: 14   411
Matt. 7: 17   183, 209,
   216, 217
Matt. 7: 24   169
Matt. 7: 25   307
Matt. 7: 26   169
Matt. 7: 27   162, 257
Matt. 7: 29   315
Matt. 8: 2   394
Matt. 8: 3   257
Matt. 8: 6   113, 162, 294
Matt. 8: 9   342, 345
Matt. 8: 13   290
Matt. 8: 15   146
Matt. 8: 20   210
Matt. 8: 24   165, 244
Matt. 8: 25   158, 167

Matt. 8: 31   285
Matt. 8: 34   384
Matt. 9: 2   350
Matt. 9: 2, 5   189, 203
Matt. 9: 5   344
Matt. 9: 5–6   349
Matt. 9: 11   146
Matt. 9: 18   260
Matt. 9: 20   413
Matt. 9: 22   119, 173,
   350
Matt. 9: 30   338, 352
Matt. 9: 36   162
Matt. 10: 6   342, 418
Matt. 10: 8   355
Matt. 10: 11   367
Matt. 10: 12   357
Matt. 10: 13   345
Matt. 10: 22   317, 318
Matt. 10: 23   333
Matt. 10: 25   281
Matt. 10: 27   351
Matt. 10: 40   183, 209,
   216
Matt. 11: 15   365
Matt. 11: 16   123
Matt. 12: 1   91, 147,
   171, 258
Matt. 12: 7   309
Matt. 12: 17   394
Matt. 12: 26   269
Matt. 12: 32   403
Matt. 12: 35   182, 209,
   216
Matt. 12: 44   418
Matt. 12: 46   308
Matt. 12: 49   290
Matt. 13: 2   308
Matt. 13: 3   192

Matt. 13: 9   365
Matt. 13: 22   411
Matt. 13: 24   268, 280
Matt. 13: 30   334
Matt. 13: 43   365
Matt. 13: 44   239
Matt. 13: 46   159, 300,
   302
Matt. 13: 52   290
Matt. 14: 9   414
Matt. 14: 18   347
Matt. 14: 27   350
Matt. 14: 29   345
Matt. 14: 31   281
Matt. 14: 36   285
Matt. 15: 11   182, 209,
   216
Matt. 15: 18   182, 209,
   216
Matt. 15: 27   147
Matt. 15: 28   173
Matt. 15: 29   171
Matt. 16: 19   322
Matt. 16: 28   417
Matt. 16: 42   382
Matt. 17: 7   348
Matt. 17: 9   336
Matt. 17: 15   166, 173,
   206, 215
Matt. 17: 17   348
Matt. 18: 12–13   224
Matt. 18: 15   269
Matt. 18: 18   322
Matt. 18: 23   268, 280
Matt. 18: 25   384
Matt. 18: 26   334
Matt. 18: 29   285
Matt. 18: 30   165
Matt. 19: 6   338
Matt. 19: 9   209
Matt. 19: 12   333
Matt. 19: 15   171
Matt. 19: 16   393
Matt. 19: 17   369
Matt. 19: 18   339
Matt. 19: 22   315
Matt. 20: 12   172, 258
Matt. 20: 18   222
Matt. 20: 28   385, 396
Matt. 21: 2   342, 346

Matt. 21: 4   394
Matt. 21: 18   347
Matt. 21: 27   290
Matt. 21: 28   365
Matt. 21: 34   187
Matt. 22: 2   268
Matt. 22: 4   113, 115,
   148, 295
Matt. 22: 7   262
Matt. 22: 18   200
Matt. 22: 21   355
Matt. 23: 2   278
Matt. 23: 3   403
Matt. 23: 13   412
Matt. 23: 37   178, 410
Matt. 24: 3   409
Matt. 24: 9   317
Matt. 24: 22   273
Matt. 24: 32–3   187
Matt. 24: 33   352
Matt. 24: 38   315
Matt. 24: 40   318
Matt. 24: 43   224, 309,
   352
Matt. 25: 5   243
Matt. 25: 8   158, 167,
   200
Matt. 25: 10   159, 257
Matt. 25: 16   418
Matt. 25: 16–22   153,
   264
Matt. 25: 18   418
Matt. 25: 20   418
Matt. 25: 24   418
Matt. 25: 35–6   138, 258
Matt. 25: 41   418
Matt. 25: 42–3   138, 258
Matt. 26: 2   225
Matt. 26: 16   146, 395
Matt. 26: 18   223
Matt. 26: 19   115, 167
Matt. 26: 26   346, 416
Matt. 26: 38   365
Matt. 26: 39   382
Matt. 26: 41   365
Matt. 26: 42   382
Matt. 26: 45   222
Matt. 26: 46   349
Matt. 26: 46–7   222
Matt. 26: 55   174, 178,

   246
Matt. 26: 56   394
Matt. 26: 58   242
Matt. 26: 62   200
Matt. 26: 63   203, 243,
   384
Matt. 26: 65   260
Matt. 26: 75   418
Matt. 27: 8   173
Matt. 27: 12   391
Matt. 27: 14   391
Matt. 27: 15   308
Matt. 27: 20   91, 153,
   264
Matt. 27: 22–3   353
Matt. 27: 33   312
Matt. 27: 34   177
Matt. 27: 35   161
Matt. 27: 40   412
Matt. 27: 49   122
Matt. 27: 50   415
Matt. 27: 52   139, 417
Matt. 27: 55   314
Matt. 27: 63   225
Matt. 28: 5   146, 200
Matt. 28: 15   185
Matt. 28: 19   369, 386

Mark 1: 6   315
Mark 1: 8   281
Mark 1: 9–11   349
Mark 1: 10   410
Mark 1: 11   278
Mark 1: 12   232
Mark 1: 13   311
Mark 1: 14–15   410
Mark 1: 15   294
Mark 1: 16   409
Mark 1: 22   315
Mark 1: 31   415
Mark 1: 35   192, 253
Mark 1: 38   346, 395
Mark 1: 40   232, 409
Mark 1: 41   414
Mark 2: 2   288
Mark 2: 3   232
Mark 2: 4   233
Mark 2: 5, 9   189, 203
Mark 2: 9   344
Mark 2: 12   391

Mark 2: 15   232, 391
Mark 2: 16   146, 165
Mark 2: 18   232
Mark 2: 19   201
Mark 2: 21–2   182, 209, 216
Mark 2: 24–7   286
Mark 3: 3   349
Mark 3: 5   88
Mark 3: 10   168, 259
Mark 3: 13   232
Mark 3: 14   152, 342
Mark 3: 21–3   286
Mark 3: 31   232
Mark 4: 1   232
Mark 4: 2   192, 288
Mark 4: 3   365
Mark 4: 10   289
Mark 4: 18   411
Mark 4: 21–30   287
Mark 4: 33   247, 287
Mark 4: 35   334
Mark 4: 37   232, 393
Mark 4: 38   199, 200, 233, 311, 313
Mark 4: 41   288
Mark 5: 1–20   191, 248
Mark 5: 4   397
Mark 5: 5   315
Mark 5: 8   289
Mark 5: 11   314
Mark 5: 15   232, 417
Mark 5: 18   285
Mark 5: 19   295, 353
Mark 5: 22–3   232
Mark 5: 23   285
Mark 5: 28   289
Mark 5: 28–34   290
Mark 5: 32   146, 166
Mark 5: 34   159, 298
Mark 5: 35   232
Mark 5: 38   232
Mark 5: 40   232
Mark 5: 41   312, 349
Mark 5: 43   290
Mark 6: 1   232
Mark 6: 7   232
Mark 6: 8   383
Mark 6: 10   367, 403
Mark 6: 12   383

Mark 6: 13   168
Mark 6: 14–16   288
Mark 6: 18   288
Mark 6: 21–9   287
Mark 6: 23   403
Mark 6: 26   177
Mark 6: 27   384
Mark 6: 30   232
Mark 6: 31   334
Mark 6: 38   414
Mark 6: 39   384
Mark 6: 40   174
Mark 6: 41   192, 253
Mark 6: 48   233
Mark 6: 50   350
Mark 6: 55–6   248
Mark 6: 56   183
Mark 7: 1   232
Mark 7: 5   233
Mark 7: 6   290
Mark 7: 9   290
Mark 7: 14   333, 365
Mark 7: 26   384
Mark 7: 32   232
Mark 7: 37   295
Mark 8: 6   233
Mark 8: 22   232
Mark 8: 26   337
Mark 8: 34   290
Mark 8: 38   393
Mark 9: 1   290
Mark 9: 2   232
Mark 9: 4   314
Mark 9: 5   334
Mark 9: 7   333
Mark 9: 16   289
Mark 9: 19   348
Mark 9: 20   146, 243
Mark 9: 21   289
Mark 9: 22   162, 173, 259
Mark 9: 28   289
Mark 9: 29   290
Mark 9: 31   225
Mark 9: 37   183
Mark 9: 38   152
Mark 9: 39   366
Mark 9: 42   162
Mark 10: 1   232, 308
Mark 10: 14   391

Mark 10: 19   339
Mark 10: 22   315
Mark 10: 33   222
Mark 10: 35   232
Mark 10: 45   396
Mark 10: 46   232
Mark 10: 48   384
Mark 10: 49   233, 349, 350
Mark 11: 1   232
Mark 11: 2   348
Mark 11: 4   233
Mark 11: 14   406
Mark 11: 15   232
Mark 11: 24   273, 274
Mark 11: 25   333
Mark 11: 27   232
Mark 11: 28   392
Mark 12: 7   366
Mark 12: 13   232
Mark 12: 15   200, 348
Mark 12: 17   355
Mark 12: 18   232, 289
Mark 12: 19   385
Mark 12: 22–3   89
Mark 12: 23   138, 259, 262
Mark 12: 26   110, 261
Mark 12: 28   289
Mark 12: 33   392
Mark 12: 41   32, 161, 168, 242
Mark 12: 42–4   257
Mark 12: 44   32, 89, 168, 259
Mark 13: 11   391
Mark 13: 13   317
Mark 13: 20   273, 274
Mark 13: 21   338
Mark 13: 25   317, 318
Mark 13: 29   352
Mark 14: 5   233, 396
Mark 14: 13   233, 345
Mark 14: 24   413
Mark 14: 32   232
Mark 14: 33   232
Mark 14: 34   334
Mark 14: 35   161, 384
Mark 14: 37   232
Mark 14: 41   232

Mark 14: 42   346
Mark 14: 44   307
Mark 14: 53   232
Mark 14: 54   314
Mark 14: 60   200
Mark 14: 60–1   290
Mark 14: 66   232
Mark 14: 72   253
Mark 15: 2, 4   290
Mark 15: 3   247
Mark 15: 6   174, 246
Mark 15: 7   306
Mark 15: 8   391
Mark 15: 10   306
Mark 15: 13–14   353
Mark 15: 16–27   233
Mark 15: 20   395
Mark 15: 22   312
Mark 15: 23   158, 250
Mark 15: 24   161
Mark 15: 26   320
Mark 15: 34   312
Mark 15: 38   159, 257
Mark 15: 40   314
Mark 15: 43   315
Mark 16: 2   232
Mark 16: 4   233
Mark 16: 6   146, 365,
   417
Mark 16: 10–15   342

Luke 1: 1   261
Luke 1: 1–4   239
Luke 1: 7   321
Luke 1: 8   401
Luke 1: 20   317, 318
Luke 1: 21   401
Luke 1: 21–2   314
Luke 1: 25   295
Luke 1: 31   123
Luke 1: 38   406
Luke 1: 41   187
Luke 1: 42   418
Luke 1: 45   148
Luke 1: 47   278
Luke 1: 51–4   273
Luke 1: 51–5   268, 274
Luke 1: 59   251
Luke 1: 62   242
Luke 1: 64   410

Luke 2: 9–10   338
Luke 2: 15   153, 334
Luke 2: 20   409
Luke 2: 26   321
Luke 2: 27   401
Luke 2: 41   174, 246
Luke 2: 43   401
Luke 2: 46   386
Luke 2: 51   245, 315
Luke 3: 9   161, 210, 224
Luke 3: 11   355
Luke 3: 14   339
Luke 3: 16   207, 223,
   224
Luke 3: 21   401
Luke 3: 22   278
Luke 4: 2   154
Luke 4: 16   321
Luke 4: 17   321
Luke 4: 18   301
Luke 4: 20   314, 416
Luke 4: 21   296
Luke 4: 25   142, 173
Luke 4: 29   306
Luke 4: 31   314
Luke 4: 36   212, 215
Luke 4: 41   168, 353
Luke 4: 43   395
Luke 4: 44   315
Luke 5: 1   322, 401
Luke 5: 3   192, 253, 347
Luke 5: 4   328, 347
Luke 5: 6   253
Luke 5: 7   99, 158, 393
Luke 5: 10   317, 318,
   365
Luke 5: 16   315
Luke 5: 17   314, 322
Luke 5: 18   146, 167,
   321, 396
Luke 5: 23   160, 294,
   344
Luke 5: 23–4   349
Luke 5: 24   342
Luke 5: 26   109
Luke 5: 34   290
Luke 5: 34–9   210
Luke 5: 36   290
Luke 6: 8   308, 349
Luke 6: 8, 10   328

Luke 6: 11   286, 395
Luke 6: 12   315
Luke 6: 23   246
Luke 6: 27–8   328
Luke 6: 30   356, 357
Luke 6: 31   328
Luke 6: 33   392
Luke 6: 34   395
Luke 6: 35   333
Luke 6: 38   356
Luke 6: 39   210
Luke 6: 40   418
Luke 6: 43   313
Luke 6: 48   307
Luke 7: 4   285
Luke 7: 5   212, 215
Luke 7: 6   171, 244, 338
Luke 7: 8   342, 345
Luke 7: 9   178
Luke 7: 13   366
Luke 7: 14   348
Luke 7: 22   334
Luke 7: 25   418
Luke 7: 35   266
Luke 7: 50   342
Luke 8: 1   174
Luke 8: 2   307, 321
Luke 8: 5   401
Luke 8: 9   289
Luke 8: 12   411
Luke 8: 20   299
Luke 8: 23   243
Luke 8: 28   337
Luke 8: 29   245, 307
Luke 8: 38   307
Luke 8: 39   353
Luke 8: 42   158, 166,
   401
Luke 8: 46   418
Luke 8: 48   342
Luke 8: 49   238
Luke 8: 54   349
Luke 9: 4   367
Luke 9: 5   403
Luke 9: 9   240
Luke 9: 11   288
Luke 9: 16   192, 253
Luke 9: 23   287, 367
Luke 9: 25   415
Luke 9: 36   138, 258,

262
Luke 9: 41   348
Luke 9: 42   165
Luke 9: 49   152, 250
Luke 9: 58   210
Luke 9: 60   333
Luke 10: 2   287
Luke 10: 3   343
Luke 10: 4   357
Luke 10: 5   351, 357,
    403
Luke 10: 7   338
Luke 10: 10   351
Luke 10: 11   352
Luke 10: 30   244
Luke 10: 37   415
Luke 10: 40   384
Luke 11: 2   345
Luke 11: 2–4   382
Luke 11: 3   356, 380,
    382
Luke 11: 7   366
Luke 11: 9   333
Luke 11: 10   183, 209,
    216
Luke 11: 14   315
Luke 11: 17–44   210
Luke 11: 21   391
Luke 11: 22   308
Luke 11: 37   384, 401
Luke 11: 39   215
Luke 11: 41   355
Luke 11: 50   395
Luke 12: 4–5   339
Luke 12: 7   339
Luke 12: 11   367
Luke 12: 13   384
Luke 12: 20   225
Luke 12: 22   367
Luke 12: 24   210
Luke 12: 27–8   210
Luke 12: 29   338
Luke 12: 33   355, 367
Luke 12: 39   309, 352
Luke 12: 52–3   322
Luke 12: 54   222, 287
Luke 12: 55   222
Luke 12: 58   397
Luke 13: 2   290
Luke 13: 6   290

Luke 13: 7   217
Luke 13: 10   314, 315
Luke 13: 11   315
Luke 13: 13   253
Luke 13: 14   392
Luke 13: 24–5   334
Luke 13: 34   178
Luke 14: 5   290
Luke 14: 7   290
Luke 14: 8   397
Luke 14: 10   417
Luke 14: 12–13   186
Luke 14: 17   345
Luke 14: 18–19   353
Luke 14: 19   223
Luke 14: 21   414
Luke 15: 11   287
Luke 15: 16   247
Luke 15: 22–3   348
Luke 15: 24   321
Luke 15: 28   285
Luke 15: 29   147, 172,
    217
Luke 15: 32   394
Luke 16: 2   240
Luke 16: 4   276
Luke 16: 9   369
Luke 16: 18   160, 417
Luke 16: 20   162, 306,
    307, 418
Luke 16: 21   411
Luke 16: 23   239
Luke 17: 2   162
Luke 17: 3   367
Luke 17: 4   166, 173,
    189, 203
Luke 17: 8   353, 365
Luke 17: 19   386
Luke 17: 27   245
Luke 17: 28   182, 315
Luke 17: 35   318
Luke 17: 37   290
Luke 18: 1   290
Luke 18: 11   242
Luke 18: 12   173, 207,
    212, 215
Luke 18: 13   242, 382
Luke 18: 14   417
Luke 18: 15   392
Luke 18: 16   366

Luke 18: 20   339
Luke 18: 22   367
Luke 18: 36   289
Luke 19: 1   152
Luke 19: 8   223
Luke 19: 10   396
Luke 19: 11   287
Luke 19: 15   306, 394,
    401
Luke 19: 27   346
Luke 19: 30   343, 346
Luke 19: 32   418
Luke 19: 33   158
Luke 19: 41   263
Luke 19: 47   315
Luke 20: 6   320
Luke 20: 7   396
Luke 20: 10   334
Luke 20: 19   147, 258,
    262
Luke 20: 25   355
Luke 20: 26   262
Luke 21: 8   342
Luke 21: 10   287
Luke 21: 17   317
Luke 21: 20   352
Luke 21: 21   338
Luke 21: 24   317, 318
Luke 21: 29   287
Luke 21: 31   352
Luke 21: 37   315
Luke 21: 37–8   245
Luke 22: 2   137
Luke 22: 10   345
Luke 22: 13   308
Luke 22: 19   333
Luke 22: 22   222
Luke 22: 34   396
Luke 22: 36   367
Luke 22: 40   353, 365
Luke 22: 42   382
Luke 22: 46   353, 365
Luke 22: 48   166
Luke 22: 49   122, 123
Luke 22: 50   162, 257
Luke 22: 51   353
Luke 22: 64   288
Luke 22: 69   318
Luke 23: 5   410
Luke 23: 10   409

Luke 23: 18   350, 351
Luke 23: 21   353
Luke 23: 23   353
Luke 23: 26   391, 409
Luke 23: 34   382
Luke 23: 43   290
Luke 23: 46   189, 203
Luke 23: 53   321
Luke 23: 55   322
Luke 24: 7   353
Luke 24: 21   245
Luke 24: 23   396
Luke 24: 32   186, 288, 315
Luke 24: 49   223

John 1: 33   308
John 1: 35   308
John 1: 38   207
John 1: 39   88, 89, 172, 258, 345
John 1: 41   119, 159, 298, 312
John 1: 42   153, 312
John 1: 46   345
John 1: 51   417
John 2: 1–10   234
John 2: 5   334
John 2: 7–8   334
John 2: 8   348
John 2: 9   234
John 2: 10   209, 216
John 2: 16   338
John 2: 17   319
John 2: 20   88, 89, 172, 258
John 2: 21   288
John 3: 2   207, 212, 215
John 3: 6   417
John 3: 7   337
John 3: 8   208
John 3: 17   395
John 3: 18   224, 304
John 3: 21   183, 209, 216, 319
John 3: 22   245
John 3: 23   315
John 3: 24   162, 321
John 3: 26   207, 215
John 3: 27   396

John 3: 36   183, 209, 216, 217
John 4: 1–38   234
John 4: 5   234
John 4: 6   418
John 4: 7   234
John 4: 8   307
John 4: 10   309
John 4: 16   345
John 4: 21   366
John 4: 24   392
John 4: 31   335
John 4: 35   224
John 4: 36   295
John 4: 38   119, 148, 295
John 4: 40   172, 258
John 4: 42   288
John 4: 47   384
John 4: 52   262
John 5: 2   313
John 5: 5   413
John 5: 6   217
John 5: 7   201
John 5: 8   349
John 5: 10   287
John 5: 11, 12   344
John 5: 14   338
John 5: 18   246, 288
John 5: 19   287, 403
John 5: 23   186
John 5: 24   160, 294, 304, 412
John 5: 29   415
John 5: 36   295, 296
John 5: 42   292
John 5: 43   296
John 5: 45   139, 292
John 6: 6   288, 410
John 6: 10   335
John 6: 13   418
John 6: 17   306, 307
John 6: 31   319
John 6: 34   355
John 6: 43   338
John 6: 45   319
John 6: 61   290
John 6: 65   290
John 6: 68   123
John 6: 71   288
John 7: 8   223

John 7: 12   288
John 7: 15   154, 418
John 7: 19   295
John 7: 22   295
John 7: 24   338
John 7: 25   288
John 7: 30   307
John 7: 32   410
John 7: 37   345, 368
John 7: 39   288
John 7: 40–1   288
John 8: 13   290
John 8: 14   222
John 8: 19   290, 309
John 8: 20   307
John 8: 21–8   287
John 8: 27   288
John 8: 28   290
John 8: 31   417
John 8: 42   240
John 8: 52   118, 139
John 9: 7   335
John 9: 9   288
John 9: 16   288
John 9: 22   307
John 9: 25   410
John 9: 36   394
John 10: 11   225
John 10: 15   224
John 10: 18   224
John 10: 20–1   288
John 10: 32   220, 223
John 10: 34   319
John 10: 37   338
John 10: 38   394
John 10: 40   315
John 11: 1–44   187
John 11: 7   346
John 11: 9–10   392
John 11: 11   118, 223
John 11: 11–12   139, 292
John 11: 13   307
John 11: 14   281
John 11: 15, 16   346
John 11: 19   307
John 11: 27   113, 139, 292
John 11: 30   307
John 11: 34   160, 296,

345
John 11: 36   245
John 11: 41   203
John 11: 44   306, 417
John 11: 57   160, 307
John 12: 2   146, 166
John 12: 14   319
John 12: 16   321
John 12: 18   396
John 12: 29   288
John 12: 33   288
John 12: 35   344
John 12: 37   418
John 12: 40   300
John 13: 1–30   234
John 13: 2   162
John 13: 4–6   234
John 13: 6   221
John 13: 7   235
John 13: 12   235, 298
John 13: 17   392
John 13: 21   235
John 13: 23   315
John 13: 24–6   234
John 13: 27   221
John 13: 31   273, 274
John 13: 34   383
John 14: 2–4   223
John 14: 7, 9   139
John 14: 9   217
John 14: 12   223, 224
John 14: 12–25   120
John 14: 18   223
John 14: 28   223
John 14: 31   346, 349
John 15: 3   148, 296
John 15: 4   370
John 15: 6   182, 270
John 15: 8   270
John 15: 9   370
John 15: 12   383
John 15: 17   383
John 15: 18   352
John 15: 24   292
John 15: 27   218
John 16: 6   296
John 16: 30   299
John 16: 33   159, 298,
    350
John 17: 1   382

John 17: 4   415
John 17: 5   382
John 17: 6   148, 296
John 17: 7   292
John 17: 11   382
John 17: 13   418
John 17: 14   296
John 17: 17   382
John 17: 23   114, 115,
    116
John 18: 2   259
John 18: 18   314, 322
John 18: 20   301
John 18: 21   418
John 18: 25   314, 322
John 18: 30   315
John 19: 3   288
John 19: 6   353
John 19: 13   171
John 19: 15   350, 353
John 19: 19, 20   321
John 19: 21   366
John 19·24   337
John 19: 28   114, 115,
    116, 160, 294
John 19: 30   187
John 19: 31   384
John 19: 33   418
John 20: 1–2   234
John 20: 1–29   234
John 20: 3–4   235
John 20: 4   146
John 20: 5–6   234
John 20: 7–8   235
John 20: 17   223, 224,
    338
John 20: 19–23   235
John 20: 23   304
John 20: 27   348
John 20: 29   414
John 20: 30–1   319
John 21: 1–14   234
John 21: 3   223
John 21: 6   162
John 21: 6–8   235
John 21: 10   347
John 21: 13   234
John 21: 15–17   299,
    333
John 21: 18   246

John 21: 19   123
John 21: 23   225
John 21: 25   401

Acts 1: 6   289
Acts 1: 10   309, 314
Acts 1: 11   140, 299
Acts 1: 12   313, 410
Acts 1: 14   315
Acts 1: 18   115
Acts 1: 21   185, 415
Acts 1: 24   382
Acts 2: 1–4   243
Acts 2: 12–13   244
Acts 2: 13   319
Acts 2: 13–14   288
Acts 2: 22   335
Acts 2: 36   352
Acts 2: 40   285
Acts 2: 41–7   183, 248
Acts 2: 42   315
Acts 3: 1–5   243
Acts 3. 2   174, 246, 413
Acts 3: 3, 5   142
Acts 3: 6   344
Acts 3: 7   416
Acts 3: 8   253
Acts 3: 12   199, 200,
    201, 418
Acts 3: 16   201
Acts 3: 17   147, 258
Acts 3: 26   413
Acts 4: 2   391
Acts 4: 18   383
Acts 4: 22   307
Acts 4: 32–5   183, 248
Acts 4: 34   412
Acts 4: 36   312
Acts 5: 1   159
Acts 5: 1–11   248
Acts 5: 3   288
Acts 5: 5   88, 257
Acts 5: 8   288
Acts 5: 12–16   183, 248
Acts 5: 20   351, 366
Acts 5: 25   313, 320
Acts 5: 26   146, 167
Acts 5: 28   154, 296
Acts 5: 36–7   184
Acts 5: 38   204

Acts 5: 39   153, 264
Acts 5: 40   167
Acts 5: 40–1   244
Acts 6: 1   249
Acts 6: 4   318
Acts 6: 7   245
Acts 7: 11   178
Acts 7: 20–5   19, 76,
    187, 249
Acts 7: 20–6   191
Acts 7: 26   83, 142, 152,
    250
Acts 7: 35   302
Acts 7: 36   153, 264
Acts 7: 47   169
Acts 7: 48   208
Acts 7: 51   174, 207,
    212, 215
Acts 7: 54   253
Acts 7: 60   262, 382
Acts 8: 1   315
Acts 8: 3   246
Acts 8: 4   410
Acts 8: 5   288
Acts 8: 13   315
Acts 8: 14   160, 294
Acts 8: 15   168
Acts 8: 16   321
Acts 8: 17   168
Acts 8: 19   392
Acts 8: 20   406
Acts 8: 25   416
Acts 8: 26–40   191
Acts 8: 27   308
Acts 8: 28   243, 314
Acts 8: 30   200, 201
Acts 8: 33   351
Acts 8: 34   204
Acts 8: 38–40   243
Acts 8: 39   159, 257, 410
Acts 8: 40   288
Acts 9: 4–5   207
Acts 9: 9   315
Acts 9: 11   201, 335, 342
Acts 9: 12   416
Acts 9: 17   171, 288
Acts 9: 21   288, 308
Acts 9: 24   172
Acts 9: 26   137
Acts 9: 28   315

Acts 9: 29   315
Acts 9: 33   321, 413
Acts 9: 34   189, 203
Acts 9: 37   414
Acts 9: 40   257
Acts 9: 42   259
Acts 10: 7–8   18, 19
Acts 10: 10   410
Acts 10: 11   239
Acts 10: 17   18, 19, 186
Acts 10: 21   240
Acts 10: 22   384
Acts 10: 29   204
Acts 10: 30   315
Acts 10: 37   260
Acts 10: 39   415
Acts 10: 41   259
Acts 10: 43   207
Acts 10: 44   410
Acts 10: 44–8   187, 249
Acts 10: 45   115, 154,
    294
Acts 11: 5   315
Acts 11: 12   91, 147,
    171, 258
Acts 11: 16   288
Acts 11: 18   260, 262
Acts 11: 20   288
Acts 11: 23   285
Acts 11: 28   122
Acts 11: 29–30   249
Acts 12: 4   415
Acts 12: 6   315
Acts 12: 8   345, 365
Acts 12: 9–10   345
Acts 12: 11   264
Acts 12: 14   396
Acts 12: 14–16   289
Acts 12: 15–16   244
Acts 12: 20   415
Acts 12: 23   162, 257
Acts 12: 25   415
Acts 13: 4   263
Acts 13: 5   167
Acts 13: 11   318
Acts 13: 13   167, 263
Acts 13: 15   351
Acts 13: 16   335
Acts 13: 18   258
Acts 13: 25   152, 186

Acts 13: 31   172, 259
Acts 13: 32   204
Acts 13: 36   165
Acts 13: 38   204
Acts 13: 39   183, 184,
    209
Acts 13: 42   285
Acts 13: 43   152
Acts 13: 45   288
Acts 14: 15   199, 201,
    313
Acts 14: 19   397, 415
Acts 14: 22   411
Acts 14: 23   306
Acts 14: 24   167
Acts 14: 24–6   263
Acts 14: 26   322
Acts 15: 11   207, 401
Acts 15: 12   138, 260
Acts 15: 13   335, 394
Acts 15: 15   207
Acts 15: 16   162, 418
Acts 15: 19   204
Acts 15: 21   218
Acts 15: 26   418
Acts 15: 27   410
Acts 15: 32   285
Acts 15: 36   174
Acts 15: 37   395
Acts 15: 37–8   75, 243
Acts 15: 38   395
Acts 16: 4   417
Acts 16: 9   315, 322
Acts 16: 10   263
Acts 16: 13–14   242
Acts 16: 17   287
Acts 16: 18   172, 190,
    204, 246, 384
Acts 16: 22   288
Acts 16: 27   397
Acts 16: 28   338
Acts 16: 34   417
Acts 17: 3   204
Acts 17: 4   153, 264
Acts 17: 6   240
Acts 17: 11   392
Acts 17: 15   258
Acts 17: 17–18   288
Acts 17: 18   391
Acts 17: 20   201

Acts 17:23   190, 204, 207, 215, 306, 321
Acts 17:24–5   208
Acts 17:27   394
Acts 17:28   207, 298
Acts 17:30   215
Acts 17:32   287
Acts 18:1   171
Acts 18:2   418
Acts 18:3–4   246
Acts 18:7   315
Acts 18:8   184, 246
Acts 18:9   339
Acts 18:11   173, 258
Acts 18:19   192, 263
Acts 18:23   411
Acts 18:27   263
Acts 19:6   287
Acts 19:9   410
Acts 19:13   207, 215
Acts 19:16   418
Acts 19:27   207
Acts 19:30   353
Acts 19:32   306, 321
Acts 19:38   365
Acts 19:40   201
Acts 20:6   167
Acts 20:10   338
Acts 20:13   321
Acts 20:13–15   263
Acts 20:22   222
Acts 20:23   207, 215
Acts 20:24   215
Acts 20:25   99
Acts 20:26   204
Acts 20:32   189, 203
Acts 20:38   307
Acts 21:4   385
Acts 21:11   204
Acts 21:12   285
Acts 21:13   201
Acts 21:21   207, 215
Acts 21:23   313
Acts 21:28   113, 160, 296, 300, 365
Acts 21:29   321
Acts 21:30   167
Acts 21:31   201
Acts 21:34   385
Acts 21:36   350

Acts 21:39   204
Acts 22:1   335
Acts 22:5   171
Acts 22:7–8   207
Acts 22:19   315
Acts 22:20   186, 322
Acts 22:22   350, 351
Acts 22:27   351
Acts 22:29   321
Acts 23:8   207, 212, 215
Acts 23:9   203
Acts 23:11   350
Acts 23:18   410
Acts 23:21   338
Acts 23:24   394
Acts 23:30   282
Acts 24:3   207, 215
Acts 24:4   190
Acts 24:10   204, 413
Acts 24:11   122
Acts 24:14   204, 207, 215
Acts 24:15   122
Acts 24:16   207
Acts 25:5   365
Acts 25:10   320
Acts 25:11   113, 148, 189, 203, 207, 296
Acts 25:14   319
Acts 25:20   391
Acts 25:22   251, 252
Acts 25:25   397
Acts 26:1   203
Acts 26:2   207
Acts 26:3   204, 385
Acts 26:5   138, 258, 262, 413
Acts 26:7   207
Acts 26:8   208
Acts 26:9   396
Acts 26:14–15   207
Acts 26:17   203
Acts 26:20   383
Acts 26:25   204
Acts 26:26   204, 319
Acts 26:28   152, 220
Acts 26:29   401
Acts 26:31   208
Acts 26:32   309, 397
Acts 27:9   397

Acts 27:10   122
Acts 27:19   162
Acts 27:22   204
Acts 27:23   207, 215
Acts 27:33   218, 285
Acts 27:34   204, 385
Acts 27:40   353
Acts 27:41   158
Acts 27:43   153, 264
Acts 28:4, 6   288
Acts 28:14   264
Acts 28:17   287
Acts 28:22   207, 215
Acts 28:23   412
Acts 28:26   342
Acts 28:30   258, 262

Rom. 1:9   172, 207
Rom. 1:13   153, 264
Rom. 1:21   259
Rom. 1:24   392
Rom. 1:29   154, 296, 418
Rom. 2:4   220
Rom. 2:21–2   383
Rom. 3:8   364
Rom. 3:21   116, 154, 295
Rom. 3:23   110, 259
Rom. 3:28   182
Rom. 4:14   160, 295
Rom. 4:19   418
Rom. 5:2   139, 292
Rom. 5:5   113, 115
Rom. 5:7   123
Rom. 5:12   89
Rom. 5:14   258
Rom. 6:1–11   360
Rom. 6:4   358, 361, 394
Rom. 6:5   123
Rom. 6:9   417
Rom. 6:13   358, 361
Rom. 6:17   246
Rom. 6:18   415
Rom. 6:19   358, 361
Rom. 7:7   309
Rom. 7:9   138
Rom. 8:1–8   361
Rom. 8:13   360
Rom. 8:30   273, 274

Rom. 8: 38   154
Rom. 9: 1   199, 201
Rom. 9: 2   418
Rom. 9: 3   251
Rom. 10: 6   364
Rom. 11: 32   396
Rom. 12: 1   358, 361, 385
Rom. 12: 2   360
Rom. 12: 3   383
Rom. 12: 9–19   386, 387
Rom. 12: 12–13   387
Rom. 12: 14   333, 338
Rom. 12: 15   386
Rom. 12: 19   355
Rom. 13: 6   313
Rom. 13: 7   355
Rom. 13: 8   154, 296, 305, 338
Rom. 13: 12   358, 363
Rom. 13: 13   359, 361
Rom. 13: 14   359, 363
Rom. 14: 1   333
Rom. 14: 5   333
Rom. 14: 8   182, 184
Rom. 14: 9   262
Rom. 14: 13   364
Rom. 14: 14   154, 299
Rom. 14: 20   338
Rom. 14: 23   154, 305
Rom. 15: 3   258
Rom. 15: 5   282, 406
Rom. 15: 7   333
Rom. 15: 10–11   364
Rom. 15: 13   406
Rom. 15: 14   418
Rom. 15: 19   397
Rom. 16: 1   189, 203
Rom. 16: 3–15   356
Rom. 16: 16   356
Rom. 16: 25   139, 417
Rom. 16: 26   116

1 Cor. 1: 4   416
1 Cor. 1: 6   187
1 Cor. 1: 10   383
1 Cor. 1: 13   160, 295
1 Cor. 1: 23   207
1 Cor. 2: 2   417
1 Cor. 2: 6–7   208

1 Cor. 2: 7   418
1 Cor. 2: 10   208
1 Cor. 2: 12   396
1 Cor. 3: 6   19, 76, 187, 249
1 Cor. 3: 18   368
1 Cor. 4: 6   394
1 Cor. 4: 8   262, 319, 394
1 Cor. 4: 12–13   410–1
1 Cor. 5: 2   319, 416
1 Cor. 5: 3   298
1 Cor. 5: 9   282, 383
1 Cor. 5: 11   282, 383
1 Cor. 6   360
1 Cor. 6: 11   246, 360
1 Cor. 6: 20   370
1 Cor. 7: 3   356
1 Cor. 7: 9   368, 394
1 Cor. 7: 11   368
1 Cor. 7: 12   368
1 Cor. 7: 12, 13   355
1 Cor. 7: 13   368
1 Cor. 7: 15   296, 355, 368
1 Cor. 7: 17   296
1 Cor. 7: 18   182, 338, 355, 368, 418
1 Cor. 7: 21   367
1 Cor. 7: 27   160, 295
1 Cor. 7: 28   220
1 Cor. 7: 39   304
1 Cor. 8: 2   397
1 Cor. 8: 5   313
1 Cor. 9: 15   282
1 Cor. 9: 26–7   207
1 Cor. 10: 2   396
1 Cor. 10: 2–4   249
1 Cor. 10: 7–10   338
1 Cor. 11: 2   140, 299
1 Cor. 11: 6   369
1 Cor. 11: 18   240
1 Cor. 11: 25   392, 403
1 Cor. 11: 26   207
1 Cor. 11: 27   403
1 Cor. 11: 28   182, 184, 333
1 Cor. 11: 33   335
1 Cor. 12: 3   190
1 Cor. 12: 8   183, 209, 216

1 Cor. 13: 2   396
1 Cor. 13: 8   178
1 Cor. 14: 4   169
1 Cor. 14: 9   318
1 Cor. 14: 14   391
1 Cor. 14: 16   391
1 Cor. 14: 17   169
1 Cor. 14: 23   391
1 Cor. 14: 39   339, 392
1 Cor. 15: 1   190
1 Cor. 15: 3–5   301
1 Cor. 15: 4   109, 110, 301
1 Cor. 15: 6   185
1 Cor. 15: 12–19   302
1 Cor. 15: 15   302
1 Cor. 15: 19   139
1 Cor. 15: 20   139, 302, 417
1 Cor. 15: 32   225
1 Cor. 15: 34   368
1 Cor. 15: 37   122
1 Cor. 16: 5   123, 223
1 Cor. 16: 9   299
1 Cor. 16: 11   335, 339
1 Cor. 16: 12   123, 285
1 Cor. 16: 20   356

2 Cor. 1: 10   139, 292
2 Cor. 1: 15   394
2 Cor. 2: 3–4   282
2 Cor. 2: 8   385
2 Cor. 2: 9   282
2 Cor. 2: 13   301, 302
2 Cor. 2: 17   313
2 Cor. 3: 18   360
2 Cor. 4: 3   319
2 Cor. 4: 11   174
2 Cor. 5: 1   225
2 Cor. 5: 10   115
2 Cor. 5: 10–11   114, 116, 154
2 Cor. 5: 11   115, 295, 397
2 Cor. 5: 14–17   360
2 Cor. 5: 17   360
2 Cor. 6: 11   299
2 Cor. 7: 1   359, 361
2 Cor. 7: 4   295
2 Cor. 7: 9   262

2 Cor. 7: 12 282
2 Cor. 8: 9 262
2 Cor. 8: 17 282
2 Cor. 8: 18 282
2 Cor. 8: 22 174, 259, 282
2 Cor. 9: 2 154, 295
2 Cor. 9: 3 282
2 Cor. 9: 5 282
2 Cor. 9: 7 208
2 Cor. 9: 12 313
2 Cor. 10: 11 313
2 Cor. 11: 5 397
2 Cor. 11: 21 292
2 Cor. 11: 24–5 174, 259
2 Cor. 11: 25 88, 89, 301, 302
2 Cor. 12: 8 285, 385
2 Cor. 12: 11 153, 264
2 Cor. 12: 21 418
2 Cor. 13: 1 223
2 Cor. 13: 12 356, 357

Gal. 1: 6 201
Gal. 1: 13–14 248
Gal. 1: 15–21 248
Gal. 1: 22–3 315
Gal. 1: 23 411
Gal. 2: 16 182
Gal. 2: 19–20 360
Gal. 3: 7 352
Gal. 3: 18 305
Gal. 4: 3 321
Gal. 4: 9 414
Gal. 4: 18 392
Gal. 4: 20 251
Gal. 4: 23 305
Gal. 4: 24 313
Gal. 5: 2 392
Gal. 5: 4 158, 220, 270
Gal. 5: 10 154, 299
Gal. 5: 11 160, 295
Gal. 5: 15–26 360
Gal. 5: 24 360
Gal. 6: 1 333, 357, 368
Gal. 6: 6 412
Gal. 6: 10 333
Gal. 6: 11 282
Gal. 6: 12 152, 167, 220, 392
Gal. 6: 14–15 360

Eph. 1: 3 416
Eph. 1: 17 385
Eph. 1: 18 396, 418
Eph. 2: 5 319
Eph. 2: 8 319
Eph. 3: 3 153
Eph. 3: 9 418
Eph. 3: 16 385
Eph. 3: 16–17 418
Eph. 4: 1 359, 361, 385
Eph. 4: 1–3 387
Eph. 4: 18–19 417
Eph. 4: 22 359
Eph. 4: 22, 24 363
Eph. 4: 23 360
Eph. 4: 24 359
Eph. 4: 25 378
Eph. 4: 25–32 360
Eph. 4: 26 339
Eph. 4: 27 356
Eph. 4: 28 412
Eph. 4: 31 359, 361
Eph. 5: 8 360
Eph. 5: 14 349
Eph. 5: 18 336
Eph. 5: 18–21 386
Eph. 5: 21 378
Eph. 6: 4 339
Eph. 6: 11–14 378
Eph. 6: 13 415
Eph. 6: 18 378
Eph. 6: 19 385
Eph. 6: 22 282

Phil. 1: 27–8 386
Phil. 2: 2 369
Phil. 2: 2–4 386
Phil. 2: 12 360
Phil. 2: 14–16 386
Phil. 2: 22 91, 147, 260
Phil. 2: 25 282
Phil. 2: 26 315
Phil. 2: 28 282
Phil. 3: 12–15 360
Phil. 3: 16 386
Phil. 3: 18 174
Phil. 3: 21 395

Phil. 4: 5 352, 368
Phil. 4: 11 153, 264
Phil. 4: 16 174, 259
Phil. 4: 18 240
Phil. 4: 21 356

Col. 1: 6 313
Col. 1: 12 417
Col. 1: 14 298
Col. 1: 16 105, 154, 295
Col. 1: 26 116
Col. 2: 5 313
Col. 2: 11–15 360
Col. 2: 21 364
Col. 3: 1 313
Col. 3: 1–4 360
Col. 3: 5 359, 361
Col. 3: 5–17 360
Col. 3: 8 359, 363, 378
Col. 3: 9 336
Col. 3: 9–10 359, 363
Col. 3: 12 148, 359, 363
Col. 3. 12–13 386
Col. 3: 16–17 387
Col. 3: 17 403
Col. 3: 18 378
Col. 3: 22 386
Col. 3: 23 403
Col. 4: 2 378
Col. 4: 8 282
Col. 4: 10 335
Col. 4: 12 378
Col. 4: 15 356
Col. 4: 16 335
Col. 4: 17 335, 393

1 Thess. 1: 4 148
1 Thess. 1: 6 416
1 Thess. 1: 10 411, 413
1 Thess. 2: 2 416
1 Thess. 2: 4 411
1 Thess. 2: 9 185, 260, 411
1 Thess. 2: 9–10 110
1 Thess. 2: 12 411
1 Thess. 2: 14 260
1 Thess. 2: 16 273, 274, 412
1 Thess. 2: 18 91, 264
1 Thess. 3: 4 183

1 Thess. 3: 11–12   406
1 Thess. 4: 1   384
1 Thess. 4: 8   411, 412
1 Thess. 4: 10–11   384
1 Thess. 4: 14   414
1 Thess. 5: 3   186, 391
1 Thess. 5: 10   416
1 Thess. 5: 12–13   382
1 Thess. 5: 14   334
1 Thess. 5: 23   406
1 Thess. 5: 24   411
1 Thess. 5: 26   189, 203,
   357

2 Thess. 2: 3   370
2 Thess. 2: 13   148
2 Thess. 2: 15   99
2 Thess. 2: 16   416
2 Thess. 2: 17   406
2 Thess. 3: 1–2   385
2 Thess. 3: 5   406
2 Thess. 3: 9   392
2 Thess. 3: 11   240, 411
2 Thess. 3: 12   384
2 Thess. 3: 13   368
2 Thess. 3: 14   357
2 Thess. 3: 16   406

1 Tim. 1: 4   140
1 Tim. 2: 1   384
1 Tim. 4: 10   139, 292
1 Tim. 4: 12   339
1 Tim. 5: 1   339, 370
1 Tim. 5: 5   139, 292
1 Tim. 5: 22   339
1 Tim. 5: 24   313
1 Tim. 6: 4   118, 292,
1 Tim. 6: 15   412
1 Tim. 6: 17   139
1 Tim. 6: 17–18   384
1 Tim. 6: 20   369

2 Tim. 1: 4   140, 418
2 Tim. 1: 8   339, 368,
   374
2 Tim. 1: 12   395
2 Tim. 1: 14   369, 374,
   375, 376, 377
2 Tim. 1: 16   406
2 Tim. 2: 2   396

2 Tim. 2: 2–3   370
2 Tim. 2: 3   374
2 Tim. 2: 6   182
2 Tim. 2: 15   374
2 Tim. 3: 1   352
2 Tim. 3: 8   418
2 Tim. 3: 11   168, 259,
   264
2 Tim. 4: 1   370
2 Tim. 4: 2   375, 376
2 Tim. 4: 3–4   370
2 Tim. 4: 5   369, 375,
   376, 377
2 Tim. 4: 6   370
2 Tim. 4: 7   298
2 Tim. 4: 8   418
2 Tim. 4: 11   346, 386
2 Tim. 4: 16   406
2 Tim. 4: 19   356

Titus 1: 15   174, 418
Titus 3: 3   311
Titus 3: 5–6   115
Titus 3: 15   356

Phile 12   282
Phile 19   282
Phile 20   406
Phile 21   282
Phile 22   366

Heb. 1: 13   298
Heb. 2: 13   322
Heb. 2: 18   119, 148,
   295
Heb. 3: 4   183, 184, 209,
   216
Heb. 3: 5   122
Heb. 3: 13   334
Heb. 3: 18   122
Heb. 4: 4   298
Heb. 4: 10   270
Heb. 4: 16   334
Heb. 5: 1   393
Heb. 5: 14   418
Heb. 6: 1   347
Heb. 6: 10   416
Heb. 7: 6   305
Heb. 7: 8   412
Heb. 7: 9   305

Heb. 7: 13   298
Heb. 7: 19   115
Heb. 7: 20   319
Heb. 7: 23   319
Heb. 7: 27   393
Heb. 8: 5   305
Heb. 8: 11   352
Heb. 8: 13   148, 296
Heb. 9: 2   153, 264
Heb. 9: 6   418
Heb. 9: 13   418
Heb. 9: 25   393
Heb. 10: 2   418
Heb. 10: 9   109
Heb. 10: 10   319
Heb. 10: 11   299
Heb. 10: 14   115, 298,
   412
Heb. 10: 15   397
Heb. 10: 22   334
Heb. 10: 29   416
Heb. 11: 6   413
Heb. 11: 7   153, 264
Heb. 11: 7, 9, 12, 13   88
Heb. 11: 9   416
Heb. 11: 13   259
Heb. 11: 17   152, 250,
   305
Heb. 11: 21   410, 412
Heb. 11: 23   258
Heb. 11: 28   110, 296,
   305
Heb. 11: 32–40   183
Heb. 11: 33–9   259
Heb. 12: 1   334
Heb. 12: 2   119, 160,
   295
Heb. 12: 12   369
Heb. 12: 22   119, 154
Heb. 13: 1–25   334
Heb. 13: 3   368
Heb. 13: 15   174
Heb. 13: 18   393
Heb. 13: 21   406
Heb. 13: 24   356

Jas. 1: 6   299
Jas. 1: 10   266
Jas. 1: 11   266, 267, 268
Jas. 1: 13–15   208

Jas. 1: 17   311, 313
Jas. 1: 21   378
Jas. 1: 23   266, 299
Jas. 1: 24   266, 267, 304
Jas. 2: 2–4   270
Jas. 2: 10   305
Jas. 2: 11   379
Jas. 2: 12   334
Jas. 2: 24   182
Jas. 3: 3   182
Jas. 3: 15   311, 313
Jas. 4: 1   411
Jas. 4: 4   394
Jas. 4: 7   378
Jas. 4: 7–10   379
Jas. 4: 8–10   374
Jas. 5: 1   375
Jas. 5: 7–8   370, 375,
   376
Jas. 5: 15   397
Jas. 5: 20   352

1 Pet. 1: 2   406
1 Pet. 1: 10   416
1 Pet. 1: 13   372, 374,
   375
1 Pet. 1: 15   373
1 Pet. 1: 17   375, 376
1 Pet. 1: 21   267
1 Pet. 1: 22   372, 373,
   375
1 Pet. 1: 24   266, 268
1 Pet. 2: 1   378
1 Pet. 2: 2   374
1 Pet. 2: 5   396
1 Pet. 2: 11–12   387
1 Pet. 2: 13   373, 378
1 Pet. 2: 15   393
1 Pet. 2: 15–16   387
1 Pet. 2: 17   373, 374
1 Pet. 2: 18   386, 387
1 Pet. 2: 25   315
1 Pet. 3: 1   386, 387
1 Pet. 3: 6   270
1 Pet. 3: 7   386, 387
1 Pet. 3: 9   386, 387
1 Pet. 3: 10–15   379
1 Pet. 3: 14   405
1 Pet. 3: 18   395
1 Pet. 3: 20   152

1 Pet. 4: 1   378
1 Pet. 4: 10   386, 387
1 Pet. 5: 2   99, 370, 373,
   375, 377
1 Pet. 5: 5   375, 378
1 Pet. 5: 5–12   379
1 Pet. 5: 6   375
1 Pet. 5: 8   374, 375
1 Pet. 5: 8–9   378
1 Pet. 5: 9   375
1 Pet. 5: 12   282, 375
1 Pet. 5: 14   357

2 Pet. 1: 2   406
2 Pet. 2: 9   393
2 Pet. 3: 4   218
2 Pet. 3: 7   319

1 John 1: 1   193
1 John 1: 5–2: 2   214
1 John 1: 7   215
1 John 1: 8–10   213
1 John 1: 10   298
1 John 2: 1   213
1 John 2: 1–12   214
1 John 2: 5   305, 319
1 John 2: 8   207
1 John 2: 12–14   282
1 John 2: 13–14   159
1 John 2: 19   309
1 John 2: 23   412
1 John 2: 27   215
1 John 2: 28   370
1 John 2: 29   295
1 John 3: 4–10   212, 213,
   214, 215, 216, 217
1 John 3: 6   212
1 John 3: 8   166, 218
1 John 3: 9   213
1 John 3: 14   160, 294
1 John 3: 20   208
1 John 3: 22   403
1 John 4: 1   339
1 John 4: 2   418
1 John 4: 7   295
1 John 4: 2   418
1 John 4: 7   295
1 John 4: 7–8   208
1 John 4: 9–14   193
1 John 4: 12   319

1 John 4: 13   296
1 John 4: 14   292, 296
1 John 4: 17–18   209
1 John 5: 15   403
1 John 5: 20   240
1 John 5: 21   369

2 John 5   383
2 John 7   412
2 John 9–11   412
2 John 10   339

3 John 3   215
3 John 9   282
3 John 15   356

Jude 1   148
Jude 2   406
Jude 9   406
Jude 14   273, 274
Jude 17   368
Jude 18   318

Rev. 1: 13   418
Rev. 1: 18   313
Rev. 2: 5   162
Rev. 3: 17   118, 139, 292
Rev. 5: 4–5   336
Rev. 5: 5   159, 257, 264
Rev. 5: 7   110, 301, 303
Rev. 7: 4   418
Rev. 7: 14   303
Rev. 8: 5   301, 303
Rev. 9: 1   418
Rev. 9: 1–11   191
Rev. 9: 6   225
Rev. 9: 15   418
Rev. 10: 4   338
Rev. 10: 7   274
Rev. 11: 2   274
Rev. 11: 6   394
Rev. 12: 15   170
Rev. 14: 3   160
Rev. 14: 8   274
Rev. 14: 13   412
Rev. 15: 1   274
Rev. 16: 4   170
Rev. 18: 2   418
Rev. 18: 3   119, 148
Rev. 18: 3, 15, 19   93

Rev. 18:15   414
Rev. 19:3   303
Rev. 20:2   173
Rev. 20:4   173, 258
Rev. 21:2   418
Rev. 21:8   418
Rev. 21:24   168
Rev. 22:17   345

Gen. 17:20   272
Gen. 22:2   278
Gen. 27:2   277
Gen. 28:16   276
Gen. 49:11   268

Exod. 20:13–16   339

Deut. 5:17–20   339
Deut. 8:10   272
Deut. 17:7   335
Deut. 24:1   354

Judges 14:16   277

1 Sam. 2:4–5   269

2 Sam. 14:21   272
2 Sam. 24:23   272

1 Kings 8:47   272

Isa. 1:3   268
Isa. 5:13–14   272
Isa. 8:17   322
Isa. 9:5   272
Isa. 11:9   272
Isa. 34:4   317
Isa. 40:7   268
Isa. 42:1   278
Isa. 43:10   278
Isa. 44:2   278
Isa. 53:8   351
Isa. 62:4   278

Jer. 4:29   272
Jer. 8:7   268

Ezek. 29:13   272

Hos. 4:6   280
Hos. 10:7   272
Hos. 10:15   272

Joel 3:12   349

Amos 5:2   272

Zeph. 1:11   280

Ps. 1:1   268
Ps. 2:7   278

Ps. 9:11   268
Ps. 10:3   268
Ps. 16:9   279
Ps. 20:7   272
Ps. 36:13   272
Ps. 49:13   268, 280
Ps. 49:21   268, 280
Ps. 84:4   268
Ps. 97:8   279
Ps. 102:3–11   268
Ps. 126:2   349
Ps. 143:4   268, 280

Prov. 1:7   268
Prov. 14:13   268
Prov. 22:12–13   268

Cant. 7:7   280

Baruch 4:5   350
Baruch 4:21   350
Baruch 4:27   350
Baruch 4:30   350

Judith 7:30   350
Judith 11:1   350
Judith 11:3   350

SUBJECT INDEX

Abbot, E. A. 374
Abel, F.-M. 95, 104
absolute time value, *see* primary tense;
   time reference
ACCOMPLISHMENTS 44–5, 91, 93, 97,
   129, 149–54, 163, 169, 170, 171,
   172, 178, 192, 200, 217, 219, 220,
   222, 242, 250, 257, 262, 263, 264,
   298, 341, 362, 376, 393, 394, 414
   criteria for identifying 149–50
   illustrations 150–1
   influence on aspect-usage 151–4
achievements 44, 127, 154
actional character, *see* procedural
   character
active voice, effect on aspect 106, 115,
   293–5, 318
ACTIVITIES 44, 129, 140–9, 163, 169,
   170, 171, 172, 178, 192, 200, 217,
   222, 242, 245, 257, 262, 264, 340
   criteria for identifying 140–3
   illustrations 144–5
   influence on aspect-usage 145–8
actual occurence, effect on aspect 31,
   34–5, 38–41, 49, 79, 84–5, 421
adverbs, effect on aspect 47–8, 141–4,
   149–50, 155, 165, 170–4, 206, 214–
   15, 217–18, 221, 246, 257–8, 264,
   300
Aerts, W. J. 310, 320
Agrell, S. 30
aktionsart 1–3, 12 n., 13–14, 29–42, 43,
   45, 69, 117, 179
allegory, perfect of 305
annalistic use of historical present 227
antecedent occurrence 17–19, 27–8, 76,
   186–7, 407, 413–14
anteriority 112–14, 290–1

Antoniadis, S. 209–10, 279
aorist aspect
   description of basic sense 97–8
   survey of suggested general meanings
   86–98
   usage with ACCOMPLISHMENTS 152–3
   usage with ACTIVITIES 147
   usage with CLIMAXES 158–9
   usage with PUNCTUALS 161–2
   usage with STATES 137–8
aorist indicative
   categories of usage 255–82
   contrasts with imperfect 9, 19, 74–7,
   176–7, 244, 282–90
aorist in commands and prohibitions
   325–32, 334–5, 335–40, 354–64,
   366–79, 380–2, 384–5
aorist infinitive, subjunctive, and
   optative 390, 393–6
aorist participle 406–8, 413–16
aoristic perfect 110, 299
aoristic present 190, 204
Armstrong, D. 65
asking, use of aspects with verbs of 282–
   90
aspect
   definition 1–5, 8, 31, 49–50, 78–85,
   86, 195, 420–1
   distinction from procedural character
   29–50; *see also* procedural character
   distinction from tenses 8–29; *see also*
   time reference, effect on aspect
   interaction with other features 8, 46–
   9, 72–7, 79–80, 84 n., 125, 126–96;
   see also listings under specific features
aspectual verbs 178–9
atelic, *see* boundedness, as element of
   lexical meaning

Bache, C. 36, 38–41, 194
background narration 74–5, 191; *see also*
    discourse features
use of imperfect in 19, 248–9
use of pluperfect in 307, 321
Bakker, W. F. 23, 64, 380 n.
BDF, *Grammar* 70, 98, 122, 175, 286,
    290, 327, 329, 375
BDR, *Grammatik* 3, 104, 282, 375
Beare, F. W. 372, 373, 374
Best, E. 377
binary opposition 56, 58, 62, 65, 69
Black, M. 268, 279, 280
Blass, F. 1–2, 89, 98, 100, 234, 283–4,
    327, 375–6
Blass–Debrunner, *Grammatik des NT*
    Griechisch 92, 375
Blass–Thackeray, *Grammar of NT Greek*
    375
'bordercrossings', as lexical type 156 n.
boundedness, as element of lexical
    meaning 99–101, 119, 130, 140,
    145, 149, 154, 217
boundedness, shown by compositional
    features 150–1, 169–70, 171
Brugmann, K. 13–14
Burton, E. De W. 2, 70, 94, 101, 104
Buttmann, A. 87
Buttmann, P. 9–10
Bybee, J. 107

Carrington, P. 377–9
catechetical material, effect on aspect
    377–9
change, as element of lexical meaning
    129–34
Chantraine, P. 105–6, 294
classes of verbs, *see* verb-types
CLIMAXES 129, 154–60, 163, 172, 176,
    178, 200, 217, 219, 220, 222, 242,
    245, 250, 256, 263, 264, 298, 340,
    393, 394, 414
    criteria for identifying 154–6
    illustrations 156–7
    influence on aspect-usage 158–60
clothing, aspect usage with verbs of
    362–3
collective plurality, effect on aspect 166–
    7

Collinge, N. E. 65
Colson, F. H. 350
combinatory variants 82 n., 97, 99, 103,
    126, 184, 194–5, 202, 334, 340–1,
    364, 390; *see also* secondary
    meanings of aspects
commanding, use of aspects with verbs
    of 282–90
commands and prohibitions, use of
    aspects in 325–88
completed action, as a general meaning
    for the aorist 89–91, 375–6
completed action, as meaning of perfect
    104
completion 14, 18, 25, 30, 38, 50, 65, 67,
    70, 79, 195, 283, 375–6
complexive aorist, *see* constative use of
    aorist
compositional elements, effect on aspect
    46–9, 163–79
comprehensive aorist, *see* constative use
    of aorist
Comrie, B. 19, 26, 36, 38, 56, 57, 60, 106,
    107, 297–8
conative 158, 167, 179, 264
conative use of imperfect 249–52
conative use of present 219–21, 366, 393,
    412–13
conditional sentences, use of aspects in
    252, 309, 400, 402–3, 405
conjunction reduction 192–4
constative, as a general meaning for the
    aorist 14, 92–4
constative use of aorist 255–61, 369–70,
    395–6, 415–16
consummative use of aorist 263–5, 368–
    9, 375–7, 394–5, 414–15
contemporaneous occurrence, *see*
    simultaneity
contextual features, effect on aspect 3,
    24, 81–3, 111, 183–4, 190–4, 196,
    206, 214–15, 219, 221, 222, 224,
    227, 250, 252, 256, 258, 264, 265,
    266, 269–70, 298, 301–2, 304, 311,
    331, 336–7, 357–63, 421; *see also*
    compositional elements
contradictory opposition 55, 66–8
contrary opposition 55, 66, 68–9
count noun, effect on aspect 47–8, 169–

70, 181–2
Crisafulli, V. S. 106
Cuendet, G. 95
current relevance, as a meaning for the perfect 107, 110–11
cursive, as a general meaning for the present 14, 101–3
Curtius, G. 10–12, 15–16, 19–20
customary occurrence 173, 178, 211–17, 246–7, 315, 332–4
customary use of imperfect 244–9
customary use of present 205–8, 211, 391–3, 410–11

Daube, D. 387–8
Davies, W. D. 387–8
definition level, in describing aspect 39–41, 79–80, 82 n., 84 n., 195, 420–1
Deissmann, A. 350
deixis 18, 109, 113, 116, 122, 198
descriptive use of aspects 161 n., 199–201, 227–9, 241–4, 285, 286–7, 304, 365, 391, 409–10
desiderative imperfect 251–2
discourse features, effect on aspect 72–7, 190–4, 231–3, 248–9, 306–7, 321
distributive 167–8, 174, 183, 185, 217, 258-9, 354–6, 367–8, 385, 392, 410–11
Dodd, C. H. 214
dramatic use of aorist 275–81
dramatic use of perfect 302 n., 304 n.
duration, as element of lexical meaning 128–9, 130, 145, 149, 152, 154
durative 9, 10, 12, 13, 14, 29, 30, 32, 35, 37, 38, 39, 41, 47, 49, 56, 62, 64, 67, 70, 79, 142, 172–3, 179, 184, 195, 200, 202, 242, 257–8
durative, as a general meaning for the present 98–100
dynamic verbs 129

effective aorist, see consummative aorist
embedded past, as a meaning for the perfect 108
emphasis of speaker in aspect-usage, see forcefulness of expression; speaker's choice; viewpoint
English, translation problems 109, 110,

201, 205, 218, 221, 242–3, 252, 260, 275, 276, 281, 302 n.
epistolary use of aorist 281
epistolary use of perfect 304 n.
equipollent opposition 56, 65–72, 124–5
Eriksson, K. 236, 237
exegesis, use of aspect in 196, 421–2
experiential perfect 297–8
expressive periphrasis 310, 311, 314, 318
'extended' aorists 33, 99, 257–8
'extended now', as a meaning for the perfect 108–9
external viewpoint 26–8, 79, 97–8, 119–20, 124, 255, 326, 364, 366, 388, 390, 393, 413, 420

Fitzmyer, J. 279–80
forcefulness of expression, effect on aspect usage 251, 289, 369, 380–1
foreground narration 19, 74–5, 191, 248–9
Forsyth, J. 49, 53–5, 57–8, 59, 65, 71
Friedrich, P. 51, 66, 69
function level, in describing aspect 39–40, 80, 195, 420–1
future tense 120–4
    as non-aspectual 122
    as temporal only 122–3
    aspectual meaning 120–1
    modal meaning 121–3
    survey of suggested meanings 120–3
future perfect periphrastic construction 322–3
future perfect tense 309
future periphrastic construction 317-18
futuristic use of aorist 269–74
futuristic use of present 221–6, 413
    portraying vividness or certainty 221, 222, 224, 225

Galton, H. 20, 25–6, 64
general precepts, use of aspects in 327–9, 332–4, 337–40, 354–64, 366–70, 371, 383–4, 386, 387
general truths 208–17, 249, 265–9, 280
general vs. specific distinction of aspect-usage in commands, exceptions to the pattern 340–79

general vs. specific reference, effect on
aspect 128, 146–7, 170, 177–8, 179–
85, 199, 206, 210, 222, 245–6, 259,
287–8, 326–8, 337–9, 383–5
generic occurrence 180 n., 209–11, 216–
17, 410–12
Gildersleeve, B. L. 200, 218, 265
giving, use of aspects with verbs of
354–6
gnomic use of aorist 265–9
gnomic use of perfect 304
gnomic use of present 208–17, 224
Goedsche, C. R. 42
Gonda, J. 51
gradable and ungradable transitions
144, 156–7
gradable or gradual oppositions 65–9,
125
Green, T. S. 100
Guillaume, G. 21–2

habitual, see customary occurrence
Haustafeln, use of aspect in 387–8
Hebrew verbs 17, 61, 267–9, 271–4,
276–81, 316–17, 387–8
Herbig, G. 16
Hermann, E. 31, 34, 35–6, 38, 41
Hettrich, H. 23, 24, 175
Hilliard, A. E. 376
Hirtle, W. H. 22
historical present 193, 226–39
Hjelmslev, L. 55
Hodges, Z. C. 214–15
Holt, J. 55, 57, 68
Hopper, P. J. 72
Hort, F. J. A. 374

imperative mood, use of aspect in 325–
82
imperfect indicative
categories of usage 240–53
contrasts with aorist 176–7, 243–4,
247–9, 282–90
frequency in NT books 253–5
non-indicative modal nuances of 176–
7, 252
used with negative in stating
resistance or refusal 176–7
imperfect periphrastic construction

313–17
with customary sense 315
with progressive sense 314–15
imperfective aspect 1, 12–14, 37; see also
present aspect
inceptive 146, 191–2; see also ingressive
inceptive use of imperfect 252–3
incomplete occurrence 14, 219–21, 222,
250–1
incompletion, as a general meaning for
the present 100–1
indefinite past, as a meaning for the
perfect 108, 109–10
indefinite past event, aorist used for
260–1, 280–1
indicative mood, use of aspect in 113,
198–324
indirect commands, use of aspects in
382–5
indirect discourse, use of aspects in
infinitive of 401
infinitive, use of aspects in 385–6, 390–
402
ingressive 93–4, 118, 137–8, 165, 179,
184–5, 195; see also inceptive
ingressive aorist, used in call for change
of conduct 361
ingressive use of aorist 261–3, 368, 371–
4, 393–4, 414
inherent meaning of verbs, see lexical
meaning of verb
instantaneous, as a general meaning for
the aorist 87–9
instantaneous, as element of lexical
meaning 88, 128–9, 149–50, 154–
62, 163
instantaneous occurrence 88, 93, 96, 97,
256–7, 263
instantaneous use of present 202–5
intensive 32, 292–3
intensive perfect 292
internal viewpoint 26–8, 79, 85, 102,
103, 124, 128, 202, 326, 329, 364,
365, 388, 390–1, 408, 420
interpretation of NT, use of aspect in, see
exegesis
intransitive verb, effect on perfect
meaning, see transitivity, effect on
aspect

invariant meaning of aspect 79–84, 86, 97, 103, 119, 123, 124
iterative 13, 14, 101–2, 142, 156, 166, 206, 212, 244, 257, 258, 315, 318, 355
iterative, as a meaning for the imperfect 244–9
iterative, as meaning for the present 98, 205–8

Jacob, A. 22
Jacobsohn, H. 31, 33–4, 35, 36
Jakobson, R. 54–5, 56–7, 61, 64–5, 66
Johanson, L. 61, 63–4
Joüon, P. 289–90

Kelly, J. N. D. 374
Kenny, A. 43, 45, 46, 127, 129, 148
kind of action, see aktionsart
Kiparsky, P. 192–3, 229–30
Koschmieder, E. 20–1, 33–4, 188
Kretschmer, P. 381
Kubo, S. 214
Kuehne, C. 95

Latin, influence on analysis of Greek 9, 10, 12, 16
Levin, S. 230
lexical meaning of verb, effect on aspect 32, 42–6, 49–50, 83–4, 88–9, 91, 93, 96–7, 99, 101, 102–3, 120, 127–63; see also verb-types
"linear" aorists 87, 93; see also "extended" aorists
Lloyd, A. L. 106–7
Louw, J. P. 95, 96, 104, 193, 336–7
Lyons, J. 18, 36–8, 66–7, 123, 194

McCoard, R. W. 107–11, 114, 116
McKay, K. L. 93, 102, 104, 121–2, 147–8, 218, 293
Mandilaras, B. 200, 203, 211, 253–4, 300–1
markedness in aspectual oppositions 55–67, 69–70, 71, 79, 96
  contrastive sense for the unmarked member 60, 63, 64
Marshall, I. H. 353
Martin, R. 22

mass noun, effect on aspect 47–8, 169–70
Mateos, J. 45–6, 98, 127 n., 159, 252
Mayor, J. B. 374
maxims, use of aspects in, see general truths; gnomic uses
Mitchell, T. F. 78
mixed opposition 66, 69–70
modified-privative opposition 60–5
Moffatt, J. 375
momentary occurrence 9, 14, 30, 37, 38, 39, 50, 67, 79, 88, 93, 120, 155–6, 160–2; see also instantaneous occurrence
momentary, as a general meaning for the aorist, see instantaneous
monolectic verb, definition of 310
mood, effect on aspect 48; see also imperative, indicative, optative, subjunctive
Moorhouse, A. C. 78, 105, 252, 275
morphology and aspect 15–16, 303, 320
motion, use of aspects with verbs of 144, 150–1, 171, 222, 263, 341
Moule, C. F. D. 87, 98, 267, 305, 373
Moulton, J. H. 2, 92, 98, 120, 336
Moulton, W. F. 67
Mourelatos, A. P. D. 107
Mozley, F. W. 380
multiple occurrences, see repeated occurrence
Mussies, G. 61, 62, 96, 101–2, 104

narrative succession, effect on aspect 146, 191, 252–3, 262–3
negatives, effect on aspect 48, 174–8
neutral member of an opposition 55, 57, 58–60, 61, 63–4, 68, 70
non-indicative moods, use of aspects in 325–88, 389–419
noun phrases, effect on aspect 47–8, 163, 180–3
number of subject or object, effect on aspect 164–9, 287
Nunn, H. P. V. 94, 98

object phrase, effect on aspect 47–8, 151, 164, 169–71, 180–3
optative, use of aspects in 390–7, 404–6

Osburn, C. 230

papyri, use of aspects in Hellenistic 203, 211, 237, 253–4, 267, 276, 281, 353, 388 n.
participle, use of aspects in 386–8, 406–18
passive voice, effect on aspect 105, 294, 318, 319, 320, 416
past action still in progress 217–18, 413
past time reference 9–10, 17–18, 198, 240–1, 255; *see also* time reference, effect on aspect
Paul's theology of "old life-new life", aspect usage in 357–63
perfect
  as non-aspectual 106–7
  aspectual meaning 117–19
  contrast with aorist 113, 114–16, 298, 300–3
  contrast with present 112–13, 292–3
  external temporal meaning 113
  general meaning 103, 119–20
  historical development 105–6, 294
  indicating state of object 106, 293–6, 299–300, 303
  indicating state of subject 105, 291–3, 293–6
  internal temporal meaning 112–14
  role of pragmatic inferences 111
  secondary place relative to present and aorist aspects 124
  survey of views of the English perfect 107–11
  traditional view 103–1111
  usage with ACCOMPLISHMENTS 153
  usage with ACTIVITIES 147-8
  usage with CLIMAXES 159
  usage with PUNCTUALS 162
  usage with STATES 138
  usage with temporal adverbs 109
  voice of perfect verb, effect on aspect meaning 105–6, 115–16, 293–5, 318, 319, 320
perfect in commands and prohibitions, limited use 326
perfect indicative tense uses 290–305
  focus on completed action 297–8
  focus on resulting state 291–7

rare uses 304–5
  with aoristic sense 299–303
  with present stative meaning 299
perfect infinitive, subjunctive, and optative 396–7
perfect participle 318–23, 406–8, 416–18
perfect periphrastic construction 318–20
  expressing previous past occurrence 321–2
  focus on completed action 319
  focus on resulting state 319
  in explanatory clauses 321
  with present stative meaning 320
'perfective' (i.e. aorist) aspect 1, 13–14, 37, 39, 76; *see also* aorist aspect
perfective use of present 239–40
performances, as a lexical class 45, 127–9, 140, 143, 145, 148, 149, 160, 161, 170
performative use of present 187–90, 202–3
periphrasis
  types of 310
  with aorist participles 310 n.
  with perfect participles 318–23
  with present participles 311–18
periphrastic tenses 309–23
phase of action 43, 107
Pistorius, P. V. 87–9
Plummer, A. 279
pluperfect tense 305–9
  expressing previous past occurrence 307–8
  focus on completed action 307–8
  focus on resulting state 306–7
  in explanatory clauses 306–7
  with past stative meaning 308–9
pluperfect periphrastic construction 320–2
  expressing previous past occurrence 321–2
  focus on completed action 321
  focus on resulting state 320–1
  in explanatory clauses 321
  with past stative meaning 322
plural number, effect on aspect 46 n., 166–9, 206, 258, 287–8
Polish 30

Porzig, W. 31, 35–6, 38, 41
Post, L. A. 381
prayer, use of aspects in 380–2, 406
prefacing, as element of lexical meaning 128–9, 155
prefixes, effect on aspect 32, 151
present aspect
  description of basic sense 103
  survey of suggested general meaning 98–103
  usage with ACCOMPLISHMENTS 152
  usage with ACTIVITIES 145-6
  usage with CLIMAXES 158–9
  usage with PUNCTUALS 160–1
  usage with STATES 137
present in commands and prohibitions 325–34, 335–40, 341–54, 364–6, 380–2, 383–4
present indicative categories of usage 198–240
present infinitive, subjunctive, and optative 390–3
present participle 311–18, 406–13
present periphrastic construction 312–13
primary tense 17–18, 122, 325; see also deixis; time reference, effect on aspect
privative opposition 56–65, 68, 70, 71, 125
procedural character 29, 41, 49–50, 99, 126–63, 179; see also lexical meaning of verb; verb-types
progressive use of imperfect 241–4
progressive use of present 199–201, 365, 391, 409–10
progressive, as a general meaning for the present 101–3
prohibitions
  traditional rule for use of aspects in 335–7
  use of aspects in 325–6, 335–9, 352, 365–6, 382–5
proleptic use of aorist 269–74
proleptic use of perfect 304
prominence in narration, effect on aspect 74–5, 191
proverbial sense for present, see gnomic use of present

punctiliar, as a general meaning for the aorist 87, 92, 95–6
punctiliar, as a meaning for the future 120–1
PUNCTUALS 129, 163, 172, 176, 178, 195, 217, 242, 245, 256, 264, 340
  criteria for identifying 155–6
  illustrations 157
  influence on aspect-usage 160–2

Radermacher, L. 95, 104
recent past occurrence 260–1, 275–81
reference point
  in defining aspect 27–8, 85
  in temporal relations 17–18, 113, 122–3
relative tense 17–19, 23–5, 26–9, 76–7, 407–8; see also antecedent occurrence; secondary tense; simultaneity
Renicke, H. 42
repeated occurrence 102, 128, 160–1, 166–8, 172, 173–4, 177–8, 179, 181–5, 195, 206–7, 258–9, 262, 328–9, 333–4, 357, 367–8, 392, 410–12; see also distributive; iterative
resultative perfect 294 n.
resulting state, use of perfect to denote 291–7, 319
resulting state, use of pluperfect to denote 306–7, 320–1
Reynolds, S. M. 193, 230
Rijksbaron, A. 24–5, 175
Robertson, A. T. 2, 70, 92, 98
Ruijgh, C. J. 23–4, 28
Ruipérez, M. S. 61, 64, 71
Rundgren, F. 61, 63
Russian aspect 53, 55, 57, 59, 60
Rydbeck, L. 5

Saussure, F. de 51–2
Schwyzer-Debrunner, Syntax 90–1, 106, 122, 200, 205–6, 226–7
secondary meaning of aspects 19, 26–8, 70, 74–5, 77, 80–2, 84, 100, 101, 102–3, 195, 325 n., 326, 339, 364, 365, 367, 383, 390, 400, 407, 413; see also combinatory variants

secondary tense 17–19, 26; *see also* relative tense

Selwyn, E. G. 373, 374

semelfactive 39, 165; *see also* single occurrence

Semitic influence on NT aspect usage 17, 239, 268–9, 273, 276, 278–81, 316–17, 387–8

sending, use of aspects with verbs of 282–4

Septuagint 231, 236, 237, 262, 267–9, 271–4, 276–80, 316, 317, 322, 349, 350, 351, 354, 362, 379, 380, 399 n.

sequence in narration, effect on aspect 76–7, 191, 262, 288–9

similes, aorist used in 266

simple aspect 94–5, 204–5

simultaneity 9–10, 17–19, 27–8, 76, 186–7, 190, 199, 201, 205, 241, 244, 288–9, 365–6, 391, 400–1, 407–10

single occurrence 164–6, 328–9, 340, 357, 367–8

singular number, effect on aspect 164–6

Slavic languages and aspect 8 n., 16, 21, 25–6, 30–1

Smith, Carlotta 40–1

Smith, Charles R. 95

spatial features in aspect 26–8

speaker's choice in aspect usage 31–2, 34–5, 38–40, 49–50, 52–4, 63, 78–9, 82–3, 84–5, 92, 149, 166, 168, 172, 195, 235, 254–5, 257, 258, 261, 285–6, 303, 399, 411, 421

speaking, use of aspect with verbs of 189–90, 202–4, 231–2, 282–90, 351–2

specific command, use of aspects in 327–32, 334–5, 337–40, 340–54, 356, 365–6, 371, 381–2, 384–5

specific reference, effect on aspect 128, 170, 179–81, 200–1, 202–5, 241–3; *see also* general vs. specific reference

Spicq, C. 373

Stagg, F. 58, 95–6, 185, 261

state or condition, as meaning of perfect 104, 114–17

STATES 44–5, 93–4, 96–7, 118, 129–40, 163, 167, 178, 184, 192, 200, 201, 202–3, 217, 220, 239–40, 242–3,

245–6, 250, 257–9, 261–2, 275, 291–2, 299, 306, 308–9, 318, 340–1, 368, 391, 392, 393–4, 403, 405, 414
  criteria for identifying 129–34
  illustrations 134–6
  influence on aspect-usage 136–40

Stork, P. 402

Streitberg, W. 12–13

structural relations between aspects 50–72, 124–5

stylistic variation among NT writers in aspect usage 161 n., 231–3, 234–5, 237–9, 247, 253–5, 284, 286–9, 297, 315–16, 330–2, 336, 344–5, 355–6, 357–64, 367, 370–9

subject phrase, effect on aspect 163–9, 170, 180–3

subjective features of aspect 31–2, 34–5, 37–40, 49, 85, 92, 149, 166, 172, 257, 258, 285–6, 303; *see also* speaker's choice

subjunctive mood, use of aspect in 325, 390–7, 400, 402–4

subsequence 17, 122–3

substitute periphrasis 310, 311, 312

summary aspect 14, 36, 40, 70, 92–4, 97–8, 138, 161, 166–8, 172, 173, 256–9, 326, 347, 365, 366, 369, 390, 413
  as a general meaning for the aorist 92–4, 97–8

suppletive periphrasis 310, 320

Swete, H. B. 348

Synoptic parallels, use of aspects in 238–9, 253–5, 300 n.

Szemerényi, O. 20

Taylor, C. C. W. 143

Taylor, V. 348

telic, *see* boundedness, as element of lexical meaning

temporal clauses, aspect usage in 18–19, 24, 76, 400–1

tendential use of present 220

textual variation 6

Thackeray, H. St. J. 231

Thomas, W. 193

time reference, effect on aspect 17–19, 113, 165, 185–90, 198–9, 202–5,

227–9, 240–1, 255, 290–1, 301–2, 306, 308, 321–2, 323–4, 325–6, 389, 400–1, 406–9, 413–14, 416 n.
traditional material, effect on aspect 377–9, 387–8
transitivity, effect on aspect 105–6, 294–5, 298, 307, 312
translation problems, Greek to English, *see* English, translation problems
Trubetzkoy, N. S. 54, 56, 65
Turner, N. 3, 69, 87, 98, 213, 289, 381–2

undefined, as a general meaning for the aorist 58, 94–6
unmarked, as a general meaning for the aorist 94–6
urgent sense for aorist command 369–70, 374–5, 380–2

Vendler, Z. 43–5, 127–8, 141, 154
verb-types 43–6, 127–63; *see also* ACTIVITIES; ACCOMPLISHMENTS; CLIMAXES; lexical meaning of verb; PUNCTUALS; STATES
Verkuyl, H. J. 47

viewpoint, as feature of aspect-meaning 26–8, 35–6, 40–1, 50, 79, 83–5, 86, 97, 99, 103, 118, 119–20, 124, 195, 255, 411, 420–1
vividness 225, 226, 230–5; *see also* descriptive use of aspects
loss of 234
voice, effect on aspect 48, 105–6, 115–16, 293–5, 318, 319, 320; *see also* active voice; passive voice; transitivity, effect on aspect

Wackernagel, J. 105–6, 294
Wallace, S. 74–5
Webster, W. 100
Weinrich, H. 73–4
Wilcox, M. 351
Winer, G. B. 67, 87, 98

Zeitart 11, 12, 30
Zeitstufe 11, 12, 14, 21, 30
zero tense 193, 229–30
Zerwick, M. 95, 101, 104, 105, 121, 213, 279